THE SS

HUNTER BATTALIONS

THE HIDDEN HISTORY OF THE NAZI RESISTANCE MOVEMENT 1944–45

D1615520

About the Author

Perry Biddiscombe is Professor of History at the University of Victoria, British Columbia, Canada. He is the acknowledged world expert on the guerrilla forces of the Third Reich. His other books include *The Last Nazis: SS Werewolf Guerrilla Resistance in Europe 1944–1947* and *Werwolf!: The History of the National Socialist Guerrilla Movement 1944–1946*, described by *The Independent* as 'the most complete history of the Nazi partisan movement'. He lives in Victoria.

PRAISE FOR PERRY BIDDISCOMBE

'Throws fresh light on the Third Reich's last days' *BBC HISTORY MAGAZINE*
'The book explores the background to the movement, its operations and its wholly negative legacy... this type of terrorism is a nasty constant in the history of the German radical-right' *HISTORY TODAY*
'Detailed, meticulously researched and highly readable... a must for all interested in the end of the Second World War' *MILITARY ILLUSTRATED*

THE SS

HUNTER BATTALIONS

THE HIDDEN HISTORY OF THE NAZI RESISTANCE MOVEMENT 1944–45

PERRY BIDDISCOMBE

TEMPUS

First published 2006

Tempus Publishing Limited
The Mill, Brimscombe Port,
Stroud, Gloucestershire, GL5 2QG
www.tempus-publishing.com

British Library Cataloguing in Publication Data.
A catalogue record for this book is available from the British Library.

ISBN 0 7524 3938 3

Typesetting and origination by Tempus Publishing Limited
Printed in Great Britain

Contents

Acknowledgements

My recent researches have resulted in a series of fascinating correspondences and exchanges with scholars working in analogous areas, whom I want to acknowledge for providing their expertise and for stimulating my own thinking. Thanks to Paltin Sturdza, Michael Jung, and especially Jeff Burds, with whom I have exchanged much information and whose insights have proven invaluable in developing my understanding of the situation in Eastern Europe. Jeff is most kind in sharing knowledge and truly regards our discipline as a collaborative effort. Thanks as well to my colleague, Serhy Yekelchyk, who provided advice on Ukrainian sources, and to Eugéne Martres, who helped me with literature on German parachutists in France.

A work of this scope – it covers twenty-four different countries – would not have been possible without the help of a number of specialists who provided me with access to literature in languages that are beyond my ken. In this regard, I especially want to thank Sonja Yli-Kahila and Chris Wojtan, who are former students of mine and graciously came to my aid. Sonja and Chris translated literature on resistance movements in Finland and Poland, and the depth of the sections of the book dealing with such matters owe directly to their contributions. My appreciation as well to Rachel Dekker, who helped me investigate rumours about Skorzeny's possible connection with Prince Bernhardt of the Netherlands. For aid with letter-writing to various archives and libraries, thanks to Pasi Ahonen, Vanetta Petkova, Bogdan Verjinschi and Sharon Willis.

A special debt of gratitude is owed to the various archivists and librarians who have helped me over a long period of time. So thanks to the archivists at the National Archives II (College Park), the National Archives of the UK, the various offices and bureaux of the Bundesarchiv, the Archives Nationales, the National Archives of Canada, the Imperial War Museum and the Archivio Centrale dello Stato. Aila Narva at the Arkistolaitos in Helsinki kindly provided me with references to Finnish literature, and the staff at the Centre d'Études et de Documentation Guerre et Sociétés Contemporaines, in Brussels, gave me material on pro-German activists in Belgium. Thanks as well to the librarians at the Library of Congress, the Staatsbibliothek zu Berlin (especially the Zeitungsabteilung, Westhafen), the Bibliotheque Nationale, the Centre Pompidou, the British Library, the Robbins Library (London School of Economics), the German Historical Institute (London), and of course the McPherson Library, which is the intellectual centrepiece of my home institution, the University of Victoria. In particular, the librarians in the Interlibrary Loans section at McPherson Library deserve commendation for their hard work and diligence.

My publisher, Jonathan Reeve, kindly showed interest in a book of this scope and gave me considerable latitude. Certainly, I am grateful for his patience and good humour. Thanks as well to the production team at Tempus, who excel at their jobs. Their ability to format a book that is pleasing to the eye makes it much easier to present a historical narrative that is not a chore to read. And thanks to one of my department's secretaries, Eileen Zapshala, who helped me with technical issues involved in preparing the manuscript.

Finally, my sincere appreciation to my wife and son, who helped with research, proofread several chapters of the manuscript and have generally acted as a sounding board for my ideas and inspirations. Through thick and thin, they have always supported me.

Perry Biddiscombe, Victoria, BC

Introduction

Readers who crack the spine of this volume will find themselves through the looking glass. They will encounter a faltering Third Reich, around 1944–1945, that attempted to field partisans and 'freedom fighters' against its enemies, promising to 'liberate' Europe from the very powers that were themselves delivering the continent from tyranny. Such efforts revolved around the central figure of Otto Skorzeny, the notorious German commando chief – and rescuer of Benito Mussolini – who created a network of special units which functioned at the intersection between military force and politics.

Although Skorzeny prided himself a simple man, his was a house of many mansions. The centre of his network was a series of SS battalions called *Jagdverbände*, or 'hunter formations', which were assigned the job of leading a guerrilla war behind the lines of the advancing Allied and Soviet armies. This volume, however, also chronicles the story of a closely related body called 'Section S', which trained saboteurs and terrorists, and it provides an account of *Abwehr* '*Frontaufklärung*' ('front reconnaissance', FAK) detachments, some of which specialised in sabotage and bore responsibilities that overlapped those of the SS-*Jagdverbände*. All three types of units were controlled by Skorzeny, at least loosely, and he planned to amalgamate them into a coherent whole. A clear recognition of the nature and function of these organisations will help us understand the legacy of their chief, perhaps in a different sense than he himself might have wanted.

Anyone who seeks to understand the real history of the Skorzeny *Leute* (personnel) must first cut through a powerful narrative created by Skorzeny himself. Even while still in post-war Allied captivity, Skorzeny convinced an American journalist to publish his account of the Mussolini rescue in *True* magazine, thus introducing himself to the English-speaking world. Memoirs followed in 1950, although these were originally greeted with a storm of controversy: French communists rioted over the serialisation by *Figaro*, while the US Government froze the proceeds from the English-language edition. Even as late as 1963, the States Attorney in Cologne initiated an investigation against the German publisher of Skorzeny's double volume autobiography on the charge that the books were inimical to the well-being of German youth. Despite such embarrassments, Skorzeny was widely credited with providing the ultimate account of his units' operations, and he did his best to present a non-political image.[1] He further influenced the literature by graciously granting interviews as he basked in exile in Franco's Spain, and his output was supplemented by the work of his sycophantic biographer, Charles Foley. In the commercially successful *Commando Extraordinary*, Foley followed his subject's preferences in seeing Skorzeny as a good soldier, 'not… like Hitler, a fanatic ready to pull the world down on its head'. In fact, in order to get preferential access to Skorzeny, Foley blithely ignored evidence of Skorzeny's Nazi convictions, including rumours about his continuing association with the post-war fascist underground.[2] Once Skorzeny had hurdled obstacles set by war crimes and denazification trials, he became highly protective of his reputation. When a fellow German veteran questioned the veracity of his stories, he challenged him to a duel, and when an American television documentary suggested that he was wanted by the Israeli Government for war crimes, he notified the programme's sponsors that he would sue for libel in the absence of a retraction.[3]

The key impression that Skorzeny sought to create was that of a politically neutral man-of-action, and he directed the public's attention toward a few of his most outstanding stunts, particularly the 'rescue' of Mussolini and the infiltration of American lines during the Battle of the Bulge. He attempted to write history in the Greek heroic vein, creating a chronicle of extraordinary events rather than an account of process or a description of structure. Skorzeny was also comfortable with being an icon of masculinity and soldierly comradeship, but not with being readily identified as a National Socialist. Similarly, he wanted to be regarded as a swashbuckler – 'a German D'Artagnan' – rather than as a plotter whose units were essentially instruments of subversion.

There are several other reasons why Skorzeny failed to provide a detailed organisational history of the *Jagdverbände*, Section S or the FAK detachments. First, he was trying to develop a reputation as a tactician of genius, perhaps even having lessons to teach the armies of the Western Powers, as the latter steeled themselves for a supposedly inevitable confrontation with the Soviet Union. In crafting this image, he was willing to exaggerate his own role in several high-profile enterprises, and he was reluctant to admit mistakes.[4] On the other hand, an honest look at many of his systematic attempts at sabotage reveals Skorzeny to have been an overextended, inefficient and often inept intriguer. Moreover, his men frequently appear in an even worse light, sometimes unable to achieve the level of sobriety or self-composure necessary to mount efficient operations, or so disheartened by the Third Reich's string of defeats they could barely rouse themselves to action. In addition, personnel from the SS and the military components of Skorzeny's network fought each other constantly. One of the by-products of this dysfunction was that Skorzeny's operations in various countries were infiltrated by enemy agents; his top agent in France, for instance, actually entered into the employ of the Allied intelligence service. The Skorzeny *Leute* were a dangerous lot, but their feckless approach to matters of operational efficiency and security made them less lethal than would otherwise have been the case.

Second, some of Skorzeny's units had perpetrated war crimes, particularly in Slovakia, Greece and Denmark, where they were trying to clear the ground of patriot resisters and thus create the 'clean slate' that they needed to launch their own operations. Since Skorzeny was tried in an Allied military court for breaches of the rules of war in the Ardennes, he hardly wanted to emphasise his association with such units, particularly where instances of foul play involved the massacre or manhandling of civilian populations. He had to admit killings of civilians in Denmark – these actions were directly controlled by his headquarters – but he had a set of convenient excuses for why he was not responsible for most of the damage in that unfortunate country. Skorzeny and his forces also murdered German and Austrian civilians late in the war, but Skorzeny naturally admitted nothing about such outrages.

Skorzeny's attempt at public relations did not leave him immune to censure, particularly from critics who felt that his self-glorification was a slap in the face to the real heroes of the Second World War, or from voices who charged that he had never engaged in a reflective consideration of his role in service of an obvious evil. Orville Prescott called his autobiography 'the proud record of the military achievements of an insensitive, unscrupulous and essentially stupid man'. However, Mary McGrory cut to the heart of the issue in contending that Skorzeny's memoirs were 'as interesting for what they leave unsaid as for what they say', and that he actually offered 'precious little'.[5] Thus, what is obviously required is a contrapuntal investigation of the role played by Skorzeny and his units during the last year of the war. The weighting that Skorzeny attached to the various aspects of his career, his depiction of the central purpose of his detachments, and the meaning and relevance that he attributed to various operations – all these are matters that should be re-examined. Engaging in such a reinterpretation of the SS-*Jagdverbände*, Section S and the FAK units is the purpose of this book.

The true role of Skorzeny's special forces was not only to carry out 'one-shot' political and military tasks, as specified by the *Führer*, but to subvert the liberation of Europe, and to do this in a systematic fashion. In later describing his adventures, Skorzeny largely ignored this second – more insidious – purpose. The historiography has unfortunately followed his lead.[6] In truth, the *primary function* of Skorzeny's force was to rouse Europeans into anti-Soviet and anti-Allied resistance. The head of the SS, Heinrich Himmler, made arrangements in September 1944 to launch pro-German rebellions in all of the territories recently evacuated by the *Wehrmacht*, and two months later Skorzeny was instructed to make use in such operations of existing nationalist guerrilla groups in Central and Eastern Europe, such as the Ukrainian Partisan Army (UPA) and the Polish Home Army (AK). Skorzeny was also told to coordinate his efforts with other SS, military and Foreign Office bodies involved in the same process.

Substantial numbers of men were deployed. The *Luftwaffe* parachuted over 450 FAK saboteurs in the summer of 1944, ninety-seven operations being carried out along the Eastern Front alone. Overall, the *Luftwaffe*'s special services squadron, *Kampfgeschwader* 200, dropped one thousand parachutists along enemy lines of communication. At least 600 men were deployed behind Soviet lines in the last part of 1944, when the *Jagdverbände* and FAK units were attempting to divine the direction of the forthcoming Soviet Winter Offensive. The bulk of the Skorzeny *Leute* were infiltrated through the main battle line, stay-behind operations accounted for another ten to twenty per cent of deployments, with the remainder (twenty to thirty per cent) accounted for by parachute drops. The *Jagdverbände* carried out twenty to twenty-five missions monthly along the Western Front, plus at least an equal number in the Balkans.[7]

Belatedly assuming the mantle of 'freedom fighters' was a difficult shift for the Nazi leadership that controlled Skorzeny. Hitler, for instance, was contemptuous of minor countries and told Joseph Goebbels 'that the rubbish of small nations still existing in Europe must be liquidated as fast as possible'.[8] In addition, one does not usually think of National Socialism as an internationalist or cosmopolitan movement: Hitler had said in *Mein Kampf* that he had no intention of putting the Nazi Party in the vanguard of a league of 'freedom movements' because he regarded the prospects of such groups as grim and because he had no intention of linking up with supposed racial inferiors, especially Russians.[9] He also regarded Pan-Europeanism with disdain, judging it a recipe for political paralysis. His vision of Europe's future, particularly in the East, was one of colonial subjugation to Germany, a project for which he did not expect much sympathy from those being subjugated.[10]

There was, however, also a rival school of thought within the Nazi Party and the SS that drew from an older sense of German imperialism and which regarded the Reich as the gravitational centre of a *Mitteleuropa* system of states. This group sought a neutralised and neutered France; a constellation of minor satellite states in Central and Eastern Europe, all of which would 'naturally' seek the protection of German arms; plus a Russian heartland that was sovereign but weak, and would serve Germany as a supplier of raw materials and food.[11] As the SS drew more foreign volunteers into its armed wing during the 1940s, its propaganda and recruitment policies increasingly shifted toward this type of view. In other words, despite originally being the staunchest proponents of *Germanisierung* and ethnic cleansing, the SS became increasingly internationalised as the war progressed, a process obviously related to the Third Reich's increasing need to augment its own strength by mobilising anti-Soviet sentiments throughout Europe. By 1944, even Himmler belatedly came around to expressing sympathy for the 'Russian liberation' project, and the Third Reich's security chief, Ernst Kaltenbrunner, argued in early 1945 that 'our policy toward the Poles must be revised immediately'.[12]

German propaganda also came to emphasise the Germany-as-protector-of-small-nations theme. The *Deutschesnachrichtenbüro* argued that the Western Powers had sold out the interests of small countries to Stalin, and that while they blamed Hitler for picking on minor powers, the *Führer* had 'waged a passionate battle to ensure peace and for cooperation with equal rights of European peoples... Germany alone is fighting for right and justice.' Danube Radio, beaming to the Balkans in February 1945, made the point even more explicitly: 'To liberate all the small nations and return to them complete economic and political sovereignty, this is the principle for which National Socialist Germany fights.'[13]

One might well question whether or not this late-blooming concern for national self-determination (and for supra-national Pan-Europeanism) was genuine: 'new right' and apologist writers have long claimed that it was, culminating in Hans Werner Neulen's contention that the *Waffen*-SS came eventually to embody a 'Eurofascist' idea quite distinct from National Socialism. However, deep doubts about Nazi sincerity are probably justified. It is certainly significant that the SS 'General Plan for 1945', which reflected the thinking of the powerful Gottlob Berger, chief of the SS Main Office, talked about luring the West into a false sense of complacency and about the inevitability of a third world war, 'Europe versus Eurasia'. Despite Himmler's well-publicised concessions to the 'Russian liberation movement', he still believed, as late as 1944–1945, that Russia's western boundary would eventually have to be pushed as far east as Moscow,[14] and in November 1944, he announced that 'sooner or later we shall again advance beyond our frontiers and borderlands, thus creating the territorial forefield and glacis of power which the Greater Germanic Empire needs'.[15]

What, then, was the point of the evolving Nazi 'Wilsonianism' (as hollow as it was)? By the last year of the war, German military strategy was increasingly designed to prevent defeat – perhaps by building solid river defence lines at the Roer, the Rhine, the Elbe, the Oder or the Vistula – until the tenuous enemy coalition had a chance to fall apart. In September 1944, Gottlob Berger called for holding the Soviets in the Carpathians and central Poland and meanwhile launching local counter-offensives that could push the Western Allies back to the Somme, leaving a central realm that the Germans could spend the next ten years securing. It was also hoped that the development of missiles, super-submarines or jets could turn the tide of battle, but it was thought that such projects would need time to mature.[16] In thinking about the means to supplement such strategies, the Germans decided that the Soviets and Western Allies had taught them a valuable lesson, namely, that the development of wireless communications and airborne methods of supply had revolutionised the waging of war behind enemy lines. Certainly, they hoped to use such techniques as profitably as they had been employed against the Third Reich. The SS 'General Plan', for instance, talked about 'mobilising groups which have been stimulated by the occupation of the enemy in both Eastern and Western Europe'.[17]

To achieve success, the amended Nazi approach to Europe obviously had to have resonance outside the Third Reich. There is good reason for doubting whether Europeans would fight for the same country that had oppressed them for three or four years, even if the latter was now claiming to fight for 'European' culture. It was one thing for the Nazis to mobilise resources and manpower from regions that they had occupied and then to tell themselves that this help was freely given. It was quite another to raise support in areas from which the Germans had withdrawn and where they had spent the previous few years brutally manhandling the population. Despite the fact that their cause had been weighed down by this recent history, there were SS and *Wehrmacht* officers who believed that nationalist elements and former collaborators in evacuated areas could still be incited into action.

With the exception of a few groups in Eastern Europe, there is not much evidence that the resistance groups mobilised by Skorzeny had a mass base or that they included more than a small cohort of misguided nationalists and rabid anti-communists. Nonetheless, the Nazis were trying to make a virtue out of necessity by 1944–1945, arguing that 'a small troop of convinced fanatics is worth more than a big party'.[18] It is also apparent, however, that the much-lauded guerrilla movements supported by the Allies and the Soviets were not mass organisations either, at least until 1943 (by which time an element of opportunism had entered into calculations). The romantic image of the resistance fighter as the manifestation of a common European spirit of freedom has been one of the most durable of wartime legends, but with the end of the Cold War and the transformation of the French and Italian communist parties, a much more critical historiography of the anti-German resistance has begun to take shape. Indeed, some studies have emerged that, as Tony Judt notes, would have been unthinkable in conception and unpublishable in form only a short time ago.[19] To some extent, this study mines the opposite side of this seam, suggesting that while the winners in 1945 imposed their own politicised and functional interpretation of resistance, they also prevented the formation of public memories about different kinds of resistance that did not fit comfortably into prevailing conceptions of the war.

It is also difficult to claim that the resistance movements supported by the Germans had much strategic or even tactical value. Authorities as diverse as Basil-Liddell Hart, John

Keegan and Alan Milward have long cast doubt on the effectiveness of pro-Allied and pro-Soviet resistance movements, arguing that such groups were usually not subjected to much command-and-control nor were they prepared to attack targets of strategic value during periods when armies in the field most required such services.[20] Certainly, as we shall see, the same caveat applies to the movements associated with the Germans. Although these groups caused limited damage to Germany's foes, they did not have the capacity to create strategic reversals. Larger and more independent groups, such as the UPA and the Chetniks, had contact with the Germans and accepted weapons from them, but there is no evidence that they took orders about which targets to attack. The benefit to the Germans came more in the form of various bits of assistance and intelligence, which often arrived unexpectedly. It was not an arrangement upon which they could rely.

Amidst the euphoria of Allied victory and the subsequent concerns of the Cold War, Skorzeny's attempts at subversion were forgotten. At the dawn of the twenty-first century, however, we are only too familiar with the damage done by ethnic nationalism, the tendencies of 'failed states' to surrender authority to warlords, and the violent potential of fanaticism. These themes bring Skorzeny to mind and they suggest new perspectives for interpretation. Unless we want to take Skorzeny's account as the final word on the role that he and his units played in the Second World War, we are merited in taking a second look at the topic. In fact, we may have to take a wrecking ball to the edifice that has been so carefully constructed by the commando chief and his admirers.

1
The Skorzeny *Leute*

Like all things, Skorzeny's sabotage units did not suddenly materialise from stardust, fully formed and absent of any progenitors. Rather, they were the product of discrete forces in German history and reflected a sense of encirclement that legitimated any means of weakening Germany's rivals, even irregular modes of warfare. Indeed, Skorzeny's network of units grew over the course of time from an unlikely seed born of the attempt to exploit Britain's traditional Achilles' Heel in Ireland. The story of how an obscure commando company evolved into a brigade-sized politico-military force with a chain of command running to the pinnacle of the Nazi state must rate as one of the more bizarre narratives from a time and place notable for outlandish events.

PRECURSORS AND ANTECEDENTS

As early as the 1880s, Otto von Bismarck had considered rousing a revolt in Russian Poland in case of war with the Tsar, and the Kaiser Wilhelm II proceeded further in the same direction, encouraging plots in Muslim countries under the domination of powers in the Entente. During the First World War, the German high command and Foreign Office encouraged guerrilla warfare throughout the empires of the Allied powers, concentrating special attention upon Morocco, India, Poland, the Ukraine, the Caucasus and Ireland. They enjoyed some success, particularly by threatening Allied interests in Persia and Afghanistan and by using these countries as bases for operations against Allied territory. By 1918, the Imperial Government had spent 382 million marks on insurgency propaganda and special operations, and the idea of 'self-determination' had become an important element in German foreign policy.[1]

Even the Weimar Republic pursued similar strategies. During the 1920s, German military intelligence, the *Abwehr*, cooperated with the borderland guerrilla service, the *Feldjägerdienst*, in organising skeletal bands of ethnic Germans (*Volksdeutsche*) living in Poland, Czechoslovakia and Lithuania.[2] With the advent of the Third Reich, even larger numbers of *Volksdeutsche* were recruited as agents. In fact, such operations were eventually organised not only by the *Abwehr*, but by the SS Security Service (*Sicherheitsdienst*, SD). Recruitment of Nazi or pro-Nazi underground groups helped pave the way for seizures of territory in Austria, Czechoslovakia, Poland, Belgium and Yugoslavia,[3] and after the assault upon the Soviet Union, the Germans were able to inspire a degree of unrest even among Soviet-Germans living in the Volga river basin, hundreds of miles behind Soviet lines. Stalin responded by dissolving the entire Volga-German Autonomous Republic and deporting its inhabitants into Asia, a process that served as a prototype for his eventual treatment of ethnic groups in which even small numbers of people showed signs of sympathy for the invader.[4]

Early attempts to exploit Nazified *Volksdeutsche* were organised on a case-by-case basis, although in the autumn of 1939 the *Abwehr* institutionalised the method by creating 'Special Building and Instructional Company 800', which was based in the old garrison town of Brandenburg and took that city's name as its moniker. The Brandenburg unit represented a crucial stage of evolution in the Third Reich's capacity to wage '*Kleinkrieg*' ('small unit warfare'), and it particularly proved its worth during the early years of the Russian campaign, when German troops in mufti seized Soviet bridges.[5] The Brandenburgers' very successes, however, resulted in problems of over-extension. By 1943, the unit had been built up to divisional size and was increasingly being diverted into regular combat duties, particularly in the Balkans, a development that resulted in the loss of some of its highly trained specialists amidst the grind of conventional fighting. Many recent cases in military history have shown that when hard-pressed generals throw specialist commandos and light infantry formations into regular combat, these units are typically cut to ribbons, notwithstanding their élan and their high degree of physical and mental fitness. Certainly this process effected the Brandenburgers, and to reinforce their capabilities for combat they were armed with artillery and tanks, which in turn further diminished their sense of particularity.

Nazi leaders also suspected that because of the Brandenburg unit's association with the largely anti-Nazi *Abwehr*, it was being cultivated as the praetorian guard of the conservative opposition within the Third Reich. This supposition was not far from wrong and as a means of pre-emption, the Nazi leadership transferred control of the division from the *Abwehr* to the *Wehrmacht Führungsstab*. Hitler and his cohorts also made arrangements in 1944 to strip the Brandenburg Division of its surviving capabilities for special operations, which went to the SS.[6]

If the use of *Volksdeutsch* commandos and partisans proved problematic, the employment of non-German-speaking foreigners was even more difficult, particularly after the advent of the Third Reich. Many Nazis showed disdain for foreign guerrillas and troublemakers, even if their causes coincidentally worked to Germany's advantage, although providing secret support for such elements would fit well into the Hitler regime's predatory foreign policy. Eventually, most Nazis decided that the amoral opportunism of Nazi statecraft had to take precedence over the disagreeable aspects of working with 'racial inferiors', particularly in Eastern Europe. In the 1920s, the main proponent of foreign resistance movements was the *Abwehr*'s sabotage bureau. Although its enthusiasms were held in check by the conservative Weimar policy of 'fulfilment', which meant avoiding direct challenges to the major powers, the *Abwehr* did contact such disparate groups as Hungarian revanchists in southern Czechoslovakia and Breton separatists in western France.[7] However, the *Abwehr*'s main cat's paw was the Ukrainian nationalist movement, which was used to threaten and destabilise Poland. Although contacts with the Ukrainians briefly terminated in 1933, due to the racial intransigence of the new regime, the Ukrainian capacity to upset potential enemies was too lucrative to ignore, and in 1937 the *Abwehr* re-established links with the Organisation of Ukrainian Nationalists (OUN) and began training the movement's members. For the Ukrainians, the result of such ties was a record of repeated betrayals by an arrogant and callous ally: when the OUN tried to grab Sub-Carpathian Ruthenia from a disintegrating Czechoslovakia, the Germans gave the land to Hungary; when the Ukrainians tried to liberate Polish Galicia during the 'September War' against Poland, the Germans handed the territory to the Soviet Union; when they tried to proclaim the independence of the entire Ukraine during the early days of Barbarossa, they were told that the western part of their country would now be part of German-dominated Poland and that the rest would be run as a colonial dependency of the Third Reich.[8] Similar betrayals were perpetrated in the Baltic states, where the Germans also cultivated local nationalists and received their help in launching anti-Soviet uprisings in 1941. As was the case in the Ukraine, the Germans eventually unveiled their own irredentist programme for the region.[9]

Despite Nazi deceit, there is no doubt that support for pro-German subversion yielded considerable dividends, especially during Barbarossa. As a result, the German machinery to encourage such activity evolved to a considerable degree of complexity. The *Abwehr's* sabotage wing, its second section (*Zweierorganisation*), was charged with equipping and training *Abwehr Kommandos* and a staff, code-named 'Walli II', was organised in Warsaw in order to coordinate these operations. The '200 series' of these *Kommandos*, that is, the formations with three digit unit numbers beginning with a two, were charged with sending saboteurs up to 120 miles behind Soviet lines. '100 series' *Abwehr Kommandos* were organised by espionage-oriented sections of the *Abwehr* and were responsible for intelligence gathering; '300 series' units were tasked with counter-intelligence and anti-partisan operations. Eventually, *Abwehr Kommandos* of all three types were attached to German forces on every front and were renamed *Frontaufklärung* (FAK) units. As before, the '200 series' retained sabotage as its special province.[11]

In order to match the pace and extent of *Abwehr* operations in Russia, the SD also organised its own sabotage agency called 'Zeppelin', which in 1942 began infiltrating and parachuting squads of pro-German Russians, who were often deployed hundreds of miles behind Soviet lines.[12] Although 'Zeppelin' originally recruited great masses of personnel from the ranks of Red Army deserters and POWs, this strategy shifted around the turn of 1943–1944, when Berlin ordered that 'numerous small groups are to be formed... for the solution of purely political questions in enemy territory'.[13] Although the Soviet security services rolled up many 'Zeppelin' groups, the SD received reports suggesting that they occasionally carried out acts of industrial sabotage and demolished railway lines, and through 'Zeppelin' the Germans learned much about the mood of the Russian people and the military disposition of the Red Army.[14]

As the struggle in Russia bogged down into an attritional campaign, the scale of German efforts accelerated. Many *Abwehr* specialists, along with officers of *Wehrmacht* combat formations, came to believe that the only way to win the war was to liberalise Nazi occupation policies, address the alienation of increasingly indignant populations behind German lines, and try to reawaken a Russian civil war.[15] The *Abwehr* and 'Zeppelin' did what they could to realise this objective and to gather any important intelligence that became available along the way. The number of agents parachuted into the Soviet rear doubled in 1942, increasing by another fifty per cent in 1943, and the number of groups infiltrated through enemy lines also rose exponentially.[16] Dozens of commando attacks caused Soviet losses that were small, but nearly always exceeded the casualties amongst the troops conducting the raids.[17] In 1942, for instance, *Abwehr* losses in sabotage attacks totalled 654 men (mostly Russian personnel), while the Soviets lost 6,700 troops, plus six trains and over one hundred vehicles and armoured cars.[18]

By 1942–1943, the German sabotage services had reached the ultimate geographical extent of their reach, operating at some points over 2,000 miles from Berlin. In the North Caucasus, German teams supported local rebellions and the mountains were alive with armed groups of local civilians and Red Army deserters. A Caucasian specialist with Army Group A reported that 'partisan warfare is burning particularly hot in the territories of Dagestan, Chechnya, Ingushetya, Kabarda and Adegeja... The fighting has assumed a severe character and even the Soviet air force has had to undertake raids against the partisans.' Stalin repaid the Chechens and Ingushi in the same way that he had dealt with the Volga-Germans: in early 1944, the NKGB violently uprooted and deported nearly the entire population of these mountain nations.[19] The roots of the present-day conflict in the North Caucasus lie partly in this horrendous outrage.

The Germans also retained contact with guerrillas even further afield, particularly in central and southern Asia. They estimated that there were 80,000 anti-communist partisans in Soviet Turkestan, to whom they sent liaison officers and advisors. Many of the operations to support these 'Basmachi' bands were run through Afghanistan, although disaster struck when the local Abwehr mastermind in that country, Hauptmann Dietrich Witzel, was expelled in 1943.[20] Afghanistan also served as a base for operations against India, where the Germans supported rebel tribal leaders in the North-West Frontier Province and had contact with a radical faction of the Congress Party.[21] To the west, in Iran, the Abwehr ceded priority to the SD, which was busy cultivating the hill tribes, elements in the army and Islamic clergymen, even as early as 1940. When Iran was militarily occupied by Britain and the Soviet Union in 1941, the Germans launched a pro-Axis underground and they had some success in organising sabotage attacks, at least until their agents were rolled up by the Allied security services.[22]

In the Arab world, the Germans had to remain alert to the sensitivities of Spain and Italy, both of which held North African territories and frowned upon Abwehr or SD operations designed to stir up Arab nationalist sentiment.[23] Nonetheless, the Zweierorganisation was suspected of complicity in an uprising by the Algerian Rifles, who in January 1941 massacred their officers and marched on Algiers.[24] The Germans also encouraged nationalist plotters in Iraq, who rose in an anti-British revolt in May 1941, and veterans of this abortive rebellion, together with Syrian and Palestinian nationalists, were later trained by Sonderstab 'F', which occasionally sent parachutists back into the Middle East.[25] In Egypt, Abwehr agents established contact with anti-British conspirators in the army, and in Morocco they made similar overtures to regional nabobs and landed airborne saboteurs in the country.[26] In Tunisia, Abwehr Kommando 210 made dozens of attempts against Allied-controlled railways, bridges and supply dumps, and they set up a stay-behind organisation.[27] The SD also participated in such activity by creating Operation 'Parseval', which had a mandate to 'deal with the direction of resistance movements in French north-west Africa', and was manned mainly by Frenchmen, Spaniards and Arabs.[28] Even after the Germans were chased from North Africa, they continued to visit secret airfields and drop saboteurs into the region.[29]

While it is obvious that the Germans had launched sabotage efforts at many widely scattered points by 1943, several fundamental changes occurred after the key turning point battles at Alemein and Stalingrad. In the first place, as the Germans began to withdraw from areas within Europe, there was a great temptation to do what the enemy had done to them in supporting the construction and growth of armed resistance movements. Thus the emphasis in German efforts increasingly shifted to defensive modes of *Kleinkrieg*, particularly through the preparation of stay-behind activities. In fact, as conventional German military capacity diminished, the importance of weakening the enemy through irregular means increased accordingly, and the scale of such efforts grew by leaps and bounds.

Just as a realisation of their defensive posture was dawning on German guerrilla warfare specialists and spy-masters, the importance of the SD in these areas also grew exponentially. Identifying what they obviously saw as a field of opportunity, SD officers no longer wanted to stake a claim just over a few remote outposts like Iran, but to dominate the entire realm. This increasingly seemed possible because the *Abwehr*'s anti-Nazi inclinations and its links to the anti-Hitler resistance movement were starting to imperil that agency's existence.

IRISH ORIGINS

Although it is a largely forgotten story, the original wedge for expanding the SD's sabotage/subversion effort was born of German attempts to exploit tension in Ireland. At first, German plans for Ireland, around 1940–1941, were fixed upon using the Irish Republican Army (IRA) to raid Ulster, or perhaps exploiting the nationalists as a medium through which to get Eire's premier, Eamon de Valera, to invade the British part of the island. Such troubles could prove a useful diversion for any prospective German invasion of Great Britain. By 1942, however, a variant of this plan, code-named 'Thousand', had replaced the original, offensively oriented version. As the opportunity to conquer Britain faded, German concerns shifted toward keeping southern Ireland free of Allied occupation and thus denying it as a base for anti-submarine warfare in the North Atlantic. Fearing that the temptation to grab control of Irish ports was increasing as the U-Boat scourge became more severe, the *Abwehr* and the Foreign Office suggested that two *Wehrmacht* divisions be held in readiness at Brest, France, so that they could be ferried to Ireland in case of a British invasion. This plan was rejected out of hand by the Armed Forces High Command (OKW), which had neither sufficient land nor sea forces to undertake the mission.

At this juncture, Edmund Veesenmayer, the Foreign Office's specialist in conspiratorial intrigue, advanced a more modest scheme that he discussed with the SD-*Ausland*. In a series of conferences hosted by the OKW's Special Staff on Commercial and Economic Warfare, and in which navy, *Luftwaffe* and *Abwehr* representatives took part, Veesenmayer proposed that aircraft and blockade-running sea vessels be reserved in order to supply the Irish with arms in case of an emergency, and that a small SD special services company be built in order to help the Irish Army should British invaders push into Eire. In case of such a *coup de main*, a small IRA-German team would be landed in order to prepare Irish opinion for a limited German intervention. This detachment would also reconnoitre drop zones for a main party to follow. Several days after the dispatch of the pathfinders, the SD unit would be parachuted or landed by sea, whence it would start guiding Irish regular and irregular forces in rear-guard efforts and in the organisation of partisan warfare, for which the Irish were felt to be suited by both temperament and tradition. The German specialists would also be responsible for training Irish soldiers and 'volunteers' with modern weapons, a supply of which would be air-dropped or landed on the coast by German vessels.

Until the middle of the Second World War, the SD-*Ausland* had no special services unit of the sort required for the prospective intervention in Eire. SD-*Ausland* regional bureaux had created their own sabotage groups on a case-by-case basis, such as 'Zeppelin' and 'Parseval', but the only SD subsection formally charged with supporting general sabotage activity was the supply office, Section F, which Himmler had ordered to form a guerrilla-warfare and subversion directorate code-named 'Otto'. Based at 6a Delbrückstrasse, Berlin, 'Otto' was run by *Sturmbannführer* Hermann Dörner, a former adjutant to Himmler and a rising star in the SD hierarchy. When the SD agreed to organise a formation for combat in Eire, it was placed under the loose purview of 'Otto', although a large role in determining the character of the unit was played by *Obergruppenführer* Jüttner, the training chief of the *Waffen*-SS. Jüttner acted as the initial liaison with SS combat formations, from the ranks of which the unit's men were recruited. In August 1942, a Dutch SS officer, Pieter van Vessem, was transferred to the SD and led one hundred *Waffen*-SS volunteers to an SD training ground at Oranienburg, near Jüttner's headquarters at Fichtergrund. At Oranienburg, the men cooled their heels for over a month, not being informed of their mission, until Dörner finally arrived and launched preparations for operations in Ireland.

Despite the fact that the Oranienburg unit was well-trained and well-armed, two Brandenburg specialists who were sent to observe the company in November 1942 were not impressed. When these officers, Helmut Clissmann and Bruno Rieger, showed up at Oranienburg, they explained that they had been ordered to provide English lessons and wireless instruction, although Clissmann was a close associate of Veesenmeyer and was also supposed to check on the unit's overall progress. Clissmann had lived in Eire before the war and was considered an expert on Irish matters. He and Rieger found the three platoons of trainees in a feisty and arrogant mood, noting that with their utter contempt for all things foreign, they would not make themselves popular in Ireland. The SD troops, Clissmann later recalled, had been 'too overbearing and spoilt by SS discipline for use in Catholic Eire'. He and Rieger issued a negative report, while at the same time Hitler began to reconsider the 'Thousand' scheme because of the changing strategic situation. In conversations with Dörner, Veesenmayer agreed to make the SD unit available for other duties, and a number of Irish nationalists recruited by Dörner were released for alternate missions.[30] In general, it was not a propitious start for a formation that was destined to evolve into the main German locus for the organisation of guerrilla warfare throughout Europe.

A HERO DESPITE HIMSELF

After plans for 'Thousand' were abandoned, the SD-*Ausland* decided to retain the Oranienburg Special Operations Unit as a permanent addition to its roster, controlled administratively by the SD but depending on the *Waffen*-SS for personnel and training. Dörner used the new organisation to train foreign agents, and in the spring of 1943 he spent considerable time preparing twenty German saboteurs, plus Persian translators and guides, for air-drops into Iran. The idea behind this project was to stir up Iranian insurgent groups. A six-man team was deployed on 29 March 1943, with the insertion carried out by a long-range aircraft from Crimea tasked by 'Zeppelin'. Two of the operatives were able to find and join Franz Meyer, an SD agent who was already on the ground, but the mission as a whole failed when its chief, Gunther Blume, was arrested.

A similar plot was developed for the Belgian Congo. With the help of Flemish fascists, a small group of missionary fathers and a few disaffected Belgian colonists, SD special forces hoped to land a ten-man '*Vorkommando*' by U-Boat and then build up an insurrectionary army of 2,000 men. The ultimate goal was to make contact with a rebellious African tribal chief, accepting his hospitality in the bush and carrying out sabotage attacks, while a radio outpost would keep SD controllers informed about operations. Oil wells were considered an especially important target. This scheme never materialised – perhaps the notion of aiding revolutionary African tribesmen caused the racists in the SS leadership to blanch – and the Portuguese Legion, which had a base in Angola, refused a request for help.

Finally, van Vessem and company were also being trained for operations in the Balkans,[31] but before they could be sent to this front the course of the unit's history was abruptly altered by the appearance of the monumental figure of Otto Skorzeny. Because of the SD's increasing concern with irregular operations, the organisation's chief, Walter Schellenberg, decided to dispense with the services of Section F and create a new bureau, Section S, which would be totally devoted to training saboteurs. The leader of this new office was *Obersturmführer* Otto Skorzeny, a 35-year-old Viennese SS man who had joined the Austrian Nazi Party in 1932 and had bloomed as a protégée of Austrian SD luminary Ernst Kaltenbrunner. At a hulking six-foot-four and 195 pounds, his heavy features and dark complexion highlighted by a duelling scar that ran the length of his face, Skorzeny was a considerable physical presence. Intellectually, he had no special abilities and was far from being a member of the Viennese literati, although he was a quick study and had a working knowledge of several languages. Like his father Anton and brother Alfred, Skorzeny was trained as an engineer. He was employed in various engineering and construction enterprises and in 1937 bought 'Otto Skorzeny Scaffolders', a firm he had been managing since 1934. From 1922 onward, Skorzeny had also been a member of various student cadet corps, eventually graduating to the ultimate right-radical gathering ground, the *Allgemeine*-SS. As an SS volunteer, Skorzeny played a role in the *Anschluss*, the Nazi-inspired unification of Germany and Austria, and in the *Kristallnacht*, a nationwide anti-Semitic pogrom that proved a precursor to the Final Solution.

In 1939, Skorzeny joined the *Luftwaffe*, but his dreams of rapid promotion faded and he began pulling strings to wrangle a transfer to the armed wing of the SS, applying even to the *Totenkopf* units that guarded concentration camps. In February 1940, he was accepted into the SS-*Leibstandarte* 'Adolf Hitler', later shifting to the '*Das Reich*' Division. Skorzeny fought on the Western Front and in Yugoslavia and Russia, being awarded the Iron Cross and rising quickly through the ranks. He became an officer in February 1941, although he was then invalided with gallstones, being detailed to a desk job at the *Waffen*-SS motor pool and driver training section in the southern suburbs of Berlin. This was a difficult period. For an action-lover like Skorzeny, relative idleness was hard to bear, particularly since it seemed to smack of shirking, and in the summer of 1942 the SS and Police Court actually accused him of absence without leave, a charge that was only dropped after investigators determined that he was genuinely ill and that he craved a combat assignment. It was from his modest post in Berlin-Lichterfelde that Skorzeny was eventually plucked by SS boss Heinrich Himmler and given a mandate to found the new 'S Section' of the SD-*Ausland*

and to coordinate SD sabotage schools ('S' initially stood for 'schools' rather than 'sabotage'). According to the paperwork, Skorzeny was chosen 'on the grounds of his technical expertise'. He reported for duty on 18 April 1943, was promoted to *Hauptsturmführer* ten days later, and then set up his offices in the SD-*Ausland* headquarters at 32 Berkärstrasse, Berlin. A considerable row surrounded his promotion because Skorzeny had recently been confined to house arrest for entering a bar in Paris during a day of national mourning, after which he had abused the military police patrol that had come to pick him up. Officers in the SS motor pool complained that Skorzeny should never have been promoted during the penalty phase of his punishment, but 'since the *Reichssicherheitshauptamt* cares nothing about regulations', they could have Skorzeny with the best of luck.

Skorzeny was a talented amateur in the field of *Kleinkrieg*, although he was not in the same league as his hero, T.E. Lawrence. Nonetheless, he did share with Lawrence a defining brand of firebrand nonconformism. Fancying himself the Viennese striver in a world governed by stodgy Prussian Brahmins, Skorzeny was at odds with the regimentation of the *Wehrmacht*, and he was interested in pursuing original tactics and new forms of military strategy, although these were not always successful. Nazi war reporter Robert Kroetz called him the 'new type of warrior... the total political soldier', and it is interesting to note that this was the way in which the Hitler regime was officially disposed to interpreting Skorzeny.[32] The 'political soldier' – a bastardised form of the Nietzschean superman – was defined in neo-conservative and SS ideology as an unflinching warrior schooled in direct action, in particular one willing to use military methods both on the battlefield and in the political or diplomatic fields. In fact, these latter spheres were understood simply as extended forums for the historic and transcendent struggle in which the Nazis believed they were engaged. This idea gave rise to a notion that we shall soon encounter as 'diplomatic direct action', that is, the romantic doctrine that a political or military leader was the incarnation of a cause, an army or a nation, and that by strengthening or hindering the individual leader his following could be either boosted to victory or mortally weakened.

Skorzeny had first shown his prowess as a 'political soldier' in Austria, where at the time of the *Anschluss* he had led an SS squad in apprehending the Austrian head of state. This episode had brought him kudos from senior Austrian Nazis like Arthur Seyss-Inquart, and as a reward he received the captaincy of a Viennese motorised formation in the *Allgemeine*-SS. It was probably this episode that made Skorzeny a credible candidate, once the time came, for the leadership of the SD's new sabotage section. Skorzeny also benefited from the fact that Kaltenbrunner's star was on the rise; after the assassination of Reinhard Heydrich, Kaltenbrunner was appointed chief of the SS security directorate, the *Reichssicherheitshauptamt* (RSHA), of which the SD-*Ausland* was a part.

With Kaltenbrunner suddenly in a position to help his friends, not only was Skorzeny now recognised as a first-rate 'political soldier', but the standing of other Viennese officers in the SD improved. Kaltenbrunner and Skorzeny, along with two of the section chiefs in the SD-*Ausland*, Wilhelm Waneck and Wilhelm Höttl, formed a Viennese 'mafia', often at odds with the chief of the SD-*Ausland*, Walter Schellenberg, and with the boss of the powerful SS-Main Office, Gottlob Berger. Skorzeny and Waneck took particular pleasure in ignoring regular bureaucratic channels. In so doing, they banked on Schellenburg's disinclination to face issues directly, and despite the fact that the latter had a superior intellect, as well as Himmler's ear, he lacked the courage to bulldoze Skorzeny and Waneck back into line.[33]

Once in the saddle, Skorzeny gathered a coterie of romantic misfits and desperadoes who regarded themselves as free thinkers. Skorzeny's right-hand man was a fellow Austrian named Karl Radl. According to Eugen Dollmann, Radl was 'intelligent and understanding… a typical Viennese' averse to pointless bloodletting. Three years younger than the commando chief, he was also a member of the Austrian SS and in the 1930s had been a close friend of Skorzeny's wife, through whom he knew Skorzeny himself. After studying law at the University of Berlin, Radl volunteered for front-line duty, but when commissioned he was attached to the SD-*Ausland*. Several years later, he accidentally bumped into Skorzeny in a Berlin restaurant and agreed to Skorzeny's request that he join him as his deputy. Made of finer clay than his boss, Radl had a mandate to move paper and to integrate Section S within the ponderous machinery of the SS bureaucracy. Popularly known as 'Skorzeny's Nanny', he provided a crucial centre of gravity in the new sabotage headquarters and attended to the red tape that his high-flying chief felt was beneath him.

Three other key recruits were Arnold (Arno) Besekow, Adrien von Fölkersam and Werner Hunke. Besekow was a criminologist from the Magdeburg police who met Radl in May 1943 and was subsequently recommended to Skorzeny. He was then appointed as head of the Fourth Bureau of Section S, which controlled the training of agents and the formation of stay-behind networks, and he also succeeded Radl as the chief of the Second Bureau, which planned and controlled small-scale operations. It was in this capacity that he was sent to the Netherlands in 1943 in order to collect reports from captured parachutists about Allied special operations. By one account, he also directed the laying of 380 sabotage dumps in areas likely to be overrun by the Soviets and the Western Allies. A thick-set and ruddy-faced cigar chomper, Besekow appeared in both uniform and civilian clothes, but was invariably well-groomed. One SD officer at Skorzeny's headquarters later remembered Besekow and Radl as 'the brains of the organisation' – 'Skorzeny himself was a heavy drinker and eater, stupid but popular', although Besekow too had a fondness for drink and for women. Although amiable, he could be brutal: he bragged of having ordered the killing of 800 men, and he threatened at least one acquaintance with death by his own hand should he ever suspect him of betrayal or obstruction.

Baron von Fölkersam was a thirty-year-old Baltic German who spoke a number of languages and was an early member of the Brandenburg detachment. The Byronic counterpoint to Besekow's loutish pug, he had garnered a reputation by slipping a commando unit behind Soviet lines near Maikop and creating havoc along Red Army lines of communication. To get authorisation for the transfer of von Fölkersam and ten other prospective Brandenburg volunteers, Skorzeny had to endure a three-hour interview with the *Abwehr* chief, Admiral Wilhelm Canaris, and even then he was only finally able to recruit von Fölkersam by slipping him through a backdoor bureaucratic channel. The young Brandenburg officer became the chief of staff in Skorzeny's commando unit.[34]

Hunke had an even more exotic background. The son of an engineer residing in Tientsin, China, Hunke lived in the Far East until he was sent to Germany in order to attend middle school. He then became an enthusiastic Nazi, studying at an elite National Socialist academy and, like Skorzeny, training as an engineer at a *technische Hochschule*. After joining the *Waffen*-SS in 1939, he spent four years in Finland and Russia and was brought back to Germany in order to serve as a China expert in SD-*Ausland*. After it became apparent that he had lost touch with the land of his youth, he become one of Skorzeny's company commanders and eventually, in September 1944, his operations officer. Hunke transmitted Skorzeny's orders, compiled reports and recruited personnel.[35]

When Skorzeny agreed to organise Section S, he got as an endowment the Oranienburg Special Operations Unit. Skorzeny felt strongly about these troops – his 'beautiful men' as he called them in one misty-eyed moment after the end of the war.[36] At first, however, Skorzeny's recruits were anything but 'beautiful', at least in moral composition, and they were hardly an elite. As the Oranienburg *Sonderkommando* was refocused away from its original concentration on Ireland, it was built up to battalion size by recruiting *Waffen*-SS convicts who agreed to undertake dangerous assignments in lieu of finishing their sentences in SS stockades. In fact, many of the inductees into the Oranienburg formation came from an SS probationary camp in Chlum, Czechoslovakia, although Skorzeny later claimed that he found ninety per cent of these personnel unsatisfactory and sent them back to Chlum. Skorzeny, however, was reluctant to give up on probationary convicts as a source of manpower, and as a result he negotiated an arrangement to improve the screening process. The chief of the SS Legal Bureau, Franz Breithaupt, agreed that his office would scour the personnel records of prisoners in SS stockades and disciplinary units and focus only upon convicts who had good records in confinement and might be persuaded to apply voluntarily for '*Sondereinsatz*' ('special action'). Breithaupt wanted Himmler to institutionalise this procedure and give him authority to make appropriate transfers of personnel.

Unfortunately for the SS, the movement was embarrassed when Skorzeny used elements of Section S – Hunke in charge – to set up joint training programmes for special services personnel from the *Luftwaffe*, the navy and the SS. Several cycles of a four-week course organised along such lines were held at the *Leibstandarte* 'Adolf Hitler' barracks in Berlin-Lichterfelde. It was not long, however, before the volunteers provided by the armed forces discovered that their SS confrères were probationary convicts. Naturally, 'unpleasantness' occurred and navy officers, in particular, complained about having to associate with such men. The matter came to Himmler's attention, and although Skorzeny and Kaltenbrunner recommended simply hiding the status of the trainees, Himmler showed a preference for recruiting future Skorzeny *Leute* from throughout the SS, not just from amongst convicts. In fact, he refused to approve Breithaupt's request for permission to automatically transfer SS convicts into Skorzeny's formation, instead instructing that cases be evaluated on an individual basis. Indeed, in the case of nine potential transfers that were sent forward for his approval, Himmler sanctioned only two, sending the other seven men to the notorious *Sonderregiment* Dirlewanger.

During the same period, Kaltenbrunner suggested issuing an appeal throughout the SS for volunteers willing to undertake '*Totaleinsätze*', that is, near-suicide missions, arguing that a similar entreaty in XI *Fliegerkorps* had raised 450 men for a special *Luftwaffe* unit. This call circulated in the late spring of 1944 and was pitched toward SS men from Russian-occupied territories, troops who had lost relatives in air raids, and soldiers 'who have nothing to hope for'. The '*Totaleinsatz*' appeal changed the nature of the Oranienburg *Sonderkommando*, although it never entirely lost its probationary character. The expanded range of recruits also caused Skorzeny's unit to grow to the point where it comprised a headquarters formation and three line companies, the last of which was formed in 1944 and consisted of Flemish and Dutch volunteers drawn from sabotage schools in the Low Countries. Skorzeny also renamed the unit *Jägerbatallion* 502 and moved its headquarters to a hunting lodge at Friedenthal, not far from its original home at Oranienburg.

With the rush of '*Totaleinsatz*' personnel, it is legitimate to begin describing Skorzeny's troops as an 'elite', and they were increasingly characterised by the usual markers of such personnel: they were subjected to gruelling standards of endurance, physical fitness and technical proficiency; they had a romantic notion of warfare and were fond of striking heroic (and often anti-technocratic) poses; they were typically alienated, ill-disciplined and tribalistic; and they were contemptuous of mass action, whether on the battlefield or in the realm of politics. Relations between officers and ranks were fraternal, a necessity for men deployed in conditions where they were often outside of their officers' immediate control. Despite this temperament, there is room for scepticism about such men's capabilities. Many of the Skorzeny *Leute* drank heavily, and a number of officers were alcoholics. One pupil at a Section S school near The Hague later remembered that the favourite pastime of the instructors was to get drunk and fire pistols in the air, a practice hardly in accord with the ascetic lifestyle promoted by the SS and which did nothing to engender respect by the trainees. We might also note that tales of derring-do aside, Skorzeny's commandos were often deployed against rear echelon troops, policemen or civilians, and that any well-trained unit of light infantrymen, given the same liberal access to radios, explosives and aircraft, probably could have achieved similar results.[37]

Such as it was, the Friedenthal Battalion had two basic duties. One was to provide raiding parties that functioned in the immediate rear of the enemy, operating from bases behind their own lines in the manner traditionally associated with commandos. One of the first places where this tactic was tried was Yugoslavia, where the Friedenthal First Company, the remains of the original Oranienburg formation, still under van Vessem, was deployed against Titoist Partisans. Van Vessem, it appears, was not a Skorzeny favourite and was dispatched far from the new centre of power. Special Friedenthal platoons were organised and their personnel disguised in civilian clothes or enemy uniforms. These '*Trupps*' were comprised of twenty-five soldiers each, usually assembled at a ratio of two Germans to each foreign volunteer, and when deployed they split up into six-man teams that infiltrated the enemy rear and camped for three or four weeks in heavily wooded areas. Typically, they roamed freely throughout their operational areas, carrying out sabotage and reconnaissance, aided by local sympathisers. When they collected information, they returned to a central rendezvous point, where intelligence was radioed back to German-held territory and fresh targets were provided.[38]

The *Jägerbataillon*'s second function exploited the propensity of special forces for putschism and conspiratorial activity, precisely the type of tendency that had created trouble for the Brandenburgers, but redirected this aptitude externally. Such quasi-military activities were described as the 'carving-out-the-brains' strategy. These tactics, much influenced by German appreciations of British attempts against Erwin Rommel and Reinhard Heydrich, were based on the comfortingly archaic notion that the health and freedom of manoeuvre enjoyed by a leader was intrinsic to the strength of the leader's following, and that by interfering with the former the latter could be fatally hindered. This type of quick-fix strategy, upon which the flailing Third Reich had begun to depend, first involved interfering with the functions of wayward pro-German diplomats and political leaders, whom Skorzeny's men were supposed to bully back into line. Operations ranged from attempts by small commando teams to steal diplomatic baggage, such as the plan in 1943 to grab documents from a Hungarian diplomat travelling through France, to efforts by whole shock platoons to kidnap or intimidate foreign leaders, such as the effort to set up pickets around the French provisional capital of Vichy and organise a swoop aimed at Marshal Philippe Pétain. *Le Maréchal* was suspected of planning a move to North Africa or of readying an announcement of his successor over radio, designs which Skorzeny was supposed to help foil by prevailing upon Pétain to relocate to Paris, by force if necessary. Many such operations were prepared but did not materialise because of political considerations.

Actions were also organised against enemy leaders, particularly by Arno Besekow. Russian historians have long contended that the Friedenthal Battalion lay behind Operation 'Long Jump', the supposed dispatch of SD paratroopers in an attempt to ambush the 'Big Three', Churchill, Stalin and Roosevelt, as they gathered in Tehran for the November 1943 conference on Allied strategy. In the West, this affair has usually been regarded as an NKGB rouse designed to convince Roosevelt to lodge in the Soviet embassy, either in order to bug his quarters or as an excuse to keep Stalin from having to travel the dangerous roads of Tehran by bringing the US president to his location. Skorzeny issued post-war denials about the existence of 'Long Jump', but if we are to grant Russian sources any credence – and the head of the NKGB's 'Special Tasks' bureau, Pavel Sudaplatov, has stuck with the standard Soviet account even in the post-Soviet era – there were at least the initial makings of an operation. Two Soviet spies, one posing as a German lieutenant in the Ukraine, the other a 'deep cover' operative in the *Abwehr*, picked up indications of the plot. The impostor in the Ukraine, Nikolai Kuznetsov, established a friendship with a German SS officer who was recruiting personnel for an operation against the Soviet high command. These men were being trained at a special camp in Vinnitsa. The key nugget of information Kuznetsov provided to Moscow was that his SS 'friend' would soon be travelling to Tehran. The 'sleeper' agent was Ilya Svertlov, who had been posing as a German since 1930 and had joined both the Nazi Party and the German intelligence service. An expert on Iran, where he was stationed at a German outpost, he had already helped betray the Nazi sabotage programme in that country before being recruited by Schellenberg for 'Long Jump'. Svetlov was given a thorough description of the plot and was sent to Tehran, along with a German radio operator, in order to prepare safe houses for SD parachutists. Although Svetlov's cover was 'blown' by fellow German agents, who became suspicious of his behaviour, he radioed to Moscow the coordinates for a parachute drop by a Ju 52 transport aircraft, which was supposed to drop a squad of parachutist-assassins. With this information in hand, the Soviets deployed a squadron of fighters to shoot down the incoming German aircraft, which crashed near the Iranian-Turkish border, littering the ground with small arms and ammunition. The German agents in Tehran were then rounded up, although the Soviets took advantage of the situation, scaring the Western Powers about the possibility of a 'back-up' plan. It is possible that Skorzeny took an early look at this operation and bowed out, determining that was unfeasible, which left it to Schellenberg to carry out the job.

In Operation 'Theodor', launched in January 1944, Skorzeny, Besekow and two of their Balkan specialists, *Hauptsturmführer* Mandl and Stüwe, made preparations for a small detachment of Croatian signals troops to grab Marshal Josef Broz Tito and then hand him over to a larger German unit. The operation, as originally conceived, was never carried out because of communications difficulties, Yugoslav Titoist advances and political strife amongst Germany's Croatian allies, although several Skorzeny *Leute* were parachuted behind enemy lines and they managed to locate Tito's headquarters. This valuable intelligence was passed on to SS paratroopers who actually carried out an abortive raid in June 1944. Skorzeny and Radl objected to later allegations that they were partly to blame for the failure of the paratroop mission, claiming that by the time it was launched they no longer had much involvement in the project. Whatever the case, several future leaders of Skorzeny's *Jagdverbände*, including *Major* Benesch of the Brandenburg Division and *Hauptsturmführer* Rybka of SS Paratroop Battalion 600, cut their teeth operationally in this undertaking.[39]

A similar plan unfolded in Italy, where Himmler was demanding evidence of vigorous activity by German special forces. Under the oversight of the SD representative in Rome, *Obersturmbannführer* Herbert Kappler, several of Skorzeny's officers developed a scheme called *Sonderunternehmen* 'Anzio', which involved blowing up the staff headquarters of the Allied theatre commanders, Mark Clark and Harold Alexander. A tank repair shop in Anzio was specified as a secondary target. With Himmler pushing the pace of preparations, *Obersturmführer* Tunnat assembled four Friedenthal parachutists under *Leutnant* Lammers, although the operation was confounded by an array of problems. One of the squad members was injured in training and Tunnat had difficulty in procuring a special boat so that he could approach the target by sea. He also had trouble in finding British uniforms with which to clothe his assassins. Three attempts to launch the team's boat were ruined by rough seas, but a fourth try, on the evening of 8 March 1944, succeeded in getting the dinghy into the water. However, the crew of the German patrol boat that had launched the small craft later heard an explosion and saw a fireball rise into the sky over enemy-held territory. They assumed that the team's boat had been spotted and machine gunned by Allied sentries, and that this salvo had detonated the commandos' supply of explosives.[40]

By far the most famous instance of 'direct action diplomacy' involved the rescue of fallen Italian dictator Benito Mussolini, a task that secured Skorzeny's reputation and made him a figure of international renown. After the Fascist Grand Council toppled Mussolini on 25 July 1943, throwing into doubt Italy's adherence to the Axis alliance, the Germans were faced with several unpalatable alternatives: they could put stock in the good faith of the new Italian regime and reinforce local German troops until the Italians showed clear evidence of disloyalty; they could pull back the *Wehrmacht* to the Alps and build a new defence line; or they could take an aggressive approach and organise SS and *Luftwaffe* commandos for a counter-coup. Hitler chose the last option and on 26 July he personally picked Skorzeny to locate and mark the key figures of the new Italian Government, thus laying the groundwork for the arrest of 120 anti-Mussolini plotters. Skorzeny was also supposed to find *il Duce*. Skorzeny, Radl and Besekow immediately flew to Rome (although Besekow was recalled in mid-August in order to deal with sabotage activity in Yugoslavia). The trio had at their disposal a complement of forty Oranienburg commandos.

Although the SD tracked the locations of the Italian royal family and leading members of the government, the notion of overthrowing the new regime was quickly overshadowed by the seemingly all-important need to liberate Mussolini. Himmler repeatedly radioed Skorzeny, ordering him to focus on this latter task, although not to forget about 'rescuing' other senior fascists as well. Finding out where the new authorities were holding Mussolini was no easy task, especially since the nervous Italians shifted his location constantly. Nonetheless, SD agents throughout Italy pricked their ears for leads. In August, an intercepted letter suggested that Mussolini was being held on the Tyrrhenian island of Ponza, and a German officer drinking with Italian sailors then confirmed that the fallen despot had been moved from Ponza to a small island north of Sardinia. After a reconnaissance flight that wound up with a crash into the sea and the near-death of Skorzeny, a joint Oranienburg-navy operation was launched. This mission, however, failed to get to the island in time. All that was found in an initial scouting expedition was an empty cell whence *il Duce* had recently been spirited to a new location by hydroplane. A disconsolate Skorzeny was recalled to Berlin for consultations, although within several days he was sent back to Italy in order to complete his task. His career hung in the balance.

By 2 September 1943, Herbert Kappler had learned from sources in the Italian Ministry of Interior that *il Duce's* jailers had recently submitted a report from a hotel in the remote Gran Sasso hills. Himmler told his local representatives to share this information with no one except General Kurt Student, whose *Luftwaffe* parachutists were supposed to carry out the actual 'rescue'. Student was contacted on 9 September. Several of Kappler's spies scouted the Gran Sasso in order to confirm Mussolini's presence, and after additional reconnaissance by air, *Luftwaffe* gliders landed a company of air force paratroopers and SD commandos in the meadows near the hotel. According to several paratroop officers, the operation was actually under the command of *Major* Harald Mors and was supposed to proceed without Skorzeny, who was regarded mainly as an intelligence gatherer, but Skorzeny insisted on tagging along in the company of thirty of his men. A 200-man *Carabinieri* guard was overrun with little fighting and was prevented from shooting its famous prisoner, which it had been ordered to do in case of a German assault. Within minutes, however, Skorzeny had begun playing the role of exclusive liberator, angering the paratroopers. Arrangements for the getaway were also complicated by Skorzeny's presence. *Il Duce* wanted to travel by staff car, but the Germans convinced him to clamber aboard a small *Storch* aircraft that they had managed to land on a perilously short makeshift runway. A second *Storch* sent for Skorzeny was unable to land, so as Student later recalled, 'great, fat Skorzeny, who weighs two hundredweight, climbed into the Storch, making the third man in it'. The *Storch* barely became airborne – only some skilful piloting prevented a crash – but the commandos were then able to fly Mussolini to a rendezvous with a Heinkel 111 and thence on to Vienna. After an audience with the *Führer*, *il Duce* returned to Italy and set up a puppet government, which immediately came under a large measure of German influence. Separate commando raids against Fort Boccea and Regina Coeli, led by *Hauptsturmführer* Eugen Wenner and timed to coincide with the Gran Sasso operation, succeeded in freeing other leading fascists with whom the Germans wanted to organise the new regime.[41]

The ballyhoo that followed the Mussolini rescue laid the first stitch in a rich and colourful tapestry called the Skorzeny myth. As early as 14 September Skorzeny was on

Radio Germany, providing what Mors later characterised as a distorted version of the mission. He was also awarded the Knight's Cross and promoted to *Sturmbannführer*. In fact, he bragged to Kappler that 'I am receiving considerable donations of money'. Skorzeny happily basked in the limelight, deputising for the *Führer* at the awards ceremony for heroes of German agriculture, which was held at the Berlin Sportspalast on 3 October.[42] Indeed, he sucked up attention like oxygen and suffocated everyone else connected with the Gran Sasso mission, including the SD intelligence gatherers, the *Luftwaffe* paratroopers, and the SS commandos who had rescued lesser leaders. Such behaviour discomforted Skorzeny's critics, such as Gottlob Berger, who saw him becoming 'a hero despite himself'. Within a week of Mussolini's liberation, the airmen and paratroopers involved in the mission had grown so disgruntled at the lack of acknowledgment that Radl called Skorzeny back to Italy in order to beat down the flames of an incipient revolt. Skorzeny met with Student on 18 September and two days later reported to Himmler:

In my opinion, Student is informed only by his officers partly of only half the story and partly falsely. There are no signs of disturbance among the men. On the contrary, they have congratulated us heartily, and some of them have asked for transfer to the SS. There is only disturbance among a few officers and the General Staff, who were always against the undertaking and, up to the last, against its execution.[43]

In a ham-fisted attempt to mend fences, Skorzeny offered to share some of the money flowing into his coffers with *Luftwaffe* men injured or wounded during the 'rescue' operation.[44]

Despite the obvious boost to Skorzeny's career, one might question the strategic and political value of his achievement. Although it was an undeniable tonic for Axis morale, saving a leader whose mystique had already been irreparably damaged was a dubious accomplishment, and it might have been better for the Germans to have based their neo-fascist satellite regime on younger and fresher faces. German officials in Rome proposed that the former Italian minister of agriculture, Renato Tassinari, serve as the leader of the new republican regime, but Hitler would have none of it, insisting that Mussolini be hoisted back into power. Subsequently, the running joke in the *Wehrmacht* was that Skorzeny had been awarded the Knight's Cross for fetching *il Duce*, but that he would have received the Oak Leaf Clusters had he brought him back.[45]

A CHANGE OF HEART

While Skorzeny was building up the Friedenthal formation and simultaneously launching his own legend, a crucial shift was beginning to reshape the overall demeanour of the SS, especially on racial and foreign policy questions. Although Himmler had long envisioned the armed strike force of the SS as a broadly 'Teutonic' enterprise, with recruits coming from areas outside Germany's frontiers, in the early 1940s the SS's restricted access to German manpower – the German Army had precedence – forced it to look for volunteers in imaginative directions. Particular attention was focused upon *Volksdeutsch* and 'Nordic' (Dutch, Danish and Norwegian) cannon fodder. After Barbarossa, this more liberal standard of recruitment was reinforced by the anti-communist hysteria stirred up throughout Europe by Nazi propaganda.

One goal was to develop Nordic SS divisions as the base of an eventual European SS army, and the sense of 'national' and racial struggle, once so central in Nazi ideology and agitprop, was increasingly subsumed within the theme of 'Europeanism'. Indeed, the SS journal *Das Schwarze Korps* talked about 'making the *Waffen*-SS into a rallying centre for all truly soldierly European forces'. As time passed and recruitment standards were further liberalised, even non-Nordics like Balts, Bosnian Muslims and Albanians were encouraged to form SS legions. This was squared with racial policy by arguing that although supposed racial flotsam was now being organised under SS leadership, such elements were not, and never could be, part of the knightly SS *Orden*. In fact, even most *Volksdeutsche* and Nordics could not match the strict standards required for membership in the allegedly elite strata of the SS movement.[46]

Despite the persistence of Nazi racial precepts, there was a cadre of radical officers in the RSHA and the SS Main Office who wanted to explore some of the implications of pragmatically working with foreigners. In particular, they saw a possible framework for an amended SS world view, in which they envisioned fellow Nordic nations not just as targets of domination, but as potential partners in a Germanic confederation, retaining some sense of their individual culture and identity.[47]

Some officers even wanted to go beyond such a limited re-conceptualisation, involving the SS in what Heinz Höhne calls 'a conspiracy of commonsense'. Although the consolidation of the 'German West' was originally aimed at more effectively conquering the 'Slavic East', by 1943–1944 some officers were advising that the latter goal be reconfigured as well, at least for the sake of public opinion. The idea of a 'Russian liberation movement' was originally developed by *Wehrmacht* propaganda officers and eastern specialists, and they had already built a movement around Andrei Vlasov, a Soviet general captured in 1942. Himmler was originally opposed, although even he was willing to countenance the formation of the SD's Russian guerrilla organisation, 'Zeppelin', and in 1943 he allowed the creation of several *Waffen*-SS units manned by peoples of the USSR (such as Cossacks, Caucasians and Ukrainians).

Most historians agree that a key role in Himmler's conversion was played by a 34-year-old intellectual and *Waffen*-SS colonel named Günther D'Alquen, editor of *Das Schwarze Korps*. Doubts about existing eastern policy had been forming in D'Alquen's mind for some time, and when he was ordered in 1944 to carry out a large-scale propaganda operation against the Red Army, codenamed '*Skorpion-Ost*', he begged Himmler to unleash potentially momentous forces by endorsing Vlasov. Since Vlasov refused to be used solely as a propaganda instrument, any SS overture would have to concede full recognition of his project. As one of the chief prophets of Nazi racialism and colonialism, Himmler was resistant, but no one could deny the logic of D'Alquen's argument that racial questions were becoming irrelevant in an environment governed by the possibility of defeat. Himmler never gave up on the attainment of Nazi goals in Russia, but for the sake of expediency he met with Vlasov and encouraged him to form the *Komitet Osvobozhdyeniya Narodov Rossi* ('Committee for the Liberation of the Peoples of Russia', KONR). From the SS point of view, it was a large concession, however captious in nature, although the whole idea clashed with simultaneous nods of approval being given by Himmler's chief deputy, Gottlob Berger, to the many ethnic separatists functioning at the fringe of the Soviet federation and who wanted, unlike Vlasov, to break up the Russian/Soviet monolith.[48] More will be said in chapter two about this paradox in late Nazi policy and how it complicated Skorzeny's endeavours.

An example of one variant in SS thinking is provided by the 'General Plan for 1945', a cynical product of SS officers involved in the training of foreign volunteers. This scheme called for a major domestic reform involving the 'substitution of Roman fascist and collectivist features in our National Structure by a Germanic National Socialism', an initiative that would in turn suggest the rise of new authorities who might look more kindly at the prospect of an armistice with the Soviets. In reality, this strategy would be an elaborate feint designed to scare the Western Allies and to draw them to the negotiating table, eventually allowing an unhindered prosecution of the war in the East. Underlying everything would be a statement of liberal German war aims, a Nazi version of the 'Atlantic Charter' that would supposedly help Germany in winning a final struggle. 'Germany is fighting the war', affirmed the authors of the document,

> not only for such negative aims as the preservation of our national life and defence against foreign powers, but also for positive aims such as the European Confederacy and the cooperative, nationalist and socialist society of the peoples of Europe. This must become the central theme of our political warfare. For years we have acted contrary to these principles and have practiced an unveiled imperialism, confusing mastery and leadership with force and tutelage.

After rallying Europe and settling with the Western Powers, the Germans were then supposed to strengthen the Vlasovites and achieve a final victory in the East.[49]

While the Germans had no doubts about their ability to raise resources and manpower in countries they still controlled – the flow of foreign Germanophiles and collaborators into the *Waffen*-SS actually increased in the last fifteen months of the war[50] – there was naturally some question about whether the Third Reich's increasingly liberal line would sell in regions which the *Wehrmacht* had already evacuated or from which it was in the process of retreating. Nonetheless, some SS and army intelligence officers believed that the Germans still had enough of a constituency, at least among collaborators, indigenous fascists and rabid anti-communists, to support limited operations. Having always conceived of resistance movements as mobilised minorities, they thought that there was no reason why they could not encourage their own supporters to form such movements and thereby harass and divert the enemy, much as foreign recruits of the *Abwehr* and the Brandenburg unit had earlier done in an offensive capacity. In addition, such tactics could serve the changing needs of German propaganda, around 1944, which was increasingly prone to suggesting that chaos and disillusionment in liberated countries would rebound in Germany's favour, perhaps by reinforcing Germany's alleged role as a guarantor of order and thereby encouraging the Western Allies to dicker.[51] For the Germans, there was no better way to emphasise the 'chaos' in liberated parts of Europe than by using their own resources to help create it.

With ideological cover for the organisation of pro-German resistance movements already developing, it is no surprise that the task was allotted to Skorzeny. Whether Skorzeny actually came up with the idea to form such movements is unclear. He later contended that he and Fölkersam had drawn up plans for the activation of such groups, and French collaborators who worked with Skorzeny recalled that as early as the spring of 1944, his people were developing plans for a Europe-wide organisation 'to fight communism after a German defeat'.

Others contend that the basic notion came from junior officers in the Brandenburg Division, particularly the young East Prussian squire Hans Pavel and the Rhineland-born Herbert Kriegsheim, the latter of whom had much experience in the Caucasus and Yugoslavia and briefly served as an instructor at one of Skorzeny's training schools.[52] Perhaps the idea, being a natural extension of evolving SS recruitment and propaganda themes, developed separately but concurrently in several different agencies. In any case, by the late summer of 1944 it had become a topic of consideration at the most senior levels of command, and Hitler authorised Skorzeny as the appropriate authority to run such a programme.[53] The official order was passed from Himmler to Kaltenbrunner on 16 September:

> The organisation and leadership of resistance movements in France, Flanders, Wallonia, Finland, all of the occupied East (also in future Estonia, Latvia and Lithuania), Romania, Transylvania, Bulgaria and Greece and any other foreign territories occupied by the enemy is the responsibility of the *Reichssicherheitshauptamt*. In Denmark and Norway, the organisation of resistance movements is to be prepared.

Himmler encouraged German officials to work with local fascist panjandrums: '…these national leaders', he intoned, 'if they are given necessary support for their secret organisations, can in each case achieve more than we can with our special groups'.[54]

An Army High Command (OKH) memo dealing with Skorzeny's new job, dated 12 November 1944, also added an important gloss on the commando chief's mandate. By this time it had been decided that in addition to organising new pro-German forces, Skorzeny was supposed to work with existing nationalist groups that had previously fought the Germans, but could presumably be convinced to confront the Red Army. The Ukrainian Partisan Army (UPA), the Polish *Armija Krawoja* (AK) and the 'National Lithuanian Movement' were all specifically mentioned.[55] This task, if it could be accomplished, would be an impressive feat: it would amount to nothing less than arranging a veritable switch of sides by a number of large-scale guerrilla groups that had formed to fight Nazism, but which had already, of their own volition, begun to assume an anti-Soviet stance. In fact, the logic of a stridently anti-communist posture had already forced some of these groups to line up alongside the *Wehrmacht*.

Finally, Skorzeny was also expected to exploit groups of bypassed *Wehrmacht* troops or escaped POWs. If possible, such bands of stragglers might be led back to German lines so that they could be put back into regular service. The SD worked closely with the high command signals unit and with experts from Jena University in order to develop easy-to-use radio sets that could be parachuted to cut-off German troops.[56] Through such means, these groups were supposed to be brought into contact with German authorities and issued with appropriate orders.

THE SS-*JAGDVERBÄNDE* AND ITS COUNTERPARTS

To carry out the daunting mission that Skorzeny had been assigned, his Friedenthal Battalion was expanded and reorganised. Brandenburg *Streifkorps*, or scouting units, were now grafted onto the Friedenthal trunk. The *Streifkorps* had been formed in the summer of 1944 in order to segregate the Brandenburg Division's specialist personnel as the bulk of the formation mutated into a regular line formation. They were recruited by *Oberleutnant* Frey, who was sent by OKW. He soon gave up on gathering volunteers and began conscripting appropriate personnel. The original purpose of *Streifkorps* troops was to filter through enemy lines disguised as forced labourers escaped from Germany, although they were expected to do this bereft of any papers, rations or radio equipment. After collecting information on Allied or Soviet forces, they were responsible for making their way back to German lines.

By order of *Obergruppenführer* Jüttner, the newly formed *Streifkorps* were transferred to Skorzeny's outfit in September 1944, with the troops being told that the *Führer*, in gratitude for their services, was incorporating them into the SS, although they could continue to wear their army uniforms and were not being asked to swear the SS oath of fidelity. Despite these concessions, some men refused to remain in the SS-incorporated units and instead transferred to regular *Wehrmacht* formations. Others endured the initial shift but later decided that they were unhappy, transferring back to the Brandenburg Division upon request.[57]

The *Streifkorps* were now called '*Jagdverbände*', literally 'hunter units', although a closer translation would be 'ranger units'; British cryptologists and translators at Bletchley Park called them 'pursuit units'. As Karen Hagermann notes, a multilayered use of the 'hunting' metaphor had already been employed by German patriotic poets for 150 years and was meant to lend a sporting image to combat, both dehumanising the enemy as game and de-emphasising the dangers of being a rifleman/hunter. Theodor Körner, writing in the revolutionary year of 1813, had said that '*die deutsche Jagd*', as undertaken by patriotic *franc-tireurs*, was aimed at bagging 'hangmen and tyrants', and from at least Körner's time, the term '*Jagd*' was associated with various freebooters and light infantry harassers.[58] Skorzeny, significantly, had his headquarters at the Friedenthal '*Jagdschloss*'.[59]

With the transfer of the *Streifkorps*, four battalion-size '*Territorialen Jagdverbände*' were formed: '*Ost*', '*Südost*', '*Südwest*', and '*Nordwest*'. These units were officially parts of the *Waffen*-SS, whose leadership staff handled personnel, discipline and administrative matters; operationally they were controlled by the SD-*Ausland* and they were attached to the *Wehrmacht* in various theatres in order to ensure local capacities for sabotage and the nurture of resistance movements in previously German-occupied regions. Individual commanders had a large degree of operational autonomy, although the fact that they depended upon the army for equipment and fuel meant that military officers had a means of influencing deployments. Most of the Friedenthal Unit became *Jagdverband* '*Mitte*', and Skorzeny also formed a headquarters staff and a special paratroop shock force called *Jäger* Battalion 600. Along with the Brandenburg *Streifkorps* came between 1,200 and 1,800 'volunteers', of whom 900 were retained and funnelled mainly into *Jagdverbände* '*Südost*' and '*Südwest*'. In November and December 1944, Skorzeny also drew 2,500 men from the SS depot troops and home staffs, plus getting permission from the *Waffen*-SS recruitment overlord, Gottlob Berger, to raise volunteers from the foreign legions under SS command. In late September 1944, Berger also gave Skorzeny permission to recruit *Volksdeutsche* from the SS training ground at Sennheim. Although Skorzeny had permission to raise as many as 5,000 men, only *Jagdverband* '*Mitte*' had achieved its full complement by the end of 1944, when the regional battalions were only about seventy per cent complete.

Volunteers for the *Jagdverbände* were subjected to a filtering process; they had to be physically fit and to speak at least one foreign language,[60] but the speed with which they were recruited, trained and deployed was sometimes brisk, a practice that hardly allowed for adequate background checks. In fact, Skorzeny's idea of secrecy was simply to tell his associates to keep quiet about their work. Security control smacked of the conventionality and caution that Skorzeny hated. Besekow was particularly guilty of security lapses, especially by admitting his sultry Belgian girlfriend, Rosita Casier, into the inner counsels at Friedenthal. Casier had first become the mistress of an *Abwehr* agent in Brussels and had then moved on to Besekow, regarding herself as a modern-day 'Mata Hari'. At one point, Besekow tried to hand Casier the entirety of 'Henriette', his Belgian stay-behind network, although this occasioned loud protests from the agents already running that organisation. Eventually, Casier came under suspicion of 'playing a double game', and she was sent south 'for her health', first to Austria and then to Italy, where she lived the last several months of the war in fear for her life.[61] Despite Besekow's romantic myopia, he knew that there was something wrong: he confessed in January 1945 that the Allies seemed well-informed about everything happening at Friedenthal.[62]

As well as being encouraged to craft an instrument like the *Jagdverbände*, Skorzeny was also given a wider mandate to coordinate all German efforts aimed at encouraging pro-German resisters. For this purpose, he appointed special local coordinators called Area Commissioners (*Länder Beauftragte*), who had the power to use various German intelligence resources in order to support foreign resistance movements. OKW noted on 12 November that the tasks of the *Jagdverbände* demanded 'close collaboration with all military, political and civil authorities', and it instructed its forces 'to support the Commanders of SS Harassing Units and the Area Commissioners... in their work and to make available to them for the preparation and direction of planned undertakings all necessary data.'[63]

Naturally, Skorzeny was told to work closely with other sections of the SD-*Ausland*, particularly the agency's intelligence bureaux, since German notions about espionage and subversion were tied together in a complicated knot. This type of collaboration involved establishing close relationships with Section B, which handled information-gathering in Western Europe and included the North African sabotage group 'Parseval'; Section C, which spied on the Soviets and ran the infamous 'Zeppelin'; and Section D, which collected intelligence in Scandinavia. Of particular importance was Section E, which organised espionage in south-eastern Europe and was run by Skorzeny's friends Waneck and Höttl. Kaltenbrunner took an inordinate interest in the affairs of Section E, which meant that the Viennese clique often worked together on problems and opportunities in the Balkans. All of these offices, B through E, formed 'invasion nets' (I-*Netze*), which were loose webs of stay-behind agents devoted to espionage, but which could also form potential starting points for efforts at subversion.

Skorzeny was also expected to work closely with the quartermasters and technical experts of Section F, who, it will be recalled, had once organised all SD efforts at sabotage, but had been stripped of this function with the formation of Section S. Skorzeny regarded Section F as 'inefficient and unproductive' and branded its commanding officer, *Sturmbannführer* Werner Lassig, with a charge of incompetence. After the transfer to Skorzeny's headquarters of Section F's most able officer, *Hauptsturmführer* Reinhardt Gerhard, relations between the two organisations were almost completely severed.

Skorzeny preferred to get weapons and equipment directly from suppliers, especially the HASAG factory 'Hugo Schneider' in Leipzig, whose director, Paul Budin, worked closely with the *Jagdverbände* in developing plastic explosives. Skorzeny also had good relations with a Nazi chemist, *Sturmbannführer* Dr Widmann, who led an SS research centre called the Criminal Technical Institute and was often seen at Friedenthal during the spring of 1945. Widmann used slave labour from the Sachsenhausen Concentration Camp in order to manufacture igniters for German plastic explosive, called Nipolit. Schellenberg disapproved of Skorzeny's shopping outside SD channels in order to fulfil his supply needs, but there was nothing he could do to stop him. Skorzeny also had little use for Section F's radio training facility, the Havel Institute, since it employed many Alsatians and Lorrainaise and was therefore regarded by Skorzeny as 'a nest of traitors'.

Skorzeny was more willing to seek help from Section G, a small SD research and cartographic office created in October 1943. Section G was the brainchild of its chief, Dr Krallert, a Viennese geography professor and another favourite of Kaltenbrunner. Krallert is on record in the spring of 1945 trying to mobilise the resources of a number of semi-private geographic and ethnographic institutes with which his bureau had contact, in particular circulating a questionnaire eliciting information about the political, physiographic and racial basis for pro-German guerrilla warfare in various areas. Krallert noted in a memorandum on 11 March:

> Behind all fronts, particularly in the East, but also in Italy and in the West, resistance movements and rebellions have sprung up on their own initiative. For a long time, attempts have been made to gain influence over these movements, to coordinate their activities, and finally to direct and extend them so as to provide decisive assistance and relief to our military efforts on all fronts. This plan can only be carried out successfully if considerable forces of our own are made available for the purpose and if these forces are fully trained and advised by experts. The making available of these forces as well as the planning and direction of guerrilla warfare is the task of VI S and Mil D. It is expected that the institutes of Gruppe VI G will afford all possible help as regards advice and training... In view of the extreme urgency of the matter, I would request you to give this question priority over all other work...

A conference on this matter was also planned.[64]

Skorzeny was also expected to deal with an office in one of Schellenberg's pet creations, the SD-*Ausland Zentralbüro*, which was set up at the end of 1944 and was responsible for the dissemination of data collected by the SD. One of the *Zentralbüro*'s subsections was '*Kleinkriegsplanung*', or the 'Brown *Maquis*' office, a small staff of four officers that was created in early 1945 at the instigation of a former *Luftwaffe* and *Abwehr* officer, *Oberfeldrichter* Dr Schoen. A legal expert, Schoen was a keen Nazi and a first-rate political schemer, having played a role in the downfall of Admiral Canaris. Although he built the 'Brown *Maquis*' office without the direct approval of Schellenberg, who argued that *Kleinkrieg* had nothing to do with the work of the *Zentralbüro*, his self-appointed task was to keep track of Skorzeny and his various projects. By mid-March 1945, Schoen was busy collating reports on the problems of *Kleinkrieg*, cooperating closely in this effort with Sections S and C, probably in the latter case with *Standartenführer* Rapp, head of 'Zeppelin' and a close confederate of

Schoen. On 5 April, Schoen hosted a conference that included domestic Nazi guerrillas ('Werewolves'), OKW representatives and *Jagdverband* officers, an achievement suggesting that he could demand some measure of compliance from Skorzeny.[65]

If dealing with colleagues in the SD-*Ausland* was a trial for Skorzeny, he had much more trouble in contending with remains of the *Abwehr*, since Skorzeny was constantly at odds with the old hands of the German intelligence service. Nonetheless, these elements were important to his purposes and an opportunity to bring the *Abwehr* to heel developed in 1943–1944. In fact, Skorzeny's rise coincided with the disintegration of the *Abwehr*, a process from which the SD benefited tremendously. Himmler and Schellenberg had long resented the dominance of the *Abwehr* in the intelligence field, as well as fearing its position as a rallying point for the conservative opposition. The chance to give form to these resentments was provided by the repeated failures of the *Abwehr* in its assigned field, and the agency's character as an old boys network around Canaris meant that it did not have the solid backing even of OKH or OKW. The final fiasco came in early 1944, when the Assistant Military Attaché in Turkey, an *Abwehr* agent, defected to the British, in the process severely damaging Germany's intelligence network in the Near East. Himmler and Schellenberg jumped at the opportunity, convincing Hitler to break up the *Abwehr* and subjugate its most important elements to the RSHA. Henceforth most of the *Abwehr* was lined up alongside the SD-*Ausland* as a constituent bureau of the RSHA called the *Militärisches Amt* (or Mil Amt), with the *Zweierorganisation*, the *Abwehr's* sabotage component, becoming the second bureau of the new Mil Amt.[66]

The army responded to this démarche with several strategies designed to maintain its influence in the intelligence and sabotage field. First, although the Mil Amt was formally subordinated to the RSHA, personnel links kept it integrated into the *Wehrmacht's* chain of command. When Canaris was retired, he was replaced by his former deputy, *Oberst* Georg Hansen, a General Staff officer. Another long-time *Abwehr* hand, *Oberst* Wessel von Freytag-Loringhoven, became chief of the *Zweierorganisation*. Within such counsels, the influence exercised by Kaltenbrunner, Schellenberg and Skorzeny was minimal.

Second, the army succeeded in detaching the '200 series' *Frontaufklärung* detachments, which instead of passing to the Mil Amt were subordinated to a new 'Army Department' formed under the military high command. Freytag-Lohringhoven, who quickly wore out his welcome in the RSHA, was transferred to the high command and put in charge of the 'Army Department', a shift that amounted to a promotion. He was replaced atop the *Zweierorganisation* by Major Fritz Naumann, a 56-year-old *Abwehr* officer who was more of a Nazi than Freytag-Loringhoven but still did not fit comfortably into the new order of things. Skorzeny was crestfallen because he badly needed the '200 series' FAK detachments to reinforce his *Jagdverbände*, and in truth, he hoped eventually to amalgamate the two forces, annexing the former to the latter. Because of the early start in the field by the FAK units, they had existing capacities for sabotage operations, plus links with potentially anti-Soviet groups such as UPA, the Ukrainian National Revolutionary Army (UNRA) and the AK. According to *Abwehr* officers, these lines of contact were threatened, not enhanced, by the involvement of Skorzeny and the bull-in-a-china-shop demeanour of RSHA fanatics who refused to make the kind of political compromises needed to make such relationships work.

New opportunities for the SD were opened up by the anti-Hitler putsch on 20 July, which implicated elements of the former *Abwehr*. Hansen was arrested and executed, while

Freytag-Loringhoven committed suicide. OKH was subsequently ordered to dissolve the 'Army Department' and Schellenberg and Skorzeny quickly rushed into the breach. Schellenberg became the new boss of the Mil Amt and he introduced a system of dual command, whereby each of the *Gruppenleiter* in the SD-*Ausland* got control of sections of the Mil Amt operating in corresponding fields. Eventual fusion of the two organisations as a 'united German intelligence service' was the final goal. Under this scheme, Skorzeny was awarded direct control of the *Zweierorganisation*, now renamed section 'D' and relocated to Birkenwerder, a mere nine miles south of Friedenthal. This arrangement was supposed to mark a great achievement for Skorzeny because Mil D now officially became the controlling agency for the '200 series' FAK units. In reality, however, a new series of roadblocks was soon set in place by the army and the best Mil D could manage for several months was to provide training and administrative facilities for FAK units, and to guide them with vague 'strategic directions'. Actual operations were still planned by the FAK formations themselves, working in close concert with army intelligence officers.

One big problem was that Skorzeny had to retain Fritz Naumann, the General Staff officer, as the deputy chief of Mil D. According to Radl, who served as Naumann's liaison with Section S, there was scant cooperation between Skorzeny and Naumann, although the latter had to submit regular reports to Skorzeny and to pay regular visits to Friedenthal or the Berkärstrasse. Skorzeny never deigned to visit Mil D headquarters or even to send a letter of introduction upon his appointment, although he did interfere with personnel appointments, purging two anti-Nazis in the late summer of 1944, and he also took work from Mil D and redirected it toward the *Jagdverbände*. Reports and proposals sent to Friedenthal took a long time to return, and were sometimes unmarked, even by a stamp, which suggested that the chief had little time for his new agency. By December 1944, Naumann was fed up and deliberately left his post without permission in order to prompt Skorzeny to dismiss him. Skorzeny was only too happy to oblige.

With Naumann shuffled off to an obscure administrative position, Skorzeny imposed in his stead Dr Roland Loos, a 53-year-old lawyer who had been in the *Reichswehr* but was considered a protégée of Kaltenbrunner, having known the RSHA boss from past times in Linz. Tall, thin, monocled and reserved, Loos was not the type of personality likely to put colleagues at ease. He had only been in Mil D since September 1944, when he began handling correspondence for Skorzeny. According to one of the section leaders of Mil D, Loos 'was clearly the liquidator of the old *Abwehr* and wanted to make Mil D a completely SS organisation... Unlike his predecessor Naumann, [he] was anxious to have Mil D swallowed up by Amt VI-S and the *Jagdverbände*, and worked hard to Nazify the personnel under his command.' Loos was constantly on the look-out for anti-Nazis in Mil D, of whom there were many, and in March 1945 he fired the highly decorated head of operations in the Balkans because he was one quarter Jewish. Skorzeny assented (despite his personal regard for the officer in question). According to Schellenberg, Loos disrupted the entire FAK control mechanism, and the SD boss later claimed that only his intervention prevented Loos from breaking up the FAK units and distributing their resources and manpower between the *Jagdverbände*.[67]

Besides struggling to gain full control of Mil D, Skorzeny was vexed to learn that even by getting the upper hand he had not yet attained firm control of the '200 series' FAK units.

After the dissolution of OKH's 'Army Department', a replacement was formed called the 'Frontaufklärung and Troop Abwehr Department', this time under the control of OKW. This new body was run by Oberst Hugo von Süsskind-Schwendi, with none other than Major Naumann doing double duty as Süsskind-Schwendi's secondary. Backed by Kaltenbrunner, Skorzeny began to shell OKW with demands to dissolve the 'Frontaufklärung and Troop Abwehr Department', and in October 1944 Schellenberg undertook a series of discussions with General Winter of the Wehrmacht Central Office, aiming to arrive at a compromise solution. A concession of sorts was eventually obtained. The generals agreed to disband the 'Frontaufklärung and Troop Abwehr Department' on condition that a single bureau be created within the Mil Amt in order to control FAK activity, that the army have some influence over staffing, discipline and administrative matters related to this new agency, and that the new body oversee FAK links with the field armies, which were determining FAK activities in the most immediate sense. Schellenberg was happy with this new arrangement, partly because it checked Skorzeny's boundless ambitions. Naturally, Skorzeny was less pleased to learn that instead of having all command functions over the '200 series' FAK units revert to Mil D, on 1 December a new rival called Mil F was formed. Mil F was led by Oberst Georg Buntrock, a career officer with Eastern Front reconnaissance experience, but also an ardent National Socialist and thus supposedly acceptable to the SS and the Nazi Party. Upon his appointment, however, Buntrock was instructed by Feldmarschal Keitel to keep FAK work 'a Wehrmacht concern'.

Skorzeny, Radl and their cohorts regarded Mil F not as a link in the chain of command, but merely as a liaison agency between Section S and Mil D. Buntrock reported to Kaltenbrunner in January 1945 that the SD was trying to 'limit the scope of the Front Aufklaerungs Kdos', and he later described Skorzeny as a malevolent force whose 'ambitions... were matched only by his blustering incompetence'. Kaltenbrunner referred the unholy mess to Schellenberg, who was supposed to work out a solution. Several German intelligence officers suggest that the Skorzeny Leute did manage to grab effective control of the '200 series' FAK formations by February–March 1945, despite the latter's desire for autonomy. On the other hand, officers close to the struggle later suggested that deep-rooted differences between Mil D and Mil F remained a problem until May 1945 and that such discord gummed up the control machinery for the FAK units.[68]

In general, Skorzeny was treated as persona non grata by the former Abwehr officers in the Mil Amt, particularly because the commando chief had remained loyal to Hitler during the July 20th putsch and had brought harm to some of their old acquaintances by helping to 'restore order' in Berlin. Note the following assessment by Oberstleutnant Werner Ohletz, the air force liaison at the Mil Amt (and himself an officer who had been briefly detained after July 20th):

Skorzeny was the most hated man in the whole Mil Amt. Skorzeny hated army officers and declared at every opportunity that for him there was no such thing as an officer's code of honour; it was only a cloak for cowardice in face of the enemy... On 20 July Skorzeny was mad with rage. If Schellenberg had not intervened, he would have seized and closely interrogated the whole Amt Abw. Oberstleutnant Randl-Semper, who knew Skorzeny thoroughly – and detested him, as did all who knew him and were not merely his yes-men – told [Ohletz] that up to March [1945] Skorzeny had done nothing but hound people whom he suspected of being connected with the 20 July affair of defeatism. Skorzeny was a complete megalomaniac and drew up the most fantastic projects. There existed no law for him; he did and permitted what he pleased.[69]

Obviously, given this type of environment, Skorzeny's ability to cooperate with his Mil Amt associates was limited.

Skorzeny had better luck with yet another military agency called 'Foreign Armies East' (FHO), which was an evaluation office of the General Staff and controlled army intelligence officers along the Eastern Front. These field officers ran their own local patrols, line-crossing operations and interrogations, all of which gathered great volumes of intelligence about the hinterland of the Russian Front. Based on such resources, the relentless Reinhard Gehlen, head of FHO, had organised a headquarters called *Sonderstab 'R'*, which coordinated resistance activity behind Soviet lines.[70] Gehlen tried to support the autonomy of former *Abwehr* officers vis-à-vis Kaltenbrunner and Skorzeny, but he was one of the losers as Mil D expanded its authority, and as a realist he tried to maintain passably good relations with the new centre of power. This policy did not stop Skorzeny from poaching upon FHO's preserves and Gehlen was eventually dismissed as chief of FHO, a move attributed by most historians to kill-the-messenger resentment by Hitler, who distrusted Gehlen's estimates about the capacities of the Red Army, although Ohletz saw the hidden hand of Skorzeny at work. On 21 April 1945, FHO itself was dissolved.[71]

Before Gehlen was pushed off stage, he made one important contribution to the Skorzeny programme. In late February 1945 he suggested that the German attempt to foster anti-Soviet guerrilla movements should be given an ideological and structural character based on the idea of 'green' activism. 'Green' was an adjective long used to denote anti-communist partisans who were not 'white', that is, reactionary, but had a strong local base, and the term had been used since the time of the Great War in both Russia and Yugoslavia.[72] Specifically, Gehlen advised that a 'Secret Federation of Green Partisans' be organised, but only loosely linked to the Germans. Moreover, this new body would be disassociated with General Vlasov, thus making it acceptable to ethnic partisans who might be suspicious of the Great Russian pretensions of Vlasov and his followers. The chief value of the operation, Gehlen suggested, would be to gather intelligence behind the façade of supporting an anti-Soviet resistance movement.[73]

It is unclear whether or not this scheme was ever formally adopted, although the guerrillas who aligned themselves with the Axis cause in 1944–1945 were frequently identified as 'greens'. One problem in the creation of such a federation was that the potential members were sometimes as much at odds with each other as with the Soviets or the communists. Many of the movements that accepted help from the Germans had contact with each other: UPA, for instance, had links to the Romanian Iron Guard and the Serbian Chetniks, and the Albanian *Balli Kombetar* and Serbian Chetniks both cultivated ties to the Greek National Republican League (EDES).[74] However, many of the right-wing partisan groups in countries neighbouring each other supported stridently irredentist claims that put them at loggerheads. It was difficult to see, for instance, how Macedonian and Serbian nationalists, or Serbian and Croatian nationalists, could ever arrive at a genuine reconciliation of aims. A German attempt to mediate an alliance between the Chetniks and Kosovar Albanian nationalists ended in failure. A FAK study in the autumn of 1944 also suggested that an understanding between the AK and UPA was impossible – the two groups had just spent the past year butchering each others' supporters in the West Ukraine – and the best that could be expected was a momentary truce so that the two bodies could each turn to face the Soviets.[75] *Sturmbannführer* Krallert's SD research desk, Section G, was tasked to study such problems,[76] but it is unlikely that it came up with any recommendations before the end of the war.

Besides contending with various army staffs such as FHO, Skorzeny also had to deal with the commando organisations of the *Luftwaffe* and the German Navy. The *Jagdverbände*'s main partner in the air force was a special unit of long-range aircraft formed in 1942, and with which Skorzeny first came into contact in October 1943. By February 1944, this outfit had evolved into a full-scale battle group called *Kampfgeschwader* (KG) 200, and it had assembled a wide range of aircraft, including Ju 252s, Ju 188s, He 111s, and captured American B-17s and Soviet TB-7s, which were stationed all over German-occupied Europe. KG 200 was under the command of *Oberst* Werner Baumbach, who answered to the home air defence force, *Luftflotte* 'Reich', although in reality the unit was controlled by Skorzeny and Schellenberg, whose patronage provided its *raison d'être*. Monthly conferences of SD, Mil Amt and KG 200 officers arranged mission priorities, with detailed planning being done directly by individual *Jagdverbände* or FAK units and the KG 200 squadrons assigned to service their needs. Bolstered by the kind of authority provided by direct access to the leadership of the Third Reich, Skorzeny, Schellenberg and Baumbach kept KG 200 well supplied and they forced other staffs and squadrons of the *Luftwaffe* to cooperate in their various projects. By the turn of 1944–1945, KG 200 was headquartered at Gatow and was flying from airfields at Finow, Hildesheim, Echterdingen, Rangsdorf, Stendal, Frankfurt, Cracow and Finsterwald, although missions were limited as fuel shortages grew worse.[77]

Skorzeny's relations with the commando detachments of the German Navy were more problematic. Patrol craft and motor boats could potentially play a large role in the waging of guerrilla warfare in maritime countries, particularly Italy, where there was nearly 5,000 miles of coastline and where the Mussolini dictatorship had created a number of fanatic and highly trained special naval units, most of which were inherited by the German occupiers and the Republican Fascist regime. Unlike the case with Baumbach, however, the chief of the *Kriegsmarine*'s '*Klein Kampf Verbände*' (KKV), *Konteradmiral* Helmuth Heye, resisted Skorzeny's desire to control his outfit, even despite the potential advantages that a close association with Skorzeny could bring. A hardy sea captain with the Knight's Cross, Heye was not fond of Nazis and on one occasion admitted that he preferred the British to 'these wild boars'. Although Heye met with Skorzeny repeatedly and could not exclude the SD from naval training and operations, the admiral retained a final say over raiding activities involving his units. According to POWs captured by the Allies, there was constant friction between Skorzeny *Leute* and KKV officers. 'We didn't get on very well with the navy', remembered one SS officer, 'but we were dependent on them for supplies'. Radl later claimed that Heye skilfully got Skorzeny to procure manpower and material for KKV training schools – a forty-man company of Friedenthal parachutists was transferred in August 1944 – but that once these resources were in hand, Heye locked

Skorzeny out of KKV operations. Navy men considered Skorzeny's SS volunteers to be lacking in nautical knowledge or to be fellow sailors 'making good' in SS uniforms because their progress through the ranks had stalled in the *Kriegsmarine*.[78]

Finally, much to his discomfort, Skorzeny was expected to work with two government agencies, the Eastern Ministry and the Foreign Office, both of which represented the type of beadledom that he despised. The Eastern Ministry had been formed in July 1941 in order to run Germany's new colonial empire in the occupied USSR. Alfred Rosenberg, the Nazi Party's not-so-profound philosopher, had been placed in charge of the ministry, with none other than Himmler's lieutenant, Gottlob Berger, serving as Rosenberg's number two from August 1943 until January 1945. Skorzeny, it will be recalled, was not friendly with Berger. Nonetheless, Skorzeny had to deal with the Eastern Ministry because it oversaw a number of embryonic émigré 'governments' claiming to represent supposedly 'freedom-loving peoples' of the USSR.

The pattern of precedence for the minuscule émigré 'governments' paralleled the system of ranking used by the Soviet political authorities: 'National Agencies' were roughly equivalent to Autonomous Soviet Socialist Republics and 'National Committees' were equal to Soviet Socialist Republics. The first such body was established in the spring of 1942 as the 'National Turkmeni Unity Committee', an initiative quickly followed by the creation of Georgian, Armenian, Azerbaijani, North Caucasian and Kalmykian 'national committees'. Finally, a largely fictional creation called the 'Smolensk Committee' was proclaimed late in 1942, claiming to represent ethnic Russians rallying behind Vlasov. The 'Smolensk Committee' had originally been backed by the army, and although the Eastern Ministry recognised it in 1943, it never controlled it to the degree that it did the separatist committees, which remained its real focus of interest. The entire initiative briefly faltered when Hitler denounced the committees in June 1943, but as noted above, Vlasov's stock rose again when he found a new ally in the form of Himmler and he was able to set up the KONR. The Eastern Ministry was cool to the KONR because of the shadow it cast over the separatist committees – only the 'Kalmyk Committee' answered Vlasov's demand for the small committees to accede to the KONR – and as a result of the ministry's opposition, the Foreign Office was able to jump into the picture and assume responsibility for the political posture and external relations of the KONR.

Nationalities living in the Ukraine and the Baltic states were late in getting their own 'national committees', partly because these were countries on which the Nazis continued to have designs and to which they were reluctant to concede autonomy (even once they no longer controlled them). The Ukrainians had also made it clear that a 'Ukrainian Committee' would never subordinate itself to the KONR. Rosenberg's attempt to form a 'Ukrainian Committee' in 1943 had already been blocked by radical Nazis and the project was only raised again toward the end of 1944. Despite the impediments, however, Ukrainian and Baltic committees were formed in the first few months of 1945.[79]

As noted, the Foreign Office claimed responsibility for the KONR, but in 1944–1945 it also assumed control of the propaganda, ideological development and military involvements of a series of so-called 'national governments' representing countries outside the USSR. With the collapse of numerous German allies and client states in 1944–1945, pro-German elements from these regions flocked to the Third Reich, mainly in order to save their skins, although some also maintained political aspirations by forming exile regimes. These bodies included the French 'Governmental Commission', a 'Liberation Committee' for Flanders and Wallonia, the 'national governments' of Romania and Bulgaria, plus the Serbian 'Government Committee' and Finnish, Albanian and Greek 'national committees'. Efforts to create Montenegrin and Iranian 'national committees' were stillborn. By 1944–1945, with the extent of German-controlled territory being constantly whittled away by the enemy, the panicky pro-German governments of Republican Italy, Norway, Croatia, the Netherlands, Hungary and Slovakia all fell into much the same category as the 'national governments'.[80]

Obviously, the importance of the 'national committees/governments' was that they provided ideological cover, however thin, for Skorzeny's project, although they also had their own intelligence services, which worked together with the SD.[81] In addition, the émigré politicians were valuable conduits to the legions of their countrymen serving in the SS or the German Army, and they played an important role in helping to shape appropriate propaganda for their homelands.[82] At the turn of 1944–1945, all German diplomatic agents accredited to the émigré governments, including the fascist regimes in northern Italy, western Hungary and Croatia, were given a '*Führerbefehl*' in which Hitler assured them that the Ardennes Offensive was a turning point and that pro-German partisan movements would be invaluable in hindering the enemy response. As a result, the *Führer* charged a veteran diplomat named von Rinteln with handling all such matters at the Foreign Office, and he instructed the various envoys to report on the measures necessary to inspire the development of powerful guerrilla movements in Allied-held territories.[83] Coordinating such efforts with Skorzeny proved difficult, particularly since the Foreign Office had poor relations with the SS. Both Himmler and Kaltenbrunner despised Ribbentrop and had long limited SS contact and collaboration with his ministry.[84]

One final Foreign Office initiative of importance for Skorzeny was the establishment of *Dienststelle* 'Neubacher'. In August 1942, Ribbentrop appointed Hermann Neubacher, the former mayor of Vienna and a possible rival claimant to the post of foreign minister, as 'Special Plenipotentiary for South-Eastern Europe'. In October 1943, he also charged Neubacher with 'unified leadership of the battle against communism in the south-east', and in December 1944, following the German evacuation of forces from the Balkans, Neubacher became boss of the 'Vienna Office for Serbia, Montenegro, Albania and Greece'. Through such means, Ribbentrop sought to isolate a competitor from the centre of power, and he assumed that even though Neubacher had been given an important job – that of squashing Balkan 'Bolshevism' and cultivating local nationalist forces – the latter would be handicapped by having his own minions interfere with Neubacher's efforts. However, while Neubacher received the cold shoulder from officials within his own ministry, he enjoyed a warm relationship with the Austrian clique that had risen to the top of the SD power structure after 1943. Like Skorzeny, Neubacher was an engineer and he had studied at the same Vienna polytechnic as the commando chief. As a result of such affinities, the 'Vienna clique' was happy to back Neubacher in his efforts to undercut Ribbentrop. Kaltenbrunner, who, it will be recalled, took great personal interest in the subversion of south-eastern Europe, considered Neubacher a brilliant political strategist, and he established an ongoing means of personal contact through the appointment of a liaison officer, the former newspaperman Theodor Wuehrer. 'Everything', Schellenberg later recalled, 'was always decided to a nicety with Neubacher'. As a result of this relationship, all Skorzeny's efforts in the Balkans had to be closely coordinated with Neubacher and his staff.[85]

A LACK OF FOCUS

Despite being charged with the coordination of a large number of agencies and military units, and with a project that could hardly be described as anything but monumental, Skorzeny was not freed from responsibilities for the type of functions that had previously been performed by the Friedenthal formation. The inevitable result was that during the last eight months of the war, Skorzeny's concentration and energy were fractured into increasingly disconnected and unproductive slivers. This was a problem that Skorzeny not only failed to avoid but actually made worse due to his self-indulgent tendency to involve himself in every endeavour that might possibly bring some measure of glory. Thus, Skorzeny not only wandered off on tangents; he lived in a constant state of digression.

After the Mussolini rescue, Skorzeny became Hitler's favourite means for the practice of politics and diplomacy by force, and the new *Jagdverbände* were quickly dragged into such operations, which were euphemistically called 'special duties'. In fact, Skorzeny created a '*Sonderabteilung*' in Section S, which was devoted to the preparation of 'operations for the *Führer*' and was led by Skorzeny's fellow Austrian, *Obersturmführer* Käfer. He also employed a similar specialist in the *Jagdverband Führungsstab*, *Standartenführer* Otto Bayer, although when 'special missions' were actually launched, most of the planning and executive control lay directly in Skorzeny's hands. Such functions were usually undertaken by *Jagdverband Mitte* and the *Jäger* parachute battalion, which consisted largely of German personnel.[86]

The first such operation involved a pre-emptive move designed to keep the Hungarians loyal to the Axis. Different factions of the Nazis had long involved themselves in Hungarian politics: Kaltenbrunner and Höttl had backed Count Fidél Pálffy, representing the slavishly imitative Hungarian National Socialists; local SS-Police commander Otto Winkelmann belatedly supported Ferenc Szálazy, chief of the Arrow Cross, Hungary's most powerful fascist party and a movement with a relatively autonomy-prone orientation; while the SD's old partner in intrigue, Edmund Veesenmeyer, now the German ambassador in Budapest, upheld the authority of the incumbent regent, Admiral Miklós Horthy. In late September 1944, when Hitler discovered that Horthy had begun to dicker with the Soviets, preparatory to pulling Hungary out of the war, he commissioned Skorzeny 'to intervene with a special unit at the fulcrum point of events in Budapest… and force a resolution in favour of the Reich'. Essential guidelines for the operation had already been worked out by Höttl. Skorzeny assembled a core of 250 men from *Jagdverband Mitte*, plus an additional 1,200 paratroopers and various *Waffen*-SS troops. The initial organisational work was done in Vienna, where Skorzeny gathered a fleet of gliders and skulked around town calling himself '*Doktor* Wolff'. In early October, he shifted his base of operations to Budapest, quartering his troops in the city's suburbs. Meanwhile, Kaltenbrunner, Höttl, Winkelmann and Veesenmeyer were called to Berlin, where they learned that Hitler had chosen to back Szálazy.

With the candidate for a new dictatorship in place and Horthy's surrender plans proceeding apace, Skorzeny was given the green light for Operations '*Panzerfaust*' and '*Maus*', neutralising both Horthy and his son 'Nikki', who was handling negotiations with the Titoist Yugoslavs. Skorzeny led a squad in carrying out '*Maus*', the abduction of Horthy junior – 'Mickey Mouse' – and his friend, the Hungarian shipping magnate Felix Bornemissza, both of whom were parlaying with Tito's representatives. Skorzeny's raiders blew up young Horthy's car, killing his chauffeur and wounding one of his guards, and then nabbed Horthy and Bornamissza, plus two Yugoslavs. Young Horthy was beaten into insensibility, bundled into a sack and then carried in a rolled carpet to a Budapest airfield, whence he was flown to Vienna. Interestingly, the Yugoslav contacts were actually SD 'plants'; one was a Croatian major recruited from the palace guard of the Ustashe regime.

Horthy elder, who had anticipated such a démarche, responded by publicly calling for an armistice with Russia and then withdrawing to his bastion on top of Castle Hill in Buda. The palace was ringed with loyal Hungarian troops and Horthy settled in to consider his options. Skorzeny subsequently threw a cordon around the castle, delivered Horthy an ultimatum calling for the regent to retract his demand for an armistice, and then overran the citadel with some Tiger tanks and a unit of SS paratroopers. Four Germans and three Hungarians were killed. In something of an anticlimax, Horthy had already surrendered to Veesenmeyer, who had been granted access to the palace a half-hour before Skorzeny's assault. Szálazy was quickly hoisted into power, and on 18 October Horthy was put on a special train bound for Germany.[87]

Like the Mussolini snatching, '*Panzerfaust*' and '*Maus*' involved disagreements with an ally of Germany that was in the process of leaving the fold, and whose soldiers and gendarmes were unlikely to relish a fight with their recent brothers-in-arms. The fact that there were nearly 500,000 German troops in the vicinity of Budapest also suggests that overthrowing the government was not exactly a magnificent feat of arms,[88] although there is no doubt that Skorzeny helped bring about this event with minimal losses.

Since Skorzeny and Besekow already had experience in making assassination attempts, it is hardly a surprise that they had a continuing mandate not only to snatch foreign military and political leaders, but to kill such people as well. According to Rupert Mandl, Skorzeny's chief of operations in the Balkans, Besekow had plans to kill Stalin, with a plot centred on a Russian courier pilot who was working for the Germans and had provided them with a valuable stash of documents. Mandl knew that an operation involving this pilot was supposed to unfold from a base in Danzig, although that was the extent of his knowledge. Whether or not this scheme matured is unknown, although Skorzeny did meet with a Zeppelin-trained Russian POW who agreed to fly into Russia – via a modified Arado 332 – and then use his array of special weapons to attack members of the Soviet high command.[89] This Zeppelin operation was actually carried out in September 1944, but the NKGB spies had already uncovered the plot, with the result that the Arado was captured on its secret landing field and the assassin was picked up while trying to flee the area around the landing zone.

After the Western Front was re-established in mid-1944, Skorzeny ordered his field commanders to attack enemy generals and senior political personalities in the territories liberated by the Western Allies. Stay-behind agents and parachutists captured in France admitted having such assignments. Hans Pavel, who had operatives in Allied-liberated Strasbourg, launched a devious scheme to murder the Catholic archbishop of the city and blame the incident on marauding Gaullists. The Allies learned of the plot when they captured a *Südwest* line-crosser, but by that time it had already been nixed by Himmler, who was aware of the political risks should the authors of the plan be exposed. Besekow was also tasked with the assassination of Charles de Gaulle, although by early 1945 he and Skorzeny had decided that De Gaulle was better alive than dead and that prominent communists, like Maurice Thorez, made better targets. In addition, Besekow plotted against the commander of the First French Army, Jean Lattre de Tassigny, although he also wanted to negotiate with the same man. At one point, he mused about putting female agents into the vicinity of various enemy leaders, who would then be attacked with 'microbes' released by his spies.[90]

The most notorious such conspiracy was a plan to kill Allied supreme commander Dwight Eisenhower. Certainly, there is no doubt that Skorzeny despised Eisenhower – he blamed him for the bombing of Berlin – and it is clear that he wished him harm.[91] The only question involves the degree to which a scheme actually matured. Many of the Skorzeny *Leute* captured during the Battle of the Bulge told their interrogators about a plot to kidnap or kill Eisenhower, and they were sometimes able to provide a startling level of detail about the assassination group's members, vehicles, disguises and likely ruses. Eisenhower's counter-intelligence chief, Colonel Gordon Sheen, thought that this information was sufficient to keep the supreme commander bottled up in Paris at the height of the German drive into Belgium, a policy that had a detrimental effect on the responsiveness of the Allied chain of command. Nonetheless, no assault against Eisenhower occurred nor were any assassins engaged en route, so when Skorzeny and Radl later struck innocent looks and denied having ever launched such a mission, they were given the benefit of the doubt by their Allied captors (and by most subsequent historians). The story was blamed on rumours that ran rife at Skorzeny's headquarters, perhaps planted by the commando supremo himself.[92]

Some evidence, however, suggests a greater level of malfeasance by *Jagdverband* leaders. A recent account by Fritz Christ, a soldier in Skorzeny's special unit and a self-confessed member of the assassination team, seems to resolve some of the mysteries. According to Christ, the Germans were aware of the route by which Eisenhower daily travelled to his headquarters at Saint-Germain-en-Laye, and they planned to cut off his jeep with a truck, force him to surrender and then drive him back to German lines. Matters did not go as planned. Several hours after the ten-man team left its assembly point at Blankenheim, its truck, travelling in no-man's-land under American colours, was strafed by *Luftwaffe* fighters. Christ jumped into a ditch and watched as his vehicle was hit a second time and burst into flames, presumably incinerating everyone still on board. The date was 13 December 1944. Clad in elements of both German and American uniforms, Christ feared being shot by either side and fled in panic to Cologne, where he was sheltered by a kindly railway station commandant and then treated for shell shock.[93]

This fiasco marked the termination of the first operation against Eisenhower, but Skorzeny was not through yet. In March 1945, the chief of the Nazi Party's 'Organisation

Abroad', *Gauleiter* Bohle, introduced Skorzeny to the redoubtable Walter Kraizizek, who had made headlines in 1943 by escaping from an internment camp in South Africa and then undertaking a cross-continent odyssey that eventually carried him back to Germany. Bohle thought that Kraizizek would make a perfect addition to the *Jagdverbände*. After listening to a description of Kraizizek's African adventures, Skorzeny launched into a tirade against Eisenhower, suggesting that Kraizizek, with his faultless command of the English language, might be the right person to infiltrate Allied supreme headquarters and kill the general. Although Kraizizek had misgivings about the mission, he subsequently reported to Neustrelitz, where he was introduced to several members of his squad. On 12 April, he saw Radl in order to pick up false identification papers and a letter stating that he was on a '*Reichsmission*' for the Security Police (Sipo) and SD-*Ausland*. Although Kraizizek's '*Einsatzführer*' subsequently ordered him to join *Jagdverband* guerrillas in the Harz Mountains, he instead headed for Dresden, and when this Saxon city was threatened by the Red Army, he fled to Aue, where he joined a municipal delegation that met with advancing American troops. His help in arranging the surrender of the town so impressed an American battalion commander, Major Fayley, that he was hired as a translator and interrogator. Although Kraizizek described his flight to Dresden as an act of desertion, officers in the Counter Intelligence Corps (CIC) suspected that he was 'a penetration agent' who had successfully wormed his way into the employ of the US Army. Whatever the case, Kraizizek soon confessed all to Fayley, claiming to be disgusted by his countrymen's cowardice in failing to accept responsibility for past misdeeds. Once Skorzeny and Radl were in American hands, they denied that Kraizizek had been assigned an assassination mission, although Allied interrogators believed the essential truth of his story.[94]

In addition to being saddled with para-political missions, Skorzeny and the *Jagdverbände* had to maintain a consistent level of commando activity, a field now totally vacated by the Brandenburg Division. *Jagdverband* raiding groups operated much like their Friedenthal precursors, focusing attention on railways, post offices and supply caches controlled by the enemy.[95] In March 1945, for instance, FHO pointed out a Soviet dump at Jaszbereny, forty miles east of Budapest, as a possible target for *Jagdverband Südost*.[96] Bridges deep in the enemy rear were also marked for *Jagdverband* teams, and one of *Jagdverband Ost*'s most significant failings was its inability to destroy four bridges over the Vistula (at Warsaw, Cracow, Deblin and Thorn), over which the Soviets were carrying material for their forthcoming offensive against Berlin and which Gehlen suggested as targets on 28 March 1945. Although the officers of the *Jagdverbände* professed to hate bureaucratic buck-passing, they responded with a textbook example of such behaviour: 'Planning re one of the bridges is in hand. Execution of [the] operation depends on fuel allocation, aircraft allocation and various personnel matters.' 'That means', Gehlen cabled back, '[that] we can't expect any action for the next six months!' All four bridges were still intact when the Red Army launched its final drive upon Berlin.[97] Skorzeny later claimed, however, that his units did step up raiding activity in the Soviet rear.[98]

Bridges and locks closer to German lines, mainly along the Rhine and the Oder, were the responsibility of Skorzeny's frogman teams and KKV detachments. In early March 1945, all maritime operations behind the Western Front, at least in interior and inland waters, were put under the oversight of *Jagdverband Südwest*, although many missions in

Italy and Eastern Europe remained under navy control.[99] Swimming saboteurs managed to damage a railway bridge at Nijmegen and they partially destroyed the Kruysschens Lock Gates at Antwerp, although twelve frogmen deployed against the American-held bridge over the Rhine at Remagen were reassigned when it finally collapsed of its own weight. Members of this group subsequently attacked Allied pontoon bridges along the Rhine, but they were scattered by small arms fire before they could cause any damage.[100] One member of the team also crept into Switzerland and reconnoitred five bridges over the Rhine at Basel, all of which were slated for demolition in case the Allies violated Swiss neutrality.[101] Along the Italian front, German swimmers made attempts against at least four bridges, including a pontoon span that was destroyed over the night of 29/30 October 1944.[102] Swimmers attached to *Jagdverband Südost* cancelled attacks against bridges along the Danube because the structures were too closely guarded, although they managed to destroy a Soviet pontoon bridge, plus sinking 10,000 tons of enemy shipping, much of it near Estergom, Hungary.[103]

Land-based *Jagdverband* detachments were typically divided into reconnaissance parties, which spotted targets, and sabotage teams, which did demolitions. Some of the cadre in these teams were expert riflemen who were furnished with telescopic sights in order to eliminate sentries at sensitive points. While sabotage troops often dressed in civilian clothes, reconnaissance detachments were usually clad in enemy uniforms, of which the *Jagdverbände* had assembled a large supply. Section S was collecting British uniforms and equipment as early as the spring of 1944, and along the Eastern Front *Jagdverband Mitte* gathered Soviet, Romanian and Bulgarian uniforms, which they used to send commandos into enemy-held territory. Once infiltrated, units maintained communications by radio and carrier pigeons. Squads sent behind enemy lines usually carried rations of canned meat, biscuits and chocolate, plus caffeine tablets. Before leaving on missions, commandos were supplied with the names of behind-the-lines sympathisers, who were expected to supply money, sabotage material and identification papers.

In one impressive action, a company of fifty-seven Germans and pro-Nazi Russians spent six weeks in Soviet-occupied Poland. Led by one of Skorzeny's protégées, *Untersturmführer* Walter Girg, this group was supposed to address the absence of adequate *Luftwaffe* reconnaissance by trekking from Danzig to the encircled German fortress of Breslau, nearly 250 miles to the south-east. Despite the fact that the band started out with inadequate rations, poor winter clothes, few maps and no transport, it quickly captured several wagons and motorised vehicles. Girg's men constantly skirmished with NKGB troops, Red Army soldiers and Polish militiamen, killing twenty-four Soviet secret police officers and destroying a number of munitions depots and security strong points. On 15 February 1945, Girg's radio operator fell through the ice while crossing the frozen Vistula, a loss that foiled the reconnaissance aspect of the mission and prompted a turn north to the Soviet-encircled bastion of Kolberg. Girg reached Kolberg on 15 March, although he and the thirty-five surviving members of his detachment were then nearly shot by the German garrison commander on the charge that they were infiltrators sent by the pro-Soviet 'Free Germany' movement. After establishing their *bona fides*, the troops joined the beleaguered Kolberg garrison, except for Girg, who was sent back to *Jagdverband Mitte*, bearing a bounty of intelligence and tips for other German groups headed behind Soviet lines.[104]

Several raiding operations were carried out at such a magnitude and length that they assumed a degree of institutional autonomy. One such extended project was developed by FAK 202, headquartered in Cracow, and was based upon a group of Russian collaborators recruited in that locality. Code-named *Sonderunternehmen* 'Jaguar', it was the brainchild of *Leutnant* Heinrich Weyde, an enterprising 27-year-old German Balt. Weyde had an excellent command of the Russian language, which accounted for the rapport that he enjoyed with Vlasovite troops. In the autumn of 1944, 'Jaguar' was transferred to the oversight of FAK 206, based in Hungary. Although Weyde was still in direct command, ultimate control was now exercised by *Hauptmann* Reinhardt, a veteran commando leader and another expert in the handling of Russian volunteers.

Under Reinhardt's guidance, a company of German, Russian and Hungarian personnel were formed into three groups that specialised in disguising themselves as Red Army troops or anti-Nazi Hungarian Partisans. The most important element was a phoney 'Red Army tank squad' that included six captured T-34 and Joseph Stalin tanks. This 'Jaguar' detachment carried out approximately one mission per month, raising havoc with Russian communications, destroying bridges and creating confusion behind Soviet lines. By the end of 1944, after several months of operation, 'Jaguar' commandos had caused seventy-five Soviet casualties for the loss of none of their own. In one instance, Weyde feigned an attack on German lines, leading Soviet tanks into a deadly ambush; in another battle, this time at Székesfehérvár, 'Jaguar' tanks disrupted an impending Russian assault, and then silenced enemy artillery with fire from their own guns. FAK 206 was told in early March 1945 that 'Jaguar' was being transferred back to FAK 202, then stationed in Bohemia, but this scheme was indefinitely postponed on 22 March.[105]

Of course, by far the most infamous example of such activity occurred during the Battle of the Bulge, the abortive German campaign in Belgium. In late October 1944, Hitler summoned Skorzeny to his headquarters and outlined the parameters of the forthcoming assault. Germany, said Hitler, could radically improve its position through a surprise offensive in the West, and Skorzeny had been chosen to play an important role in this operation. Through infiltration, shock tactics, and the illicit use of enemy uniforms and markings, German commando teams could seize several vital bridges over the River Meuse, as well as performing reconnaissance. A special commando unit would be organised for the mission, which would be independent of the *Jagdverbände* and Mil D, although it would be run by Skorzeny. The subterfuge was code-named Operation 'Greif'.

By mid-November, a training camp had been set up at Grafenwöhr, and the unit, dubbed '*Panzer* Brigade 150', quickly took shape under the command of *Oberstleutnant* Hardick, pending Skorzeny's arrival to lead the unit in battle. Skorzeny almost cancelled his involvement when Field Marshal Keitel authorised a widely distributed order calling for English speakers and captured equipment to be gathered for a special action; Skorzeny quite properly suspected that a copy of the order would fall into the hands of the enemy. The Allies did in fact capture the directive, but fortunately for the Germans, Allied intelligence either failed to decipher the proper nature of the order or they failed to impress its importance upon senior Allied echelons. Meanwhile, at Grafenwöhr, 1,000 volunteers from the *Wehrmacht* and SS were led through a programme of special training, and when this number proved insufficient, Skorzeny added four companies of men from the *Jagdverbände*, plus recruits from several army and *Luftwaffe* units. Overall, the unit eventually mustered 2,400 personnel. American uniforms were purloined from POWs, despite complaints from the Inspectorate for Prisoner of War Camps, which even protested to the Foreign Office about such breaches of the Geneva Convention. The best trainees were also infiltrated into a POW camp for Americans near Limburg, where they mingled with US soldiers and studied their slang and customs.

The plan for 150 *Panzer* Brigade's operational use was to deploy most of the personnel as shock troops, divided into three Battle Groups that could infiltrate the American front, partly disguised in American uniforms and with vehicles marked with a white star. After penetrating the American-controlled hinterland, teams could then grab and protect bridges over the Meuse coveted by OKW. To augment the operation, several hundred of the best English speakers were formed into a commando company, called *Einheit* 'Stielau', after its commander. This formation was supplied with enemy vehicles captured in Normandy and the best American uniforms on hand, and would be deployed mostly as four-man jeep teams. Several larger squads of eight men would also be dispatched in three-quarter-ton trucks. Overall, forty-four such squads were organised. When Skorzeny's recruits became acquainted with the nature of their mission and grew wary – many had volunteered thinking that they would be assigned as translators – they were told not to worry about their honour nor about their safety if captured. Infiltration methods were supposedly 'modern tactics' and the Allies were employing the same devices, although it was unsettling that some members were issued with vials of cyanide to use in case of capture.

Skorzeny assumed direct control of 150 *Panzer* Brigade on 14 December, bumping Hardick down to command of one of the Battle Groups. Almost immediately, the plan went awry. In the first place, the Battle Groups were never deployed against the Meuse bridges because German detachments that were supposed to grab a jump-off point in the Hohes Venn Mountains never secured their objective. On 18 December, Skorzeny called off the operation, although he later led his unit into battle as an infantry brigade at the town of Malmedy. The results were mediocre, and Malmedy itself was never taken.

As for the *Einheit* 'Stielau' jeep teams, Skorzeny deployed at least eight of them, plus some of the larger pioneer teams loaded into ¾ ton trucks. Within a week, the teams had sustained heavy casualties, particularly since the Americans quickly discovered their presence, and guards at roadblocks developed trivia questions about the World Series, Hollywood movie stars, and other bits of Americana. Skorzeny later claimed that twenty-three of the Stielau *Leute* were killed, captured or went missing during the offensive, although Allied figures suggest that fifty Germans were captured in American uniforms and shot.

Despite their losses, the *Einheit* Stielau teams enjoyed considerable success. They cut wires, altered road signs, blew up two bridges and an ammunition dump, and laid mines along Allied supply routes. At Liège, one bold agent, disguised as an American MP, took charge at a busy crossroads and methodically sent traffic in the wrong direction. Skorzeny gave the Stielau squads strict instructions not to fire on American forces while in enemy uniform, part of a vain attempt to protect the teams under the Hague Rules of War, although in at least one case shots were fired. In this instance, a jeep team commanded by *Leutnant* Kocherscheidt got stuck in a mud hole, and when two US MPs helpfully offered to push the vehicle out, Kocherscheidt and company panicked, shot at the bewildered solders, and then scattered into the woods.

For the Germans, the main advantage offered by the jeep teams was the tension they caused on the American side of the front. Troops going to and from the battle zone kept their guns trained warily on each other, and scores of men who forgot the winner of the World Series found themselves in jail. An entire British reconnaissance squadron, sent to aid in police duties, was taken prisoner and incarcerated by suspicious Americans. Nervous MPs at road crossings carelessly reported major troop movements by radio with little or no attempt to code the communications, which was a bonanza for *Wehrmacht* signals intelligence. The result of this sloppy breach of security was that the Germans were able to keep track of the disposition and strength of *all* major Allied units, which certainly would have led to heavy American losses had the *Wehrmacht* still been able to exploit such knowledge operationally.

After the German offensive sputtered, Skorzeny withdrew his Battle Groups in late December, followed in mid-January by the last of the Stielau jeep teams. About 1,500 men returned to Grafenwöhr. *Panzer* Brigade 150 was officially dissolved on 17 January, without much ceremony and in the absence of any Ciceronian oratory. In fact, the entire enterprise was thought to have fallen short of expectations, perhaps because the Americans had gained prior knowledge of the operation. Most equipment and personnel were returned to their original units, although some supplies and uniforms were redistributed to the *Jagdverbände*,[106] with eleven truckloads sent to *Jagdverbänd Südwest* and two to *Südost*.[107] A Skorzeny representative, *Obersturmführer* Gölling, also turned up at Grafenwöhr, making a call for volunteers willing to join the *Jagdverbände*. This appeal produced thirty recruits for Skorzeny's units, including several outstanding officers.[108]

As if Skorzeny did not have enough to do, he also developed an obsessive interest in special weapons, something that derived partly from his technical background and training, partly from a broader Nazi assumption that German racial superiority would yield technological answers to tough military and strategic problems. Working closely with special naval units, Skorzeny formed some of his volunteers into one-man torpedo squads, explosive vessel teams and assault boat units. In the summer of 1944, he also established liaison with an air force experimental unit, *Transport-Kolonne* XI *Ost*, and he sent recruits to the *Luftwaffe* as 'self-sacrifice men' willing to ride V-1 projectiles to their targets. In particular, Skorzeny worked on Project 'Reichenberg', the development of a steerable V-1. This idea, however, ran afoul of Hitler's insistence that 'the German soldier must have some chance of survival, however small', as well as being spoiled by an internal KG 200 study suggesting that the cost in life would not be worth the likely successes of the programme. Fuel shortages provided a further disincentive.[109]

Closely related to such projects was an operation to attack Soviet industry, a scheme that passed through several permutations. The notion first came either from the Air Ministry or the Armaments Ministry, and the original suggestion, code-named 'Ulm', was to use special long-range aircraft to drop German commandos into the Ural Mountains so that they could attack Soviet steel and tank production facilities, especially at Chelyabinsk and Magnitogorsk. After initial study, the focus was shifted to the destruction of electric power circuits supplying the target factories, especially since the Soviets had no grid system to provide alternate power sources for damaged transformers. Although Skorzeny was involved with this plan from the outset, most of the initiative lay with 'Zeppelin'; Skorzeny later claimed that he had turned down an opportunity to have the Friedenthal Battalion provide the requisite manpower for the project. In the early autumn of 1943, reconnaissance agents collected information about the location of transformers, and a company of saboteurs was formed and trained under *Hauptsturmführer* Semenov at the main 'Zeppelin' training camp in Sandberge. A thirty-man supply group was also formed in early 1944. Although some of the Semenov *Leute* were moved to forward points in northern Russia, the Soviets almost immediately forced them to retreat to Latvia, and a shortage of Ju 252 and Ju 290 aircraft prevented their deployment until a jumping off point near Minsk was lost in the Soviet Summer Offensive of June–July 1944.

After the Germans were chased out of Byelorussia, 'Ulm' was reconfigured as Operation 'Iron Hammer', with the new target being fourteen power plants that supplied electricity to armaments factories around Moscow. Skorzeny spent long hours working with Professor Steinmann, a Berlin University academic hired by the *Luftwaffe*, mainly with the intention of sending manned V-1s against the targets. Aerial photography was completed, but the plan was complicated by Hitler's reluctance to sanction suicide missions and by the eventual loss of the launching sites in East Prussia. Nonetheless, the project was still receiving attention as late as 1945. In February, Skorzeny met with Himmler, Baumbach and armaments chief Albert Speer in order to discuss the plan, with Speer concluding that 'the verdict must soon be delivered'. By this time, equipment was being gathered at airfields in Parchim and Rostok in order to send special piggyback aircraft – 'Mistel' – against the targets. Elaborate scale models had been built and precise calibrations for bomb loads had been calculated. The project was only finally shelved in mid-April, after it had provided a tremendous drain on time and resources and had yielded practically no results.[110] In a final irony, Baumbach later helped the US Air Force recover the reconnaissance photos of Moscow, which were hidden at the end of the war but eventually provided data for projected American bombing runs against the Soviet capital.[111]

Compounding the distractions around Skorzeny was the fact that the commando chief, like the Brandenburg officers who preceded him, found it impossible to refuse entreaties from embattled officers at the front who needed any kind of trained manpower to hold the massive tide of enemy troops and machinery welling against the Third Reich. Skorzeny and Radl were aware of the dangers of being dragged into regular combat and had deliberately avoided organising the *Jagdverbände* on a regimental or divisional scale in order to make the units less attractive to resource-starved battlefield commanders.[112] Nonetheless, when the Soviet Winter Offensive brought Red Army forces all the way to the River Oder, a mere fifty miles east of Berlin, Army Group Vistula began a desperate effort to construct a final defence line. On 30 January, Skorzeny received an order from his SS boss, Heinrich Himmler, who was commander of Army Group Vistula: 'Immediately march all available units of the *Jagdverbände* to Schwedt an der Oder and build a bridgehead east of the Oder. This must be big enough to serve as a base for later offensive operations. During the march, relieve the troops of the Russian-occupied town of Freienwalde.' While Skorzeny was left wondering how to relieve the garrison of a city that had already been lost, he did quickly assemble three battalions of commandos and sent them to Schwedt, forty miles north-east of Berlin, where the Soviet Fifth Guards Army was preparing operations against a bridgehead on the eastern bank of the Oder. Appended to the *Luftwaffe's* 9th Parachute Division, Skorzeny's assemblage consisted of *Jagdverband Mitte*, under *Obersturmführer* Fucker; Parachute *Jäger* Battalion 600, under *Hauptsturmführer* Milius; and part of *Jagdverband Nordwest*, under that unit's commander, *Hauptsturmführer* Hoyer. During fighting in February, Hoyer was badly wounded and was replaced by *Hauptsturmführer* Dethier. Forces from *Nordwest* were available because alone of the regional *Jagdverband* battalions, much of its field of operations (the Low Countries and Scandinavia) had not yet been occupied by the enemy. In addition, its training centre at Neustrelitz was not far from Schwedt. Trained sabotage specialists were not required to go to the front, although some volunteered for action. In mid-February, for instance, ten Belgians showed up 'looking for a bit of excitement', which they found. Of this group, three men were wounded and two killed, including *Oberscharführer* Edouard Op de Beeck, a *Nordwest* trainer and recruiter. At one point, the entire *Nordwest* contingent was trapped behind Soviet lines on a hill near Königsberg-in-der-Neumark, although they succeeded in making an overnight escape.

After his less-than-stellar performance at Malmedy, Skorzeny again got the opportunity to prove himself as a field commander, and again he showed himself capable but not brilliant. As many of his precious language and technical experts were chewed up in conventional fighting, Skorzeny banged away hopelessly at the Soviets. Being who he was, of course, he could not operate entirely within the bounds of conventionality. In February, he landed *Jagdverband* parachutists along the communication lines of attacking Soviet forces and had some success in cutting off enemy supplies. In addition, he encouraged reconnaissance patrols to range thirty or forty miles into Soviet-held territory, where they gathered reams of tactical intelligence and kept the Soviets off balance. SS paratroopers in one village ambushed and destroyed sixteen Soviet tanks, using only bazookas and machine guns. Skorzeny also set up a thirty-man 'Sharpshooter Cadre' led by Odo Willscher, a Sudeten German who had been a sniper in the Czechoslovak Army. Willscher later claimed that his squad killed 1,500 Soviet troops and even stopped a tank attack by wiping out supporting infantry. In positional fighting around the bridgehead, Skorzeny's forces lost ground but managed to hold the bulk of the enclave, eventually leading Skorzeny to report that the Soviet flood-tide had ebbed, at least locally. This conclusion was supposed to imply that the combat deployment of Skorzeny's special forces was no longer necessary.

By March 1945, Skorzeny had finally had enough. He first withdrew himself and some of his staff officers from the bridgehead, and then pulled back the *Jagdverbände* to Friedenthal and Neustrelitz. The extraction of *Obersturmführer* Fucker was particularly difficult, as it involved a long exchange of correspondence that lasted into April 1945. Most of the remains of the parachute battalion were folded into a nearby SS *Panzer* corps, although Skorzeny won the right to separate fifty selectees and form a special storm platoon under *Obersturmführer* Hubert Schürmann, a unit which was then withdrawn to Neustrelitz. According to Skorzeny, this flight was ordered by *Führer* headquarters; according to Radl, it lacked consent or direction from any superior authority, something of an embarrassment since Skorzeny had shortly before shot a small town mayor because he had made an 'unauthorised withdrawal' from his district. Whatever the case, Skorzeny's reputation had, by this stage of the war, made him practically immune to censure or discipline, and such freebooting was increasingly tolerated as the integrity and structure of the *Wehrmacht* began to collapse. At Schwedt, for instance, Skorzeny refused an order from Martin Bormann to rescue several truckloads of Nazi Party papers stranded behind Soviet lines, and he also rejected Himmler's demand to have one of his officers tried for failing to hold a position. Skorzeny had become, literally, the overindulged brat of the Third Reich. Hitler thought about stationing him along the south-western front in Baden, which was about to face an onslaught from the French and Americans, but instead Skorzeny pulled his forces southwards, into the fabled Alpine Redoubt. As for the situation at Schwedt, the eastern bridgehead collapsed shortly after Skorzeny's troops withdrew, and the town itself was overrun on 26 April by forces of the Second Byelorussian Front, which were sweeping forward to Berlin. The SS paratroopers left behind were obliterated in this final maelstrom.[113]

No one would deny that Otto Skorzeny was charismatic, that he enjoyed a rocket ride to a position of fame and influence, or that he was willing to face danger. He also had a sense of chivalry, almost of a Victorian character, which he demonstrated in December 1944 by defying a direct order from Kaltenbrunner to execute a British prisoner of war. Michael Obladen, the deputy chief of the KKV and a strident anti-Nazi, argued that Skorzeny was a 'congenial companion [and]... might have a good and soft heart',[114] although there is also no doubt that he often demonstrated a capacity to be as hard as granite.

It is also undeniable that Skorzeny had a chronic inability to say 'no' to demands upon his time or that his faults often outweighed his virtues. Even once he was charged with a mission that could have had an important (although not decisive) impact on the course of the war, and certainly could have fully consumed his time, he could not – or would not – free himself from a wide series of distractions. Having tasted celebrity after the Mussolini rescue, he was attracted to anything that would again have comrades slapping his back and the grateful *Führer* bestowing thanks. Thus, a responsibility no less daunting than the subversion of liberated Europe was insufficient to draw Skorzeny's attention away from various para-political missions, commando actions, experiments in high technology and regular combat assignments. Having so many things to do, Skorzeny was left without much time to provide the territorial *Jagdverbände* with central direction or a singular sense of purpose. In the final analysis, it was a situation that did not serve the interests of the Third Reich, but it was a fortunate turn of affairs for the Soviets and the Western Allies.

2
East is East

Since Russia had always lain close to the heart of the Nazi enterprise, and the Red Army provided the Third Reich with its biggest opponent, it is no surprise that *Jagdverband Ost* was one of the largest and most important of Skorzeny's regional battalions. According to Skorzeny, *Ost* was eventually built to a strength of 800 to 1,000 men (including 400 Germans, 200 Russians, 160 Balts, 50 Poles and 10 Caucasians), although Radl advised that a total complement of 200 to 300 troops was probably closer to the actual mark. *Ost's* field of operations ran from the Caspian and Black Seas in the south to the Baltic in the north, an area in which the Germans counted between 390,000 and 650,000 anti-Soviet partisans. *Ost* also had a high-profile commander in the person of Adrien von Fölkersam, who had been unhappy as Skorzeny's chief of staff and had demanded an assignment with more chance for exercising command.

There were, however, three obstacles faced by Skorzeny in building an effective instrument for partisan warfare behind the Eastern Front. First, *Jagdverband Ost*, more than any of its sister units, had the job of winning over nationalist guerrilla bands that were already in the field. The racists and political dunderheads who came to *Ost* as part of its SS inheritance were scarcely qualified for the delicate acrobatics involved in convincing enemy formations to switch sides, a reality well illustrated by events in Latvia (which will be discussed below). As a result, much of the important work on the Eastern Front was done by units of the *Zweierorganisation*, which were under a looser degree of Skorzeny control than the favoured *Jagdverbände*. Former *Abwehr* officers in the FAK units later recalled that the anti-communist inclinations of many Ukrainians, Byelorussians and Cossacks made their work in Russia 'comparatively easy', and that it was 'only SS stupidity and unwillingness to arrive at political compromise with some of the anti-Soviet groups in Russia and Poland [that] ruined this fertile ground'. Skorzeny himself saw Slavs as the ultimate 'other', masochistic and cruel, albeit technically savvy. 'Obviously', he mused, 'the westerly White Russians, Ukrainians, and so on, are more like us than the rest, but for some reason history seems to have tarred the whole two hundred million of them... with the same brush – and they are just Orientals.'

A second obstacle involved the fact that the Brandenburg Division had not had sufficient time to organise Russian, Ukrainian or Polish *Streifkorps* that could be transferred *en toto* to the *Jagdverbände*, nor did it bequeath to Skorzeny a central training school for eastern saboteurs. *Jagdverband Ost* was thus left as the only one of Skorzeny's regional battalions that never had a fully developed battle school. As a result, the bulk of *Ost* had to be built from scratch, largely by recruiting maverick Russians, Ukrainians and Poles. Most of this human material was organised as an inchoate mass, not being divided up into regionally or nationally based companies (*Jagdeinsätze*), as was the model of organisation in the other *Jagdverbände*. This lack of internal segregation probably owed to the fear that any attempt to organise such companies would offend either the Great Russian nationalists, who wanted all things Russian treated by the Germans as a whole, or the various Ukrainian, Byelorussian and Caucasian separatists, who were eager to see German political and military policy reflect their own desire to see the Soviet state dismantled.

The exception to this rule consisted of a company of nationalist Balts that had been organised by the Brandenburg Division and had originally gone into action in the summer of 1944, attached to Army Group North. German authorities had at one time considered making this unit the base for an independent *Jagdverband*, but instead it was folded into *Jagdverband Ost*, whence it came under the command of *Sturmbannführer* Manfred Pechau, a protégée of Arno Besekow and a veteran of the Mussolini rescue. A sporty type with an athletic frame and a glass eye, Pechau was 'a violent Nazi' who hated the *Wehrmacht*. He had previously served with the SS-Police headquarters in Riga, but came to the *Jagdverbände* from Section S, where he had run Skorzeny's agent school in The Hague. Like many of his fellow Skorzeny *Leute*, Pechau was a heavy drinker. While in The Hague he had been shot by one of his own sentries while drunk and disorderly, thereafter spending several weeks in hospital. According to Karl Radl, Pechau beefed up his Baltic contingent by recruiting from a circle of Latvian, Estonian and Lithuanian informers who he had cultivated during his tenure in Riga. The new unit was dubbed *Jagdeinsatz Baltikum*.[1]

A third problem in making *Jagdverband Ost* was that the entire unit was overrun and nearly annihilated during the Soviet Winter Offensive. When it was formed in the autumn of 1944, *Ost* was based at the ancient trading town of Hohensalza, situated in a portion of northern Poland once governed by the Prussians and re-annexed by Germany in 1939. As advancing units of Third Byelorussian Front thundered toward Hohensalza in January 1945, von Fölkersam was ordered to stay put and organise a self-sacrificial stand, probably in order to protect the retreat of *Panzerdivision Grossdeutschland*. Only a few of von Fölkersam's personnel were allowed to leave when the last train westwards left Hohensalza on 20 January, and even this convoy was run off the rails by a Soviet tank pack. The best Skorzeny could do was send a few truckloads of arms and ammunition. By all accounts, the battle in Hohensalza from 20 to 22 January was not especially fierce: German troops and gendarmes were not prepared to defend the town, and they had only a single tank that was soon knocked out by Soviet fire. They quickly retreated to a German artillery barracks near the market square, whence they were surrounded by Soviet armoured forces and came under fire that eventually destroyed their bastion. On 21 January, *Jagdverband* officers radioed Friedenthal to report that their position was 'untenable' and that they were organising a break-out at nightfall. Von Fölkersam was subsequently killed by a bomb, and only a few *Jagdverband* troopers ever reached German-held territory. Skorzeny numbered this remnant at only eighty men (forty Russians, thirty Balts and ten Germans), although it included some of the unit's leaders, such as Pechau, chief of the Baltic Company; *Untersturmführer* Rinne, the formation's intelligence officer; and *Sturmbannführer* Heinze, the unit's deputy commander and its liaison officer with General Vlasov. One junior officer only reached the German front in early March 1945, suffering from exposure.[2]

In early February, Skorzeny appointed as von Fölkersam's successor *Sturmbannführer* Alexander Auch, a 33-year-old Russian *Volksdeutsch* from the Brandenburg Division.

Characterised by a powerful build, a swarthy complexion, bushy eyebrows and a hoarse voice, Auch radiated a 'wild man' aura. Fölkersam was hard to replace and Auch had not much to exploit in reviving the unit, but he began to rebuild bit by bit. According to Skorzeny, he received fifty Germans, including at least two officers, plus seventy Russians who were brought to Berlin-Schoenweide in mid-February by Heinze. Mil D also contributed two camps of Lithuanian and Byelorussian trainees, who were transferred in March 1945 and were used to rebuild *Jagdeinsatz Baltikum*. Under Auch's leadership, *Jagdverband Ost* was effectively split into a number of subsections, thus implementing a plan that predated the Hohensalza disaster but now became easier to undertake because of the need for a wholesale reconstruction of the unit. The new subsections were distinguished by Roman numeral indicators, and although there were at least four such units, the two most important were *Jagdeinsätze Ost* I and II.

Jagdeinsatz Ost I had originally been activated on 7 January 1945 and was based at Nuremberg. It was under the command of *Untersturmführer* Riedl, a veteran of FAK intelligence work along the Eastern Front. *Jagdeinsatz Baltikum* was subordinated to *Ost* I, and the unit consisted mainly of pro-German Balts. According to Riedl, the formation's mandate was to execute 'undertakings in areas where pressure on the front can be relieved directly. Under this category fall also Kommando undertakings with Estonians, Letts and Lithuanians. Recruitment of members of the Baltic nations and training camps B are run by *Ost* I.' *Untersturmführer* Adolf Engelmann, a Bavarian language teacher, was assigned the task of running a series of missions, codenamed 'Wildcat', at least ten of which were planned and which were coordinated closely with FHO and OKW. With several exceptions, bureaucratic and logistical difficulties prevented much progress until March 1945, although 200 sabotage packs, consisting of Nipolit bombs and charges, were distributed in order to support 'Wildcat' operations. By this point in the war, the Allies were effectively harassing German sabotage efforts through bombing and strafing attacks. In late February, 'Wildcat' organisers travelling to Skorzeny's headquarters took four hours to get from Berlin to Friedenthal by commuter train: chaos had been caused by air-raid alarms and power outages. One of *Ost* I's non-commissioned officers, *Oberscharführer* Schwertner, was wounded by a low-flying aircraft on 2 March and supply problems had become so severe that fifty Baltic troops training at Nuremberg got lousy because of a simple lack of soap.[3]

The main 'Wildcat' operation was undertaken *not* in the Baltic region, but in central Poland. Skorzeny had received evidence that groups of German soldiers bypassed by the Soviet Winter Offensive were still near the city of Łódz, where there was a sizeable *Volksdeutsch* population and a community of 10,000 Baltic refugees. German stragglers in the area had established telephone contact with OKH – special efforts had been made to secretly repair the lines – and they claimed that the Soviets had not made a systematic effort to occupy territory behind the front. In Łódz itself, there was not even a minor enemy garrison; one bewildered *Volksdeutsch* industrialist in the city actually phoned Berlin, wondering what he should do in this surreal situation – should he resume production? Always fascinated by the prospect of cut-off German soldiers with potential freedom of action, Skorzeny dispatched a dozen of Pechau's Baltic commandos on a wild goose chase intended to round up these stragglers and harass Soviet lines of communication. Parachuted near Łódz, none of the commandos ever returned to

German lines, and it seems likely that they took their last breaths in a place a long way from their homelands and for a cause far removed from their own.[4]

According to Radl, another thirty-man fragment of *Jagdeinsatz Baltikum* was deployed at the front near Opava, Bohemia, where there was also a *Skorpion* unit. Radl suggested that some of Pechau's agents debouched for Sweden, where large numbers of Baltic refugees, mostly Estonians, arrived by sea in 1944–1945. Some of these agents established contact with the British Secret Service (SIS), which was already operating against the Soviets in the Baltic states. By the summer of 1944, Swedish military intelligence, the *Mileter Tgänst* (SMT), had begun launching intelligence-gathering operations along the Soviet Baltic coast, employing former SS men as members of its teams, and it was sharing information with the British. Such contacts were of potential value to the Germans because they suggested that the British might recognise the need for a more comprehensive alliance against 'Bolshevism', the establishment of which had become one of the main interests of German foreign policy. The Germans would have been less intrigued had they known that the chief Soviet mole in Whitehall, Kim Philby, was reading the operational reports from Stockholm and then sending appropriate warnings to Moscow.[5]

Jagdeinsatz Ost II was comprised of the Russians drafted into the *Jagdverbände* in February 1945, most of whom were former POWs drawn from the Vlasov movement. The unit was colloquially called *Einheit* 'Giel', after its commander, a 47-year-old army *Hauptmann* and commercial banker of Latvian origin. Giel had earlier been attached to the *Jagdverband Führungsstab* and had once been posted with Army Group Centre, where he had been responsible for preventing communist subversion of Russian personnel working for the SS. Members of this unit were trained in a chalet in the Riesengebirge, a range of mountains in south-eastern Germany, where they were instructed by German Baltic SS officers who had earlier been deployed on long-range commando actions around Leningrad. Their training culminated in the execution of elaborate 'dummy' missions, such as attaching phoney explosives to closely guarded German bridges (although the sentries were not informed of such exercises and had shoot-to-kill orders). *Ost* II was built up to a strength of several hundred men until April 1945, when Auch led 150 Russians to the vicinity of Opava, where they joined members of *Ost* I and were stationed at Janske Lazne. They subsequently went into action behind Soviet lines. One team from either this formation or 'Zeppelin' was flown by KG 200 over a thousand miles into Soviet territory, where they parachuted and then blew up a factory along the Volga. Ironically, German POWs held by the Russians were forced to work on rebuilding this structure. It is also likely that members of the unit fought partisans; Skorzeny is on record during this period complaining about a band of Soviet parachutist-guerrillas in the Ostrava district, offering a price on the head of the leader of this detachment. A remnant of the battalion also stayed at Friedenthal and was eventually sent to the Oder Front under Skorzeny's supply officer, *Hauptsturmführer* Reinhardt Gerhard. This fragment was overrun or destroyed as the Red Army smashed its way into Berlin in late April 1945.[6]

While it is true that *Jagdverband Ost* was hobbled before it ever hit its stride, Skorzeny had access to other resources upon which he could rely. Since the bulk of the *Wehrmacht* was deployed on the Eastern Front, the theatre was a primary point of concentration for the *Zweierorganisation*, which specialised in laying supply dumps for guerrillas, cultivating local nationalists and conducting propaganda operations (*Zersetzungsunternehmen*).

'200 SERIES' FAK UNITS ON THE EASTERN FRONT

UNIT	COMMANDING OFFICER	COMMAND STRUCTURE	HEADQUARTERS	RESISTANCE MOVEMENTS
FAK 202	*Hauptmann* Witzel takes command after the death of *Oberstleutnant* Seeliger	Army Group South (later A)	Lvov (summer 1944), later moved to Cracow and then to Frankenstein, Salzbrunn and Kollin	Russians, Ukrainians, Poles
FAK 203	*Oberstleutnant* Arnold, released from command in late January 1945; replaced by *Hauptmann* Tanner, who was killed in mid-March 1945	Army Group Centre, later transferred to Army Group Vistula	Lentschutz (Western Poland), later Brandenburg (February 1945)	Russians, Estonians, Byelorussians, Poles, Lithuanians
FAK 204	*Major* Rönnecke (spring 1944 onward)	Army Group North, later transferred to Army Group Vistula	Riga, later moved to Insterburg, then Danzig and finally to Prenzlau (March 1945)	Balts, Poles
FAK 212	*Hauptmann* Reuter (summer 1944 onward)	Transferred from Italy to Silesia (Army Group South, later A)	Breslau, later Bad Lengenau	Poles, Slovaks

After the disaster caused by the Soviet offensive in January 1945, FAK 203 was subordinated to 204 and FAK 212 was similarly subjected to directives from 202.

In November 1944, a meeting was held in Bischofsfelden in order to work out spheres of responsibility between *Jagdverband Ost* and units of the *Zweierorganisation*. Wolfram Heinze was the delegate for *Ost* and Alexander Auch for the *Jagdverband* central staff, while FAK 202 and 203 were represented by their unit commanders. Fritz Naumann's right-hand man, Gotthard Gambke, was sent to represent the interests of the Mil D headquarters. These officers agreed that control of anti-communist resistance movements ought to lie in the hands of *Jagdverband Ost*, and that the latter would maintain liaison with Vlasov. FAK units could continue direct relations with anti-Soviet insurgents, but had to forward all information to the *Jagdverbände*. Future operations deep behind Soviet lines would be the responsibility of *Ost*, while the *Zweierorganisation* was confined to organising activities closer to German-held territory.[7]

In addition to collaborating with the FAK units, *Ost* was supposed to cooperate with other intelligence agencies that were still outside Skorzeny's sphere. Section C of the SD–

Ausland contributed crucial resources, especially the information and contacts provided courtesy of 'Zeppelin', and personnel in Skorzeny's units were occasionally seconded to or from 'Zeppelin'.[8] The various 'national committees' also had intelligence and infiltration networks of interest to Fölkersam, especially Vlasov's 'Smolensk Committee' and its successor the KONR, both of which trained men to cross Soviet lines and spread propaganda. The 'national committees' were particularly valuable in indoctrinating *Jagdverband* and FAK trainees and providing propaganda material.[9]

'GREENS' AND REDS

When the *Jagdverbände* were activated in the autumn of 1944, Skorzeny's attention was directed toward two kinds of resisters in the Russian Soviet Federative Socialist Republic (RSFSR), that is, Russia proper. The first of these categories was 'anti-Soviet resistance groups in the Soviet hinterland as far as the Caucasus, built from enemies of the system, deserters, etc.', and the second was 'other Soviet resistance groups of non-Russian elements (prisoners of war, deportees, prisoners)'.[10] Through 'Zeppelin' and other agencies, the Germans had collected a huge volume of data on anti-communist groups behind Soviet lines,[11] and they knew by 1944 that there were hundreds of partisan bands active from the River Don to the Pacific, although they were especially numerous in non-Russian areas, particularly the North Caucasus, Kalmykia, the Crimea and Tartaria. Despite evidence of anti-Soviet activity, a German report on 15 August 1944 noted that the guerrillas were ineffective because of their lack of coordinated leadership and planning: 'If anything could provide a greater chance of success in combat it would be help from the outside, which would mean not only added material strength but would also provide individual units with a greater sense of consciousness.' It was also known that some 'green partisans', such as the bands of deserters and locals near Yaroslavl, sought cooperation with the Germans; others were in desperate straits because they were not supported by nearby populations and had not been able to establish or re-establish contact with the *Wehrmacht*.[12]

Some of the 'national committees' were eager to stir up resistance in their homelands, particularly Vlasov's 'Russian Liberation Movement', which had encouraged guerrilla warfare in the 'Smolensk Declaration' of December 1942. Although Vlasov claimed at his post-war trial that he had never sent seditionists behind Soviet lines, he told the Germans that his group had no hope of success unless it was active inside Russia, and his second-in-command, Georgi Zhilenkov, said that the movement 'depends mainly on peoples living on the other side of the front'. Certainly, Vlasov's staff helped run courses for infiltrators, which were provided at a facility in Dabendorf bei Berlin,[13] and the staffs of several 'partisan brigades' made plans for the dispatch of three-man groups into Russia by parachute. These squads were charged with instituting a four-stage strategy that began with the agitation of the members' families and friends and was supposed to culminate in the waging of guerrilla warfare, the organisation of anti-Stalinist cells in the Red Army and the encouragement of regional revolts.[14]

As the Germans retreated from Russia, they made the best effort possible, given shortages of manpower and resources, to leave stay-behind groups and to support bands sympathetic to the Axis cause. 'Zeppelin' was ordered 'to make every effort to leave activists with wireless transmitter sets in regions evacuated by the Germans',[15] although it faced difficulties in carrying out such tasks. *Sturmbannführer* Röder explained in September 1943:

> All pro-Germans suitable for our purposes are definitely leaving, and any remaining behind who are suitable for us are afraid of the Reds and lack faith in German affairs... [It is] extraordinarily difficult to leave groups behind; the Caucasian and Turkestan activists here are conspicuous through their accents, appearance, etc. They also refuse to remain behind in areas unfamiliar to them.

It was also difficult to leave or infiltrate agents because of the tight system of Soviet passes and controls.[16]

Despite myriad problems, 'Zeppelin', the *Abwehr* and the German Army did attend to matters of stay-behind placement and infiltration, particularly in areas inhabited by non-Russian minorities. As the *Wehrmacht* pulled out of the North Caucasus, it left weapons for local populations, plus deploying scattered German detachments that joined 'green' partisans as they fled to the hills. Caucasian paratroopers trained at Oranienburg were formed into platoons or small companies and dropped into the mountains in the company of German officers. The *Abwehr* dispatched similar units throughout 1942–1943, and as late as September 1944, 'Zeppelin' groups in the Caucasus were being ordered to establish contact with local partisans.

In Kalmykia, the 16th *Panzerdivision* made efforts to set up a network of 'green bands', and after the German retreat, daily *Luftwaffe* flights over the area east of Elitsa suggested that these partisans were being re-supplied. This programme, however, ended badly. In June 1944, a Ju 290 flew out of an airfield in Romania with thirty uniformed Kalmyk guerrillas, all refugees who had fled with 16th *Panzerdivision* during its retreat. After landing its passengers near Elitsa, the Ju 290 was supposed to be camouflaged and then fly back to Romania on the following night, although this plan was ruined when Red Air Force fighters spotted the aircraft and Soviet ground troops overwhelmed the crew. The Soviets then forced the German radio operator to send out a rescue call, which lured a second Ju 290 and led to the capture of that aircraft and its crew. After losing two machines (and their crews), Berlin came to suspect a Soviet 'radio game' and they also assumed that their Kalmyk guerrillas had fallen into Soviet hands.

Generally, Stalin's response to anti-Soviet resistance was brutal. He moved security regiments into the effected areas, equipped with artillery and sniffer dogs. Eighty per cent of the paratroopers dropped into the Caucasus were tracked down and annihilated. Although the hard-pressed Kalmyks managed to wipe out a company of Soviet secret police, the NKGB eventually rallied to defeat the guerrillas in both the North Caucasus and Kalmykia, and they destroyed the partisans' support bases by deporting whole nations and tribes into Asia.[17] As late as 1944–1945, however, Mil D could still report that 8,000 armed Chechen and Ingush horsemen had retreated into the mountains, where they were keeping their herds and raiding Soviet transport.[18]

Of course, the real prize was comprised of Russian-speaking bands which, if properly cultivated, could undercut the war effort of the Russian population, or at least call the loyalty of that population into question. The most important of these bands were made up of locally recruited *Wehrmacht* auxiliaries, labour troops and gendarmes who had been bypassed in Soviet advances. Most of these men had at least a passing familiarity with the pro-German stance of Vlasov and were therefore called 'Vlasovites'. The political nature of such bands varied: some behaved like marauder gangs, particularly in areas where German civil and Nazi Party officials had earlier exercised control and had given everybody, even those willing to collaborate, a good look at the true nature of Nazism; others assumed a more decidedly political hue, mainly in regions that had formerly been under control of *Wehrmacht* authorities and where Vlasovite propaganda had been liberally disseminated; some groups, particularly along the boundary of the Ukraine and the RSFSR, were defined by the Nazis as being 'pronouncedly pro-German', having only 'weak nationalist tendencies'. A few such groups were led by escaped German POWs. In the more easterly territories never occupied by the Germans, guerrilla groups were comprised mainly of draft dodgers and deserters, although these groups were not as well armed as their western Russian counterparts because they could not scavenge weapons from the battlefield. Their main points of concentration were the regions around Kalinin, Kirov and Tambov (the latter of which had been a gathering ground for anti-Soviet guerrillas in the early 1920s), although as far east as Yakutsk there were bands raiding the Trans-Siberian Railway. All these groups, both in previously occupied and unoccupied territory, distinguished themselves by ambushing Soviet military and civilian transports, shooting local communist officials and Kolkhozy leaders, and blowing up bridges and rail lines.[19]

By the time that Skorzeny received his mandate for waging guerrilla warfare, a number of efforts in Russia were reaching a point of fruition. In August 1944, the *Luftwaffe* dropped three radio-equipped squads of parachutists into central Russia. These Russian legionaries, trained by FAK 204, were code-named 'Borgia' I, II and III. Although 'Borgia' I and II never contacted their German controllers, 'Borgia' III reported several successful sabotage actions and was reinforced through parachute drops. By the beginning of 1945, however, the guerrillas had begun to show a diminishing appetite for action and in March communications were severed.[20]

A particular flow of manpower and resources was directed toward the Central Russian Highlands, a range of low hills and forests between Smolensk, Briansk and Orel. While this area was under German occupation, the Nazis had encountered considerable anti-Stalinist sentiment and Second *Panzer* Army had enjoyed success in mobilising an anti-partisan militia called the 'Russian National Army of Liberation' (RONA).[21] Although 50,000 RONA troops and supporters withdrew with the Germans, a number fled to the local woods and accounted for the anti-Soviet marauders frequently reported to be prowling the region. These groups blew up bridges and rail lines, cut communication wires and shot at Soviet aircraft, although as a 'Zeppelin' report noted, their activity was motivated more by fear of capture than by dedication to any specific political programme.[22] In the summer of 1944, a 'Zeppelin' station in Danzig made contact with RONA and began parachuting technical specialists, supplies and radios to guerrillas near Briansk, asking that they organise reception areas and burn signal fires in order to designate drop zones. The morale of these guerrillas was buoyed up with promises of extraction, although this was complicated by the retraction of German lines during the 1945 Soviet Winter Offensive.[23]

FAK 203 also began training Russian volunteers in order to deploy them in the Central Highlands, where they could support existing guerrilla groups and carry out sabotage. This operation was dubbed *Insurgierungsunternehmen 'Mob Tag'*. Efforts were closely coordinated between Mil D and Major Pavlov of the Vlasov Army. In late August 1944, the first dozen *'Mob Tag'* trainees, heavily armed and dressed in Red Army uniforms, were flown to a contact point east of Chernigov, in the northern Ukraine, but the Ju 290's spotter saw so many blazes in the woods around the drop zone that he could not distinguish the signal fires that guerrillas on the ground had been instructed to light. Thus, the *'Mob Tag'* parachutists were returned to base and the nationalist guerrillas were instructed to burn green flares so that future signal fires would be discernible. In a return flight on 4 September, the crew of the Ju 290 found the drop zone and the parachutists were successfully deployed, being met on the ground by a reception committee. Three tons of dynamite were also dropped. In all, fifty *'Mob Tag'* volunteers were dropped in successive waves, and they subsequently reported the demolition of railways, enemy vehicles and supply dumps. The *Luftwaffe* re-supplied these forces in December 1944 and April 1945.

The *'Mob Tag'* groups were also reinforced by further parties of parachutists, code-named 'Wolf', although Project 'Wolf' failed for a number of reasons. An initial ten-man group was dropped east of Toropets on 31 August 1944, but as the KG 200 aircraft veered away from the drop zone, the crew observed a ring of vehicle headlights converging upon the field, suggesting that the Soviets were waiting and that 'Wolf' had been betrayed. A second group was dropped near Briansk in the autumn of 1944. This team managed to report by wireless, although the Germans came to feel that its leaders were more concerned with banditry than in waging guerrilla warfare.

FAK 202 was also interested in the Central Highlands. In 1943, two partisan warfare specialists, Hans Raupach and Walter Hösch, drew up a scheme called 'Aurora', which they subsequently developed in coordination with an ex-Red Air Force squadron leader, A.N. Kusnetzov, who was in close contact with Vlasov's staff. Planners hoped that 'Aurora' would activate Vlasovite cells behind Soviet lines and that anti-communist militants would conduct propaganda. An initial group of fifteen Russians began training in May 1944 at a FAK 202 camp near Cracow. National Solidarists (NTS), a network of Russian fascists originally based in the exile community, were the dominant force amongst the recruits, although the SD distrusted the NTS because of suspicions that they had been infiltrated by the Soviet intelligence service. Police restrictions imposed on NTS members made the training and indoctrination of such elements problematic.

In mid-August 1944, three former Soviet air force officers trained as part of 'Aurora' were parachuted into the Briansk Forest with the mission of causing sedition and winning converts to the German cause. In late October, an additional squad was dropped into the Upper Desna region, where it had orders to set up NTS cells and reinforce *'Mob Tag'* and 'Wolf'. Since the Germans were poor at coordinating operations run by different elements of the *Zweierorganisation*, this attempt to link FAK 202 and 203 formations wound up in a typical fiasco. When the 'Aurora' and 'Wolf' detachments first came into contact, each regarded the other as a Soviet militia unit and heavy fighting broke out before the situation could be clarified. German controllers in Cracow rolled their eyes and decided not to reinforce 'Aurora'.[24]

How 'Aurora' and its sister detachments ultimately fared is not clear. They were probably overrun by the Soviet authorities, at least eventually, although right-wing Russian exiles continued to insist as late as 1946 that there were nationalist partisans still holding out in the Briansk Forest.[25]

Despite occasional successes, there were two outstanding problems hindering Skorzeny's efforts in Russia. First, the *Zweierorganisation* had always feared that many of its Russian volunteers were simply opportunists who wanted a way to return home or, worse yet, that they were playing a double game in favour of the NKGB. In the later years of the war, the Soviet victory at Stalingrad increased Stalin's prestige and the creation of a more liberal and patriotic atmosphere in the USSR led even resolute enemies of the regime to reconsider their opposition. The answer to the challenge, according to the Germans, was *not* to recruit mercenaries or desperados, but to attract ideologically charged anti-Stalinists, which naturally brought them to Vlasov's doorstep. By 1944, the *Abwehr* was telling Vlasovite operatives that their leader was the most recent in a line of socialist heroes who had quarrelled with Stalin – Lenin, Frunze, Blücher and Tukachevsky had all supposedly fit into the same category – and that their German patrons were 'national socialist', *not* 'fascist'. Even with Vlasov as an asset, however, the Germans still assumed that most Soviet POWs who expressed interest in 'Russian liberation' had 'volunteered' under a measure of duress and that many simply reported to the Soviet authorities after deployment behind enemy lines. The Germans also favoured Caucasians or Tartars, but their faith in such elements was thrown into doubt when a Muslim detachment being trained for parachute operations deserted to Soviet Partisans near Vinnitsa.[26] KG 200 crews worried about carrying heavily armed groups of parachutists who were surly and some of whom were suspected of being double agents. What would happen, they wondered, if one of these agents decided to toss a live grenade back into the fuselage as he jumped out of the hatch?[27]

Another problem with late-blooming operations against the RSFSR involved shortages of aircraft. Some of KG 200's limited range machines, like the Heinkel 111, could barely reach Russian territory by the autumn of 1944. The four-engine Junkers 290 could make round trip flights from East Prussia to Central Asia, but Hitler had never shown much interest in this aircraft and only sixty-five were built. Captured American B-17s could also reach deep into Soviet territory, and they were flown on such missions from an airfield near Cracow, but again, KG 200 had only a small number of such aircraft. Some Russian teams were deployed along the non-Russian fringe of the Soviet Union, which was still within range of *Luftwaffe* aircraft. Such was the case, for instance, with a Russian squad dropped in April 1944 and another that parachuted in December 1944, both in the Transnistrian territories that had been claimed by Romania but were later re-conquered by the USSR.

The lack of air power impinged especially upon the deployment of Caucasians, Tartars and Central Asian Turks, the very people in whom the Germans had invested much of their trust. So although the Kabardine 'National Committee' encouraged the Germans to field an entire 'Caucasian National Army' by parachute, the *Luftwaffe* barely had sufficient capacity to drop small groups and supply packages into the mountains. In fact, the loss of airfields in Crimea hindered even those limited operations.

One casualty of the aircraft crunch was collaboration with the Vlasovites. Vlasov was acutely aware that hundreds of Soviet transport planes had been deployed to help communist Partisans and he was disappointed by the German failure to match the scale of this effort. In fact, the *Luftwaffe* seemed unable to array any more than several dozen aircraft in guerrilla warfare operations. German officers attributed Vlasov's thinking to a supposedly unfortunate Slavic tendency to consider matters only in terms of mass, but try as they did, they could not assuage his scepticism. His willingness to cooperate disappeared completely after the German retreats in the winter of 1945.[28] Rather, after the proclamation of the KONR, Vlasov built his own small Russian nationalist air force, which was used to drop agents and propaganda material behind Soviet lines.[29]

Since the lack of aircraft prohibited the dropping of many Russian operatives into their homeland, such agents were increasingly deployed close to the fronts in Poland and the Balkans. In the Küstrin bridgehead, thirty Russian nationalists were led into battle by FAK lieutenants Hirschheydt and Erben, and in Pomerania, Waldemar Göttler, one of the masterminds behind '*Mob Tag*', tried to get a detachment of Russian legionaries across Soviet lines. East of Warsaw, five teams of Russian adolescents parachuted behind Red Army lines. Their task was to destroy railway locomotives by putting explosive coal in the tenders, a mission that scored some successes and caused alarm among Soviet security forces. Two similar teams, heavily armed and disguised in Soviet uniforms, were dropped near Lublin on 18/19 January 1945. In Yugoslavia, a company of Russians trained by Section S was sent to the front, and a company of Kasachs – *Einheit 'Pfeil'* – was mustered to fight Titoite Partisans.[30]

In the final analysis, the military worth of Russian guerrillas was a trifle, but the movement did yield some propaganda value, which both Goebbels and Himmler attempted to exploit. It was stressed in Nazi media that 'millions' of Russians had risen against Stalin, particularly in the North Caucasus, the Lower Volga basin and the Central Russian Highlands. The purpose of making such claims was fourfold. First, they implicitly excused Hitler's 1941 invasion of Soviet Russia, which was increasingly regarded by Germans as a monumental error. Propaganda suggested that the 'Russian Liberation Movement' had long been latent, and that Germany's attempt to 'liberate' the USSR had actualised it. Second, news about 'Vlasovite' guerrillas was a morale-booster in Germany's remaining Slavic satellites, and it played well in liberated countries with Russophile traditions, such as Serbia and Bulgaria, where Skorzeny was attempting to support anti-communist resistance movements. Third, the message was meant to scare Germans, who were led to think that if even Russians regarded 'Bolshevism' as a mortal peril, their own defensive efforts ought to be correspondingly more intense.[31] And finally, such propaganda was supposed to provide hope that Soviet military momentum might be slowed by internal disruptions, although this line of argument backfired when the Red Army cut deep into the heart of eastern Germany in early 1945, apparently undeterred by hostile guerrillas. Despite the fact that Nazi claims had thus been contradicted by the course of events, German propagandists kept hammering away at the theme until the end of the war.[32]

FACT AND FANCY IN BYELORUSSIA

Because the RSFSR was so far afield, Skorzeny's attentions were more focussed upon the western borderlands of the USSR, which were inhabited by Slavic ethnic groups that were increasingly coming to identify themselves as something apart from Russian. Byelorussia was not specifically mentioned to Skorzeny as a possible field of operations, probably because the country was remembered as a recent hotbed of Soviet Partisan activity and was regarded by Nazis as a racially inferior backwater. Upon consideration, however, Skorzeny saw several opportunities to threaten the peace and security of the newly liberated republic.

During the German occupation, Nazi hysterics had created a two-dimensional picture that did not do justice to the true complexity of the Byelorussian situation. Although the region's great forests and marshes provided bases for numerous Soviet Partisan detachments, they also gave cover to various 'green' and anti-Jewish bands. Beyond their anti-Semitism and doubts about Stalinism, such groups had only vague political tendencies, which reflected the fact that the Byelorussian people generally lacked a distinct sense of themselves vis-à-vis the Great Russians. While this ambiguity might seem a problem in the potential organisation of an anti-Soviet resistance movement, the few Germans who bothered to explore such issues believed that it could actually be an advantage, making it easier to turn ideologically inchoate bands toward German purposes. On the other hand, the nebulous nature of the bands had also meant that the proper measure of propaganda and duress by Soviet Partisans could lure the guerrillas back toward the Soviet side, something that had been repeatedly demonstrated.

There was a Byelorussian nationalist movement, but it was relatively weak. Like its Baltic and Ukrainian counterparts, the movement had been exploited by the Germans in 1941 in order to mount diversionist operations against the Red Army, only to find its hopes for Byelorussian autonomy crushed by the subsequent reality of German occupation. Nonetheless, many of the movement's veterans were drafted into German auxiliary units, and after the tide of the war shifted in 1943, the Nazis began to reconsider their treatment of the nationalists, allowing them to form a 'Byelorussian Central Council'.[33]

For the Germans, there was even more to consider as Byelorussia fell into Soviet hands. The Red Army had grabbed control of the eastern part of the country by early 1944, but there was evidence that not all was well behind enemy lines. Large bands formed in the south-eastern corner of the republic, where there had been 'white' partisan activity in the early 1920s. Numbering 20,000 men, these groups attacked Soviet headquarters and damaged railways, highways and bridges.[34]

After a massive Soviet offensive in June 1944, the Germans lost their last footholds in Byelorussia, although cut-off eastern auxiliaries and German soldiers formed new guerrilla groups. Rural folk in wooded regions complained that they could hardly sleep at night because of constant firefights between Soviet patrols and *Wehrmacht* stragglers. As the Red Army advanced through central and western Byelorussia, policemen and functionaries of the German puppet regime, many of them Byelorussian nationalists, fled to the forests for safety. The Soviets claimed that such 'forest fugitives' were controlled by the Germans and had belonged to pro-German organisations, particularly the NTS. According to the Soviet 51st Army, remnants of the 'Byelorussian Home Defence' and SD auxiliaries were roaming the forests north and north-west of Minsk, some in bands as large as 8,000 men. Beginning in July 1944, such groups began attacking the railway between Pinsk and Sarny, and they also forced the Soviets to put a heavy guard on the line between Baranovice and Brest. German reports suggested a degree of lingering popular loyalty to the pro-German puppet regime.[35]

Encouraged by such news, Skorzeny arranged a meeting with the leaders of the former administration in Byelorussia, all of whom had beat a hasty retreat to Berlin in June and July 1944. These men, Radislav Ostrowsky, V.I. Rodko and Mikolai Abramtchik, agreed to cooperate in finding recruits and staff for several sabotage schools that could train infiltrators. Such line-crossers, it was felt, could serve as rallying points for partisans who had already fled to the woods. Two SD facilities were established, one at Dahlwitz, near Berlin, and a second at Walbuze, in East Prussia. Radio communications, encoding, demolitions and assassination techniques were taught at these schools. FAK 203 also established a Byelorussian camp at Insterburg, which was run by *Major* Gerullis. This facility was later evacuated to Boitzenburg, in Pomerania, and was eventually transferred to *Jagdverband Ost*.

In the late summer and autumn of 1944, FAK 203 sent several teams into Soviet-liberated areas of Byelorussia, and these detachments were followed by a thirty-man paratroop unit codenamed the 'Black Cats' and led by Michael Vitushka. A number of groups with radio transmitters were also air-dropped into the area east of Vilna, where they operated so effectively that the Germans made plans for large-scale parachute drops in the region, although such operations were impossible to execute because of the shortage of aircraft. Other detachments filtered through the dense Bielavieza Forest, near Bialystok, and such squads had considerable success in rousing the 'forest fugitives' to greater levels of insurgency. German intelligence reports suggested lively anti-Soviet partisan activity in the Marijampole area and in December 1944 nationalists disguised in Soviet uniforms attacked a Minsk airfield, blowing up an ammunition dump and destroying several planes.

The Soviets, of course, provided a brutal response, particularly since they needed to protect vital transport arteries leading to the front in Poland and eastern Germany. A fifty-mile border strip was forcibly evacuated, and a fierce purge burned through Byelorussian towns and villages as the Soviets arrested pro-German collaborators. The NKGB was willing to deploy an entire division in order to chase several infiltrators through the woods or question several hundred thousand people for leads. Deployment of manpower on this scale made life for the guerrillas very difficult. The presence of seasoned Soviet Partisans who had functioned in the area also provided the authorities with an invaluable local auxiliary. Finally, it was rumoured that a small number of NKGB informants had wormed their way into the woodwork at Dahlwitz and other camps, so that the Soviets may have had prior knowledge about where nationalist infiltrators would cross the lines or how they would be deployed. Some of the *Jagdverband* and FAK paratroopers were able to break back through to German lines, particularly while their bases in East Prussia were still available, but most were tracked down and killed. Within three months, the German network in Byelorussia had been all but eliminated; the chief of the underground in Minsk was arrested and shot in early March 1945, his body being dumped on the street, along with those of six of his comrades. The last guerrillas were almost certainly liquidated by 1946, and Vitushka himself was hunted down, captured and executed, although he continued to live on in Byelorussian nationalist hagiography.[36]

Another opportunity involved the tens of thousands of German stragglers trapped in the woods of the Byelorussian republic. Some of these soldiers broke up into small groups and attempted a return to German lines. Although most were captured by the Soviets, 800 succeeded in reaching the German front, where they had interesting stories to tell. Byelorussian civilians, they said, were often friendly and had provided provisions. Red Army prisoners taken by the Germans also told of attacks on Soviet outposts by bypassed German troops still holding out in Byelorussia. Civilians living east of Brest reported the existence of a band of German and Hungarian stragglers.[37]

For Skorzeny and his cohorts, however, the most important fragment of information came from Aleksandr Demyanov, a member of the pre-1917 gentry who had deserted to the Germans in 1941, had been recruited by the *Abwehr*, and had then parachuted back into the Moscow region in February 1942. Demyanov had used his Moscow contacts and his skill as an electrical engineer in order to get a job as a junior communications officer at Stavka, the Red Army high command, thus becoming the *Abwehr's* most important agent behind Soviet lines. In 1944, Demyanov visited the communications department of the Red Army headquarters in Byelorussia, whence on 19 August he sent a message to Berlin suggesting that a huge concentration of bypassed German troops had been stranded along the Berezina river. Led by the former commander of *Landeschützen* Battalion 675, Heinrich Scherhorn, this group allegedly occupied a camp formerly used by Soviet Partisans, and provisioned itself through foraging raids. In September, Scherhorn established a link with Army Group Centre via Demyanov. He claimed that his group was constantly accumulating more men, as cut-off troops gravitated to the central mass, and that as a result of these additions his troop strength had risen to 2,700 men, including 200 eastern auxiliaries. He also had a small force of tanks and artillery. Morale, however, was supposed to be declining, and Scherhorn claimed that it could be resuscitated only by a breakthrough drive to the west, for which he needed supplies.

Officers at Army Group Centre were uncertain about what to do. The *Ostheer* usually made it a point of honour (and of practical necessity) to break such forces out of encirclement. The Scherhorn group, however, was more than 100 miles behind enemy lines, which made any rescue a daunting task. Moreover, the intelligence officer at Army Group Centre, Hans-Heinrich Worgitzky, was suspicious of Scherhorn's story. How, he wondered, could such a large force survive in an area dominated by Soviet Partisans, who would surely wipe out any foraging parties and report the unit's location to higher headquarters? Worgitzky speculated about an NKGB ploy to collect weapons and food, and perhaps divert German energies in an unprofitable direction, a suspicion further piqued when several Vlasovite radio agents parachuted into Scherhorn's vicinity never reported back. Officers at Army Group Centre finally decided that although they were willing to commit more supplies and radio agents, they also wanted to verify the group's authenticity before launching a major effort to lead it to safety. Scherhorn was told, meanwhile, to break up his battalion into smaller march groups and to move his wounded to former Red Partisan airfields, where they could be picked up by German aircraft. A number of KG 200 transport planes were deployed to drop supplies and maintain contact.

The issue of an independent investigation of the Scherhorn band was referred to FHO, which in turn requested von Fölkersam to send a number of teams to the Berezina area, without telling Scherhorn, in order to determine the group's true nature. On direct orders from Himmler, four paratroop squads were formed, each comprised of ten to fifteen German, *Volksdeutsch* and Russian personnel and each equipped with a radio transmitter. The operation was codenamed '*Freischutz*'. During the autumn of 1944, all four teams were flown into action from airfields in East Prussia, two with orders to search areas east of the drop zone, and two with orders to scour areas to the west. The first radio message from these teams was disturbing: the paratroopers had not yet found Scherhorn, but there was heavy fighting in the area, including operations by Soviet aircraft. They noted: 'Enemy have seen us. Machine guns firing.' – and then the radio fell silent. Such evidence of Red Army units in the region contrasted with Scherhorn's reports of general serenity, and doubts began to resurface. However, Scherhorn unknowingly reassured the Germans by reporting on 19 October that some of his outposts were skirmishing with local civic watch guards and Soviet militia. Although two of Skorzeny's squads disappeared and a third thrashed its way back to German lines, the fourth, led by *Untersturmführer* Schiffer, enjoyed apparent success: on 4 November it radioed back, informing its controllers that it had found the Scherhorn unit and that it was prepared to vet its authenticity. German plans then called for Schiffer to return by land, but since his men were exhausted, arrangements were made to supply the party by air. Ten packages of food, medicine and ammunition were dropped. Plans to evacuate the detachment from former Red Partisan airfields were abandoned due to the Soviet offensive in East Prussia, and the squad made its last contact with Friedenthal in early 1945.

Meanwhile, Schiffer's confirmatory message sealed a decision to extract the Scherhorn *Leute*. The matter was placed before Hitler and Göring, who agreed to an operation run by FAK 103. The interests of *Jagdverband Ost*, however, lay elsewhere. Its deputy commander, Wolfram Heinze, saw a huge, ready-made partisan formation in the Soviet rear, and he showed signs of wanting to use Scherhorn's men to conduct guerrilla warfare. Skorzeny and company hoped, noted one officer, 'that this centre of guerrilla warfare would develop into a more general revolt against the Soviet regime', an idea apparently piqued by information that Byelorussians were helping the Scherhorn band. After Schiffer's 4 November message, Heinze and Worgitzki worked out a compromise. Overall, the Scherhorn group would not be deliberately employed for partisan activity, but the *Jagdverband* could satisfy at least some of its objectives through use of vacant space aboard *Luftwaffe* supply flights and it would also be given access to Scherhorn troops who *voluntarily* agreed to serve in the Soviet rear.

While German leaders were making up their minds about what to do, Scherhorn had been advised to send half his march columns toward the lakes district north-east of Vilna, and the other half toward the forested territory west of Naliboki. The eventual plan was to remove some of the troops by means of aerial landings on frozen lakes or airfields formerly used by Soviet Partisans. Those forces not evacuated by such means were supposed to slash their way through to the front, where local German counterattacks would facilitate attempts to cross the lines. At the same time, KG 200 did its best to keep the march groups supplied – although the aircraft were frequently grounded by bad weather and mechanical difficulties, particularly in November 1944 – and a regular trickle of German experts were dispatched in order to help with various medical and technical issues, especially the repair of airfields. One supply operation was abandoned when circling aircraft saw the reception committee involved in a firefight with Soviet pursuers. A similar attempt on 8 December was cursed with aircraft mechanical problems, and the commander of FAK 103 was killed when he was hit by a propeller blade after a forced landing. Two other planes also experienced engine problems, and when bad weather rolled in, this operation was also cancelled.

Scherhorn reported that he was faithfully following Army Group Centre's instructions, although all existing plans went awry at the time of the 1945 Soviet Winter Offensive. The Soviet advance destroyed any likelihood of a successful Scherhorn breakthrough because of the westward retreat of German forces, which put them far out of reach of any Germans still trapped in Byelorussia. New *Jagdverband* and FAK teams were sent to Scherhorn in February 1945, but by that time it was clear that the optimistic assumptions that originally lay behind the rescue effort were no longer valid. In fact, since the entire unit could not be extracted by air, the *Wehrmacht* now decided to abandon a lost cause to the intrigues of *Jagdverband Ost*, particularly since it was known that Skorzeny, who also knew that any chance of evacuation was finished, nonetheless persuaded Hitler to maintain the flow of airborne supplies. In March 1945, the operation was transferred to *Jagdverband* control, with the rationalisation that fuel shortages were preventing realisation of the extraction effort. SS commandos were supposed to maintain the pretence of rescuing the Scherhorn Battle Group, or at least the wounded, and the bulk of the battalion's men would retain their military ranks. Troops 'who *voluntarily* put themselves at the disposal of the SS-*Jagdverbände*' were henceforth to be regarded as SS men, as were the Russians with Scherhorn's unit. Supply dumps, aircraft and a FAK 103 administrative staff were all transferred to the command of *Jagdverband Ost*. FHO radioed Scherhorn and encouraged him to hold out, as well as informing him that he had been promoted and awarded the Knight's Cross.

Polish commandos were subsequently sent to help Scherhorn march columns as they supposedly approached Poland, and a plan to dispatch a team led by Skorzeny himself was cancelled only because of severe German military reverses in April 1945. Only on 5 May 1945 was Scherhorn informed that the war was lost and that he would have to rely on his own resources.[38]

If this affair gives the impression that Skorzeny was a ruthless exploiter, it is a rich irony that, in the final analysis, he was himself masterfully manipulated. The truth is that Worgitzky's original fears about Scherhorn had been entirely correct. The Scherhorn band had once been real enough, but it had been whittled down to a size of 1,500 men and then overrun by the Soviets in July 1944. About 20,000 German troops had gathered in the woods west of the Berezina after being bypassed by the Red Army, but in truth the condition of these men had been desperate. Most had become demoralised and could be controlled by their officers only through imposition of the harshest type of discipline. By the time these Germans were rolled up by the Soviets in early July, they had been without food for ten days and had thrown away their weapons. Soviet loudspeaker trucks working at the edge of forests to encourage surrenders experienced unprecedented successes, convincing groups as large as 800 soldiers to capitulate. In addition, many Germans had been so pliant after capture that they had not required guards while marching to POW assembly points.[39]

The advantage exercised by the Soviets was that they knew about the full extent of this collapse, while the German leadership was not so aware. At the same time, Stalin also suspected that the Germans were eager to exploit forces trapped behind Soviet lines. With these factors in mind, Stavka developed an ingenious plan to capitalise on the situation and outfox the Germans. Their main asset was Demyanov, who had been recruited as a Soviet spy in 1929 and since 1942 had been performing brilliantly as a double agent, supplying the *Abwehr* with great reams of carefully crafted disinformation. Demyanov's NKGB and Soviet military handlers were told to let the Germans know that Demyanov had visited the Red Army in Byelorussia, and once the Soviets had captured Scherhorn they ordered Demyanov to spin a tale about the supposed Scherhorn battalion. Scherhorn was held in strict isolation in Moscow, where he was forced to write his original messages to the Germans, and in late October 1944 he was moved to a forest hut in Slaboda, near the supposed location of the Scherhorn unit. He and his radio operators then sent radio messages to Berlin with the muzzles of Soviet machine pistols pointed at their temples. Members of the 'Free Germany' movement were also recruited to act as background scenery, particularly since it was necessary to allow occasional *Luftwaffe* transport aircraft to land and take off if the ruse was to be kept alive.

Scherhorn never thought that his compatriots would be duped into believing that such a large force could roam freely along the Soviet lines of communication, but as we know, the radio reports, skilfully written by Scherhorn's controllers, Leonid Eitingon and Yakov Serebryansky, found an eager audience, including Skorzeny. As a result, the Soviets captured twenty-five German agents and confiscated 150 tons of supplies, thirteen radio transmitters and ten million rubles in cash (Scherhorn had told Berlin that he wanted to maintain the sympathy of Byelorussians by paying for his supplies). Not only were these men and resources thrown down the drain, but they were denied to real German and Byelorussian nationalist bands that could have benefited from such help. Soviet Chekist Pavel Sudaplatov, who worked on the operation, later described it as 'the most successful radio deception game of the war', while Worgitzky, a future deputy chief of the West German secret service, called it 'the greatest disaster of my career in intelligence'.[40]

'DOWN WITH HITLER! – DOWN WITH STALIN!'

While attempts to encourage guerrilla warfare were a bust in Byelorussia, Skorzeny and his cohorts had more success in the Ukraine. For Nazis who bothered to draw distinctions amongst Slavic '*Untermenschen*', Ukrainians were regarded as a cut above Great Russians or Byelorussians. More importantly, the Germans were aware that the Ukraine was the home of a nationalist movement much more powerful than its Byelorussian counterpart, particularly in West Ukraine, birthplace of the Ukrainian national idea. Ukrainian nationalists had worked closely with Germans since the Great War, and as will be recalled, OUN had collaborated with the Nazis. After the Germans conquered the Ukraine, however, this tendency to cooperate gradually deteriorated, mainly because of the genocidal nature of German occupation policies and anti-partisan measures. The leader of the radical OUN faction, Stefan Bandera, was imprisoned by the Germans, followed in time by the more conservative Andrei Melnyk. Both men continued to support OUN involvement in the recruitment of pro-German gendarmeries, but after several years even this policy had become impossible to stomach. Forced to take part in brutal anti-partisan razzias against their own people, more and more of the OUN Janissaries fled to the woods, and in early 1943 they were joined by Roman Shukevych, the Banderist security commander in the Ukraine. These Banderist deserters declared themselves in favour of full-scale guerrilla warfare against the German occupiers, having grown so disillusioned that any process of mending fences would be most difficult.

Meanwhile, because the OUN was initially hesitant about the formation of anti-German guerrilla groups, such activity was dominated initially by a figure *not* closely associated with the OUN, or at least with its Banderist faction. After the Germans had swept through the West Ukraine in 1941, a Volynian businessman, 'Taras' Borovets, established a minuteman organisation called the Polesian *Sich*, the mandate of which was to round up Red Army stragglers and partisans. The German civil administration dissolved the *Sich* in November 1941, but its remnants, renamed the Ukrainian Partisan Army, then fled to the woods. It was this group that subsequently mushroomed into a huge complex of guerrillas by the spring of 1943, the size of which has been estimated at between 20,000 and 40,000 men. Borovets's relationship to the Germans was ambiguous: although his bands attacked SS and police units, they also accepted help from the *Wehrmacht*, in return for which they guarded German Army supply lines and participated in raids upon Soviet and Jewish resistance groups. In fact, a German intelligence report noted in the spring of 1943 that Borovets was 'pronouncedly friendly' and held as his ultimate goal 'the erection of an independent Ukrainian state with a strong dependence on Germany'. In June 1943, Borovets met with several *Abwehr* agents with the hope of forging a closer relationship to the *Wehrmacht*, although he still wanted no connection to the Nazi police.

Meanwhile, the new Banderist guerrillas had themselves stolen the title 'UPA', hoping to secure some of the prestige secured by Borovets's early start in the field. In the summer of 1943, they also forcibly annexed almost all the non-Banderist partisan groups, including the Borovets UPA, in a savage campaign of consolidation. Borovets and a rump of his group, estimated at 6,000 men and renamed the Ukrainian National Revolutionary Army, were chased by the Banderist usurpers into communist-infested territory, and in November, he met with *Sonderstab* 'R' at Rovno. When the discussions turned to political matters, however, *Abwehr* officers handed the talks over to the SS, who thereafter 'escorted' Borovets back to Warsaw and brought his offer of collaboration to Hitler, who promptly refused it. Borovets was then held in Warsaw for over half a year. Although some of his UNRA bands remained active in the rear of the advancing Red Army, the Germans realised that they had become insignificant. When Borovets was released in August 1944, he remained in German-held territory and formed a 400-man parachute brigade.[41]

Guerrillas of the Banderist UPA, or 'Green Cadre', were a tougher nut to crack. The Germans themselves were increasingly willing to dicker, realising that they might have to give up the western Ukraine and that the UPA, in such an instance, might prove a valuable stay-behind force.[42] As late as January 1944, however, FHO suggested that there was no Banderist inclination to collaborate, rather venturing that such bands might gravitate to the Soviets and that it would be easier for the Germans to work with Polish nationalist guerrilla groups.[43] Nonetheless, even the Banderists eventually made their peace, especially in view of the increasing Soviet threat. Since the Banderist formations had been created originally as German security units, it is no surprise that they had already gone back to this source in 1943 in order to deal with a shortage of trained officers and platoon leaders, which was the guerrillas' main deficiency. When the Germans formed a Ukrainian SS combat formation, the 'Galicia' Division, Shukevych was originally opposed, but he eventually decided that the force could be turned to UPA's advantage by using it as a vehicle for training partisan leaders. With this purpose in mind, he released many young guerrillas for training in the new *Waffen*-SS unit. By the spring of 1944, the 'Galicia' Division was stationed along the front in the West Ukraine, at which time its officers negotiated mutual aid deals with local UPA detachments, including promises not to recruit each other's men. UPA units, however, soon began to break this agreement, especially since their principal reason for sending men to the division had been to retrieve them and exploit their newly acquired skills. After the SS 'Galicia' Division was chewed up during the Battle of Brody, an estimated 7,000 survivors fled to the woods and joined (or rejoined) the UPA.[44]

Meanwhile, as the Soviets began pushing through the West Ukraine, UPA detachments ceased most of their attacks against the Germans and refocused attention upon Soviet Partisans and conventional military forces. The idea of negotiating a provisional UPA-German alliance seems to have started in the north-western Ukraine, where the Volhynian UPA was weaker than its south-western (Galician) counterpart. The first local negotiations involved XIIIth Army Corps, SS Battle Group 'Prützmann' and regional bands under control of UPA-'North'. In January and February 1944, a number of arrangements were made for UPA troops to cease attacks on German supply lines, return captured German soldiers, turn over Red Army POWs and share reconnaissance information with the *Wehrmacht*, in return for which the Germans agreed to supply the guerrillas with ammunition for specific operations (although they would not provide a stock that could be accumulated). These agreements worked well and by May–June 1944, the relationship had progressed to the point where UPA detachments were helping FAK 105 radio reconnaissance groups in return for having a 300-man UPA infiltration unit armed with German ammunition and medical supplies. According to the Soviets, the commander of UPA-'North', Dmytro Kliachkivskyi, was able to call in a *Luftwaffe* airdrop of 500 submachine guns, ammunition and clothing when he found himself in a tough spot behind Soviet lines.[45]

Elsewhere, German-UPA cooperation was more sporadic, but tended to follow the pattern set in the north-western Ukraine. In February 1944, UPA bands fought alongside the *Wehrmacht* in the Tarnopol region, and near Lvov and Stanislav, UPA detachments helped the Germans against Red Partisan units. In Lvov, exploratory talks were held between *Hauptsturmführer* Pappe and Dr Ivan Hrynokh, who had been given a mandate to negotiate by the UPA leadership. The last skirmishes between UPA and the German Army were in the late spring of 1944, although UPA continued to harass the German civil administration in eastern Poland and guerrilla units continued to circulate anti-German propaganda. These events were, nonetheless, ripples in an increasingly placid relationship. In several cases, UPA troops withdrew with the *Wehrmacht* and subsequently fought communist partisans in Hungary or Slovakia, or they organised guerrilla warfare in anticipation of a Soviet advance into northern Romania (Operation 'Chmara'), although they found it difficult to work with the Romanian 'greens' because the latter lacked adequate directives from Vienna. In eastern Poland, two groups that had withdrawn from the Ukraine contented themselves with battling Polish partisans and helping to smuggle food to their confrères on the other side of the front. The bulk of UPA, including its leadership staff and the high command of UPA-'West', withdrew into the Carpathian Mountains, with the expectation that from this remote redoubt they could keep open lines of contact to Hungary, Slovakia and Germany. FAK 202 estimated on 20 September 1944 that over 95% of UPA units had remained in the rear of the Red Army.

The Germans also reconciled themselves to meeting UPA's material needs, at least as far as possible. It was not unusual, one guerrilla commander later recalled, finding an abandoned farmhouse deliberately stocked by the Germans with supplies. By July 1944, FAK 202's Operation 'Lydia' – the laying of sabotage dumps in the Chernovotsy-Stanislav area – had been completed and the Ukrainians requested access to these stocks as soon as the Soviets had overrun the region. While FAK 205 was headquartered in Lvov, its personnel buried a large amount of captured Soviet and British equipment throughout the surrounding district. One German officer later remembered establishing forty dumps of arms and ammunition in the forests of Galicia, and another later recalled supplying 20,000 boxes of arms and a large quantity of ammunition. About fifteen tons of equipment, including 800 rifles, 200 machine pistols and fifty machine guns, were sent to the Czarny-Las, a UPA stronghold, and UPA battalion commander Maksym Skorupsky obtained 300 rifles, six heavy machine guns and 100,000 rounds of ammunition. According to one report, the *Luftwaffe* left at Stryy eighteen captured British Mosquito aircraft, plus ground and flight personnel.[46] The scale of such aid was obviously substantial and helped keep UPA in the field during a difficult period.

By the time serious negotiations between UPA and the Germans got underway, army intelligence officers realised that they required a formal nod from the RSHA in handling such matters, and in July 1944 UPA leaders encouraged Mil D to mediate relations with the Nazi security apparatus. UPA was, they pleaded, no longer an anti-Nazi resistance movement and ought not to be treated as such. Himmler, meanwhile, had been convinced by Günther D'Alquen to take a second look at the Ukrainian guerrilla movement, and he eventually approved German overtures. This policy adjustment was complete by September 1944.[47]

Shortly afterward, as we know, von Fölkersam and Skorzeny assumed responsibility for all matters involving behind-the-lines subversion. The *Jagdverband* chiefs seemed to realise, however, that while it made sense for the SD to cease persecuting the UPA, rushing to the opposite extreme and assuming responsibility for support of the guerrillas would be uncomfortable, given the nature of the SD's past relationship with the nationalists. Skorzeny thus decided that the existing lines of contact between FAK 202 and UPA should be maintained, and when the FAK 202's commander, *Oberstleutnant* Seeliger, was killed in action in the late summer of 1944, Skorzeny replaced him with the redoubtable Dietrich Witzel, who had recently returned from adventures in Afghanistan and was sure to undertake a vigorous approach in helping the Ukrainian partisans. Although the initiative remained with FAK 202, Skorzeny arranged for fortnightly reports and he closely followed the course of operations. In fact, he regarded promotion of a Ukrainian insurrection as one of the most important functions of his organisation.

After FAK 202 was forced to evacuate its headquarters at Lvov, it relocated to Cracow and, under Witzel's direction, sent 100 Ukrainian volunteers for training at a Mil D camp in Sohl, Upper Silesia. Together with KG 200, FAK 202 began to airdrop supplies, radio agents and technical specialists into friendly areas, starting with the mid-summer delivery of 200 Russian guns and 20,000 rounds of ammunition. Medical corpsmen sent to the Ukrainians helped save the life of *Sotnia* leader Stephen Khrin, who was eventually destined to become a famous UPA sector commander. FHO eventually called for the dispatch of even more weapons, medical supplies and radio equipment, but attempts to get material from the quartermasters at OKH were not encouraging. All that was still available were 2,000 captured Soviet semi-automatic weapons (without requested silencers), 3,000 Russian machine pistols, 500 Russian mortars, and a number of hand grenades, explosives and mines. The machine pistols were missing their drums and lacked sufficient ammunition. OKH suggested that further weapons would have to be obtained from the army groups or from Vlasovite units at the front, formations not likely to withdraw material from their own precious stocks. In addition, available German aircraft were in short supply and a *Luftwaffe* plane was reportedly shot down while trying to supply UPA bands near Lvov. FHO admitted on 1 November 1944 that airdrops of weapons had been 'modest', although the dispatch of radio equipment in return for behind-the-lines intelligence was yielding substantial dividends. By late November, UPA functionaries were complaining: the Germans, they said, 'had left UPA behind Russian lines with almost no support', and the Nazis had supposedly failed to appreciate what large-scale assistance for a partisan movement could accomplish, even though this lesson had been aptly taught by the Soviets.

Some of the agent-dropping operations undertaken by the Germans were a waste of time and resources; others yielded good results. An example of the first category was the experience of three Ukrainian parachutists, two men and a woman, who were dropped into a forest near Tarnopol. Upon landing, they were immediately arrested by Soviet militia and then evacuated to Chertkovo, in the eastern Ukraine, where they were interrogated and executed. Their radio equipment also fell into Russian hands.

Hauptsturmführer Josef Krieger had a similarly short sojourn behind Soviet lines. Shortly after landing, he begged a ride from a Galician peasant and was deposited at the front door of the local NKGB headquarters. Krieger had been sent to the Chernovotsy area, at the edge of the Carpathian Mountains, where he was supposed to contact a stay-behind agent named Mazepa and a local guerrilla chief named Lugovoy. Before the Germans had evacuated eastern Galicia, Mazepa had trained Lugovoy and had helped him form a sizeable band, supplying weapons and food. Krieger was supposed to further build up the band to the size of a regiment and lead four columns of guerrillas into the eastern Ukraine, where the nationalists had less of a presence than in their western stronghold. Krieger's capture helped foil this plan and much of the Lugovoy group was destroyed in fighting during September 1944.

Better results came from two parachutists dropped by the *Luftwaffe*, both anti-tank specialists who joined Ukrainian partisans in Galicia. On 24 October 1944, these parachutists tried to mine a bridge near Trostyanets, although this action led to a running battle with a large contingent of Red Army troops. When the Soviets deployed two tanks in order to lead their forces toward a UPA concentration point, the parachutists were ordered to confront the armour with anti-tank grenades and Molotov cocktails. Along with a squad of six UPA riflemen, they ambushed the tanks, although one of the paratroopers was so badly wounded that he shot himself with his service pistol rather than await capture by the enemy. The overall battle was a success for UPA, particularly since the guerrillas caught Soviet troops charging across an open field. The partisans claimed only seventeen dead, while the district committee of the Communist Party later admitted that over 200 Red Army soldiers had been killed.[48]

The most important behind-the-lines mission involved the establishment of a more secure line of communication between UPA and FAK 202. Although UPA had dispatched a negotiating team, which in August 1944 met with German officers at Krynica, most contact between the two sides was indirect, passing either through a network of German spies in the Ukraine or through OUN agents in the Nazi system of camps for eastern labourers. As early as September 1944, the Germans considered sending envoys directly to the UPA leadership, but they were awaiting the unlikely chance of a political settlement between Germany and the Ukrainian nationalist leadership. Witzel soon tired of this course and decided to act without the supposedly requisite improvement in the political climate. Assembling a seven-man unit of Germans and Ukrainians, he personally led this squad across the front near the Uzsok Pass on 6 October 1944, thus launching Operation 'Sonnenblume'.

Within four days, Witzel and company had found a UPA unit near Suchy Potok, about thirty miles behind the front. Witzel knew the Ukrainian commander from earlier negotiations and he managed to reschedule, via radio, a *Luftwaffe* airdrop of supplies that had earlier been cancelled because the UPA band had been forced to abandon the drop zone in anticipation of a Soviet raid.

The march resumed after a sojourn at Suchy Patok, albeit under increasingly uncomfortable conditions. By this time, the detachment had buried some of its supplies, including its blankets, in order to make better speed under the weight of its weapons, ammunition and wireless equipment. Team members suffered from the cold – they were by now travelling at heights of over 3,000 feet in the chilly and moist Carpathian Mountains – and they took ill from eating mouldy bread. Nonetheless, they persevered, and after following a circuitous route designed to avoid Soviet positions, on 16 October they reached Bubniszcze, headquarters of the UPA leadership. They gave the UPA chiefs a wireless transmitter in order to ensure communications with FAK 202, although exposure to the damp forests of Galicia had caused the radio batteries to deteriorate. This problem necessitated a raid on a Soviet airbase at Orov, where the commandos managed to steal the batteries, although they suffered the injury of one of their officers through a grenade blast. By 30 October, secure radio contact with the German base in Cracow had been established. During their residence at Bubniszcze, the visitors carried out reconnaissance and trained UPA officers in espionage and *Kleinkrieg* techniques.

On 31 October the expedition headed eastwards, with Witzel and a UPA guide running ahead in order to find a suitable landing strip for an aircraft that would pick them up and return the party to Cracow. On 5 November a German plane flew over the proposed airfield, dropping supplies for UPA as well as a *Luftwaffe* officer with orders to inspect the proposed landing site. Two days later, a Ju 52 landed at the makeshift airfield, over 110 miles behind Soviet lines. Witzel's squad, plus five German stragglers and two UPA representatives, climbed aboard the aircraft and flew back to Poland. Although the team had suffered various torments, Witzel regarded the operation as a tremendous success, noting that good treatment by Ukrainian civilians and guerrillas suggested that future German infiltration parties would be well received. Witzel was subsequently awarded the Knight's Cross.

One of Skorzeny's responsibilities was to count and activate German soldiers behind Soviet lines, and it was with his encouragement that Witzel also undertook this task. By the autumn of 1944, a considerable body of intelligence suggested that thousands of German troops left in the Ukraine had either joined the UPA or had been captured by the guerrillas and were thereafter integrated into their ranks. Many had also been liberated through UPA raids on Soviet POW camps and march columns. The UPA leadership had decided in June 1944 that German officers should be permitted to run the movement's schools and training camps, and German non-commissioned officers soon found themselves in charge of UPA *Sotnia*, or 100-man battle companies. Skorzeny later claimed that as late as 1946–1947, there were more than 10,000 Germans fighting alongside UPA troops, and certainly German stragglers played a role in organising a 3,000-man partisan column that terrorised the Sanok region of Galicia in 1946.

During his trek behind Soviet lines, Witzel was able to get the names and ranks of several hundred UPA Germans. He also negotiated the release of Germans who were ill or needed to return to German lines for pressing reasons – a courier system of shuttle aircraft was supposed to retrieve such troops – and contemporary reports confirm that there were several occasions where UPA groups assisted German stragglers or escaped POWs in breaking through to German lines, particularly around Lvov. In addition to 'Sonnenblume', another ten-man German task force, codenamed 'Kolibri', slipped through the lines and cooperated with UPA forces near Stanislav, mainly in conducting a count of German stragglers. This detachment remained a month in Soviet territory and like the 'Sonnenblume' unit, it was picked up by a German plane after completing its mission. Despite the success of such roll-taking operations, Skorzeny later claimed that UPA headquarters resisted releasing most of its German troops. The UPA, said Skorzeny, leaned so heavily on German 'volunteers' that its chiefs had no intention of passively waving goodbye as many of their best soldiers flew off toward German lines, although they were willing to trade sick and wounded men in return for weapons. They prepared makeshift airfields for landings, although the *Luftwaffe* lacked the necessary fuel to support such operations.[49]

Most news from the Ukraine, around autumn 1944, was positive, suggesting the availability of a vast and only partially tapped resource. Some intelligence estimates claimed that UPA-'West' had 100,000 troops and two million sympathisers, and that UPA-'North' had nearly as many cadres and supporters. The fact that the Soviets killed or captured more than 165,000 men in the first year of operations against the UPA also suggests the scale of the movement. On an almost daily basis, guerrilla groups blew up rail lines and bridges, as well as attacking Soviet aerodromes. *Jagdverband Ost* reported that they were especially active in the regions around Lutsk and Lvov, where they were grouped in 500-man units. In late August and early September 1944, First Ukrainian Front was forced to launch a large-scale sweep of such areas and German intelligence estimated that fifteen to twenty NKGB regiments were diverted, plus several cavalry divisions and a number of small Red Army tank units. In 1944 and early 1945, nearly 5,000 Soviet troops were killed or wounded in engagements with the partisans. According to the Germans, highlights of the UPA campaign included the destruction of twenty-three Soviet vehicles and five tanks in a raid near Vladimir-Volyniskiy, an attack on a Soviet troop train at a station south of Lvov, and the ambush of a Soviet regiment near Stryy, which reportedly resulted in the deaths of forty Soviet soldiers. The UPA had popular support in parts of Volhynia and Galicia; thus, the advancing Soviets were faced with UPA-inspired graffiti that read 'Down with Hitler! – Down with Stalin!'

FHO claimed that the UPA actually got stronger after the Soviet onslaught, and that the Soviets had shown, with their own partisan movement, 'the worth of a uniformly organised guerrilla war… if we support and control it in the same way'. Certainly, the guerrillas had high hopes for supply via airdrops. After returning from behind Soviet lines, Witzel gushed that the UPA was the most powerful resistance movement in the Soviet Union and that Vlasovite bands were often getting unmerited credit for its achievements. A captured Red Army colonel suggested that the Soviet front would collapse if guerrilla activity was not contained, a report that Himmler sent to Mil D and FHO.

The only disturbing part of this assessment was that much of the UPA's power represented potential that was not fully actualised. Although there were numerous reports about sabotage, which forced the Soviets to redeploy troops for guard duty and prompted the stationing of strong NKGB units in effected areas, the UPA often treated the Red Army in the same way that it had handled the *Wehrmacht*. The bulk of Red Army formations had been allowed to sweep across the Ukraine unmolested, while the UPA regarded its real enemies as the Soviet secret police and civil administration. Thus, according to Witzel, much UPA time and energy was invested in killing Soviet officials and liberating Ukrainian nationalist prisoners and German POWs. A particularly important function involved destroying local records and other resources needed for Red Army recruiters to muster men into the Soviet armed forces. Direct attacks on Soviet military outposts and transports were intended mainly to disrupt such manpower drafts. Otherwise, the main way in which the UPA challenged the Red Army was through the circulation of propaganda, and one of the Eastern 'experts' in FAK 202, Dr Hans Raupach, noted that UPA spent much of its time organising passive resistance.[50]

The Soviets, of course, also interfered with the UPA's operations through their typically ferocious reaction to any kind of opposition. Fire and steel comprised the essence of their response. By the early autumn of 1944, NKGB troops were burning down villages thought to support the guerrillas and they also parachuted agents, disguised as German radio operators, into areas sympathetic to the UPA. This trick had already been used in the Volga German Republic and in the North Caucasus, and it had the double advantage of drawing out potentially anti-Soviet elements as well as scaring the population about the authenticity of German parachutists in their midst. The punishments for failure to respond in an appropriate fashion were severe; the populations of three villages near Brzezany were deported *en masse*.[51] Some sense of the threat is suggested by the fact that one of Stalin's main deputies, Nikita Khrushchev, was sent to Kiev in order to suppress the nationalists, and that Khrushchev burned a swath through Ukrainian society that rivalled the purges of the 1930s.[52]

Witzel's programme to support the UPA was interrupted by the 1945 Soviet Winter Offensive, which forced FAK 202 to decamp from its headquarters in Cracow. It first relocated at Gorlitz, in Silesia, and then settled even further afield, at the Bohemian town of Kollin. In late January and February, FAK 202's range of operations was restricted mainly to Silesia, and the UPA had to carry on its fight without outside help (such as it was). Worse yet, the Germans were deprived of the sole remaining ground link with the Ukrainians at the Carpathian town of Krynica, and this loss occurred at a time when aerial supply of the UPA was a difficult option. There was also depressing news from behind Soviet lines: OKH noted on 8 March 1945 that as severe NKGB repression began to restrict the UPA's popular base, guerrilla operations were being increasingly curtailed. On the other hand, a report on 7 March also suggested that partisans had made the western Ukraine so impassable that the Soviets found it difficult to resupply their forces in Hungary. Some degree of German-UPA contact was eventually restored, and before the end of the war additional Ukrainian cadres were parachuted into the Soviet rear, most of them graduates of special courses at the Luckenwalde and Sohl training camps.[53]

It is important to note that even as the German-UPA relationship matured, Skorzeny and Witzel never controlled the UPA; they merely established a tenuous alliance with it. As Skorzeny and Radl later admitted, 'UPA distrusted the Germans' and there were good reasons for this wariness, given Germany's past record of betrayals. Veterans of FAK 202 also conceded that their unit's relations with the UPA 'were not very good' and 'that the Ukrainians proved uncooperative although very willing to receive arms and ammunition'.[54] One group of parachutists, recruited from amongst Ukrainian labourers in Germany, was disarmed by the suspicious guerrillas, apparently because it was felt to be working for German, rather than Ukrainian, purposes.[55] When Witzel returned from the western Ukraine, he claimed a 'close personal relationship' with UPA leaders and asserted that they were ready to meet the German need for more direct attacks against the supply lines of the Red Army. However, even he admitted that the Germans would never run the Ukrainian resistance movement and that the best they could expect was the stationing of a permanent German liaison officer in order to orient operations in favour of the Nazi war effort. Specific demolitions desired by the OKH would be most effectively handled by German '*Jagdkommandos*' assembled for such purposes, although such detachments would probably be able to rely on the support of the Ukrainian people.[56]

This discussion calls to mind much literature on pro-Allied abcresistance during the Second World War. Most historians have concluded, as Werner Rings notes, 'that [partisan] operations acquired real value only when they were systematically incorporated into overall strategic planning'.[57] The Germans certainly realised that this was true, although there is no evidence that they ever managed to encourage significant integration of UPA operations. Efforts in this direction were further upset by the 1945 Soviet Winter Offensive.

Military collaboration between the Germans and the UPA might have developed along more fruitful lines had the two sides come to a political understanding, but this never happened. Talks between FAK officers and UPA representatives were held in the summer of 1944, but a deliberate decision was made to keep politics off the table. Any discussion of fundamental policy issues, it was thought, could throw light on differences so wide that the existing state of co-belligerency might be threatened. In September, however, FHO advised that the UPA would be more effectively exploited 'if its political goals could be supported through an appropriate change in the German political position', and FAK 305 recommended the same, noting that Germany should recognise 'Ukrainian claims to political and military equality'. The Eastern Ministry also conceded that with the German withdrawal from the Ukraine, the last obstacle to an alliance with the Ukrainian guerrillas had been removed, and it advised that the partisans be asked to spread propaganda about Germany's supposedly benign intentions in the Ukraine.

There were, however, three obstacles that stood in the way of consummating this evolving relationship. First, there was a simple lack of trust caused by horrendous events so recent that they had been neither forgotten nor forgiven. The Ukrainians were convinced that a recovery of German military strength would be accompanied by a reincorporation of eastern Galicia back into the 'General Gouvernement', the German colonial regime in Poland. This administrative arrangement, dating to 1941, had been deeply resented by Ukrainian nationalists and was a continuing source of ill will. UPA representatives suggested that General Governor Hans Frank had been too quick to make concessions to hostile Poles while ill-treating the more pro-German Ukrainian population. This was an interpretation that would have surprised most Poles, who quite rightly regarded Frank as a savage oppressor.

On their side, the Germans had also come to distrust the ultimate overlord of the Ukrainian partisans, Stepan Bandera, whose release was required by the UPA as a condition of any reconciliation. In June 1944, the SS reluctantly agreed to honour this demand, although the Gestapo dragged its feet and Bandera was only finally released in the autumn of 1944. Mil D officers believed that only Dietrich Witzel's constant harping secured this concession. In SS and Nazi Party circles, Bandera was popularly thought 'to be more against Germany than against Bolshevism', and the most that was said in his favour came in the form of an assessment by Gottlob Berger on 5 October: Bandera, wrote Berger, was potentially dangerous – he hated Germans as much as Russians – but he was on a short leash and could be considered an asset. 'At the moment he cannot do much against us', Berger reasoned, 'while if activated on our side he can seriously endanger [enemy] communications.' Bandera's release, however, had no discernable impact on UPA behaviour.

Another problem, not entirely separate from the first, was that SS policy in the autumn of 1944 began to swing sharply in favour of Vlasov's 'Liberation Movement', particularly with the declaration of the KONR. Vlasov's organisation was based upon a maintenance of the Greater Russian union, a policy that was anathema to the Ukrainian separatists. UPA representatives made clear that they would under no circumstances support Vlasov, or even condone him. In fact, they warned that if a recovery of *Wehrmacht* strength ever brought Vlasovites into the Ukraine, they would fight these 'Muscovite' forces just as surely as they were resisting the Soviets. Skorzeny and Radl later admitted that any chance of a true rapprochement with the Ukrainian nationalists was shattered the moment that the KONR was proclaimed.

A final sticking point arose from Bandera's belief that the Western Allies were about to emerge triumphant in the war, and that the real future of the Ukrainian independence movement lay in this quarter. Bandera had accepted help from the SIS in the 1930s and his intelligence chief, Mykola Lebed, was once again trying to cultivate British support. The corollary of this policy was that UPA collaboration with the Germans had to be carefully disguised in order not to prejudice the movement's hopes for relations with the Western Allies. A clear signal was given by the fact that two UPA regional commanders were court-martialled and executed in the spring of 1944 because their cooperation with the Germans had become too open. This factor limited the manner in which the Germans could treat the UPA. In the negotiations during the summer of 1944, the UPA made the Germans promise that they would not favourably mention the movement in propaganda, lest the Soviets get the chance to portray the guerrillas as 'fascist mercenaries'. The UPA wanted to remain formally illegal and conspiratorial (although Army Group North Ukraine did order its staffs in August 1944 to stop referring to UPA groups as 'bands' and start calling them 'units'). In view of the UPA's posture, the Germans knew that they could not be seen giving UPA officers specific combat or intelligence assignments. German staffs were told that UPA offers of help could be accepted, but never forced or cajoled.

Given such myriad problems, the best the Germans could accomplish politically was the belated erection of a 'Ukrainian National Committee', which was created in March 1945. The chief of this body, Pavlo Shandruk, bore the support of Bandera (although he had a more ambiguous relationship with Melnyk). He visited FAK 202 on 24–25 March 1945 in order to 'inaugurate active work in the enemy hinterland' and to meet with the liaison staff of the UPA, although by that time it was too late to get much accomplished. As Alexander Dallin notes, the Germans fiddled with the matter of a 'national committee' until the war was nearly over 'and contact with UPA in the field was all but lost'. In addition, although Bandera backed Shandruk, he would not issue a formal declaration of support and not all factions in the UPA followed his lead in recognising Shandruk's authority. In short, the 'national committee' did not develop as an effective instrument of German policy nor as a valuable channel between the Germans and the UPA, at least in the short time that it existed.[58]

THREE BALTIC BRUSH-FIRES

If the political implications of the German-UPA alliance were complicated, Skorzeny's attempt to cultivate Baltic guerrillas was equally strewn with political and cultural pitfalls. Shortly after the end of the war, Skorzeny and Radl admitted that 'difficulties arose' when their Baltic partisans requested guarantees of future political independence for their countries. Although not a deep thinker, even Skorzeny realised that his guerrillas needed more than their daily bread if they wanted to think of themselves as anything better than mercenaries. As a result, the SD got permission from the Rosenberg Ministry to extend concessions to the Baltic activists, but these sanctions were quickly retracted by Erich Koch, the newly appointed Nazi commissioner for the Baltic. Koch had already forged an evil reputation as civil commissar in the Ukraine, and he was infamous as a genocidal opponent of all manifestations of local identity and autonomy. Koch's small-minded actions, Skorzeny later recalled, 'caused great resentment'.[59]

German approval for Baltic nationalism was tied up with the related issue of the Baltic 'national committees', a matter that eventually aroused such concern that it wound up on the *Führer*'s agenda. In the original Nazi view, the Baltic States were a key point of focus for German irredentism, particularly since the area had traditionally been the home of a large *Volksdeutsch* population and Estonians and Latvians were believed to contain a high proportion of Germanic racial stock. In this view, the Baltic States were well suited to emerge as a German province rather than as a frontier colony of the Greater Reich. Such a perspective implied, in turn, that the Baltic peoples should be treated marginally better than their unfortunate Slavic neighbours, although it also suggested a measure of direct rule and boded ill for local forms of Baltic nationalism. For a long period, even as the formation of 'national committees' became standard practice for other peoples of the Soviet Union, the occupiers resisted the extension of such prerogatives to the Balts.[60]

It was only after the *Wehrmacht* had been ejected from most of the Baltic region that the Rosenberg Ministry considered major reforms. In November 1944, it served notice of an intention to set up 'national committees' for all three Baltic republics, a concession that came as welcome news to Skorzeny's commandos, although Koch and his powerful ally, party chancellery boss Martin Bormann, soon got in the way. The main source of debate was the creation of a Latvian committee, since the *Wehrmacht* still occupied a sizeable portion of the Latvian coast and any acknowledgement of Latvia's right to national existence would have more than symbolic consequences. Hitler expressed a typical disinterest in the issue and thus gave a free hand to Himmler, who was trying to find a middle ground between pro-separatist liberals and Nazi irredentists. His solution was to call the new Latvian body a 'freedom committee', thus avoiding use of the supposedly objectionable adjective 'national', although his deputy, Gottlob Berger, complained that subsequent efforts to assemble the committee still involved him in a bruising bureaucratic struggle with the Eastern Ministry and the Foreign Office. Berger, a supporter of Pechau's *Jagdeinsatz Baltikum*, suggested that interdepartmental skirmishing over Latvia was having adverse affects on the construction of Estonian and Lithuanian committees and was disheartening to 'all pro-German activists on the Eastern Front'.[61] Once authorised, the Latvian committee never had the favourable impact that was hoped,[62] but it did eventually realise the fears of its opponents by seeking recognition as a provisional government in early May 1945.[63]

After the three 'national committees' were established, 'political advisors' were sent to *Jagdeinsatz Baltikum* under cover of the SS Main Office, although these individuals also represented the interests of the new 'committees' and were supposed to signify their influence in helping to 'liberate' their homelands. The three delegates were *Standartenführer* Juuling for the Estonians, *Oberleutnant* Ziukas for the Lithuanians, and *Untersturmführer* Grapmanis for the Latvians.[64]

Given this political background, it will come as no surprise that *Jagdverband* attempts to cause trouble in the Baltic states were relatively straightforward in Estonia and Lithuania, but much more complicated in Latvia. In Estonia, the *Abwehr* had already experienced success in encouraging anti-Soviet partisan warfare during the early days of Barbarossa. Nonetheless, when Estonian nationalists had floated the idea of organising veterans of this guerrilla campaign, Operation 'Erna', into the core of a national army, the Germans answered with a flat 'no'. Still, some of the 'Erna' guerrillas later turned up in *Waffen*-SS units or in Border Guard regiments organised by the Germans, and some also volunteered for special formations that served in the Finnish Army as light infantry detachments. When the Red Army overran Estonia in the summer of 1944, most Estonian auxiliary units were forced to withdraw with the *Wehrmacht*, although a few of their members volunteered for German commando operations. Some 10,000 men who did not retreat, and who were not captured by Soviet forces, escaped into the underground and began to wage partisan warfare. Some of the volunteers who came back from Finland also fled into the forests, particularly since the reason that they had joined the Finns was to learn the skills necessary to defend their homeland against a resurgent Soviet threat.[65] Two of these men were Finnish Army lieutenants Rosenberg and Kello, who offered to serve as training officers in a FAK 204 camp at Keilajoa. When the Germans withdrew from Estonia in September 1944, these officers stayed behind in order to conduct guerrilla warfare.[66]

There is no doubt that the Germans provided support for Estonian *Kleinkrieg* efforts. In the spring and summer of 1944, FAK 204 ran Operation 'Eiche', the burying of sabotage caches in northern Estonia and on the islands of Saaremaa and Hiiumaa, which were envisioned by Estonian nationalists as possible redoubts. During the fighting in the summer and autumn of 1944, FAK 204 ran ten missions behind Soviet lines, collectively codenamed Operation 'Eestimaa'. In July 1944, ten Estonian militants were also trained at a Mil D facility in Kamenz and then dispatched on a separate operation called 'Kater', which involved the infiltration of Soviet lines near Lake Peipus in order to carry out reconnaissance and sabotage. This exploit, conducted by *Oberleutnant* Kubit, was an experimental foray intended to develop the stratagems necessary for large-scale deployments. The main lesson was that the Soviets were deadly and vigilant opponents; all the members of the team were either killed or captured and they never got a chance to report to German controllers via their radio transmitter.[67]

Once the Germans had withdrawn from Estonia, *Jagdeinsatz Baltikum* assumed responsibility for most sabotage efforts. Manfred Pechau left thirty stay-behind agents in the country, and a squad of Estonians was being trained at Friedenthal as early as September 1944. Despite the disruption of *Jagdverband Ost* at Hohensalza, a platoon called *Jagdkommando Estland* was eventually organised and managed to send three groups into the homeland in late January 1945. By early March, two more operations had been planned by the *Baltikum*'s forward headquarters. Codenamed 'Ulme' and 'Ahorn', these missions involved the parachuting of two squads into Estonian territory, both equipped with radio transmitters. It is not clear whether or not these drops were undertaken before the end of the war, although a sixteen-man Estonian wireless *Trupp* was being trained in Nuremberg and personnel were moved forward to Elten and Greifswald, presumably in order to aid in active operations. Another seven-man Estonian squad was running operations out of Schleswig and Denmark as late as May 1945, apparently using submarines in order to reach their destinations.[68]

In Lithuania too the Germans launched anti-Soviet resistance preparations with their usual mix of half-hearted enthusiasm and bad faith. Their main asset in the country was the interwar fascist movement, the 'Iron Wolves'. In 1941, Lithuanian nationalists had greeted the German invasion of the USSR with an anti-Soviet insurrection, although like the Ukrainian nationalists, they made the mistake of issuing a precipitate declaration of independence, thus incurring the wrath of their Nazi 'liberators'. After disbanding the nationalist partisan formations, the Germans eventually allowed the establishment of 'Litauische Sonderverbände' under General Povilas Plechavicius, with the promise that these battalions could train under the Lithuanian flag, although the project went awry when the Germans tried to incorporate the units into the Wehrmacht. The local SS-Police commander, Friedrich Jeckeln, was determined to rein in Plechavicius's forces. Plechavicius reacted by ordering his men to desert amass. Whole detachments fled into the woods and degenerated into guerrilla bands, although the main aim of these groups was to confront the Soviets.

Although Nazi officialdom regarded the Plechavicius deserters as enemies and there were armed clashes between the two sides, the formations received a continuing measure of succour from the German Army, which refused to take offence at their manifestations of national sentiment. The Wehrmacht armed and supplied these 'illegal' units and tried to convince them to send volunteers to East Prussia for training as wireless operators. By August 1944, one of the detachments had been rebuilt to regimental size; another was completing its formation and armament at a base near Telsiai.[69] As the Soviets advanced through Lithuania in the late summer and early autumn of 1944, German intelligence reports suggest that many Lithuanians remained 'loyal' to the German side – supposedly the lesser of two evils – and that bypassed German troops were readily accepted into nationalist partisan bands.[70] FAK 103 noted in mid-September that the woods around Raseiniai were already full of German stragglers, Red Army deserters and Lithuanian draft dodgers, all of whom were being helped by the population.[71]

Skorzeny was ordered to help the 'National Lithuanian Movement', which was thought to number 30,000 guerrillas, but with the disruption of the 'Wild Cat' project the Jagdverbände failed to launch any serious efforts. Although Jagdverband Ost inherited a training camp for Lithuanians, and although Jagdeinsatz Baltikum was separately training units containing seventy-two Lithuanians, described as 'serviceable groups', only several small Jagdverband detachments were dispatched into Soviet-occupied Lithuania. The first was a radio-equipped team of seven Lithuanian volunteers sent on a mission in the autumn of 1944. A major action was planned for March 1945, but it is not clear if this operation ever came to pass.[72]

Much of the initiative was left to units of the Zweierorganisation, which had good contacts with the Lithuanians and had cached supplies during the spring and summer of 1944. As a result, they were ready to operate at a time when the Jagdverband programme was still in its infancy. It was they who organised Korvettenkapitän Laurinat's training camp at Rummelsburg, Pomerania, which was originally run by FAK 203. In a single two-month period, Laurinat dropped forty-seven heavily armed commando teams behind Soviet lines. Despite their enthusiasm, most of these detachments were eliminated within a year. Line-crossing operations were launched by *Leutnant* Waldemar Göttler, who planned a series of undertakings codenamed '*Libinan*' I to IV. Göttler proposed to send guerrilla squads into Lithuania, using supplies earlier cached in Latvia in order to rearm and provision these detachments. '*Libinan*' I and II were actually carried out.

Even historians sympathetic to the Lithuanian partisans admit that they received German help and that parachutists provided access to plentiful German stores of arms. Several hundred German-trained operatives were infiltrated or dropped into Lithuania, mostly communications specialists and demolition experts. Lithuanian nationalists claim, however, that such elements were strictly subordinated to the guerrilla high command and that after the beginning of 1945, guerrilla bands were increasingly comprised of persons of Lithuanian ethnic origin.[73]

The story of the Lithuanian Freedom Army (LFA), the largest of the nationalist movements, provides a good example of the Lithuanian-German relationship. Originally formed in 1941 as a means of resisting the Germans, the LFA remained largely dormant during the Axis occupation, although it roused itself as the Red Army approached Lithuania's borders. Deciding upon the necessity of armed struggle, the LFA leadership sought help both from the Germans and from senior officers of the pre-war Lithuanian Army, one of whose number, General Motiejus Peciulionis, agreed to lead the movement's military wing. The Germans provided weapons before they retreated, and in the spring of 1945 they also sent a three-man party to join Peciulionis's staff and maintain liaison with the *Zweierorganisation*. This team parachuted near Baisogala. Although its radio operator immediately surrendered to the Soviets, two remaining members succeeded in contacting the Lithuanian guerrillas.[74]

Lithuanian partisans interfered with Red Army lines of communication and with Soviet pacification efforts – FHO noted that they were active around the turn of 1944–1945 north-east of Vilna and between Raseiniai and Panevežys – although the Soviets answered this challenge with their standard response to partisan warfare: the punitive laying to waste of whole villages, mass deportations, and the air dropping of NKGB *agents provocateurs* into areas effected by guerrilla operations. As happened in the Ukraine, the Kremlin dispatched one of the rising stars of the *Nomenklatura*, in this case Mikhail Suslov. Equipped with a mandate to eradicate the nationalist guerrillas, Suslov relied heavily on the services of Lavrenti Beria's right-hand man, NKGB general Sergei Kruglov.[75]

Compared to Lithuania and Estonia, the situation in Latvia was complicated, at least from a German perspective. Unlike its neighbours, Latvia had a large pro-Soviet proletariat, which traditionally had been hostile to the Baltic German elite, and whose hostility met with the mutual disdain of the latter. Despite this tension, there was no country in the region that meant more to German irredentists. During the First World War, when German forces had occupied Latvia, they had tried to establish it as a duchy (or duchies) under the German crown, particularly the coastal peninsula of the Courland, where ten per cent of the population was ethnic German and the high culture was Germanic.[76] Naturally, the Nazis were the heirs to such sentiments. During the retreat from the Soviet Union, they made an extra effort to hold on to Latvia, and they managed to form an unconquered pocket in the Courland, the lines of which were manned by a German army group that held out until May 1945.

Given this history, riding the tiger of Latvian nationalism seemed a risky proposition. The Latvian nationalists could put up a good fight and by the autumn of 1944 the Germans were already hearing reports about anti-Soviet guerrilla warfare in the eastern Latvian province of Lettgallia. Indeed, one NKGB officer who was stationed in the area in 1945–1945 later recalled that Latvian guerrillas were the most fanatic of all the anti-communist partisans in the western USSR. However, it was precisely this intensity of national spirit – based in a country of historic and current interest to German expansionists – that rendered Latvia a special case. In fact, it caused such tension that security jitters eventually got the better of the occupiers and caused them to botch the development of a coherent anti-Soviet guerrilla programme. This story also reveals, perhaps more clearly than any other episode, the depth of animosity between the former *Abwehr* elements that Skorzeny had inherited and the SS thugs to whom he was introducing the subtleties of political warfare.

The main point of contention was Janis Kurelis, a former general in the Latvian Army who was deeply concerned about the recovery of Soviet fortunes after 1943, although he disclaimed any political ambitions. Like Plechavicius, Kurelis was one of a generation of senior warhorses whose names were associated with the golden age of Baltic independence and who counted for a great deal in the organisation of popular resistance. In late July 1944, Kurelis got German authorisation to form a counter-guerrilla corps that was technically independent of the occupiers, although it shared many of the same military objectives. Kurelis's fondest wish was to form the nucleus of a force that could possibly hold an unoccupied fringe of Latvia even if the Germans evacuated their armies (which they were widely expected to do). He hoped that the Western Powers would eventually send help against the Soviets, as they had done in 1919. With these objectives in mind, he set up his headquarters in Skriveri and appointed Captain Kristops Upelnieks as his chief of staff. Upelnieks was a covert member of the 'Latvian Central Council' (LCC), which had been established late in 1942 and had close contacts with the Latvian émigré community in Sweden. The LCC regarded the Kurelis corps as a sort of home guard in service of the patriot resistance movement. By August 1944, Kurelis's troops were already busy fighting Soviet Partisans and parachutists.

Kurelis's reputation drew to his banner a number of evolving nationalist guerrilla units, made up largely of forest-bound fugitives from a number of German bodies, including the labour service, Latvian militia detachments and the two Latvian SS formations, the 15th and 19th divisions. In October and early November 1944, droves of deserters fled from both SS units, in the first case because the division was being transferred to Germany, and in the second because it was assumed that Hitler was getting ready to evacuate his beachhead in the Courland and would leave the Latvians in the lurch. Because Kurelis was not officially in German service, his movement looked attractive to the deserters. On the other hand, since Kurelis was trying to stay loosely within the bounds of the law, he could not afford to organise runaway SS legionaries who were regarded by the Germans as having put themselves beyond the pale. Thus, the general's control over these groups was loose, although the fugitives regarded themselves as 'Kurelians'. Because of the indeterminate degree of control exercised by Kurelis over many of his followers, estimates on the size of his movement vary. The 'Kurelians' told the Germans that they numbered 500 volunteers, although they informed Peter Klibitus, their liaison officer at the LCC outpost in Sweden, that they had 1,000 men in their ranks. Visvaldis Mangulis cites estimates running from 1,200 to 16,000 men, the range of which depends on how finely the term 'Kurelian' is interpreted.

Since Kurelis was involved in organising the nationalist guerrilla bands that were already engaged against the Soviets in Lettgallia, he was of immediate interest to various FAK officers. *Leutnant* Hasselmann, chief of *Trupp* 212, saw a splendid opportunity to re-enlist in German service many highly capable men who were sitting in the woods, or at least to channel the energies of these men with the help of Kurelis. Hasselmann prevailed upon Kurelis to reserve the best of his volunteers for FAK sabotage and combat missions, and also to facilitate the security of Latvian partisan units that *Trupp* 212 was itself organising. These operations, undertaken in October 1944, yielded good results, and when central Latvia was overrun by the Soviets in late September, forcing Kurelis to shift his headquarters to Stadze, in the Courland, he agreed to leave behind 150 men to function in the rear of the Red Army. This company was called *Einheit* 'Lobe', in honour of a much-admired Latvian colonel in the *Waffen*-SS.

With Kurelis's support, Hasselmann launched Operation '*Latvija*', throwing a dozen teams of parachutists into action around Riga, probably with the hope of using sabotage caches that *Trupp* 212 had buried in the district. Only several of Hasselmann's groups managed to return to German lines, although several reported by radio, which prompted a follow-up operation called '*Nachschub* Riga'. Five parachutists sent out to make contact with surviving elements of '*Latvija*' discovered that members of the unit had fallen into Soviet hands and were operating their transmitters under duress.

Operating from a base in East Prussia, FAK 203 also dispatched a number of sabotage teams in order to demolish stretches of the Riga-Daugaupils railway. Inspired by the night sky, the Germans called the four parachute groups 'Mercury', 'Venus', 'Mars' and 'Jupiter', while the detachments slipped through the front were called 'Neptune', 'Uranus' and 'Orion'. Aerial reconnaissance suggested that these missions were partially successful.

In evaluating such activity, it is crucial to re-emphasise both the constantly shifting configuration of Kurelis's organisation and the tenuous nature of his relationship with the Germans. Unfortunately, Kurelis was not successful in balancing himself at the edge of the law. For their part, the Germans had little contact with him, except through a few low-level officers like Hasselmann, and despite the fact that Hasselmann was eager to sing his praises, Kurelis was little understood in senior echelons of the German Army and the SS. The Gestapo reported that he was in contact with deserters from the *Waffen*-SS, and rumours swirled that he was also dickering with communist bands. Hasselmann largely conceded the first charge, but denounced the second as Soviet disinformation.

After considerable effort, Hasselmann succeeded in sponsoring negotiations at Talsen on 2 November, with Kurelis and Upelnieks representing the 'Kurelians' and the vicious mass murderer Friedrich Jeckeln representing the Germans. Everything seemed to go well: Kurelis and Upelnieks agreed to place three companies of guerrilla hunters within the SS-Police framework, to screen deserters so that they could be forwarded to frontline service and to raise a corps of volunteers for service in *Jagdverband Ost*. In addition, plans were made for propaganda calling upon Latvians to fight for a 'free Latvia', naturally on the German side.

No sooner had this agreement been put on paper, however, than matters began to deteriorate. Some of the men loosely under Kurelis's control were reported to be looting small towns and villages, and a special unit of Soviet parachutists, the 'Red Arrow', had been ordered by Moscow to act as *agents provocateurs*. They undertook various crimes disguised as 'Kurelians'. In addition, some of the Latvian SS deserters, upset by rumours of a German retreat from the Courland, staged attacks upon German troops. The proverbial straw, however, was provided by increasing evidence that Kurelis's links with Sweden led ultimately to the British. Unknown to the Latvian nationalists, the SD had long been monitoring the radio communications of both the 'Kurelians' and the LCC, and the Germans suspected that Swedish officers providing help to the nationalists were backed by the SIS station in Stockholm. By this stage of the war, the Germans were usually delighted to have the British supporting the same resistance groups as themselves – such convergences seemed to suggest a community of interests – but in this case they worried because they were still on hand in Latvia and local resistance forces could potentially be turned against them. In the final analysis, they decided not to take a chance on Kurelis.

The key agent in this evolving shift of allegiances was Jeckeln, who was described by acquaintances as 'unintelligent and extremely loathsome', and was never famous for his Solomonic sense of judgement. Just as he had reacted negatively to the Plechavicius legion, Jeckeln once again could not bear the idea of an armed force operating on an autonomous basis. Within days of meeting with Kurelis, he was already telling his army opposite number, Baron von Gersdorff, he intended to dissolve Kurelis's private army. On 14 November, he launched a three-day operation euphemistically referred to as a 'levying' of Kurelis's forces. On the first day, 680 men were arrested, including Kurelis and Upelnieks, and two days later the bulk of these men were forced aboard a ship and sent to Germany, where many eventually wound up at the Stutthof Concentration Camp. The elderly Kurelis was eventually released to the care of his family, but Upelnieks was not so lucky. He was brought before a military court and executed at Liepaja on 19 November. One of Kurelis's companies, under Lieutenant Rubenis, engaged in a three-day running battle until it was finally wiped out and Rubenis was killed. In all, about 500 'Kurelians' died in combat or were executed, but the German Army and the SS had at least won peace of mind.[77] 'The successful levying of the "Kurelis" Resistance Organisation', reported FHO, 'has removed a latent danger to the security of our troops.'[78]

Hasselmann was aghast. His plans for anti-Soviet resistance lay in ruins and he predicted an immediate increase in the flight of nationalists to the timberlands, plus a rise in nationalist guerrilla attacks against German forces. Moreover, he charged that the leaders of *Jagdverband Ost* had engineered the blow against Kurelis, presumably as a means of denying Kurelis's base of power to their rival, *Trupp* 212, and clumsily 'levying' it for themselves.[79]

German *Kleinkrieg* policy in Latvia never recovered from the Kurelis affair. Even an SD assessment later admitted that Kurelis had been extremely popular and that his arrest had inspired widespread discontent, perhaps constituting a turning point in German-Latvian relations.[80] Many of Kurelis's troops evaded the SS 'levying' and fled into the woods, taking with them their weapons. They subsequently reported to Sweden that there were 10,000 like-minded partisans living in the heavy forests of the Courland, and refugees streaming out of Latvia confirmed that the woods were literally crawling with nationalist guerrillas, now committed to fighting both the Germans and the Soviets. To the extent that such forces still had contact with the outside world, they looked toward the Swedes and the British as possible patrons. Some nationalists argued that it was better to flee to Sweden than to act as cannon fodder for the Germans.

Hasselmann also complained that the 150 Latvian volunteers working for his unit 'lost all appetite for service' once they saw how the 'Kurelians' had been treated. Only one major FAK operation was conducted after the Kurelis affair. Codenamed '*Bärenfang*', it involved the assassination of a Soviet intelligence officer, who was killed near Riga by an eleven-man German team.[81]

As for *Jagdverband Ost*, it apparently got little from the loutish 'levying' of the Kurelis legion. *Ost* had originally started 'Wildcat' activity in the autumn of 1944, running operations from a base in Kabile. Agents operated in the Soviet-occupied provinces of Zemgallia and Vidzeme, and plans were made for the launch of an underground newspaper, tentatively titled *18 November* (the date of Latvia's independence). The initial leadership cadre consisted of eager Latvian officers from the *Waffen*-SS, who believed that they had an opportunity to once again demonstrate Latvia's right to exist. However, there were problems evident from an early date. 'Wildcat' officers treated the Germans as a necessary evil, arguing that they were the only current source of weapons and supplies, but that it was a mistake to pin hopes on the Third Reich. Indeed, some elements were already looking to the British, and at least one 'Wildcat' leader, Robert Sebris, was already working for the SIS, at least indirectly. The Kurelis affair deepened this antipathy, since the 'Kurelians' were broadly seen as patriots who had served the national good despite a lack of leadership and adequate weapons.[82]

Having fouled the recruitment pool in Latvia, *Ost* had to scramble to find recruits among Latvian refugees and labourers in Germany. This difficult task was assigned to *Untersturmführer* Arvid Janevics, a former Latvian army officer who had been posted with the German security police in Riga. By January 1945, Janevics was organising a *Jagdeinsatz Baltikum* battle school at Hohensalza. No sooner had this project been launched than the Soviets overran Hohensalza, in the process killing much of the manpower that had been assembled. Janevics survived and according to one report he slipped behind Soviet lines, whence he sent radio messages back to his German controllers. By March 1945, however, he was back in Germany, where he was eventually captured by the advancing Americans. One of Janevic's chief recruiters, Edouard Sowers, also managed to escape the vortex at Hohensalza, slogging his way through to German lines with a small band of troops, only to find out what the Nazis really thought of him. Transferred on 25 January to Skorzeny's command post outside Berlin, he was treated so shabbily that he eventually threw up his hands and defected to 'Zeppelin'. Pechau's Latvian political counsellor, Gunars Grapmanis, an officer in the 19th *Waffen*-SS Division, was also dragooned into searching for 'Wildcat' recruits, although he had severe doubts about the nature of this task. Seeking inspiration from Skorzeny, he and his aides visited Friedenthal in mid-

February 1945, but no one could get a sense of what Skorzeny planned to do or how he aimed to further their cause.[83]

By all accounts, it was difficult to stir up Latvian enthusiasm for service in SD ranks. A *Jagdverband* mustering report on 20 March 1945 mentions nine volunteers being trained as part of a Latvian wireless group, and an eyewitness at Friedenthal in late February and March 1945 recalled seeing a sixty-man '*Lettischer-Verband*' that passed through the camp, although this unit also included Estonians. By February 1945, Latvian radio operators were being moved to Stolp and thence on to the Courland, but after the Kurelis affair, there is only one reference to a *Jagdverband* team actually being sent into Soviet-occupied territory: a small detachment deployed in late January 1945.

By March 1945, 'Wildcat' officers had built a guerrilla structure called '*Laima*', a reference to the ancient Latvian deity of good feelings and positive thought. The name reflected a sense that only the most wildly optimistic of Latvian cadres could still be expected to see purpose in resisting the Soviets. Although '*Laima*' was supposed to coordinate existing partisan groups, the fact that *Jagdverband* officers had alienated such elements led them to make the questionable claim that Latvian resistance existed mainly in spirit, rather than reality, and that '*Laima*' would have to start from the ground up, developing an 'illegal' network that could eventually support sabotage and guerrilla warfare. Like many German enterprises, '*Laima*' was highly organised, being developed around a small headquarters – five people, including two radio operators – which was responsible for training, distribution of supplies and issuing directives. The main idea was to provide a central direction for guerrilla warfare and intelligence-gathering in Soviet Latvia, although '*Laima*' was also supposed to organise stay-behind preparations in Courland and even to function in Germany, where Latvian refugees could be deployed in enemy-occupied portions of the country. Naturally, the organisation was 'independent' in name only, since it was actually subordinated to Pechau.[84] It is unclear whether or not such efforts had any practical effect.

'THE ONLY COUNTRY WITHOUT A QUISLING'

The problems that the Germans faced in trying to exploit anti-communist Baltic and Ukrainian partisans were tame compared to the difficulties of negotiating with the Polish underground movement. Although Skorzeny was charged with reaching out to the main Polish resistance organisation, the *Armija Krajowa*, or 'Home Army',[85] the recent history of German-Polish relations did not bode well for such a project. Hitler hated the Poles, and although he had once been willing to gain a momentary advantage in the balance of power by dickering with the dictatorship of Marshal Pilsudski, he did not recognise the long-term legitimacy of Polish national existence, something that became painfully apparent when Poland was overrun in 1939 and the SS began systematically destroying the Polish leadership class. Since the Nazis were interested only in exploiting Poland as the gateway to a future eastern empire, they did not bother even to create a puppet regime with which to run the country. Instead, they imposed a colonial administration called the 'General Gouvernement', which was staffed at senior levels by German Nazis. Polish nationalists never tired of bragging that their nation 'had not produced a single

Quisling and did not raise a single unit on the side of the Germans',[86] but the cruel truth is that this situation was based less on any particular merits of the Poles than on the fact that the Germans long did not cultivate or accept any such help.

Given the nature of German policy in Poland, the AK quickly assumed many governmental functions, acting as an underground state and being sanctioned in this endeavour by the Polish Government-in-Exile, which eventually situated itself in London. In 1942, the émigré government ordered all armed groups in Poland to submit to the AK's authority. Supported by the Western Allies, the AK was a conservative group and took as its mandate the preparation of a mass uprising, which was expected to occur near the time of German defeat. Occasional sabotage acts were carried out to maintain morale and deflect communist charges of inactivity, but the AK could not embrace a strategy of constant confrontation because of fear of reprisals.[87] The initial German feeler to the AK came as early as September 1941, when the crusade in the Soviet Union first showed signs of becoming a protracted fight. AK commander Stefan Rowecki reported that the Gestapo had suggested a 'quiet arrangement' whereby the resistance movement would suspend its operations, while the Gestapo would provide a reciprocal suspension of repression.[88]

However, it was from 1943 onward, with the rapid retraction of the Eastern Front, that the Germans began to reconsider their Polish policy, although the shifts were not important enough or quick enough to win them credit. Several opportunities were thrown into their laps and squandered. It is true that in the spring of 1943 propaganda chief Joseph Goebbels masterfully brought to light a Soviet massacre of captured Polish officers that had taken place in the Katyn Forest in 1940, thus inducing a break in diplomatic relations between the London Poles and the Kremlin. Shortly after this breach, Rowecki ordered his resisters to concentrate armed attacks on the Nazi administration in Poland and to leave alone *Wehrmacht* lines of communication. However, the Katyn revelations made less impact than the Germans had hoped, partly because of the inability of Polish peasants and toilers to identify with the upper-class officers who had been murdered by the Soviets. In the wake of the Katyn controversy, Hans Frank, the Nazi viceroy, also began to advocate a more enlightened policy toward the Poles and he even talked about arming a Polish 'home guard'. However, Frank was blocked by Hitler and Himmler, who continued to regard Poland as a German colony.[89]

The failure of the Warsaw Rebellion in August–September 1944 provided a second chance to shift Nazi policies, given that the absence of any significant Russian help for the insurgents once again threw Soviet goodwill into doubt. German propaganda assumed a more liberal tone, calling up the image of Pilsudski, and admitting that wartime Poles had 'fulfilled [their] duty towards Europe', but there were still no concessions in the way that Poland was governed. Himmler had already begun to come around to a more reasonable way of thinking – he toyed with the idea of re-establishing an 'independent' Polish state – but he was too timid to bring his mounting concerns to Hitler.[90]

The Yalta Conference in February 1945 provided a third opportunity to forge a new Polish policy, particularly since Polish nationalists were outraged by arrangements that shifted Poland's eastern boundary in favour of the USSR and seemed likely to leave the entire country in the Soviet sphere of influence. Moreover, because the Germans had recently been shoved out of their last toeholds in Poland, there seemed little to lose by befriending Polish nationalists. The Germans played up the 'betrayal' of Poland and rushed to congratulate the London Poles on rejecting Yalta. However, when Frank suggested organising a Polish 'National Committee', he could find no support. Indeed, when Kaltenbrunner pressed Hitler to 'immediately revise' policy toward the Poles, all the latter would concede was that Polish workers in Germany should receive a status equal to other foreign labourers.[91]

Despite equivocations about Polish policy, the Germans did start reaching out to right-wing portions of the Polish resistance movement. According to the SD, Polish nationalist bands had a 'correct' attitude toward communism and the supposed Jewish peril, and FHO noted in February 1944 that the Polish underground was caught hopelessly between the Germans and the Soviets. The movement, they predicted, would eventually bifurcate, with one half resolving to cooperate with the Germans and the other making its peace with the Soviets. In August 1944, they suggested that this split was beginning to appear. As the London Poles attempted to dicker with Moscow, right-wingers attempted to move the AK away from a course of compromise.[92]

The Germans occasionally had success in arranging informal truces with right-wing regional commanders in the AK, and in the Novogrodek area the *Abwehr* supplied local AK units with weapons in order to support operations against Soviet Partisans. Despite the value of these arrangements, it was the central headquarters of the AK that the Germans most wished to convert to a path of collaboration (as they were doing with the central mechanisms of the UPA and the Yugoslav Chetniks). In this regard, they had little success, at least until the Warsaw Rebellion and the Yalta Agreement further shifted Polish attitudes. Despite the fact that the Germans captured General Rowecki in June 1943 and they tempted him with offers of collaboration, Rowecki remained stubborn and was of no value in bringing over the AK to a pro-German outlook. In fact, the London Poles were still willing to stick with the Allies and ordered the AK to carry out Operation 'Tempest', a large-scale attempt to create disorder behind German lines and thereby facilitate the advance of the Red Army. In connection with 'Tempest', AK officers in negotiation with the Germans were instructed to terminate such contacts. Local leaders who opposed 'Tempest' were accused of fomenting fratricidal conflict and dismissed. The Novogrodek battalion commander was charged with mutiny and stood in front of a court martial. There is no doubt, however, that many AK commanders retained doubts about the wisdom of 'Tempest', particularly when they learned that introducing themselves to the advancing Soviets often resulted in arrest and the break-up of their forces.

During the talks between the Novogrodek AK and the *Abwehr*, the Germans explained that they wanted contact with the AK central command and that to secure its help they were willing to be 'flexible', even to the extent of liberalising the nature of German rule and allowing the AK to control elements of the Polish administration. Although Rowecki's successor, Tadeusz Komorowski, had already pondered armed resistance behind Soviet lines, he had committed himself to 'Tempest' and refused to consider any German offers: the official line, he said, was that there could be no understandings or agreements, even if they brought local benefits. Rather, victory was still the final goal and AK leaders would have to remain committed to the launching of a last-minute rebellion against the occupier.[93]

As is well known, this ultimate revolt, the Warsaw Uprising of August–September 1944, was a costly disaster, and it created the impression – rightly or wrongly – that Soviet forces in nearby Praga had twiddled their thumbs and allowed the flower of the Polish nationalist movement to be annihilated. A Mil D study in September 1944 hinted that until the revolt, chances of converting the AK to German purposes had been slim. The AK's main discourse, it claimed, had revived an age-old hatred of Germany and had portrayed the war as a life-and-death struggle in which one side, the Germans, wanted to destroy the 'biological substance' of the other. The Soviets, on the other hand, had supposedly benefited from a semblance of pan-Slavic sentiment and from the influence of Polish elements sympathetic to their cause. With fresh evidence of Soviet betrayal, however, the AK was no longer treating the USSR as an ally, and resentments about likely Soviet domination, the shift of the eastern frontier and the drafting of Poles into pro-Soviet armies came bubbling to the surface.[94] Such realisations, Mil D reported, would be exploited in 'Zweier-sphere' propaganda work, and one can see subsequent evidence of an approach that was cognizant of Polish hatred of Germany, but nonetheless tried to turn Poles in an anti-Soviet direction. Pamphlets designed for AK fighters conceded that Poles might never feel affection for Germany, but urged them to think strategically because Germany had become 'a purely secondary enemy'.[95]

Naturally, the Germans did everything possible to encourage the AK's sense of abandonment, starting rumours and using underground channels for propaganda, and there is some evidence that by the last phase of the revolt, opinion in the AK had begun to shift. The Germans were pleased to find anti-British leaflets in rebel-held areas, and they encountered surrendering AK troops who told them that more struggle against the *Wehrmacht* was pointless, but that the future lay with a German-Polish-British-American coalition against the USSR. In truth, the fact that the Warsaw rebels capitulated at all came as a surprise. Most senior Nazis had expected Komorowski to go down fighting and the AK had borne the capacity to have extended the fighting for several more weeks.

Had the Germans known about everything that Komorowski had done during his last few weeks in command of the AK, they would have been happier yet. With Warsaw collapsing around his ears and the Red Army sitting across the Vistula, Komorowski organised a limited measure of resistance behind Soviet lines, and he also recommended the practical termination of 'Tempest' and the cancellation of further offensive operations against the Germans. These orders, however, were restricted to officers and not shared with men in the ranks. After some to-and-fro, the regime in London approved these arrangements, although it noted that the AK could not wholly cease the struggle against Germany. 'Otherwise', it pointed out, 'the international position of Poland would greatly deteriorate and the further existence of the Home Army, dependent on Allied supplies, would be jeopardized.'

Despite the fact that the Germans were not current on Komorowski's doings, they suspected that he might be open to an overture. Although the Germans who captured Komorowski claimed that he cursed his allies and regretted having ever started the revolt, they could not pry from him any significant concessions. One of these generals, *Obergruppenführer* Erich von dem Bach-Zelewski, offered to leave Komorowski at liberty and to work with him against the Soviets, but Komorowski huffily responded that he (von dem Bach) could 'expect nothing from me which would be opposed to my conception of honour or to my allegiance and fidelity to my own authorities', and he also hinted that with the Third Reich approaching defeat, it would be folly to switch sides at such a late date.

In spite of this rebuff, von dem Bach arranged for his prisoner to be held in the company of his staff and for most of his troops to be taken captive under the terms of the Geneva Convention, rather than being summarily shot, which had been the standard Nazi treatment for partisans. Von dem Bach was no humanitarian, but Komorowski and his men were obviously valuable assets from which some future utility might still be gained. There was even talk of appointing Komorowski as a 'secret counsellor' to the 'General Gouvernement'.

Not to be dissuaded by a simple 'no' from Komorowski, the Germans launched another initiative in early November 1944, hoping that he could be persuaded to become a Polish Vlasov. This time the German delegate was Harro Thomson, an RSHA officer who told Komorowski that he had come at Himmler's personal request. Thomson had earlier worked on the Rowecki interrogation, which he told his captive, although he declined to mention that the Germans had since executed Rowecki. A North German lawyer who knew little about Poland, Thomson tried to get his way through bluff and bluster. He assured Komorowski that the Axis still had enormous reserves of men and material, that war-winning weapons were being developed, and that victory was in sight. As a result, it would be a mistake for the Polish resistance movement not to accept German help against the Soviets. Komorowski, who had seen bomb damage in Berlin and knew which way the wind was blowing, abruptly repeated his earlier refusals to work with the Nazis.[96] Thus, although Komorowski had already done much of what the SD was requesting, even before he had surrendered his command, he refused to give his interrogators the pleasure of knowing about such matters.

Although Komorowski remained stubborn, by November German field reports were beginning to suggest that the general had already conceded a great deal, at least in *de facto* fashion. Although the Gestapo warned that the AK was preparing a new revolt, FHO claimed that there was a modest shift of power toward the right-wing of the movement and that operations in German-occupied Poland had largely ceased.[97] The Germans also saw Polish guerrilla activity behind Soviet lines growing steadily more intense. According to German sources, there were 6,000 AK resisters hiding near Bilgoraj, and in the Bialystok area strong Polish and Vlasovite groups were blowing up rail lines and attacking Soviet troop columns. There were similar accounts from the area around Lublin, and south-east of Warsaw a regiment of pro-Soviet Polish troops reportedly deserted to the AK. A few guerrilla units even included bypassed German troops; at Nacza, near Radun, a German-Polish band had been active in the summer of 1944, even as the Warsaw Rebellion was underway. Three hundred Red Army soldiers were killed in clashes in the last four months of 1944, and Stalin began to fret about the possibility of full-scale civil war in Poland.

Even more important than reports of such activity, the Germans had reason to believe that some of it was coordinated. Since German signals intelligence intercepted and decrypted the radio communications of the exile Polish Government, the Germans knew that a January

1945 instruction by the London regime to dissolve the AK was a canard, and that Polish Prime Minister Arciszewski had issued a secret counter-order that directed AK elements to maintain contact, hide their weapons, and harass Soviet lines of communication.[98] In early 1945, a nationalist emissary suggested that AK units in eastern Poland were willing to accept German help, particularly 'the dropping of weapons and explosives'.[99]

Not only did such news work to the advantage of the Germans, but political and international developments over the winter of 1944–1945 pushed in the same direction. In Soviet-liberated Poland, the pro-Soviet 'Lublin regime' took the 'October Turn', a drastic swing to the left in which it all but abandoned the effort to bring centrist and nationalist forces into a Soviet-supported coalition, thereby unintentionally laying the groundwork for the survival of anti-communist resistance.[100] In a corresponding move in the opposite direction, the London government veered sharply rightward, a shift marked by the resignation of moderate premier Stanislaw Mikolajczyk and his replacement by the stridently anti-Soviet Tomasz Arciszewski. The British were outraged by this change and Whitehall dropped the AK almost as completely as it had abandoned the Yugoslav Chetniks, postponing the departure of a British military mission, banning further supply flights and imposing pre-censorship upon the exile government's wireless transmissions to German-held territory.[101]

Although it seemed to the London Poles that nothing worse could happen, the Yalta Declaration provided an ultimate moment of agony. The provisions of the agreement were regarded as a betrayal by patriotic Poles of all stripes, and on 13 February the London Poles denounced the arrangement as 'a fifth partition of Poland… accomplished by her Allies'. As a result, they refused to recognise the agreement's legitimacy. Komorowski called it 'our most painful blow'.

Naturally, the Germans sensed that they had yet another chance with the Polish nationalists, and they rushed *Haupsturmführer* Karl-Otto Benninghaus to the Colditz POW camp, where Komorowski was being held. Unlike the brutal von dem Bach or the bombastic Thomson, Benninghaus was a man of some sensitivity: a 41-year-old Rhinelander, he had studied law and was a student of German culture in Eastern Europe, having served with the *Volksdeutscher* Central Office. Until 1944, he had also recruited Polish 'volunteers' for 'Zeppelin'. Benninghaus professed to come to Komorowski as a friend and admirer, representing a group of relative liberals associated with the pre-war German-Polish Association. He admitted that bad treatment had been meted out to the Poles, a policy he professed to have always opposed, but he suggested that Germany was now ready to make amends by helping the Poles deal with the Soviet occupation that had recently been imposed upon their homeland. There was no talk of wonder weapons bringing German victory; just a claim that Poland and Germany were part of the West, and that they were now facing a threat from 'an alien civilisation'. In these circumstances, Komorowski would no doubt want to return to his primary task of fighting for Polish independence, and if he so wished, Germany was ready to release such officers as he needed, transport them to the Soviet rear, and supply them with money and weapons. It was a persuasive pitch.

According to Komorowski's memoirs, the general steadfastly refused to be lured by this more subtle appeal for his help, and he told Benninghaus that he had not changed his mind since speaking to von dem Bach and Thomson. Komorowski's officers also later affirmed that he never wavered in refusing to cooperate with German requests for a joint front against the USSR.[102] However, the evidence from the German side is more ambiguous. Gerhard Teich, the chief intelligence officer of 'Zeppelin' and a man in a position to know about the nature of German intrigues along the Eastern Front, later described Komorowski as having 'deserted to the Germans after the fall of Warsaw'. This description of the general's course of action is frighteningly close to that provided by the Soviets and the 'Lublin Poles', who always suspected that Komorowski was 'a traitor sold to the Germans'. In addition, Benninghaus led a special bureau in Section C, which Teich described as 'a *Referat* formed in March 1945 to deal with Polish volunteers under Bor-Komorowski'. The fact that this office was formed *after* Benninghaus had spoken to Komorowski suggests either a greater degree of *attentisme* by the general than he was later willing to admit, or a considerable amount of wishful thinking by the Germans. It is significant, however, that 'the *Referat* never actually functioned',[103] and it is also true that Komorowski was never released from German captivity, which would have been the precondition to any deal.

The Germans thought they might have better luck with Komorowski's successor, Colonel Leopold Okulicki. Although Okulicki assured the British that he was still an opponent of the Germans, even the British could see that he was an ardent critic of the Soviets and that he expected an imminent East–West confrontation.[104] The Germans were encouraged when their spies reported that Okulicki was reorienting AK opinion for a possible change of course. In early 1945, they received a verbatim transcript of his New Year's Day address:

Today the Polish people are threatened with absolute annihilation from the East. Therefore, we must direct our attention in this direction. I am no soothsayer, but the moment approaches in which the AK will emerge from the underground and serve as a Polish Army, side-by-side with Germany, against the Bolshevik wave, the centuries-old foe and enemy of Christendom. Since political matters are still momentarily unresolved, I ask you, AK soldiers, to avoid all unnecessary sabotage against Germany because no one knows whether today's enemy will be our friend tomorrow.[105]

Not surprisingly, the Germans found Okulicki's remarks encouraging.

On 25 February 1945, Reinhard Gehlen delivered an assessment that must be judged as crucially important, given the reports of informers and German successes decrypting Polish wireless traffic:

According to impressions that seem certain, the intelligence service and the Polish resistance movement are prepared – with the official approval of the émigré government – to enter into cooperation against Bolshevism without political conditions. They are also prepared, if the need exists, to supply the necessary weapons for battle-worthy *Agenten-Aufklärung*. It would therefore be possible… to get a foothold in broad form with a *Frontaufklärung* agent net in all of Poland. Since the London Polish Government has officially disbanded the resistance movement, it will secretly reconstruct it in the Soviet-occupied sector.

Gehlen realised that problems of camouflage were crucial to the London Poles because of their relationship with the British, and that any joint German-Polish projects also had to be disguised in order to avoid offending Nazi irredentists. He proposed to deal with such problems by using his 'Federation of Green Partisans' as a circuit breaker. 'Such cooperation with the Poles', he explained, '[would] not be carried out on the German side, but rather on the side of the anti-Bolshevist Russians. This would also avoid the chance that cooperation could somehow radiate into the political sphere.'[106]

As the London Poles began exploring such lines of contact, the split in the resistance movement predicted by the Germans finally occurred. After Mikolajczyk left the government-in-exile, he called upon his followers in the AK to approach the 'Lublin Poles', and in February 1945 the domestic political body controlling the AK, the Council of National Unity (CNU), also broke with the Arciszewski regime, recognising Yalta and ordering talks with the 'Lublin Poles' and the Soviets. Even Okulicki reluctantly agreed to cooperate. The final result of this approach was a disaster: in March 1945, sixteen senior AK and CNU officials involved in negotiations were snatched by Soviet security forces and sent to Moscow, where they were locked up in Lubianka Prison and accused of fighting a guerrilla war in the rear of the Red Army.[107] Naturally, this outcome delighted the Germans.[108]

There were right-wing elements of the AK still engaged against the Soviets, and the Germans tried to court these elements, despite their obvious reluctance and the associated difficulties of camouflaging the relationship, which meant that the results were mixed (at best). Nonetheless, the SD had been relatively quick off the mark in trying to recruit anti-communist Poles. Section S was training Poles as early as 1943, particularly at its sabotage school near The Hague and at a specialised facility near Berlin. In addition, AK radio agents were trained by an SD unit in Prague. It is interesting to note, in conjunction with the Gehlen memorandum cited above, that members of the 'Polish Group' in Prague were recruited by a Russian intermediary.[109] In the late winter of 1945, the SD-*Ausland* told its constituent sections to approach the AK, and a Polish agent was slipped into Poland from Slovakia, equipped with orders to contact an AK headquarters and – if possible – lead a Polish guerrilla negotiator back to German-held territory.[110]

As was the case with the Ukrainians, however, the main initiatives toward Polish nationalists were left in the hands of Mil D officers, and there is no doubt that some FAK units made progress in bringing Poles under their colours. We know, for instance, that FAK 203 set up Polish sabotage groups and that it also launched a Polish propaganda unit under *Hauptmann* Schlegel. It organised a training camp near Łódź, mobilising at least sixty-four Poles captured while serving in units with the Red Army. These men were trained to blow up rail lines and contact anti-Soviet comrades operating as partisans behind Russian lines. In one case, two Polish volunteers were passed through enemy lines along the River Oder and then travelled to the Silesian town of Liegnitz, where they destroyed sensitive documents stored in the billet of a Soviet general. Both agents succeeded in fleeing back to German lines, bringing with them evidence of their success. In another instance, a six-man group parachuted into the district around Lublin. Members of this squad could not find the anti-communist guerrillas whom they were supposed to contact, but they did use their explosives to blow up a rail line and derail a train. Meanwhile, the German front had been pushed far westward, although one of the Polish guerrillas, Josef Rajezkowski, succeeded in reaching the Oder, where he crossed back into German-held territory. He managed this feat while disguised in the uniform of a Russian soldier whom he had shot.

The soul of FAK 203's effort was a 25-year-old officer named Machnik, an anti-Nazi who had formerly been posted with the espionage component of the *Abwehr*. A native of Upper Silesia, Machnik spoke Polish and had excellent contacts in 'the national Polish movement'. In early 1945, he and another FAK 203 officer, *Leutnant* Erfling, were transferred to the oversight of FAK 204 and their training camp was shifted to a site in Pomerania. Machnik and Erfling were each given charge of Polish '*Streifkorps*', or raiding parties, and in March both men were sent into Soviet-held territory with the aim of causing as much trouble as possible. Machnik managed to unite his group with AK detachments and remained behind enemy lines. Erfling did not fare so well. The personnel of his detachment deserted to the Soviets, although Erfling himself escaped and then struggled back to German lines.[111]

Lev Kopelev provides a Polish perspective on these '*Streifkorps*'. He tells the story of Tadeusz Ruzanski, an AK soldier who had fought in Warsaw and was taken into captivity near the end of the battle. Ruzanski and his fellow prisoners could never quite believe that the Germans were attempting to cultivate them for special operations, and they certainly never reconciled themselves to carrying out such tasks. After a month of horrific treatment, Ruzanski and a number of his compatriots were shifted to a special camp, where they were happy to find plentiful rations, good medical care and clean barracks. Within several weeks, the prisoners were issued 'training' weapons (rifles with the locks removed), and they were given Polish uniforms and German boots. They spent their time training for guerrilla warfare under Polish officers captured in 1939, and they were also formed into military units. Ruzanski was part of a thirty-man platoon under the command of a Polish major.

In January 1945, the camp was visited by a German *Oberst*, who announced that the time had come for the Polish 'volunteers' to rejoin the battle, although they would now be fighting on the German side.

Gentlemen, up to now we have been enemies. But the German army knows how to respect the military valour of its enemies...

[We are] being forced to leave the territory of your Fatherland. We know that many of you have reason to be dissatisfied with us, and with what you have experienced during the occupation. But, gentlemen, you are all soldiers, and I don't have to explain to you that this is war, a war unprecedented in scale and intensity. After the victory of the German Empire, a reasonable and just order will be established over all of Europe, an order worthy of the traditions of our all-European culture. Because, no matter how much we may have fought each other, we are all Europeans. And now, Asiatic hordes are moving against your Fatherland...

Yesterday, we were enemies, but today, history has decided otherwise. By the will of history, in the interests of all the peoples of Europe, in the interests of your Fatherland, we have become allies. And because of that, we are giving you our best weapons and our best equipment and are presenting you with the opportunity to defend your long-suffering Poland against the Soviet invasion with the same valour with which you fought against us.

After this rousing address, Ruzanski's platoon climbed into two waiting trucks – a third truck was loaded with automatic weapons, bazookas, explosives, food supplies and medical equipment – and the party set forth under the direction of four FAK troops. However, when the platoon camped in a woods west of Bydgoszcz, immediately behind the front, the Poles disarmed their German escort and gave themselves up to the advancing Soviets.[112] Yet more light is thrown on this incident by the account of a Nazi civil official, who later confirmed that the German retreat from Bydgoszcz was protected by Polish guerrilla rear guards, although the relationship with these forces was tense, particularly when a German commander threatened to shoot the population if they would not evacuate in timely fashion.[113]

While FAK 204 ran Polish 'Streifkorps' in eastern Pomerania and Kashubia, the opposite end of the country, Upper Silesia, was under the purview of FAK 212, which had been transferred from Italy. FAK 212 officers already had some experience with Polish issues, since they had been trying to subvert Polish field forces in Italy, but after they arrived in Upper Silesia they were reinforced with several FAK 202 specialists, all of whom had practice in recruiting and training Polish volunteers. The intention behind these shifts of personnel was to prepare Operation 'Weissdorn', which involved the construction of a local stay-behind network. In October, one of the recent transferees to FAK 212, Joseph Lazarek, set up a recruitment centre in Katowice, employing thirty recruits seconded from the army, and during the same month Leutnant Ramdohr organised a training school at the Schloss Stolz, near Frankenstein.

Although the Katowice region had been annexed by the Third Reich and its inhabitants were now formally German citizens, Lazarek's idea was to abandon this pretence and appeal to Poles on patriotic grounds, emphasising the threat posed by the USSR. With this object in mind, he secured the transfer of a 43-year-old non-commissioned officer named Larish, who spoke fluent Polish and had been employed in German Stalags as a welfare officer for Polish prisoners. Deeply sympathetic to the Polish cause, Larish was given charge of 'Weissdorn' propaganda, which he was supposed to orient toward intellectuals and students. Yet another German officer, Leutnant Weissweiler, was ordered to secure the support of the Catholic Church, allegedly an essential prop for any project built upon a Polish nationalist base. Weissweiler was supposed to bring local priests into the conspiracy, which he was initially able to do, although as it became apparent that their activities might have a military aspect, many lost nerve and withdrew. Weissweiler even had difficulty prying an anti-Soviet pastoral letter from the archbishop of Breslau, who explained 'that he took his orders from the Vatican, not from the RSHA'.

As was often the case with such delicate projects, the main danger was one of Nazi politicisation. Lazarek and Weissweiler worried that Ramdohr, who was a Brownshirt officer, would contaminate 'Weissdorn' schooling with elements of National Socialist doctrine, although to give Ramdohr credit, he resisted this temptation. Complications arose, however, when organisers were told to recruit Germans for the project. Most of these men were poltroonish Nazi Party officials who had awkward relations with the Polish nationalists and could only be expected to bolt upon the advance of the Soviets. At the turn of 1944–1945, an effort was also made to contact Nazi women's and girls' auxiliaries in order to recruit radio operators.

The course at Schloss Stolz eventually graduated 150 battle-ready volunteers, mostly miners and industrial workers who had been run through drills in weapons handling, sabotage and guerrilla warfare. Even before the Soviets arrived, however, Lazarek had given up the notion of fielding full-scale bands, planning instead to send out individuals or small teams in order to murder Red Army officers. FAK 212's commander, *Hauptmann* Reuter, had also given orders to prepare 'scorched earth' demolitions for mines and industrial facilities, but Lazarek thought such things not only undesirable but unachievable, given shortages of explosives and equipment. As a result, little was done. When the Soviets arrived in January 1945, moving at an unexpectedly quick pace, not enough men had been trained nor enough equipment distributed to make a difference to the situation, even tactically. Neither had the radio apparatus for the female signals network yet arrived.[114]

The most important approach to the Poles was left in the hands of FAK 202, which had a number of staff officers, such as Walter Hösch, who were sympathetic to the Poles and had close contacts with Polish nationalists. FAK 202 officers decided to depend neither upon individual Polish recruits nor upon the AK; rather, they cultivated the AK's right-wing rival, the '*Narodowe Siły Zbrojne*' ('National Armed Forces', NSZ). When Polish resisters had been ordered into the AK in 1942, 20,000 ultranationalists had refused to join, opting instead to fuse with Polish fascist guerrillas and form a new extremist movement. Although NSZ activists were intensely anti-German – their version of Polish irredentism called mainly for the westward shift of boundaries at Germany's expense – their anti-communism and anti-Semitism created a community of interests with the Nazis. One captured NSZ officer told interrogators that if Germany had created a '*Judenfrei*' Polish government after the September War of 1939, Polish 'nationalists' would have cooperated closely with the Third Reich. German Army and Gestapo officers were holding exploratory talks with NSZ regional chiefs as early as 1943, although at that time Himmler still disapproved of such contacts, as did NSZ commander Tadeusz Kurcyusz. By 1944, however, many NSZ leaders were arguing that the USSR had emerged as the main threat to Polish liberty, and unlike the AK headquarters, the NSZ high command became increasingly willing to countenance tactical cooperation with the Germans, although they realised that this had to be disguised in order to foil communist and AK propaganda. Thus, the Germans could report in late 1944 that 'NSZ has presently taken up the struggle against Soviet bands, paratroopers and Jews and hereby seeks to cooperate with German authorities'. German weapons and equipment were provided on a limited basis, particularly to NSZ units in the Lublin district. Some of these formations continued to fight even after the Soviets overran Lublin, carrying out sabotage and harassing Red Army efforts to draft men for a new Polish Army.[115]

The Germans also had a close relationship with NSZ bands in the Kielce area, particularly because of the brokerage of Hubert Jura, a one-time NSZ field commander. Recruited by the Radom Gestapo over the winter of 1943–1944, Jura formed a pro-German militia called 'Tom's Organisation', which established close contact with local NSZ detachments and acted as a middleman for the provision of German weapons and supplies. Jura also got German passes and petrol in order to facilitate the mechanised movement of NSZ forces around the Kielce region. The local Gestapo chief, Paul Fuchs, was a keen advocate of cooperation with NSZ and backed Jura enthusiastically. By the early summer of 1944, the Germans had established a relatively smooth relationship with local NSZ contingents, and several months later the Radom Gestapo reported that the guerrillas had impressed it with their fight against communist partisans and their ability to end local train robberies.

The interests of the Kielce guerrillas and the Germans also converged in another way. In answer to the emerging Soviet 'menace', NSZ leaders considered moving thousands of men into territory controlled by the Western Allies, a project that could hardly proceed without the tacit assent of the Germans. Fuchs and Witzel dreamed about levying much of this westward-bound manpower as a 'Polish Volunteer Brigade', which would be similar to Polish phalanxes organised by the Central Powers during the First World War and would be capable of supporting partisan warfare behind Soviet lines. Although some elements of the RSHA feared that such a force would be unreliable, transit plans for the Kielce guerrillas were negotiated between German and NSZ officers, and in August 1944 a mobile NSZ formation was organised with the object of preparing the guerrillas for redeployment in case of a Soviet advance into south-central Poland. The Poles called this unit the 'Holy Cross Brigade', after the mountains in which it was based; to the Germans it was the nucleus of the 'Polish National Legion'. By the turn of 1944–1945, the 'Holy Cross' formation had grown to a strength of 1,200 men. It was run militarily by Lieutenant-Colonel Antoni Dabrowski and politically by Władysław Kołacinski.

As was often the case in relations between the Nazis and their guerrilla collaborators, the German-NSZ alliance was hardly absent of friction. Despite repeated attempts in the autumn of 1944, Fuchs could not persuade NSZ leaders to set up an anti-communist radio station, and even at this late date there were complaints about occasional assaults by 'Holy Cross' partisans upon small German detachments, the aim of which was to gather weapons. NSZ members probably also constituted most of the Poles being trained at an SD camp in Tomoszów, where German officials complained about repeated desertions. According to Okulicki, there were skirmishes between the 'Holy Cross Brigade' and the Germans in early January 1945, mainly owing to the fact that the guerrillas resented being treated as German auxiliaries.[116]

Fences were mended, however, once the Soviets launched the massive January 1945 offensive, which quickly reached the Holy Cross Mountains. With the cooperation of Fuchs and a local German field officer, *Leutnant* Mrotschy, the 'Holy Cross Brigade' was issued with permits and letters of recommendation for its march *nach Westen*; the Poles in turn agreed not to attack any Germans and promised that their column would avoid large towns. Stay-behind elements were left to harass the advancing Red Army. On 19 January, Dabrowski announced that 'we have entered into a state of non-belligerency with the Germans for an undetermined period of time'. The brigade's flight was a minor military epic that involved dodging Soviet pursuit columns and occasionally skirmishing with German checkpoints along the line of retreat. On 17 January, the unit crossed the border of the 'General Gouvernement' with no difficulty, although it was threatened with being disarmed when it reached German-held Bohemia. On 19 January, the Poles barely made it across the River Oder: with Soviet forces closing in, the Germans allowed *Wehrmacht* units and civilians to cross on a surviving bridge before finally permitting the Poles to cross the span. On 27 January, a German field commander at Zabkowice Slaskie tried to redirect the brigade to the front, although Dabrowski argued that his men were not yet ready for conventional fighting and that their intention was to report for training. Berlin finally intervened and the Poles were allowed to proceed in the direction of Prague.

By mid-February, the 'Holy Cross' guerrillas had reached their designated assembly point at Kosseck, Bohemia. This was the location of a FAK 202 training camp commanded by *Hauptmann* Heilmann. Although the Poles were disconcerted by the constant presence of German officers and sergeants around the training grounds, they now had to offer their pound of flesh, agreeing to prepare forces for deployment under German command. On 7 February, Dabrowski's men were ordered to participate in guerrilla courses, although Dabrowski refused German entreaties to place the entire unit under German control and he was also reluctant to allow his troops to receive parachute instruction. In March 1945, Hubert Jura suddenly appeared at Kosseck, having been evacuated to Berlin at the time of the Soviet Winter Offensive. Under his direction, members of 'Tom's Organisation' seemed more willing than NSZ troopers to undergo parachute training.

By March, the Germans were demanding the re-establishment of contact with 'Holy Cross' elements in southern Poland, which were now believed to be concentrated twenty-five miles east of Kielce. An agent with orders to contact the guerrillas was infiltrated through the front south-east of Frankfurt on the Oder, but he was arrested at a Soviet checkpoint. Three 'Tom' detachments were dropped by air, each equipped with orders to carry out reconnaissance and establish radio communications between the Holy Cross Mountains and Kosseck. A group led by Captain Zygmunt Rafalski was parachuted on 23 March, but Rafalski was soon picked up by the Polish Militia in Kielce. A second squad, headed by a Polish lieutenant, was left leaderless when its chief stepped on a landmine and was killed.[117]

Meanwhile, the 'Polish Legion' steadily grew larger, perhaps because it benefited from the recruitment of a steady stream of Polish refugees pouring into Bohemia. According to one FAK 202 officer, there were 5,000 members of the unit by April 1945, and the Germans were intent on making the formation bigger yet. In early April, they released Major S.W. Kozlowski, an NSZ leader whom they had arrested in 1943. On 13 April, Kozlowski was brought to Kolin, near Prague, where he met with Fuchs and a contingent of FAK 202 and *Jagdverband* officers led by *Obersturmführer* Wolf. On 17 April, Wolf got permission to draw Polish POWs from German prison camps for 'a special operation of the Polish Brigade', and Kozlowski was immediately dispatched to *Stalag* Murnau and to Dachau Concentration Camp in order to recruit Polish 'volunteers'. The Germans hoped for a yield numbering in the thousands, but they were sorely disappointed. Kozlowski met at Murnau with officers who had survived the Warsaw Uprising, but they refused to throw in their lot with the Germans. After several weeks of fruitless efforts, he returned to the brigade empty-handed.

This brief history of the 'Polish Legion' is clearly one of mixed messages and ambiguity. Although no Polish unit of comparable size came so close to wholesale collaboration, neither the officers of the formation nor its German handlers considered the Poles loyal to the German cause. In fact, by mid-April there were signs that German patience was wearing thin and rumours flew around Kosseck about an ambush being prepared by a nearby SS division.[118] Since neither side bothered to feign friendship, the threat of violence was never further away than a single misstep or misinterpreted signal. Whether or not the Germans got any value from such an affiliation is an open question.

Why did groups like the 'Holy Cross' resisters take help from the Germans? Such willingness was the almost inevitable outcome of the three-way fights that had broken out behind the Eastern Front by 1943, pitting German security services against communist partisans, communist partisans against nationalist guerrillas, and nationalist guerrillas against the Germans.

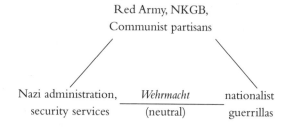

Three-way fights are unstable configurations because once one party to the conflict begins to emerge as the winner, the other two antagonists are usually drawn together, despite their mutual hatred. This stage of the conflict had arrived by 1944–1945, as the Red Army and its communist guerrilla allies came close to securing final victory. There is no doubt that some of the right-wing partisans who gravitated toward the Germans in 1944–1945 did so extremely reluctantly. One UPA commander, in writing to a German military headquarters in April 1944, confessed that 'we harbour great doubts…'; the Germans, he said, seemed beaten and demoralised, they had a record of leaving their allies in the lurch, and 'the ludicrous policies of the slavedriver Hitler and his criminal party clique' had alienated all of Europe.[119] Nonetheless, Germany was still a great power and the groups that did not yet have firm assurances of British backing – or, like the Polish guerrillas, were losing such support – needed friends wherever they could find them. As Nicholas Vakar later noted, 'In Eastern Europe a political compromise… involves no concession of principles and no change of ultimate objective. The parties are fellow travellers, not partners.'[120] The real hope of the Ukrainian, Baltic, Byelorussian and Polish nationalists was that Germany still had enough capacity to severely weaken Soviet Russia, creating a relative vacuum between the two giants that would allow for smaller countries to exercise their independence. In other words, they hoped that the geopolitical pattern characteristic of the period 1918–1920 would re-establish itself.

If the guerrillas grudgingly accepted German support – and the Germans, incidentally, just as grudgingly supplied such aid – one must ask whether such relationships had any impact on the course of the war. Certainly the Germans gained new sources of intelligence and they ensured the sporadic harassment of the Red Army. An FHO study concluded that from August 1944 to February 1945 there were over 600 battles and skirmishes behind Soviet lines, mostly involving Soviet security forces and the UPA.[121] Stalin himself railed about stay-behind agents 'drawn from Latvians, Lithuanians, Poles, Roumanians and Ukrainians... The[se] agents were surprisingly well-trained and organised, and well-equipped with radio sets.' If such elements were allowed to function, he claimed, the Red Army could never hope to keep its strategic intentions a secret. As a result, on 18 December 1944 Stalin authorised the formation of five NKGB divisions, each comprising 5,000 men and armed sufficiently to defeat the resistance movements that had recently appeared behind Soviet lines.[122]

Although the Soviets had to devote numerous counter-guerrilla units to fighting the partisans, they had the support of a majority of the population in the RSFSR, and even during the large-scale combing operations in the Baltic region, West Ukraine and Poland, there were elements of the population willing to help the Soviet authorities. Moreover, the ranks of the nationalist organisations were penetrated with NKGB and SMERSH agents and the Soviets kept tabs on German reconnaissance and sabotage parties by monitoring their communications.[123] Skorzeny eventually concluded that the establishment of a Russian 'Maquis system' had proven incredibly difficult, and he later described Soviet security measures as 'fabulous'.[124]

Soviet counter-insurgency operations required considerable manpower, but as noted above, most of it came from forces specifically devoted to security. Several Red Army divisions were diverted for limited lengths of time, but considering the massive preponderance of the Red Army over the *Ostheer* by 1945 – along the crucial Vistula front, it had a fivefold advantage in manpower and armour[125] – the effect was not decisive. In the race by each side to outdo the other by decoying men and equipment, it was probably the Soviets who won the game in Byelorussia, considering the resources that the Germans threw into the Scherhorn sinkhole. In the final analysis, only in Hitler's never-never land, where the Red Army was bled white and on the verge of collapse, would the effect of the anti-Soviet guerrillas have made a difference, but the final irony is that the *Führer's* political and racial prejudices kept him from showing any enthusiasm about helping such forces.

If the work of *Jagdverband Ost* and the FAK units did not keep the Third Reich intact any longer than would have been the case in its absence, it nonetheless had some effect. Many of the groups helped by the Germans stayed in the field far longer than their Nazi patrons, particularly since they had been spared from having to rely solely on scavenging weapons or training their own personnel. Remnants of UPA and the Baltic guerrilla groups survived into the early 1950s, although it is true that by 1947 they had been reduced to bands of fugitives hiding in underground bunkers.[126] Guerrilla efforts hindered the full incorporation of the West Ukraine and the Baltic republics into the USSR and they complicated the collectivisation of agriculture. The Polish nationalists waged a virtual civil war from 1944 to 1948, a conflict that eventually resulted in the deaths of nearly 34,000 supporters of the 'Lublin regime', plus untold numbers of partisans and nationalist sympathisers.[127] At the very least, the activity of Polish bands obstructed the organisational and agitprop work of the pro-Soviet Polish Workers' Party (PPR) and thus favoured the fortunes of the Peasant Party, which functioned in independent form from 1944 to 1947 and re-emerged an important force in the political life of the country.[128]

Such events, in turn, prompted a quick revival of the power of the Soviet Communist Party within the USSR and the suppression of all possible rivals in the recently incorporated western territories, including the nationalist intelligentsias and the local churches. The liberal climate associated with the Soviet war effort ended as the Kremlin scrambled to deal with these new problems, which provided the Anglo-Americans with a rationale for denying recognition of the acquisition of new territory and also threatened to give the American and British intelligence services a toehold along the western fringe of the country. According to Stalin, any successful defiance of Soviet power could spread unrest throughout the entire Soviet population, which he saw as a potential powder keg of disaffection. Thus, the power and responsibilities of the Security Ministry were expanded, and Jeffrey Burds suggests that 'in its essence, the *Zhdanovshchina* was a Soviet state effort to destroy the opportunities of foreign espionage services to find willing recruits among the Soviet people'. Burds also suspects that the questioning of FAK 212's Joseph Lazarek, who was captured by the Soviets, increased Russian worries about the situation in the western borderlands. Lazarek admitted to his interrogators that key players in the *Ostheer* intelligence agencies had made preparations to hand over their contacts to the Anglo-Americans.[129]

In Poland, underground violence provided the PPR with a golden opportunity to contend to its Soviet backers that it was the only force in the country in which the Soviets could lodge their trust, and that it should therefore be quickly and fully vested with dictatorial power. Links between the Peasant Party and remnants of the AK and NSZ were used to discredit the legal opposition. In the next chapter, we shall see this interplay re-enacted again and again in various East European settings, with the details of the story governed by diverse national situations and the strength of various individual resistance movements.

Finally, the threat of armed opposition was met everywhere by the Stalinist panacea: mass deportations. Entire nations of Caucasians, Kalmyks and Crimean Tatars were dispatched into Asia, as were substantial populations of Ukrainians and Balts. In eastern Poland, ethnic Ukrainians were transferred amass to the USSR, partly in order to deprive UPA of a regional base. And these events of an historical scale eclipsed the tens of thousands of individual burnings, lootings, arrests, beatings and killings that were the by-products of guerrilla warfare, but which have been forgotten as the great sweep of history is recorded. Thus not only did the Nazis bring to Eastern Europe a culture of racial terror and destruction, but they created a legacy that allowed for a continuation of such conditions long after the Third Reich itself had collapsed.

3
The Balkan Cockpit

Skorzeny's strategies for south-eastern Europe varied between two basic formulae. While operations in the USSR and Poland were based on converting established resistance movements to a pro-German course, in the Danubian lands to the south-west there were no large anti-communist guerrilla bands. Four of the countries in this region – Slovakia, Hungary, Romania and Bulgaria – were German allies, and in each of these the state security apparatuses had fought domestic communism with a great measure of success. Communism itself was anathema to Romanians and Hungarians, who shared an antipathy toward all things Russian (although many Slovaks and Bulgarians did not feel such revulsion). In Slovakia and Hungary, which were forced to stick with Germany until the bitter end, Skorzeny's mission was to develop wholly new anti-communist resistance movements that would function in case of a Soviet invasion, mainly by using native fascists, fanatic soldiers and secret policemen as a recruitment base. Bulgaria and Romania were different cases again. In the late summer of 1944, both of these countries abandoned the Axis and then declared war on Germany, which naturally led the Germans to seek the help of local political and paramilitary organisations that had been considered hostile by Sofia and Bucharest during wartime, but were now suddenly in German good books because they were still willing to 'fight communism'. The Internal Macedonian Revolutionary Organisation (IMRO) and the 'Legion of the Archangel Michael' – also known as the Iron Guard – were the two most important of these agencies. Skorzeny also expected assistance from local *Volksdeutsch* communities and from bypassed contingents of German troops, although the only country where this strategy proved its worth was Romania.

In contrast, the Aegean, Ionian and Adriatic coasts of the Balkan peninsula – Greece, Albania and Yugoslavia – provided political environments similar to western Russia and Poland and were therefore suitable for implementing a similar strategy, that is, the conversion of existing guerrilla groups to a pro-German stance. The grand architect of this course was Kaltenbrunner's collaborator Hermann Neubacher, head of a maverick Balkan *Dienststelle* in the Foreign Office. Neubacher and kindred spirits in the *Abwehr* were the original authors of a plan eventually taken up by Kaltenbrunner, which was to cultivate local nationalists, such as Napoleon Zervas, Draza Mihailovic and Vlodko Macek, mainly on the assumption that these men were '*bundnisfähig*' (cooperative) and would collaborate in a campaign against 'communism'. On 14 September 1944, Hitler's operations officer, *Generaloberst* Jodl, ordered German forces in the Balkans to cooperate with Neubacher in exploiting existing strife between right-wing and left-wing partisan movements in order to ease the burdens of the *Wehrmacht's* retreat from the peninsula. German troops were also told 'to promote, if possible, clashes between both groups after our retreat'.

Given the historic character of the Habsburg Empire, Carpathia and the Balkans were of great interest to the 'Vienna clique' that controlled the RSHA. Kaltenbrunner was obsessed with the notion that the Austro-Hungarian Empire could be refashioned under the banner of the Third Reich, and he acquainted his agents in the Danubian Basin with the need for a specifically Austrian approach to the area. Kaltenbrunner's *éminence grise* in such affairs was SS-*Obersturmbannführer* Wilhelm Waneck, a long-time Viennese Nazi. After participating in a premature attempt to overthrow the Austrian Government, Waneck had fled to Germany and was given work with the administration of Dachau Concentration Camp. He eventually joined the expatriate 'Austrian Legion' and was recruited by the SD in 1937, whence he began to organise Nazi mischief in south-eastern Europe. In 1943, he was appointed chief of Section E. Balding, short-sighted and poor of hearing, Waneck was famous not for his technical competence, but for his abilities as a bureaucratic infighter and for scoring victories in the RSHA's interminable turf wars. He had been able to defy Schellenberg in having Section E's headquarters transferred to Vienna, where it was isolated from the remainder of the SD chain of command and became an available instrument for the whims of the 'Vienna clique'.

With Kaltenbrunner and Waneck calling the shots, Skorzeny's instrument for south-eastern Europe, *Jagdverband Südost*, was brought under a large measure of Section E influence, as were local units of the *Zweierorganisation*. Waneck was jealous of Skorzeny and had no qualms about interfering with the autonomy of his sabotage units. Section E had long helped the *Jagdverband* select its personnel and had asked to be kept informed of all operations 'in order to avoid conflicts in planning', but this arrangement was formalised on the basis of an order from Himmler in early March 1945. Thereafter, *Südost*'s operations were officially organised under Section E oversight. Waneck later suggested that this arrangement made joint operations simpler and was necessary to prevent overlapping commitments of men and material.

According to Schellenberg, there was no rhyme or reason for the direction of SD policy in south-eastern Europe, except that it was diametrically opposed to the initiatives undertaken by Ribbentrop. Kaltenbrunner, understandably, took a kinder view of his work. His inspiration, he said, was the enlightened despotism of Maria Theresa, which to Kaltenbrunner meant centralising authority but giving each nationality the means for self-development. He also later claimed that he tried to forge broad anti-communist coalitions rather than relying solely on local fascists. Thus, he favoured working with such centrist leaders as Iuliu Maniu in Romania, apparently realising that in a region where the bulk of the population was still comprised of peasants and rural labourers, winning the allegiance of peasant parties would offer a lasting political advantage. Nonetheless, quizzical Allied interrogators noted in June 1945 'that the groups in which [Kaltenbrunner] still places his hopes are not the moderates whose favour he courted, but such movements as the Macedonian IMRO, the Iron Guard and the Zbor'.

It was in such a hothouse atmosphere of intrigue and amateur political scheming that *Jagdverband Südost* developed into an organisation of considerable size. According to Skorzeny, *Südost* had a complement of 2,000 men, and even the conservative Radl, whose post-war estimates of *Jagdverband* strength were always lower than Skorzeny's, counted 500 to 800 men in *Südost*'s ranks. Either way, *Südost* was the largest of the territorial battalions and it was also central to the *Jagdverbände*'s sense of purpose. As will be recalled, elements of the Friedenthal Battalion had been deployed in the Balkans as early as 1943 and many of the unit's tactics had been developed in the Partisan-ridden territories of occupied Yugoslavia. *Südost* was first based at Jaidhof, near Krems, although when Vienna fell to the Soviets in April 1945, the headquarters were withdrawn to the Lower Enns region, further up the Danube valley. The unit was commanded by Ernst Benesch, a forty-year-old *Obersturmbannführer* who had been chief of the Brandenburger '*Streifkorps Kroatien*'. Its primary mission, as described by one officer, 'was to build-up pro-Nazi partisan movements in South-East Europe'. Another officer said that it was responsible for the maintenance 'of Germany's interests in the Balkans after the withdrawal of the armies'. One of Skorzeny's young acolytes later called such efforts 'Brown Hand operations', which he described as 'killing and carrying out sabotage… with Hungarians, Roumanians, Bulgarians, everyone imaginable'. Huge stores of weapons were accumulated in Vienna in order to support these missions. In the winter of 1944, the Germans began preparing for a major counter-offensive in Hungary, an undertaking in which their special operations units were supposed to play a large role.

Jagdverband Südost had a huge field of operations that included all of the Balkans, plus Hungary and Slovakia. Four of *Südost*'s companies covered the Danubian countries and the eastern Balkans: *Jagdeinsatz Slowakei*, under *Untersturmführer* Pawlowsky; *Jagdeinsatz Ungarn*, based at Acs-Teszer, later Dabrony, under *Hauptsturmführer* Kirchner; *Jagdeinsatz Rumänien*, based at Jaidhof under *Hauptsturmführer* Müller; and *Jagdeinsatz Bulgarien*, based at Jaidhof under *Obersturmführer* Werg. The *Jagdverband* also controlled *Jagdeinsatz Donau*, a unit of frogmen that was deployed along the Danube. *Slowakei*, *Rumänien* and *Donau* were all descended from Brandenburg *Streifkorps* of 60 to 100 men.

Südost also devoted much of its manpower and resources to the Dinaric Balkans, particularly Serbia and Croatia. The Zagreb-based '*Streifkorps Kroatien*' became *Jagdeinsatz Kroatien* and Benesch was succeeded as company commander by *Obersturmführer* Schlau. *Jagdeinsatz Serbien* was cobbled together from Section S and Section E sabotage programmes, while efforts in Greece were handled mainly by *Sonderkommandos* that Skorzeny had inherited from Section F of the SD-*Ausland*. After the German evacuation of Greece in October 1944, a *Jagdeinsatz Griechenland* was organised in Austria, although it probably remained minuscule. There is no record of any *Jagdverband* unit being organised to cause trouble in Albania, from which the Germans withdrew in November 1944.

It should be noted that the wild dynamics of the western and southern Balkans appealed to Skorzeny's action-loving sensibility, and that he treated the region like a glorified training ground and weapons testing range. In fact, he situated the eastern school of Section S in the Partisan-infested Fruska Gora, in northern Yugoslavia, specifically so that trainees could engage guerrillas in order to gain combat experience. He later waxed sentimental in revealing how the school and the local Partisan bands had shared the same doctor, who divided his time between the two sides. Less quaint was the way that the *Jagdverband Führungsstab* issued poison bullets for use in the Balkans, apparently because this was a more effective means of testing than firing the projectiles at hapless concentration camp inmates. These bullets, illegal under the rules of war, contained ampoules of hydrocyanic acid and could induce death in five seconds.[1]

In addition to collaborating with Section E and with *Dienststelle* Neubacher, the Skorzeny *Leute* were supposed to cooperate with FAK 206, which covered Slovakia, Hungary and Romania, as well as FAK 205, which ran missions in Bulgaria and Macedonia, at least until it was withdrawn to Slovakia in the autumn of 1944. In the western Balkans, much of the workload was assumed by FAK 201, which was based in Belgrade (and then Vukovar and Zagreb). Its chief was Otto Modriniak, a veteran of the Austro-Hungarian Army and an anti-Nazi who was 'disinterested' in the war. Because of a profusion of officers like Modriniak, the remnants of the *Abwehr* steadily lost authority and personnel, particularly after the abortive putsch against Hitler, and the FAK formations in south-eastern Europe became closely monitored by Waneck. Had the war lasted several more months, local elements of the *Zweierorganisation* probably would have been folded into *Jagdverband Südost*.[2]

A CARPATHIAN FIASCO

By the summer of 1944, as the Red Army approached Central Europe, the Germans were already beginning to think about Slovakia as a redoubt for pro-German guerrillas. The mountainous interior of the country was a perfect theatre for partisan warfare and the Germans believed that emotionally too, the Slovaks were suited for guerrilla activity. Moreover, the Germans had helped the Slovaks win their autonomy in 1938–1939, and since that time Slovakia had been a staunch ally of the Third Reich. Internally, the country was governed by the clerico-fascist regime of Father Josef Tiso, an arrangement that had a considerable base of support.

With such factors in mind, the Germans began making preparations for guerrilla warfare in a potentially Soviet-occupied Slovakia. The Brandenburgers got off to a quick start by organising 'Einsatzgruppe Slowakei', alternately called 'Streifkorps Südost', which was set up on the basis of verbal orders. 'Slowakei' was under the command of its eventual SD chief, Dr Pawlowski, who originally was an *Oberleutnant* in the Brandenburg Division, and 100 men, mainly Slovakian *Volksdeutsche*, were recruited and trained by Alexander Auch. The group was the original core of what later became *Jagdeinsatz Slowakei*. Unlike many of his fellow company commanders in *Jagdverband Südost*, Pawlowsky was a man with a sense of political discretion and tact, and his forces were thus able to make a considerable impact upon the situation in Slovakia.[3]

Mil D efforts were divided between FAK 205, which conducted Operation 'Sirius', FAK 212, which organised *Unternehmen* 'Harbig', and FAK 201, which ran Operation 'Tatra'. A 'Sirius' training camp was set up Podhradie, although early in 1945 it was relocated to Senica; a month later, it was transferred to the oversight of FAK 206. Under a succession of commanders, Camp 'Sirius' trained at least thirty-six Slovak volunteers, mainly for guerrilla warfare. These men were eventually transferred to the control of FAK outposts and were deployed throughout the country, although it is possible that not many saw action. From September 1944 to early April 1945, FAK 205 also buried 111 dumps in order to supply the needs of future guerrillas. Nearly thirty Slovak volunteers were recruited in order to tend these caches, although there had been inadequate time to properly train these personnel.[4]

FAK 212's contribution was Operation 'Harbig', which was named for a Teschen lawyer who had a wide circle of contacts in the Silesian-Polish-Moravian-Slovak border region. Harbig and a small team of recruiters, mostly Slovak *Volksdeutsche*, signed up a number of Slovak and Slanzak recruits, particularly in the region around the Beskid Mountains, and these recruits were then sent to Camp Kreuz, a training facility in a hostel near Glatz, Silesia. Camp Kreuz was commanded by *Leutnant* Bargel, who ran groups of twenty trainees through two-week courses that focussed upon weapons training, sabotage and partisan warfare. About sixty volunteers eventually completed the programme and were posted back to Slovakia, although Harbig and Bargel made a mess of the affair. Despite the fact that it had originally been intended to induct thousands of men, Harbig faced difficulties in finding recruits. In fact, the later sessions of the course sometimes included as few as ten men and the entire programme might have petered out had the Soviets not overrun the training camp in early February 1945. Harbig's Mil D superiors thought him incompetent and suspended him in December 1944, although he was reinstated due to Bargel's influence. He also had difficulties in keeping the recruits who actually reached Glatz, partly because he could not compensate trainees for lost wages nor could he feed them at the level of rations common in Slovakia. Bargel also insisted that the recruits be fascists friendly to Germany, and he insisted on providing ideological instruction, although the training schedules were already too short. In addition, German trainers lacked requisite equipment and Camp Kreuz was so heavily snowbound that it was difficult to get outdoors for field training.

Operation 'Harbig' was supplemented by an attempt to plant underground dumps in northern Slovakia. These boxes were prepared at Special Camp Luckenwalde and were each supposed to support a ten-man partisan unit. Containers typically held a dozen Russian or Dutch rifles, German machine pistols, Soviet hand grenades and 2,000 rounds of ammunition. They were called '*Ostereier*' ('Easter Eggs'), which implies that they were meant to provide a spring surprise for the Soviets, and they were planted by two German combat officers seconded to FAK 212.[5]

A similar project was launched by FAK 201 and was based in the Tatra Mountains, south of the 'Harbig' zone of operations. The 'Tatra' mission was led by veterans of *Trupp* 221, which had earlier fought in the southern Balkans and whose survivors were either shipped north during the winter of 1944–1945 or were attached to *Trupp* 219, which was withdrawing from Greece. It was led by *Leutnant* Bührmann, a romantic figure who had been active in *Kleinkrieg* in Macedonia and was recovering from a shoulder wound when he was appointed to lead the operation. A German radio message on 22 December 1944 describes Bührmann's task as '[an] urgent large-scale operation'. In February, 1945, Bührmann was joined by *Leutnant* Katz, a young explosives and sabotage expert seconded by FAK 206. The 'Tatra' *Gruppe* was supposed to be reinforced in April by a *Jagdverband* unit, which began training in the Austrian Alps, but this force was redirected against the Western Allies before it could be deployed.

Two recruitment pools served the German effort to field guerrillas in Slovakia. First, there was the local *Volksdeutsch* community, 130,000 strong and led by Franz Karmasin. The Nazified leadership of this group had helped to engineer the Slovak declaration of independence in 1939, and during this affair a *Volksdeutsch* auxiliary had been armed by the SS and had busied itself in creating as much trouble as possible. The Carpathian *Volksdeutsche* were further bonded to the Third Reich in 1944 when they became targets for anti-Nazi rebels and responded by forming a special minuteman unit called the *Sturmgeschutz*. Members of the *Sturmgeschutz* formed natural cannon fodder for operations 'Sirius', Harbig' and 'Tatra'.

Of equal importance were the stalwarts of the Slovak Popular Party's armed wing, the Hlinka Guard (named for yet another priest, Andrej Hlinka, who had been the leader of the Catholic autonomists during the interwar period). Although the Popular Party was originally a conservative movement not given toward brash or violent gestures, an anti-German Slovak revolt in 1944 was met with the countervailing emergence of militants who were keen on the full fascistisation of the country and the merciless punishment of the rebels. This group willingly encouraged the training of 'special Slovak units' – some at Camp Kreuz – and it supported the cultivation of a capacity for armed resistance to a revived Czechoslovak republic, should the Third Reich lose the war. One of the most powerful of these fanatics was Otomár Kubala, the last chief of staff of the Hlinka Guard and the boss of state security during the final days of the Tiso regime.

Given their extensive preparations, the Germans were shocked to find that it was pro-Soviet Partisans, rather than their own friends, who first managed to turn Slovakia into a theatre of guerrilla warfare. Communist Partisans too had been stockpiling supplies, and after they increased the scale of their insurgency in the summer of 1944, they managed to coordinate their activities with a dramatic mutiny of Tiso's Slovak Army, about one quarter of which went over to the rebels. In late August, these anti-German Partisans and mutineers grabbed control of a large part of central Slovakia. The *Wehrmacht* was forced to contend with this uprising for two months, until it finally collapsed amidst a rebel flight to the mountains. Unlike the case with the revolt in Warsaw, the Germans made little effort to convert their deflated opponents, even though some of the insurgents remained advocates of Slovak autonomy. Several hundred 'white partisans' who later rallied in the High Tatra to fight the communists were veterans of the 1944 Rising, but there is no evidence that the Germans did anything to encourage the conversion of such elements or to bring about such a result.

When the Slovak Revolt broke out, German plans for their own guerrillas had to be re-calibrated, particularly because the rebels were occupying some of the same ground on which the Germans hoped to launch their own programme. In the autumn of 1944, several Mil D officers, including Ernst zu Eikern, Gotthard Gambke and Hans Raupach, gathered in Cracow in order to deal with this problem. They decided to create a FAK *Sonderkommando*, called 'Edelweiss', which could foray into the mountains and clean out pockets of enemy Partisans, thus clearing the ground for implementation of 'Sirius', 'Harbig' and other German programmes. The erstwhile chief of FAK 212, Erwein *Graf* von Thun-Hohenstein, was assigned to run the 'Edelweiss' project. Thun was a 48-year-old Tyrolean noble who had fought in the First World War and had later participated in Wolfgang Kapp's infamous march upon Berlin. After trying his hand as a farmer in Argentina, he had joined the *Abwehr* in 1940, his linguistic abilities and knowledge of Eastern Europe proving a tremendous asset. Thun was also a romantic daredevil who had launched a series of raids behind Soviet lines, including one celebrated exploit that resulted in the death or capture of 660 Russians. Since 1943, however, he had been drifting. He had been charged in a court martial with making 'frivolous statements' about the Nazi Party and began going to seed in Italy, where he spent his time drinking and carousing. Mil D hoped to refocus his energies.

Much of the manpower for 'Edelweiss' was provided by North Caucasian nationalists being trained at the Mil D facility in Sohl, Upper Silesia. These men had originally been drawn to the Nazi banner by a promise of independence for their mountain nations. Having booked passage on that vessel, they were forced to stay onboard as it careened back through Eastern and Central Europe. These forlorn souls eventually found themselves in northern Italy, a full 1,800 miles from their homelands. The German intention was to train such men for deployment by parachute in southern Russia – this was the reason they were sent to Sohl – but a shortage of aircraft prevented such operations. With the approval of Gambke, fifty of these Caucasians were sent to Slovakia and became the mercenary core of Thun's *Sonderkommando*, to which was also added a coterie of forty-five Cossack volunteers. A contingent of 130 Slovak auxiliaries completed the roster. This unit was contributed by Kubala and consisted of Hlinka Guardsmen and Slovak soldiers (including a few rebels who were captured but wanted to avoid sentences in a concentration camp). The Russian elements of 'Edelweiss' were run by officers from *Trupp* 218; the Slovak detachment was commanded by Ladislav Niznansky, a Slovak nationalist who had fought on the Eastern Front and was then captured by the Germans after the decomposition of the Slovak Army.

Shortly after being fielded, 'Edelweiss' troops scored a significant success. During a raid of suspected Partisan hideouts near Polomka, they stumbled upon a detachment of thirteen American intelligence officers, plus several British agents, who were serving as an Allied liaison mission to the Slovak Partisans. By coincidence, they had come across a mountain cabin occupied by the Allied officers. After directing a fusillade toward the building, they captured all of its inhabitants except a single member of the Czechoslovak Parachute Brigade, who jumped through a window and hid. Although these prisoners were taken in uniform, they were transferred to the control of the Gestapo and then sent to Mauthausen Concentration Camp, where – at Kaltenbrunner's command – they were shot on 23 January 1945. After capturing the Allied liaison officers, Thun pushed deeper into the hills, encountering several Slovak Partisan emissaries who tried to deter him from pressing further, although by that time he had already spotted a second mountain hut, which bore investigation. This action precipitated a three-hour battle with Slovak Partisans, which permitted a small party of surviving Allied personnel to escape. Thun eventually burned down both buildings and brought the skirmish to a close by calling in a barrage from German field guns in Polomka.

Although 'Edelweiss' recruits had been promised a quiet tour of duty guarding bridges and tunnels, passivity was not part of Thun's nature. By early January 1945, he was launching regular forays into the mountains near Banska Bystrica, which resulting in heavy fighting with pro-Soviet Partisans. He favoured tactics of subterfuge and infiltration, making use of Soviet uniforms in order to gain the confidence of enemy Partisans and facilitate the approach of his forces. Although Thun often donned the garb of a gentleman hunter, dressing for operations in a cloth jacket and knee breeches, he was willing to clothe himself as a Soviet officer and to exploit his excellent command of the Russian language in order to complete the deception. This practice led to some hair-raising climaxes in which 'Edelweiss' troops unsheathed their knives and surprised the foes who had been drawn into their vicinity. Thun readily participated in such hand-to-hand fighting, wildly swinging his favourite stick.

Frequently, the 'Edelweiss' unit gave no quarter. Of seventeen Slovak partisans overrun near Kremnica, eleven were later found buried in a mass grave. Six Soviet partisans apprehended by Thun and Niznansky 'disappeared', as did a group of American fliers who had bailed out of their aircraft and were captured near Senica.

As is sometimes the case in counter-insurgency warfare, operations deteriorated into bloody massacres of civilians. As a result, many of the 1,000 people killed or captured by the 'Edelweiss' unit were relative innocents. After receiving reports of guerrilla activity and sniping in several mountain villages, heavily armed 'Edelweiss' troops surged into the hamlet of Ostry Grun in the early morning of 21 January 1945. They were accompanied by vengeance-prone *Volksdeutsch* minutemen from the *Sturmgeschutz*. Although the young men of Ostry Grun had already taken flight at the sound of approaching vehicles, the troops managed to round up sixty-two people, mostly women and children. Only light opposition was encountered from pitchfork-wielding farmers. The assemblage of villagers stood waiting for several hours, after which a motorised troop of white-clad SS men arrived and mowed down the townspeople with their machine pistols. The 'Edelweiss' and SS troops then moved on to the neighbouring village of Klak, where an additional eighty-four people were chased down and massacred. Adding insult to injury, 'Edelweiss' and *Sturmgeschutz* men plundered houses and stole cows, and in Klak the church was destroyed (perhaps by Muslim Caucasian militiamen).

Thun was also ordered to hunt 20,000 fugitive Slovak Jews, the last remnant of a community once numbered at 90,000 people. In February, an 'Edelweiss' patrol in the Ksina Valley discovered eighteen Slovak Jews, mostly women and children who were hiding in earthen bunkers. These unfortunates were flushed out of their subterranean haven and shot, apparently on Thun's direct orders.

Despite the fact that Thun did as he was told, he was not an enthusiastic Nazi and was reportedly ashamed of his unit's operations. He felt particular guilt for the treatment accorded to the American and British prisoners captured near Polomka, telling a fellow officer that had he anticipated their fate, 'I would have let them go… They should have been sent to a POW camp.' Skorzeny was suspicious of his subordinate's sympathies and when Thun was recommended for the Knight's Cross, he stopped the recommendation from going forward, arguing that Thun's wife had a partly Jewish ancestry. Only when investigation revealed that it was Thun's brother who was married to an Austrian Jew did Skorzeny allow the recommendation to proceed.

As the Soviets surged through Slovakia, the 'Edelweiss' unit was steadily pushed westwards. By March 1945 it was operating in the West Slovak hills around Vrutky. In one of its last engagements it overran a small detachment of French Partisans who were caught in bunkers near Martin. One Frenchman was killed and three more were handed over to the tender mercies of the SD. By the last days of the war, most members of the 'Edelweiss' unit had deserted. Thun was eventually captured by the Soviets, who presented him before a military tribunal and then had him shot. Niznansky too was captured, but he was subsequently recruited by the Czechoslovak security service in order to root out Hlinkite remnants and uncover the external centres of organisation supporting these elements. Sent into the US zone of Austria in the autumn of 1947, he promptly defected to the Americans.[6]

By early April 1945, most German special units had been forced to flee Slovakia, as had Father Tiso, who carried his regime into exile at Kremsmünster, Austria. Karmasin and his Carpathian *Volksdeutsch* leadership cadre also moved to Kremsmünster. Contact between the FAK units and their Mil D controllers all but collapsed, although two-way wireless communications were maintained with ten SD outposts behind Soviet lines. Father Tiso was also convinced to make radio broadcasts to the occupied homeland.[7]

Efforts to inspire resistance had some impact in eastern Slovakia, where refugees reported a wild campaign of looting and rape by Red Army troopers. Men in Prešov were forcibly inducted into the Czechoslovak Army and pro-German Slovaks were stood before a wall and shot.[8] One of Pawlowsky's *Jagdkommandos* provided a considerable flow of intelligence about such matters, which was forwarded to Section E and was used to shape appropriate propaganda. There is no doubt that Soviet outrages provided perfect fodder for the German and Hlinkite information services, which claimed that a 'Free National Slovakia' movement had developed. Two goods trains were allegedly blown up near Prešov and there were other manifestations of hostile activity.[9] However, as Soviet forces pushed into central and western Slovakia, some degree of discipline was restored and the comportment of Soviet troops improved markedly, a process that interfered with German plans to conduct atrocity propaganda. In March 1945 the Germans air-dropped a million leaflets into occupied zones of the country, but such material had relatively modest messages, advising Slovaks to remember the sixth anniversary of Slovakia's independence and to remain loyal to 'their' state.[10]

There was some evidence in the post-war period of resistance by Hlinkites calling themselves 'white partisans',[11] and there is no doubt that when UPA bands began operating on Slovak soil in the summer of 1945, they got a good reception.[12] Externally, remnants of the Tiso regime continued to insist that the Slovak State remained legally in existence and they made broadcasts from secret radio transmitters in Austria and Italy, as well as establishing courier contact with the Slovak separatist underground. The leader of these elements was the one-time Slovak foreign minister, Ferdinand Durcansky, a figure who had been involved in last-minute Hlinkite propaganda schemes and was evacuated to Germany in order to set up a 'black transmitter', which was supposed to beam misinformation back into the homeland. After the end of the war, Durcansky claimed that Tiso had vested executive authority in his hands.

The continuing activity of such forces had serious consequences. By 1947, Hlinkite remnants had become riddled with Czechoslovak police informants, who discovered that Durcansky had established links even with Jan Ursiny, the deputy chair of the Slovak Democratic Party. As a result, Ursiny was forced to resign from the Czechoslovak coalition government in November 1947. From this point, it was easy for Czechoslovak communists to claim, amidst an increasingly strained international atmosphere, that the Prague regime was threatened by nefarious internal and external forces, and that despite the government's friendliness toward the USSR, only a fully 'Sovietised' Czechoslovakia could be prepared to meet such challenges. Unfortunately, Stalin was open to this logic and he approved a communist seizure of power in February 1948, using the government's alleged inability to deal with Slovak underground resistance as part of the excuse. Durcansky, having contributed to the incrimination of non-communist political forces in his homeland, slunk off to exile in Latin America.[13]

THE LAND OF THE WHITE TERROR

There were few places in Europe where there should have been an atmosphere more conducive to anti-Soviet resistance than Hungary. Alone of the countries in Central Europe,
Hungary had been controlled after World War One by a communist regime, which had
taken shape under the leadership of Béla Kun. This brief foray into radical politics had
resulted in an invasion by the hated Romanians and was also followed by a ruthless White
Terror, organised by bands of Hungarian army officers and veterans, the *Tiszti Különítmény*.
Resurgent right-wingers also propped up the 25-year dictatorship of Miklós Horthy, and
the domestic environment in Hungary provided a perfect medium for the spread of rac-
ist chauvinism and romanticism. The Depression gave Hungarian fascism a mass base, and
its impact, combined with the anti-Trianon revisionism of the ruling strata, led Hungary
directly into the arms of Fascist Italy and Nazi Germany. Indeed, Hungary's position as
a German client state paid dividends between 1938 and 1941, when Hungary recovered
much of the territory that had been lost to Czechoslovakia, Romania and Yugoslavia.

Despite such gains, the cautious Horthy was lukewarm about the Barbarossa Campaign
and he largely dropped out of the war in the East after heavy Hungarian losses in 1942–1943.
In fact, Horthy began secretly exploring means of restoring Hungary's neutrality without
losing face or exposing the country to a harsh German response. When the Germans
learned about the full measure of Hungarian contacts with the Allies, they militarily
occupied the country, although Horthy was momentarily kept in office as regent. The Red
Army's conquest of eastern Hungary in October 1944 was met by a white-hot resolution to
defend the Hungarian homeland – or at least Hungarian fascists displayed such doggedness
– but moderate strands of opinion thought it better to follow the example of Finland and
Romania, that is, to dicker with the enemy. As will be recalled, Horthy was pursuing this
option when he was overthrown in mid-October by a Skorzeny-orchestrated putsch. With
Hitler's backing, Hungarian fascist maestro Ferenc Szálasi took power and mobilised all
available resources and manpower for a fight to the finish with the Red Army. Meanwhile,
senior elements in the military and political establishment, regarding Horthy's removal as
illegitimate, moved to the Soviet-occupied part of the country and built a rival regime that
declared its existence in December 1944 and then signed an armistice with the USSR.[14]

Since the Germans had anticipated at least part of this sequence of events, Skorzeny
had begun training Hungarians at his special sabotage schools even before the formation
of the *Jagdverbände. Jagdeinsatz Ungarn* was organised in October 1944, originally based at
Acs-Teszer, although it was later moved to Dabrony in order to maintain contact with
partisans being organised by the Hungarian Army. The commanding officer was a 28-year-
old officer named Wolfram Kirchner, who had been a leader in the Hitler Youth and was
an ardent Nazi. Kirchner was also a veteran of the Brandenburg Division and had extensive
experience in the Balkans, eventually joining 'Streifkorps Kroatien' in 1944. *Jagdeinsatz Ungarn*
was organised into three *Kommandos*, plus a training camp at Ebreichsdorf, Austria, which
was commanded by *Obersturmführer* Jaksch. This facility began functioning in December
1944 and offered courses in wireless operation, demolitions and espionage. A small number
of Hungarians were also trained at Skorzeny's battle school in northern Yugoslavia, at least

until that site was overrun by the Red Army in the autumn of 1944. Survivors continued their training at Mürz Zuschlag, in Lower Austria. Yet another platoon, led by a Hungarian lieutenant, attended a demolitions course at Neustrelitz toward the end of 1944, and a Hungarian *Sonderkommando* was also trained at a ski school near Berg Gammschtein.

The personnel of *Ungarn* were drawn from 'Streifkorps Kroatien' or were Hungarians and Hungarian *Volksdeutsche* sent by the *Waffen*-SS recruiting office in Budapest.[15] Many of the Hungarians were members of the Arrow Cross Party, which was the ruling power in Hungary after October 1944. Formed in 1935, the Arrow Cross was the only fascist party able to attract a mass following. Although the 'Hungarianism' of the Arrow Cross had fostered a relatively independent attitude toward Germany, party functionaries had been accepting aid from the SS since 1938, when the Germans had arrived next door in Austria.[16]

The position of the Hungarian *Volksdeutsche* was another matter. Numbering 500,000 souls, they should have comprised a major resource for the *Jagdverbände*, but the recruitment potential of the group was never realised, particularly if we compare it to the robust role played by the *Volksdeutsch* community in neighbouring Romania. Although the Hungarian-Swabian *Volksbund* had a long relationship with the SD, the group had provided far fewer recruits to the *Waffen*-SS than its Romanian or Yugoslav counterparts, and Hungarian *Volksdeutsche* were typically more assimilated than ethnic Germans in other parts of south-eastern Europe. Even the *Volksbund's* chief, Franz Basch, had poor relations with the *Waffen*-SS, which he thought was putting impossible recruitment demands upon Hungarian-Germans.

By the end of 1944, Kirchner was pressuring Basch to dissolve a home guard that he had set up several months earlier and to redirect its manpower toward *Jagdeinsatz Ungarn*. In one example of the *Volksbund's* ongoing reluctance to help in organising such efforts, *Untersturmführer* Friedrich Kauder, one of Basch's home guard commanders, carried out an unauthorised withdrawal of his 400-man battalion to Altmünster, Austria. Kauder had been forced to hand over thirty men to *Jagdeinsatz Ungarn* and was threatened with having the remainder of his complement drafted by the *Waffen*-SS.[17]

Where the *Volksbund* did make an occasional show of guerrilla resistance, the results were horrific. In the portion of the Banat recovered by Hungary from Yugoslavia, 150 Hungarian-Swabian civilians were shot in reprisal after a round of sniping resulted in the death of a Soviet lieutenant. 'There were no more outbreaks', noted a British observer.[18]

Despite recruitment difficulties, *Jagdeinsatz Ungarn* managed to mount a number of operations. Beginning in October 1944, the unit undertook a series of combat and reconnaissance missions codenamed for stars, the largest of which, 'Evening Star', involved 100 Hungarians and ten German instructors left behind in Szeged in order to harass enemy supply lines. Through the autumn and winter of 1944–1945, *Ungarn* regularly ran 'Star' missions every several weeks, mostly probing operations looking for weak spots in Soviet lines through which men and supplies could be sent to the Hungarian resistance movement. Thus, ten men were left behind in the Hungarian Banat in October 1944 (although they were never heard from again); half a dozen patrol missions were undertaken near Lake Balaton around the turn of 1944–1945; eighty Hungarians were deliberately stranded in the Bakony Forest, whence they maintained radio contact with German stations (March 1945); two squads of a dozen men each were left behind enemy lines south of Lake Balaton (March 1945); and a company of seventy Hungarians was infiltrated through Red Army lines near Lake Balaton.

A major operation was also launched on New Year's Eve, mainly at the request of *Brigadeführer* Jochen Rumohr, an old Skorzeny chum who was chief of the German garrison in the surrounded bastion of Budapest. In an attempt to get 500 tons of weapons and supplies to Budapest, an eight-man crew was recruited to sail a ship down the Danube. This craft floated to within eleven miles of the city, but ran aground on 2 January 1945. One commando succeeded in slipping through to the Hungarian capital, where he secured a launch and returned to the vessel. The crew had plans to offload as many supplies as possible, via the launch, but they eventually decided to abandon the vessel and individually infiltrate the ring around Budapest. This announcement, radioed to Vienna, was the last that was heard of the crew. A week later, a *Südost* patrol reached the area and found the ship, which had been looted by local civilians but was, remarkably, not yet confiscated by the Soviets.

After February 1945, a dozen paratroop teams, each including an officer and five men, were dropped into liberated Hungary. The men of these '*Fern Einsatz Gruppen*' were equipped with pistols, submachine guns and sabotage material, and their job was to mix with the population, disseminate propaganda and line up recruits for guerrilla bands. One third of the teams were equipped with radios, although none ever reported back to German lines.[19]

Finally, it should be noted that Skorzeny established a close relationship with Károly Ney, a wealthy Hungarian-Swabian industrialist and army officer. A militant fascist, Ney returned from the Eastern Front in 1943 and formed a tightly knit fraternity of anti-communist veterans. In the summer of 1944 he entered the service of Winkelmann and Höttl and was officially inducted into the *Waffen*-SS, being given command of a 1,500-man brigade attached to the 'Maria Theresa' Division. Since Ney wanted to field guerrilla units behind Soviet lines, he was put in contact with Skorzeny, who was happy to provide arms, weapons and supplies for a 'suicide unit' carved out of Ney's brigade. Ney used his contacts with Hungarian veterans to raise personnel, and in September 1944 he officially established the *Halafejes Legro*, or 'death's head' detachment. Training was conducted at a camp in the Bakony Mountains, where German SS officers and enlisted men acted as instructors.

Unhappily for the Germans, Ney proved both operationally incompetent and needlessly vicious with his own people, who were abused by the thieves, rapists and murderers who found their way into the ranks of his brigade. Perhaps because of these indiscretions, Ney had a falling-out with Skorzeny, who eventually withdrew his support. Ney then offered several hundred commandos to the SS 'Florian Geyer' Cavalry Division, which reportedly dropped many of them behind Soviet lines. The rest of *Kampfgruppe* 'Ney' was depleted in conventional fighting with the Soviets, although a remnant withdrew into Austria. In the post-war period, Ney wrangled support from the American and Italian espionage services and set up a camp at Grausen, where he trained survivors of his battle group in guerrilla warfare.[20]

Several other German formations aligned with Skorzeny played an important role in Hungary, particularly FAK 206, which was assigned the task of training and equipping anti-Soviet partisans. This detachment controlled a supply dump at Tat, which contained huge quantities of captured Soviet rifles and machine pistols, plus explosives suitable for sabotage work. Numbering 110 men and ten officers, including its commander, *Hauptmann* Reinhard, and its liaison man with the Hungarians, *Leutnant* Schlegelberger, FAK 206 was based originally at Budapest, although it shifted headquarters in the face of Soviet advances, first to Györ and eventually to Kapuvár, near the Austrian border. Hungarian commandos and guerrillas were trained at a small village south-east of Kapuvár. FAK 206 specialised in front reconnaissance and sabotage, although it also supplied Hungarian partisans being moved through the front and into enemy territory. In addition, the unit ran parachute missions behind Soviet lines, such as Operation 'Uranus', plans for which were developed by a Mil D officer, *Leutnant* Alfred Piff.[21] Radio messages from late November and early December 1944 suggest that FAK 206 officers were already training Hungarian parachutists for action behind enemy lines, but that they needed wireless sets before they could deploy personnel at Kaposvár, a town in south-western Hungary that fell to the Soviets on 2 December.[22]

Apart from FAK 206, several other elements of the *Zweierorganisation* also supported Hungarian resistance. In an operation to augment 'Uranus', FAK 205 laid 110 supply dumps in Hungary, especially in the south-western part of the country, which was added to its sphere of responsibility in early December 1944. FAK 205 also ran Camp Hubertus, a training facility that was established at Malachy, Slovakia, by *Major* Friedrich Vatter. Twenty men were trained at this camp before it was dissolved in March 1945.

In addition, several of FAK 201's units were active. *Trupp* 214, which operated largely in Yugoslavia, organised a Hungarian stay-behind network while the detachment was temporarily stationed in Budapest during the summer of 1944. This project, codenamed Operation 'Maier', focussed upon recruiting nationalist students at St Stephen University in Gyöngyös, some of whom were supplied with radio sets.

Trupp 215 organised an independent unit of 'volunteers', *Freikorps* 'Drautal', which, as the name suggests, was meant to defend the central Drava Valley (the 'Drautal'), an area that had been annexed by Hungary in 1941. *Freikorps* 'Drautal' was also supposed to protect, or in the case of retreat, to destroy the Hungarian oilfields at Maort, west of Nagykanizsa. The unit was initially formed of 4,000 men, mostly Croats and Hungarians, although the structure of the formation was unstable. In early March 1945, 2,800 of its men were impressed into the Hungarian SS while they were training at Dubrava and Nedelisze. In addition, the unit's commander, *Oberleutnant* Giersch, was barely capable of running a formation of this scale. A dishevelled and nearly illiterate Brownshirt, Giersch had comported himself like a medieval warlord while stationed in Crimea, notching his gun for each of the lives that he had taken and gathering around him a bodyguard of fierce Cossacks. Although a brutal Nazi, he was also a coward who rarely appeared on the battlefield, a failing that made his appointments of company and platoon leaders crucial. Unfortunately, these men were not good choices either. One non-commissioned officer was accused of killing Croats under his command; another junior officer fled from a battle with Titoite Partisans and was then brought before a court martial.

Trupp 215's main task was to organise caches and hideouts for future saboteurs, especially those of the *Freikorps*'s stay-behind unit, *Überrollungskommando* 'Lovasci'. Stationed in the Maort oilfield, 'Lovasci' was supposed to sabotage oil pumping installations that were still intact after a retreat by the *Wehrmacht*. The *Sonderkommando* was run by two fanatical officers named Schniggenfittich and Sturm. The former was a crafty Hanoverian who had been a commercial draughtsman in civilian life; the latter was a Hungarian *Volksdeutsch* who had fought on Tito's side but had defected to the Germans, mainly because of the entreaties of his young Croatian fiancée.

In general, the Germans skilfully exploited Hungarian delusions about retaining a claim to the country's newly annexed territories, arguing that the best means of maintaining a presence in these areas was to organise pro-Hungarian resistance. One of the *Trupps* of FAK 202 managed to strand Hungarian agents in the region around Košice, which fell to the Red Army in late January 1945. Košice had been a Hungarian town until it was incorporated into Czechoslovakia, although the Czechoslovaks had returned the city to Hungary in 1938. Eight teams of Hungarian stay-behind agents were deployed around Košice in late 1944. They had instructions to cross back into Hungarian- or German-held territory and report on their operations, although the rapid retreat of Axis armies subsequently made it impossible for any of the infiltrators to return.[23]

The Germans also encouraged Hungarian intrigues in northern Transylvania, another traditionally Hungarian territory that had been reclaimed in 1940, much to the chagrin of the Romanians, who controlled it during the interwar period. The main Hungarian group in the region was the 'Guard', which was descended from a larger resistance movement called the 'Neighbourhood'. The 'Guard' was originally the paramilitary wing of the 'Neighbourhood' and had been launched as a self-defence organisation for Hungarian families – twenty to a unit – although it also developed a capacity to spread rumours and launch terrorist attacks. In November 1944, Hungarian propaganda organs claimed that there was already active resistance in parts of northern Transylvania overrun by the Soviets and the Romanians. They contended that Hungarian-Transylvanian villagers were fleeing to the mountains in order to escape labour drafts and that these elements were forming guerrilla groups. These bands supposedly armed themselves by raiding enemy convoys.

The 'Guard' was partly controlled and financed by the Hungarian embassy in Bucharest, a practice that continued even once this outpost transferred its allegiance to the pro-Soviet Hungarian regime, and by the spring of 1945 the Germans were attempting to exploit this legation in order to re-establish links with Hungarian-Transylvanian irredentists. On 10 March 1945, the SD told its Romanian collaborators that 'in northern Transylvania we are taking steps to contact Hungarian circles', although such news was hardly likely to impress the ardent Romanian nationalists still working with the Germans. A month later, the Romanians responded that Hungarians in Transylvania could not be trusted: 'We advise you against action [in] northern Transylvania because loyalist feeling there is too strong. Hungarians are being misused there by the Soviets as oppressors of the Rumanians. [There is a] danger of treachery owing to local disputes.'[24]

The most important element of the anti-Soviet underground consisted of an independent guerrilla organisation conceived and created by the Hungarians, although the Germans provided material and spiritual support. After the shift of power from Horthy to Szálasy, the government ordered the Hungarian high command to organise a resistance movement 'on a large scale'. The new creation was called the Hungarian Democratic Youth Movement, although it was actually neither democratic nor youthful, considering that it was recruited among right-wing Hungarian troops and gendarmes, as well as among adult members of the Arrow Cross. It is likely that the 'Hungarian

Democratic Youth' was descended from a similar group called the 'Anti-Bolshevik Youth' (ABI), which had been organised in 1944 as a juvenile guard for the fascist parties in Hungary and had played a role in the October putsch, when its members served as message-runners and spread right-wing leaflets. In fact, the 'Hungarian Democratic Youth' may simply have been the ABI operating under a new name. The armed wing of the movement was called the *Kopjás* ('Pikemen'), a reference to the late medieval forces that had protected Hungarian frontiers against the Ottoman Turks, the 'eastern scourge' of an earlier era.

The chief of the 'Democratic Youth' was Brigadier General Zákó, a former boss of the ABI and a confederate of Emil Kovarcz, a leader of the *Tiszti Különítmény* and Szálazi's 'Minister of Total Mobilisation'. According to one account, Zákó stole the idea for the *Kopjás* movement from Karl Ney, who had already approached Szálasy with the proposal to build an anti-Soviet guerrilla group, which Zákó then proceeded to organise. Zákó's chief of staff was Captain Korponai, an officer in the Hungarian General Staff's Second Bureau. Korponai was no friend of the Third Reich, but he undertook his assignment with the idea that the movement could be developed on the basis of 'purely Hungarian... ideals', and that it would have a pro-British appreciation of Hungary's place within the larger matrix of European politics. According to Korponai, if the Germans still wanted to provide help despite such an understanding of the movement, that was their choice and aid would be accepted from any quarter. Korponai and the other *Kopjás* staff leaders met several times with Skorzeny after the movement was activated in January 1945, presumably in order to extract promises of help.

ORGANISATION OF THE 'HUNGARIAN DEMOCRATIC YOUTH MOVEMENT'

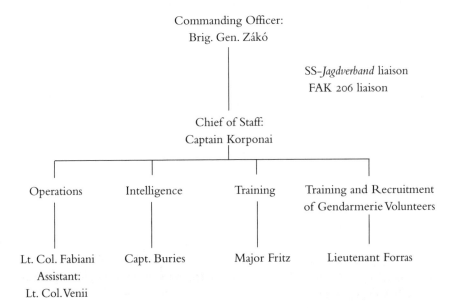

In addition to the *Kopjás* central staff, guerrilla quartermaster and training units were built in order to create a proper capacity to conduct operations. Food was provided from Hungarian stocks, although most weapons and special equipment came from FAK 206 and *Jagdeinsatz Ungarn*. Late in the war, supplies ran short and operations were restricted. Guerrillas were regarded as members of the Hungarian Army and wore uniforms while training. When a company of gendarmerie volunteers was ordered by Korponai to attend a course in Ebreichsdorf, Austria, mainly in order to learn how to use silencer-fitted rifles provided by *Jagdverband Südost*, the trainees wore white sheepskin tunics, the traditional uniform of Hungarian mountain troops. After the start of 1945, most of the guerrillas were trained in the Bakony Mountains of western Hungary.

Kopjás forces were usually deployed by allowing themselves to be bypassed by Soviet advances, a tactic that rarely involved activity by the Germans. Such operations were underway in January 1945 at Valenceto and near Lake Balaton, where guerrillas were ordered to come out of concealment as soon as the Soviets had passed and then to move to the immediate rear of the Red Army's battle line. After the abortive German counter-offensive in March 1945, which was followed by a Soviet push all the way to Vienna, large groups of Hungarian guerrillas were left in western Hungary, and others were passed through Soviet lines by retreating Hungarian forces.[25]

The effectiveness of the *Kopjás* movement, and of related SS and FAK operations, is difficult to gauge. A FAK report in late November 1944 suggested that Hungarian volunteers 'are full of keenness and determination, though not willing to work directly for Germany', and there is also evidence that they were already running afoul of the Soviet occupiers. By the end of 1944, the NKGB had eliminated three resistance groups, comprising a total of eighty-five guerrillas, and on 21 December Soviet trackers engaged in a prolonged shoot-out with a band near Sugafe, a battle in which six guerrillas were killed. As the Soviets rolled up to Lake Balaton, *Jagdverband* patrol detachments blew up several Red Army munitions dumps, and German intelligence reported that 'in [the] hilly country [of] Mecsek Hegyseg, north of Pecs, [there is] constant skirmishing between Arrow Cross men and communists'. Army Group South also noted that as it attempted to relieve the besieged 'fortress' of Budapest in early 1945, its forces were well received in re-conquered territory and that the population in the path of SS Division 'Viking' was rising up against the Soviets. Indeed, there was evidence of a stiffening attitude toward the turn of 1944–1945. By February, German spies were reporting considerable resentment in Soviet-liberated Hungary, a feeling mainly related to food shortages. FHO also suggested that unrest was caused by the pro-Soviet government's attempt to draft manpower for an anti-German army, which prompted many Hungarians to flee to the woods, and that 'anti-Soviet bands received a strong influx toward the end of the month [January] due to countless cruelties of the Soviet occupation troops'. An intelligence summary on 11 January predicted an upsurge of guerrilla warfare in response to the Soviet military regime. In February, an NKGB report suggested that while Hungarian guerrillas had not yet developed into a serious problem, their main activity was establishing contact with civilians and recruiting manpower in order to expand partisan bands. These recruits were being trained at secret camps deep in the woods, and were to be deployed in the spring 'when the German Army is supposed to switch over to the offensive'.

On the other hand, there is some evidence that the relative passivity of the *Kopjás* movement did not please the Germans, nor was it entirely intended. Both German and Soviet documents suggest that some *Kopjás* guerrillas simply used the infiltration of enemy lines as a means of returning to their homes in the Soviet-occupied zone, and certainly many of the bands or parachute teams equipped with radio transmitters never reported back. Some Hungarians deployed through such means hid their supplies or saved them for a later date. FHO complained in early March 1945 that disaffected Hungarian civilians were surging into the bands, but that they suffered from lack of leadership and that many of their uncoordinated sabotage acts were worthless. According to a Hungarian gendarmerie officer, the *Kopjás* guerrillas were encouraged by the Hungarian leadership merely to engage in passive resistance, and since the Germans had a more active view of their role, the already delicate relationship between the *Wehrmacht* and the Hungarian Army was further strained. FAK 206 was so distrustful of the guerrillas that it would not allow partisan infiltrators to proceed to the front without an armed escort, which was similar to German handling of AK commando groups in Poland. Despite the fabled Hungarian support for White Terror, Wolfram Kirchner told the Allies in 1945 that 'the attitude of the Hungarian people offered little promise for the success of any [anti-Soviet resistance] movement', and one *Kopjás* staff officer later admitted that the Germans 'mistrusted all Hungarians because they never achieved any results'.[26] In addition, the broad Danubian plain that made up the bulk of Hungarian territory was unsuitable for supporting partisan warfare.

As the Soviets advanced across the last significant stretches of German-occupied territory, the Szálasy regime abandoned its provisional capital at Sopron and headed into Austria, accompanied by elements of *Jagdeinsatz Ungarn*, FAK 206, the Hungarian intelligence service and the *Kopjás* staff. Although the Germans claimed that they made a special effort to get the Hungarians to safety, moving the headquarters of the resistance movement to Pöllau, one of the members of the *Kopjás* staff, Lieutenant Ernö Forras, later remembered the evacuation much differently. According to Forras, both he and Korponai had hoped to use Austria as a channel through which to reach Udine and hook up with the victorious British Army advancing northward through Italy. The suspicious Germans, however, stopped the party at the Austrian frontier, disarmed them and took away their transport. Forras, Korponai and a company of Hungarians – about 120 men in all – then withdrew into the Styrian Mountains, where they joined elements of the Austrian anti-Nazi movement 'Red-White-Red' and went to war with isolated groups of German Army and SS troops.[27]

After the end of the war, remnants of the *Kopjás* movement established links with officers of the St Laszlo Division, who were interned in the British-occupied sector of Austria, and they also tried to establish a sense of common cause with the London Poles, the Chetniks and sympathetic elements in the British occupation regime.[28] The impact of such activity was significant, although the Soviets, in remembering the White Terror of 1919, had anticipated even more violent resistance to the occupation of the country. Such expectations had led them to take a relatively liberal line, defining Hungarians as a misled people to be 'freed from fascism', and to reward the population with humane treatment if no resistance was offered. Arrangements were made to bring marauding Red Army troopers under control – usually without much effect – and the Soviets also promised to release Hungarian POWs if their homes were more than sixty miles in the rear of the main battle line.[29] It is true that when the Soviets authorised the creation their own anti-Szálasi regime, they foisted upon it a harsh armistice agreement, but they also allowed this government to take shape as a relatively representative coalition of centrist and leftist elements. Elections in October 1945 were won by the Smallholders Party, the Hungarian equivalent of the peasant parties that were popular in most of east-central Europe. Had the *Kopjás* movement managed to threaten Soviet forces in a significant fashion, it is hard to imagine that the occupiers would have assumed such a non-interventionist stance.

Unfortunately, the *Kopjás* movement and other similar organisations remained active. For several months after the end of the war, there were Hungarian bands roaming the Alps; one such group was trapped by US forces near Berchtesgaden in early August 1945. Operating from Austria, such resisters maintained a courier service with Hungary and they managed to smuggle a prominent right-wing politician out of the country. The British called such remnants 'a considerable security threat', and wondered if they had managed to establish links with the Smallholders, particularly with the party's leader, Ferenc Nagy, and its general-secretary, Béla Kovacs. After a series of attacks in the Gyöngyös area, which resulted in the deaths of three Soviet officers and several Hungarian policemen, 100 anti-communist militants were arrested, some with connections to the Smallholders Party. Evidence suggested that the propaganda chief of the Smallholders was an accomplice in such outrages and arms were being stockpiled at party headquarters. More plots were uncovered toward the end of 1946, again implicating Smallholder activists, as well as a number of military officers. Béla Kovacs fell under a particular degree of suspicion.

The result of these developments was ultimately the same as in Czechoslovakia. Hungarian communists were quick to take advantage. They labelled the conspirators as 'fascists' and used incriminating information to attack their Smallholder rivals, although Ferenc Nagy promised to purge the party of armed troublemakers. Communist boss Matthias Rákosi met Vyachaslav Molotov in the spring of 1947, warning the latter about predatory 'fascist reactionaries' who wanted to invite the Western Powers into Hungary and hinting that the ongoing presence of the Red Army was fully warranted. Molotov agreed that Soviet troops were still needed in Hungary and it is also likely that the Hungarian communists were given Soviet ascent for a full seizure of power.[30] Thus, the anti-communist resistance played into the hands of local communists by giving them an excuse – and an opportunity – to grab power.

IN TRANSYLVANIA THERE'S A TRIBE

While the Hungarian *Volksdeutsche* were not enthusiastic about anti-Soviet resistance, their compatriots in north-western Romania were much more eager. This group was comprised mainly of Robert Browning's 'Transylvanian tribe', descended from German settlers who had arrived 700 years earlier – the legend of the Pied Piper is probably a metaphor for the way that Hungarian recruiters had once cleared Lower Saxon towns of young men and women by inducing them to settle Hungary's wild frontier – while an adjacent cluster of *Volksdeutsche* in the Romanian Banat came along in the eighteenth century. Both the Transylvanian Saxons and the Banat Swabians developed as colonies of self-sufficient farmers and townspeople, numbering over 500,000 people by 1930, and maintaining their own churches, cultural bodies and newspapers. Most of this community had supported the transfer of Transylvania from Hungary to Romania in 1918–1919, and in the 1930s a Nazified 'revitalisation' movement began to tie together the different fragments of the *Volksdeutsch* community, creating a sense of ethnic kinship stronger than traditional class, confessional or regional loyalties. By the 1940s the Nazified leadership of the '*Volksgruppe*' had fallen under the control of its youngest and most radical elements, who negotiated a corporate autonomy agreement with the Romanian Government.[31] When the Soviets eventually knocked Romania out of the war and began to overrun Transylvania and the Banat, Himmler ordered the RSHA to form a *Volksdeutsch* resistance movement, regarding the territories as a separate entity, at least for organisational purposes.[32]

When Romania defected from the Axis on 23 August 1944, and then declared war on Germany two days later, the situation of the Romanian *Volksdeutsche* quickly grew desperate. The German Sixth Army, which conceivably could have protected the community, or at least covered its evacuation, was itself in deep trouble, as it suddenly found itself cut off in a country that had switched sides. Small Romanian Army and Border Guard units, now aligned with the Soviets, tried to secure southern Transylvania and the Banat against disorganised remnants of the German Army streaming toward the Carpathians, and they also awaited the arrival of the Red Army, which was lumbering westward from Bessarabia.

In this awkward and confusing situation, Himmler appointed SS-*Obergruppenführer* Artur Phleps as his trouble-shooter. Phleps was a native Transylvanian who had organised a *Volksdeutsch* home guard in 1918 and had thereafter acquired command experience as an officer in the Romanian Army and the *Waffen*-SS. In late August, he was transferred to northern Transylvania, which was under Hungarian sovereignty, and he received the title of Higher SS and Police Commander (HSSPf) 'South Transylvania'. Phleps's mandate was to mobilise German scratch forces and to convince the Hungarians to move troops into southern Transylvania and the Banat, thereby creating an environment in which the *Volksdeutsche* could take flight, although the chance of organising such an evacuation looked slim. He was also told to encourage the Transylvanian Saxons and Banat Swabians in forming a resistance movement, and on 1 September 1944 he assured Himmler that he 'had started up the *Volksdeutsch* partisan organisation that had been charged to him as a special task'.[33] This effort benefited from the fact that the *Volksgruppe* had already organised semi-secret facilities for the pre-military training of *Waffen*-SS volunteers and from the fact that units of Mil D had cached weapons near the passes at Turnu-Rosu and Predeal.

At the crucial hour, many Romanian *Volksdeutsche* remained loyal to the Third Reich and were opposed to Bucharest's switch of sides. They frequently hid scattered remnants of the German Sixth Army that drifted into the Civin, Agnita and Fagaras mountains, and they warned these elements about enemy patrols, although the Soviet response to such activity was typically to line up the offenders in front of a firing squad. City-dwellers also helped small 'cells' of German officers who hid in urban areas. These support networks were mainly female in composition and were led by Albertine Hönig, the leader of the women's section of the *Volksgruppe*. Many of the cut-off German troops remained armed, although always short of ammunition, and they retained momentary radio contact with German units in Hungary and Yugoslavia.[34] The stragglers and *Volksdeutsch* civilians also cooperated in the maintenance of an intelligence network. Both groups were led by Fritz Cloos, head of the German-Romanian Labour Front and chief of a number of small SD stay-behind teams in Transylvania. Aside from Hönig, Cloos was the only major figure in the *Volksgruppe* leadership with sufficient pluck to remain behind enemy lines. According to the German citation recommending him for the Knight's Cross, Cloos 'on his own initiative… called a resistance movement into being. That the morale of the *Volksgruppe* did not collapse is to be ascribed to his activity. It is thanks to him that nests of resistance exist throughout the entire country.'[35]

Phleps also assembled manpower and resources on the German side of the front. He rallied several thousand *Volksdeutsch* refugees, Romanian 'Legionaries' and SS men, and these formations, together with the Hungarian Army, managed to occupy most of the Banat, where they formed a home guard and evacuated 30,000 *Volksdeutsch* refugees, before retreating in the face of overwhelming Soviet force.[36] Some of the *Volksgruppe*'s Banat cadre, including district chief Josef Komanschek, escaped from a Romanian transport bringing them to a detention camp in Wallachia. After a brief period in the underground, they fled to German-occupied Yugoslavia.[37]

Skorzeny's initial contribution to this evolving guerrilla war was Operation '*Waldläufer*', for which Besekow held a secret conference at Friedenthal in August 1944. The goal was to beg help from Mil D in organising an attempt by the nebulous *Jagdverband Südost* against a railway bridge captured by the Soviets. The operation was never carried out, albeit for reasons that are unclear.

'*Waldläufer*' was replaced by an even more ambitious project codenamed '*Landfriede*', which involved the dispatch of Walter Girg and two platoons from *Jagdverband Mitte*. On 26 August, Skorzeny ordered Girg to fly into the Banat and either distribute weapons, so that local civilians could fight the Soviets and Romanians, or evacuate *Volksdeutsch* refugees to German-held territory. Girg and his men first travelled by rail to Vienna, where they got extra orders from Waneck and Girg spent a day in the headquarters of Section E, studying intelligence reports from Romania. Six aeroplanes were standing by to fly the group into action. Skorzeny's original plan had been to airlift Girg's commandos to Timisoara, but since the latter location was threatened by the enemy, Girg decided to take his ninety *Jagdverband* troops and forty Romanian *Volksdeutsch* volunteers to Phleps's command post, hoping to get permission for a revised raiding and sabotage scheme. Girg found Phleps in a small frontier village, and the general endorsed the young officer's amended programme.

Girg's new intention was to divide his force into three groups and infiltrate these units deep behind the Romanian-Soviet Front, mainly with the hope that they could discover Red Army intentions and sabotage the Soviet route of advance. An eastern troop under *Oberscharführer* Fritsch was told to operate forty miles south of Brasov; the middle group, under Girg himself, was supposed to commit sabotage and reconnaissance from Sibiu to the Turnu-Rosu Pass; and the western unit, run by *Oberscharführer* Hahn, was intended to function as far as Cluj and the terrain a dozen miles to the south. All three platoons were armed with knives, pistols and British Sten guns, plus large supplies of plastic explosive, and the eastern and western groups were clad in uniforms resembling those of Allied paratroopers. Members of Girg's unit wore civilian clothes tailored in the local style. Two of the groups had transmitter-receiver sets similar to the types used in Me 109s. Three day's rations were supplied, but the formations were expected to stay another ten days behind enemy lines, living off the land.

The infiltration groups crossed the Romanian frontier on 31 August and accomplished a great deal. The area was so lightly held that some of the platoons travelled by train to their operational zones. The eastern troop destroyed the water main in Brasov, blew up five bridges and collected 500 *Wehrmacht* soldiers who were fleeing the Soviets, while the western force gathered important tactical and strategic intelligence. Girg's own platoon lost contact with two of its sub-groups at Holtau, and on 4 September it moved toward the Turnu-Rosu, stealing Romanian Army uniforms from a patrol that it had ambushed. Girg and company arrived at their destination after a ten-hour climb. After gathering information from local Romanians, who were not always hostile, Girg and company were attacked by a Soviet unit, escaping only after heavy fighting. They then moved toward the main Soviet line of advance, but they were mistaken by a Romanian patrol for deserters. Their equipment was searched and their machine pistols were found. Although one of the commandos escaped, the remainder were beaten with rifle butts and were eventually handed over to a Soviet officer, who promptly lined them up in front of a tree and fired his weapon. Girg was hit in the foot but was able to flee the scene and stagger twenty miles back to German lines, dodging enemy patrols and checkpoints along the way.

Girg's mission ascertained that the Soviets intended to push quickly through Cluj with fresh armoured forces, information that reportedly allowed an entire Germany army corps to escape encirclement. It was an achievement for which Girg received the Knight's Cross. By 1 October 1944, sixty per cent of Girg's company had regained German lines, although some of those left behind were not necessarily dead or captured. Rather, a few *Jagdverband* men went to ground among friendly *Volksdeutsch* civilians, joining Cloos's resistance nests. Girg later learned that nine of these men had joined a wireless transmitter unit, which kept operating in Transylvania until the end of the war.

Despite Girg's accomplishments, Phleps was unable to build a solid defence line or even to evacuate most of the Romanian *Volksdeutsche*, a fact becoming obvious by the third week of September 1944. On 21 September, as his forces in the Banat were pushed back, Phleps was killed near Arad under mysterious circumstances. According to some accounts, he was hit by 'friendly fire' from German Stukas, or was overtaken by a Soviet patrol, although German reticence about releasing the details fed a proliferation of theories, suggesting that Phleps had actually fallen on his sword, in the old imperial tradition, or that he had displeased Himmler and been arrested. Moscow Radio later claimed that he had hidden in the Banat and was leading a resistance movement.[38]

Phleps's removal from the scene allowed for the political and military emergence of Andreas Schmidt, who since 1941 had been the chief of the Nazified *Volksgruppe*, and was in the process of emerging from a mid-career funk. Born in a Transylvanian farming village in 1912, Schmidt had experienced a meteoric rise, becoming head of the German-

Romanian Labour Front in 1939 and advancing from there to the *Volksgruppe*'s top job. Schmidt managed to climb the ladder by aligning the *Volksgruppe* with the *Waffen*-SS, in the process helping to recruit 60,000 volunteers for SS ranks, and his reputation at the SS Main Office was sealed by the fact that he literally married the boss's daughter: in 1941, Schmidt wed Krista Berger, whose father Gottlob ran recruitment for the *Waffen*-SS. Although Krista died in 1943 and Schmidt then remarried, the sense of kinship between Schmidt and his powerful father-in-law remained intact. For Schmidt, the tie linked him directly to a major centre of power in Berlin; for Berger, it ensured his control of a large recruitment pool that was also being eyed by internal competitors within the SS. By early 1944, the private war between Berger and Kaltenbrunner was starting to cause splits within the *Volksgruppe* leadership staff. Although Schmidt had performed valuable services for the SD, recruiting agents and providing information, his promotion of Berger's local interests eventually forced members of his staff identifying with the SD to draw away from their leader. The two most important dissidents were Kurt Auner and Matthias Liebhardt, and in 1944 they launched a persuasive smear campaign against Schmidt, largely focussed on his personal quirks. Schmidt threatened to have Auner and Liebhardt arrested, but they were protected by Kaltenbrunner.[39]

When Romania deserted the Axis on 23 August 1944, Schmidt's enemies found a perfect opportunity to throw darts at their nemesis. Because Schmidt was a careerist who had banished all thoughts of defeat, he had made few preparations to evacuate the Romanian *Volksdeutsche* in case the Red Army neared Transylvania and the Banat. As a result, the population was unprepared for the rapid change of affairs in the late summer of 1944. Worse yet, Schmidt had left for Berlin on 21 August, and his chief deputies, Walter May, Erich Müller and Hans Ehrmann, had also debouched for Vienna, convenient absences that made it look as though Schmidt and company had received advance warning of the 23 August coup that precipitated Romania's plea for an armistice, and that they had fled in anticipation of this catastrophe.[40] Schmidt himself later admitted that the *Volksgruppe*'s information service had for weeks been predicting Romania's imminent about-turn.[41] Compounding matters, on 24 August Schmidt phoned his headquarters from Berlin, issuing a stay-put order that destroyed any chance of a last-minute evacuation, and when he did return to Transylvania, he withdrew from the front so quickly that he had to arrest some of his own staff members in order to force the retreat. He also tried to bully the North Transylvanian *Volksdeutsch* Nazis, now attached to the Hungarian *Volksbund*, into launching a commando raid in order to rescue his new wife Adele, whom he had gallantly left in the homeland. The North Transylvanians refused 'to undertake the role of partisans', although they were then mercilessly reproached by one of Schmidt's representatives. On 3 September, Schmidt turned up at Phleps's command post, but he seemed unsure of himself and devoid of his typical braggadocio. Rather than cooperating with Phleps, he fought with the general and complained that nothing was being done, either through radio or leafleting, to challenge the call for peace issued by Hans Otto Roth, the chief of a denazified version of the *Volksgruppe* organised by the Romanians. Appeals for help flew out to Berger, who pressured Phleps to coordinate his efforts with Schmidt.[42]

After Phleps's untimely demise, Schmidt and the *Volksgruppe* staff retreated to Budapest in order to explore the remaining options for 'helping' the Transylvanian Saxons and

Banat Swabians. Although some constructive ideas were floated, such as *Sturmbannführer* Rimann's proposal to dispatch welfare and pension payments via neutral channels,[43] Schmidt was interested in a more grandiose scheme that had the double advantage of reversing negative impressions that his earlier behaviour had generated as well as putting him in a position to challenge Roth for control of the Romanian-German community. The basic idea, apparently developed by Schmidt himself, was to put members of the Nazi *Volksgruppe*'s staff at the disposal of Skorzeny, who would train them as commandos and then parachute them back into Transylvania and the Banat. The final goal, inspired by the example of the Girg raid, was to launch a partisan war and prepare for a projected German counter-offensive, which Schmidt hoped would carry the *Wehrmacht* back into the eastern Balkans. Schmidt saw himself leading the parachute teams back into the homeland, an act of contrition and self-sacrifice that he felt was sure to strike a chord with Himmler. Even Schmidt's supporters later saw this plan more as a product of the *Volksgruppenführer*'s id than a well-reasoned scheme to aid his people.

When Schmidt's proposal was first circulated, most senior Balkan Nazis turned thumbs down. The leaders of the Hungarian and Yugoslav *Volksgruppen*, Franz Basch and Josef Janko, were both opposed – perhaps they saw the setting of a precedent that they would be expected to repeat – and officers of the *Volksdeutsch* Central Office were also sceptical. Even elements in the SD wondered how Schmidt was going to do undercover work when he had such a widely recognised face. Most of Schmidt's staff had doubts, feeling that a few inexperienced novices could not accomplish much of military value. 'A senseless undertaking', noted one contemporary observer, 'doomed to failure from the start!' Critics also argued that partisan operations in *Volksdeutsch* regions would prompt Soviet and Romanian reprisals, particularly against the families of *Waffen*-SS paratroopers involved in the project. Such parachutists knew, as one Foreign Office official delicately observed, 'partially from their own experiences in Russia, that partisan warfare means the obliteration of whole villages'. Schmidt and his backers blithely dismissed such concerns, assuring critics that the Transylvanian Saxons and Banat Swabians would need someone to protect them from Soviet atrocities, particularly once the *Wehrmacht* returned to Romania in a forthcoming offensive.

Since Schmidt had the encouragement – probably the insistence – of Himmler in pursuing his chimeric quest, he bulldozed the remainder of the *Volksgruppe* leadership into offering themselves as the manpower needed to make the project a reality. By October 1944, Schmidt had 250 *Volksdeutsch* SS men in training, 150 of whom were led by propaganda specialist Hans Kastenhuber and were stationed at the *Jagdverband* school near Neustrelitz. Others were being trained at the Seebarn camp outside Vienna. Matthias Liebhardt and Erich Müller were appointed as Schmidt's liaisons with Skorzeny. Müller, as chief of the *Volksgruppe*'s local version of the SS, the *Einsatzstaffel*, was also put in charge of *Jagdeinsatz Rumänien*. At the turn of 1944/1945, seventeen senior figures of the *Volksgruppe* parachuted back into the homeland: on Christmas Eve, Walter May and Willy Depner parachuted into the Brasov area and on 3 January, Hans Kastenhuber and Richard Langer jumped into the same region. In late January, yet another plane carrying Banat-Swabian leaders Christian Bloser and Josef Komanschek crashed near the front in Hungary, killing Bloser and injuring Komanschek, who was captured. All these men were former leaders of the *Volksgruppe*'s various bureaux and had been hastily inducted into the *Waffen*-SS.

Schmidt himself spent most of December and January in Transylvania, a sojourn that started and ended with aviation misadventures. After repeated postponements of the mission, which miffed Himmler, Schmidt and company parachuted over eastern Hungary and took several weeks to trudge on foot to Transylvania. By late December, Schmidt had been given up for dead, so SS officers were overwhelmed when news reached Berlin suggesting that he had finally arrived in Sibiu. 'In spite of everything', they told Schmidt by radio, 'we can scarcely contain ourselves for joy at your turning up. Our work commenced in the spring will bear fruit despite setbacks… We are proud of you and will drink shortly to your good health.' Berger arranged for his son-in-law's promotion to *Hauptsturmführer* in the *Waffen*-SS Reserve.

During this period, as Schmidt shuttled between Sibiu, Brasov and Bucharest, he continued to display the jarring mixture of gallantry and blatant egotism that had characterised his tenure at the helm of the *Volksgruppe*. He spent much time arguing with local SD agents, particularly Roland Gunne; he doted on his young wife in Brasov (although he failed to move her out of harm's way); and he blustered about German military capabilities to quizzical *Volksdeutsch* civilians.[44] One member of the Sibiu Anti-Fascist Committee who caught up with Schmidt in Bucharest told him to head for Hungary 'because his presence put a burden upon the entire *Volksgruppe*', but Schmidt assured his censor that he had met with senior German officers and was sure that the fortunes of war would once again turn in Germany's favour.[45]

In late January 1945, Schmidt was ordered to return to Vienna in order to re-evaluate operations, a development prompted by the failure of the Ardennes Offensive and by a general sense of gloom that had descended over the *Volksdeutsch* group. Unfortunately for the *Volksgruppe* leader, arrangements for the trip were put in the hands of his arch-rival, Roland Gunne, the blond and blue-eyed *Volksdeutsch* SD officer who had been left in Romania to sabotage the Ploesti oil fields, but instead had begun using his local knowledge and contacts in order to infiltrate the Romanian Army. One of Gunne's main projects was to identify potential deserters in the Romanian Air Force and to convince such crews to fly their Ju 88 aircraft from Oradea to German-held airfields in Slovakia and Austria, thereby creating a rudimentary shuttle service for Nazi and Legionary agents. Gunne proposed to arrange for several Romanian bombers to run himself, Schmidt and Romanian fascist leader Constantine Stoicanescu back to Vienna, but when the time came to leave, there were repeated delays in securing aircraft, and the three men were forced to spend two weeks loitering around the airfield, waiting for aircraft to become available. Access to several machines was finally procured on 9 February, but Gunne's plane experienced 'motor problems' and could not make the flight. Schmidt and Stoicanescu touched off in a separate warplane.

Vienna was already worried about the three men because the SD cell in Bucharest had incorrectly reported their departure on 26 January. As a result, Cloos, the acting chief of the resistance movement, had already been directed to carry out an investigation. 'Who can have committed treachery?', asked Vienna. Originally, there was some suspicion that Gunne, Schmidt and Stoicanescu had deserted, but this thesis was not supported by the *Volksgruppe*'s contacts in the Romanian secret police, the *Sigurantza*. 'A trap is not possible', the resisters reported. '[The] pilot has returned and is in Miskolz. [A] courier [is] on the way there to ascertain precise facts.' Cloos suggested on 12 February that the Romanian bomber had 'probably [got] stuck somewhere and could not get on', but two days later Gunne reported by radio, claiming that he had not left on 9 February, but was still attempting to find an Me 109 to fly him to Vienna or Bratislava. Meanwhile, he said, he was staying near the front with his collaborators in the Romanian Army. Soon after receiving this news, the guerrillas' courier returned to the '*Führungsgruppe*' and Cloos was forced to report that Schmidt and Stoicanescu had been located, although their fate was not a happy one. The duo, it seemed, had been shot out of the sky over Romanian lines in Hungary and were presently in an enemy military hospital in Debrecen, recovering from injuries suffered during the crash of their aircraft. On 28 February, Gunne showed up in Bucharest, although suspicions about his role in the affair were already crystalising. A week later Moscow Radio announced that a Romanian aircraft carrying two German agents had been shot down near Debrecen, and that a Romanian Air Force lieutenant, Tandafirescu, was being held on charges of having procured the aeroplane for the enemy. Gunne's SS controllers told him (via radio) that the Soviets seemed '[to] know all about Schmidt and Stoicanescu'.

On 10 March, Gunne provided a detailed account of the affair, supplemented by information he had supposedly received from a Romanian contact. Schmidt and Stoicanescu had been shot down by a Romanian fighter 'given [a warning] by [the] NKVD three days beforehand. Treachery [is] excluded according to what has been discovered so far. Denunciation by ground personnel in Oradea [was] likely by reason of [several] weeks stay, two attempts to take off, and return with engine trouble.' This account was accepted as the official version, although Schmidt's patron, Gottlob Berger, would have none of it. Berger firmly believed that Kaltenbrunner and Skorzeny had betrayed Schmidt to the Soviets, and that Gunne was the implementer of this plan. Cloos later claimed that a Romanian radio operator, supposedly a Soviet double agent, had betrayed Schmidt.

Efforts were made to keep the identities of Schmidt and Stoicanescu from becoming known to their captors, as well as to buy the two men out of Romanian captivity, but both attempts failed. Schmidt was later transferred to Soviet jurisdiction and was tried and sentenced to twenty-five years at hard labour. He died in 1948 at the infamous Vorkuta camp in the Soviet far north.[46]

The rest of Schmidt's leadership cadre fared little better. Walter May was arrested twice, and although he managed to bribe his way from captivity in the first instance, he met with his death – probably through shooting – after being picked up a second time. Willi Depner was arrested in May 1945 and during a long and painful process of interrogation he probably revealed much about the guerrilla movement. Like Schmidt, he was eventually carried off to the Soviet Union. Josef Komanschek was also grilled by the *Sigurantza* at Oravitza, and the guerrillas heard that he had given up crucial knowledge under torture, although such accounts were unverified. One report suggested that Komanschek was subsequently shot by the NKGB; another that he had been transferred to the USSR. Of a leadership cadre of seventeen parachutists, two were killed and eleven captured by the Soviets. Only Kastenhuber and Langer managed to survive the war in control of their battle groups. The chief of the stay-behind network, Fritz Cloos, was also arrested in mid-March 1945, while in the process of trying to save a radio outpost from a Romanian raid. He too was handed over the Soviets, after which he passed through Lubianka Prison and eventually ended up at Vorkuta.[47]

While the fate of the *Volksgruppe* leadership forced the parachutists to hunker down, they were still able to function sporadically. Skorzeny-trained paratroopers dropped into Transylvania in four-man teams, beginning in the autumn of 1944, when twenty-five men from *Jagdeinsatz Rumänien* were deployed. Once on the ground, these commandos were helped by friends who provided them with identity cards bought from Romanian soldiers or railway clerks. Although many parachutists could not speak Romanian and were picked up when their identities were challenged by Romanian gendarmes, others successfully went to ground in Transylvanian Saxon granaries or in subterranean bunkers, generally living outside villages and towns inhabited by sympathetic countrymen.[48]

Aerial supply drops began in early 1945, first near a guerrilla camp at Cuicas and then, after that position was abandoned on 12 February, near a partisan base at Heldenburg (although operations there too were suspended on 21 February). In order to facilitate supply flights, the guerrillas set up ground beacons and maintained five meteorological stations: 'Weather in Transylvania', noted Vienna, 'is basic for our operations'.

None of these activities were undertaken readily. The resisters complained on 8 March, with regard to weather observations, that

> if take-offs do not take place on the basis of our reports, the reports will be discontinued as these are obtained… with the greatest difficulty. It is incomprehensible to us that *Luftflotte* 4 could carry out dropping of men here in the past, but the same be impossible for us owing to alleged bad weather conditions.

Similarly, the resisters were hesitant to light ground beacons because of a fear of Romanian and Soviet patrols, particularly if they could not be sure that an aircraft would make a drop at the set time and place. They often cursed their controllers for 'putting us off with promises', and they were not above threatening to quit operations in the absence of adequate arms, equipment and medicine. A radio message on 22 February said tersely: 'You are once again reminded that if supplies and remittances do not arrive by March 1st work will be stopped at this end.' Despite the fact that the *Luftwaffe* was put on notice, a transport aircraft dispatched on the night of 26/27 February could not make a drop because of local ground winds in excess of forty miles per hour, although the air force promised to have supplies in the hands of the guerrillas by 7 March. Matters were further complicated when a Ju 88 assigned to such operations crashed and its highly trained crew was killed. As a result, it subsequently became impossible for the Germans to use specially constructed boxes that they had developed for the safe dropping of men and equipment. Vienna controllers, for their part, took offence at the accusations that coursed so freely over the airwaves. 'Everything has been done here', they noted on 9 March, 'to enable supplies to start'. Men, material and money had been sitting at a *Luftwaffe* airfield for weeks, awaiting favourable weather conditions. They hinted that bogus meteorological reports had been fed to the partisans and that these were responsible for delays.[49]

Because of the difficulties involved in sending money to the guerrillas by parachute, the *Volksgruppe* leadership queried Vienna about the possibility of routing funds through

Switzerland or Sweden, noting on 7 February: 'We shall find ourselves in a catastrophic position if the money does not arrive.' The main financial channel was Account 930 at the Société Générale de Surveillance S.A. in Geneva, and Rudi Stärker, a member of *Dienststelle* Neubacher, was charged with telegraphing money to Bucharest via this account. Procedural problems delayed the development of the system, and Vienna told the resisters on 5 March:

> With regard to [your] remittance, please have patience since the matter is extremely difficult by reason of the situation in the neutral states and any breakdown must be avoided. For the rest, supply of money for your end has largely been procured and was hitherto only dependent on technical difficulties, which can now positively be eliminated. [The] remittance will be affected by 16/3.

Indeed, money began moving along this pipeline in late March 1945 and eventually totalled 600,000 Swiss francs, paid out in Bucharest as more than 1.5 million lei. Thus, money began flowing just as the war was ending, a stroke of good fortune for the Soviets and their allies.[50]

The main mission of the parachutists was to organise *Wehrmacht* stragglers and *Volksdeutsch* sympathisers into combat groups, and by all accounts, they had good material with which to work. A radio report noted in January 1945: 'German defence forces which were partly overrun in the first onslaught continue to offer stiff resistance and thereby hinder the enemy advance, so that German forces can re-form in the arranged area for a counter-offensive which is planned.' By the spring of 1945, Hans Kastenhuber had organised 1,500 guerrillas in the Brasov region, who sat awaiting a successful *Wehrmacht* counter-strike that never came. Reports collected by the Germans also suggested that the Transylvanian Ore Mountains were 'a nest of partisans'.[51] However, an attempt to liberate German POWs, of whom there were 100,000 in Romanian camps, fizzled. A four-man team, *Einheit* 'Prinz Eugen', was dropped near Resita on 16 December 1944, equipped with a mandate to contact senior officers amongst the POWs and organise an uprising, which would be facilitated by *Luftwaffe* airdrops of weapons. Although well-armed and provided with extensive help by the Romanian fascist underground, the 'Prinz Eugen' group could only get close to a relatively minor camp near Sinaja, which housed 180 German officers. Much larger camps near Jassy and Focsani were in areas sealed off by the Soviets and which the parachutists were unable to penetrate. The team's leader, Klaus Tüscher, reported this failure to Vienna and the group was reassigned to reconnoitre Soviet lines of communication.[52]

Many 'green' groups – as they were called by 1945 – came to blows with the Romanians and Soviets, particularly as the guerrillas lashed out at patrols sent to track them down. Near Sibiu, two Romanian gendarmes were killed when they attempted to check the identity of a man on horseback wearing a *Volksdeutsch* paramilitary uniform. In February 1945, a battle broke out in the woods near Nimesch when young *Volksdeutsche*, mostly soldiers on leave who had fled to the forest, were spotted collecting supplies and carrying this material back to their underground bunkers. Romanian policemen and soldiers surrounded the partisans and forced their surrender after pummelling them with automatic weapons fire and hand grenades. The guerrillas told Vienna on 21 February that there had been 'various unforeseen, violent arguments between green camps and collecting points with gendarmerie and police'. Near Brasov there were 'wounded, prisoners and dead'.

Although 'green' guerrillas appeared to undertake few actions of an offensive character,[53] they contended that major operations were supposed to await the launch of a German offensive in south-eastern Europe,[54] and Mil D documents suggest that the partisans had orders to blast railway lines and that they took occasional jabs at enemy lines of communication. In January 1945, four heavily armed parachutists clothed in Romanian Army uniforms were caught trying to blow up a railway bridge over the Olt river, and near Lugoj, members of Einheit 'Prinz Eugen', also clothed in Romanian Army uniforms, derailed a train carrying Soviet T-34 tanks, damaging a number of wagons. In Brasov, a Red Army convalescent was shot twice and dumped into a ditch, an outrage that was one of a number of bushwhacking in the city, and on 28 February the Soviet headquarters in Brasov was blown up.[55] Hans Kastenhuber also met German staff officers who were planning attacks in the mountains, and in February 1945 an operation codenamed 'Red Tower' was staged near Turnu-Rosu Pass, where the guerrillas had a major base. 'Green' reports admitted that the action cost casualties, but a refugee later suggested that it was the Soviets who were on the warpath at Turnu-Rosu, having intercepted German radio messages that they were attempting to trace to their point of origin.[56]

The resisters were also charged with a range of tasks that could best be described as para-political. They were supposed to run an underground pipeline through which to spirit cut-off Wehrmacht personnel back to Germany, and to create a tracking service in order to find people of interest to the SD. On 27 February, the resisters were ordered to ascertain the condition and whereabouts of German embassy and consular personnel who had been overrun in Romania, plus 'details about [the] extent to which other Reichsdeutsche have been interned'. Leaders of the Volksgruppe who had fled into exile, such as Hans Kaufmes, Hans Ehrmann, and Rudolf Sonntag, used this tracing service to check on the condition of their families.[57] The resisters were also supposed to secure the parole of various sympathisers who had already been apprehended. In mid-February, for example, they were 'trying to effect [the] release' of an engineer named Sywonowsky, a former fire brigade chief who had been arrested and handed over to the Brasov Army Corps.[58] In addition, the partisans were supposed to distribute propaganda leaflets. On 22 December 1944 the Romanian gendarmerie captured two parachuted boxes full of printing material, both of which were found in a village near Sibiu.[59]

Despite doubts about the effectiveness of the Red Army and the determination of the Romanians, who were felt to be helping the Soviets only under compulsion, the guerrillas had little to buoy their spirits by the spring of 1945. The capture of Schmidt and the ascension of a pro-Soviet government in Bucharest caused morale to deteriorate, and 'green' leaders no longer put stock in Vienna's assurances of 'wonder weapons' about to turn the tide. By April, contact with controllers in Austria was becoming sporadic – in fact, the Jagdverband and FAK control centres were scurrying into the Alps – and when the war ended, the surviving leaders of the organisation decided to abandon their mountain training camps, bury their weapons and concentrate solely on getting Wehrmacht stragglers back to Germany.[60] As late as the autumn of 1947, there were still Wehrmacht troops hiding in the woods around Agnetheln, waiting for their turn to travel along the underground railway, although many other stragglers had already been tracked down by the Romanian secret police.[61]

Unfortunately, the ultimate results of *Volksdeutsch* resistance in Transylvania and the Banat were predictable; in fact, it prompted exactly the kind of catastrophes that had been foreseen by critics of the Schmidt plan. After forcing German-Romanians to register with the authorities, the Soviets on 8 January 1945 began to deport nearly 100,000 Transylvanian Saxons and Banat Swabians to the USSR, which they claimed to have the right to do under the terms of the Soviet-Romanian armistice. This process was focussed on men aged 17 to 45 and women 18 to 30, many of whom eventually wound up in the Don and Dnieper basins, although small groups were dispatched as far east as the Urals. Conditions of transport and employment were so severe that fifteen to twenty per cent of the deportees did not survive long enough to return home. In addition, Romanian agriculture and industry were badly disrupted. The governments of Romania, Britain and the United States protested the deportations, both on humanitarian and practical grounds, but the Soviets responded by claiming that the measure was *not* a mass population transfer but a temporary labour draft, and that the subjects were Nazi sympathisers who were threatening Soviet lines of communication.[62]

Although the 'green' guerrillas reported that the deportation had caused a desperate situation,[63] they would not accept blame for the measure nor would they let it dissuade them from their activities. In fact, since thousands of young *Volksdeutsch* civilians fled to the woods to escape Romanian and Soviet patrols, the ranks of the guerrillas actually swelled.[64] Schmidt requested the intervention of the Red Cross and Catholic Church, although he sneered at contemporary efforts by Hans Otto Roth and Bishop Viktor Glondys, who were attempting to moderate Soviet policy. According to Schmidt, Roth and Glondys were regarded as traitors by the *Volksdeutsche* because they had encouraged *Wehrmacht* stragglers to surrender.[65] In February 1945, the guerrillas asked Vienna to tone down propaganda about the deportation; apparently, the less said about the matter, the better the effect. They also tried to capitalise upon the situation, reporting that deported members of the 'green' movement '[had] begun organising among the deportees', especially in the southern Ukraine, and that when sufficient funds arrived, they would be in a position to exploit these contacts.[66]

No discussion of guerrilla warfare in Transylvania would be complete without mention of the peculiar set of circumstances in northern Transylvania. Because of the Vienna Award of 1940, northern Transylvania had been detached from Romania and returned to the control of Hungary (of which it had been a part until 1919). The fact that the territory had a separate administrative history, if only brief, meant that the balance of forces and cast of characters was different than in the south. Although there was a considerable population of *Volksdeutsche* in northern Transylvania, and reports from *Wehrmacht* stragglers suggested that these people were still sympathetic to the German cause,[67] there were two factors that limited the scale of pro-Nazi partisan activity.

First, local Transylvanian Saxon officials were attached to the Hungarian-German *Volksbund* rather than to Schmidt's Romanian-German organisation, and as part of this group they had been encouraged to develop evacuation planning, in marked contrast to the case in southern Transylvania and the Romanian Banat. Moreover, northern

Transylvania's geographic removal from the scene of the *Wehrmacht*'s debacle in late August meant that there were three to six weeks longer than in the south in which to organise evacuations. Thus, an estimated 48,000 men, women and children were able to flee during September and October 1944,[68] leaving not many of their compatriots behind. When the deportation began in January 1945, Soviet patrols were able to snatch only about 8,000 *Volksdeutsche* from the Carei district, 7,000 from Satu Mare and a mere 150 from the regional capital of Cluj.[69]

A second factor inhibiting guerrilla warfare was that the Soviets installed a direct Red Army regime in northern Transylvania, specifically with the intent of keeping order in the territory. At the time of Romania's early defection from the Axis, the sole lure that the Soviets were able to dangle before Bucharest was the promise of help in recovering northern Transylvania, a concession that they formally offered in article nineteen of the Soviet-Romanian armistice. Soviet and Romanian armies then conquered northern Transylvania in the next two months, but Romanian avengers – 'national guards' – also surged into the territory, terrorising ethnic Hungarians and generally causing disorder. Even according to Romanian tally, thirty-five people were killed, and more liberal estimates place the number of fatalities in the hundreds. In late October and early November 1944, the Soviets retaliated by crushing the 'national guards', and they then suspended Romanian governmental authority in the recovered parishes, claiming that the Romanian regime had turned a blind eye to paramilitary vigilantes. In place of Romanian institutions, the Soviets appointed local authorities who were Hungarian – local Hungarians suddenly discovered the merits of the Communist Party – or Romanian leftists.[70] This regime remained in power until March 1945, when it was displaced by the restored authority of the Bucharest government, albeit in the form of a pro-Soviet structure that had just come to power.

The imposition of direct Soviet rule in northern Transylvania, combined with the near-total evacuation of the local *Volksdeutsche*, made it difficult for the Germans to launch a guerrilla war. Nonetheless, the Romanian Government reported on 24 January 1945 that the enemy had returned to northern Transylvania with heavy and light armament:

> Anti-military and enemy political formations make their appearance and carry out unchecked activities against Roumania and the Allied Powers. Thousands of German and particularly Hungarian soldiers are still in that territory who are in possession of arms and who are organising resistance. These elements and the consequent atmosphere of unrest and worry, contribute greatly to the sufferings of the population and are detrimental both to Roumanian and Allied interests.

Northern Transylvania, said the Romanians, was internally defenceless and civil guards organised by the local regime were 'undisciplined and unpaid… more of a menace than a defence for the public'.[71]

American officers who visited Cluj in early 1945 confirmed this assessment, reporting that the *Luftwaffe* was busy dropping weapons and other materials. 'German underground resistance', they reported, 'is growing in the section of Transylvania formerly occupied by Hungary. The German Army is attempting to organise guerrillas in the Transylvanian hills by parachuting all kinds of supplies to areas predominately German.' Several small groups were caught attempting to blow up the Turda-Cluj railway, which was a crucial line for the provisioning of the front in Hungary. *Jagdverband Südost* and units of the *Zweierorganisation* had long thought that Romanians, Ruthenians and Szeklers would make better guerrillas than the local *Volksdeutsche*, and they had recruited manpower accordingly. One team of parachutists captured near Turda was comprised of Romanian POWs taken by the *Wehrmacht* and then 're-educated' to make them suitable candidates for deployment in their homeland. When caught, members of this group were clothed in civilian garb and were holding 460,000 lei and over 300 pounds of TNT and fuses. Their instructions had been to act only against the Soviets. Having completed their sabotage assignments, they were supposed to report to the Romanian Army and claim to be POWs who had escaped from the Germans.

Although the Americans reported such difficulties, the Soviets responded by saying that the Romanian Government had been instructed to intensify countermeasures.[72] The Romanians claimed, in turn, that they could hardly accomplish anything of worth if their administrative authority in the north was restricted, and that trouble in the region owed to the fact that such powers had been limited. The Romanian Government, they contended, was not even able to maintain the degree of order to which it had committed itself in the September armistice. As noted above, the Soviets restored full control of northern Transylvania to Romania in March 1945, which was obviously an attempt to prop up a newly installed regime in Bucharest, although the official line was that the new government was more capable than its predecessor in dealing with 'fascist' opposition. Nonetheless, the SD continued to send agents into the disputed province – one such mission in late March was coordinated with the Hungarian Army – and the Soviets continued to complain of pro-German activity.[73]

A STORM BREWS IN ROMANIA

While ethnic Germans and *Wehrmacht* stragglers dominated the resistance movement in Transylvania, elements of native Romanian character were prevalent in the rest of Romania, although they were supported by Roland Gunne's German agents in Bucharest. At first blush, Romania might not have seemed a natural forum for pro-Nazi partisan warfare. Unlike Hungary and Bulgaria, the country had been on the Allied side in the First World War and during the interwar period it had been part of the French-supported 'Little Entente'. On the other hand, Romania's geographic position and the expansion of the country at the Paris Peace Conference had fostered the growth of a romantic brand of ultra-nationalism. The addition of Transylvania, Bessarabia and Bukovina had made Romania one of the sizeable powers along the western fringe of the Soviet Union and had thereby determined the country's status as a pillar of the anti-communist *Cordon sanitaire*. The Romanians also added a racial element to this dynamic, re-emphasising their foundational myth as the surviving remnant of an ancient Roman colony in Dacia. This sense of identity was reconfigured to fit modern circumstances by suggesting that Romania was the eastern lynchpin of Latinity, holding the line against Asiatic Slavdom, and that the country had a natural community of interests not only with France, but with Fascist Italy. In addition, the inclusion in an expanded Romania of relatively wealthy Jewish, Hungarian and ethnic German minorities reinforced a persecution complex. Romanians were left trying to fathom how the core of the country, rich in grain and oil, had remained a rural backwater while other peoples in the region had advanced materially.

Not surprisingly, this environment proved a seedbed for the growth of various forms of fascism. From amidst a crowded field, it was the romantically and religiously inclined 'Legion of the Archangel Michael' that made the most progress. Founded in 1927, the Legion had within a decade negotiated an electoral alliance with one of the two mainstream political forces in the country, the National Peasant Party, and with such legitimation it emerged as the third biggest vote-getter in the 1937 elections.[74] After Romania's despot, King Carol, failed to prevent the country's neighbours from stripping away its newly acquired borderlands – the 1940 cessation of northern Transylvania was the final straw – the royalist dictatorship was overthrown and replaced by a joint fascist-military government, led by Legionary chief Horia Sima and army supremo Ion Antonescu. In 1941 the two partners in this regime fell out in a brief civil war, in which the Legion was defeated and then forced to return to clandestine modes of operation.

German Government and Nazi Party agencies divided their sympathies during the 1941 fracas, with the Foreign Office supporting the Romanian military and the SS backing the Legion. After the Legion's defeat, various SS and *Volksgruppe* functionaries managed to smuggle the Legion's 'captains', including Horia Sima, into Germany, where they were treated initially as guests of the *Reichsführer*-SS. Although the Legionary leadership was thus delivered safe and sound – it even had time to organise an informal cabinet for a prospective Legionary government – Sima embarrassed his hosts by bolting to Rome in an attempt to get full backing from the Italian Fascists. Inevitably, he was caught and retrieved, whence he and his cohorts were incarcerated in the Sachsenhausen and Dachau concentration camps, although even there they were housed in special quarters and they remained a handy counterweight with which the Third Reich could keep Antonescu's regime in line.[75]

As one might expect, Romania's rapid disengagement from the war and subsequent switch of sides led to the release of Sima and company. The Legionaries now anticipated that they would be allowed to convert their shadow cabinet into a pro-German regime, perhaps based in Transylvania, Sima's home province. Alas, these expectations were not borne out, at least in the short term. Although Germany's knee-jerk reaction to Romania's 'betrayal' was to announce the creation of a Romanian 'National Government', at the time of this declaration the Germans had not the slightest idea about who would actually lead such a regime. German military and Foreign Office officials hoped that sympathetic Romanian generals would cross to the German side, but they gradually became disabused of this notion. German officers were shocked to find that none of their Romanian friends deserted the new regime in Bucharest, not even avowedly pro-German generals. For a while Sima played coy, making radio speeches for the Germans but claiming that he was not eager about the prospect of a 'National Government' unless the Germans could hold on to a significant patch of Romanian territory. This display of feigned disinterest soon passed, however, particularly as it became clear that the Germans were still holding chairs at the table for prominent Romanian conservatives and that they did not want to scare off such elements by handing the entire 'National Government' to the Legion.

By October, Sima and three of his 'captains' had wheedled 'provisional' and unpublicised appointments in the 'National Government', but they then had to fend off a challenge from General Ion Gheorge, the former Romanian ambassador in Berlin, whose lukewarm endorsement of the Axis cause provided the Foreign Office with the conservative Romanian ally whom it desired. However, Sima and his new Foreign Minister, Prince Michael Sturdza, managed to get the ear of Himmler. Sturdza reported that Gheorge did not support resistance in the homeland – the general apparently thought that the Anglo-Americans would soon displace the Soviets – while the Legion provided the only real basis for violent opposition to the new regime. Sima admitted, for his part, that the Legion had been badly mauled during the Antonescu dictatorship, but he argued that 'the humiliations and destruction' wrought by the post-Antonescu regime had inspired 'a powerful turn-around in favour of the movement. Credible reports suggest that years of Legionary propaganda could not have achieved the results that these weeks have yielded…' Sima and company also complained that the provisional status of their émigré regime was insulting, especially compared to the official standing of the Bulgarian 'National Government', and as a result the regime was formally and publically recognised in a ceremony at Vienna's Palace Lobkowitz on 10 December 1944.[76]

Even before being feted in Vienna, the 'National Government' had begun to take shape as a body of three distinct parts, although these were all run by Sima. The regime itself controlled propaganda: 'National Government' radio began broadcasts on 15 September and transmissions on various wavelengths continued until nearly the end of the war. The main transmitter, the 'Free Voice of Romania', heaped scorn on both the Romanian middle class parties and the communists, lauding the Legion as 'the soul of the nation', and the programme grew markedly better in the late winter of 1945, mainly because of the improved capacity of the Nazi information service in Romania.

The second component of the 'National Government' was the Legionary movement, which assumed the airs of being a state party. In an obsequious letter to Himmler on 8 September, Sima pledged that the Legion's 'living goal' was to maintain 'organisational and permanent connections to the National Socialist movement', and in keeping with this intention, a liaison officer, Professor Gamillschek, was posted to the SS.

The third element of the 'National Government', and the one of principal interest to us, was the 'Central Office for the Action in Romania', which had its command post in Vienna and an important sub-headquarters in Budapest.[77] By order of Himmler, the Legion was assigned control of the Romanian resistance movement and was 'to be supported under the wing of the Reichssicherheitshauptamt by all means available'. Sima met in Budapest with the RSHA's guerrilla specialists and he also visited the headquarters of Army Group South Ukraine, where he convinced generals von Grolmann and Friessner that the various army, SS and *Volksdeutsch* bands in Romania should be subordinated to a single authority (presumably his own 'Central Office'). He also arranged exchanges of political and military intelligence.[78]

As Skorzeny was brought into the picture, he considered the resources that he had on hand. His mainstay was '*Einsatzgruppe Rumänien/Siebenbürgen*', which had been formed by the Brandenburgers in the summer of 1944 and had been attached to Army Group South Ukraine as part of '*Streifkorps Karpaten*'. This group of sixty men was transferred to *Jagdverband Südost* in September 1944, becoming Erich Müller's *Jagdeinsatz Rumänien*. A number of SD stay-behind teams under *Volksdeutsch* leaders had also been organised before the German evacuation of Romania, mostly under purview of a counter-insurgency agency called the '*Oel Sabotage Abwehr Organisation*' (OSAO), which was supposed to prevent damage to the key oil refineries at Ploesti. The ASAO was set up on the basis of direct orders from Himmler and was run by the nefarious *Hauptsturmführer* Gunne, a *Waffen-*SS officer who had been transferred to the SD. Gunne's organisation was subordinated to Skorzeny's Section S and was supposed to operate *against* Romanian oil fields should the Germans ever be forced to evacuate the eastern Balkans. Gunne had submitted plans for the possible sabotage of Romanian oil facilities well before the 23 August coup, and Skorzeny was familiar with his resources and methods. Although the Romanian putsch cut short the further development of such plans – a surprise attack by the Romanian Fifth Army Corps prevented German demolitions in the oil fields – several six-man groups were left in Ploesti at the time of the German retreat and Gunne began work on reassembling his network.[79] Gunne also served as the intelligence officer of a 2,000-man *Kampfgruppe* consisting of German headquarters and service personnel from Bucharest, who broke through a Romanian Army ring and retreated north-west into the mountains.[80]

A number of Romanians had been trained at Section S camps as early as the spring of 1944, although after the formation of *Jagdeinsatz Rumänien* a larger number of recruits was enrolled at the unit's facility in Korneuberg. Romanian paratroopers were also trained at the Section S facility in Mürz Zuschlag, at a Legionary camp in Neukarenburg, at Special Camp Luckenwalde, at two FAK 206 schools near Kapuvár, at Section E facilities in Vienna and, for a short time in early April 1945, on a boat moored in the Danube at Durenstein. For the most part, recruits were Legionaries, Romanian Army POWs and deserters, or Romanian students and labourers resident in Germany. The records of a group of twenty trainees, who were schooled at Luckenwalde, suggests that they were usually aged between eighteen and forty-five and that they came from towns and villages scattered all over Romania. They were told that they would be the 'occupation forces' when Romania was eventually recovered by the *Wehrmacht*. Their supreme leader was the Legionary 'captain' Constantin Stoicanescu, who was one of the instigators of the 1941 Legionary uprising and had prepared Sima's wartime flight to Italy. Stoicanescu, as will be recalled, eventually shared the same fate as Andreas Schmidt. The paratroopers' mission, according to Sima, was 'to organise teams of Legionaries to perform terrorist acts and sabotage in the rear of the front and in [the interior of] the country. The purpose is to restrict [the supply] of armaments and war material.' The interdiction of rail traffic was supposed to contribute to the success of a forthcoming German counter-offensive in Hungary, which was expected to gain momentum in the spring of 1945. In addition, parachutists were instructed to score political advantages from the poor deportment of Red Army troops and alert people to the imminent dangers of communisation.

Plans for specific operations were being drafted as early as September 1944.[81] Although Army Group South Ukraine suggested keeping Sima's guerrillas out of Transylvania as long as conventional operations in the region were still underway, after October 1944 the Legionary leadership was free to send its infiltrators wherever it wished, with the eager support of the army. Many parachutists were actually dropped in Transylvania, where they were supposed to organise resistance 'in loose cooperation' with the *Volksgruppe*. Primary zones of deployment included the Apuseni Mountains, the Banat, Oltenia, the Brasov region, the Sibiului Mountains and Bukovina.[82] Operations were organised by *Jagdverband Südost*, Section E and formations of the *Zweierorganisation*, sometimes acting in concert, and KG 200 dropped the first nine teams between October and December 1944. These operations were codenamed 'Steinbock' I–III and 'Regulus' I–VI,[83] the latter of which included Germans as well as fascist Romanians. 'Regulus' was run by *Leutnant* Alfred Piff, the Mil D's expert on Romania and an officer fanatically determined to carry out his mission. He gathered a cadre of fifty-two Romanian volunteers, whom he formed into seven teams, each equipped with a wireless set. By the end of 1944, a number of radio operators had been landed in Romania, including Sima's personal secretary Ilie Smultea.

It was disconcerting, however, that several key agents were captured by the Romanians and handed over to the Russians, particularly since this created a suspicion that the movement's chain of command and training apparatus had been penetrated by Soviet informers. Several leaders of the 'greens' believed that a Romanian radio operator, Dr Taranu, was a Soviet agent and that he had provided the Russians with inside accounts of the Legion's plans and methods of operation. Suspecting such penetration, the resisters in Romania wanted further parachute operations suspended. On 28 January 1945, a radio agent codenamed 'Ludu' delivered a tart response to German suggestions about the deployment of more parachutists: 'I protest against renewed dropping of men in spite of repeated warning[s]. A new traitor may uncover part of our network. In agreement with [the] Green Command here we demand cessation of all action.'[84]

It is unclear whether or not this rebuke had any effect, although there is no doubt that by March 1945 matters were back in full swing. In addition to the fact that the *Wehrmacht* was on the offensive in Hungary, an operation for which it desperately required a diversion, the weather during the last half of March 1945 was perfect for airborne operations. On 17 March a German plane dropped parachutists and leaflets around fifteen villages near Deva, and on 20 March more paratroopers were dropped near Arad and Bihor. On the night of 24 March, eight men from *Jagdeinsatz Rumänien* were flown into the Giumalau region of Bukovina, equipped with radios and a sum of 35,000,000 lei. All of these operations went smoothly, but a major fiasco occurred on the evening of 26 March. Three Romanians, together with a large amount of medical supplies and five radio sets, were supposed to be dropped near Brasov, although *Luftwaffe* pilots could not find the ground beacons and apparently dropped the men and supply containers in the wrong location. This was a serious mistake because the leader of this team, Michael Farsh, was carrying a large amount of money strapped around his chest. Two weeks later, Legionary guerrillas were still searching for Farsh and his team, who were not at the drop site and had failed to turn up at a designated safe-house. According to a Romanian source, the Soviets on 29 March captured supplies, arms and 72,500,000 lei, all of which had been dropped into the Brasov area. This may have been the forlorn Farsh and his consignment.[85]

Whatever the fate of Farsh, there were already so many '*Einsatztruppe*' being set down in Romania that Roland Gunne had to appeal to Vienna for up-to-date listings in order for the SD station to keep track of incoming personnel.[86] By April 1945, the Soviets had begun nocturnal patrols of Romanian airspace because, according to Gunne, 'they fear the dropping of airborne troops of the Rumanian National Army'. We also know that from mid-March to mid-April 1945, Skorzeny's time and energy were consumed largely with Romanian matters.[87] By this period, there were several radio outposts and literally hundreds of SD and FAK agents operating on Romanian soil.[88]

Although SD officers had a difficult time mounting *Luftwaffe* flights during April and early May 1945, they continued to make plans for parachute operations or nocturnal landings on secluded airstrips, and they communicated such intentions to the Legionary guerrillas. The last hurrah was a resupply of radio equipment and technicians called Operation 'Piff'. This enterprise, the sequel to 'Regulus', was launched in March, when Sima seconded twenty-five men for wireless training in Breitenfurt. Even as Piff and his confrères were chased out of Vienna and retreated high into the Alps, they continued to organise operations as if it were the high noon of the Third Reich. Supplies, manpower and aircraft for Operation 'Piff' had been collected by 30 April 1945, with the intention of re-supplying the Romanian resisters at a secret airfield south-west of Brasov. The guerrillas were notified on 3 May: '24 men will be set down under the command of *Hauptmann* Gill, including Iosef Dumitru. Gill is himself an excellent wireless technician. The undertaking is finely equipped technically. Gill is to form a central wireless station and to coordinate all lines hitherto established by *Frontaufklärung*'.[89] Although *Wehrmacht* forces in the Alps were literally days away from a final capitulation and KG 200 was short of fuel, two aircraft allotted to Operation 'Piff' took off from an airfield near Linz, where unit members were given a personal 'send off' by Sima. The plane carrying Gill never arrived at its destination – perhaps it was shot down – but the second machine crash landed, disgorging survivors who established contact with the underground.[90]

Despite such reinforcement, there were relatively few instances in which the Legion interfered with enemy communications, and when Radio Danube did occasionally report such successes, the resisters rebuked the propagandists, saying that the claims prejudiced their efforts.[91] In the western Wallachian town of Craiova, where Iron Guardists enjoyed some success in harrassing a Red Army staging area for the supply of arms and ammunition to the Titoite Yugoslavs, the Soviets quickly swept up the saboteurs and seized their wireless sets. Sima himself frowned upon 'uncoordinated individual actions', which he argued caused Soviet reprisals and eroded civilian support for the resistance movement.[92] Thus, much of the Legion's attention was directed toward reorganising Legionary cells, called 'nests', and a British military observer in Moldavia noted that 'Legionaries are armed but do not intend to use arms for some time to come'. Nonetheless, such units collected intelligence and carried through various para-political tasks, such as the attempted rescue of Colonel Palius Ionescu, the former director of Romania's military intelligence service. Ionescu was being held in detention by the new authorities.[104] In addition, Legionaries inspired resentment of the Soviets through exploiting news about the undisciplined behaviour of Russian troops.[94] Although reports from Romania suggested the Legionary underground was small – the group directly under Sima's control numbered 600 men – Kaltenbrunner estimated that the movement was capable of rallying 200,000 people.[95]

In late February 1945, Vienna instructed the underground that 'the preparation and military direction of the resistance movement' would henceforth be codenamed '*Schmetterling*', and by early March, Gunne was pressing his controllers for a clear indication about what was expected of the movement:

We await [a] basic order, so that we can make our plans, working from this, bearing in mind conditions and possibilities at this end. We can only give our opinion about supplies of men and material when we have been informed of the general intentions of the *Führung* and [an] assignment has been given, especially concerning the USSR.[96]

Two days later Gunne was told that Section E had assumed control of all operations in Romania, and that projects would henceforth be more organised than had been the case:

Hitherto only small scale agent operations in the sphere of *Frontaufklärung* have been carried out before coordination. Assignments will be issued shortly, especially in the military sphere. [97]

On 10 March, a clear directive – the 'basic plan' requested by Gunne – was provided to Nicolae Petrescu, one of Sima's paratroop commanders in Romania. Petrescu was told that as a result of discussions in senior echelons, several fundamental matters had been determined:

First, no acts of sabotage are to be undertaken for the present. Make all preparations, however, so that they can be carried out at a given moment with maximum success. Second, the Legionary movement must work underground. Under no circumstances must it become prominent, not even by written propaganda. Third, the camps and quarters must be as small as possible, so that they do not extract [*sic*] attention. They are to become the rendezvous for the coming operations. Fourth, as far as possible, battle groups must remain within the framework of local organisation, camouflaged as well as can be, both in town and country, and nevertheless so organised that they can be controlled with ease at the given moment. Fifth, make good use of the time we still have to complete the organisation of the Legion. Do not forget that the main aim is not only information, but the formation of a fighting organisation. Sixth, tactics hitherto [are] very good. Establish contact with all dissatisfied elements which feel themselves threatened by Bolshevism – army, parties, church and crown. Seventh, the masses must be drawn into the coming battle. Establish a front of the Rumanian nation against Bolshevism. The Communists must be isolated from the rest of the masses of the people. Likewise the Jews, so that the distrust of the mass of [the] workers grows.

The coming revolt would, Petrescu was told, 'be either launched from this end or determined by events at your end'.[98]

It is likely that the Germans encouraged direct action at the time of their offensive in Hungary, and certainly by April 1945, with the Third Reich reeling from a succession of heavy blows in both east and west, the SD had begun requesting a more active display of resolve by Legionary guerrillas. '[The] situation here', controllers noted on 11 April, 'demands urgent and violent action or [the] employment of the prepared groups in your area'.[99] Even in the wake of this appeal, however, there was little evidence of heightened guerrilla or sabotage activity in Romania. Apparently the Legion had no intention of sacrificing its valuable underground organisation for a state that was obviously on its last legs, even if it was a patron and an ally.

If parachute operations and sporadic resistance marked the ultimate extent of Legionary activity in Romania, the effect would have been no more notable than that of the parallel effort by the *Kopjás* movement in Hungary. The Legionaries, however, also carried out a form of subterfuge far more insidious than partisan warfare, namely the widespread penetration of the new order, especially the infiltration of rival political parties and the establishment of a channel of influence within the Romanian Army. It was particularly through these means that Sima sought to organise a revolt in Romania, hopefully so weakening the Soviets that he could move his 'Romanian National Army' to the western border of the country. Nicolai Petrescu, the former secretary-general of the Legion, had the mandate to run infiltration operations and was sent to Romania by air in November 1944.[100]

The conditions for such activity were opportune. The putsch against Antonescu had saved the Soviets the bother of setting up either a military government or a minority communist regime,[101] and for six months Romania was run *not* by Soviet puppets, but by a succession of relatively conservative coalition governments. These regimes were led by two Romanian generals, Constantin Sanatescu (August-December 1944) and Nicolae Radescu (December 1944-February 1945). Sanatescu had a pro-Western orientation and an anti-Legionary reputation that owed to his role in crushing the 1941 uprising. Radescu, however, was a nationalist with a distinctly harder edge. During the 1930s, he had been chief of the 'Crusade for Romanianness', a fascist rival to the Legion and a movement that Radescu's enemies feared he was seeking to revive.[102]

Unfortunately, neither Sanatescu nor Radescu did much to purge right-wingers from the civil or military bureaucracy, nor did either bother to arrest many Legionaries. Even the British, the most sympathetic of the Allied Powers, warned that the Romanians were 'riding for a fall'. In early October 1944, the British Political Representative in Bucharest informed a Romanian colleague that 'it was not "Communism" but "anti-Communism" which would bring down the present national government', and he later told Whitehall that 'none will be able to blame the Russians if they impose a military government, disastrous as that would be for Rumania and indeed for the Balkans as a whole'.[103] When there were instances of sabotage at Ploesti, the Soviets sealed off the oil-producing region, and when there were attacks against Red Army troops in Bucharest, generals Vinogradev and Vasilev complained to Sanatescu and threatened to maintain order directly unless countermeasures were undertaken.[104]

Radescu came to power in December 1944 amid much sound and fury, pledging to pick up all Axis nationals and fascists, and to purge the Romanian administration, but Ministry of Interior figures in early January 1945 showed that only 183 Legionaries had been arrested.[105] In addition, Christmas leaves for internees had resulted in more than one hundred escapes of pro-German individuals who had been incarcerated in earlier waves of arrests, a fiasco that nearly cancelled out the effect of the new arrests and became the source of a national scandal.[106]

In this sort of environment, even the Romanian communists were not immune to Legionary manipulations. Desperate to increase the size of the minuscule party, the

Muscovite leadership faction led by Ana Pauker recruited numerous Legionaries into communist ranks, even despite the reticence of a nativist faction of party leaders, which was concerned about the doubtful loyalties of Pauker's recruits. Teohari Georgescu, representing Pauker, met with Nicolae Petrescu and negotiated the entry of whole fascist bands into the Communist Party. Even Georgescu seems to have worried about this arrangement, ruefully noting in the summer of 1945 that while some Legionary 'workers and peasants' had been 'redeemed', others were not true converts. 'They simply put on another coat', said Georgescu, '[but] even if it is red they will not avoid the punishment which they will receive if they continue their treacherous policy.' A British military observer also got the impression that Moldavian 'Legionary-communists' were still fascists at heart and that they were taking orders from their old masters:

> They are apparently chiefly concerned in efforts to disturb Anglo-Russian relations. Their directive seems to be to infiltrate into leftist groups and to propaganda against Britain and sow suspicions among the Russians of our good faith. Germany's only long-term hope of recovery is friction between ourselves and the Russians... [The Legionaries] may use [their arms] to provoke incidents between Russian and British elements if occasion is offered. I was told by two Jews at Galatzi that these Legionary elements in the leftist groups have already had some success in spreading anti-Jewish propaganda among the Russian soldiery.[107]

Surviving records of radio messages reveal Legionary reports about successful penetration of the Romanian Communist Party.[108]

The National Peasant Party (NPP), led by Iuliu Maniu, was of equal interest, although it also posed something of a threat. One of Romania's two traditional parliamentary parties, the NPP had supported the 1944 putsch against Antonescu, and in the sunny afterglow of that event it had negotiated a pact with one of the Legion's most powerful underground 'captains', Horatiu Comaniciu, with whom Maniu had been in contact since 1942. Comaniciu genuinely believed that the Legion was finished as a political force and on 1 September 1944 he declared 'the end of our mission', recommending that his followers join the NPP (as well as the other parties).[109]

Seeing much of the Legion's strength leached by the NPP, Sima stewed in resentment in Vienna. Although he and Maniu had once been political allies, he warned his Nazi patrons that pro-German elements in the centre of the political spectrum were 'very rare', and he added that even if 'bourgeois democratic elements' might once again cast an eye toward Germany because of their fear of Russia, they would be unreliable friends. Such circles, he warned, were dependent on 'Anglo-American Free Masonry'.[110]

Despite these assumptions, Sima was forced to change his outlook as he spent time at the Section E headquarters in Vienna, in the process coming under the influence of Kaltenbrunner. The RSHA boss was interested in the NPP because it had a mass base and could serve as a powerful centre of resistance in Romania. Kaltenbrunner viewed Maniu as 'a vacillating politician' who at times had courted the Bulgarians, the Russians and the French, but now was ready to woo the Legion in order to build a bridge to the Germans. SS intelligence suggested that Maniu had painted himself into a corner through supporting the 23 August putsch, particularly since he had expected the Western Allies to arrive in Romania, but was now left facing the Red Army. Although currently 'playing along' with the Soviets, he was actually planning an anti-Soviet uprising, a project in which he hoped to interest senior echelons of the Romanian Army, as well as the SIS. His greatest hope was for a German-British peace so that both powers could combine against the Soviets and liberate Romania. According to Kaltenbrunner, the NPP needed Legionary support to achieve its goals, so he convinced Sima that it was he, not Maniu, who was in the stronger position. In Kaltenbrunner's own terminology, he 'trained' Sima (rather like one would train a dog) and made him a 'politically respectable' partner for the NPP, although Sima never ceased to argue that the Legion was the true rallying point for anti-communist forces, and that support from other quarters was 'canalising' toward it.[111]

By early 1945, the PNN was extending feelers to the Legion and the SD. According to a guerrilla report, '[the] Zaranists [National Peasants] have approached the Greens and enquired how many men they could provide for a counteraction in case of an attempted Communist coup. [The] issue of weapons in barracks is planned. [The] enquiry [was] alleged to have been made with knowledge of Radescu. [The] Green Command has replied with caution, namely [saying that] if the Army strikes the first blow the Greens will join the Zaranists undercover.'[112]

In a message from Vienna on 2 February, the Foreign Office reported that 'Maniu is in contact with nationalist circles', although the timing of a revolt was problematic:

First, Soviet repression in Roumania has resulted in plans for [an] uprising with support of circles close to the present government. Nationalist circles close to Germany… believe [that the] movement [is] insufficiently prepared but are nevertheless willing to participate in [a] general rising. Failure would mean the loss of Green 'points d'appui' in Roumania. [It is] preferable to make [the] attempt simultaneously with [a] counter offensive on [the] Eastern Front.

Three days later, Ribbentrop advised that the date of the uprising be left to the Romanian conspirators or to Sima, and 'not to force the pace'.[113]

After the Russians imposed a pro-Soviet government upon Romania in March 1945, another proposal was raised: 'Maniu has carried on all discussions with a group of Romanians concerning organisation of a resistance movement. A council of leaders has ordered one of its members to get in touch with the Legion.'[114] In May 1945, Kaltenbrunner told the Americans that 'the latest news from Roumania was that cooperation of the Iron Guard with the other parties was quite feasible… The Iron Guard and Maniu can be combined at any time.'[115]

Sima also ordered Nicolae Petrescu to negotiate with the National Peasants and thus take the initiative away from the maverick Comaniciu, although Comaniciu restored some of his credibility, at least in Sima's eyes, by re-embracing the cause of anti-communist resistance. Petrescu met with PNN leaders Ion Mihalache and Nicolae Panescu: 'These men', he later claimed, 'requested collaboration in order to put Legionaries at their disposal for the protection of National Peasant meetings.' Petrescu also had a conversation with Iuliu Maniu.[116]

The Legion had even more success in courting the Romanian Army. Reports about the Romanian troops in Hungary and Slovakia revealed widespread desertion and poor morale.[117] As a result, the Legionary leadership told Petrescu to 'establish contact with the Rumanian divisions at the front, building up your organisation for that purpose. The Army must be persuaded not to let itself be slaughtered, but to go over to the Germans. In the case of a German offensive, the Army must take up arms against the Soviets.'[118] At the most basic level, the execution of this task meant converting Romanian POWs and convincing them to return across the front lines in Slovakia. Their mission was to return to their original units and stir up trouble. Similar teams were dropped behind Soviet lines as part of Operation 'Regulus'. Some of the infiltrators secretly intended to surrender once across the lines, although they often found that when they followed such a course, they were still incarcerated by the suspicious Russians and sentenced to twenty-five-year terms of imprisonment.[119]

Leaflets signed by the Romanian 'National Government' were also dropped along Romanian lines of communication, particularly in Transylvania, where there were supposed to be two battalions of Romanian troops hiding out in the Apuseni Mountains, mainly because they were refusing to fight the Germans. Soldiers in Romanian home garrisons were warned that the Soviets intended to send them to Siberia: 'Save yourself so that you may save later your women, your children and your property. Resist the Russians! Don't you know that the Russian Army has trampled upon the armistice terms?'[120]

More serious was the Legionary and SD attempt to convert senior Romanian generals. It was felt that after Romania's rapid switch of sides, the generals had remained loyal to the new regime because they had been lured by the promise of recovering northern Transylvania from Hungary, although within half a year 'the officer corps consider[ed] itself betrayed and cheated'.[121] Northern Transylvania's full recovery had been postponed and armed Romanian communists had undertaken land seizures and other forms of revolutionary activity. On the other hand, the German recognition of the 'National Government' provided an alternate pole of loyalty and the Germans also got a hearing for their promise of a large-scale offensive in the spring of 1945. The consequent shift of sympathies was dramatic. Legionary agent 'Ludu' reported by radio on 11 February 1945 that contacts with the most senior echelon of the army had been re-established:

A Roumanian general of the reserve staff stated to me that the supreme general staff has worked out a strategic plan in the event of the Russian army retreating through Roumania, should a German counter-offensive be successful, for the purpose of employing the Roumanian army against the Soviets and protecting the country. In the general's opinion, the Royal House would agree to this action if the eventuality should arise, but treat the information with caution.[122]

One week later, an SD agent reported that senior military leaders were disturbed by communist demonstrations 'and are seeking to cover their rear, even by using the Legion'.[123]

A particular source of hope was General Gheorghe Avramescu, who had once been a keen advocate of the anti-Soviet crusade but had stayed loyal to Bucharest after 23

August. In fact, Avramescu was given command of the Romanian Fourth Army, which fought in Transylvania and Hungary, and he was personally cited by Stalin for meritorious service. Nonetheless, he was attracted by the call of the 'National Government' and in the autumn of 1944 he put out feelers, indicating that he might defect if he could find a way to bring his family through the lines. On 5 November, he sent Prince Sturdza, his son-in-law, to negotiate in his stead, and there was speculation that a successful German offensive might enable Avramescu to bring over part of the Fourth Army to the German side. Sima promptly appointed Sturdza as his foreign minister, while OSAO chief Roland Gunne was posted to Avramescu as a liaison officer. A report by Gunne on 14 February was full of praise:

> General Avramescu has been promoted to army general and at the request of Malinovsky is once again employed as C in C of the 4th Army. He is off to the operational area tomorrow. Avramescu's behaviour is unimpeachable. He is ready for any collaboration. The government intended to put Avramescu in the forefront of politics; on the advice of the Legion, he preferred a command at the front. He is ready, if necessary, to take over political duties also. Close contact is maintained from this end by a permanent contact man with Avramescu.[124]

The predatory Gunne treated the affair with an intense sense of proprietorship: when the Legion proposed sending Prince Sturdza back to Romania in order to dicker with the Fourth Army, Gunne discouraged the dispatch of this potential rival. Sturdza, he said, 'is not to come as he is too well known and the undertaking would be endangered'. Given the fact that Avramescu was such a centre of attention, it is hardly a surprise that his treachery was uncovered by the Soviets. He was arrested on 3 March 1945, on orders of the local theatre commander, Marshal Malinovsky, and he later died in a Soviet prison camp.[125]

As suggested by the Avramescu affair, German endeavours in Romania did not escape Soviet attention. Reports from the Second Ukrainian Front were rife with references to 'Green Guards', to the persecution of pro-Soviet officers and to the fact that Nazi agents had penetrated the staffs of several frontline divisions. One report suggested outright Romanian harassment of the Red Army, including the machine gunning of Soviet vehicles. A number of senior Romanian officers were also blasted in such evaluations, particularly General Mikhail, head of the Romanian General Staff.[126]

As a result, and as a consequence of Soviet foreknowledge about the forthcoming *Wehrmacht* counter-offensive in Hungary, the Russians moved to reign in the Romanian Army and to force Radescu out of power. In mid-February 1945, Malinovsky claimed that the Romanians were mobilising men and setting up unauthorised emplacements in Bucharest, and he sent three Romanian regiments to the front. The Romanian Army in Bucharest was eventually ordered to dismantle machine gun nests, disarm troops and disband unit depots,[127] prompting *Sigurantza* officers to tell their German friends that the Russians were neutralising the Romanian Army 'for fear that it may attack them in the rear if the Germans do bring off an offensive'.[128] By the turn of February/March 1945, Soviet troops had arrived in Bucharest in force, including two NKGB divisions, and the

Soviets informed King Michael that Radescu would have to be dropped and replaced by Petru Groza, leader of a Transylvanian farmers' party closely allied to the communists. The Soviets told the Western Allies that Radescu had been caught conspiring with the Legion and that plans had been made to attack Soviet forces in Bucharest.[129] Groza's pro-communist regime came to power on 6 March, promising to cleanse the bureaucracy and to more thoroughly police the country, and over the next month there was a wholesale drive against surviving Legionaries and Germans, a campaign that damaged the 'green' network. Gunne reported on 12 March that 'throughout the whole country [the] arrest of Legionaries [has] begun', and five days later he added that 'important material and files [have been] exposed'. The arrest of radio operator Nicu Popescu forced Gunne and other leadership elements to shift base, since Popescu knew the location of their hideout, and by 19 April 1945 most of the wireless stations in Bucharest had been lost.[130]

It will come as no shock to learn that the Groza government laid the basis for the communisation of Romania, as it was likely to do once in a position of authority. The question at hand, however, is why the regime came to power when it did. Many Western historians have portrayed Groza's appointment as the consequence of an unmerited Soviet intervention in Romanian affairs. According to conventional wisdom, this process involved the displacement of a democratic and relatively unblemished regime, and was motivated *not* by short term military or political calculations, but by a premeditated Marxist-Leninist scheme for the seizure of power – a 'prefabricated revolution', as it was described by Hugh Seton-Watson. It is clear that this stereotypical view really had little to do with the facts of the case. In fact, Soviet directives recently unearthed in the Russian archives show that the Soviets had no long-term plans to change the Romanian social or economic system.[131]

The German leadership was satisfied with the course of events in Romania, particularly since its agents had helped bring matters to a head. The guerrillas were told on 15 February 1945 that Kaltenbrunner was 'extremely pleased with the work hitherto done', and several weeks later, Gunne was informed that a summary of his reports was being given to Hitler – 'The *Führer* is extremely interested in developments at your end'.[132] If Romania had been won back to the German side through such machinations, it would have been rated as an important gain, but prompting a Soviet intervention was just as valuable – perhaps more so – because it caused a split between the Soviets and the Western Allies. Senior British and American statesmen claimed that the Soviet intrusion into Romania's affairs was unwarranted and Gunne noted on 1 March that 'there is more and more confirmation… that the conflict of Bucharest is a fight for power between the Anglo-Americans and the Russians'.[133] Goebbels gleefully remarked in his diary that the political impact of Legionary activity was an added dividend:

The Iron Guard is dealing out terror and provocation and the Soviets are concluding therefrom that they must make tabula rasa in Rumania. There is talk of fascist impudence, the worst vice in Soviet eyes, and Rumanian politicians who tried to make common cause with the British and Americans are being accused of this. There is little love lost between the Russians and London over all of this, but the British are now too intimidated and too impotent to dare oppose the Soviets openly.[134]

Despite this sneering evaluation of British political courage, the Germans were happy to find themselves on the same side as the United Kingdom, with both nations now standing in opposition to Moscow. In fact, at the end of January 1945, Gunne reported that he had established contact with British and American officials posted with the Control Council in Bucharest, and he was authorised by Waneck to make reports to the Anglo-Americans about 'national resistance circles'. According to Gunne, the Western Allies refused to intervene in the Romanian-Soviet stand-off, although at the height of the crisis in early March 1945 they unofficially encouraged King Michael, Maniu and other non-communist leaders to oppose Soviet intervention.[135]

Ironically, some Legionary elements had never wanted to realign with the Germans but to solicit the support of the Western Powers, a preference also expressed by the Comaniciu Group.[136] Although Sima stuck with the Germans, there is some evidence that he explored the alternative course, particularly near the end of the war, when he realised that his only chance of playing a role in Romanian affairs lay with the Allies. SD agents in Madrid reported in late April 1945 that Legionary leaders were cooperating with Vlasov in attempts to contact the British and Americans and that Sima was 'inimical to Germany at heart and allied to us only because of the common antagonism to the Soviet Union'.[137]

Meanwhile, the 'National Government' was in the process of dissolving as it was chased into the Alps, along with its SD and Foreign Office contacts, and communication with Romania grew more sporadic.[138] A message on 3 May 1945 instructed the resisters to check in periodically even if regular communication temporarily ceased: 'If contact is lost for more than a month, [the] out-station will call on the 1st, 10th, 15th, etc. until [it is] re-established. Contact will in any event be resumed.'[139] Even after the collapse of the Third Reich, secret SD control stations in the Alps remained in contact with the 'green' resisters and the Legion was also able to establish direct contact with a radio outpost in Timisoara, having apparently gained access to Mil D frequency and code data. In July 1945, the 'green' movement in Bucharest was advised that financial resources in Switzerland were still available, and it was told to maintain contact with the Legion, but to exercise a great care. Sima told his agents in Romania: 'Continue activity as before. The forwarding of material will take place in a short time.'[140]

It was the strategy of political infiltration that eventually doomed the Legionary underground. As one Legionnaire noted, the movement's strength was so widely dispersed between contending groups that they no longer had the trust of any single side, and anti-communists within the Legion regarded the infiltration of the Communist Party with deep suspicion. Indeed, by 1946 the Romanian communists and the Interior Ministry were doing a better job of using Legionaries to infiltrate the Iron Guard than vice versa. Pro-communist Legionaries were used to form 'Shock Units', which violently broke up cells of the underground, and even Petrescu agreed to help uncover resistant Legionary cells and encourage Legionaries not to join the NPP. Apparently, this strategy entailed a desperate effort to win a place for the Legion – or its former elements – in the new order. Such efforts were eventually repaid with Petrescu's arrest and his trial by the communist regime. By this time (1948), the regime had also arrested or interned tens of thousands of active Legionaries or former members of the movement.

Meanwhile, Sima attempted to reassert control by dispatching another of his lieutenants, Eugen Teodorescu, with orders to subordinate Petrescu. However, by the time Teodorescu arrived in Romania, the Legionary underground was disintegrating or was heavily infiltrated by communist agents. Naturally, this prejudiced Sima's ability to interest American, French or British intelligence agencies in his network, although as late as 1950 he was still claiming to have small guerrilla bands operating in the homeland. Abroad, Sima reconciled himself to working more closely with Radescuite and NPP centres of resistance, and he even attempted to mend fences with King Michael, who was now in exile, but the Legion never regained the trust of other anti-communist elements.[141]

THE MACEDONIAN GAMBIT

The Third Reich's treatment of a wayward Bulgaria was markedly different from policy toward Romania. German strategy was predicated upon the assumption that if trouble arose with Bulgaria, it would be important to draw military assets in Bulgarian-annexed Macedonia toward the German side. The agency chosen to fulfil this function was the infamous Internal Macedonian Revolutionary Organisation, whose gunmen were brutal enough to serve as fit collaborators for the Nazis.

By the time that the SD began to cultivate the IMRO, the organisation already had a half-century of experience in bloodletting and revolutionary skulduggery. Formed in 1893, the IMRO had compiled a record that included a major revolt against the Turks, plus decades of raiding into Vardar and Aegean Macedonia from bases in western Bulgaria. The Bulgarians supported IMRO bands, called *Komitadji*, because they coveted the portions of Macedonia that had been incorporated into Yugoslavia and Greece, and IMRO in turn became a huge factor in Bulgarian affairs, the proverbial tail wagging the dog. In the 1920s and early 1930s, IMRO dominated the Pirin district – that is, Bulgaria's portion of Macedonia – although the movement also split into warring factions consisting of autonomists and pro-Bulgarian irredentists. The latter of the two fragments, led by Ivan Mihailov, accepted help from revisionist powers hostile to Yugoslavia, especially Italy and Hungary, and it also developed an alliance with the Croatian Ustashe. In 1934, after a coup in Sofia led by the *Zveno*, a group of military technocrats, the Mihailovists were reined in and their faction of IMRO was banned, mainly because the new leaders of Bulgaria were no longer willing to countenance the damage done to Bulgaria's reputation by IMRO terrorism. The Mihailovists subsequently went underground and retained an informal network of contacts.[142]

The Germans only became interested in IMRO after the Balkan Campaign of 1941. The Bulgarian Government did not enjoy the full trust of the Germans, particularly since Tsar Boris was a lukewarm ally. Boris had refused to join the crusade against the Soviet Union, and had entered the war against Yugoslavia and Greece only so that he could grab the bulk of Macedonia. Thus, Bulgaria hardly looked ready to repeat its Herculean performance in the First World War, when it had bled itself white containing an Allied expeditionary force at Salonika. As Field Marshal von Weichs noted dryly, the Bulgarians were no longer 'the Prussians of the Balkans'. Kaltenbrunner and Neubacher shared this assessment, feeling that it was the Serbs, rather than the Bulgarians, who would make the best anti-Soviet resisters in the region. One of the results of this perception was that the fascist parties in Bulgaria, notably the 'National Legion' and the *Ratnitsi*, received no German help in their schemes to overthrow Tsar Boris.[143]

Thus we are returned to the matter of the IMRO, the repository in which the Germans decided to invest their hopes. Since 1941, Mihailov's surviving organisation had been based in Zagreb, where its Ustashe friends had come to power. Mihailov also became a factor in Bulgarian-occupied Macedonia because he formed a number of committees that campaigned for Bulgarian annexation of the province, and because veterans of his organisation held important posts in the occupation regime. The SD used Mihailov as an informant as early as 1942, and in the autumn of that year it had sent six IMRO guerrillas into Yugoslavia in order to infiltrate the Chetniks. However, it was after the *Wehrmacht* failed to eliminate Tito's Yugoslav Partisans in 1943 that Mihailov truly began to cut a larger profile in Berlin and Vienna. By this time, the SD believed that it was necessary to coordinate all available anti-communist forces for an extended fight in the Balkans, and Mihailov had long impressed the Germans by steadfastly resisting pressure for the subordination of his faction of the IMRO to the Comintern.

By the middle of 1943, Section E's station chief in Bulgaria, *Sturmbannführer* Kob, had come into contact with a lawyer named Zilev, who was running the Mihailovite underground propaganda apparatus in Sofia. In October 1943, Kob asked Zilev to come to Berlin for a chat with Schellenberg, and within a week of these talks direct negotiations between Mihailov and Schellenberg had been arranged. Schellenberg later recalled that when the 47-year-old Mihailov arrived in Berlin, he lacked a sense of physical presence, being small, slim, bald and pale, but that his eyes shone with the light of a fanatic. Kaltenbrunner also received Mihailov in Berlin, although he was flat on his back – bedridden with swollen veins – and it was only during a later meeting in Vienna that he was able to take proper account of his visitor. Both Schellenberg and Kaltenbrunner prevailed upon Mihailov to form counter-insurgency *Ohrana* (Guards), which could be deployed in northern Greece, but they also asked him to perform two clandestine services. First, they suggested that he help set up an intelligence service and stay-behind network in Bulgaria proper; and second, they requested that he build a pro-German movement and lend his prestige to German political schemes for Macedonia, although the precise nature of those schemes was still unclear. Schellenberg and his cohorts already desired the creation of a Macedonian 'Free State'; Kaltenbrunner, Neubacher and Waneck wanted to keep Macedonia as part of Bulgaria. Mihailov agreed to these proposals and was thereafter supplied with SD money and resources.[144]

Subsequently, much time and investment was directed to Bulgaria. As part of Operation 'Triton', German planners divided up Bulgaria and Macedonia into five operational zones, in each of which they cached arms and food, usually near main thoroughfares. They also began recruiting and training Bulgarian guerrillas, and by April 1944, at least seven Bulgarians were being trained at Skorzeny's eastern battle school in Yugoslavia. The Germans also strengthened Mihailov's existing network by providing four million lewa for the financing and training of a number of wireless operators who were infiltrated into Bulgaria. Some of these men were supposed to begin operations immediately; some were told to lay low and act as future stay-behind agents; some would be withdrawn with the Germans, in case of an evacuation, and then dropped back into the country by parachute. IMRO functionary Vladimir Kurtev was appointed to run the cells from Sofia, while it was expected that after any prospective Bulgarian defection, the network would be controlled by Kob and Zilev.

This system of agents performed well as long as Bulgaria was still ostensibly part of the Axis, but after the Red Army arrived in Bulgaria and helped to hoist its local sympathisers into power, the network collapsed. It is probably no coincidence that many of the principal figures connected with the project, Kob and Zilev among them, were killed when Bulgaria switched sides. At Neurokop, two dozen IMRO men were slaughtered, and many others were imprisoned or interned. Amidst this chaos, only two agents survived and continued to radio political and economic data back to Vienna. They remained active until April 1945. It should be noted, however, that the repression of 1944–1945, while bad, was not as severe as the punishment meted out to other parties. During this period, Bulgarian communists set their sights mainly on the bureaucratic and police remnants of the royalist regime, and IMRO, which had been in opposition for the last decade, received only secondary attention.[145]

IMRO also tried to activate *Komitadji* within Bulgaria in order to help the beleaguered Germans, but these bands never functioned at the scale that was anticipated. Records of German radio messages from late August and early September 1944 mention the mobilisation of bands by 'national committees' in western and northern Bulgaria. In the northern town of Ruse, a Danubian river port lying directly in the path of Soviet forces slicing through Romania, the local 'committee' organised about eighty guerrilla groups. The intention was to send these units 'into all endangered zones, wherever they might be in Bulgaria, in order by diversionary actions to assure the German forces a peaceful withdrawal'. Four similar groups dispatched by the SD had reached the Bulgarian frontier by 1 September, but the remainder were still begging arms and money from the Germans. In the main, these resources were not available. The SD asked the army if it could provide material, but military officers claimed on 31 August that deliveries were 'not possible from here', although they were willing to release one of the stay-behind depots that had recently been laid by Mil D.[146]

IMRO also failed in its attempt to establish an independent political force to dominate Macedonia. Part of the fault lay with the Germans. The German Army was not as fond of the IMRO as the SD, which meant that they were reluctant to arm it, and Schellenberg and Kaltenbrunner were at odds over Macedonia's political future. According to Schellenberg, Hitler began mulling the possibility of Macedonian 'independence' as early as 1943, but he only provided full authorisation in the summer of 1944, by which time it was too late to properly organise such a project. Schellenberg also pointed a finger of blame at Mihailov, saying that the latter had accepted German help to establish 'a Bulgarian Opposition Party', but that he had actually done little to create such a force.

At the vital hour, reports reached Vienna and Berlin suggesting that influential Macedonians were hesitant about supporting Bulgaria's pending switch of sides, although intensified attacks by Yugoslav communist Partisans were causing tension within Macedonia. Bulgarian-Macedonian police and army officers had begun feeling out the Germans about the possibility of remaining loyal to the Axis, and General Kotsho

Stoyanov, commander of the Bulgarian occupation force in Macedonia, thought that perhaps a third of his force could be won over to the Germans. Hitler believed that two or three Bulgarian divisions could be convinced to continue collaborating with the *Wehrmacht*. SD officers in Tirana reported that 'the will to resistance [*sic*]' was more intense in Macedonia than in 'Old Bulgaria', and that it could be further encouraged if Bulgarian officials were dismissed and replaced with native Macedonians. They also suggested that the 'ideal solution' was the proclamation of an autonomous Macedonia under German protection. 'The time for active intervention by Ivan Mihailov has come', they noted. 'It is now or never!'

The Germans did indeed unsheathe Mihailov, supposedly the ultimate weapon, sending him to talk to Stoyanov about the possibility of issuing a Macedonian declaration of independence and then re-clothing Stoyanov's men in IMRO uniforms. Nonetheless, Schellenberg admitted that 'the situation... seems hopeless'. Mihailov lacked either the firepower or the political machinery necessary to win over the bulk of the population. Failing a major application of force by the *Wehrmacht*, which was impossible, 'the wishes of the *Führer*, can no longer be translated into action on the basis of political means alone'. On 6 September, the pro-IMRO 'Macedonian Committee' told Mihailov that a declaration of independence was impossible because both its membership and the general population had become progressively demoralised. Indeed, Mihailov's long absence from Macedonia had deprived him of support at the key hour and his committee in Skopje lacked adequate authority.[147] The Bulgarian Government ordered its occupation forces to return home, an instruction that was largely obeyed, and Stoyanov was dismissed by the 'neutrality government' that held power in Sofia from 2–9 September 1944.[148] Mihailov fled into exile in Vienna and was eventually driven into the Alps, where he set up his headquarters in Alt Aussee.

The subsequent fate of the IMRO bears an uncanny resemblance to the late history of the Iron Guard. Like Horia Sima, Mihailov fled into hiding in 1945 and was able to retain contact with clandestine IMRO cells in both Bulgaria and Yugoslav Macedonia. However, Vladimir Kurtev, Mihailov's man-in-Sofia, made the same mistake as Nicolae Petrescu in Bucharest. Instead of waging a struggle against the pro-communist government, he tried to negotiate, specifically with Interior Minister Anton Jugov. For several months, the new regime showed interest. Until 1946, it was still interested in foiling Yugoslav objectives in Macedonia, for which IMRO might serve as a handy weapon, and communists in the regime were locked in a power struggle with the *Zveno*, which was a sworn enemy of IMRO. The communists and IMRO thus had a common foe. This deadly dance continued until June 1946, by which time the Soviets had cracked the whip – the bulk of Macedonia would remain part of Yugoslavia – and the Yugoslav Titoists were pressing for action against IMRO. On 8 June, Kurtev and a dozen IMRO leaders were arrested when they arrived at a 'negotiating session', and this swoop was followed by a police campaign that resulted in the apprehension of 150 additional activists. Except for some disconnected fragments, the IMRO underground was destroyed.[149]

Since the Mihailovite IMRO had failed to prove its worth, the Germans began looking at a number of alternative options, most of which involved desperate forms of irregular or unconventional military action. In the late summer of 1944, all the news from Bulgaria was bad: on 17 August, the government declared Bulgaria neutral; on 25–26 August, as the disaster in Romania began to unfold, Sofia demanded the evacuation of all *Wehrmacht* troops and arranged to disarm German soldiers streaming into the country from Romania; on 5 September, the Bulgarians broke diplomatic relations with Berlin; and on 8 September, the Bulgarian Government officially declared war on Germany, even though the Soviets had recently declared war on Bulgaria and had then invaded the country, directly precipitating a coup by the pro-communist 'Fatherland Front'. The government of Bulgaria after 9 September 1944 was a coalition dominated by communists, Left Agrarians, Social Democrats and the *Zveno*, and was heavily influenced by the occupying Red Army. Bulgaria officially signed an armistice with the Soviet Union in October 1944.

While the pace of this shift was dramatic, it did not occur so quickly that the Germans were not able to concoct a number of harebrained schemes, all of which were intended to limit the damage of Bulgaria's about-face. Such was FAK 201's Operation 'Cosinna', an attempt to retrieve a fleet of Tiger and Panther tanks that Germany had recently provided to Bulgaria. The 'Cosinna' shock force managed to push to Niš, in the Bulgarian occupation zone of Serbia, but then had to withdraw under heavy fire, battering its way back to Belgrade.[150] A plan for a mass uprising of 14,000 *Wehrmacht* internees – the Bulgarian equivalent to Operation 'Prinz Eugen' – fits into the same category of pipedreams. After restoring freedom of action, these troops were supposed to form guerrilla bands and fight their way to German-occupied territory, a scheme that was also connected with an order to destroy German emplacements and supply stores in Bulgaria. Little came of this affair, and the most von Weichs could later say was that 'the Bulgarian people aided German soldiers… with their attempts to escape to Serbia'.[151]

Yet another German fancy was Operation '*Hundesohn*', an attempt to foist Bulgarian right-wingers into power, perhaps with the help of an SS police division. This plan focussed on indigenous Bulgarian fascists, a faction that the Germans had long abjured in favour of the IMRO. Mihailov's anaemic performance suggested that other Bulgarian die-hards might now have to merit consideration. In early September, Schellenberg advocating the arming of Bulgarian militants and the launching of *Wehrmacht* probes from both the north and the south, if only symbolically to support the Bulgarian fascists. The German ambassador in Sofia, Heinz-Adolf Beckerle, disagreed with this strategy, arguing that Bulgarian right-wingers were weighed down by a sense of defeatism and by the fear that a putsch would prompt Allied air attacks, from which Sofia had already suffered badly.[152]

Because of such considerations, Beckerle recommended sending 'nationalist' leaders to Vienna, where they could escape the clutches of the 'neutrality government' and start organising an exile regime. The most important figure to follow this course was Aleksandûr Zankov, one-time prime minister and organiser of the crypto-fascist 'National Social Movement'. Hitler regarded Zankov's flight as an event of historical magnitude, comparable to De Gaulle's defection to London in 1940, and Zankov was sworn in as head of the Bulgarian 'National Government' in a ceremony at Vienna's Hotel Imperial on 9 September 1944. His main deputies were General Nikola Žekov, the First World War Bulgarian commander and head of the 'National Legion', and Asen Kantershiev, head of the *Ratnitsi*, although Kantershiev was still fighting his way out of Bulgaria. One of Kaltenbrunner's Vienna flunkies, Erich von Lüttgendorf, was appointed as RSHA liaison officer to the new 'government'. Originally, there had been some notion of basing Zankov's regime in German-occupied Macedonia, where it could function on the convenient fiction that Macedonia was still Bulgarian territory, but that intention evaporated because of the *Wehrmacht*'s precarious hold on the province.[153]

In the end, the Germans were reduced to applying the same strategy as they were concurrently developing for Romania: probing and subverting the country from the exterior, mainly with Skorzeny-trained agents operating under cover of the 'National Government', and hoping through such means to start a revolt. Unlike the case in Romania, however, there was no *Volksdeutsch* community in Bulgaria and the native fascist movement was based in the country's small intelligentsia, which showed little capacity for fighting a guerrilla war. One bright spot was that there was evidence of spontaneous right-wing resistance in the wake of the 9 September Coup. Near Plovdiv, there were skirmishes between Fatherland Front Partisans and Bulgarian 'nationalists', and according to British liaison officers with the communist guerrillas, 'Fascist leaders and army officers are fleeing to the hills and encouraging their men to become partisans'. On 12 September, anti-communist saboteurs poisoned the water supply of Plovdiv.[154] In Sofia, members of the fascist youth group, the 'Branik', posed as communist militiamen and carried out raids and house searches in order to gather the weapons that they needed for a flight to the hills. In a village near Novo Selo, a small band of 'National Legionaries' tried to incite peasants and made plans to blow up a bridge over the River Iskar, although they were rounded up before causing much damage.[155]

Zankov was not slow in exploiting such news and encouraging unrest. Within a week of the creation of the 'National Government', the *Luftwaffe* began dropping leaflets, signed by Zankov and appealing for Bulgarian officers, soldiers and civilians to disobey the new regime in Sofia. Zankov also installed himself as a regular feature on radio, calling for insurrection in the homeland.[156] In early October 1944, the 'nationalist' station reported that policemen, soldiers and peasants – so-called 'National Bulgarian Free Guards' – were organising frequent attacks on the Plovdiv–Sofia highway and throughout the Rila Plateau. Zankov claimed that such activity had hindered the progress of Soviet armies and disorganised their communications.[157]

Naturally, Zankov sought to send small units into liberated Bulgaria in order to gather intelligence and support insurgent activity. Originally, Macedonia was used as a base for such operations, although that territory was so infested with Titoist Partisans that whole groups of *Ratnitsi* were being cut off and overrun even within the region itself.[158] When FAK 201 enquired on 1 October about sending 8,000 kilograms of special rations to Skopje, they were advised that the intended route was impassable and that the supplies would have to be airlifted.

One group of *Ratnitsi* did manage to get through to 'Old Bulgaria'. Recruits for this unit had assembled in Vienna and had been trained by SD officers, who were assisted by Asen Kantershiev's deputy, Dmitri Belchev. One of the eight team members was the former assistant chief of the 'Commissariat of Jewish Affairs', Ivan Georgiev, and the group was led by Vladimir von Cherkasky, an expatriate Russian who had lived in Bulgaria. Two Azerbaijani radio operators were also attached to the unit. The Cherkasky *Gruppe* was flown into Skopje on 2 November and then driven to its infiltration point near Strumica.

Heavily armed and supplied with hundreds of thousands of *leva* and gold coins, they managed to slip across the lines disguised as Titoist Partisans. Six of the guerrillas went to ground at an Eastern Orthodox cloister near Neurokop, although their presence was quickly discovered and they were all killed – save one – when communist militiamen surrounded the monastery. A note found on one of the dead *Ratnitsi* fighters revealed that Cherkasky had gone on to Sofia, where he was making arrangements to set up a radio outpost. Following leads in this document, the Bulgarian authorities were able to capture Cherkasky, plus a small cabal that he had recruited in the Bulgarian capital.[159]

The famous *Leutnant* Bührmann was also based in Skopje, along with front reconnaissance *Trupp* 221, which enlisted Macedonian-Albanian tribes to wage 'large-scale partisan warfare'. Bührmann always managed to secure first-rate equipment for his bands and was tremendously popular. He also recruited Bulgarians living in Macedonia and used them for operations against Bulgaria proper.[160] By the late autumn of 1944, however, the Germans could no longer hold their base in Macedonia and they had to evacuate Skopje on 13 November, bringing covert operations against 'Old Bulgaria' to a momentary halt.

Mil D was lucky to leave a radio operator in Skopje, and this agent thereafter sent back a series of harrowing news items about starvation, Titoite repression and the large-scale shooting of German prisoners and former FAK collaborators. The Skopje outpost reported on 19 February: 'The population here is in panic. If the population had anything to hope for, it would take to the mountains without waiting for the fine weather. If a single transport aircraft were to appear from any quarter to help the hungry forest folk, the population would flee *en masse*, even including many anti-Germans, who were disappointed in liberation in such a form.'[161] Certainly, there were some Macedonian-Albanian elements already in the woods, whom the Germans perceived as friendly, and the Germans did try, fitfully at least, to start trouble. In early 1945, they parachuted a commando group into the mountains north of Skopje, although this unit, which had been trained at the Kaiserfeld camp near Graz, lost its way and then had to be re-supplied by air. Wireless communication failed several days into the operation.[162]

By the turn of 1944–1945, the *Wehrmacht* had been pushed as far north as Bosnia, and the best the Germans could then manage were a series of airborne missions against Bulgaria, collectively codenamed '*Bär*'. Such tasks were organised by lieutenants Tummler and Bauer, the officers who had run *Unternehmen* 'Triton' and were now supposed to coordinate ongoing operations in Bulgaria. In the autumn of 1944, a cadre of agents was recruited from the ranks of the 'National Legion' in Vienna. Once trained, the volunteers were parachuted into three of the five regions demarcated during Operation 'Triton'. The first undertaking involved three men, led by *Leutnant* Boris Nedelkoff, who parachuted into the mountains south of Sofia, an area that had once provided sanctuary for Fatherland Front Partisans. Nedelkoff scouted the terrain and was charged with constructing an anti-communist movement, a task in which he had considerable success, eventually assembling a group of several thousand members. On 22 February 1945, Nedelkoff's men crept into Sofia and spread pamphlets urging a Bulgarian insurrection. The leaflets were signed by the ostensible leader of the 'Army of Liberation from Bolshevism', Dotsho Christovs, although the Legionaries had not actually been able to contact the elusive Christovs.

Several additional teams were also dropped by parachute. They were supposed to collect intelligence but were not responsible for supporting the 'nationalist' underground. Such elements re-established contact with Vienna and they reported on Soviet troop movements and on the attempt of the new regime to draft manpower for the Bulgarian Army.

'National Government' parachute units were forbidden to undertake sabotage without specific instructions, although Mil D was interested in blasting Bulgarian rail lines and its saboteurs occasionally carried out such actions. The parachutists reported, for instance, that they had tried to dynamite the railway between Sofia and Sopot on the evening of 28 February, but that the explosives had detonated prematurely and killed two saboteurs. If activity by such elements achieved anything, it did force the Soviets to concentrate special troops around Sofia, where they ran patrols constantly, and the Russians also moved forces into southern Bulgaria in order 'to protect… citizens from Bulgarian fascist elements in [the] hills'. The new Bulgarian government also organised a 'People's Militia', partly to quell potential unrest and maximise its authority. Not surprisingly, the Germans were pleased with the results of 'Bär', particularly since the environment in Bulgaria was believed to be exceedingly difficult.[163]

Part of the problem was that so much of the Bulgarian bureaucracy and political establishment was purged, either through legal or extralegal means. This was quite unlike the situation in Romania. While the first post-Antonescu regimes in Bucharest remained relatively unconcerned about Legionary and *Volksdeutsch* machinations, there was no such flimflam in Sofia. Unlike its Romanian counterpart, the Bulgarian Communist Party had long been a force in Bulgarian national life and it actually profited from its association with the Soviets. Russophile sentiments in Bulgaria were widespread and ordinary folk still appreciated Russia's aid in the liberation of the country in 1878 (although there was some deterioration of this sentiment due to the pillaging and drunkenness of Soviet troops). In general, there was a much broader base in Bulgaria for a relatively quick seizure of power by pro-Soviet elements, although the absence of attrition on the Eastern Front and the failure of the communists to cause losses through wide-scale partisan warfare also meant that there were still numerous 'nationalists' who could oppose a communist take-over. In addition, the Bulgarian communists felt a degree of urgency in dealing with this problem. The Red Army had not seemed eager to overrun Bulgaria, nor even to displace the pre-Fatherland Front government, and the Bulgarian communists feared that were the Soviets to evacuate the country at the end of the war, the pro-communist regime would face intense 'nationalist' opposition.

The answer to this dilemma was radical purges. Over the autumn and winter of 1944–1945, Bulgaria experienced the most rapid and proportionally severe purges carried out anywhere in Eastern Europe.[164] In April 1945, the US political representative in Sofia estimated that 20,000 people had been killed by militiamen or communist partisans since September 1944, and that hundreds more had been sentenced to death by 'People's Courts', including some of the country's most senior political figures. Obviously such conditions made it difficult for 'National Government' resisters to operate. Indeed, there is no evidence that the SD and Zankovites managed to penetrate the Bulgarian Government,[165] although the Left Agrarians were accused of liaising with 'fascists' and were duly persecuted by the communists.

Although purges were an effective means of eliminating pro-German sympathisers, they offered a propaganda advantage to the 'National Government', which referred to the process as a 'St Bartholomew's Day Massacre'. 'National' broadcasts called upon Bulgarians not to permit the 'dishonour' of unfair trials, and in early February 1945, when there were death sentences imposed on a number of former cabinet ministers, Zankov tried to shame the nation into an insurrection:

> Bulgarians! Death sentences on 100 Bulgarian citizens have already been pronounced... Never have you been so dishonoured. Bulgaria and its intelligentsia have to be murdered!... Do not protest! Your voices will be like a voice crying in the wilderness! Fight! Fight with every weapon, with sabotage and destruction. Take your rifle and go to the forest! Defend your liberty, your right to be free!

Not much came of this appeal. The 'National Government' claimed a few assassinations of Bulgarian officials and a supposed surge in transport sabotage, which they called 'a worthy answer to the People's Courts', but there was no wide-scale insurgency.[166]

In the long term, Bulgarian right-wingers in exile fared better than their cohorts in the homeland. Like the other 'national governments', the Zankovites were eventually chased into the Alps and wound up at Alt Ausee. Kaltenbrunner last saw the key figures of the regime in early May 1945. After Germany's defeat, Zankov went into hiding, although he was picked up by the CIC in April 1946, not far from Salzburg. Sentenced to death in absentia by the Fatherland Front government, he was lucky to eventually find sanctuary in Argentina.[167]

CHAOS THEORY IN GREECE

In considering the southern and western Balkans we first come to Greece, a country whose location belied the fact that its liberation fit a standard Western European model, that is, it was accomplished by the Western Allies, who pre-empted a local communist seizure of power. Nonetheless, the violent interplay between rival resistance groups fit the usual East European pattern. Greece was originally overrun by the Axis Powers in 1941, after which a number of native guerrilla bands (*andartes*) began to assemble, most of them under the banner of the National Popular Liberation Army (ELAS), which was the strike force of the pro-communist National Liberation Front (EAM). In addition, small nationalist bands also began to take shape, particularly after the Greek exile government reluctantly authorised the fielding of such forces in 1943, especially in the old royalist bastion of the Peloponnese. The Germans made peace with many of these groups, such as the '*Ethniki Drasis*', the 'X' bands and the Panhellenic Liberation Organisation, although the only such group remotely capable of challenging ELAS was the staunchly anti-monarchist and anti-communist Greek National Republican League (EDES), which had been formed in 1941 and had launched its first *andartes* in 1942. By 1943, EDES had 5,700 men in the field, mostly in the Epirus region of north-western Greece. Although EDES and ELAS made initial attempts to work together, the collapse of the Italians, which was accompanied by a concurrent attempt by ELAS to expand into Thessaly, Macedonia and the Peloponnese, marked the onset of a period of heavy fighting between the two groups.[168] This development alerted the Germans to the depth of animosity between their Greek opponents and suggested various opportunities.

EDES is of interest in our story largely for negative reasons, since it was a potential partner for the Germans, although the latter were never able to establish an alliance secure enough to make EDES available for exploitation by the time that Skorzeny entered the picture. There is no doubt that the SD succeeded in subverting and controlling the Athens-based Central Committee of EDES, into which they inserted Gestapo agent Ionnis Voulpiotis. With Voulpiotis acting as a channel, the EDES headquarters began receiving funds from the pro-German government of Ionnis Rallis, and its leading figures also gradually came to accept official appointments in the puppet regime, particularly with its anti-communist auxiliaries, the 'Security Battalions'. For the Germans, however, the real prize was the EDES field force in Epirus, which was commanded by a bearded and gregarious adventurer named Napoleon Zervas. Although Zervas worked independently of the EDES Central Committee, and although he retained close links with the British, he too entered into relations with the occupier. In late 1943, when EDES came under a series of brutal ELAS assaults, Zervas sent emissaries to the German XXII Mountain Corps, explaining that he desired 'serious cooperation'. A cease-fire was arranged, prisoners were exchanged, liaison officers scurried back and forth, and there was a subsequent synchronisation – if not coordination – of operations against ELAS. Indeed, German documents from this period repeatedly cite Zervas's 'loyal attitude', and in return for his cooperation, his staff was given free run of the district around Yannina, the capital of Epirus, and his intelligence service was allowed to function within the city. Naturally, Zervas revealed none of these unpalatable facts to the British, and after the Germans publically proffered their friendship, his liaison officer warned that 'Zervas requires secrecy... in order not to lose the supplies from the Allies upon which he depends'. Even in this limited regard, Zervas eventually began to stray, buying fuel and ammunition from General Vasilios Dertilis, chief of the 'Security Battalions', although he had sufficient gumption to refuse direct offers of supplies from the Germans.[169]

After a half year of relative peace, Zervas's relationship with the Germans began to unravel. This parting of the ways owed to two factors. First, there was an important segment of the German command in Athens, led by Sipo boss Walter Blume, which never trusted Zervas and hoped to invest exclusive German support in Greek fascists willing to align themselves openly with the occupying power. Despite the fact that this policy flew in the face of the Neubacher-Kaltenbrunner desire to conciliate moderate nationalists, Blume upset the equilibrium with Zervas by arresting Dertilis and shutting off Zervas's flow of munitions and petrol.[170] Second, Zervas came under increasing British pressure to create grief for the *Wehrmacht*, and at their urging he began raiding German supply routes in May–June 1944, particularly since the Germans were concurrently busy fighting ELAS. As it became obvious that the British were preparing landings in Greece, Zervas thought it wise to reassert ties to the Allies and to rely upon the British to fend off an eventual communist revolution.

Throughout the summer of 1944, there were a number of efforts to save the EDES-*Wehrmacht* relationship. Staff officers at XXII Mountain Corps argued that increasing EDES hostility was orchestrated by the British and that Zervas was actually doing his best to stay out of fights. In mid-July, the Germans put out new peace-feelers, using a Yannina gendarmerie officer as an intermediary. The Germans now wanted Zervas to cut all ties to the British or, failing that, to renew the truce until British forces arrived in Greece. In return, Zervas would be allowed to take Yannina at the time of any forthcoming German withdrawal from Epirus. Zervas, who had suddenly rediscovered his uncompromising attachment to the British, refused to respond without consulting Cairo and London, although he did discretely authorise a representative to meet in Yannina with the chief of FAK 311, *Major* Fritz Fuhrmann. The Yannina negotiations ensured the safe withdrawal of the German Army from Epirus and a FAK unit later reported that EDES guerrillas were helping to fight Albanian communists along the Greco-Albanian frontier. In general, however, EDES feistiness had caused local German generals to lose patience and officers at XXII Mountain Corps decided that EDES and ELAS would henceforth have to be treated in the same fashion, a point that even Neubacher was forced to concede. He noted on 30 September that there was no longer a 'question of supporting one group or the other… the point is not to save Greece from Bolshevism but exclusively to sharpen the Anglo-Russian conflict'. As a parting shot, the occupiers inserted an article in the Yannina daily *Epeirotikos Keryx*, claiming that after ten months of excellent relations, Zervas had chosen to throw in his lot with the British and 'the Bolsheviks'.[171]

Since Zervas was never completely weaned from the British, he hardly rated as a reliable agent for post-occupation German intrigue in Greece. In fact, as Skorzeny came into the picture, the looming arrival of the British made it difficult for the Germans to argue that anyone credible ought to accept their help as a means of preventing a communist take-over. The British seemed willing to fight communism themselves, and in actuality, anti-communist forces that had earlier served the pro-German regime, such as the 'Security Battalions', rallied to the banners of the British expeditionary force that landed in October 1944. The subsequent purge of collaborators was milder than anywhere else in Europe and only a few right-wing republicans attempted to resist the restoration of the royalist regime.[172]

As a result of this sequence of events, which was unique in Eastern Europe, Skorzeny was denied the continuing cooperation of the sort of mainstream nationalists represented by Zervas and he abandoned the notion of successfully 'turning' a major anti-communist resistance group. In any case, Skorzeny's main agents in Greece belonged to the Blume school of thought. They had already issued a critical report on Zervas, arguing that he should be captured and turned over to the regional *Wehrmacht* garrison commander.[173] As an alternative, they focused efforts upon the same type of fascist misfits and oddballs who provided the source of manpower for German sabotage projects in other territories liberated by the Western Allies, and who they imagined would play an integral role in the 'chaos strategy' of turning all against all.[174] Preparations for such efforts began in 1943 and were channelled through two special agencies that were first organised by SD-*Ausland* F, but had been annexed by Section S. These bodies, *Sonderkommandos* 2000 and 3000, were originally intended to support sabotage all over the eastern Mediterranean, but they eventually became focused upon Greece, with *Sonderkommando* 2000 organising sabotage preparations in the German-dominated north of the country, and its sister agency in the Italian-occupied south. Accordingly, *Sonderkommando* 2000 was based in Salonika and *Sonderkommando* 3000 in Athens.

Sonderkommando 2000 forged close links with an extremist republican and anti-Semitic group called the National Union of Greece (EEE), which was also one of the recipients of Blume's patronage. Although suppressed in the 1930s, EEE re-emerged to play a role in anti-Jewish outrages in Salonika, its main base, and it sprouted an anti-Bulgarian façade, which gave it a degree of popular appeal. *Sonderkommando* 2000's chief, Walter Ried, established a close relationship with EEE's regional leader, Colonel George Poulos. Ried and Poulos made a strange pair, the one a hard-drinking Tyrolean womaniser, the other a short and plump army reserve engineer given to launching political harangues, but they shared a common ground of fanatical anti-communism. They formed six-man stay-behind teams that were heavily armed and funded with British and American currency. By the autumn of 1943, for instance, one such group was set up at Kozáni, sixty miles south-west of Salonika. By the spring of the following year, arrangements had been made with the Havel Institute to provide for the creation of a wireless reception post and the distribution of radio sets.

Ried and Poulos realised, of course, that to launch their stay-behind guerrillas they would need to first clear Greek Macedonia of ELAS *andartes* and to suppress supporters of the communist Partisans. For this purpose, Poulos formed a 'Greek Volunteer Corps' of 800 anti-communist gunmen. There is no doubt that the 'Volunteer Corps' caused damage to ELAS, but it was also responsible for much villainy in western Macedonia, raping women in Verria, shooting passers-by in Skylitsi, and slaughtering dozens of villagers in Hortiatis. In Giannitsa, more than seventy-five people were shot or beaten to death and a third of the town was reduced to ashes. A British assessment noted that Poulos's men 'behaved with greater ferocity than the Germans themselves toward the local population'. ELAS reacted by launching a desperate assault upon Poulos's headquarters in April 1944, infiltrating a unit of twenty men into the neighbourhood around Poulos's command post and then opening fire with automatic weapons, although Poulos was able to slip away. His second-in-command and 200 of his fighters were not so lucky.

In the spring of 1944, Skorzeny decided to replace Ried as head of *Sonderkommando* 2000, although he had difficulty in finding a suitable replacement. By July he had recruited Hugo Willsch, who presided over a final expansion of the *Sonderkommando's* range of operations, although during the same period, personnel were being transferred south in order to reinforce *Sonderkommando* 3000. As a result, by the time that the German evacuation of Greece began to loom, Willsch had to recall his main radio operator from Athens, asking that room be reserved on an emergency flight. In early October, Skorzeny told Willsch to 'go on working on the same lines as 3000', and to report by air mail 'on the present final staff of the resistance movement of 2000'. Shortly afterwards, Willsch was ordered to fly to Berlin and describe these arrangements in person. It is likely, however, that any sense of resolution in *Sonderkommando* 2000 had dissolved by this final hour. A FAK unit in Salonika reported in September 1944, that German *Dienststellen* in the city were already in full flight, as were most special agents: all were terrified by the prospect of an ELAS victory. Poulos cleared out in timely fashion. He fled to Slovenia, where he formed a Greek 'volunteer police battalion', and he eventually joined the 'Greek National Committee' in Austria.[175]

As for *Sonderkommando* 3000, it was dominated by the colourful figure of Otto Begus, whose personality and mode of operation constitutes a story in itself. A 43-year-old veteran of *Freikorps* 'Oberland', Begus had originally arrived in Greece as the commander of a military police unit, but was later transferred to the SD. Corpulent and stooped, he was a chain-smoker with an excessively nervous temperament. In addition, he and his adjutant, Walter Reiner, were drinking buddies who imbibed throughout the day and then frequented nightclubs in the evening, which meant that they had an unparalleled acquaintanceship with barkeepers and racketeers throughout mainland Greece. This aspect of their social lives influenced the relationships that they established as an operational necessity. Begus, for instance, supplemented his SD funds by running two casinos, and he was not shy about soliciting help from anti-communist Greek merchants. On one occasion, he accepted a 20,000-Reichsmark bribe from a black marketeer who desired release from German confinement, and he then took advantage of the occasion to force the contrabandist into his sabotage network. A dissolute lifestyle, of course, also had costs. Reiner was hollow-cheeked and greenish and could barely keep his uniform neat. During one raucous evening, he passed out in a nightclub and the proprietor took the opportunity to search his pockets, gaining valuable information about the nature of his posting and assignments. Since security was lax and Begus and Reiner were frequently befuddled, it is no surprise that *Sonderkommando* 3000 was penetrated by a British agent, Andreas Diamandopulos, who kept the SIS *au courant* on developments and was only uncovered in the spring of 1944, when he was arrested by the Sipo.

In April 1944, Skorzeny instructed Begus to return to Berlin for consultations. Shortly after these talks, Begus was replaced by Franz Neumann, although he briefly returned to Athens in order to orient Neumann. He was eventually re-posted to Verona. Neumann was a former naval engineer who had served in Italy and had a powerful and stout composition, his face marred by a dagger scar. One acquaintance later recalled that he 'gave the impression of great physical strength but was not a sympathetic character'. He was usually sober.

While the chiefs of *Sonderkommando* 2000 focused upon the EEE as their preferred instrument, Begus and Neumann cultivated the Organisation of National Forces of Greece (OEDE), which was based in Athens. This outfit was comprised of working class thugs who received German stipends and felt empowered by being allowed to carry pistols and store rifles in their headquarters on Academy Street. At first, the OEDE had mainly propaganda value – Goebbels addressed members of the group when he visited Athens – but by the spring of 1944 it was also being considered for stay-behind tasks. In fact, *Sonderkommando* 3000 applied for radios from Section F and there was a spurt of organisational activity, particularly since it was rumoured that the Allies were planning an airborne invasion of southern Greece. A number of foreigners resident in Athens, especially Italians, were added to the Greek core of the network. After Neumann's appointment, he came under heavy pressure to expand the *Sonderkommando's* manpower, lay stores and identify future sabotage objectives, although Section S carped in late July that it '[had] so far not received the necessary documents', and it also noted that Schellenberg now wanted weekly activity reports. Neumann claimed that he had expanded the unit's intelligence network on Lesbos, Crete and the Peloponnesian peninsula, and that he was sending relevant details to Berlin, although he also made an appeal for extra operating funds, arguing that without such money 'all the work conducted so far will be useless'.

Throughout 1943–1944, Begus and Neumann built up three closely related structures, which were collectively called the 'Sabotage and Resistance' network, or *Zernetz* (Demolition Net). The most westerly part of this complex was organised along the Ionian coast from Corfu to Patras. This organisation was the brainchild of Begus's translator, Sergio Kanarin, who recruited many of the key agents. Once Kanarin had set the wheels in motion, responsibility for the formation and deployment of the groups devolved to Lavrentios Lavrentiades, an Athenian merchant of Levantine origin. Lavrentiades began drawing demolition supplies from SD depots over the winter of 1943–1944 and he visited Athens monthly in order to draw his men's pay, last being seen in the capital in July 1944. He established cells in Patras, Agrinion, Lamia and Yannina, although by some accounts he also disposed agents to additional locations all over the western mainland of Greece.

More important yet was the Athens-based sabotage group founded and run by a 41-year-old Westphalian named August Ludewig. As a member of the French Foreign Legion from 1925 to 1942, Ludewig was in bad odour with the Nazis, who hauled him off to Berlin in January 1943 and threatened him with a concentration camp sentence unless he was interested in performing some sort of dangerous work. It was under such conditions that Ludewig reluctantly agreed to become a saboteur. He was subsequently trained in Berlin and then posted to Athens, where he was charged with arming and preparing sabotage cells recruited by the SD. This organisation was eventually expanded to a level of 150 men, mostly Greeks or Italian renegades who had refused repatriation to their own homeland. This manpower was divided into fifteen member groups and scattered throughout eastern and northern Greece, with twenty-five men based in Athens and ten in Salonika. In the mid-summer of 1944, Ludewig returned to Germany in order to inspect bomb damage at his home, although he also stopped by the Berlin headquarters of Section S in order to get last-minute instructions. Ludewig was intended for stay-behind deployment in Athens and as a result he was provided with a radio and with four trained operators who would maintain communications with Vienna. In September 1944, he also drew from SD stocks seven suitcases full of explosives, plus £5,000, enough financing to last for several months. Ludewig's job was to blow up the Marathon Dam and demolish utilities and transport facilities in the Athens-Piraeus area, as well as harassing British officers with assassination attempts.

A third network was also founded by Begus in 1943 and was intended to be a resistance movement (as distinct from the western and eastern demolition groups). Begus assigned this organisation to the control of Greek fascist leader George Panteloglu and it was built around a core of Greek collaborators and OEDE members. Despite some teething pains – three members of the movement were arrested by the Greek police for armed robbery – the group slowly took shape and elite OEDE activists were trained by Ludewig. A nucleus of fifty novices was built up to a cadre of 150 volunteers, who were broken up into battle groups of a dozen men each and were prepared to decamp for the hills and wage partisan warfare. The point was for the guerrillas to act as a rearguard for the retreating *Wehrmacht*, blowing up bridges and detonating demolition charges already lain by German Army sappers. It was also hoped that when the guerrillas fled to the mountains they would be joined by 500 to 600 additional OEDE cadres, and that

3,000 sympathisers would go to ground in order to protect themselves from anticipated anti-fascist purges. In addition, Lieutenant Papageigorakis of the Greek barracks police was expected to convince 260 pro-German gendarmes to join the guerrillas. A radio link to Vienna was provided by Hans Becker, a Dutch SS wireless operator, and five low-powered sets were distributed in order to provide contact between the guerrilla detachments. These sets were manned mainly by Italian operators.

ZERNETZ (SOUTHERN GREEK SABOTAGE AND RESISTANCE NETWORK)

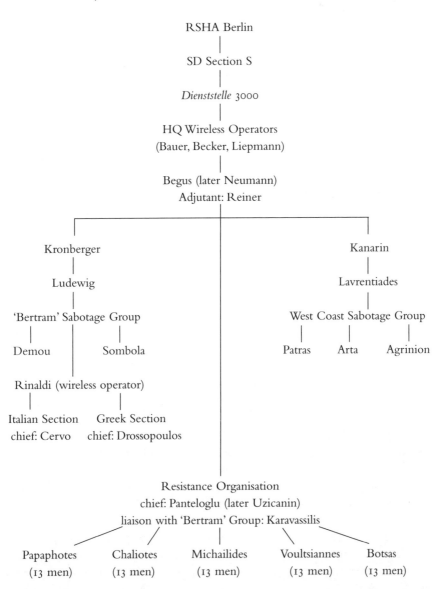

RSHA Berlin

SD Section S

Dienststelle 3000

HQ Wireless Operators
(Bauer, Becker, Liepmann)

Begus (later Neumann)
Adjutant: Reiner

Kronberger   Kanarin

Ludewig   Lavrentiades

'Bertram' Sabotage Group   West Coast Sabotage Group

Demou   Sombola   Patras   Arta   Agrinion

Rinaldi (wireless operator)

Italian Section   Greek Section
chief: Cervo   chief: Drossopoulos

Resistance Organisation
chief: Panteloglu (later Uzicanin)
liaison with 'Bertram' Group: Karavassilis

Papaphotes   Chaliotes   Michailides   Voultsiannes   Botsas
(13 men)   (13 men)   (13 men)   (13 men)   (13 men)

As was usually the case with SD stay-behind projects, little went according to plan. Several radio messages were received at Vienna after the various groups were activated, but no sabotage was reported, even from Lavrentiades's Ionian group, which was little effected by British counter-insurgency operations. The two main organisations, those under Ludewig and Panteloglu, began to misfire even before the British arrived in force. Both groups were hobbled when the quartermaster of *Dienststelle* 3000, Georg Kronberger, entered into contact with a British spy. Kronberger handed the British a long list of German agents and since he was already suspected of treason by his colleague, Hans Becker, he eventually defected. He provided British Middle East intelligence (SIME) with detailed information on the *Zernetz* and he also described numerous SD personalities in Greece. On 8 October, Skorzeny ordered that he be 'removed', should he turn up, but two days later SIME wisely evacuated Kronberger and his Greek girlfriend, flying them both to Cairo.

Despite Kronberger's defection, Ludewig was ordered to activate his sabotage cells and he and his Italian wireless operator, Alberto Rinaldi, were posted on a twenty-four-hour radio watch. Around the time that the British entered Athens, Ludewig was instructed to start sabotage in the Athens–Piraeus–Phaleron region, although in reality he was already considering giving himself up. As matters unfolded, he never got the chance to pursue that option. Several days after the arrival of British forces, two of Ludewig's chief operatives, Dimitrios Dimou and Georgios Somboulas, both defected to the enemy, placing in British hands detailed knowledge about the leadership of the group. Ludewig and his Greek mistress were arrested on 20 October and Rinaldi and his radio set were captured on the same day. Subsequent interrogations led to the arrest of twenty-seven further agents and to the recovery of the group's explosives.

The disintegration of Panteloglu's resistance movement was even more dramatic. Although the leaders of OEDE were aware that EAM was interested in penetrating their organisation with spies – they had already caught and killed an infiltrator in early 1944 – they were not able to prevent communist Partisans from eventually inserting several informers. The most important agent, Spiros Thiakos, was picked in the late summer of 1944 to serve as the interpreter for a Bosnian named Muhamed Uzicanin, who was Panteloglu's paymaster and chief lieutenant. A Muslim who did not speak the Greek language, Uzicanin had been a strange choice to help lead the OEDE and he was unhappy about the posting. In early September, he speculated about killing Panteloglu and destroying the OEDE arms cache stored in Panteloglu's home, a notion in which Thiakos took interest. In fact, Thiakos revealed that he was an ELAS agent and he introduced Uzicanin to his commander, Captain Lamis, who also showed interest in Uzicanin's idea. By 14 September, Thiakos had obtained the keys to Panteloglu's residence, which he turned over to his confederates, and twelve days later an ELAS detachment showed up at Panteloglu's door, dressed in SS uniforms and identifying themselves as members of *Sonderkommando* 3000. The squad surprised Panteloglu in bed, shot him to death, and then killed at least nine other OEDE members, including the group's quartermaster. The Partisans also stole a number of machine pistols before they were engaged by a party of SS men belatedly coming to Panteloglu's rescue. Three communist commandos were killed in the subsequent fight, and they failed to destroy most of OEDE's sabotage equipment and explosives.

Panteloglu's murder precipitated the collapse of the resistance group, with Becker advising on 28 September that the organisation was 'completely blown'. Sniffing vulnerability, Ludewig – who was at liberty for another three weeks – tried to seize the resistance movement's fund of foreign currency, which consisted of £2,600 in gold, 1,000 gold sovereigns, 600 gold Napoleons and £1,000 in paper currency. Its surviving sabotage material was transferred to the Athens artillery park. Becker sent a series of desperate radio signals to Radl, Besekow and Neumann, pleading for new orders. Section S couriers were sent to Athens with additional funds, but there was no response to Becker's messages until 8 October, when Skorzeny finally took time to respond. In his usual style, he grandly announced that both the 'HZ [sabotage] and HW [resistance] Gruppen in the Greek area are being directed by me'. He authorised Ludewig to take control of the resistance organisation and its finances, as well as giving him permission to recruit the 'best men' from the resistance group and to make use of its sabotage material. On the other hand, he noted, both organisations were to be sharply delineated, presumably to prevent the collapse of one from dragging down the other. 'Becker', Skorzeny added, 'is to remain with Ludewig as link man.' Lieutenant Papageigorakis was to be evacuated at the first available opportunity.

Such arrangements did not save the day. Several radio operators remained active in Athens and the Greek mountains, but not much else was heard of the movement and it apparently caused the Allies little trouble. A British report at the end of 1944 noted that the 'organisation has possibly deteriorated and may degenerate still further into a band of brigands'.

Britain's real problems in Greece were with ELAS, and given the fact that bitter fighting eventually broke out between these erstwhile allies, Skorzeny's instructions to Uzicanin are of some interest. Becker reported on 7 October that Uzicanin was implicated in the betrayal of Panteloglu, but despite this warning signal, Skorzeny ordered Uzicanin to infiltrate the ELAS. In the spirit of the Jodl directive of 14 September, Skorzeny noted that 'differences between the communists and the nationalist circles supported by the English are unbridgeable, [so] Uzicanin is to penetrate the communists without fail... in order to bring differences to a head by provocation'. Part of the Athens network was supposed to support this project.[176]

The British intercepted this order and became curious about the lengths of German-ELAS complicity, especially as British soldiers in Athens began dropping from ELAS bullets. What happened is unclear. Uzicanin showed up at the door of an ELAS headquarters in Sariyanni, but it is uncertain what he was trying to accomplish. According to a radio message from Neumann, the resistance network in Athens was still looking for the errant paymaster three days after Skorzeny's orders were transmitted on 8 October – 'Find Uzicanin at all costs' was Neumann's injunction – so it is possible that Uzicanin never received his instructions to penetrate ELAS. Nonetheless, he absconded with most of the funds that were supposed to be transferred to Ludewig and he then paid ELAS functionaries to hide him until British forces reached Athens. Once he reported to officers of the newly arrived SIME, he also emptied his pockets for them, although this final disposition of funds offended Thiakos, the erstwhile communist spy. Thiakos raided Uzicanin's house while the latter was in British custody and made off with the balance of OEDE money, which probably ended up in ELAS coffers. Whether Uzicanin's loyalties were really with the ELAS or with the Germans, the British felt he was a security risk and they evacuated him to a POW camp in Bari.

While Uzicanin ended up in British hands, SIME noted in early November 1944 that ELAS was protecting 'various enemy agents who surrendered with arms, W/T sets and gold before British troops arrived', suggesting that Uzicanin was only one of a number of operatives. In December, when a full-scale war broke out between ELAS and British forces in Athens, an American intelligence observer noted that 'a German Officer was captured quite early in the fighting, leading a group of E.L.A.S. fighters, in an attack on the police station... This man has long been known as a German saboteur organizer.' Certainly, the chief of MI6, Sir Stewart Menzies, believed that the Germans had taken a hand in events. In November 1944, an SD defector had warned the SIS about 'German participation in [communist] activities in Greece', and on 16 December Menzies noted that 'the actual situation in Greece was foreseen by Skorzeny who prepared to exploit it... [A]t least one of his S.D. networks has still not been broken up.'

On the other hand, Neubacher reported to Ribbentrop that there was no chance for the Germans to intervene in the renewed EDES-ELAS fighting that accompanied the revolt against Britain, and the British high command in Athens eventually concluded that the German captive mentioned above had fled to ELAS as a genuine deserter. Although they conceded evidence of other German soldiers serving with ELAS – there may have been as many as 600 such men, organised under the aegis of the 'Free Germany' movement – available data did not suggest 'that German post-occupation agents are playing any material part in support of the insurgents'. When Skorzeny and Radl were later interrogated by their Allied captors, they meekly disclaimed any responsibility for the street battles that had occurred in Athens. The initiative for such disturbances, they claimed, came from sources other than their network.[177]

With the Zernetz in tatters, a few SD elements fled abroad and tried to regroup. Neumann flew back to Germany in late September 1944 and was posted to Friedenthal, where he continued to train Greek agents and facilitated their deployment. In Austria, the Skorzeny Leute began the difficult process of organising a Jagdeinsatz Griechenland, although little is known about the size or composition of this organisation and it probably remained minuscule. Kaltenbrunner could later remember only four or five Greeks who were still working for the Germans by the end of the war, at which time these few volunteers were discharged at Kremsmünster.[178] The requisite political foundation for continuing efforts was provided by the establishment of the 'Greek National Committee', led by a Neubacher protégé, the former vice-premier of the Rallis regime, Hector Tsironikos. The creation of the 'national committee' was announced in January 1945, but by the time it began to take shape, its members had been chased into the Alps and were counting the days until the end of the war.[179]

For all extensive purposes, the SD had shot its bolt in Greece, and after the turn of 1944–1945 the initiative was seized by a Frontaufklärung unit attached to FAK 201 and led by Dr Krautzberger, a Sudeten German who had once served as German liaison officer to Zervas. Like the SD, Mil D had attempted to leave a network in Greece, which consisted of five sabotage cells. In this case, the Germans had so little luck in finding suitable agents that they dissolved two of the cells before the summer of 1944, and they then had to dismantle the remainder when the desertion of a German non-commissioned officer, Hans Wassilewski, created a critical security breach. Two small demolition teams were eventually formed in order to operate in Athens, but once deployed in the Greek capital, the leader of one of the teams, Hans Kirchner, gave himself up to Greek police. Hans Bauer, who led the other squad, was believed by the Germans to have retained his operational autonomy.

After elements of FAK 201 had retreated from Greece, Krautzberger decided to make use of mercenaries drawn from ethnic minorities in the Epirus–Macedonia–Thrace region. Such groups had fallen under Greek authority in the 1910s, but had generally been unenthusiastic about the northern extension of Greece's boundaries. As a result, these minorities formed a natural fifth column for Greece's enemies and had worked with the Italians, particularly since the events of 1941 had reawakened a regional tradition of semi-political banditry. After 1943, such bands were armed by the Germans. Some 2,000 to 3,000 Greek Albanians led by Ismail Haki operated in Epirus, probably under the loose purview of the *Balli Kombetar*, and with the benefit of German-supplied weapons. A group of Aromans (Romanian Macedonians) assumed even greater importance in German plans, being trained by a FAK lieutenant, Ludwig Schwanzer, at a special camp near Veroia. They were politically subordinated to the Legion of the Archangel Michael and deployed with great success on the Chalcidice peninsula and the Sporades Islands, often while disguised as ELAS Partisans. When *Frontaufklärung* forces were withdrawn from Salonika, they withdrew forty Aromans, flying them to Belgrade in military transport. The local FAK commander argued that if the Aromans were not evacuated in timely fashion, they would be drafted by junior *Wehrmacht* commanders and sent to the Romanian Front. Once these Aroman Legionaries reached Vienna, they were sent to nearby concentration camps, which were used to house sabotage agents being trained on German soil.

Toward the end of 1944, FAK officers developed a plan, code-named 'Pollux', which was supposed to prompt the formation of an anti-Allied resistance movement in the northern part of the country. The fundamental idea was to assemble several squads of Greek Albanians and Aromans and drop them by parachute into their homelands, where it was expected that they would be received by friendly tribes and would establish radio contact with Vienna. Their ultimate mission was to spread propaganda and 'provoke discord between Greek factions and the British'. A number of such parachutists were deployed in early 1945. In January, eighteen Greek Albanians were dropped into the region around Vola, where they went to ground and apparently escaped the attention of the Allied or Greek authorities. The Aromans were not so lucky. On the night of 13/14 February, *Luftwaffe* pilots dropped a squad of thirteen Aromans a full 200 miles away from the intended drop zone near Veroia, so that they floated to ground in the heart of the Peloponnese. Set to roost in unfamiliar territory and amidst a hostile population, eight of the paratroopers were quickly captured by the British and the Greek National Guard, and another three had been nabbed by early March. The last three members of the unit were believed to have been caught by ELAS. Although the leaders of the group were equipped with radios and explosives, most were unarmed and dressed in civilian clothes.

The airdrop was so far off target that when the Germans heard that the enemy had captured parachutists in the Peloponnese, they had a difficult time believing that these were the Aromans whom they had dispatched.

Despite this fiasco, the *Zweierorganisation* did not give up. Mil D pinned particular hopes on a twenty-year-old Corinthian woman, Panajota Wrigli, who had already proven her worth by carrying out sabotage in Piraeus. Wrigli was rumoured to have been left with a child by a British father, an experience that gave her an antipathy for her errant lover's countrymen, and she was a strident anti-communist. She was supposed to disguise herself as a man and contact the Bauer team in Athens, as well as the Greek Albanian parachutists dropped near Vola. The plan was to attach Wrigli to a four-man party of Germans, *Einheit 'Kino'*, which was supposed to sabotage Anglo-Iranian oil facilities at Abadan, using German-occupied Crete as a jumping-off point. It was intended to have Wrigli leave the '*Kino*' group on Crete and then make her way to Piraeus on a Cretan fishing boat. The scheme miscarried because of the Soviet invasion of Austria, which resulted in the loss of the '*Kino*' airfield at Wiener Neustadt. An attempt to launch the party from Radelfing failed, mainly because the aircraft's fuel supply had been confiscated by Sixth SS *Panzer* Army, and Wrigli was evacuated into the Tyrolean Alps.[180]

Although a few German spies remained in Greece in 1945, the sabotage/resistance network can hardly be rated as anything but a bust. The British were able to lay bare the complete German organisation, apprehending seventy agents, killing six, chasing twenty-five from the country, and turning ten into informers. In addition, two groups of parachutists were overrun, totalling twenty-six men, and caches of sabotage equipment were uncovered.[181] Although there was a round of 'white terrorism' in immediate post-war Greece, as surviving right-wing groups like 'X' flailed away at a seemingly defeated ELAS, there is no evidence that the Germans had induced such behaviour, nor is there proof that they had managed to provoke the British-ELAS embroilment of December 1944. The most that can be said is that after failing to turn EDES toward their purposes, at least in the long term, the Germans had a 'fallback' option in the form of the *Zernetz*, although the latter proved a futile endeavour.

ALBANIAN HEARTS AND MINDS

Germany's role in the 1941 invasion of Greece had left the Nazis in a position where they could hardly deny that they were enemy occupiers, but they were not saddled with so heavy a burden in Albania. Hitler's ally Mussolini had annexed Albania in 1939, deposing the native King Zog, although the Italians were never popular. By 1943, when Italy capitulated and its occupation armies in the Balkans withdrew from the war, the Germans had finally learned a lesson about how to deal with countries that seemed to require the presence of *Wehrmacht* troops but might otherwise be friendly. Albania was one such case, particularly because the Habsburg Empire was fondly remembered locally and the Austro-Hungarians had not made themselves unpopular during their brief occupation of the northern and central sections of the country during the First World War. With Neubacher encouraging a liberal stance, Hitler decided to take the same approach that had worked for the Austro-Hungarians and to portray his forces as liberators, rather than moving to crush Albania under the Nazi jackboot. As the Italians collapsed, the Germans sent *Wehrmacht* units into Tirana and the coastal plain, but otherwise they proclaimed Albania independent and neutral, arguing that troops would remain only until the war ended. Perhaps the most important concession was to maintain Albania's annexation of Kosovo, which had been proclaimed by Italy in 1941 at the expense of Yugoslavia. This policy was popular among the tribal Ghegs of northern Albania, for whom Kosovo served as a granary.[182]

The relative ease with which the Germans were able to attract collaborationist elements depended on social and cultural relations in the different parts of 'Greater Albania'. In the south, where impoverished Tosk peasants favoured land reform and supported the pro-communist Partisans of the National Liberation Movement (LNC), the Germans established contact with the nationalist and anti-Zogist National Front (*Balli Kombetar*, BK), which was backed by landowners, intellectuals and southern merchants. Founded in 1942 by Midhat Frasheri, the BK had deployed guerrilla bands (*chetas*) against the Italians, but with the arrival of the Germans Frasheri ordered his bands not to engage the new occupiers, an arrangement that became cosier after an LNC offensive in November 1943 drove BK *chetas* out of the hills and into the lowlands dominated by the *Wehrmacht*. By the end of 1943, a special *Abwehr* unit, *Sonderkommando Albanien*, was arming BK irregulars and German officers were leading them into the hills against LNC Partisans and members of the British Military Mission (BMM) serving with the LNC. In January 1944, a BK unit ambushed the head of the BMM, Brigadier E.F. Davies, who was captured and handed over to the Germans. Fearing a total breach with the British, Frasheri, like Zervas, began to reconsider his options, although he was not as sure as Zervas that the British would send an expeditionary force to his country and that they would therefore be of any worth in a future standoff with the LNC. Nonetheless, in early 1944 he dispatched a Valona lawyer and BK centrist, Skender Muço, to patch up relations with the Allies, although the Germans responded by tracking down Muço and killing him and two of his lieutenants. Before his unfortunate demise, however, Muço had convinced the British to resume a limited flow of money, food and sabotage equipment.[183]

Obviously, tensions between the BK and the Germans made the Ballists a risky instrument for German stay-behind operations, an assessment reinforced by the fact that BK capacities against the communists seemed limited. After the LNC overran southern Albania in the summer and early autumn of 1944, a few hundred Ballist guerrillas continued to hold out, particularly in the hills around Valona, and in late December 1944 a stay-behind agent launched a revolt near the one-time BK bastion of Berat, although the uprising was crushed by LNC forces. Midhat Frasheri escaped to Italy, where he portrayed himself as an uncompromising friend of the Western Allies.[184]

There is some evidence that the Germans never gave up on southern Albania. In the last months of the war, an Albanian 'Vorkommando' was assembled by Mil D's energetic head of Albanian affairs, *Leutnant* Tummler, and on the evening of 6 April 1945 this unit was flown out of Radelfing aerodrome in a KG 200 aircraft. The group was dropped near Flórina, in the Greek-Albanian frontier region, and was comprised of two German wireless operators, four Albanians and four Vlasovite Cossacks. They carried plentiful supplies for the waging of partisan warfare.[185] Their activities, if any at all, have left no trace.

While any measure of trouble in southern Albania came as welcome news to the Germans, they focused more upon cultivating the support of the Gheg tribes in the central and northern parts of the country, particularly as these areas came under the pressure of a northward drive by the LNC's First Partisan Division. Even here, however, there were only limited chances for causing grief to either the LNC or the Western Allies. Although tribal leaders had ready-made retinues of armed men willing to organise raids or engage in general insurrections, the type of sustained effort necessary for guerrilla warfare threatened to draw these men away from farms and sheep herds that they could ill-afford to leave untended. Any chance for leading the Ghegs into guerrilla warfare would demand resolute leadership and the ability to protect tribal fighters from reprisals.[186] In addition, the Germans inevitably saw such matters in racial terms: their local 'expert' noted that the 'oriental mentality, lack of independence as well as lack of responsibility and courage do not permit of individual operation by natives'.[187]

Such factors notwithstanding, there were five Gheg chieftains in northern Albania who attracted the interest of both the Germans and the British. Unfortunately for the Germans, only two of these men were solidly committed to their side. One was Jon Markojoni, 'captain' of the Mirdita, the largest Catholic tribe in Albania; the other was Fiqri Dine, a Muslim who dominated the Dibra area east of the Black Drin river and served as premier in the puppet government assembled during the summer of 1944. Of the other Gheg grandees, Muharrem Bajraktar, 'Lord of Liuma', was neutral; Gani Kryezu, a Kosovar who dominated the Kukes district, was pro-British; and Abas Kupi, boss of the Mati region and chief of the Zogists, was conditionally attached to the British, although he maintained relations with various collaborators, particularly Fiqri Dine. The SD reported in April 1944 that the North Albanian 'guerrilla chiefs' were biding their time and would 'assist whoever is stronger from a military standpoint'.

Kupi was the real prize because his 5,000 fighters comprised the largest anti-communist force in Albania. Although Kupi accepted a British Military Mission in April 1944, the northern drive of the LNC, which began in June, forced him to mend fences with the Germans. While *Wehrmacht* authorities remained suspicious of Kupi, Neubacher set four conditions for his entry into an anti-communist coalition with Markojoni, Dine and Frasheri, insisting that he make a clean break with the British, engage in direct discussions with the Germans, accept a German liaison officer, and agree to receive ammunition in controlled quantities. Kupi was allowed to pass 400 men directly through Tirana – they were on their way to fight the communists – and he began to get material help from the Germans, although this channel of supply was restricted in August when Kupi refused either to break relations with the British or to show up in Tirana for direct talks. At this stage, Kupi's thinking was focused by the collapse of the *Wehrmacht* in Romania and the realisation that a German evacuation from the southern Balkans was imminent. Although Kupi continued to ask the Germans for ammunition, he also recommitted himself to the British by organising an uprising in order to hinder the German retreat. In fact, he even managed to encourage the defection of Fiqri Dine, who bolted from Tirana with 500 troops and joined Kupi in the hills. An SD appreciation on 17 September noted: '[A]mong the Albanians the last doubt has disappeared that Germany's defeat and withdrawal from Albania is imminent… [The] influence of [the] English Military Mission and [the] desire not to miss their share of booty make the attitude of the Nationalists doubtful.' During this period, only Jon Markojoni stuck with the occupiers.[188]

One thing that Kupi's anti-German revolt accomplished was the disruption of Operation 'Panther', a FAK 201 stay-behind project in central Albania, particularly because 'Panther' was dependent on the reliability of local Gheg nationalists. 'Panther' was the brainchild of *Hauptmann* Eggers, commander of *Sonderkommando Albanien* and a former Hitler Youth leader and Brandenburger. A brutal and manipulative officer, Eggers was the potential 'Mr Kurtz' of the Albanian boondocks. By the summer of 1944, he controlled twenty bands of Albanian irregulars, totalling 10,000 men, and he apparently assumed that the independent *chetas* of central Albania could be manhandled as ruthlessly as the mercenaries who suffered under his direct command. By late August, he had *Sonderkommando Albanien* toiling solely on 'Panther', which called for laying enough supply caches to support six months of fighting and the funnelling of gold into Albanian banks in order to cover the operational expenses of future guerrillas. Large amounts of supplies were allotted by the *Sonderkommando's* parent unit, FAK 201 – 10,000 special ration packs and five radios were set aside in Belgrade – and by September Eggers had assembled a 100-man stay-behind *Kommando*. Arms and ammunition were also being provided to local Gheg chieftains, although such contacts were 'camouflaged'. The eventual goal was to have one of Eggers's deputies, a German Balt named von Moritz, lead an eight-man parachute squad of expatriate Albanians, who would be dropped back into the mountains after a prospective German withdrawal. It was anticipated that von Moritz's team would be greeted by friendly Albanian tribes and would help lead a guerrilla war against an LNC regime.

While this plan sounded fine in theory, Eggers was not the right man for the job. Unable to lead but only to bully, he was a harsh taskmaster and had poor relations with both his enlisted men and officers. This meant that difficulties in organising 'Panther' inevitably came to the attention of senior echelons because junior officers regularly went over Eggers's head in order to complain. *Leutnant* Keller delivered a devastating report to Army Group F, which had ultimate control of *Sonderkommando Albanien*, and *Leutnant* von Moritz also gave a critical account to officers at Mil D. According to Eggers himself, the only trouble was that LNC roadblocks and raids were delaying preparations and costing precious time.

Eggers's staff officers had rather more substantial concerns. First, they pointed out that since Eggers lacked appreciation of Albanian culture – it was he who had referred to 'oriental mentality and lack of independence' – he had not paid sufficient attention to distinguishing conscripts from volunteers, the latter being the only suitable candidates for behind-the-lines work. When *Major* Modriniak, the commander of FAK 201, challenged Eggers to estimate the percentage of his *Kommando* manned by genuine volunteers, Eggers admitted that only forty men could be categorised as such, and he then asked to send the remaining sixty to FAK 201, since they were supposedly degrading the morale of his unit. A week later, Modriniak asked Eggers what he could accomplish should transport bottlenecks prevent the timely delivery of the rations and wireless transmitters allotted to 'Panther' by FAK 201. 'Take into consideration', Modriniak added, 'the *Kommandos'* own resources, [the] willingness of the *Überrollung* people, [and] how much risk can be run.' Eggers's response did not inspire confidence: under such conditions, he conceded, he could station only two men in Tirana, eight in Durazzo, four west of Elbasan and four in the Librasht-Struga district, although with more time he could build up each unit to a strength of ten men and equip each with two radio transmitters.

Second, Eggers thought that the role of Albanian anti-communists was to fight for German purposes, which they would be happy to do. While the SD was submitting grim assessments of Albanian nationalist morale, Eggers's reports had Albanian levies in high spirits and fighting well as long as they were in contact with German troops. He admitted that in LNC-dominated regions, nationalists 'are compelled by the brutal behaviour of the enemy to hide their arms and, whilst waiting for German help, to work in residential areas or hide themselves'. Nonetheless, he told Modriniak that 'if there is an English or Russian occupation of Albania it would be possible successfully to unite and direct the guerrillas against the occupying forces, to carry out sabotage attacks on traffic routes and [to disseminate] disruptive propaganda'.

Again, Eggers's own officers disagreed with this optimistic assessment. *Leutnant* Flagel, an experienced authority on guerrilla warfare, argued that 'Panther' could be activated *only* if the Soviets occupied Albania. 'In the event of a landing by the English', he noted, 'prospects for an operation are extremely slight on account of too great a feeling of friendliness for England', although this scenario would not obviate the deployment of small sabotage squads numbering two to four men. In addition, Flagel pointed out that 'the dropping of groups with a considerable quantity of material in the mountains is not possible, as all approaches are barred by communist bands'. Von Moritz worried that Eggers had made some facile assumptions about the degree to which he could expect compliance from nationalist *chetas*, and Mil D concluded, after hearing von Moritz's report, that 'we at this end have grave misgivings about the feasibility of undertaking Panther in its present large scale, considering how the Nationalist Albanian tribes [have] changed their attitude'.

By the end of September 1944, both Army Group F and Mil D had grown weary of Eggers's antics. On 1 October, he was suspended from service, although this dramatic move stoked fears that 'Panther' was in danger of collapse since it was, in essence, Eggers's creation. In fact, Eggers was difficult to dislodge from command: four days after his dismissal he was still answering radio messages and his provisional successor, *Leutnant* Flagel, was ordered to keep Eggers from attending to his duties and looking at incoming wireless signals. The rumour mill suggested that Eggers was prepared to act as a maverick, carrying out 'Panther' with his own private resources and volunteers, and it was only with some effort that he was convinced to report to Tirana on 14 October. By the end of the month, Eggers had worked his way back to *Sonderkommando Albanien*, although he was supposed to be serving with an engineer battalion in Scutari. To further complicate matters, Flagel was eventually won back to Eggers's corner, arguing that morale had fallen even further since his dismissal and that it might be worthwhile to have him officially re-employed with his old *Trupp*. There was no chance of Army Group F reversing itself, particularly since its chief intelligence officer was the spit-and-polish *Oberst* von Harling, an old-school Prussian officer who had little appetite for insubordination. In early November, Eggers was called before a court martial at XXI Mountain Army Corps and charged with fraud and brutality against enlisted men.

Meanwhile, 'Panther' disintegrated. An officer sent to check on the operation reported that 'under present circumstance it seems impossible to carry out Panther', although it might have been feasible to deploy 'I *Gruppe*', which consisted of two men and a wireless operator. Von Moritz's Albanian paratroop team was never brought into action by the *Luftwaffe* and von Moritz himself was reassigned to the Eastern Front.[189] Flagel barely reached Croatia in February 1945 and was subsequently posted to the infamous *Freikorps* 'Drautal'.[190] The only worthwhile result of 'Panther' was that some of the arms cached by Eggers were later used – possibly – by nationalist *chetas* fighting the LNC.

Although 'Panther' had failed to set central Albania alight, the Germans had a further card to play. 'I am fully convinced', noted the SD station chief in Tirana, 'that decided action by Germany vis-à-vis [the] Albanian feudal lords can hold things back long enough to gain time in this area'.[191] After Kupi realigned the Zogists with the British, Jon Markojoni proposed a turn in the opposite direction, namely, the conducting of an anti-communist guerrilla war supported by the Germans, and he was joined in this endeavour by Muharrem Bajraktar, whose fief of Liuma had come under LNC pressure in September 1944. Bajraktar had been negotiating with the LNC, but the talks had stalled and Bajraktar had scrambled away from the last session with barely his life intact. Heavy fighting broke out and Bajraktar was forced to retreat across the Drin, bringing with him a portion of his retinue. He thereafter took refuge with Markojoni and agreed to throw in his lot with the Germans. Political cover for this new coalition was provided by the erection of a 'national committee', which was based in Scutari and was run by Markojoni's friend and ally, Father Anton Harapi.[192]

According to a British report, the nationalists were supplied with arms and ammunition left behind by the Germans as they evacuated Albania in November 1944 (although they claimed to be perennially short of weapons). It is also likely that the Germans left agents and small detachments from SS Division 'Skanderbeg', and that men from this unit, mainly Kosovar Albanians, were added to the chieftains' forces.[193] The Germans attempted to 'help' the nationalists in another way too. In March 1944, they launched a programme to bring Albanian students to Germany, and in September they encouraged the flight of Albania's elite families, whom the Germans promised to house in holding camps in southern Austria. While this policy had the unintended effect of dampening Albanian morale – the proverbial rats scurrying from the ship was not a congenial sight – the main aim was to provide FAK 201 with a recruitment pool of potential saboteurs and radio operators.

In early 1945, instructors from Mil D began training a group of seventeen Albanian volunteers billeted in a FAK 201 facility in Trofaich, near Loeben. In March, Neubacher picked ten activists from this 'Albanian *Gruppe*' and infiltrated them into Albania via Italy. According to Kaltenbrunner, the operatives were all noblemen or beys, and Neubacher 'had thoroughly indoctrinated these men in anti-Soviet ideology'.[194] However, at least one of these agents, an Albanian Army officer named Dod Ujkaj, deserted while en route to his deployment.[195]

The Markojoni-Bajraktar coalition was probably also connected to the 'Albanian Volunteer Corps', which was raised by Army Group E and described as 'a force of national Albanian guerrillas'. In November 1944, FAK 201 encouraged the surviving remnant of *Sonderkommando Albanien* to contact Army Group E with an eye toward joining the 'Volunteer Corps', but

Flagel threw cold water on the proposal, arguing this his northward-bound march groups had no idea of where the 'Volunteer Corps' was located and that joining its ranks '[would] not promise success in view of the constantly worsening situation'.[196]

German intelligence reports in November 1944 suggested that Markojoni and Bajraktar were vigorously recruiting for their forces – Bajraktar was able to call up 400 nationalists from Kalimosh – and that small groups of Albanian gendarmes were fleeing to the hills.[197] In addition, some communist Partisans were reported to have defected to the Gheg nationalists. There is no doubt that the LNC faced stiff resistance in northern Albania, even once its troops had secured the major towns and highways, and the North Albanian guerrilla war must rate as one of the most vigorous efforts supported by the Germans. Feudal chieftains fighting for their social existence provided the communists with tough opponents and the rebels were largely supported by public opinion, particularly in the Catholic regions where the clergy was hostile to the new regime. Winter conditions in the hills also strengthened the position of the feudal chiefs, and although the LNC was able to crush outright revolts, partisan warfare was a more difficult threat to contain. In late 1944, the number-two man in the new communist government, Mehmet Shehu, was sent north along with five brigades of troops and strict orders to quell resistance. The Scutari region was sealed as 'an operational zone' and an intense series of repressive measures were undertaken, including mass reprisals. Eight hostages were executed and left lying in the streets of Scutari on 26 January 1945. Desperate to save their lives, some tribal leaders entered into negotiations with the new authorities.[198]

Eventually, Jon Markojoni debouched for Zagreb, leaving in a German Army 'march group'. His sons were left to carry on the fight in Mirdite. Muharrem Bajraktar stayed in Albania until 1946, but he too was finally compelled to flee. Many of the nationalist resisters were lured into the open by a government 'amnesty', after which they were promptly shot, but small bands of right-wing fugitives were still roaming the mountains as late as the end of the 1940s. In one of the darkest chapters of the Cold War, the British eventually decided to help these elements, making arrangements to land expatriate Albanians by sea or drop them by parachute, but this programme failed badly, partly because Kim Philby kept the Soviets informed about operational details.[199]

Aside from northern Albania, a neighbouring region where the Germans managed to cause trouble was Kosovo, the northern march of 'Greater Albania'. As will be recalled, Kosovo had been added to Albania through the handiwork of the Italians, although the Germans made themselves popular by endorsing the transfer and promising to fight 'Yugoslav irredentism'. The Germans found an important ally in the person of Xhafer Deva, a Germanophile scion of the most powerful family in Mitrovica. A long-time agent of the *Abwehr*, Deva had helped German sabotage units bury arms even before the Italians collapsed in 1943, mainly with the intention of facilitating a swift transfer of power.[200] As a reward for such cooperation, the Germans appointed Deva as interior minister in the first post-Italian government of Albania. He subsequently served their interests in an embarrassingly open fashion.[201]

After German troops occupied Albania, units of FAK 201 and *Sonderkommando Albanien* were stationed in Kosovo, where they were ordered to treat the population as potential friends and to recruit levies to fight Yugoslav communist Partisans. Arms were handed out to local tribal leaders and the Germans supported operations of 'the Second League of Prizen', an anti-Slav organisation set up by Deva in order to campaign for the unity of ethnic Albanian regions (as had the first 'League of Prizen' in the nineteenth century). Founded in September 1943, the league raised its own volunteer detachments, which eventually numbered between 12,000 and 15,000 men and which disgraced themselves by carrying out anti-Serb atrocities. After the Yugoslav communists made their 'irredentist' aims clear by moving the Second Partisan Corps into Kosovo, the Germans had success in stirring up concerns about 'a Serb-Montenegrin invasion', particularly amongst elements who already had Serb blood on their hands and feared Yugoslav reprisals.[202] As the hour of reckoning drew near, Deva and the Kosovar Albanian notables withdrew from the government in Tirana and retreated homeward in order to consolidate their forces, bringing with them 1,000 men as reinforcements. Deva sought treatment in Germany for a medical condition and then showed up in Prizen, eager to prepare a guerrilla war against the Titoists.

Unfortunately for Kosovar Albanian nationalists, preparations for a war of resistance had not advanced very far. Aside from abetting the general militarisation of Kosovar Albanian society, German special forces were never able to arm Deva and his followers at the scale necessary to mount a serious challenge to the Titoist Yugoslavs. Little material or money were cached before the German flight from the province and no arrangements were made for radio contact between Albanian Kosovar stay-behind agents and the retreating FAK 201. A partisan warfare course was run at the Pancevo camp near Belgrade for a small number of Kosovar Albanians, mostly men from Urosevac and Mitrovica who were clients of Xhafer Deva's brother, Xhassim. However, none of these volunteers had completed training by the autumn of 1944 and once the time came for their deployment, their recruiter and training instructor, *Unteroffizier* Staretz, promptly deserted, leaving his charges in the lurch.[203]

Despite myriad problems, the Germans derived much more value from anti-communist and anti-Slav resistance than they had any reason to expect. In fact, as the Titoist Yugoslavs invested Kosovo, helped by their LNC allies, a bloody free-for-all broke out. 'Second League' and SS 'Skanderbeg' fighters, now called 'National Albanian Forces', served as a rearguard for the *Wehrmacht's* retreat, helping the Germans withdraw large forces from Greece and Albania through Kosovo. In addition, several thousand of Deva's gunmen remained behind Titoist lines, creating a diversion for the completion of the German retreat to Bosnia. As noted, there is scant evidence of a planned effort, but the shooting of a Titoist Partisan sentry in late October 1944 was followed by Yugoslav reprisals that cost the lives of 300 Kosovar Albanians and created the conditions for a largely spontaneous revolt. An LNC brigade deserted to the rebels, and by the turn of 1944–1945, there was heavy fighting at Gjilan, Drenica and Trepça. A British report suggested that insurgents overran the Yugoslav 17th Brigade near Presovo, killing 1,500 Titoist soldiers. By early 1945, 30,000 Yugoslav troops were involved in crushing the uprising, while the number of rebels has been variously estimated at between 2,000 and 20,000 men. In February, Marshal Tito placed Kosovo under martial law and organised a military government for the province. Kosovar Albanian *chetas* were holding out as late as the autumn of 1945, and anti-communist fugitives were said to be still prowling remote forests and hills until the 1950s.

For local civilians, the disastrous results of such activity were the same as in other parts of Eastern Europe. Estimates on the number of Kosovar Albanian casualties during World War Two range widely, but it is clear that a high percentage of these deaths occurred during the 1944–1945 uprising. According to one eyewitness, 'when many illiterate and bewildered Albanians had been found without documents… [they were] shot out of hand'. Although the conquerors bragged of their magnanimity – they supposedly released forty-eight captured rebels after a battle at Maliq – they executed large numbers of prisoners and compelled other captives to make forced marches to the Adriatic. As Michelle Lee notes, the entire affair comprised 'one of the least glorious chapters of the Yugoslav revolution', and it provided part of the psychological backdrop to the Kosovo War of 1998–1999.[204]

While Kosovar Albanians were suffering and dying, the author of these events, Xhaffer Deva, bolted for German lines in Croatia, which he and some disorganised remnants of his units reached in December 1944.[205] The Kosovar Albanians were well-received by the Croatians, who showed signs of wanting to levy the fugitives in order to augment their own special forces. One detachment of Kosovars was attached to the Croatian *Obrana* as the 'Skanderbeg Legion', while another band still cut off behind Titoist lines was dubbed the 'Prekodrinska Group' and provided with supplies. This unit was commanded by Omer Pasha.[206]

As for relations between the Kosovar Albanians and the Germans, Deva cursed the latter for not providing him with adequate help, although he did consent to a continuing degree of cooperation and he eventually ended up in Vienna, the gathering point for Balkan expatriates. A few of Deva's men were recruited into the 'Albanian *Gruppe*', which was trained in Austria, and Deva also became interested in Operation 'Algol', a FAK 201 scheme to parachute a squad of volunteers into the Sar Planina mountains, and also to airdrop anti-communist leaflets. The originator of this plan, Heini Brüggeboes, was a fanatical Nazi and friend of Skorzeny, and he knew Kosovo well. He believed that Kosovar paratroopers would stand a good chance of establishing radio contact with Vienna and that they would be able to urge local tribes to greater efforts against the Titoists. Deva was so taken with this idea that he offered to participate in the jump. In fact, he was assigned his own radio operator, a police official named Marco Berani, but 'Algol' was still in a preparatory stage when the war came to an end.[207]

After the war, Deva went to ground, although he still claimed presidency of the 'Second League of Prizen' and he remained in contact with nationalists in the homeland. He eventually secured Italian and American support for the dispatch of infiltrators into Kosovo, but the Yugoslav-Soviet breach in 1948 threw matters into flux. While the Western Powers were eager to destabilise Albania, they became more circumspect about dropping parachutists or Kosovar nationalist propaganda into Tito's 'white communist' federation. The high attrition rate for agents also began to weigh upon Deva, who eventually conceded that his countrymen were better under Yugoslav control than being ruled by the radical hermits governing socialist Albania.[208]

THE GALE OF THE WORLD

While Germans rated Albanians as friends, much SD and *Abwehr* attention in the western Balkans was focused upon their putative enemies, the Serbs. For many Germans and

Austrians of Hitler's generation, the Serbs comprised the sum of all things objectionable. Serbia and Montenegro had been thorns in the side of the Austro-Hungarian Empire and a Serb-dominated South Slav state, Yugoslavia, had subsequently served as an ally of the French and a resolute opponent of Germany's two key partners, Italy and Hungary. Although Yugoslavia acceded to the Axis in March 1941, Serb nationalists seemed to compound the error of their ways by overthrowing the government that had signed the accords, an act that resulted in Yugoslavia's violent subjugation by Germany and Italy. However, while there is no doubt that Germans and Serbs had long stood on opposite sides of the geopolitical fence, a condition that fanatics like Hitler could never transcend, there was a sense of stubbornness in the Serbs that impressed some Germans. Hermann Neubacher, who had commanded South Slav troops during the First World War and had travelled widely in Yugoslavia, was convinced that the Romanian and Bulgarian regimes were unstable, and that the doggedness of Serbian nationalists made them a more reliable bulwark against the Balkan ambitions of the Soviets and their local communist friends. Ernst Kaltenbrunner became convinced of this same conclusion.[209]

As far as the Germans were concerned, the assets in Serbia and Montenegro consisted of the same brand of native fascists and conservative military officers who typically offered their services in every occupied country. The main fascist leader was the chief of the Zbor, Dimitrji Ljotic, whose movement had been financed by the Germans before the war and who immediately stepped forward in 1941, pledging his fealty.[210] Ljotic's supporters were the driving force behind the 'Serbian Volunteer Corps' (SVC), a 15,000-man unit that was formed in 1942 upon the basis of earlier volunteer detachments that had agreed to 'fight communism'. FAK 201 appointed a liaison officer to the SVC headquarters, and toward the end of the German occupation this officer, *Leutnant* Skoberne, convinced SVC volunteers to offer their services as anti-Titoist agents and saboteurs. These men were trained at the *Lager* Pancevo, despite the scepticism of FAK 201's chief, Karl Strojil, who considered the arrangement a waste of time. SVC recruits also accounted for many of the Serbs sent to Section S and *Jagdverband* training camps. A *Frontaufklärung Trupp* at Mostar noted in February 1944 that most of the stay-behind volunteers it had recruited were Ljotic supporters, and that in accordance with a decree from the Serbian Government, it was sending these people to Belgrade, where they were supposed to be planted for future operations. When the Germans evacuated Serbia in the autumn of 1944, 4,000 SVC members fled northward, eventually gathering in Istria and Slovenia. Here they re-established radio contact with Mil D and received funds from Heini Brüggeboes, who was in charge of Mil D's forward command post in Vienna. Their numbers were inflated by the addition of repatriated Yugoslav POWs and slave labourers, who formed some of the manpower behind pro-German sabotage missions in 1944–1945.[211] In November 1944, Himmler subordinated the SVC to the *Waffen*-SS, although Neubacher pleaded that its distinctive character be preserved, lest 'its political influence in its homeland be reduced'.[212]

Another Serbian personality willing to help the Germans was General Milan Nedic, the Yugoslav equivalent of Philippe Pétain. After the Germans realised that Nedic had been a leader of the peace-at-any-price faction during the April 1941 crisis, he was foisted into power as chief of a Serbian puppet regime. Although Nedic's authority was undercut by German attempts to win-over Draza Mihailovic and his Chetniks – of which more anon – Nedic, like Ljotic, stood by the Germans until the bitter end. In October 1944 he evacuated his regime to Vienna, and the small strike force that the Germans had allowed him to assemble, consisting of 9,000 men, was also withdrawn into German-held territory and put under SS command. Although these troops were unsure about whether they wanted to remain aligned with Nedic or join Mihailovic, they were all devoted royalists, and when a rumour circulated in December 1944 about King Peter's supposedly imminent return to Serbia, many expressed a desire to break through to their homeland and support their king. Like members of the SVC, some of the Nedicites were willing to volunteer for German infiltration and parachute operations, if only to carry them a step closer to kith and kin.[213]

After Nedic reached Vienna, he appealed for the Germans to maintain a Serbian government-in-exile, arguing that it would encourage the capacity for anti-communist resistance and that Serbia had proven a better than German ally than Bulgaria, which had betrayed German interests but had already been allowed to build a 'national government'.[214] Although Neubacher endorsed his argument, Ribbentrop allowed only the formation of a 'national committee'. Nedic was permitted, however, to control a powerful radio transmitter, 'the Voice of National Serbia'. This station claimed to represent the exiled King Peter, and while such propaganda was initially weakened by Peter's attempts to reconcile with Tito, it was reinforced in 1945 by the king's obvious reluctance to sanction the formation of a coalition government including Tito and the émigré premier, Ivan Subašic.[215]

More important than Nedic was the elusive Draza Mihailovic, who was estimated in late 1944 to control a force of between 80,000 and 100,000 men. Unlike Ljotic and Nedic, Mihailovic was not a supporter of the occupation regime; rather, he was formally an enemy and a self-declared friend of the British. He was the leader of a number of Yugoslav Royal Army stragglers who had fled to the hills in 1941, usually under regional chiefs, of whom Mihailovic was but the most powerful. These straggler bands adopted the old Serbian guerrilla designation of 'Chetnik' and obtained a nod of recognition from the Yugoslav exile regime in Cairo, unlike their communist Partisan rivals under Josef Broz Tito. Although Mihailovic and Tito cooperated sporadically in the summer and autumn of 1941, this alliance soon collapsed and the Chetniks moved to mend fences with the occupiers. Mihailovic himself met with German officers in November 1941, but the two sides failed to come to an understanding and Mihailovic preferred to deal with the Italians and with Nedic's puppet government. Sporadic German-Chetnik clashes continued, but as was the case with the AK in Poland, the Chetnik movement saw itself primarily as a self-defence force with a mandate to protect the social order and conserve its armed capacities until the moment of Axis collapse or withdrawal.

The arms-length relationship between the Chetniks and the Germans was shifted by a number of dramatic events in 1943. First, the Allied invasion of Italy reduced the likelihood of Allied landings in the Balkans, much to the chagrin of the Chetniks and the relief of the Germans. Second, the collapse of Italy drew German units into poorly policed areas, such as Montenegro, that had been previously dominated by the Italians. These were the zones where the largest and most powerful Chetnik formations had developed. Third, the Italians were removed as mediators, leaving the Germans face-to-face with Serbian nationalist forces. And fourth, after Yugoslav communist Partisans survived a series of Axis 'extermination campaigns', the British established direct contact with Tito's headquarters and began treating Tito as Mihailovic's equal, suggesting that the latter no longer had a privileged status in the eyes of his major Allied patron. All these factors created a stronger impetus for establishment of a direct Chetnik-German alliance and it was not long before local commanders on both sides were negotiating a series of non-aggression pacts and mutual aid agreements. Many of these arrangements involved the exchange of liaison officers and the controlled supply of German ammunition to Chetnik units. Ernst Benesch, soon-to-be commander of *Jagdverband Südost*, was involved in negotiating at least one of these deals.[216]

It was at this moment that Hermann Neubacher was posted to Belgrade. Neubacher promised to provide form and structure to the bewildering patchwork of Chetnik-German agreements. Assembling a staff of experts on Balkan affairs, he began arguing for a formal coming-to-terms with Mihailovic, in the process angering Ribbentrop's staff, senior *Wehrmacht* officers and Croatian officials, all of whom warned him about Mihailovic's pro-British proclivities.[217] Neubacher admitted in the spring of 1944 that political approaches to the Chetniks had failed and that the only thing restraining the latter from open hostility was the unfavourable set of military circumstances. Nonetheless, he contended that a solely military relationship with Mihailovic was feasible, and that because of 'the present distribution of forces in the South-Eastern area, it is desirable for the Reich to transfer from its own shoulders the burden of the struggle against Tito's red bands on to nationalist forces as far as possible'. Neubacher's staff suggested that the Germans make systematic use of Chetnik bands, rather than getting incidental help, and that an expanded effort would involve the furnishing of munitions, the extension of medical services and the willingness to provide 'corset-bones', that is, *Wehrmacht* stiffening at key points, particularly with heavy weapons. Once again, however, such a relationship did not suggest that Mihailovic was friendly and it 'involve[s] no political obligations whatever from the German side' – '[It] has neither the character of a peace nor of an actual reconciliation of political attitudes.'[218]

Understandably, the British did not see the increasing coordination of Chetnik-German interests as the kind of relationship that usually existed between enemies, and since London was supplied with Ultra intercepts and reports from SOE officers in Yugoslavia, it was hard for the Chetniks to hide the duration and scale of collaboration. In 1943, the British decided to steer all future aid toward Tito and in the spring of 1944 they withdrew their liaison officers from Mihailovic's headquarters, also convincing the Yugoslav exile government to drop Mihailovic as its agent.[219] Meanwhile, as the German position in Serbia crumbled – the Soviets approached Belgrade in September 1944 – Mihailovic gamely launched his long-awaited final recoil against the weakened occupiers. This episode marked the same kind of last-minute uprisings launched by the EDES in Greece, the Zogists in Albania and the AK in Poland, and it had the same intention: to impress the Western Allies and hinder a seizure of power by the communists. In the great scheme of things, however, the revolt was barely noticed. A few FAK officers reported a breach in their relations with Chetnik units and there was skirmishing in some locations,[220] but the advance of the Soviets and Titoists forced Mihailovic to reinforce his relationship with the Germans rather than cutting such ties. In August 1944, Mihailovic met secretly with Nedic and he agreed to accept the latter's political leadership, while reserving the right to handle military matters independently. Mihailovic also met Neubacher and over the autumn and winter of 1944–1945 he entertained Rudi Stärker, Neubacher's deputy, on a number of occasions. Neubacher also set up an SD wireless post at Mihailovic's headquarters – radio communications began in early March 1945 – and in February two German representatives, Fridolin and Boiger, were dispatched as liaison officers. Since Mihailovic had complained of a lack of German supplies, the Germans made their first allotments of direct aid – 150,000 rounds of infantry ammunition – to Mihailovic's headquarters unit, and they arranged to evacuate 120 Chetniks wounded in battles with the Titoists. Mihailovic's only stipulations about such deals were that agreements remain oral, that the Chetniks not be clothed in German uniforms, and that he himself stay formally 'illegal', all of which he hoped would preserve a measure of his mystique.[221]

Naturally, none of this cooperation was undertaken without pitched resistance from Chetnik-haters in the senior German and Croatian leadership, and in truth there was some cause for concern, since Mihailovic's affinity for the British was well known and it was feared that he was preparing to aid possible Allied landings in Dalmatia and turn German weapons against the people who had provided them. As late as January 1945, the Germans were unsure if Mihailovic was yet in contact with the British or if he was still being supplied by Allied airdrops. Naturally, Hitler led the chorus, warning on 27 August 1944 of the dangers of 'Greater Serbian nationalism', a supposedly greater curse than communism, and several days later he also seized upon evidence of the sporadic Chetnik revolt in order to discredit Mihailovic, sending an incriminating report to Neubacher as a means of unveiling 'the true intentions of Draza Mihailovic'. The Chetniks, he ordered, should only be given limited supplies of weapons and be employed in small-scale actions.[222] Neubacher, however, had the final word. 'A collapse of Mihailovic power or his dropping out of the anti-communist front is not acceptable for us', he warned, 'unless the proven battle strength of these bands in Serbia-Sandjak-Montenegro can be replaced by German divisions.' Mihailovic's troops, he added, had to be reinforced and re-supplied; otherwise, an increased rate of desertions to the Yugoslav Partisans was inevitable.[223]

The main resource that interested Neubacher was an estimated 50,000 Chetnik guerrillas who had gathered in eastern Bosnia after the Soviet and Titoist liberation of Serbia. Unlike the UPA, the bulk of Chetnik forces withdrew to German-held territory rather than remain behind the advancing enemy. These bands established contact with German field commanders and did their best to patch up relations with the forces controlled by Ljotic and Nedic. In fact, one Chetnik officer in Slovenia, Captain Mitic, officially joined the SVC in the autumn of 1944 and he was enthusiastically promoted by the Germans as a possible bridge between Mihailovic and Ljotic. Similarly, three brigades of North Bosnian Chetniks, consisting of 3,000 men, were reported to be considering formal subordination to Nedic. Although the Germans never came to control the Mihailovic movement nor did they have a say in the deployment of most Chetnik units – in fact, they disarmed such formations if they retreated toward Croatia – they did profit from the combat between these bands and the Titoists. They also made use of small

Chetnik patrols for reconnaissance activity. Intelligence about the Chetnik groups in northern Bosnia was encouraging, suggesting that these formations wanted the *Wehrmacht* to stay in Bosnia and that they were steeled for a 'fight to the death against the Reds', although news about units to the south, in the Goradze area, was not so positive. These poorly supplied and typhus-ridden detachments were rumoured to be in contact with both the communists and the British, and to be biding their time until they could risk a rising against the Germans. As a result, FAK 201 launched a 'black operation', starting a number of rumours that were attributed to British sources but were supposed to ensure compliance with German defence efforts. It was whispered, for instance, that Tito was killing reserve officers in Belgrade, a claim sure to make Chetnik blood boil.[224]

Although most Chetnik forces had withdrawn into northern Yugoslavia, the Germans knew that stay-behind elements had been left in Serbia. In fact, Neubacher put extensive effort into determining how to help Mihailovic support and sustain these bands. Chetnik units close to the Drina river tried to break through to German-held territory,[225] but those further afield made a conscious decision to stay and fight. Neubacher noted in November 1944 that 'regional forces in Serbian territory lead a guerrilla war in Red-occupied areas. Particularly the bands of Commander Pasarac (Homolje Mountains), [Major] Rakovic in the area of Ravna Gora, and the Resistance Movement in Belgrade are working together with us.'[226]

Each of the personalities and groups mentioned in this synopsis were significant. Pasarac was a Chetnik 'captain' who had assembled a considerable force in the Homolje hills. The Germans worried, however, about the fortitude of Pasarac and his guerrillas. When they heard that some of these men were considering a Titoist amnesty offer, a rumour spread as part of FAK 201's 'black operation' suggested that twenty-six men who had surrendered ended up as slave labour in the coal mines of Kostolac, supposedly their just deserts for a voluntary capitulation.[227]

Predrag Rakovic was one of the Chetnik regional commanders most willing to accept help from the Germans. As early as 1941, he had put himself formally under Nedic's authority in order to get weapons and supplies, and in February 1944 his emissaries appealed directly to the Sipo for help, noting that they were eager to 'fight together against the communists'. Rakovic also announced that he was ready to allow the Titoist-Soviet tide sweep past him and maintain a Chetnik presence in western Serbia, the original cradle of the Mihailovic movement. Army Group E estimated at the turn of 1944–1945 that Rakovic had 5,000 guerrillas in the Cacak–Kraljevo area. Rakovic also persuaded one of his German liaison officers, *Leutnant* Egon Krieger, to stay behind enemy lines. As part of Operation 'Kara', FAK 201 gave Krieger a Brandenberg radio operator and he was ordered to report to Rakovic in the Ravna Gora. 'Kara' came to an abrupt end when Rakovic was killed in December 1944 and Krieger returned to German-occupied Sarajevo, where he subsequent fell apart in an episode of post-traumatic dissolution. He squandered his operational funds and 'his behavior with women gave rise to complaints', in Ferid Murad's polite phraseology. As a result, he was recalled to Army Group F and tried in a court martial, receiving a twelve-year prison sentence.[228]

The stay-behind unit in Belgrade was run by Saša Mihailovic, who had long been the main Chetnik agent in the Serbian capital and had previously infiltrated Nedic's security forces. Mihailovic was probably in contact with a German radio post, 'Rajko', which was run by *Trupp* 128. Throughout the winter and spring of 1944–1945, 'Rajko' sent Vienna detailed information on Titoist Partisan and Bulgarian Army deployments, as well as confirming that shootings and violence remained part of the norm in liberated Belgrade, a fact 'attributed to the activity of small Draza bands'.[229] In May 1945, the Yugoslav Government announced that it had overrun the Chetnik underground cell in Belgrade and that Saša Mihailovic had been killed.[230]

In December 1944, Neubacher proposed using the forthcoming winter to prepare behind-the-lines Chetnik units for cooperation with a possible German counter-offensive in the Balkans. 'By the onset of spring', he noted, 'such a movement will be worth reckoning, particularly if we again have offensive capabilities in the south-east', although he pointed out that it required support from outside.[231] Indeed, at the time of the German counter-offensive in Hungary, arrangements were made to drop supplies to the Chetnik 'AVALA *Gruppe*', although such efforts were crippled by transport, personnel and supply problems. A FAK *Trupp* in Nova Gradiška noted that it was attempting to help the Petrovic group of Chetniks in the Serbian Banat, but that it had no radios for potential wireless hubs, as well as lacking sets for five parachutists whom it was otherwise ready to deploy. Likewise, FAK 201 complained in early March 1945 that it 'very much desired' collaboration with cut-off Chetnik bands, but that it was short of sabotage equipment.[232] An SD intelligence report admitted that many anti-communist bands had formed in territory held by Tito and that they were seeking control by either Mihailovic or Ljotic, although in the meantime they had accomplished little.[233]

Despite Neubacher's increasing doubts about the adequacy of German efforts, he advised Mihailovic to send Chetnik commando teams across into Serbia,[234] a proposal that Mihailovic embraced. Although the Chetniks had already begun harassing Titoist Partisans with small 'disturbing units', focused mainly on looting and pillage,[235] in the autumn of 1944 they began to organise this effort and consolidate their raiding forces. In November 1944, Mihailovic toured Bosnia promoting 'an operation in Serbia', although he found few recruits. Bosnian Chetniks were willing to defend their local districts, but they had little desire to fight in Serbia. Serbian Chetniks, on the other hand, were more eager to volunteer, although Mihailovic was less willing to accept Serbs into his 'royal commandos' because of fear that many of them wanted to infiltrate the front in order to return home. Thus, Serbian volunteers had to demonstrate 'the right kind of character and moral qualities', and on 13 January 1945 the Chetnik chief suggested that 'these persons must know that if they do not accomplish their tasks they will be sentenced to death'.

Despite such exacting standards – Mihailovic himself later admitted that 'there were many who were really not fit for this' – he was able to set up two training schools, one at Srednji and the other at Modric. German-trained instructors, provided to the Chetniks as part of Special *Gruppe* 'Gara', were employed at these schools, where they showed recruits how to handle sabotage materials and organise propaganda, particularly through leaflet distribution and the scrawling of slogans ('The King'). In late 1944, the Srednji and Modric graduates were placed under the command of one of Mihailovic's deputies, Colonel Dragoslav Pavlovic, and another of Mihailovic's most trusted aides,

Colonel Keserovic, was assigned to keep scouring northern Yugoslavia for additional volunteers. The commandos were also authorised to cross into Serbia in order to sabotage communications and spread propaganda, and by the turn of 1944–1945, large numbers of Chetniks were busy infiltrating the front. In December 1944, a group of 700 infiltrators was surrounded by two Titoist brigades while attempting to reach Serbia. Members of this group ended up being forcibly levied into Yugoslav communist forces. Another unit of 700 well-equipped volunteers was dispatched in late March 1945, including the commander of the Podrinska Brigade. This unit crossed the Drina at Trsic, mainly with the intention of spreading propaganda in the Brasina region and laying the groundwork for an anti-communist uprising. Many smaller groups were also infiltrated; one such unit, under Mihail Nikodijevic, was caught in an ambush along the Kragujevic–Topola highway.[236] A German intelligence report suggested that by February 1945 Titoist Partisan units were being called back to Serbia in order to deal with such threats, although the Titoists themselves bragged that they were 'mopping up the bandits, who will soon be exterminated'.[237]

The Germans also conducted a number of operations directly under control. All Serbian/Montenegrin operations run by Mil D were codenamed '*Vuk*' and were organised by *Oberleutnant* Brüggeboes and *Sonderführer* Kostic. Matters were closely coordinated with Neubacher's office and with KG 200, which was responsible for dropping the teams into place. '*Vuk*' missions depended heavily upon the services of SVC cadres, some of whom were volunteers – in April 1945, for instance, an SVC lieutenant stepped forward, requesting parachute deployment for himself and four of his men – although others were not so willing. Consequently, there was a problem with desertions. One of the German liaison officers with Mihailovic told Mil D on 25 March that 'of the Serbian sabotage groups which were assembled by you in the Reich for the Serbia area up to now, according to my own observation, 16 men have deserted together with their equipment'. Officers of FAK 201 also groaned about the lack of radio equipment and sabotage material – in mid-January, demolition experts complained that they could not get explosives, fuses and ignition cartridges from the army's pioneer battalions, even though they had been assigned a special mission by Army Group E – and they also grumbled about *Jagdverband Südost* getting preference in the allocation of supplies.

In early 1945, a thirty-man '*Vuk*' *Gruppe* was airdropped into the region north-west of Skopje, and although the Germans never succeeded in establishing radio contact with this unit, they did arrange to keep it supplied. In addition, Mil D deployed a number of small paratrooper teams, called 'troikas', which KG 200 began dropping into Titoist-held territory in March 1945. Trained at the Kaiserwald camp in Austria, these guerrillas were short of food but were well-equipped with small arms, explosives and wireless transmitters. Their task was to sabotage communications, incite peasant revolts and assassinate Yugoslav communist functionaries, all of which was intended as a diversion for the Balaton Counter-offensive, although commandos were still being deployed after the much-heralded attack in Hungary had failed. One group had orders to repair 'Rajko's' wireless transmitter in Belgrade; another was supposed to contact pro-Allied Croats in Dalmatia and discern British intentions. A unit of Nedic supporters under Dragutin Manojlovic departed from Wiener Neustadt airfield on 6 March, dressed in British uniforms and equipped with orders to contact Chetnik bands. Members had been told that Serbian peasants were ripe for revolt and that the Titoists only controlled villages and towns. They got a nasty surprise after deployment, telling Vienna by wireless that they had been unable to establish contact with Chetnik remnants. Shortly afterwards, they were overrun by the OZNA, the dreaded secret police. Overall, the Yugoslav militia captured most of the groups and their equipment, including four wireless transmitters, although the Germans refused to cease operations. Even during the last days of the war, thirty Serbian nationalists being readied for a parachute drop were given ten days of infantry training and deployed on a mission in Istria.[238]

Mil D officers did not forget Montenegro, where they infiltrated a '*Vuk*' platoon. This combat mission was carried out by a Serb officer, Lieutenant Parezanin, who left Belgrade shortly before the city fell to the Soviets, travelling southward just as everyone else was headed north. Parezanin successfully went to ground and waged guerrilla warfare against the advancing Yugoslav Partisans. Because of a lack of radio contact, however, the detachment was evacuated in January 1945, being withdrawn to the SVC headquarters in Istria. Amazingly, it had suffered not a single casualty.[239]

Serbian missions run by *Jagdverband Südost* all bore the name of serpents, such as 'Sandviper', 'Slow-Worm', 'Adder' and 'Hornviper', thus lending the entire project the cryptonym 'Snake'. From November 1943 to September 1944, Section S trained forty-five Serbian nationalists, many of them SVC men selected by *Sturmbannführer* Rexeisen, the Sipo chief in Belgrade. Skorzeny and Radl later remembered these recruits as 'good material, eager to learn and [to] act'. With such manpower in hand, Skorzeny began to organise a joint Section S/Section E network for three of the ten districts into which occupied Yugoslavia had been divided, the other seven being the responsibility of the Brandenburg Division. When the Brandenburg *Streifkorps* were transferred to the *Jagdverbände*, the stay-behind programmes were amalgamated, and in September and October 1944 all existing groups came under the control of *Jagdeinsatz Serbien*. *Oberleutnant* Rowohl was put in charge and *Hauptsturmführer* Ulbricht was ordered to maintain links with the Serbian nationalists, which meant getting help from Mihailovic. The 'Snake' operations launched by this heterogeneous outfit involved assembling, training and equipping ten groups of twenty men each, which then allowed themselves to be overrun by the Red Army or the Titoists. After being cut off, they were supposed to establish radio contact with the staff of *Jagdverband Südost*. Although the groups were told to maintain radio silence for four weeks, even after that time none reported back to their German controllers.[240] Thus, the 'snakes' either never slithered from their holes or they were mercilessly ferreted out by the OZNA before they could cause much damage.

Such undertakings were less successful than had been hoped, not only because of supply and personnel problems, but also because of the vicissitudes of Balkan politics, which were superimposed upon the usual failure of the Skorzeny *Leute* to coordinate their operations. There were a number of difficulties, for instance, with basing Serbian raiding forces on territory that was officially part of the Croatian state, and it was difficult to get Ustashe authorities to help move Chetnik or SVC personnel to their staging areas. The worst incident occurred in December 1944, when a company of SVC volunteers under the control of *Jagdverband Südost* was intercepted while passing through a Zagreb railway station. The group was on its way to deployment in Serbia. According to the official report:

> The men of the 5th SFK [5th SVC Regiment], under the leadership of Kilorad Majic, who were on their way to the SFK, were arrested in Zagreb and shot an hour later. Ustasche Colonel Luburic carried out the shooting, justifying himself by saying [that] they were Chetniks and that Tito books were found on them. Altogether on 7/12, forty persons, including four women, were arrested and shot. Twenty-two men escaped. Pavelic has expressed his regrets. This incident was reported to Minister Ljotic by Minister Neubacher.

According to Radl, this fiasco owed partly to the incompetence of *Südost*'s commander, Ernst Benesch, who had negotiated with Luburic to guide the SVC volunteers to the Serbian frontier. Had Benesch taken the time to consult with Rupert Mandl, head of the Section S outpost in Yugoslavia, he would have learned that Luburic had a homicidal antipathy toward all Serbs. Thus, putting Luburic in charge of the escort was tantamount to having the proverbial fox guard the henhouse. In typical SD fashion, however, Benesch and Mandl were locked in a personal feud, and Radl later claimed that such infighting contributed to the overall inability of the *Jagdverbände* to properly activate its Serbian stay-behind network. The Zagreb incident also had an obstructive effect on Mil D operations, since news of the attack naturally made '*Vuk*' personnel 'agitated about their deployments'.[241]

An equally illustrative example of such backstabbing involved the disposition of Special *Gruppe* 'Gara', which the Germans sent to Sarajevo in early January 1945 and which was recommended to Mihailovic by his representative with the Germans, Colonel Borota. *Gruppe* 'Gara' consisted of a company of well-equipped nationalist guerrillas who had been trained at Mil D facilities in Austria and were sent to Mihailovic dressed in British and German uniforms. The formation was led by a renegade Ljotic supporter named Gašparovic, who told Mihailovic that he had a mandate to infiltrate his men into Serbia and then wage an anti-communist guerrilla campaign. Several key figures were not impressed by Gašparovic's 'volunteers': Fridolin pointed out in March 1945 that the Bosnians among them were turning on their heels and deserting – nine had already fled – and Mihailovic suspected that Gašparovic's Serbs, who were mostly recruited from POW camps in Germany, were well-intentioned peasants looking for a means to get home. Mihailovic announced that he would integrate the 'Gara' *Gruppe* into his 'royalist commandos', which was done by adding thirty Chetniks to the company and bringing it under the command of a Mihailovic loyalist, Captain Dragoslav Topalovic, but in truth he had no intention of welcoming it into the brood. Rather, he secretly ordered Topalovic and his second-in-command, Milovan Nedeljkovic, to bring Gašparovic as far as the Lim river, one of the tributaries of the Drina, and then to kill him, disarm his men and seize his equipment, which included special weapons and wireless sets. According to Mihailovic, Topalovic tried to disarm Gašparovic's men before they were moved near the front, which 'caused a great quarrel'. Apparently, Topalovic was then removed from joint command of the Chetnik/Mil D group, which left Nedeljkovic in charge. In the subsequent confusion, which was caused partly by a Yugoslav Partisan offensive in March 1945, Mihailovic lost contact with Gašparovic and the latter was apparently never drawn close enough to the front for the assassination plot to become operative.[242]

Another problem was that the security of German and Chetnik operations was thoroughly compromised. Serbian nationalists put great faith in the reports of a secret 'Chetnik' radio station in Serbia, which sought to 'help' nationalist commandos cross into the province. It was eventually revealed that this secret transmitter was a bogus station established by the OZNA, which was using captured Chetnik radio operators and a code-book taken from the body of guerrilla commander Rakovic after he was killed. As a result, many 'royalist commando' teams and Skorzeny detachments were wiped out or captured after they reached Serbian territory.[243]

By April 1945, the Germans had begun retreating from Bosnia and the war in the Balkans was reaching its appointed end. By this stage, Ljotic had formed an alliance with two Chetnik commanders, Father Moncilo Djujic and Dobroslav Jevdjevic, and these three men were proposing to hold Slovenia/Istria with a combined SVC/Chetnik force and to provide a forum for the return of King Peter, an increasingly attractive option for some Chetnik officers. In February 1945, Neubacher described this new centre of power as being more important than Nedic's 'national committee' and more deserving of German help. The network was placed under the supervision of a Mil D unit, *Trupp* 214, and a representative of OKW, *Hauptmann* Rosenow, who was supposed to form 'flying columns' from Djujic's men. Rosenow, however, was suspected by the Germans of coming under too much Chetnik influence, 'as [happens to] all German officers in the same circumstances'. In truth, there was a continuing lack of trust between the two sides. The Chetniks were disappointed by the failure of the Germans to deliver promised weapons, while the Germans suspected that Djujic and Jevdjevic were still dominated by Mihailovic. In the spring of 1945, Montenegrin warlord Pavel Djurišic tried to reinforce the Ljotic-Djujic-Jevdjevic concentration point with his own 20,000-man cohort, the 'Montenegrin Volunteer Corps', but this force was ambushed by the Croatians and most of its survivors were co-opted into their forces. Slovenia declared its independence on 3 May 1945, opting for King Peter, but its White Guard/Chetnik/SVC forces were swamped by fourteen Titoist divisions.

As for Mihailovic, he opted to hold out in the region south of Brod, where he was promised arms and equipment by the Germans, and he also put great stock in the preparations that had been made to support a Serbian insurrection against Tito. In the final analysis, he decided to lead this effort personally by directing his own retinue – perhaps 10,000 men – back into Serbia. In mid-May 1945, most of this small army was destroyed by the Titoists south-east of Sarajevo, although Mihailovic escaped and held out for another year. He was eventually captured in March 1946, after which he was brought to trial, found guilty and executed, although not before he delivered one of the most eloquent and painfully self-critical reflections of the Second World War era.[244] 'Destiny was merciless', he told the Belgrade tribunal, 'when it threw me into the most difficult whirlwinds. I wanted much, I began much, but the whirlwind, the gale of the world, carried away me and my work.'[245]

THE CRUSADERS

German efforts to spur anti-communist resistance were also focused upon Croatia, yet another fragment of dismembered Yugoslavia. Croatia's situation shared much in common with that of Hungary, its old imperial master. As was the case with Hungary, German patronage had allowed Croatia to expand beyond its core area, so that it included the lion's share of Bosnia-Herzegovina; like Hungary, it was an ally of Germany to the bitter end; like post-Horthy Hungary, it was run by a government of enthusiastic fascists, in this case the anti-Serb zealots of the Ustashe. It is true that there was a rising degree of tension between the Croatia and Germany as events sped toward the point of final collapse, but the Germans believed that the Croatians wanted to build a strong anti-Titoist stay-behind movement and they assumed that their own fifth columnists in the region would benefit from the help of sympathetic Croatian authorities.

The Germans' main Croatian clients, the Ustashe, seemed well-suited to functioning in an environment where they were under pressure. Founded in 1929, when a group of radical Croatian nationalists seceded from the mainstream Croatian Peasant Party, the Ustashe had always represented the principle of violent opposition to a Serb-dominated Yugoslav state, and graduates of its infamous Hungarian training camp, Jankapuszta, had tried to reduce interwar Yugoslavia to a state of anarchy. The pro-German wing of the movement had come into contact with the *Abwehr* and the SD, and during the April 1941 war, it mounted a brief insurrection against the Yugoslav authorities. On 10 April 1941, Ustashe rebels proclaimed the Independent State of Croatia, and although they numbered at most a few thousand activists, they literally built the new country from the ground up, permeating every aspect of its military and bureaucratic organisation.[246]

Steeled in such a crucible, the Ustashe state never experienced a time of peace. In fact, sections of Dalmatia, Bosnia and Herzegovina quickly came under hostile Titoist Partisan or Chetnik control, and the Croatian military began developing a capacity to cause trouble in such enemy-occupied regions. This initiative was left to one of the most skilled terrorists of the interwar period, Colonel Vjekoslav Luburic, a one-time student – and eventual commandant – at Jankapuszta. Luburic controlled the *Obrana*, a militia that had responsibility for organising resistance in Tito-controlled districts and, as Luburic later noted, 'employ[ing] against the Partisans the same guerrilla tactics used by the Reds themselves in the areas that we controlled'.[247] Ustashe guerrillas operating in Titoist territory are occasionally mentioned in contemporary documents and in memoirs, although some of these bands appear to have been cut-off stragglers from the Croatian Army who perhaps bore no connection to the Luburic programme.[248] Detachments that infiltrated behind Titoist lines in mid-March 1945, mainly at Prozor-Tomislavgrad and Rakitno, were definitely part of the *Obrana*, and the general region west and south-west of Sarajevo seems to have been of great interest to Luburic.[249]

Once it became clear that the Titoist push was likely to swamp the Ustashe state, Luburic began planning the creation of a 'Croatian National Resistance', which he envisioned carrying out widespread ambush and sabotage attacks as a means of covering the retreat of the Croatian Army and the *Wehrmacht*. Initial measures for such a campaign were undertaken and Luburic made contact with like-minded Albanian, Montenegrin and Macedonian guerrillas, all of whom he hoped would cooperate. Despite such preparations, the civilian authorities, led by Ante Pavelic, decided that resistance on such a scale would cause massive casualties, particularly in cities like Zagreb, where a contained population would be exposed to Titoist reprisals and Allied air raids. Rather, they resolved to evacuate huge numbers of civilians to Austria. On 1 May 1945, Luburic was ordered to abandon the guerrilla strategy and instead use his *Obrana* detachments as rear guards for the northward retreat of Axis forces.

Many Croatian generals believed that retreating Croatian troops would eventually get British support – there were already rumours of RAF airdrops to Ustashe forces – but Luburic thought such a turn of events was unlikely. As a result, he got permission to assemble his own personal followers, the so-called 'Luburicevci', and to do as much damage as possible *after* the bulk of Croatian forces had reached a point of safe haven. The Jankapuszta alumni, Luburic told Pavelic, were not used to surrendering, and he arranged contact points so that couriers could retain communications between himself and Pavelic after the latter had fled into exile.[250] These arrangements marked the origin of a post-war anti-communist movement called the *Krizari*, or 'Crusaders', a name that recalled the fight against an earlier 'eastern peril'.

Relations between the Luburicevci and the Germans were problematic. Units of FAK 201 had often helped the Chetniks against the Ustashe in the fratricidal warfare that flared away in 1943–1944. Matters got so bad that Otto Modriniak became a *persona non grata* in Zagreb.[251] Nonetheless, on 18 March 1945, Luburic approached a FAK 201 officer, code-named 'Merlin', asking if he was interested in jointly sending an Ustashe wireless *Trupp* into the Zimlje area, east of Konjic, where the group would be tasked with keeping track of Titoist traffic from Dubrovnik and Trebinje toward points north. 'Merlin' contacted his superiors, requesting permission to participate in the mission and asking 'whether the continuance of [such] relationships is desirable'. He also noted that 'personal relations with Luburic are good'.

Jagdverband Südost also had contact with the *Obrana*, although the fact that Luburic was the instigator of the 'Zagreb incident' – the 7 December 1944 massacre of forty *Jagdverband*-trained SVC cadres – did nothing to warm relations between the two parties. Nonetheless, a twenty-two-man unit under Viktor Sokolov was attached to various Ustashe formations, particularly the Ninth Brigade in Herzegovina, and they served as instructors and advisors. Starting in October 1944, these men accompanied Ustashe patrols on a number of anti-Partisan operations. In addition, *Sturmbannführer* Rexeisen recruited Ustashe members for Skorzeny, and *Obersturmführer* Baumann asked the headquarters of *Jagdverband Südost* if he could send Besekow a squad of ten Ustashe activists who required radio training for a mission. Several months later, the *Jagdverband* attempted to insert a group of Ustashe harassers behind enemy lines near Rikitno, although the undertaking failed. This operation had been jointly conceived and planned with the Luburicevci, and its lack of success may be what drove Luburic to knock at the door of Mil D, looking for more competent help in organising infiltrations.[252]

The Germans seldom backed a single horse and it was the same in Croatia, although the situation there was complicated by the fact that different German factions each had their own proxies. Kaltenbrunner despised Pavelic and thought that the Germans had erred by hoisting him into power. Rather, Kaltenbrunner and the 'Vienna clique' were sympathetic to the Croatian Peasant Party (HHS), which had much in common with similar movements throughout Eastern Europe, except that it was radicalised by autonomist inclinations that had pitted it against the Serbian establishment in Belgrade. The HSS leader, Vladko Ma ek, had refused to run an Axis-dominated state in Croatia, but he was so horrified by the emergence of the Yugoslav Partisan movement that he eventually told the Germans 'that his peasant party could restore order in the country'. Kaltenbrunner believed that Ma ek was the only person capable of checking the northward extension of Tito's influence, presumably because the HHS had a wide base of support.[253] According to reports reaching the Germans, Ma ek eventually conceded the need, in a country full of warring factions, to form his own armed bands, authorising the formation of a 'white' guerrilla movement that could seize power upon the eventual retreat of the *Wehrmacht*.[254] Neubacher had liaison with Ma ek and Hans Messow, chief of a FAK *Trupp* at Metkovic, also had contact with Ma ek's followers. Messow and his fellow officers bribed Peasant Party guerrillas to leave German installations alone, supplying them with the guns and ammunition that they needed for skirmishes with the Ustashe. This was an effective tactic, although it led to tension with elements of the *Zweierorganisation* that had decided to back the Croatian regime.[255] The Germans also recruited stay-behind agents from the ranks of Ma ek's followers. The head of the SD fifth column in Split was a former HHS member named Vlavkovic.[256]

Apart from the 'whites', another party of interest was the 'greens'. The 'green movement' that formed in 'Greater Croatia' is one of the more interesting phenomena of the period. It was comprised of peasants who were fed up with being exploited by all sides and had resolved to form apolitical bands devoted solely to the defence of patriotic interests and the protection of the population. Recruits came from both sides of the front. According to an Ustashe officer, Tito's forces near Split were wracked by defections to the 'green' cadre, and many Croats and Muslims in the Titoist army became convinced that their kinsmen were being sacrificed to 'Greater Serbia' aspirations, albeit under communist cover, and that the appropriate response was to head for the woods and resist. A 1,000-man 'green' group in the Zaba highlands consisted of Croats, Slovenes, Italians and Titoist deserters, all assembled under the command of escaped German POWs and a Fascist Italian officer. In the Dubrovnik-Kotor region, a band of 1,500 'green' guerrillas consisted of Ustashe and HHS supporters. Behind German-Croatian lines, 'green' formations were comprised mainly of deserters from the Croatian Army and Ustashe units. North-west of Bihac, fifty Muslims formed a 'green' band so that they could protect the population from the Chetniks without having to support the Titoist Partisans.

The term 'green' was a German and Croatian imposition, presumably remembered from usage by the Austrians late in the First World War, when it designated deserter bands of various provenances, which were united only in their determination not to fight for any cause. The various 'green' groups that took the field in 1944–1945 actually used a variety of names that reflected the heterogeneity of the movement. They were called '*Jikipari*' in southern Dalmatia, '*Skrivaci*' in the Tanca Gora, and '*Krizari*' in the Prozor-Tomislavgrad area.[257] The use of the latter term in a region where Luburic was active with his *Obrana* detachments suggests that the term '*Krizari*' may have spread from this area, where the 'greens' were in contact with the Croatian authorities.

'Greens' north of the front in Bosnia-Herzegovina had ambiguous relations with the Ustashe government and its military forces. In some areas, they refused to report to the authorities, although they usually avoided clashes with Ustashe units. In other regions, such as the Brcko-Tuzla district, where the 'greens' were commanded by a Colonel Shvaba, they joined forces with the Ustashe and the Chetniks in order to fight the Titoists, raiding the Partisan-held town of Koraj and 'pursuing and plundering' a company of Titoist troops defeated in battle near Raslani. They also guarded key stretches of road and railway. Their numbers were significant (at least locally). German reports suggested that there were 3,500 'green' irregulars in the Zavala-Gobela area, 6,000 in a valley near Sarajevo and 4,000 in the Trebava-Majevica region, the later of whom were withdrawn in early April because of Titoist pressure.[258]

News about 'green' guerrillas behind enemy lines was regarded with great interest by the Germans. Such groups were especially active in the zone west of Mostar, where 1,500 'green' partisans attacked Pozor on 23 November 1944, reportedly capturing a large amount of booty. Several months later, well-armed bands numbered at 700 to 800 men and commanded by Ustashe officer Kapulica managed to overrun the town of Imotski, where they chased away the Titoist garrison of 150 men. 'Greens' led by Kapulica had been harassing Titoist traffic between Imotski and Split, and they were also in courier contact with a large guerrilla band ensconced in the mountains south-east of Makorska Mijet.[259]

Early Mil D impressions of the 'greens' were not positive. In mid-December 1944, one German agent was ambushed and killed by 'green' guerrillas near Mostar, and another spy reported that the 'green cadre continues to be highly unreliable politically and militarily. [A] large stock of [their] arms comes from Handja [Muslim *Waffen*-SS] deserters.' Nonetheless, the Mil Amt headquarters was willing to make at least semantic concessions to the new movement, ordering that 'green' forces in areas evacuated by the *Wehrmacht* should officially be called 'Croat National Militia', and once FAK 201 officers learned that Imotski had been overrun by 'green' guerrillas, they began to show a degree of enthusiasm. 'Try to establish contact at once', they ordered a local agent. They also began to develop a more sympathetic understanding of the insecurities felt by their prospective partners: '[The greens are] favourably inclined towards [the] Ustascha', they informed Vienna, 'but distrustful, on the other hand, of the German Army, since they have been inflamed by enemy propaganda. They are told that if they are taken prisoner by the Germans, they will be dragged into a camp and will have to perform forced labour. Counter-propaganda [is being disseminated].' Within a week of this appraisal, the 'green cadre' agreed to send twenty men to Vienna for sabotage training, and local FAK officers promised that upon the return of these men, they would be employed as part of *Zugschwalben*, the FAK 201 stay-behind effort in Bosnia. On 19 February 1945, Mil D reported that 'there is a chance of incorporating a wireless operator at once into the green cadre', and they announced that they were looking for a Serbo-Croatian-speaking radio specialist and a wireless set.[260]

The evolving relationship with the 'greens' was threatened by the 'Simic Affair', which occurred on 25 March 1945 when Simic, the commander of 700 well-equipped guerrillas near Kiseljak, paid a visit to the local German garrison. Since the 'green' partisans had been getting *Wehrmacht* support, Simic and his aide had come to ask the town commandant, an officer named Meier, for a consignment of arms and ammunition. Unknown to Simic, the Croatian prefect had ordered his arrest, probably because 300 Ustashe troops had recently deserted and fled to the open arms of his band. Thus, the local Croatian authorities grabbed Simic and his adjutant and ordered their immediate execution. Once the guerrillas heard that their chief had been arrested and was facing death, they stormed into Kiseljak and announced that unless their leader was released, they would shoot the entire population of the town, including any Ustashe officials who might be present. Under pressure, Meier assumed responsibility for the two detainees, but before he had a chance to rectify the situation, a powerful Ustashe officer, Colonel Sudar, showed up in Kiseljak and with authority to transfer the two prisoners to Sarajevo. Burdened with an inordinate respect for authority, no matter what its source, Meier handed over Simic and his aide to the not-so-tender mercies of Sudar, which naturally caused great bitterness among the 'green' irregulars.[261]

How successful was the SD sabotage service in making use of the generous resources available in Croatia? Unfortunately for the Germans, the Skorzeny *Leute* seemed to have been plagued by as much dilettantism as characterised these personnel behind other fronts. The Section S attempt to build a Croatian 'S *Trupp*' can serve as an example. This project was launched in 1943 and by the spring of 1944 Skorzeny specialists were holding courses for trainees in Zagreb, a process closely coordinated with Ustashe officers Theodor Hartl and Al Grozdic, both members of Pavelic's personal guard. A contingent of eight volunteers was also being trained at The Hague and at a special facility in the Berlin neighbourhood of Tempelhof. Six groups of five men each were sent to ground in Kotor, Dubrovnik, Metkovic, Split and Sibenek, all towns along the Adriatic coast that were threatened by Partisan and British military activity in the Dalmatian islands. Each of the cells was supplied with a wireless set, 65 pounds of explosive and incendiary material, plus 500,000 kuna as a reserve fund, and the recruits were provided with civilian occupations in order to disguise their identities. Preparations were also underway to set up similar cells in fourteen additional locations, including Mostar, Makarska and Ogulin.

While this sounds like a well-organised effort, in truth the programme had been penetrated by a Titoist agent who was steadily feeding information to the Titoists. Thanks to a spy with the cell in Split, the OZNA gathered a list of cell members in Metkovic, Split and Dubrovnik, and by early May 1944 they even knew that the radio and sabotage materials of the Metkovic group were stored in a house at Capljini, ten miles north-east of the city.[262] One can assume that once the 'S *Trupp*' was activated in the autumn of 1944, it scored few success against the Titoist Partisans, particularly since the latter focused with a deadly intensity upon security matters.

Given such problems, it might be expected that *Jagdeinsatz Kroatien* would move into the breach and become a central factor in the organisation of anti-communist guerrilla warfare, particularly since this unit had a considerable pedigree, having evolved from an eighty-man Brandenburg '*Streifkorps*' based at Kraljevo. *Kroatien*, however, took a while to get its footing. When the *Streifkorps*' commander, Ernst Benesch, was promoted to command *Jagdverband Südost*, he stripped his old formation of manpower in order to form his headquarters staff. In addition, a *Kroatien* platoon was wiped out when it was caught in Sarajevo during an Allied air raid in March 1945.[263]

Whatever the reason, *Kroatien* took it a long time to become battle-worthy. It did establish a command post in Zagreb, disguised as 'Economics Staff 85', and its forward elements were stationed in Bosnia, where they advised small Croatian and Serbian units. Detailed reports on the morale and reliability of such units were also prepared. One twelve-man detachment, '*Einheit* Gerhard', was attached to the Fifth SS Mountain Corps and after the turn of 1944–1945, when functional control passed from the Brandenburg Division to the *Südost* headquarters staff, it began to engage in operations. Elements of *Kroatien* were also deployed in the Karlovac district. Such troops often joined with the Croatians in small battle groups of mixed composition. Missions included the failed infiltration effort at Rakitno, as mentioned above, and the destruction of several bridges near Prijeboj, where the spans were threatened by the Yugoslav Fourth Army. Some valuable intelligence was gleaned from the field formations and sent to Mandl, who then forwarded the data to Section E.[264] Nonetheless, the local *Wehrmacht* command noted on 8 March that Skorzeny's units were not yet ready for full service in Dalmatia or in Croatia proper, and that they 'would not be [available] for some time'.[265] By April 1945, *Jagdeinsatz Kroatien* had begun to address the problem of imminent retreat, and although the unit's officers layed sabotage dumps before leaving northern Yugoslavia, lists of the locations and contents of these caches were later captured by the British and handed over to the Titoist Yugoslavs.[266]

As was his wont, Skorzeny spent this period jealously tussling with local German raiding detachments that were more successful than his own formations, trying either to shove these units out of the picture or gain control of them. Skorzeny's old nemesis, Admiral Helmuth Heye, enjoyed considerable success in 1944–1945 by deploying KKV units along the Adriatic coast, where they raided British- and Partisan-controlled islands and stretches of shoreline. 'Naval Special Unit 71' carried out several successful operations by moving small landing detachments into place with E-Boats and then putting the saboteurs ashore in rafts and collapsible dinghies. These squads destroyed power generating stations, fuel dumps, radar facilities and lighthouses, and they caused a small number of British and Italian casualties. In addition, Unit 71 made arrangements to work with the Brandenburg '*Küstenjäger*' companies and to share the forward base that they had grabbed on the island of Peg. It was all too much for Skorzeny. By late February, 'Naval Special Unit 71' was being forced to scale back its operations because of Allied countermeasures and bombing runs on its base at Pola, and Skorzeny took advantage of the situation to ask Heye 'for [a] conference to delimit respective tasks in [the] south-eastern area'. Since Heye was relocating two thirds of 'Unit 71' to La Spezia until matters in the Adriatic settled down, Skorzeny suggested that he might as well clear out entirely, leaving responsibilities for special assignments to himself or to his friend *Oberst* Baumbach, chief of KG 200. Heye's staff responded by saying that it wanted to keep a small detachment at Pola in order 'to observe operational possibilities', and that it was supported in this intention by Army Group South, which doubted that Skorzeny's units were up to the task and recommended that collaboration '[would] only [be] possible if [the] direction of affairs [stays] in [the] hands of [the] navy'.[267] Presumably, Skorzeny then had to retreat with his tail between his legs, firing a few choice oaths at Heye.

Since the *Jagdverbände* were not winning accolades for their work in 'Greater Croatia', some of the slack was taken up by FAK 201. In late 1944, FAK 201 authorised its *Trupps* in Bosnia to start laying sabotage dumps and preparing volunteers for stay-behind duty. On 16 December, *Oberleutnant* Müller was told to get busy:

> The stress of present work is to be placed on the recruitment of… agents who are suitable, after retreat, to organise resistance groups and carry out *Verpflegsaktion* [caching operations] as *Zugschwalben*. When the *Trupp* withdraws, it is to take with it *Zugschwalben* [personnel] from its present area for employment later. *Verpflegsaktion* is also to be carried out in your operation area. [268]

The code-word *Zugschwalben*, 'or Flock of Swallows', was probably meant to indicate that resistance groups would make their appearance in the spring, at the time of the German offensive in Hungary.

Although the *Zweierorganisation* encountered the usual problems with shortages of material, they did get some help from Vienna and from the fact that the remaining personnel and supplies of *Sonderkommando Albanien* were folded into their units. Ten dumps of sabotage equipment were laid in the Mostar region, and on 21 January 1945, Müller got approval to expand the programme to include Sirokibreg, Japlanica, Sarajevo and other points where it would be possible to harass Titoist Partisan traffic. As the possibility of retreat began to loom large, FAK 201 ordered an acceleration of '*Verpflegsaktion*' and the preparation of *Zugschwalben* personnel, especially the establishment of future contact points. 'In case of military engagements', they added, 'operate in a body; sabotage tasks [are to be undertaken] as far as possible.' A number of operations were carried out, such as '*Heinzelmännchen*' or 'Z' Operation 'Ivanovic', most of which involved the deployment of Ustashe infiltrators in Titoite uniforms. [269]

In Croatia proper, Hans Messow tried to recruit paratroop radio operators from the 'Croat Legion', which was comprised of three Croatian divisions attached to the *Wehrmacht*. [270] However, the bulk of the stay-behind effort was assumed by *Oberleutnant* Dr Zawadil, a veteran of the SS raid against Tito's headquarters. [271] Like FAK officers in other parts of the Balkans, Zawadil faced horrendous shortages of supplies, and by November 1944 his cupboard was so bare that he reported 'all sabotage training and sabotage actions… are at a standstill'. An emergency consignment of fuses and explosives was flown from Vienna to Zagreb in late November, but it was still insufficient to meet his unit's needs. [272] Zawadil also had to fend off the SD, who were keen interlopers. On 18 February 1945, he warned Skorzeny's agent Mandl to stay away from a squad of trained volunteers on whom Mandl had staked a claim. Mandl's demands, he said, were 'absurd', and 'only in the eventuality of a retreat will the approximately 18 men agreed upon [be turned over]', [273] although Mil D did provide Ustashe personnel for a *Jagdverband* mission in the Karlovac area.

Units of the *Zweierorganisation* carried out a few operations – in mid-March, for instance, a party south of Cakovec captured five Titoite Partisans, including an officer – but there is reason for doubt about the effectiveness of such actions. An officer with FAK *Trupp* 216 later admitted that undertakings were amateurish and that personnel were more interested in gathering loot than in harassing the enemy. Exaggerated reports of successes were passed up the line of command. In addition, *Trupp* 216 typically got better results from fielding Chetniks rather than Ustashe fighters, but this policy was frowned upon by the Croatian authorities.[274] Modriniak later claimed that his units were starved of supplies because these were rerouted toward the *Jagdverbände*, and that once it was realised Benesch was setting up a rival stay-behind organisation, FAK 201's efforts were largely abandoned.[275]

It is true that there was a considerable spate of anti-communist guerrilla warfare in Croatia, although the liberation of the Croatian heartland came too late for such outbreaks to serve German purposes. Two weeks after the Americans and Soviets had joined hands at Torgau and a week after the Red Army had captured the Reich Chancellery building in Berlin, Ustashe forces were still holding out in Zagreb. It was mid-May before the Yugoslav Army had overrun all of Croatia, and it is likely that subsequent anti-communist partisan warfare owed less to German or Ustashe preparations than to a creeping suspicion that British forces in southern Austria – the ultimate point of Croatian Army and Ustashe retreat – were ready to hand back any surrendering Croatian troops who fell into their hands. Thus, a small part of the Croatian armies clustered in Slovenia and Carinthia never surrendered to the British Eighth Army, but instead fled to the woods and crept back to their own country, hoping that the Western Allies would eventually support them in an anti-communist struggle. This was the course followed by Luburic in May 1945 and he was joined by several other Ustashe and Croatian Army officers, including General Rafael Boban.

One of the brutal ironies of the First World War is that the Titoites pursued their Croatian antagonists because they suspected that the latter might get help from the British, and they also dealt with surrendered columns of Croatian troops in near-genocidal fashion because they feared that these men would become the rank-and-file of a fascist resistance movement. More than 100,000 men died in 'death marches' into the interior of Yugoslavia; in the Ponje Mountains, groups were shot amass and fell dead into huge pits. In thus indulging their worst assumptions, the Titoites prompted the very resistance that they feared. Indeed, thousands of Croatian stragglers and escapees assembled in the beech and oak forests of their homeland, and foreign intriguers, particularly the SIS and the Vatican, soon provided a degree of aid, partly because they had seen the worst of what the Titoites could do. The desperados of 1945 formed the original '*Krizari*' and their numbers were significant, with a British tally in November 1945 fixing the figure as high as 35,000 men. Some '*Krizari*' bands survived as late as 1947, but the new authorities soon whittled down their numbers with a carrot-and-stick approach, offering amnesties for opponents who had grown weary of a guerrilla existence, while at the same time shooting hostiles on sight and executing hostages from villages that helped such bands.[276] On the whole, it was an ugly final chapter to the civil war that had begun with the Axis subjugation of Yugoslavia in 1941.

So what are we to think about German efforts to subvert the Soviets, and their friends, in south-eastern Europe? Several points come to mind. First, it is clear that the original aim of German machinations was to touch off a revolt in conjunction with the Lake Balaton Offensive, an operation that was supposed to break the *Wehrmacht* out of western Hungary and threaten the Soviet Union's new empire in the Balkans. By March 1945, however, Germany no longer had the capacity to conduct strategic offensives without abetting irregular forms of military activity that could augment the *Wehrmacht's* increasingly meagre capacities.[277]

The Soviets, meanwhile, do not seem to have had a clear idea about how much control they sought to exert in Eastern Europe. They might have dreamed about the rapid communisation of their new client states, and they might even have believed that such a course was inevitable, but for the time being they were content to maintain coalition governments in the minor enemy states that they had overrun, if only to preserve passably good relations with the Western Powers. This point is now conceded by many historians,[278] and it was recognised by the Germans, much to their chagrin. The SD admitted on 23 April 1945 that 'the Soviets are trying to make the countries under their influence not Russian but independent; experiments to this end are being made in the Balkans and Finland'.[279] This policy made it more difficult to stir up fascist opposition or to split the Western Allies from the Soviets, although the saving grace was that local communist parties often felt less constrained than the Red Army by the demands of Soviet foreign policy. Some of these parties stood a good chance of topping the poll in a free election – the Yugoslav, Albanian, Greek and Bulgarian parties were the outstanding cases – but the Romanian and Hungarian communists were in a much weaker position. Their principal means of grabbing power, at least in the short term, was to present themselves to Moscow as the only reliable elements in an environment otherwise ruled by right-wing opposition and violence. And, of course, pro-German resisters provided them with a golden opportunity to cast themselves in such a light.

Perhaps the most tragic aspect of the anti-communist campaign in Germany's allies – current and former – was that it created a pattern of Soviet expectations and responses. From a Soviet perspective, the relative independence given to Romania, the first of Germany's eastern allies to switch sides, backfired and had to be retracted through a Soviet intervention. In fact, Romania was the first country overrun by the Red Army that had been allowed, even briefly, to maintain its own political and economic system. The Soviets were hardly happy to find their new ally taking a lacklustre attitude toward security, nor were they pleased to discover that senior Romanian officials were still in contact with the enemy. Not only did such matters provide ammunition for the Romanian communists and thereby seal the country's fate, but they made it easier for Hungarian and Czechoslovak communists to make similar claims about their alleged need to seize power. Unfortunately, Bulgaria provided the counter-model, and the experience of the Fatherland Front suggested to the Soviets what could be accomplished by a relatively quick seizure of power and a brutal purging of opposition forces.[280]

After the Soviets encountered difficulties with *Volksdeutsch* civilians in Transylvania, such turmoil also reinforced the supposed lessons of their earlier experience with the Volga Germans, suggesting that German-speaking populations had to be uniformly neutralised and kept away from Red Army lines of communication, even through means as radical as mass labour drafts and/or deportation. Not coincidentally, in every other occupied area where the Soviets encountered *Reichsdeutsch* or *Volksdeutsch* populations – western and southern Hungary, northern Yugoslavia, Silesia, East Prussia – there were also expulsions and large-scale levies of forced labour. Over 270,000 German speakers of this category, which the Soviets called 'mobilised and interned Germans', eventually passed through the Soviet camp system.[281] Stalin himself worried about such issues, warning his Western Allies to replicate his standard of vigilance in their own 'Germanised' areas, such as Alsace-Lorraine and Eupen-Malmedy.[282]

In the western and southern Balkans, there is no doubt that almost all the nationalist guerrilla groups were attracted by German lures, at least momentarily, and that they engaged in forms of quasi-collaboration. This relationship did not mean that guerrilla leaders shared political and strategic goals with the Germans, and it did not prevent a continuing level of tension, which sometimes resulted in violent quarrels. It was also obscured by the last-minute rebellions undertaken by nationalist groups as rehabilitative devices. However, it was a mistake for post-war apologists to ignore evidence that nationalist partisan leaders were implicated in forms of collaboration, or to focus on the sometimes laudable aims of such leaders at the expense of an honest examination of their methods. We might continue to debate the merits of nationalist leaders who accepted limited help from the Germans or we might examine why they agreed to such a policy, but the fact itself seems indisputable.

Finally, one cannot help but notice that the Nazis once again exported their own toxic brand of xenophobia and that their divide-and-conquer tactics increased the sum total of hatred in the Balkans. Skorzeny, Benesch, Neubacher and Kaltenbrunner helped write yet another chapter in the history of bile and vitriol that would eventually contribute to the Balkan Wars of the 1990s. Indeed, such an environment contributed to the atavistic dissolution of their own men, cut loose on the fringe of a rapidly shrinking empire. Eggers and Krieger, in particular, are classic cases of military/colonial egos disintegrating from a sense of loneliness and unrestrained hubris.

4
South of the Alps and West of the Rhine

Since the mere threat of Allied landings greatly complicated the task of German special forces in the Balkans, one can imagine the challenges that faced *Jagdverband* and Mil D officers in areas where they stood toe-to-toe with the vast armies assembled by the Western Powers. In Italy and France, there were no Red Army units or pro-communist governments that the Germans could use to scare anti-communists into a form of belated collaboration, and the American and British liberators were so popular that there was little spontaneous resistance against them. Axis diatribes about the nature of enemy 'plutocracy', 'aerial savagery', or 'cultural barbarism' lacked much resonance in a world governed by the crucial issues of food, coal and accommodation.

From a Nazi perspective, a far more effective approach – and the one increasingly employed in 1944 – was to point out that the Allies were unable to meet the material needs of Western Europeans. Thus, instead of attacking the supposed beastliness or spiritual vapidity of the Western Powers, the new line was that the Anglo-American armies brought chaos in their wake and that this condition had a political cost in the form of 'Bolshevism'. In other words, communism was still posited as the main threat *not* because it had arrived immediately, but because the door to it was being propped open by supposedly derelict and heedless powers. The leaders of Western Europe, Ivanoe Bonomi and Charles de Gaulle, were portrayed as Kerenskys, that is, transitional figures sliding down the muddy slope toward communisation. As evidence of such a course, German propaganda repeatedly emphasised several key themes: hunger and coal shortages, the loss of Italian and French imperial territory and naval strength, the allegedly unnecessary call up of armies for action against the Third Reich, and the inability of the new authorities to disarm communist guerrillas and prevent their activities from deteriorating into vigilantism.[1] The rise of a pro-German *Maquis* in France was interpreted as 'proof of the underlying justice of National Socialist ideas', and it was argued that such groups would proliferate in circumstances of German defeat.[2] Italians were presented with an 'Italy-for-the-Italians' argument about the supposed horrors of miscegenation and there was some evidence of genuine 'fraternisation' tensions upon which German propaganda could feed.[3]

Skorzeny was assigned responsibility for fishing in these troubled waters. Since social and political chaos served Germany's strategic needs and provided meat for Nazi propaganda, the more trouble in evacuated areas, the better it suited the Germans. Thus, Skorzeny was encouraged to split the anti-fascist underground movements, drawing conservative elements toward Germany and provoking the left into brigandage; he was charged with organising uprisings in order to divert British and American military attention and aid German counter-offensives; he was told to damage Allied forces by interfering with their fuel supplies and communications; and he was supposed to assemble commando teams tasked with capturing or killing Allied officers in the immediate rear of the front. And, as always, the *Jagdverbände* were entrusted with developing fascist resistance movements in Italy and France; new recruits were told that 'reliable men were needed to remain in Allied occupied territory in order to carry out fighting by special means'. The ultimate goal was to gain vengeance against Italian and French patriots and to destabilise the Bonomi and De Gaulle governments.[4] Potential saboteurs and guerrillas were told that the Germans had fabulous secret weapons yet to be deployed, a claim that was supposed to give them some reason to believe in eventual German victory.[5] It Italy, royal military intelligence speculated that the steady retreat of German conventional forces had forced the Nazis to fix upon irregular operations as their last thread of hope, particularly as the SD came into the foreground.[6]

The opportunities available to Skorzeny constituted a mixed bag. German sabotage efforts in Allied-occupied Italy were relatively more successful than those behind the Western Front, particularly because historical, political and strategic factors helped the Germans get beyond the failure of their initial stay-behind networks and cause some limited damage. Italy had a long history of romantic banditry and guerrilla warfare, a tradition that had been absorbed by such nineteenth-century nationalists as Mazzini and Garibaldi. The collective memory of such antecedents helped to legitimise unconventional forms of combat and the nationalist irregulars of the *Risorgimento* were claimed as precursors by both the anti-fascist resisters of 1943–1945 and by their pro-German opposite numbers.[7] Another factor of great importance was that Italy had been the base for the world's original (and paradigmatic) Fascist Party, which had been formed in 1921 and had become the state party in 1925. Although Mussolini was unpopular by 1943, his refurbished Republican Fascist movement, formed after his overthrow and subsequent rescue, still had a considerable constituency. Moreover, the Republican Fascists did not have to operate from exile (unlike the 'national governments') because the Germans retained control of northern Italy as the Allies slowly slogged their way up the peninsula. Thus the Germans and their Republican Fascist allies had a superb base from which to infiltrate the Allied-occupied south and islands. Naturally, the Germans and Mussolinian Italians made use of Italy's extended coastline in order to achieve this purpose.

The situation in France was rather more difficult, at least from a German perspective. Violent purges at the time of liberation had wiped out most of the SD and *Abwehr* stay-behind organisations; ninety-five per cent of the network was destroyed by 1945 and the few survivors were thoroughly discomposed. This process left intact only a few radio agents, plus depots of hidden sabotage material that had been laid in 1943–1944. In addition, the Allies felt that they could trust nearly the entire population; Paul Farmer suggests that ninety-eight to ninety-nine per cent of the country was happy to see the day of liberation. Thus, Eisenhower's headquarters could boast that

> while the Russians are faced with the problem of encountering stay-behind organisations in countries such as the Baltic states and Roumania, whose nationals have for many years been accustomed to espionage work and where many anti-Soviet groups remain, the Western Allies are more fortunate in having liberated countries practically the whole of whose population is violently anti-German.[8]

Such estimates might have been slightly optimistic: positive feelings about the liberation tended to vary in intensity between different regions in France and they also diminished over the winter of 1944–1945, mainly due to resentment over shortages of food and heating material. There may also have been some residual affection for a certain brand of Pétainist neutralism, although there is no doubt that a strong majority of the population remained opposed to any actions by the few Frenchmen still willing to serve the German cause.

The main SS instrument for involving itself in the post-liberation affairs of Italy and France was *Jagdverband Südwest*. This unit was cobbled together from several Brandenburg *Streifkorps* that were transferred to Skorzeny's oversight in September 1944 and which Skorzeny put under the control of his one-time operations officer, Hans Gerlach. A fair-haired 40-year-old, Gerlach was a former Hitler Youth leader and a Brandenburger who had served as the commander of the division's Fourth Battalion, Fourth Regiment. He was an acknowledged expert in guerrilla warfare, having written numerous articles on *Kleinkrieg* tactics and infiltration. Gerlach enjoyed a wide degree of independence because Skorzeny lacked much interest in Western Europe and allowed Gerlach to conduct business as he saw fit. He remained in constant radio contact with Friedenthal, but he submitted few written reports and the *Jagdverband Führungsstab* had only the foggiest idea of his activities. The negative side of this equation was that Gerlach was ignored by the quartermasters and comptrollers of the *Führungsstab*, who shrugged their shoulders at his indents for supplies and forced him to go begging to the *Wehrmacht*. The fact that Skorzeny was occupied elsewhere also meant that he was unaware of Gerlach's increasing uncertainties about the Nazi regime and the war that it had started. Gerlach had once been a loyal follower of Hitler, but he later described himself as 'a conscientious but… disillusioned Nazi', albeit still a strident nationalist. In fact, Gerlach increasingly saw his mission as pointless and he believed by the spring of 1945 that the only hope for the Germans was to come to terms with the Western Allies in forging a common front against 'Bolshevism'. Certainly, this was not the optimal frame of mind for the main SS officer charged with destabilising Italy and France, particularly considering the fact that he had carte blanche authority.

Whatever his views on the war, Gerlach was able to build up a substantial unit that eventually numbered 600 men. The core was comprised of 300 Brandenburg personnel, plus recruits from army replacement battalions, *Waffen*-SS units and Italian and French fascist parties. In November–December 1944, forty-five *Luftwaffe* wireless operators were added, and in the spring of the following year, a *Südwest* officer was dispatched to Bavaria in order to recruit additional personnel. Late in the war, Gerlach managed to attract sixty extra French soldiers from the SS 'Charlemagne' Division.

Despite his supposed struggles of conscience, Gerlach was a bureaucratic empire-builder. As noted, *Südwest* was designed to cover Italy and France, although the boundary line between *Südwest* and *Nordwest* was unclear and *Südwest* began running agents as far north as the Netherlands, poaching on the territory of its sister formation. This responsibility was assigned to Richard Golombiefski, a vigorous young officer who had grown up in an orphanage but exuded an 'aristocratic demeanour' (some thought that it was more the aura of a head waiter). In October 1944, Golombiefski assembled a thirty-man unit of Dutchmen, mostly veterans of the Brandenburg Division, although the contingent also included ten Dutch volunteers from the German Navy. These latter individuals had been trainees in the coastal patrol for France and Belgium, but were available for service once the Germans were forced to retreat from the Atlantic shore. Gerlach suggested that *Jagdkommando* 'Holland' was shifted eventually from *Südwest* to *Nordwest*, but there is no written evidence to prove that this was the case.

Thinking big, Gerlach also built a Spanish platoon, although Spain was technically outside the purview of the *Jagdverbände*. In the autumn of 1944, reports reached Germany about Red *Maquisards* of Spanish origin, who, having finished with the Germans, were gathering in the Pyrenees in order to launch a guerrilla war against the Falangist regime in Madrid. Such activity had the potential to cause Franco–Spanish tension, which Gerlach thought would suit German interests, diverting French manpower away from the Western Front. Fostering such a crisis seemed worth the training of a small corps of infiltrators who could be sent to the Pyrenees in order to act as *agents provocateurs*. Indeed, Gerlach had an existing base upon which to build since the Brandenburgers had assembled Spanish 'legionaries' and Spanish-speaking Germans into a platoon commanded by *Leutnant* De Metrio. It had originally been intended to use the 'legionaries' as the core of a projected '*Einsatzgruppe Pyrenäen*', but after the manpower was transferred to the SD, Gerlach formed a special unit called 'Roland', hoping to call to mind Charlemagne's legendary paladin, who had refused to call for help when the rear guard of a Frankish army was attacked while retreating from Spain. 'Roland' consisted of twenty-five men, eight of whom were veterans of the Spanish 'Blue Division', which had fought on the Eastern Front. The volunteers were trained at *Südwest*'s main battle school under *Hauptsturmführer* Hettinger, a veteran of the Condor Legion and a former Brandenburger.

At least one member of 'Roland' was sent on a reconnaissance mission to Spain, but as a whole the unit was never deployed in its intended theatre of operations. Perhaps this owed to the fact that Spanish *Maquisards* suffered a disastrous defeat in October 1944, when they tried to occupy the Aran Valley, after which the magnitude of their threat seemed to diminish. The Mil Amt is on record in early December as saying that reports on the 'Spanish Reds' had lost their importance, and several *provocateurs* already sent into the Pyrenees were refusing to encourage guerrilla warfare, arguing that such tactics were 'inexpedient since [they] will destroy prospects for later bigger undertakings'. In any case, Gerlach's Spanish troops were deployed in minor reconnaissance operations, making appearances in Italy, Belgium and Alsace. Two were seconded to the *Werwolf* and sent to the American-occupied city of Metz, although they disappeared after crossing Allied lines. Most members of the platoon were sent to Kirchhofen, where they were attached to the 265th Infantry Division and told that they would spearhead a German advance back into southern France. Requests for reinforcements were fobbed off with empty promises.[9]

Südwest's Italian wing was shaped from *Streifkorps Italien*, which had been set up shortly before its sixty men and command staff were put under Gerlach's oversight. Its nucleus was a group of Italian Fascists in the Second Battalion of the Third Brandenburg Regiment, most of whom had been tasked to work behind Allied lines in Italy. Since Gerlach was interested mainly in France, he allotted considerable autonomy to *Jagdeinsatz Italien*. The unit was run by Alfred Sölder, a mountain *Jäger* and Brandenburger who had been severely wounded in the autumn of 1943. Sölder and his fellow officers were South

Tyroleans who spoke the Italian language fluently. Some had experience in the Italian Army and were familiar with Italian military methods. Sticking close to home, they established the company's headquarters at Val Martello, near the South Tyrolean town of Meran. *Italien* had five subordinate platoons, one of which, *Jagdkommando* 'Fischer', was devoted to fighting anti-fascist Partisans.

Southern France was covered by *Streifkorps Süd Frankreich*, a Brandenburg unit that had originally been formed in late 1942 as the Eighth (Legionary) Company of the Third Brandenburg Regiment. Part of Battle Group 'Felber', this unit had participated in the occupation of southern France and was used to fight French Partisans and smugglers along the Spanish border. When Allied landings in Provence forced the retreat of Battle Group 'Felber' into Italy, *Streifkorps Süd Frankreich* lagged behind and then retreated north into Alsace, along the way shedding stay-behind sabotage groups. In Gironde, it left a small detachment run by the Brandenburg chief in Bordeaux, *Leutnant* De Metrio, although this unit eventually fled to the German-held pockets along the Atlantic coast. In the neighbourhood of Nice, six men also remained behind under the leadership of the French-speaking *Hauptmann* Feldmann, codenamed 'DeValera'. By the time the surviving rump of *Süd Frankreich* reached the Alsatian town of Altkirch, it numbered only forty men, having suffered heavy losses during the northward march. After being re-christened SS *Jagdeinsatz Süd*, the formation was withdrawn to Baden, where it was organised as three platoons, two based at Oberprechtal and one at Münsterhalden. *Süd* was commanded by *Hauptmann* Reinhold Träger, a French-speaking Berliner sent by the *Jagdverband Führungsstab*. Träger's two key lieutenants were the Frenchmen Battesti and Romains. Battesti specialised in recruiting French workers from German factories and training them as parachutists; Romains's job was to locate suitable drop zones and sabotage targets.

Jagdeinsatz Nord was a more spontaneous affair. It was formed after the Allied landings in north-west France and was originally a battle group – the 'Commando Normandie' – attached to the *Parti Populaire Français* (PPF), a French fascist movement. The detachment's first chief was the boss of the PPF's secret service, Albert Beugras, and its members were sent on sabotage actions behind Allied lines. Reports reached the Allies that a group of 100 to 200 'SS men' had been deployed as guerrillas in Normandy – perhaps this was a reference to the PPF 'Commando' – and there is no doubt that the Allies suffered from a bout of wire-cutting and sniping behind the beachhead, although this activity was often attributed to the girlfriends of German troops. During the *Wehrmacht*'s retreat through northern France and the Low Countries, the PPF 'Commando' continued to collect new recruits and it was used on missions against anti-German Partisans, particularly at Stavelot, where several Belgian patriots were arrested. In late August, it was reorganised as a Brandenburg unit, *Streifkorps Nord Frankreich*, and it was absorbed into the SS on 20 September 1944. After reaching Germany, the detachment was based at Selters, in the Westerwald, and later was relocated to Schörn, near Nassau. *Nord* was commanded by a gregarious and hard-drinking Aachener named Hofen, who was the son of a wealthy chalk maker and was a specialist on Celtic nationalist movements. Hofen had been an officer in the Brandenburg unit and had helped spearhead the 1940 advance into the Low Countries, thereafter serving as a regimental adjutant in Yugoslavia and Hungary. Badly wounded in the Battle of the Bulge, he was eventually transferred to the *Werwolf* and *Nord* came under the command of Ernst Berndt, a former Hitler Youth instructor and Brandenburg officer. Berndt was personally recruited by Gerlach.

The *enfant terrible* of *Nord* was the 28-year-old *Obersturmführer* Hans Pavel, the commander of one of *Nord*'s six platoons. Pavel was a German aristocrat at home in high society and his influence far outweighed his subaltern rank. By some accounts, he had devised many of the ideas for the basic method and organisation of the *Jagdverbände*, and he claimed to be in direct contact with OKH, the headquarters of the *Reichsführer*-SS and the Foreign Office. Pavel was blindingly ambitious and had undertaken numerous parachute missions behind Allied lines, once reportedly being disguised as a British officer. Although a close acquaintance of Skorzeny, he was intensely jealous of the latter and wanted to replace him as the main German commando leader. This aspiration made Pavel a dangerous character because it left him constantly searching for exploits through which he could win the Knight's Cross.

Although French members of the *Streifkorps* only numbered one hundred troops when the detachment was transformed into a *Jagdeinsatz* – and many of these men had been selected without much discrimination – the manpower pool was rapidly built up to a level of 300 to 360 recruits by the end of 1944, mainly by assembling volunteers from the ranks of the PPF and SS Division 'Charlemagne'. Some of the recruits were hoodlums with criminal backgrounds. The numbers were then scaled back as second-raters were weeded out through a vigorous selection process, which was based partly on getting trainees to undertake imaginary – albeit difficult – missions. Survivors of this process were sent on relatively easy operations behind Allied lines and upon their return they were considered ready for more advanced tasks. Full-scale missions were extremely dangerous and tested the mettle of even the most stalwart of the French right-wingers, who felt they were 'being sent to an almost certain death'. Many members of the unit had already been wounded in battle, some seriously. One *Jagdverband* officer later recalled a French agent who was caught while on operational deployment and was hanged by members of the Red *Maquis*, although he was cut down barely in time by pro-German sympathisers. He was then wounded in the hand in a subsequent skirmish and during a later mission he was shot through the stomach while crossing the Franco-Swiss frontier. As German controllers conceded, only the roughest and most cold-blooded of men could handle this kind of work.

Jagdverband officers also later admitted that many of the French volunteers – or 'legionaries' – mistrusted each other and that they only reluctantly accepted the authority of their superiors. As a result, German officers were their warders and nursemaids as much as their commanders. The legionaries generally lacked interest in operations and many were reluctant to return to France since they had previously been employed in brutal counter-insurgency operations against communist and Gaullist *Maquis*, and therefore could not expect much magnanimity if captured. Many of the same few volunteers repeatedly stepped forward for individual operations, so that in the Black Forest, the bulk of *Jagdverband* manpower was rarely employed in combat, but was used for such banal purposes as timber cutting. A few French *Jagdverband* members thought about deserting while on an assignment and then fading back into French society – they had ready access to phoney identification documents and plentiful stocks of currency – but they were deterred by fear of French punishment (if discovered in their homeland) or German punishment (if discovered before they crossed the lines). Indeed, one French legionary in *Jagdeinsatz Süd* was led out into the woods and shot when his German commander suspected that he had become 'unreliable'.

We should note, finally, that *Jagdverband Südwest* received from the Brandenburg Division the personnel and physical structure of a battle school, which was comprised of eighty men and located in the Gallwitz Barracks at Freiburg im Breisgau. At the end of September 1944, this facility was moved to Kloster Tiefenthal, a vacant monastery in the woods near Wiesbaden, mainly so that the school would be more conveniently located for the *Werwolf* training that would also go on within its walls. Gerlach also set up his headquarters at Tiefenthal. After the monastery was heavily damaged in an Allied bombing raid on 13 February 1945, the school was relocated to Würzburg. From October to December 1944, when the facility was functioning at peak capacity, over 260 students were run through its three-week programme, which included map reading, night marches, weapons training, plus instruction on demolitions. Pre-jump parachute training was eventually abandoned due to a shortage of aircraft as well as the development of a three-man drop container, the *Personenabwurfgerät* (PAG), that allowed KG 200 to provide a relatively safe descent for untrained parachutists.[10]

Because the Germans realised that they were not in possession of reliable or up-to-date information from France, *Jagdverband Südwest*, even more than its sister units, was supposed to work with the Mil Amt, including the intelligence and counter-espionage FAK units that were not concerned with sabotage but were expected to provide operational and political intelligence. During the autumn and winter of 1944–1945, line-crossers attached to FAK units 120 and 130 were frequently charged with gathering information on Allied fuel pipelines and French transport systems vulnerable to attack by saboteurs, and they were also told to collect political intelligence, particularly on the growth of the French Communist Party.[11] In return for providing such services, FAK intelligence officers were not shy about approaching the *Jagdverbände* if they needed special equipment or weapons, such as silencer-fitted pistols, and they also got *Jagdverband* help in slipping agents through Switzerland.[12] The most successful Mil Amt counter-insurgency unit on the Western Front, FAK 313, also got permission from Himmler to send its own saboteurs and intelligence agents behind enemy lines. Shortly after the Normandy invasion, FAK 313 helped the PPF set up a small stay-behind network in Paris and Orléans, codenamed 'Arminius', and after the retreat to Germany it organised several camps in order to train parachutists. Three teams of agents were dropped into northern France, although the zeal behind such efforts diminished after the failure of the Ardennes Offensive. One agent in this programme later recalled being told that his mission was to reinforce anti-communist and anti-Gaullist *Maquis* and that in performing this task he was doing his 'European duty'.[13] FAK 313 also sent parachutists to eastern France with orders to gage the strength of pro-German *Maquis* in Savoy and Vercors, although several of these operatives fell into Allied hands and were used as double agents.[14]

Südwest's main stablemates were units of the *Zweierorganisation* situated in the Italian and French theatres of war. The principal formation covering Italy was FAK 211, which had been formed in Klagenfurt in September 1943 and was then moved into northern Italy. Until September 1944, FAK 211 was responsible for organising anti-partisan warfare, but it was then shifted closer to the front and replaced FAK 212, which was transferred to Upper Silesia. After September, FAK 211 was responsible for sending agents into Allied-occupied Italy, building up a stay-behind network in the northern part of the peninsula, and laying demolition caches, of which 600 were hidden. FAK 211's main sabotage school was code-named *Sonderkommando* 'Magnus' and was based at Longone, although in the autumn of 1944 this institution was split into two subsections and moved to Fai and Corredo. Attendees were drawn from Mussolini's Republican Army and from Fascist paramilitary organisations such as the Black Brigades and the *Guardia Nazionale Repubblicana* (GNR). About forty-five paratroopers from a mutinous Italian airborne company were also recruited. The unit was commanded by Hans von Uslar, a 34-year-old specialist in anti-tank warfare and a man of great energy, although it was unfortunate that he had little respect for the Italians.[15]

Sabotage in France was the responsibility of FAK 210, which was led by a corpulent, scar-faced *Hauptmann* named Wilhelm Gragert. FAK 210 had once operated in Tunisia, where it had enjoyed considerable success before being withdrawn in order to start preparations for enemy landings in France. With nearly a year to make arrangements, the unit managed to lay one thousand stay-behind dumps, a project that originally shared one of designations used behind the Eastern Front, 'Easter Egg', although by the spring of 1944 it had been given the more straightforward title of '*Verpflegungsaktion*'. For caching, the Germans used waterproof wooden boxes that the RAF had dropped as part of supply packages for British agents and *Maquisards*, although by the summer of 1944 they were forced to fall back upon crates of French manufacture. The number of dumps laid was no mean achievement, especially considering that the population was not trusted to keep the locations a secret, so all digging had to be camouflaged with various excuses for tearing up the earth. Gragert also set up several training schools, one at the formation's headquarters in the Rocquencourt château outside Paris; another at La Montagnette, near Avignon; and a third at the Château Maulny, near Le Mans. While the PPF and the Vichy security service, the *Milice*, provided recruits, personnel were also drawn from one of the smaller collaborationist organisations, the *Francistes*, who were in the process of preparing their own '*Équipes bleus*' for sabotage and guerrilla warfare. Many of these trainees were used initially in operations against the French *Résistance*, but as soon as the fighting began in Normandy they were also employed behind Allied lines. Once the main battle line reached Paris, FAK 210's headquarters were withdrawn to Gimmeldingen, near Kaiserslautern, and the formation was attached to Army Group G. New training schools were organised in western Germany and the unit continued to run reconnaissance and sabotage missions in eastern France, although these yielded few results.

Brief mention should also be made of FAK 213, which was under the command of a stiff and arrogant Hanoverian police inspector named Gerken. FAK 213 was concerned mainly with the Low Countries and Scandinavia, but also had a subordinate unit at Lille, where it entered into close contact with French collaborationist parties and trained recruits at a school in Thumeries (later withdrawn to Mulheim). The original cadre of Thumeries graduates, called the 'White *Maquis*', was formed largely from the Pas de Calais propaganda unit of the *Légion des Volontaires Français* (LVF). Although there were some genuinely rabid pro-Germans in this force, it was also raised partly by press-gang methods; when one recruit tried to desert, he was mown down with sub-machine gun fire. Other trainees were told to regard the incident as a warning. In August 1944, members of the 'White *Maquis*' had success in infiltrating the French *Résistance* near Reims. These operations resulted in several arrests and summary executions, although the group subsequently had difficulty in penetrating Allied lines and suffered a horrendous rate of attrition. FAK 213 *Maquisards* managed to lay mines and they killed an American sentry in Luxembourg, but most of their operations miscarried and one raider lied to his German controllers, telling them that he had successfully blown up the railway tracks that he had been sent to destroy. Unit members sent to assassinate 'enemies of the Third Reich' in France and Belgium were all captured, tried and executed.[16]

Although the FAK units, Section B and *Jagdverband Südwest* were supposed to work together in a fraternal spirit, such expectations were dashed by the petty bickering and intramural jealousies that afflicted all German sabotage efforts. In Italy, SD latecomers tried to poach upon FAK 211 projects, transforming them into 'semi-political undertaking[s]' in which Mil D officers could provide only operational assistance, a process that led to 'constant friction'. Former *Abwehr* officers later described such interventions as the work of 'party fanatics who were little more than dilettantes'. Nevertheless, in several cases where Gerlach attempted to bulldoze Mil D into compliance with his wishes, he was usually checked. He tried, for instance, to get access to FAK 210's system of stay-behind caches in France, only to be refused point blank by Mil D officers. In late 1944, when Skorzeny tried to centralise the recruitment of sympathetic Frenchmen through a single channel, Gerlach refused to cooperate because final authority would lie in the hands of a Mil D officer, whom he felt would siphon off the best people for use of FAK formations.

There were also internal stresses within *Jagdverband Südwest* itself. Gerlach resented the fact that the SS-Police commander in Wiesbaden, the vicious mass murderer Jürgen Stroop, sent to his staff two SD 'Politruks', apparently with a mandate to further politicise the unit, and the pressure on *Jagdverband* troops to adopt SS rank grew so intense that many officers demanded a transfer back to the Brandenburg Division or to army combat units. Rumours flying around Tiefenthal suggested that *Südwest* lost seventy per cent of its contingent of Brandenburg officers because they refused to swear allegiance to the *Waffen*-SS. Gerlach's own adjutant, *Leutnant* Eckhoff, adamantly refused to put on an SS uniform and eventually had to be replaced by *Untersturmführer* Hass.[17] Obviously, such incidents did little to encourage the development of a healthy *esprit de corps*.

ITALIA LIBERATA/ITALIA INVASA

Italy had a special meaning for the Skorzeny organisation because it was the scene of the chief's greatest triumph. Long before Skorzeny had set foot in the country, however, the Germans had been preparing sabotage and stay-behind operations, a job originally assigned to the German police attaché in Rome, *Obersturmbannführer* Herbert Kappler, and to Kappler's aide, *Sturmbannführer* Loos. In the spring of 1943, as Allied military successes in North Africa provided a springboard for operations against Italy, Kappler and Loos began making stay-behind preparations for Sicily and Sardinia, sometimes in cooperation with Italian military intelligence, sometimes independently.[18] These operations failed for reasons that Kappler's superior, *Brigadeführer* Harster, believed had nothing to do with Kappler's competence,[19] although the fact that the Germans devoted more time and resources to Sicily than to Sardinia may help to explain some of the trouble that subsequently plagued that unfortunate island.[20] After the overthrow of Mussolini, Kappler expected that the Italians would soon switch sides and he began to dicker with the new Fascist underground and to send a number of 'nationalist' students to Germany for wireless and sabotage training, although Skorzeny was so busy with the Mussolini venture that he had given no orders for the reception of such elements at his schools. This endeavour was halted momentarily on 26 August.[21]

After Italy dropped out of the Axis alliance and declared war on Germany, a sequence of events accompanied by the flight of the post-Mussolini regime to Allied-controlled southern Italy, Germany assumed the status of an occupier in the central and northern parts of the peninsula. Himmler believed that since both sides were now sitting in Italy as occupying powers, the Germans were on a level playing field and thus had finally found a forum where their attempts to launch underground resistance could potentially be as successful as those of the enemy. On 5 October, Himmler ordered that all stay-behind operations be placed under a single chain of command, which Harster chose Kappler to run. Kappler was supposed to work with *Sturmbannführer* Hass, a Skorzeny man who replaced the ineffective Loos, and with *Obersturmbannführer* Schubernig, who was given special responsibility for '*Zer-Arbeit*' (stay-behind demolitions). Ten commandos employed in the Mussolini rescue were seconded to this new system. Nine of these men had been recalled to Berlin by late October, but the tenth, *Obersturmführer* Schrems, was claimed by Kappler as 'indispensable', although he too was eventually ordered to return to the Reich. An independent agent, Dr Hammer, was also supposed to work with Republican Fascist 'action groups' in order to organise a 'fifth column', a job in which he was supposed to collaborate with Kappler and Hass.

In September 1943, Skorzeny's sabotage schools were once again opened up to Italian volunteers, some one hundred of whom were trained over the course of the following year. These men came from the security organs and armed forces of the Mussolini's new 'Social Republic', particularly the GNR and the Harbour Militia. The commander of the latter, General Visconti, seemed especially willing to hand over men to the SD. Many of these 'volunteers', however, were not suitable for deployment behind enemy lines, and even though some substandard recruits were weeded out during a screening process in Italy, Skorzeny and Radl were left grumbling about the poor quality of the students reaching their facilities. The trainees showed up late; their papers were not in order; and the southerners amongst them were thought to be looking for a roundabout means of returning home. Worst of all, they frequently complained that they had been inadequately informed about German expectations and that they would not undertake sabotage assignments 'in distant territory', something they claimed to have explained to their recruiters in Rome. SD officers in Italy responded by saying that they had taken great pains to make clear the nature of sabotage operations, and Kappler groused that his volunteers were 'being treated in the wrong way, especially the officers'.

In January 1944, the first cohort of Skorzeny-trained saboteurs arrived back in Rome and a truckload of special fuses and explosive material concurrently arrived from Berlin, so Kappler was able to launch his initial infiltrations of Allied-occupied territory. The potential for sabotage was felt to be good since Allied patrols were functioning mainly in the vicinity of the front, controls were lax and the guarding of supply dumps was poor. Several teams slipped through the front over the course of the next month, most equipped with captured British demolition supplies, but nothing was heard back from the infiltrators, although Himmler began demanding reports on the operation. At least one party, a reconnaissance agent and two saboteurs, was betrayed to the enemy soon after it crossed the front. In fact, this detachment's scout led the two demolition specialists straight to a British outpost near Alfedena, after which the two captured saboteurs were tried and executed. Worse yet, the Action Party, one of the driving forces behind the anti-fascist Partisan movement, managed to infiltrate four agents into the SD training cadre. These spies were eventually responsible for the capture of several SD saboteurs. One small blessing for SD officers in Rome was that heavy snowfalls delayed operations and provided an excuse for not producing any results. A report about eleven saboteurs attempting to blow up a bridge at Termoli did force the Allies to post heavier guards along their lines of communication, but otherwise there was little yield for the sacrifice of thirty SD saboteurs who had been captured by the Allies by the mid-summer of 1944.[22]

The saving grace for the SD was that its *Abwehr* counterpart, FAK 212, also performed poorly, so that the SD barely paled by comparison. FAK 212 was formed in the summer of 1943 as an amalgam of newly formed sabotage units sent from Germany and formations retreating from North Africa. Its failure was largely the responsibility of its commander, *Graf* von Thun, whom we have already encountered in Slovakia. Thun liked to travel throughout Italy and drink, a style that he considered a rudimentary form of 'networking', but which was unappreciated in the intelligence department of Army Group C, which would have nothing to do with him. Under Thun's leadership, FAK 212 laid numerous sabotage caches in central Italy, some of which were professionally buried, but many of which were poorly weatherproofed, so that the contents were destroyed by moisture. As in Yugoslavia, this '*Verpflegungsaktion*' was intended to support stay-behind units codenamed *Zugschwalben*. As early as November 1943, Thun was passing sabotage agents into Allied-controlled territory, which was originally done from a forward base in the mountains of Abruzzi, but there was little to show for such efforts. One apparent success was reported on 15 August 1944, when three Allied bombers crashed and a fourth blew up in mid-air, all within several minutes, a significant occurrence if we consider that the Allies had discovered altitude-sensitive detonators in FAK sabotage caches.

For the most part, Thun seemed interested in subverting the Allied field forces on the Italian peninsula. He formed a detachment of twenty Indians raised from POW camps, members of which were sent across the front in order to spread anti-British propaganda in the Indian Army, and he also established a close relationship with a SS propaganda unit, '*Südstern*', which beamed pro-German propaganda to Polish forces in Italy. He planned to send a group of Polish activists into Allied-held territory in order to support such propaganda, but when he appealed to Berlin for suitable specialists, he was provided with three Byelorussians. Thun then decided to undercut Polish forces through appeals to ethnic minorities in Polish ranks, and the Byelorussians were told to ascertain how many of their countrymen were serving in Italy, as well as being dispatched to POW camps in order to round up more of their kind. Little came of this project, although several agents were captured behind Allied lines. The commander of the Byelorussians, a Polish-speaking officer named Ohl, was killed by anti-fascist Partisans.[23]

Thun's only stroke of genius was to forge an alliance with the famous Italian naval raiding detachment, Xth *Flottiglia* MAS. After negotiations between *Grossadmiral* Dönitz and the commander of Xth MAS, Prince Valerio Borghese, Thun convinced Italian naval officers to give him the services of a twenty-man cadre of marines who would operate on Italy's Adriatic coast. Several months later a similar platoon was seconded to the *Abwehr*/Mil D in order to function along Italy's Ligurian and Tyrrhenian shorelines. A training camp was organised at Capena. The eastern group was led by Captain Rodolfo Ceccacci (and was reinforced in May 1944 by squads under lieutenants Zanelli and Kummer), while the western platoon was run by Lieutenant Giuseppe Mantini. After training, these Italian marines were thrown straight into action. Ceccacci undertook a two-month reconnaissance sojourn behind Allied lines, and in April a dozen-man team led by Sergeant Tonin was sent on a sabotage mission near Pescara. In May, Tonin led another detachment on an operation in the town of Monte di Maiela, where they were supposed to interfere with British lines of communication. A member of this detachment was arrested and confessed everything under interrogation, causing the capture of the remainder of the unit, although it is possible that these men laid some of their mines before being overrun. A British report from the period suggests that a tank transporter was damaged by mines in the rear of the Eighth Army. In the summer of 1944, Xth MAS officers operated in Rome and Perugia, spreading anti-Allied rumours. One tactic was to tell stories about the supposedly impending arrival of food stuffs, which created resentment when the expected supplies did not appear. In August, Ceccacci launched two attacks against the British-held highway between Riccione and Rimini. Small teams of infiltrators destroyed several trucks and a tank.[24]

Despite a few successes, by the mid-summer of 1944 Thun had worn out the patience of his superiors. The result was his transfer to Slovakia. He was replaced by *Hauptmann* Reuter, a young officer who knew little about Italy and arrived to find a terrible state of disorder. In late August, shortly after Skorzeny had assumed command of the *Zweierorganisation*, the commando chief called Reuter to a conference in Salzburg. Skorzeny was apparently unimpressed by what he heard about FAK 212 because several days after the meeting the unit was transferred to the Eastern Front. Its subordinate formations were taken over by FAK 211, which henceforth became the sole Mil D unit responsible for sabotage and insurrection in *Italia liberata*.[25]

Meanwhile, the SD leadership – Kappler, Hass and Schubernig – continued to blunder along, arranging a stay-behind network for central Italy. By the time of the Allied victory at Cassino, which exposed the central peninsula to invasion, they had half a dozen stay-behind cells that were ready to function. The most important of these detachments, 'Gruppe Filippi', was made up of a dozen Harbour Militia volunteers under Captain Filippi, who had been working with the Germans since the summer of 1943. Additional squads of saboteurs were supposed to fan into the south, and one group was scheduled to return to German lines, whence its members would be parachuted onto the Catania Plain in Sicily. Unfortunately for the SD, none of these men were well trained, usually because of a lack of time and a shortage of wireless transmitting equipment, and their names were mentioned in radio messages that were intercepted and decoded by the British. As a result, the entire Rome network failed. Only one agent reported back after Rome was overrun by the Allies and even she – a Dutch woman trained by Skorzeny – was suspected of being controlled by the Allies. By the end of July 1944, the Allies had captured sixteen SD saboteurs in Rome, as well as discovering seventeen wireless sets and nearly all the stay-behind caches prepared by the Germans. The most important of these was in the German Embassy to the Holy See, which was partially destroyed when sabotage material extracted by the Allies caught fire and started a conflagration.[26]

In addition to the Rome fiasco, Kappler also failed to establish contact with the Republican Fascist resistance movement that had begun to form in southern Italy. Kappler reported on 16 February 1944 that there was growing disillusionment in the south owing to food shortages and that Germany's stock was on the rise, although '[the] Fascist resistance movement [has revealed itself] only in isolated actions'.[27] This was true – the Allies too noted that the Fascist underground was more notable for its organisational efforts and its propaganda than for tangible actions[28] – but there was the nucleus of a movement that could have been developed. For the first half-year of the Allied occupation, the only physical evidence of resistance was wire-cutting and the theft of Allied weapons by over-heated Italian youths. Most of the small groups involved were infiltrated by the *Carabinieri* and destroyed. The Allies also responded with promises of 'instant death' for anyone tampering with wire and threats of collective fines for nearby communities. By the spring and summer of 1944, however, resisters were also suspected of launching occasional acts of rail sabotage and firing potshots at Allied troops, and the Eighth Army noted that some wire cuts were now booby-trapped. Near Benevento, 'decapitation wires' caused injuries to Allied signals personnel riding in jeeps, and at Arpino Republican Fascist demonstrators overthrew the municipal government appointed by the Allies, although the ringleaders were then arrested and tried by an Allied court. Although teenage boys and young men continued to cause such trouble, there was also increasing evidence of involvement by former civil servants, legal officials and militia officers, who were working to link together resistance groups in Bari, Taranto and Naples and to send couriers to Republican Fascist territory. In addition, southern Fascists were attempting to stir up trouble in units of the Italian Royal Army, particularly on Sardinia, where fascistised elements of the military had fled from Sicily, Corsica and the southern mainland. Several officers on Sardinia formed an underground cell of the *Partito Fascista Repubblicano* (PFR) and were caught trying to make their way to German-held territory, carrying with them valuable documents and radio codes.[29] Kappler largely sat on the sidelines as these events unfolded and he later admitted to the Allies that he knew little about the Republican Fascist underground.

Aside from the spontaneous resistance in southern Italy, the Republican Fascists had created a stay-behind organisation, although Kappler was in the dark about this initiative as well. This group was the brainchild of the Fascist Party secretary, Carlo Scorza, who had requested Mussolini's permission to make plans for guerrilla warfare and espionage in any part of the peninsula that came under Allied control. Scorza called this network the '*Guardie ai Labari*', or 'Guards of the Gonfalon', and he nominated as its chief a former *Arditi*, Prince Valerio Pignatelli, a maverick who had recently been readmitted to the Fascist Party after suffering the effects of a poisonous rivalry with Roberto Farinacci. Pignatelli was a 57-year-old adventurer who had contacts around the world. After launching operations in Calabria, he moved his headquarters to Naples so that he could encourage Fascist remnants in Campania and situate himself closer to the front. Over the next several months, he held court in a villa near the Piazzetta del Calascione, entertaining lavishly and establishing contacts with Italian royalist officials and Allied officers, from whom he gathered reams of intelligence.

By the spring of 1944, Pignatelli and his fellow conspirators believed that they were approaching the point where guerrilla warfare was a feasible option, and they particularly wanted to attack 'collaborators' working with the Allies. One scheme involved kidnapping Benedetto Croce in order to avenge the murder of Fascist philosopher Giovanni Gentile, who had recently been killed by Florentine Partisans. In order to discuss such matters, Pignatelli sent his wife, Princess Maria, as an emissary to the north. The princess was helped by monks and priests during a hazardous passage through the Apennines – she had to cross a minefield near Cassino – but she succeeded in reaching German-held territory and in meeting with a series of senior officials. The German theatre commander, General Albert Kesselring, was an advocate of anti-Allied partisan warfare and promised to give the princess all the equipment necessary for a guerrilla campaign. She also met with Mussolini and with senior Republican Fascist officials. After her return to Naples, news of the affair reached the ears of British Field Security and Italian military intelligence, which then arrested both the princess and her husband. Although Princess Maria later escaped from confinement, active leadership of the *Guardie* was assumed by its local chief in Naples, Nando di Nando, whose *nom de guerre*, 'Scugnizzo', received a huge build-up in Republican Fascist propaganda, but who actually presided over the slow decomposition of the movement, as it was increasingly crippled by Allied countermeasures and lack of supplies.[30]

Kappler, again, was woefully unable to keep up with such developments. News of the Pignatelli mission was the talk of German circles in Italy before he was even belatedly alerted to the princess' presence. He was snapped out of his reverie by an order from Harster telling him to check up on Princess Maria and her contacts. Since Kappler had never heard of the woman he phoned Himmler's representative in Rome, Eugen Dollmann, only to be told that Pignatelli had arrived from southern Italy and that she had already met with a number of Army Group C and *Abwehr* officials. By the time that Kappler had contacted the *Abwehr* in order to wrangle an interview with the princess, she had already returned to Allied-occupied Italy.[31]

By the summer of 1944, the failures associated with the Kappler-Hass-Schubernig trio heavily outweighed the tally of their successes. As a result, Kappler was reassigned as a police attaché to Mussolini's new regime, and Hass and Schubernig were given a final chance to prove themselves by exploiting the remnants of their organisation, now renamed *Einheit* 'Ida'. This unit was based in Parma and was charged with building a stay-behind network for Florence, the main town in Tuscany. The result was once again a bust. Three groups were hastily assembled for work in Florence, but two were wiped out by the Allies and the third never tried to contact its controllers after the fall of the city, perhaps because its members had surrendered. This disaster was blamed on the betrayal of a female interpreter who was already suspected of disloyalty by the SD, a mess that reflected unfavourably on Hass and Schubernig. By mid-September 1944, more than twenty German operatives in Florence had captured by the Allies.

After the fall of Florence, the RSHA began to insist on dramatic changes. In fact, a number of new people were brought onboard the German intelligence/sabotage apparatus, including *Sturmbannführer* Klaus Hügel, who was appointed to represent Section B, and *Sturmbannführer* Otto Begus, who was transferred from Athens to Verona, becoming the Section S boss in Italy. It was these new faces who imposed the doctrine of political warfare that so raised the hackles of old hands from the *Abwehr*. Himmler and Kaltenbrunner told Hügel in the autumn of 1944 that sabotage attacks in southern Italy should continue, even accelerate, but that 'political espionage' and subversion were more important. They claimed that the multinational nature of the Allied expeditionary force offered chances to stir up trouble between the individual states of the Allied coalition and that the presence of communist partisans in the north could be similarly turned to advantage. The Italian royal government was not of interest in itself, but could be regarded as a 'mirror' reflecting the greater state of Allied interrelations and should be subverted. The black market was also supposed to offer an important target that would provide opportunities for German propagandists and *agents provocateurs*.[32]

Given the new set of priorities, German missions to the south during the last eight months of the war revealed an increasing level of politicisation. The Allies noted that FAK 211 and SD agents captured in March 1945 often had orders to spread alarmist rumours and distribute propaganda flyers. Four agents dropped near Viterbo in early March, three of them in a PAG, were charged with such activity, although they also had sabotage tasks. Parachute operatives dropped into the region of Lake Bolsena around the turn of 1944–1945 had combined sabotage and propaganda missions, as did an SD parachutist who was dropped near Caserta and then made his way to Florence. Line-crossers bound for Florence were ordered to spot sabotage targets and one was told to find a location where the *Luftwaffe* could drop explosives by parachute. One agent, Livio Luzzato, was so successful in gathering political intelligence in Rome and Florence that he was presented to Mussolini in a ceremony in February 1945. On the other hand, the Germans continued to recruit a fair proportion of washouts, such as the drug-addled Renato Bruno, whose main concern after crossing into Allied territory was to procure a supply of cocaine. Around the same time, the Germans made arrangements to airdrop recent works by Mussolini, such as *Storia di un anno* and *Il tempo del bastone e della carota*.[33]

Not only was there an expanded range of missions in Allied-occupied territory, but the number of such operations increased. From October 1944 to April 1945 there were approximately five hundred German-trained agents sent into central and southern Italy, about one quarter of whom were saboteurs, although the remainder had subversive tasks that did not directly involve demolitions. The bulk of these operatives were infiltrated across the front, although small teams of saboteurs were sometimes parachuted into place, particularly around the turn of 1944–1945, when Allied ground patrols forced KG 200 to make more active use of the two aircraft that – after heavy losses – it kept operational in the Italian theatre. Contemporary Allied documents describe the German surge as a 'powerful line-crossing offensive', or a 'mass assault' of agents, and even though the Allies claimed to capture eighty per cent of the manpower headed across the lines, there were so many agents that some were bound to have an opportunity to function. The main sabotage targets were Allied fuel pipelines and dumps, and there is no doubt that sappers managed to blow up several petrol lines. Near Ancona, a pipeline was twice damaged in the autumn of 1944, once by a bomb explosion, and Allied officers noted that an SD sabotage party had already been intercepted while on its way to blow up this length of pipe. Near Viserba, an Italian civilian was arrested near the pipeline in possession of explosives. Another two attacks occurred near Rome in February 1945, the first of which succeeded in puncturing the line through the force of a grenade blast. Unfortunately for the Germans, such damage was not a serious problem because it did not occur at guarded choke points, like pumping stations. There were also several disturbing incidents in early 1945, including an explosion and fire at Orvieto railway station, where a saboteur attempted to blow up a diesel engine, and several bomb attempts on trains and rail tracks in the switching yard at Orte.[34]

The stepped-up rate of attacks against Allied-occupied southern Italy, combined with the politicised nature of the new dispensation, meant that the Germans also showed an increased interest in Fascist underground resistance. Indeed, evidence of such activity in the south continued to reach the Germans. There was ongoing wire-cutting as well as various forms of rail sabotage. In Naples, where there was a rash of sabotage incidents in December 1944, several homemade bombs were found on rail tracks. The real impetus behind such events sometimes involved the theft of wire or the desire to derail trains in order to loot them, but German propagandists made of such news what they chose, arguing that 'the fascist movement in the enemy-occupied Italian territories is becoming... ever stronger and more active'. In several towns, there were killings of Allied soldiers, either by Republican Fascists or by gangsters, and in Florence the '*Desperato*', led by one of the original founders of the Fascist Party, Enrico Breschi, were blamed for a number of murders. The royal government was also worried by the circulation of underground newspapers and pamphlets, as well as by 'Viva Mussolini' graffiti, which proliferated on the 22nd anniversary of the '*Marcia su Roma*'.[35]

The news from Rome was particularly encouraging. On 5 March 1945, Mario Roatta, the ex-chief of the Italian general staff, escaped from Italian custody while being tried for war crimes. Roatta's escape shook the nation and nearly brought down Bonomi's government, particularly because it was aided by sympathisers outside the military hospital where Roatta was being held. Despite the fact that Roatta had been *persona non grata* in the 'Social Republic' – he had helped arrange the armistice of September 1943 – Mussolini's propagandists quickly took advantage of the incident, unfolding a dramatic narrative in which Roatta was supposedly spirited to safety by a Republican Fascist submarine.

Three days after Roatta's escape, the *Carabinieri* attempted to redeem itself by rounding up an underground group of thirty-five Fascists headquartered in the Italian capital. Led by a 41-year-old architect, Antonio Bigi, this organisation had been in contact with various criminal gangs and small private armies that had terrorised the southern outskirts of Rome, and it had also received a visit from Blackshirt General Brandimarte, who had secretly landed an aircraft in the countryside and 'inspected groups in Rome'. Italian police subsequently fretted about the possibility of thousands of Republican Fascists launching a second '*Marcia su Roma*', and the Allied garrison commander in the capital, Brigadier Thorburn Brown, admitted that the resistance movement constituted 'a real danger both to the Italian administration and to the conduct of Allied military operations'. Remnants of the underground responded to Bigi's arrest by trying to assassinate Mario Berlinguer, High Commissionaire for the Punishment of Fascist War Crimes.[36]

As the Fascist resistance movement began to loom larger in German calculations, the SD and Mil D made more active efforts to encourage such opposition to make contact with existing cells. Agents sent into Allied-occupied regions were told to gather evidence of Republican Fascist underground activity and to watch for chalk signs or scrawls that might indicate Mussolinian revivalism. A premium was placed on finding clandestine political publications and returning such materials across German lines.[37] Parachute agents were told to provide use of their radios to Republican Fascist cells.[38]

Several southern towns and districts were of special interest to the Germans and the Republican Fascists. In Naples, the original German stay-behind network had been shattered and the Germans had not made themselves popular by carrying out scorched earth demolitions, nor by their last-minute release of gangsters held in the Poggioreale jail. Nonetheless, SD officers knew that chaos reigned in the starving and typhus-ridden city, and in October 1944 they dispatched a three-man team charged with spreading propaganda and making contact with Neapolitan Fascist groups. This detachment was passed through the front with the aid of FAK 211, although its members were captured by the Allies before doing any damage.[39]

Unknown to the Germans, some progress was already being made by a member of their forlorn post-occupation network in Rome. After the fall of the Italian capital, this agent had recruited a partner and then headed to Naples in order to harass Allied occupation of the port city, although this task was made difficult by the absence of sabotage materials or a radio set. However, the two saboteurs did contact the Neapolitan Fascist underground headed by Rosario Ioele, and this outfit rendered them valuable assistance. Over the winter of 1944–1945, one of the transplanted agents succeeded in returning to German-held territory, where he gave SD officers a detailed description of the situation in Naples. Seeing an opportunity unfold, the SD at once ordered their agent to return to Naples and to start developing Ioele's group into a large-scale movement; a radio operator would soon follow. This promising enterprise met with disaster when the wireless specialist – a man recruited and trained by FAK 211 – parachuted near Salerno on 6 March 1945 and immediately surrendered to the Allied authorities. His interrogation laid bare the Naples network, which resulted in the capture of twenty-five conspirators, including six German agents, plus the seizure of a clandestine press. Ioele was arrested in Taranto.[40]

Florence also seemed to offer possibilities for anti-Allied resistance. As was the case in Naples, the German stay-behind network had been overrun and the retreating *Wehrmacht* had been shocked by the strength of an anti-German insurrection that had broken out as they pulled their units across the River Arno and into the Tuscan hills north of the city. On the other hand, Florence offered opportunities because it had been the base of a syndicalist opposition group in Fascist Italy, the *Movimento dei Giovani Italiani Repubblicani* (Movement of Italian Republican Youth, MGIR), which had been formed in 1941 from a coterie of students and civil servants attracted to the theories of Luciano Stanghellini. Although dormant by 1942, the group reappeared after the proclamation of the 'Social Republic', this time led by a short, stout and heavily whiskered Florentine named Gino

Stefani. In addition to students, the MGIR now also had an important following in the Xth *Flottiglia* MAS, and a number of dissidents or deserters from this unit entered into MGIR service, thus providing the group with a capable shock force. The most important of these figures was Lieutenant Domenico Ferreri, the MGIR boss in Milan and its chief liaison officer with the Germans. The group's goal was to organise a coup against Mussolini, who was to be replaced with patriots of a supposedly purer strain, and Stefani also wanted to reconcile the Republican Fascist Army with the Partisan movement, a goal toward which he claimed to be making progress. The ultimate aim was to keep Italian communists out of power.

Naturally, the Germans were *not* supportive of many MGIR objectives, but they realised after the loss of Florence that Stefani and company were desperate to infiltrate agents across the main battle line so they could resume contact with their Florentine stay-behind network, the *Associazione Giovani Repubblicani Italiani del Sud* (AGRIS). Such operations required German help, so FAK 211 took the opportunity to recruit and train MGIR volunteers for its own sabotage missions, apparently with the assurance that such men could look after MGIR business while behind enemy lines. Von Uslar called Stefani's outfit 'the Blues', and a number of operations were run behind enemy lines, all codenamed for variations of the colour blue (for example, '*Blau*' I, II, IV, XXII, '*Azur*', '*Kobalt*'). After a number of sorties, Stefani began to feel abused – he still had not been able to secure contact with the AGRIS – so he shifted his loyalty to the SD and began sending agents to Hass and Begus, mainly on the recommendation of Hügel. Harster was enthusiastic about the MGIR's potential and granted an interview to Stefani. Some of Harster's officers, however, were not so sure about the group's value. An assessment in the autumn of 1944 suggested that the MGIR was poorly organised and that it leaned too far to the left. In addition, Ferreri admitted begging weapons from a British-backed 'white partisan' leader, Count Edgardo Sogno Rata del Vallino. This approach failed, although the Germans suspected that this was because Sogno resented the MGIR's crypto-socialism rather than its affiliation with the SD.

With regard to Florence, MGIR infiltrators found that the AGRIS had disintegrated under Allied pressure and that the enemy, after encountering remnants of the MGIR in August 1944, had immediately identified them as sources of trouble. As a result, AGRIS members had been sent to internment camps; contact agents had been scattered or their homes had come under police surveillance; and at least one person had been seized by the Allies as a hostage. It was difficult to contemplate reassembling this worn-out flotsam into a coherent movement. A double-agent working for the *Carabinieri* and British Field Security was told by a Florentine MGIR sympathiser that 'Stefani [should] try and rehabilitate himself by going into hiding with the Partisans because many of his companions would probably be shot because of him'. The entire fiasco came to an abrupt halt around the turn of 1944–1945, when Stefani and several of his cohorts were arrested by Mussolini's secret police and charged with treason. The SD requested Stefani's release, but Mussolini would not relent, opting instead to send him to the Republican Fascist concentration camp at Lumezzana.[41] Thus ended hopes to activate a Florentine underground and to support the control of such an agency from German-held territory.

1 *Waffen*-SS troops in France.

2 *Waffen*-SS troops in street fighting in Russia.

4 Mussolini, in a photograph taken minutes after his 'liberation' by German paratroopers, September 1943.

3 An aerial photo of the Tiefenthal sabotage school after being hit by Allied bombers, February 1945.

5 German paratroopers watch over captured Yugoslav Partisans after the raid on Tito's headquarters, June 1944.

6 German paratroopers float to the ground during the raid on Tito's headquarters, June 1944.

7 A midget submarine operated by special naval forces.

Dem erfolgreichen Einzelkämpfer der Kriegsmarine, Schreibermaat Walter Gerhold, wird durch
Admiral Heye das Ritterkreuz zum Eisernen Kreuz
verliehen. Er versenkte mit dem Einmann-Torpedo
einen Kreuzer aus der Invasionsflotte in der Seine-Bucht

Above left: 8 *Waffen*-SS soldier carrying a *Panzerfaust.*

Above right: 9 The head of the KKV, Helmut Heye, presents the Knight's Cross to one of his sailors.

Left: 10 English translation of an intelligence note from a Republican Fascist underground group in Lecce. It was captured by the Allies while being carried to German lines by a courier.

From Arturo to BIANCHINI

1. GALATINA airfield dispersed on landing ground about 500 four-engined American bombers.

2. Reference point H.Q. building on entering: First hangar on right: American plans being repaired. Second hangar on right: 50 Italian transport planes. Second hangar on left: 50 American fighters. 30 metres behind hangars on right: 5 petrol dumps.

3. Oil pipe line from TARANTO airport to GALATINA at present under construction.

4. Intend bringing plan airfield Galatina provided by LECCE organisation.

CANESSA.

```
9850    GROUP XIII/52
        ROME TO BERLIN
        RSS 163/9/2/44
        GGL on 10895 kcs        1155 GMT    9/2/44
        0902/1215/78

        To Ostubaf. BERNHARDT. Gruppe Hauptmann FILIPPI with
        12 men and 2 other men are not intended for slipping-
        through to enemy territory, but instead they are to stay
        in the ROME area, as agreed, and carry out their sabotage
        activity only after the occupation of this area.  The men
        concerned have expressed their readiness also to do this.
        Technical details of the assignment have been prepared here.
                                                KAPPLER.
```

11 An ULTRA intercept shows Herbert Kappler reporting to Heinrich Bernhard about a stay-behind group intended for deployment in Rome.

```
10144   GROUP XIII/52
        BERLIN to ROME
        RSS 119/25/2/44
        QGL on 10287 kcs        0853 GMT    25/2/44
        2502/0515/71

        In the secret newspaper AZIONE GARIBALDINA an
        article has appeared which seems to have been
        influenced by General SOLETTI.  It is also stated
        that SOLETTI has succeeded in getting his mother
        and sister away from ROME and in escaping himself.
        Please ascertain whether SOLETTI is still working
        [?] in ROME, then watch him closely, because to
        judge from the article he is not straight.
                                                SKORZENY.
```

12 February 1944: an ULTRA intercept shows Skorzeny continuing to take an interest in Italian affairs and security issues.

Above: 13 Members of the Ragnar's AK guerrilla band, Nowodrodek, 1943. This unit accepted help from the Germans.

Right: 14 Lieutenant-Colonel Usko Sakari Haahti, organiser of the Finnish arms caching operation.

```
11928    GROUP XIII/58
         BERLIN TO ATHENS
         RSS 159/8/10/44
         IDE on 9045 kc/s at 1125 GMT on 8/10/44
         C710/0935/34

         In re 2 couriers from this end. Both couriers
         who delivered money have so far not yet returned
         to this end. Request immediate investigation and
         information to ISHA 6 S.
                     Sgnd. BESEKOW Hstuf.
```

15 An ULTRA intercept: Besekow barks out orders to *Sonderkommando* 3000 shortly before the German evacuation of Athens.

```
12830    GROUP XIII/246
         NUREMBURG AREA TO ?
         RSS 287/11/3/45
         PTG on 5054 kcs          1153 GMT        10/3/45
         0803/31

         To Ostuf RIEDL. "There are now only the following
         ration categories: G, fighting troops and N, normal
         consumers. To which category is the SS Jagdverband
         entitled? Have the new arrangements been
         inaugurated? [Continuation]
```

16 An ULTRA intercept reveals an interesting query from a *Jagdverband Ost* officer: do *Jagdverband* fighters qualify for combat or civilian rations?

Hungerdemonstrationen in französischen Städten
Paris seit drei Monaten ohne Fleisch und Fett

Stockholm, 22. März

In einer aus Bern datierten Meldung von „Aften Tidningen" wird über schwere Hungerdemonstrationen in zahlreichen Gemeinden und Städten in Frankreich berichtet. Besonders ernsten Charakter hätten diese Demonstrationen in Annemasse und Saint Julien getragen. Ein Demonstrationszug in Grenoble habe aus 30 000 Personen bestanden. Die Versorgungslage sei am schlimmsten im Departement Isère gewesen.

Im einzelnen meldet der Reuterkorrespondent Harold King aus Paris, daß die Ernährungslage in den großen Städten der französischen Regierung große Sorgen verursache. Sieben Monate nach der „Befreiung" sei die Lebensmittelzufuhr, die Paris und andere große Städte erreiche, geringer denn zu irgendeinem Zeitpunkt seit Beginn des Krieges. Seit drei Monaten habe niemand seine Fleischration erhalten und seit drei Monaten praktisch kein Fett mehr. Es werde bereits von einem kommenden Brotmangel gesprochen. Die Presse kritisiere scharf die verantwortlichen Regierungsstellen, vor allem das Ernährungs- und Transportministerium. Der Schwarze Markt blühe, aber die große Masse, die sich ihm nicht leisten kann, müsse hungern.

Die Sicherheit in Frankreich sei nicht besser als die in Rom, schreibe der Berichterstatter der spanischen Zeitung „Madrid" von der französischen. Grenze. Der „Figaro" habe berichtet, daß mehr denn je Pistolen und Maschinenpistolen ungehindert angewendet würden. Schwärme falscher Polizisten überfielen Straßenpassanten und räumten Wohnungen aus, während die wirkliche Polizei nach Autofahrern, die nicht

sofort hielten, geradezu ein Scheibenschießen veranstalte.

Hunderte von Polizisten erwarteten die Züge aus dem Landesinnern auf den Pariser Bahnhöfen, um nach gehamsterter Butter zu fahnden, die die Hamsterei dann aus den Fenstern werfen. Gleiche Durchsuchungen fänden in der Untergrundbahn statt, wo man die Pakete aufmachen müsse.

Daß man sich in Frankreich auf kleine Hamsterer stürze und nicht auf das Banditenwesen geschehe aus Wahlgründen, an denen auch die Kommunisten Interesse hätten. So gehe man nicht etwa mit Waffengewalt gegen den Diebstrikt Correrza vor, der keine Lebensmittel an die Städte abliefere, sondern man stoppe nur die Brotzuteilung, da es sich um eine Hochburg der Maquis handle.

Polnischer Nationalausschuß in London aufgelöst

Stockholm, 22. März

Wie aus London gemeldet wird, ist der sogenannte Polnische Nationalausschuß auf Vorschlag des Ministerpräsidenten Arciszewski vom Präsidenten Raczkiewicz aufgelöst worden. Ein neuer Ausschuß soll demnächst einberufen werden. Als Gründe für die Auflösung bezeichnete Raczkiewicz die Notwendigkeit, durch Hereinnahme neuer Vertreter eine größere Leistungsfähigkeit angesichts der neuen Probleme zu gewährleisten, denen sich Polen jetzt gegenübersieht.

Der aus 24 Mitgliedern bestehende Ausschuß wurde im Februar 1942 ins Leben gerufen.

17 German propaganda on food shortages and unrest in liberated France. From *Völkischer Beobachter*, 23 March 1945.

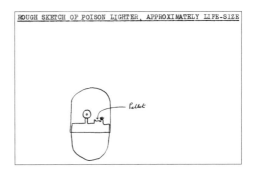

ROUGH SKETCH OF POISON LIGHTER, APPROXIMATELY LIFE-SIZE

Pellet

18 Rough sketch of poison lighter used
by Skorzeny *Leute*.

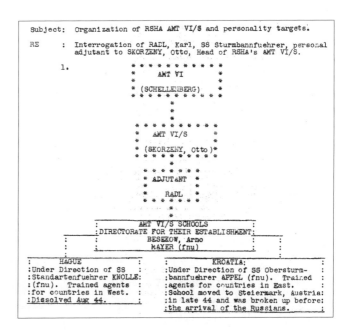

114518 GROUP II/539
        VIENNA TO BELGRADE
        RSS 408,406,400/4/9/44
        ZMB on 3650 kcs   2257 GMT   3/9/44
        XZ 92

        7. For GUSTL for KOFUB. RUDO radioes on 29/8: The
        National Committee in RUSCHUK yesterday decided to
        send groups armed and equipped by SAMUM into all
        endangered zones, wherever they be, in BULGARIA, in
        order by diversionary actions to assure the German
        forces a peaceful withdrawal. I await orders, money
        and weapons.
        RUDO No. 7 of 30/8: The National Committee in SOFIA
        has issued orders to its groups to assemble at points
        through which German units pass, in order to protect
        them from attacks and sabotage. The National Committee
        in RUSCHUK has organized about 80 groups. They are,
        however, short of weapons and money. Despatch these
        [for them]. Report SERENADE.
        RUDO no. 8 of 1/9: Today the secretary of the Russian
        consulate in SOFIA visited the chief of the district
        administration RUSCHUK and asked for the names and
        places of residence of all prisoners of war.
        RUDO no. 9 of 1/9: Yesterday evening the Communist
        Regional Committee announced itself in RUSCHUK:
        Chairman: DIMITER NEJKOFF, Secretary DIMITER SAVOFF
        and Regional adviser ALEXANDER KOVATSHEFF, sent from
        SOFIA.
        RUDO no. 10 of 1/9: The staff of the National Legion
        has its H.Q. at present in ELENA. The first 4 groups
        despatched by SAMUM are already on the frontier.
                                WALTHER.

19 Reports about the
attempted activation of pro-
German Bulgarian guerrillas,
as intercepted, decrypted and
translated by British listeners at
Bletchley Park.

Subject: Organization of RSHA AMT VI/S and personality targets.

RE   : Interrogation of RADL, Karl, SS Sturmbannfuehrer, personal
          adjutant to SKORZENY, Otto, Head of RSHA's AMT VI/S.

       1.
                        * * * * * * * * * *
                        *   *
                        *   AMT VI   *
                        *   *
                        * (SCHELLENBERG) *
                        * * * * * * * * * *
                                *
                                *
                                *
                    * * * * * * * * * *
                    *   *
                    *   AMT VI/S   *
                    *   *
                    * (SKORZENY, Otto)*
                    * * * * * * * * * *
                        * * * * * * *
                        *   *
                        * ADJUTANT *
                        *   *
                        *   RADL   *
                        * * * * * * *
                              *
                              *
           ....
           :   AMT VI/S SCHOOLS   :
           :DIRECTORATE FOR THEIR ESTABLISHMENT:
           :   BESEKOW, Arno   :
           :   MAYER (fnu)   :
           :....:..............................:.......:

   ....
   :   HAGUE   :   :   KROATIA: :
   :Under Direction of SS :   :Under Direction of SS Obersturm-   :
   :Standartenfuehrer KNOLLE: :bannfuehrer APPEL (fnu). Trained   :
   :(fnu). Trained agents :   :agents for countries in East.   :
   :for countries in West. :   :School moved to Steiermark, Austria:
   :Dissolved Aug 44.   :   :in late 44 and was broken up before:
   :.......................:   :the arrival of the Russians.   :

20 Organisation of
Section S according
to Karl Radl.

```
138292   GROUP II/3520
         SESSLACH (WILJA) TO ?
         RSS 4/1/4/45
         WUT on 3641 kcs              0020 GMT        1/4/45
         16/102

            Circular msg. for all. No. 164. Immediate. Foreign
            W/T operators, if possible artisans, who were originally
            intended for operation outside GERMANY, are to be called
            on to let themselves be installed and over-run in
            the area now near the front. Install them in concerns
            in the closest collaboration with authorities
            remaining at their posts and also, in order to secure
            cover, with some who have withdrawn. Employers must
            not be informed. Secure supplies of every kind.
            Position with regard to sets makes it necessary that
            priority be given to installations near the front.
                                      HERDER.
```

21 ULTRA reveals the Mil Amt attempting to secure foreign radio operators for Werewolf activity in occupied portions of Germany.

```
139574   GROUP  II/1
         MADRID  TO  BERLIN
         RSS 350,353/7/1/45
         LRI on 9390 kcs.      1536 GMT        7/1/45
         109

            No. 175. For BABETTE - MATE.  V 154 BACUS 29/12
            via FERNANDEZ from PICADOR worker coming from PARIS.
            1) USA airfields FRANCE: ORLY exclusively North
            Americans; LE BOURGET complement of 4-engined
            bomber and a great number of fighters and fighter-
            bombers;  Département EURE near CONCHES airfield
            restored.  2) PARIS AVENUE KLEBER Allied HQ [approx.
            40 letters missed] resident CHAMPS ELYSEES. 3) Near
            IVRY recently a passing ammunition train exploded.
            200 killed  The PETAIN Militia carrying on a great deal
            of sabotage, mostly in barracks and offices of the
            Gendarmerie and Garde Civique [sic]. Activity of
            sharpshooters in PARIS at night; their victims are
            Allied soldiers.
                          ELCANO  -  GUTIERREZ  5940.
```

22 In an ULTRA intercept, a German agent in Spain reports on news of anti-Allied activity in France, January 1945.

```
                         S E C R E T

M.G.I.R. Plans:


    1. Organization of the Youth of Italy, particularly
students during the current war.

    2. Avoidance of further strife and bloodshed among
Italians. Avoidance of further losses of men needed for
postwar reconstruction.

    3. Convoy to all Italian military personnel that the
war in Italy is strictly between the Allies and the Germans.

    4. Fusion of Partisans and members of Republican Fas-
cist Army; then diversion from combat against any Italians.

    5. A coup d'etat against the Fascist Government of
Mussolini.

    6. Construction of a new Republican Government formed
of fresh individuals for all Italy, based on free and equal
voting privileges.

    7. Prevention of a Communist revolution in Italy after
the war; neutralization of Communist propaganda to avoid
Italy's becoming a vassal state of Russia.

    8. The return of the country as a new Italy to the
Italians and for Italians.
```

23 'MGIR Plans' according to captured Mil Amt agent Eugenio Cesario.

24 An ULTRA intercept: Romanian agents are given instructions for guiding a parachute drop, April 1945.

To LULATSCH. There is only one of the type of aircraft in question in this area, so that in accordance with a discussion with the appropriate Kommando a landing must be refrained from as otherwise no further operations can be flown. The risk consists less in capture than in a crash, so that you will have to prepare the dropping. When the engines are heard the letter L meaning "drop immediately" or K meaning "do not drop" should be given clearly as proposed. Other arrangements made, flarepath etc. in excellent order.

STROLCHI.

BALISSAGE D'UN TERRAIN POUR PARACHUTAGE ALLEMAND

3 balises

60 m.

Direction du vent

800 L. MAXIMUM.

Direction de l'avion

30 m.

Longeur MAXIMA.

3 balises.

Above: 25 German arrangements for the marking of landing spots in liberated France, as provided by three *Milicien* parachutists captured in the Tarn, January 1945.

Right: 26 An English translation of a letter seeking funds to support 'Operation Skorzeny', 1948.

For the operation SKORZ./B. – Berlin? about one Million D-Mark is still needed, to be ready by 15 December 1948. You take over the collection of the highest sum possible for the district of MUNICH. Pick from among our people those who have not suffered too much financially and (who) above all things are absolutely reliable. Obligate everyone to silence with personal word of honor.

On 25 November 1948 send the money in a little package registered to:

Gerhard PONNEREWITSCH, WENDLINGEN/Neckar, General Delivery, as sender, Alexander HUBER, MUENCHEN.

You are requested not to confide in any one of your relatives, so that the knowing are few.

Long live the Fuehrer.

"When I brought the subject of means of communicating
with SKORZENY in Dachau up again, BEURER told me that he had
found a different way on how to forward the letter on to SKOR-
ZENY (Agent's Note: This was at a time when the SKORZENY trial
was still on). He introduced me to a Mlle. ANDREE, lnu, a
French woman of approximately 38 years of age who is supposed
to be a secretary/interpreter in Dachau camp and who offered
herself to forward a letter to SKORZENY. In this connection
BEURER told me that, while Mlle. ANDREE was willing to be of
help she could not be compared with her predecessor in office
in Dachau camp, namely, Miss WILSON, an American citizen
who had been connected with him before and who had been much
more eager in cooperating with him. Miss WILSON, according to
BEURER, is now in Augsburg. This was all he said about her and
her present activities.

SOURCE: "Peter"   EVAL: Not Given

File in dossier No. 4763

27 A CIC infiltrator in Skorzeny's post-war prison circle reports about the commando chief's arrangements for maintaining contact with the outside world.

Skorceny entflohen „aus persönlichen Gründen"

Darmstadt. In der Nacht vom 25. zum 26. Juli entfloh der ehemalige SS - Obersturmbannführer Otto Skorceny, bekannt durch die Entführung Mussolinis vom Gran Sasso im Jahre 1943, aus dem Interniertenlager Darmstadt, in das er im März des Jahres von Dachau überwiesen wurde. Nach Ansicht des Lagerleiters dürfte der dreifache und von Scheinwerfern angestrahlte Stacheldraht für den Entführungsspezialisten kein Hindernis gewesen sein, zumal sich Skorceny nicht in Einzelhaft befand, sondern mit etwa 400 Mithäftlingen zusammen untergebracht war. Es konnte noch nicht festgestellt werden, ob die Flucht durch Mithilfe anderer Personen gelang.

Wie der Leiter des Interniertenlagers Darmstadt, Kosmetschke, erklärte, sind Vermutungen nicht begründet, daß Skorceny einem ausländischen Staat ausgeliefert werden sollte.

Ein Mitinternierter richtete am Tage nach der Flucht dem Leiter des Interniertenlagers im Auftrag des Geflohenen aus, Skorceny würde an den Vorsitzenden seiner Lagerspruchkammer eine ausführliche Erklärung über die Gründe seiner Flucht senden. Er habe das Lager „aus dringenden persönlichen Gründen" verlassen müssen. (Eig. Ber. — P. M.)

Schiffe bleiben unter Wasser

Hamburg. Die Hebung deutscher Schiffe unter 1500 BRT, die im Vereinigten Wirtschaftsgebiet oder vor dessen Küste gesunken sind, wurde, nachdem erst kürzlich die Genehmigung dazu erteilt worden war, vom Bipartite-Control-Office (Transport-Group) wieder verboten. Diese Maßnahme hat in deutschen Schiffahrtskreisen starkes Befremden ausgelöst. (HK)

Kasseler Zeitung 28 July 1948

"B"

28 Skorzeny's escape from confinement as reported in the *Kesseler Zeitung*, 28 July 1948.

29 A French view of the Alpine *Maquis* in Germany. From *Le Canard Enchaîné*.

30 A French view of *Milicien* saboteurs, examining a message from Marshal Pétain. One parachutist says 'They must be part of psychological warfare'. From *Le Canard Enchainé*.

Above right: 31 18 December 1944: the SD arranges support and supplies for Jacques Doriot's White *Maquis*, which Doriot has assured Ribbentrop can 'stand on its legs'.

Below left: 32 German propaganda on a number of Indian rebels supposedly killed in operations against the British colonial power, 1942.

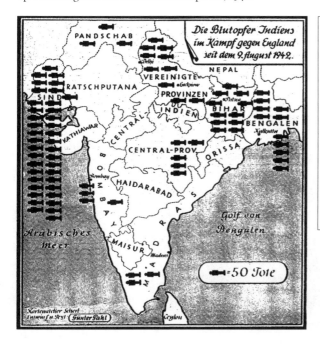

33 Republican Fascist propaganda leaflet celebrating the semi-legendary guerrilla leader 'Scugnizzo'.

Above: 34 Two Fascist Republican infiltrators about to be executed by the Americans in Santa Maria, Italy, 30 April 1944. While tied to the stake, both men sang Fascist songs and when the order to fire was given, the one on the left shouted 'Viva Italia Fascista!'.

Left: 35 German swimming saboteur captured along the Rhine near Remagen, 18 March 1945.

Left: 36 Gotthard Gambke, one of the officers of the Eastern desk of Mil D. Gambke ran operations in Russia and Poland, and helped launch *Unternehmen* 'Edelweiss' in Slovakia.

Middle: 37 Hans Raupach, an officer with FAK 202. Raupach was one of the officers behind operation 'Aurora'.

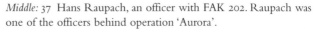

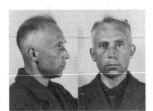

Below left: 38 Road guards of the US 84th Division check vehicles entering and leaving Marche, Belgium, January 1945. American troops were on the look-out for Skorzeny's 'jeep team'. Note the wire-cutting bar welded to the front of the jeep.

Below right: 39 Members of the CIC screen civilians at Recht, Belgium. Nazi sympathisers gave a cheery welcome to German troops who retook the town on 17 December 1945.

Above: 40 American and Belgian soldiers inspect the identity cards of Belgian civilians before they cross a bridge near Namur. During the Ardennes Offensive, guards were on the alert for German saboteurs and parachutists.

Right: 41 Italian saboteurs dig up a demolition cache for their American captors in Campo Tizzoro, 4 February 1945.

Left: 42 Skorzeny in Berlin, October 1943.

Above: 43 Skorzeny at Schwedt an der Oder, February 1945.

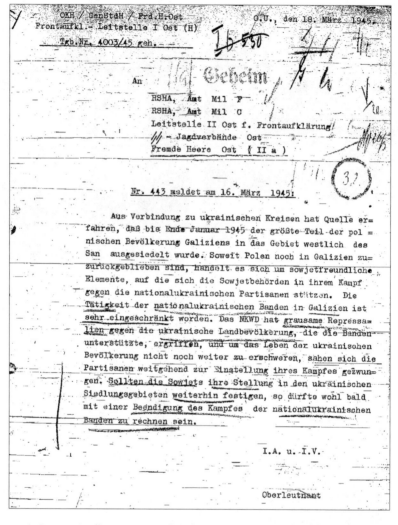

OKH / GenStdH / Frd.H.Ost
Frontaufkl.- Leitstelle I Ost (H)

O.U., den 18. März 1945.

Tgb.Nr. 4003/45 geh.

Geheim

An

RSHA, Amt Mil F
RSHA, Amt Mil C
Leitstelle II Ost f. Frontaufklärung
/// - Jagdverbände Ost
Fremde Heere Ost (II a)

Nr. 443 meldet am 16. März 1945:

Aus Verbindung zu ukrainischen Kreisen hat Quelle er=
fahren, daß bis Ende Januar 1945 der größte Teil der pol =
nischen Bevölkerung Galiziens in das Gebiet westlich des
San ausgesiedelt wurde. Soweit Polen noch in Galizien zu=
rückgeblieben sind, handelt es sich um sowjetfreundliche
Elemente, auf die sich die Sowjetbehörden in ihrem Kampf
gegen die nationalukrainischen Partisanen stützen. Die
Tätigkeit der nationalukrainischen Banden in Galizien ist
sehr eingeschränkt worden. Das NKWD hat grausame Repressa=
lien gegen die ukrainische Landbevölkerung, die die Banden
unterstützte, ergriffen, und um das Leben der ukrainischen
Bevölkerung nicht noch weiter zu erschweren, sahen sich die
Partisanen weitgehend zur Einstellung ihres Kampfes gezwun=
gen. Sollten die Sowjets ihre Stellung in den ukrainischen
Siedlungsgebieten weiterhin festigen, so dürfte wohl bald
mit einer Beendigung des Kampfes der nationalukrainischen
Banden zu rechnen sein.

I.A. u. I.V.

Oberleutnant

44 A German intelligence report describes intense pressure against Ukrainian national partisans in Soviet-occupied Galicia, March 1945.

45 Part of a German propaganda leaflet airdropped into Soviet occupied regions of Slovakia, March 1945. The sketch shows the hammer and sickle looming over a representation of the Carpathian Mountains.

United States Department of Justice
Federal Bureau of Investigation
Washington, D. C.
March 27, 1951

IN REPLY, PLEASE REFER TO
FILE No. _____

CONFIDENTIAL
BY SPECIAL MESSENGER

MAR 20 1963

DOC. MICRO. SER.

To: Director
           Central Intelligence Agency
           2430 E Street, N. W.
           Washington, D. C.
                Attention: Major General W. G. Wyman
                            Office of Special Operations

From: John Edgar Hoover - Director
           Federal Bureau of Investigation

Subject: COLONEL OTTO SKORZENY, was.
           INTERNAL SECURITY - GE

           You will recall that captioned subject was Commanding
Officer of a German Military Unit during World War II which kidnapped Mussolini after his capture by the Allies, and that subject
engaged in sabotage and espionage missions against the Allies.

           Information has been received from a confidential
informant residing in the United States, whose reliability has not
been established but who is in a position to furnish information
concerning subject, that subject is residing in Madrid, Spain, with
Countess, Ilse Von Finklestein. Informant advised that recently
Countess Von Finklestein had gone to a clinic in Hamburg, Germany,
for treatment and she was accompanied by subject.

           It will be appreciated if you would furnish this Bureau
information in your files or information which you may develop
concerning subject.

46 J. Edgar
Hoover helps trace
Skorzeny's post-war
movements.

WAR ROOM SECRET 3
363

INCOMING TELEGRAM.

Sent   6. March 1945
Received 13. March 1945
Channel   OSS SAINT

Reference PARIS 50984
          W.R.C.
Case Officer
File

WR B. informed
MG
15/3/45.

                    P R I O R I T Y

URGENT   215-12th. and STRAS

To : CRUSADE   4 MAR 1945

Info : SPEARHEAD, 12th.AG TURNIP, 6th.AG(STRASBOURG)

From : BLISS

Further our 165   not Received

1.   US. B-17 plane with GERMAN markings shot down by night fighter at
L U V I G N Y 40 Kms east of L U N E V I L L E 0630 hours 3 March

2.   Plane transport for parachutists.

3.   Crew of eleven. One apprehended. Five dead. Five unaccounted for.

4.   Sergeant K U R T   B O T T C H E R, turret gunner, at 19th.
General Hospital N A N C Y.

5.   Four agents reported captured. In hands of 1st Tactical Air Force.
Not yet interrogated. Our comment: May be mission crew members.

6.   Seargeant B O T T E C H E R, under interrogation by FRENCH states
plane left S T U T T G A R T 2315 hours 2 March. One agent dropped
approximately 0100 hours 3 March.

DISTRIBUTION   /Contd.

2.SIS (VB VF)   1.W.R.F.
3.W.R.C.   3.Spares
1.W.R.E.   2   ACTION COPY

131

47 Part of an Allied
description of the
destruction of a
Luftwaffe B-17, 3
March 1945.

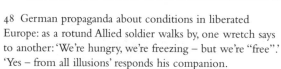

49 On the right is Arno Besekow, one of Skorzeny's right-hand men; on the left is Ludwig Nebel, Skorzeny's main agent in France. Nebel deserted to the Allies and 'blew' Skorzeny's operations in France.

48 German propaganda about conditions in liberated Europe: as a rotund Allied soldier walks by, one wretch says to another: 'We're hungry, we're freezing – but we're "free".' 'Yes – from all illusions' responds his companion.

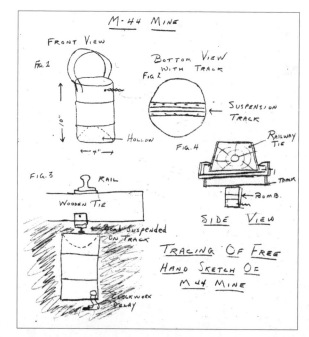

50 An M-44 bomb, designed for blasting railway tracks, as sketched by Christoph Theumer of *Jagdverband Ost*.

ENCLOSURES

COPY NO. _____
(For Record Section only)

MILITARY INTELLIGENCE DIVISION W. D. G. S.

MILITARY ATTACHE REPORT ___SICILY___
(Country reported on)

Subject ___SUBVERSIVE ACTIVITY, FASCIST.___   I. G. No. ___3020___
(Brief descriptive title)

From ~~RUBK~~ ___JICANA___ Report No. ___6602___ Date ___6 January 1944___

Source and degree of reliability:
Allied General Military Court record given this office by
1st Lt. Correa, prosecuting officer at the trial.

SUMMARY.—Here enter careful summary of report, containing substance succinctly stated; include
important facts, names, places, dates, etc.

M-5368

       During the latter part of September and early part of
October, the C. I. C. discovered a plot to reorganize Fascism
in Sicily. (See JICA Detachment Sicily Reports Subject "Weekly
Stability Report" dated 2 November and 7 November 1943 respectively.)
Approximately thirty young men and one young woman were arrested and
confessions were obtained from more than half of those in custody.
The trial of these individuals has just been completed and fifteen
of the accused were convicted. Salvatore BRAMANTE was given the
death penalty, the rest were given varying sentences from ten years
to six months.

       Following is a chart listing the accused, the offenses,
pleas, the court verdict and the sentence.

Prepared by: GORI P. BRUNO,
            Capt., Inf.,

          BYRON R. SWITZER,
          Colonel, A. C.,
          Chairman, JICANA.

JICA Detachment SICILY
NO. SIC-43.

POUCH NO. _____
JIARC NO. _____
A _____
N _____
AAF _____
OSS _____

SIGNATURE: _____

REF. 2 Feb '44
    (SE)

Auth:J.E.Bakeles

No.of copies 16

SE   x
Hist.   x(cover only
RS
Special Br. 2
Div. Af. 2

Distribution by originator ___JIARC; G-2,AFHQ; OSS: Civil Affairs___

Routing space below for use in M. I. D. The section indicating the distribution will place a check mark in the
lower part of the recipients' box in case one copy only is to go to him, or will indicate the number of copies in case
more than one should be sent. The message center of the Intelligence Branch will draw a circle around the box of
the recipient to which the particular copy is to go.

AGF	AAF	ASF	AC of S G-2	Chief IG	Eur.-Afr.	Far East	N. Amer.	Air	Dissem.	AIC	FLBR	OSS
	2											x

M A Sec.	CIG	Rec. Sec.	DNI	BEW	CWS	ENG.	OPD	ORD	Sig.	State	QMG
	2		3							2	

Enclosures:

JWP/arc

WAR DEPARTMENT
O.C.S.17 (2nd Rev.)

51 American report on a Republican Fascist resistance group broken up in Sicily.

NOTES FOR FSS/CIO.

13. The following information obtained from (   ), a
Kilo 212 parachutist saboteur arrested on 3 March, is of interest
as typifying current enemy methods.

14. His task consisted of: -

(a) Sabotaging high-tension pylons by placing plastic
charges of 250 grams each at three of the corners
of the base of a pylon, each to be connected by
a quick-burning fuze and the whole to be exploded
by a delayed action fuze.

(b) Sabotaging railway lines by placing two plastic
charges each of 250 grams 1 metre apart in the groove of the rail,
and connecting them to an explosive capsule on top of the
rail which would be detonated by a train passing over it.

(c) Sabotaging telephone wires by cutting as opportunity
offered.

(d) Changing road signs and notices.

(e) To obtain information of the Allied treatment
of Italians. (Obviously to be used as propaganda
material).

15. He also revealed that students at sabotage courses were taught
to conceal ignition capsules in the tops of their fountain pens, or
in the lining of a hat or beret.

(Extract from letter, Office of the AC of S, G-2, Allied Force Headquarters,
file GBI-389.701, 2 April 1945, subject: AFHQ Counter-Espionage and Counter-
Sabotage Summary for March 1945.)   (TOP SECRET)

Left: 52 An Allied report on the objectives of an Italian parachutist-saboteur captured in March 1945.

Below: 53 Training sheet for use of German sabotage devices.

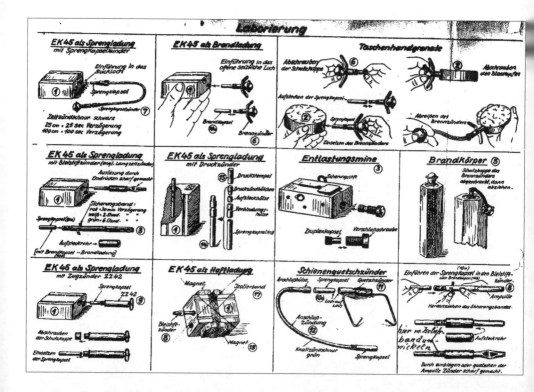

Right: 54 Walter Kraizizek, escaped prisoner-of-war and adventurer. In March 1945, Kraizizek was recruited by Skorzeny to kill General Eisenhower.

Below: 55 Material from a German sabotage cache unearthed in Rome, 29 June 1944. Contents include waterproof charges, detonators and a plastic case for carrying detonator caps.

Below: 56 German radio set and technical instructions captured near Lyon, France, February 1945, in the possession of two parachutists. The radio consisted of a five-watt transmitter, a receiver and a power supply, each housed in a galvanised iron case.

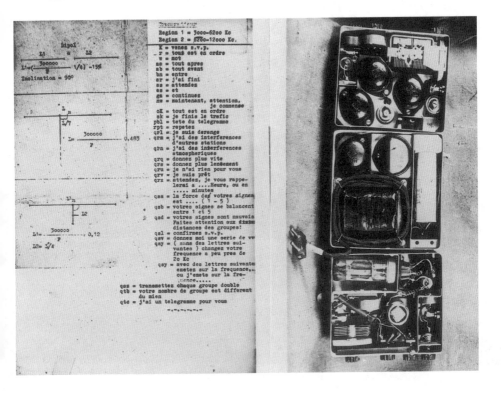

Far left and left: 58 & 59 Joseph Verstraeten and Delphine Lagrou, leading members of the 'Henriette' underground organisation.

57 Wilhelm Waneck, after being captured by the Allies. Waneck was the mastermind behind SD intrigues in the Balkans.

Above left and left: 60 & 61 Belgian parachutist-saboteurs Henri Morael and Anita Preloger. They were captured by the Allies after being mistakenly dropped into France.

In the main, the Allies were impressed by how little sabotage occurred in Allied-occupied Italy, especially considering the resources that the Germans were devoting to the effort, and they could rightly claim that most demolition agents were captured by checkpoints or patrols before they had a chance to operate. Such was the destiny of two FAK 211 parachutists who landed near Cassino and were supposed to attack a fuel pipeline with locally cached supplies, and of three paratrooper-saboteurs caught near Ravenna in January 1945. It was also the fate of fourteen saboteurs who were arrested while attempting to make use of demolition dumps hidden in the Lucca–Pistoia region. Given the overall deterioration of Germany's strategic position by March 1945, Allied counter-intelligence officers started to wonder why their foes were still bothering to destabilise Italy and harass Allied efforts on a front that had become a distinctly secondary concern for both sides. They attributed the effort to an over-optimistic German appreciation of their own powers to cause dissension, as well as a desire by German intelligence and commando officers to justify their own existence and protect relatively comfortable jobs that were usually performed at some distance from the front.[42]

One type of operation that did reward the exertion consisted of seaborne raids by small units of saboteurs landed in rubber rafts. The shape of Italy made it advantageous to use maritime routes around the front, particularly along the stretch of Adriatic coast from Ravenna to Ancona, where shallow beaches facilitated landings by sabotage parties moved into location by KKV vessels. Targets included the Allied fuel pipeline, the east coast highway, road and railway bridges and enemy military traffic. Missions were planned and organised by one of the sub-units of FAK 211, *Trupp* 257, which ran operations from Porto Garibaldi and Venice and had its own Lilliputian fleet of motor-boats and dinghies. Recruits were drawn mainly from marines of Xth *Flottiglia* MAS, whom the Germans called 'mules'. According to a German officer familiar with FAK operations, *Trupp* 257 carried out fifteen raids in the last half-year of the war, although only six made a significant impact.

In October and December 1944, Xth MAS volunteers made three landings in the Rimini area. On the night of 13/14 October, a seven-man team rigged explosive charges to British vehicles and laid land mines before retreating by means of the same motor launch that had brought it ashore. In a repeat performance several nights later, five saboteurs blew up several trucks and again laid mines, although their boat was damaged when it struck an obstacle upon landing. The men fled on foot, although only two managed to return to German lines. Several months later, yet another detachment of thirteen Italian marines landed at Rimini, operating in parties of four men each. They cut communication lines, blew up four British trucks parked outside Bellaria airfield and then dispersed into the interior of the country. Most were captured by the Allies around the turn of 1944–1945, four being turned in by their own countrymen after they had appeared at a farm looking for food and accommodation.

On the night of 9/10 January 1945, saboteurs operating near Porto San Giorgio blew up a railway bridge, something of an irony since Allied counter-intelligence had boasted before the incident that no bridges had been destroyed by enemy sabotage action. Measures to guard such structures had thus been relaxed. The commando unit responsible for the demolitions had been ordered to operate against bridges near the mouth of the

Tenna river, but had been accidentally put ashore eight miles south of its intended landing zone.

On 16 March, German E-Boats moved three detachments of saboteurs within several miles of the Italian coast, but operations were hindered by fog and the sinking of a recovery vessel, which sprang a leak. One unit, codenamed 'Wotan', was put ashore near Ancona. Another eight-man detachment, 'Brieftaube', had a combined sabotage/subversion/propaganda mission and was launched near Civita Nova. Because of radio intercepts deciphered by the Allies, the arrival of 'Brieftaube' was expected. Retreating E-Boats heard explosions and from a distance of twenty-four miles they spotted a tongue of flame shoot into the sky above Ancona. All eight operatives were captured by the Allies.

On 18/19 April, two landing parties were ferried by E-Boats into position off Senigallia and were put ashore in rubber dinghies. Both groups fixed explosive and incendiary charges to the Allied fuel pipeline, placed bombs underneath rail culverts and attached plastic explosive to the cable shafts, points and masts for railway overhead wire. The saboteurs also laid tyre-bursters and mines in order to damage rescue vehicles and hamper firefighters. The delay mechanism attached to some of the pipeline charges exploded prematurely, and amid alarms and searchlight beams, the E-Boats offshore could see bright flames lighting up the horizon. Although Allied crews were able to disarm the bombs under one of the rail culverts, another bridge was destroyed and rail service was delayed for sixteen hours. The charges clamped to the fuel pipeline also caused fires in two spots seven miles apart, thus dividing the attention of firefighting crews and cutting off the fuel supply to the eastern half of the Italian front for six hours.

The KKV Command, under Nazi Party pressure, ordered such attacks to continue until the bitter end, but by April 1945 fuel shortages and the increasing hours of daylight were making sabotage expeditions more difficult. At the very least, such undertakings forced the Allies to set up a special service to guard the coast (manned mainly by Italians from the *Guardia di Finanza*) and the Allied air forces had to increase aerial reconnaissance patrols along the shore of the Adriatic. The raids also had propaganda value, raising a sense of alarm in the rear of the Allied front.[43]

Operations along Italy's north-western coast were more problematic. Allied-controlled harbours along the Ligurian shore were brightly illuminated and maritime approaches were closely guarded, while the execution of tasks against more remote objectives, such as Elba or Corsica, was possible only with underwater craft or with long-range vessels of considerable speed. In addition, the absence of many islands or appropriate coastal features made it difficult for boats returning from missions to hide, particularly from aerial reconnaissance or attack.[44] Despite these impediments, several operations were launched out of La Spezia, although none were successful. On 16 March 1945, an E-Boat dropped off four agents on a combined sabotage/espionage sortie into Livorno, but the party was picked up by the Allies while still in the water.[45] A number of missions organised by Xth *Flottiglia* MAS were also abortive. Three Italian frogmen were captured off the pier in Livorno on the night of 18/19 November 1944, attempting to tow a supply of mines into the harbour. This team was supposed to mine enemy ships and then change into civilian clothes and set up a forward base, making preparations for a second detachment and making aggressive use of the remainder of their explosives. On 16 March, an Italian patrol boat was sunk by enemy action off Cape Ferrat, with the loss of a small Italo-German crew and three Italian agents. A trio of Xth *Flottiglia* MAS saboteurs was also captured at Viareggio on 18 April 1945, after they had been landed by dinghy. They were equipped with a machine gun, a hundred pounds of dynamite and a supply of plastic explosives. Their job was to harass Allied traffic on the Via Aurelia, but even though all the men were ardent Fascists, they had dumped their equipment and given up the mission even before bringing their raft to shore.[46]

Such operations caused severe stresses in German–Republican Fascist relations. By 1944, 120 men from the elite swimmer-parachutist battalion of Xth *Flottiglia* MAS had been seconded to service with Mil D, which created a distinct sense that the Germans were exploiting their Italian allies. Many Italian officers believed that Mil D's demands were exceeding the bounds of the Borghese-Dönitz agreement. Indeed, by the summer of 1944, FAK officers were press-ganging Xth MAS troops for special tasks or they were encouraging enlisted men to desert and were then recruiting the deserters. In July, the commander of the swimmer-parachutist battalion, Captain Nino Buttazoni, arrested one of his officers for aiding German-inspired efforts 'to desert the Italian flag', and in November, after failing to renegotiate the Borghese-Dönitz agreement, Borghese repositioned the entire unit along the Yugoslav frontier. The obvious purpose for this redeployment was to put distance between the battalion and the avaricious officers of Mil D, although the official rationale was that it encouraged the formation of an 'anti-Slav front'. It should also be noted that Borghese put the training elements of the swimmer-parachutist unit, henceforth called the 'Vega Battalion', under the command of Captain Mario Rossi, who was ordered to resist the depredations of Mil D and to run his own independent sabotage operations. Indeed, one veteran of the Xth MAS later recalled that these detachments carried out stay-behind espionage and sabotage actions. The *Zweierorganisation* formally retained the option to withdraw 150 extra volunteers from Xth MAS ranks, but neither Borghese nor Buttazoni would release further men.[47]

Efforts to encourage guerrilla warfare in *Italia liberata* were left largely to the Republican Fascists, although the Germans appreciated the potential for such activity and were eager to help. Initial efforts were directed largely toward propaganda. As early as 25 September 1943, a radio appeal to the southern population called for 'hinder[ing] with every means the movement of the English and Americans'. In addition, the National Authority for Assistance to Refugees, which was set up to aid tens of thousands of Fascists streaming north, provided select refugees with training in guerrilla warfare, and it also prepared airdrop leaflets providing 'instructions for conducting a partisan struggle'. Most importantly, Republican Fascist press and radio carried a profusion of stories about guerrillas operating in '*Italia invasa*', particularly the celebrated 'Scugnizzo', who was described as a young lieutenant from the Italian Army. Such content was meant to serve as a morale booster by suggesting that there was a southern Fascist force analogous to the rising anti-Fascist partisan movement in the north. The media campaign, however, was the fruit solely of journalistic imagination, which entailed risks for credibility should the myth diverge too far from reality. Even Mussolini was disappointed to learn that 'Scugnizzo' was fancy more than fact. With some exceptions, such propaganda was scaled back in 1944, mainly at the behest of the Ministry of Popular Culture, which wanted more credible claims.[48] In reality, early examples of Fascist guerrilla warfare were almost nonexistent: the most that the Allies could find was *one* Italian guerrilla fighter, who was wounded near Torino di Sango, and four German stragglers living in a remote mountain village near Avellino. In the latter case, Canadian Field Security raided the village in February 1944 and found evidence of a recent parachute drop, although they missed their quarry.[49]

A different approach was taken by the secretary of the PFR, Alessandro Pavolini, who opposed exaggerated claims about Fascist guerrilla warfare because he felt that they merely raised ironical eyebrows, as well as disappointing the Germans. He adopted the opposite tack, organising real opposition by '*franchi tiratori*' (*franc-tireurs*) and Fascist partisans, while trying to maintain a modicum of secrecy. With the German defeat at Monte Cassino, Pavolini realised that the *Wehrmacht* would have to withdraw to the 'Gothic Line', which it had prepared between Pisa and Rimini. This process made central Italy the staging ground for a more systematic attempt to wage partisan warfare. Von Uslar backed Pavolini enthusiastically.

Rome fell within three weeks of the German loss at Cassino, so there was little time to make preparations for the Italian capital. On 3 June 1944, the local chapter of the PFR was informed of the forthcoming German evacuation of the city, and it made preparations to leave behind a 'political assistance organisation', which was supposed to diffuse propaganda and provide help for Fascists left in the capital. This network was led by Filippo Dell'Agli, a prominent syndicalist who had been head of the agricultural workers' union in Naples. Dell'Agli was provided with 500,000 lire, a printing press and a supply of pistols and ammunition. His organisation was based on a cellular structure and included three elements: first, a group of loyal Fascists who had never been members of the Fascist Party or had been expelled, and thus were expected to escape enemy scrutiny; second, young Fascists of the *Gruppi d'Azione Giovanile*; and third, party workers with the district organisation of the PFR.[50] A PFR report from the capital two weeks after its occupation suggested that there had been anti-Allied ambushes and sabotage attacks. However, the authors of these events were not members of Dell'Agli's stay-behind network, but 'republican Mazziniani', that is, dissident socialist and communist youth under the leadership of a Dr Cola. Underground Fascists in the capital reported that Cola, for all practical purposes, backed the northern republic and therefore deserved support in his struggle against 'Anglo-American capitalism'.[51]

Learning from the Roman experience, Pavolini made better preparations for Tuscany, Umbria and Marche, militarising part of the PFR's bureaucratic machinery. He toured central Italy in the summer of 1944, forming '*nuclei di fascisti repubblicani*' – immediate precursors of the Black Brigades – which he argued would 'maintain order' and eventually be transformed into 'rebel Fascist bands'. On 11 June, he issued a directive ordering that Fascist *Gerarchi* be evacuated from threatened areas, but that lower echelon officials were to go underground: 'Specially chosen elements, especially those fit for inclusion in bands, must spark a fascist rebellion or even, in accord with the German authorities, make themselves available for terrorist attacks, clandestine radio operation, etc.' He also demanded the nomination of underground PFR bosses – 'secret *Federale*' – in order to create cellular party structures, and he told party leaders to do their utmost in begging arms and transport from the Germans. Convincing Kesselring to contribute weapons was difficult because an entire Republican Fascist army battalion had recently defected to the Allies, so it was clear that only the most loyal elements could be equipped. Nonetheless, Pavolini reported to Mussolini on 19 June: 'Particular care is being devoted to the organisation of activist groups that will remain in place or radiate into the south. Very sound initiatives have been undertaken already in Terni, Arezzo, Grosseto, Florence, Livorno and Pisa: clandestine wireless posts, secret printing presses, bands and political movements.'[52] Five days later, Pavolini reported that anti-fascist patriot attacks were being met through 'the action of special elements that we will leave in Tuscany'.[53]

This programme bore fruit. In Pavolini's home town of Florence, he recruited 400 workers, students and militiamen to act as *franchi tiratori*. Armed with Italian and German rifles and deployed in small teams, these fighters had orders to subvert the Allied conquest of the city, holding positions as long as possible and then withdrawing along tactical lines of retreat. Their goal was to shoot anyone who appeared on the streets and thereby paralyse the restoration of civil life. When the Germans evacuated the southern part of Florence on 11 August 1944, the *franchi tiratori* sprang into action, providing severe opposition for patriot resisters trying to affect the city's liberation. Heavy fighting broke out, especially in the Porta Romana district, and troops of the 8th Indian Division had to be diverted in order to reinforce anti-Fascist partisans. Officers at Allied military government headquarters had to strike the British and American flags above the building because the banners were attracting fire. One Allied observer noted: 'Fascist parties fully armed stood fast from balconies and windows – sniping and machine gunning the defenceless population and their opposite numbers, the Partisans of the Italian Liberation movement. Fanatical fire fights ensued from the house tops, church towers and in peaceful parks.' After a week of such mayhem, the *franchi tiratori* went to ground or were captured by anti-fascist Partisans, whence they were typically stood in front of a wall and shot. More than 120 snipers met this fate. Even after the suppression of sniping, resistant Fascist elements continued to skulk about the town, and the incident provided a model for later outbreaks in the great northern industrial cities, particularly Turin.[54]

In the countryside of central Italy, a few embryonic Fascist bands also appeared, particularly since the Allies had swept so swiftly to the 'Gothic Line' that there was hardly time for their troops to visit, much less occupy, remote stretches of the Apennine massif. From Tivoli came a report that many outlying villages had never seen a single Allied soldier, but were providing refuge for German troops and Republican Fascists clad in civilian clothes. A few of these Germans were deserters who had joined anti-fascist Partisan bands, but others were clearly still on the Axis side, being kept alive by Italian girlfriends who carried them food and clothing at night. There were several small groups hiding in the region around Saltara, including a pair of fanatics who were suspected of murdering a Canadian soldier on 25 August 1944.[55] British military police combed the hills north of Florence in a search for Republican Fascist bands suspected of killing two Allied soldiers and stealing their identity documents.[56] An Allied report also described such guerrilla activity in the central part of Umbria:

Daily reports arrive at this office to the effect that in the mountains in this area there are still to be found many Fascists in the company of German soldiers who have stayed

behind to participate in various acts of sabotage. In one area in particular, near the town
of Spoletta [sic] and Foligno, there is reported to be at present a band formed as well
as being in the process of expanding, under the guidance of one Proff Coppo, former
founder of the Fascio Repubblicani in the Terni area. The people of this town are alarmed
that no action is being taken by the Allies to apprehend these persons… The partisans of
this area are willing to band together under the leadership of an Allied representative and
go out in search of this party.

Several high-profile Republican Fascists, including Pietro Faustini and Umberto Capatti,
had returned to Umbria and were working in league with Coppo. In a nearby district,
a GNR captain was reported to be hiding in the mountains and spreading anti-Allied
propaganda. An Allied raid on 3 September narrowly missed capturing this fugitive. The
British did manage to arrest at least fifty 'green' guerrillas, but the latter were hardly
popular, their prison compound being repeatedly besieged by Red Partisans intent on
causing them harm.[57]

After August 1944, the organisation of guerrilla bands fell under the purview of
Pavolini's pet creation, the Black Brigades. Presented as a return to the *squadrismo* of early
Fascism,[58] the 'Auxiliary Corps of the Blackshirt Action Squads' entailed a militarisation
of the PFR, whereby the district chapters became the Black Brigades and the *Federale*
became the commanders of these regional paramilitary formations. Although the Black
Brigades were formed in German-held territory, Pavolini began working on a plan to
form 1,200-man underground brigades in every *compartimento* in central and southern
Italy (except for Sicily and Sardinia). Each brigade was supposed be divided into 200-man
groups that would function as *franchi tiratori* or guerrillas, although specialist squads would
infiltrate the southern political parties, spread propaganda, murder opponents and carry
out sabotage. Pavolini planned to man these units with volunteers from the northern
Black Brigades, the sabotage squads being raised from soldiers in the Xth *Flottiglia*
MAS. Members of the political and sabotage squads were supposed to be controlled by
underground staffs in Rome and Florence and parachuted into place by KG 200. The
rank and file were supposed to be infiltrated through the front or be bypassed in rugged
country near Bologna and Pavullo.[59] The logical conclusion of this drift was to turn the
entire Republican Fascist movement into a conspiratorial organisation, 'the PFR *Segreto*',
which would eventually withdraw into an Alpine Redoubt in the Val Tellina and control
Fascist guerrilla bands throughout Italy.[60]

Although individuals from the Black Brigades were running missions behind Allied
lines as early as August 1944,[61] it was only in 1945 that the first full-scale bands were
organised. FAK 211 offered technical and training assistance, but the results were not
encouraging. The initial guerrilla group failed because its members were unfit for the
job. Although personnel of the clandestine brigades were supposed to be kept in line by
a severe penal code, which aimed at preventing looting and common crimes, this cadre
managed to get into trouble even before reaching Allied-held territory. The Germans
arrested the leader and two of his associates, while the remainder were dispersed,
although four were sent to the agent school at Fai. A second group was trained in Milan
by the commander of *Trupp* 255, Kersting, who worked closely with Pavolini's aides

Puccio Pucci and Aniceto del Massa. Part of this unit was deployed in the south and the remainder was awaiting transport at the end of the war. Two further groups were also being prepared by the Black Brigade in Milan but were still on Republican Fascist soil at the conclusion of the conflict.[62]

The activities of the Black Brigade/Marche also reveals Pavolini's plan in operation. Two groups of this formation were trained by the Germans at Padua and were parachuted at Osimo on 27 December 1944, with orders to conduct operations in various districts of Marche and in the neighbourhood around Rome. Two of the saboteurs, Angelini and Capotosti, were supposed to carry out demolitions in the Ancona area and then perform reconnaissance, while three others were supposed to go to Rome and blow up an Allied fuel line. Once these elements had returned to base, two further agents were supposed to leave 'with the task of organising bands of *fascisti* and blowing up the station in Pedaso'. The task of organising bands was also charged to a Sammarinese lieutenant who was dropped separately into the Ancona–Rimini area. Matters went awry when Angelini and Capotosti were captured by the Allies, blowing the operational security of the mission.[63]

As the Germans and Republican Fascists showed increasing interest in rousing southern Italians into rebellion, they dispatch a number of agents charged with such tasks. In October 1944, the Allies captured a pair of SD operatives responsible for organising guerrilla warfare and three additional emissaries of the same type were nabbed in January 1945. These latter had the mission of recruiting men for bands that they promised would be reinforced and re-supplied by air. In their desperation, the Republican Fascists also went back to the time-tested technique of wireless propaganda.[64] In the spring of 1945, *Radio Repubblicana* launched 'the Movement for the Insurrection of *Italia Invasa*', which involved the broadcast of a series of bulletins to sympathisers in liberated Italy. 'Fascists of Calabria', for instance, were informed that they had 'already formed numerous and powerful bands, which seriously trouble the invaders and the traitors who are his accomplices'. Listeners were then advised to strengthen such groups:

> assemble the young; wrench the weapons from the hands of Bonomi's henchmen; whenever you meet an isolated enemy soldier, suppress him; whenever an enemy vehicle stops, attack it and set it on fire… Act as guerrillas by day and by night; be the first to bring about the mother country's insurrection.[65]

The desire to inspire insurgency in southern Italy came closest to realisation on the troubled island of Sicily, which is ironic since Sicily had never provided a strong base for Italian Fascism. Indeed, when the Republican Fascist Interior Ministry first began recruiting Sicilians for 'political missions' on their home island, most of the volunteers happily accepted passage home and were then never heard from again.[66] On the other hand, food shortages, the rise of regional separatism and the re-emergence of the Mafia created severe tensions in Sicilian society, and when the Bonomi regime tried to call up draftees for service at the front – Italy, it will be recalled, was now on the Allied side – there was a huge outburst of anti-conscription sentiment. Obviously, this issue had little to do with Fascism, but because conscription was an issue involving young people, students were in the vanguard of the opposition, and the Republican Fascists had an active following among students at the universities in Palermo and Porto Empedocle. Even before the anti-draft crisis, a Republican Fascist youth group had already provoked strikes and student brawls, and members of other cells had scrawled graffiti and engaged in sabotage.[67] Republican Fascist agents parachuted into Sicily over the autumn and winter of 1944–1945 attempted to make contact with such elements and they were frequently cited as a factor in inciting public discontent. The *Carabinieri* in Ragusa complained about the role of 'enemy agents' and described Comiso, Vittoria and Giarratana as 'nests of sedition' where well-armed rebels had been stirred up by seditious elements. Although Italian military intelligence failed to prove a concrete link between Sicilian insurgents and the Republican Fascist underground, officers suggested that the latter had established ties to the Sicilian separatist movement, particularly since ex-Fascist *Gerarchi* felt that a declaration of Sicilian independence would protect them from anti-Fascist purge and restitution measures radiating from Rome. Signs praising Mussolini and Hitler were frequently seen in separatist processions.[68]

Anti-draft disturbances in Sicily over the autumn and winter of 1944–1945 approached the level of a general revolt. Agitators roused crowds by arguing that it was folly to fight for occupying powers that were about to impose a harsh peace agreement upon Italy and would probably strip the country of its colonies and of north-eastern borderlands. Signs hoisted at the University of Palermo on 12 December read 'no more arms, but bread and peace'; a manifesto circulated in Catania on 14 December accused a 'cowardly monarch' of fighting other people's wars so that he could keep his throne. Graffiti in Palermo read '*Duce, Duce, Duce, ritorna!*' and posters threatened to punish 'traitors' who agreed to serve in the army. Republican Fascist sympathisers were also assured that the Allies were in headlong retreat on the Western Front, and that the 'Social Republic' would soon be in a position to help southern rebels. 'Republican Italy is about to launch an effort to liberate [the south]', announced the '*Gruppo* B. Fratelli' of the PFR, which was based in Palermo. 'Do everything you can to aid our forces… Young men, don't report for induction.'

The sense of outrage was not confined to rhetoric: in Palermo, violent riots in October 1944 led to the deaths of twenty-nine people after Italian troops opened fire on a crowd. At Catania, the entire town was overrun by a mob that burned government buildings, destroyed public records, firebombed a number of Italian military vehicles and disarmed soldiers and *Carabinieri* officers. One rioter was killed and a dozen people were wounded. In Agrigento Province a full-scale rebellion broke out in January 1945, resulting in the deaths of at least thirty-six people, and in Giarratana an Italian officer was killed and ten more soldiers went missing. Yet another uprising at the village of Palazzo-Adriano, in the southern part of Palermo Province, necessitated the deployment of government troops and armoured cars. Watching from vantage points in the north, the Germans and their Italian friends could not have been more pleased, particularly since a few of the rebels signalled their affiliation with the Fascist Republic.[69]

As the SD's newfangled political notions were increasingly interjected into the discourse on guerrilla warfare, the Germans and Republican Fascists decided that it would also be good idea to subvert the anti-fascist resistance groups that had taken shape in the northern section of Italy. Behind German lines, Fascist volunteers were recruited to infiltrate the underground parties on the centre and left of the political spectrum, and agents were encouraged to establish 'anti-Fascist' credentials so that they would later be in a position to cause dissension within the organisations that they had penetrated. According to Hügel, the war ended before such activity could be planned in detail, although he did deploy a special agent, Kurt Caesar, who infiltrated a communist Partisan group in the Milan–Como region.[70] Since the Republican Fascists were eager to expand such projects, they created a special group, 'Organizzazione V', in order to penetrate partisan bands with agents, obtain arms, and eventually keep these weapons once the Allies arrived. The 'V' organisation recruited members from the Republican Army and the Black Brigades, and it had its headquarters in the old Fascist stronghold of Cremona, with regional branches in Turin, Milan-Novara and Ferrara. There were arms dumps and training facilities at the latter location. Volunteers left Milan for the Alpine hills above Como and Varese, and in May 1945 such elements were reported to be causing trouble and refusing to disarm. By April 1945 a number of 'white partisans' in the north-western and north-eastern corners of Italy had also entered into negotiations with the Republican Fascists, particularly with Xth Flottiglia MAS, in order to oppose French and Yugoslav irredentism.[71]

As was usually the case with the Germans, there was no effort to build a single stay-behind organisation to function in case of a German withdrawal from northern Italy. Rather each body associated with Skorzeny's network launched its own separate effort.

The Section S boss, Otto Begus, launched Operation 'Zypresse' (perhaps because the cypress, the quintessential tree of Mediterranean Europe, is a symbol of durability). The unit was run from the SD headquarters near the Piazza Bra in Verona, which actually had a plaque on its door marked 'Zypresse'. Although Begus had cut his teeth in Greece, he was better suited to operations in Italy, being a native South Tyrolean and a veteran of the Italian Army. However, since Begus continued to play the role of the bibulous night owl, detailed work was done by his staff. Begus manned 'Zypresse' with volunteers from the Xth Flottiglia MAS, although as noted, he also accepted recruits from the MGIR, mostly men in whom Section B had no interest and were thus sent on to Verona. Agents were prepared for missions in a small training camp near Verona, where occasional assistance was rendered by Hügel (although relations between Begus and Hügel were strained). Further help was provided by seven instructors sent to Italy by Jagdverband Mitte. The school was supposed to be run jointly with local elements of Mil D, but as Hügel later recalled, FAK 211 and Operation 'Zypresse' fought constantly over which organisation was subordinate to the other. 'Zypresse' ran saboteurs into Allied-occupied territory and also fielded eight stay-behind cells in the Po Valley, each consisting of two to three men. These cells were bereft of radio equipment but may have had access to transmitters belonging to the 'Ida-Netz'. Begus also worked with Lieutenant-Colonel Maurizio Bassi, an Italian air force officer who organised Republican Fascist propaganda for southern Italy and was eager to drop saboteurs and leaflets into Allied-occupied territory.

Begus developed several clever subterfuges, although these schemes typically ended in failure. One such project involved the establishment of a printing press that could produce not only forged documents, but currency notes of the sort used by the southern regime. This counterfeit money could then be supplied to agents or used to undercut the financial stability of the royal government as it extended its authority northwards.

To run this operation, the Germans turned to Professor Polidoro Benveduti, a librarian and archivist who was an expert in reproduction techniques and document verification. Unfortunately for Begus, Benveduti was a poor choice. German and Fascist Republican officials lied to him in order to ensure his participation, telling him that he would have time to indulge his own research in a modern laboratory, but when he learned of the real purpose of 'Zypresse', he grew wary. Thus began nearly a year's worth of stonewalling and foot dragging, as Benveduti lurched from one technical 'problem' to another, facilitated by German demands that he constantly shift the location of his print works, which allowed him to claim a steady series of difficulties. In July 1944, he assembled a small team and was sent to Como, where he claimed that his printing machinery was incomplete and that parts had been 'lost'. When told by the SD that his facility would be relocated to Germany, he protested and was able to get the latter to agree to a location in the South Tyrol. In October 1944, his team was moved to Brixen and in December to Ostisei, although he claimed that some of his equipment had been stolen in transit. He then went to Milan in order to purchase replacement material and chemicals, but upon his return, he observed that the chemicals were inferior and consequently were of little value. By April 1945, his machinery had been mounted and was ready to operate, but the press' electric motors would not work without transformers. Begus, suspicious and annoyed, told Benveduti that he bore full responsibility for any future mishaps. By this point, however, Benveduti and his principal assistant, a former Partisan officer named Amilcare Zelioli, were stockpiling arms and had entered into contact with the patriot resistance. When the retreating Germans eventually ordered the printing press destroyed, Benveduti and Zerioli dismantled the machinery and hid parts for future recovery.

Another 'Zypresse' project was Operation 'Andreas', which was launched in the summer of 1944 and was built around Andreas Zolyomy, a charismatic Hungarian-Jewish water polo champion. Zolyomy had originally worked for Italian military intelligence and later became an agent of the SD. Begus employed him on a special task in Milan, with a local SD officer, Guido Zimmer, acting as liaison. The plan was to form a small 'communist' underground that could be used to infiltrate the Italian Communist Party and could also be employed against the Allies when they reached northern Italy. Zolyomy was suitable for such a mission because he had a close relationship with the Marini family, which owned a Milanese pharmaceuticals company that provided medical supplies to anti-fascist Partisans. After spending weeks in the library, reading about communism, Zolyomy began distributing recruitment leaflets in the vicinity of Corso Sempione. Eventually, he gathered a group of 26 members who thought that they had joined a communist organisation and who included a locally renowned veteran of the International Brigades. Begus provided hand grenades, twenty rifles and machine pistols and over 500 pounds of dynamite, and Zimmer tried to get the Verona headquarters to supply propaganda material. Meanwhile, Zolyomy began toying with the ideological preconceptions of his followers, contending that Italian communism was 'too Christian', and that there was room for another creed, a line of argument that was supposed to open a door to the right, perhaps to the MGIR.

It was all for nought. In December 1944, MGIR boss Ferreri reported to Zimmer that one of his contacts in the 'white' underground had exposed Zolyomy as an informer who was keeping anti-fascist Partisans abreast of goings-on in the SD. Circumstantial evidence also accumulated – Zolyomy, for instance, suddenly no longer needed German stipends – and when Zimmer teased him with the suggestion the Germans and British should be fighting on the same side, he (Zolyomy) revealed that he had friends who might be able to facilitate the creation of such an alliance. Convinced that Zolyomy was playing a double game, Zimmer had him arrested on 2 January 1945, although he was subsequently released on the condition that he remain in contact with the German authorities. Under suspicion and in fear for his life, Zolyomy went into hiding in February 1945.

Jagdeinsatz Italien's stay-behind project was organised by one of the unit's companies in north-eastern Italy, *Jagdkommando* 'Sölder', and was run in coordination with Republican Fascist minister Host Venturi. In fact, the entire network was called 'Moretti', after Venturi's codename. *Hauptmann* Sölder is on record in late 1944 enlisting Italian policemen and members of the Black Brigades for this venture, although in recruiting policemen he ran into the ubiquitous Herbert Kappler, now liaison officer with Mussolini's secret police. Ever the vigilant anti-Semite, Kappler blocked the transfers because one of the personnel requested – a line-tapping expert – was an Italian Jew. It was only after Sölder's brother appealed to Hügel that the *Jagdkommando* received the men it wanted (minus the Jewish telecommunications specialist). It is likely that a Republican Fascist cell set up in Bologna by *Federale* Torri was part of 'Moretti', particularly since this group got its radio equipment from the SD-*Ausland*.

Another of *Italien's* sub-units, *Jagdkommando* Kieswetter, developed elaborate plans for blowing up bridges across the Po after the area had been occupied by the Allies, but this was apparently a separate enterprise from 'Moretti'. *Obersturmführer* Kieswetter and his unit were attached to the Tenth Army in December 1944.[72]

Finally, mention must be made of FAK 211's stay-behind effort, which was launched in September 1944 and was intended to leave wireless equipped cells all over northern Italy for the combined purposes of sabotage, subversion and espionage. Agents were signed up by a Milan recruiting office, whose most dynamic figure was Hamburg businessman Reinhard Reme, a figure with longstanding commercial contacts in Milan. Reme arranged for his operatives to be trained at *Sonderkommando* 'Magnus' and since they were members of the Italian Republican armed forces, he secured their release papers from Marshal Graziani's staff. Much of the subsequent effort was organised through an enterprise of *Trupp* 255 called the 'Gibim Prodotti Corporation', based in Milan. The word 'Gibim' was a play on the German term '*Gib ihm*' ('give it to 'em'). The Gibim Corporation was disguised as a cosmetics firm, but in reality it distributed sabotage material and provided twenty-two agents with cover as company salesmen. All these operatives had been recruited from a Republican Fascist anti-aircraft unit at Monza. FAK 211's commander, *Major* von Uslar, intended to leave the Gibim company in Milan during a prospective German retreat through northern Italy, whence it would sabotage road and rail traffic between Milan and Genoa. The unit was commanded by Amedeo Torres and Guido Belloni.

Like *Jagdeinsatz Italien*, FAK 211 made plans to destroy a number of railway bridges over the Po and Ticino rivers, a project codenamed '*Nachtigall*'. Not only were FAK troops responsible for the tactical destruction of these bridges as the *Wehrmacht* retreated, but their demolitions expert, *Leutnant* Hubert Güldenpfennig, laid supply caches near the bridges so that they could be blown again, even after the Allies had repaired them. About eighty agents were also equipped with floating mines and sent to live in the small towns along the Po. Their job was to blow up Allied pontoon bridges. After months of living in quiet country villages, however, many of these operatives began stealing from the natives and otherwise disturbing the peace, which in turn necessitated their recall.[73]

Although the Germans put much time and effort into their Lombard stay-behind networks, they performed no better than their pluckless southern and central Italian antecedents. The Germans faced the usual technical difficulties, such as getting sufficient equipment or procuring wireless sets that could beam a signal over mountainous terrain. As well, training of stay-behind operatives was undertaken hastily and was hindered by inevitable language difficulties. Despite a rigorous screening process, the recruits do not appear to have been qualitatively better than the self-interested or unintelligent characters who had manned the network's precursors. By the winter and spring of 1945, some of the agents had started black market activities with their operating funds or had otherwise got into trouble with the police. Others spoke to outsiders about the nature of their work — two trainees at the Longone school were reportedly sent to concentration camps in Germany after they had become too talkative — or they simply abandoned their assignments. Such was the case with a husband-and-wife pair in Bologna, who happily accepted their pay and reported to the local *Platzkommando* over the winter of 1944–1945, although they had no intention of making use of their explosives after the Allies arrived in the city. A few volunteers deserted to the anti-fascist Partisans, which naturally imperilled the security of the stay-behind groups.

Of course, even had the networks suffered from none of these problems, they still would have been unable to rise above the set of circumstances surrounding the German retreat in northern Italy, which occurred at the same time as Berlin was overrun and the Third Reich had begun to crumble. All stay-behind operations were predicated on the assumption that German and Republican Fascist forces would withdraw into the Alpine Redoubt and provide resisters with a degree of external control, but this sequence of events never occurred.[74] Rather, the German armies in Italy capitulated on 2 May 1945 and the Republican Fascist movement disintegrated as the party's hierarchs made a dash for a redoubt in the Val Tellina, where they expected to make a last stand.[75] Mussolini and Pavolini were both caught and executed by communist Partisans.

There were several solely Italian efforts to set up stay-behind cells, including initiatives by the Black Brigades and Xth *Flottiglia* MAS, although operations by the latter, which Borghese assigned to Mario Rossi, also had an anti-German caste and were meant to hinder scorched earth measures.[76] Ominously, the Rossi network established cosy relations with certain non-communist resistance groups, which reflected its desire to become the focal point for an anti-communist bloc. Fifth Army CIC saw Xth MAS agents as the most dangerous of neo-Fascist remnants because they were a highly respected elite and had a potentially popular programme of anti-communist activism, thus containing 'all the seeds of a new fascism in Italy'. Indeed, Pavolini's *franchi tiratori* sniped in Turin and small Republican Fascist bands fled to the Alpine foothills,[77] but it was the remnants of Xth MAS who were worth watching. The Rossi stay-behind groups were broken up in May and June 1945, although the men behind such units had considerable potential for action, especially if they avoided tipping their hands through open resistance or terrorism. By 1946, fragments of Xth MAS were trying to reorganise and there is no doubt that they had a conducive environment. One Allied report noted:

> there are some 50,000 ex-fascists in northern Italy who are unable to find employment owing to their political past, and many of whom are unable to return to their homes for fear of partisan vengeance... Their main activities probably consist of clandestine meetings at which the name of Duce is repeated ad nauseam and burning deeds of heroism are planned. Little results beyond writing on walls...

The Allies felt that their security measures, combined with the force of Italian opinion, held these elements in check, but they worried about the possibility of a charismatic leader coalescing such discontented masses.[78] Fortunately, Borghese was in confinement during the early post-war period, although he did re-emerge in the late 1940s, forming anti-communist 'action groups' that played a violent role in the disputed border town of Trieste, fighting Yugoslav irredentism. Most importantly, he helped lead the neo-Fascist *Movimento Sociale Italiano* (MSI), which became a considerable presence on the Italian political landscape and served as the heir, if not the lineal descendant, of the Xth MAS stay-behind network.[79]

THE TABLES TURNED

Conventional wisdom suggests that France was an Allied nation during the Second World War – De Gaulle and the *Résistance* (rather than Pétain and Vichy) represented the country's real character – and that as a logical consequence of this fact, German attempts to subvert liberated France were doomed to ignominious failure. While there is undoubtedly much truth in this depiction, the reality was somewhat grainier than a picture painted in such broad strokes would suggest. There is no doubt that people in northern France welcomed the Allies with great acclaim; Allied reports in late August and early September 1944 speak of 'flowers, wine, kisses and embraces'.[80] The reception, however, was not so positive in Normandy (which suffered horrendous damage because of heavy fighting), nor in western France (where Catholic conservatives had mixed feelings about the collapse of Pétainism), nor in southern France (where the Nazi occupation had not been as long or as dense as in the north), nor in Alsace-Lorraine (where part of the population was ethnically related to the occupiers and had been subjected to pervasive Germanification measures). There were also temporal limits to the positive response accorded to the Allies. According to Jefferson Caffrey, the US ambassador, 'American popularity zoomed to an all-time high in France for one month preceding and one month following the liberation of Paris', although he was forced to concede that by the turn of 1944–1945, 'the emotional glow of liberation has dimmed'.[81]

There were several components to this post-liberation neurosis. First, the Americans failed to guarantee food supplies any more effectively than the Germans. Foodstuffs ran so short that city-dwellers found themselves on the brink of starvation and food riots broke out in towns such as Nancy. Vichyite and French fascist exiles in Germany were only too happy to provide demonstrators with their slogans: 'Liberation', they proclaimed, 'is famine'.[82] Resentment of requisitioning also dampened French enthusiasm for the Allies, as did a perception that Americans 'don't know the Germans' and were not fighting hard enough during the mid-winter German offensives in Belgium and Alsace. These last-minute German blows prompted 'a very violent reaction' in public opinion, and for a short time French civilians began to recalculate their expectations of Allied victory. As for the deportment of the De Gaulle government, many French critics thought that it was too focussed on restoring external 'grandeur', particularly at the expense of domestic priorities, while others believed that the round of extensive purges that had occurred – both summary and judicial – were either too light or too severe.[83]

The purges, or '*épuration*', played a special role in energising an anti-Gaullist and anti-communist backlash, particular since the process had the unfortunate effect of encouraging a flight to the *Maquis* by implicated right-wingers. The summary nature of the early purges was enough to terrorise anyone with reason to feel guilty, although many people who were arrested were eventually released if no specific charges could be brought against them. In southern France, prefects, mayors and officers of the French Forces of the Interior (FFI) complained about the 'cavalier' approach of the *Services de Sécurité Militaire*, which often released people arrested by the French *Résistance*, and there were particular gripes about acquittals of high profile collaborators, such as the chief of the Corsican PPF, who was released amid warnings about 'a reinforcement of the Fifth Column'. Indeed, although the authorities were holding 32,000 internees by the end of 1944, there were a number of dangerous men and women still roaming loose, and of this number a small percentage had begun to arm themselves for resistance to the new order, or at least to mount opposition to the more anarchic elements of the French *Résistance*, which were still active. One CIC observer noted that the tables had turned: 'Before the Germans had the Gestapo; the French had the Maquis. Now the French have the Gestapo and the Germans have the Maquis.'[84]

Actually, there were a few pro-German bands in the *Maquis* even before D-Day. The Germans and Vichyite security forces had already launched operations to penetrate anti-German guerrilla groups and in one of the strongholds of the 'Red *Maquis*', the Dauphiné-Savoy region, former Vichy minister Jacques Chavalier had formed a 'secret organisation' that was charged with constituting a counter-*Maquis* and stopping 'brigandry'.[85] Certainly such bands had already formed in Corsica, which had been freed of Axis control in the autumn of 1943. American officers in the south-western corner of the island reported in the spring of 1944 that 'former collaborationists are hiding in the maquis and may be receiving aid from local sympathisers or feudal dependents of wealthy fascist-minded Corsican families'; such elements were suspected of signalling *Luftwaffe* aircraft. Four SS men, including one of Skorzeny's raiders, were captured on Corsica in November 1943.

After the liberation of mainland France, the size of the collaborationist *Maquis* increased as the virulence of the purge prompted right-wingers to seek refuge in the woods and hills, and a few bypassed German troops also swore to keep fighting. By November 1944, police reports from the Pyrenees suggested that fugitive groups of Vichyite security troops – *Miliciens* – were gathering in the hills and receiving help from Spain, a process that elicited a stiff French complaint about the 'large-scale smuggling of arms' to pro-German *Maquisards* along the Bidasoa river. Police investigations in the Loire *département* suggested the same type of phenomenon, citing a number of farms that had been put to flame, and in the Haute-Loire, the prefect noted the presence of a band of *Miliciens*, French fascists and escaped German POWs, which was receiving supplies parachuted by the *Luftwaffe*. *Comités Départementaux de la Libération* also reported that German arms and food were being dropped to former collaborators in a forest near Clamecy and that a *Maquis* of *Miliciens* and ex-Gestapo agents was forming in the Haute-Savoie. Regional leaders of the movement included Blaise Agostini, former intendant of the LVF in the Haute-Savoie, and Maurice Durame, a Rouen lawyer who was arrested by the French around the turn of 1944–1945. Initially, both advocates and opponents of the movement called it the 'White *Maquis*', a term that evoked memories of Bourbon counter-revolution, although French fascists eventually preferred to distinguish the bands by reference to the colour of their shirts – that is, 'Blue *Maquis*' – while the opponents of the bands developed the more derogatory appellation of 'Brown *Maquis*', which linked the bands with the shirt colour of the hated Nazis.[86]

In addition to the White *Maquis*, there were a number of urban resistance cells scattered across France. These were typically small organisations that were covered by the generic term 'Fifth Column', which French men and women remembered from the days of the great subversion panic in May–June 1940. In the Pyrenean town of Tarbes, for instance, the local *Épuration* Commission uncovered a group of five conspirators, led by a seminarian and including a gendarmerie officer. This group was preparing to attack prominent militants of the French *Résistance*.[87] At Lille, police arrested members of a small movement of former collaborators who had been circulating leaflets defending the policies of Marshal Pétain. The moving spirit of this group was Edmond Duhamel, one-time local chief of the *Parti Social Français*, and the band was of some interest to the Vichyite exiles in Germany, who were gratified to learn that anti-Gaullist and anti-communist resistance was spreading into the north of the country.[88]

The White *Maquis* and the Fifth Column were active in trying to destabilise the new order, especially in southern France. From September 1944 to February 1945, there were nearly thirty raids upon militia barracks, police stations, post offices and prisons, usually by carloads of desperados who raked the installations with gunfire. These attacks left at least thirty-six people dead and fifty wounded, mostly victims of an explosion at a militia cantonment in the Vaucluse.[89] There were also bombings of barracks and gendarmerie posts at Aix-les-Bains, Castres and Valence, all of which resulted in casualties.[90] In Corsica, American communication lines were cut and there were cases of sabotage against Allied aircraft; a B-17 based at Ajaccio had to make a forced landing after a charge exploded when the plane was airborne, and at Calvi airfield sugar was discovered in the gas tanks of several Spitfire fighters.[91] In the Albertville region of Savoy, wire-cutting and signalling to nearby German artillery gunners was blamed partly on ethnic Italians.[92]

Aside from the existence of violence-prone groups and individuals, another advantage for a German sabotage campaign consisted of the western and northern bases of Royan, La Rochelle, St Nazaire, Lorient and Dunkirk. The Germans also retained a small piece of occupied Britain in the form of the Channel Islands. Even after the *Wehrmacht* was chased to the German frontier, these 'Atlantic Fortresses' remained intact against pressure from weak American and Free French forces attempting to contain their garrisons. From such strong points, the Germans retained a capacity to raid the surrounding regions: as late as March 1945, 200 commandos briefly overran the Norman port of Granville, liberating fifty-five German POWs and destroying harbour facilities and supply ships, and on the night of 4–5 April, a force of eighteen saboteurs attacked the coastal town of Dielette, being put ashore in rubber rafts. Both assault groups were dispatched from the Channel Islands and were under the command of the fanatic Vice-Admiral Hüffmeier.[93]

The 'Atlantic Fortresses' also served as starting points for agents on intelligence and sabotage operations, and there is evidence that each of the pockets were employed for such purposes. In the early autumn of 1944, the Germans used the Crozon Peninsula as a base to harass the Allies at Châteaulin, and attacks in this area were attributed to Breton nationalists working with the Germans. By the beginning of 1945, the Germans were excited about the prospect of using the Atlantic bases to restart dormant agent networks, a project that Mil B described as 'a task of extreme importance for the immediate future' and towards which it was collaborating with Mil D, Mil F and naval special forces. French agents working on the scheme suggested reviving PPF groups and attempting sabotage, although Mil B forbade any of its radio agents from taking part in active resistance. A German naval officer, Friedrich Kaulen, was sent to the Gironde pocket in March 1945 in order to oversee the operation, although he was subsequently lured into Allied-held territory by a contact serving as a double agent for the Americans. On 6 April, Kaulen and two other German officers were ambushed and killed near Pauillac, which naturally put a damper upon the project.[94]

One final asset for a prospective German sabotage campaign consisted of the 20,000 Vichyites and French fascists who in the late summer and early autumn of 1944 descended upon Germany, where they organised an émigré regime, still with Pétain, now a virtual prisoner, at its apex. In early September, the Germans authorised Fernand de Brinon to form a 'Governmental Delegation' – later called a 'Governmental Commission' – and to concentrate Vichyite émigré forces in south-western Germany. It was an embarrassment that Pétain would not acknowledge the new arrangement, but the aged *Maréchal* was brought to the exile capital at Sigmaringen and his name was used to issue decrees. Fittingly, he was based in a 'fairytale' castle that provided the perfect environment for his regime's optimistic fantasies. The Vichyites also organised a radio outlet called '*Ici la France*', which broadcast from a station near Stuttgart.[95] This transmitter found a certain audience in France, at least among the curious.[96]

The main strike force of the 'Governmental Commission' was Vichy's one-time counter-insurgency service, the *Milice*, which had been formed in 1943 and was involved in heavy fighting against the French *Résistance*. In several mad dashes in August and September 1944, nearly 10,000 *Miliciens* and their dependents succeeded in reaching Germany. Of this group, half were subsequently deployed as labour, several thousand were sent to the SS 'Charlemagne' Division, and nearly 1,500 were retained as a personal army by Joseph Darnand, the chief of the organisation. Darnand was a veteran of the French Army and during the 1930s had served as head of the Nice chapter of the Cagoule, a gang of fascist terrorists and bombers who had tried to destabilise the Third Republic. As Vichy's interior minister and head of the regime's shock troops, Darnand was the

Vichyite equivalent of Himmler, and as such he was charged with forming a pro-German resistance movement.

In order to accomplish this task, Darnand held a number of conferences with French and German advisors and in October 1944 he announced the formation of a special service called the '*Organisation Technique*' (OT), which consisted of 150 to 250 volunteers drawn from Darnand's retinue. German liaison was maintained by *Leutnant* Schubert, and later *Hauptmann* Kurrer, whose office was codenamed *Stelle* 'Gunther'. Supreme command of the OT was assigned to the former director of Vichy police, Jean Degans – another one-time member of the Cagoule – while day-to-day control was exercised by the OT's training chief, Jean Filliol, a small wiry man with an Adolf Hitler moustache, an ever-present pipe and a crippled right hand that he kept gloved. Filliol was also a former Cagoulard. When charged with his new task, Filliol announced his intention to train sixty parachutists, with another one hundred to come later, and he sent a telegram to Skorzeny requesting help. Within several weeks, he had set up headquarters at Wilflingen, in the Sigmaringen district, and he had also organised three training camps – Hausen, Wald and Mengen – in the same vicinity. The training regime at Hausen, the sabotage school, included courses in reconnaissance, map reading and the use of explosives, although SD advisors complained that the discourse at all three camps was mainly political.

Morale in the OT was poor, particularly since some of the activists fancied themselves anti-German nationalists, although the prospect of surrendering to the ascendant Gaullists seemed sure to result in execution or a prolonged prison sentence at hard labour. Compliance with OT rules and objectives was also enforced by the Gestapo, which sent recalcitrants to concentration camps; one reluctant parachutist was threatened with death unless he made his jump.[97] Because the *Milice* resented being seen as a simple instrument of the Germans, and because Skorzeny was hoping to heighten its enthusiasm,[98] it was allowed to run a number of independent operations aimed at provoking right-wing resistance in France. Four three-man groups of agents from the OT's sabotage and propaganda section were parachuted behind enemy lines in early 1945, two on 6 January (in south-western France) and two on 9 February (in the northern part of the country). The members of these groups were equipped with wireless transmitters, small arms, sabotage material and large amounts of currency. The groups deployed on 9 February were dropped in PAGs and they had a small printing press and copies of a tract called '*Frère Scout*', which pointed to an attempt to infiltrate the French scouting movement. The duty of the groups was to establish contact with Vichyite sympathisers, particularly in Paris, as well as spotting future drop zones for parachutists and sabotaging targets specified by German or OT controllers. Members of the two later groups were charged with ascertaining the whereabouts of their predecessors and they were supposed to make contact with Filliol's agents in Spain, establishing a 'chain' of contacts across the frontier near Perpignan. Although some of the parachutists briefly remained in contact, they did little to carry out their assigned tasks or to communicate with their radio contacts in Germany. After a few months, most were tracked down and arrested; one committed suicide after he was apprehended on 29 March 1945. More misfortune struck when eighteen *Milicien* agents headed for Paris were killed in an air crash just after take-off. Only two *Luftwaffe* crew members managed to crawl from the wreckage.

One of the chief problems for the parachutists was that there was no ground organisation to welcome them back to France and lend support. All the OT could provide were lists of likely sympathisers, plus the assurance that if the parachutists got in trouble, they could seek the help of '20,000 pro-German *Maquisards*' reputed to be operating in the Castellane district of the Basse-Alpes. Eventually Filliol conceded that parachutists were facing 'reception difficulties' and that it might be a good idea to land them in La Rochelle and infiltrate them into Allied-held territory.[99] It is unlikely, however, that there was sufficient time for this scheme to unfold.

One peculiarity of the German effort to subvert liberated France is that the SS and Foreign Office did not assign responsibilities for raising manpower solely to the pro-German exile regime in Sigmaringen. Rather, they also looked to an independent force in the form of the stridently fascist *Parti Populaire Français*, led by Jacques Doriot. A 47-year-old ex-communist, Doriot cared little for the legality of the de Brinon government, thinking it too conservative, and he was sometimes wont to say that he shared more with the militants of the French *Résistance* than with the 'defrocked collaborators' of Vichy and Sigmaringen. As was the case with Stefan Bandera and Valerio Borghese, Himmler and Kaltenbrunner were impressed by Doriot's fiery – albeit unorthodox – activism, and in the *Reichsführer*'s September 16 order activating various pro-German resistance movements, Doriot was specifically mentioned, along with Darnand, as the future nucleus of an underground in France. Since Doriot would not acknowledge the authority of the regime at Sigmaringen, Ribbentrop tried to prevent political fragmentation by arguing that Doriot ought to focus his efforts on liberated France, specifically by forming a 'nationalist *Maquis*'. For this purpose he would be allowed to form a 'Liberation Committee', which would come under Pétain's suzerainty in only loose fashion and would be empowered to pool the resources of the French fascist parties. This proposal interested Doriot because he saw the suggested committee as the cornerstone of a 'revolutionary exile regime'.

This much-touted body was formed in January 1945 as the *Comité de Libération Française* (CLF), and it immediately issued a call for armed opposition much more insistent than any previous appeal by the 'Governmental Commission'. Doriot talked about uniting the White *Maquis* and Fifth Column under a single banner, and he boasted of leading a 'liberation struggle' for 'a united Europe capable of resisting Bolshevism and Anglo-American imperialism'. Not surprisingly, enemies of the PPF in the French émigré community argued that the CLF was really just the Doriotiste party in glorified form. Although its creation weakened the standing of the 'Governmental Commission', even De Brinon and Darnand eventually gave grudging nods of approval by subscribing to the committee's charter.[100]

Just as Doriot had managed to crawl to the top of the émigré heap, he was killed when his staff car was strafed by hostile aircraft near Mengen. The Germans announced that Doriot was the victim of Allied 'aerial gangsters', but the identity of the perpetrators – it could also have been the *Milice* or the SS – has never become clear.[101] Doriot was replaced by the secretary-general of the CLF, Lucien Estève, a French Tunisian who had earlier led a PPF-dominated liberation committee for French North Africa.[102]

Since Doriot wanted little to do with Sigmaringen, he developed a separate infrastructure in south-western Germany. He initially established his headquarters at

Landau, near Neustadt, and later shifted his base to a castle on the island of Mainau in Lake Constance. Like the 'Governmental Commission', the PPF organised its own wireless transmitter, 'Radio Patrie', which beamed from atop the mountain height of Bad Morgentheim in Württemberg. This station described alleged French suffering under 'American occupation' and its theme song, played by Jean Hérold-Paquis, was 'Libère-toi, France, libère-toi!'[103]

The PPF had a vigorous intelligence service called the 'appareil secret', which was formed in 1941 and came under the control of the party's leader in Lyon, Albert Beugras. The 'appareil secret' cut its teeth on organising resistance to the American and British forces in North Africa, even to the extent of using its Marseilles mob contacts in an attempt to peddle narcotics behind Allied lines.[104] When the possibility of an Allied invasion of the metropole began to loom, the PPF proved willing to organise opposition. By mid-1943, the SD had set up a camp at Château de Vaucelles, north of Paris, in order to train PPF agents for North Africa, but also to prepare personnel for infiltration of the French Résistance and for stay-behind tasks in case of Allied landings. The German liaison officer at this facility was Roland Nosek, a 38-year-old Sipo man who had a personal friendship with Doriot and directed huge sums of money into PPF coffers.[105]

Once 5,000 PPF men and their dependents descended upon Germany, demoralised and bedraggled by their ejection from their homeland, they provided recruits for an expanded version of the 'appareil secret'. As early as September 1944, Beugras was whispering about the need for a partisan war. 'It was a question', Hérold-Paquis later recalled, 'of schools, illegal work, clandestine parties, parachutages. It all had an aftertaste of civil war, a whiff of adventure that seduced the young...' Within weeks, a number of facilities had been organised, including a training camp for leaders near Wiesbaden and special schools at Reutlingen and Mainau. Doriot's friend Nosek was appointed as German liaison officer and was given a small staff dubbed 'Sonderkommando Konstanz'. By early November 1944, at least 110 men and women were being readied for action and it is possible that as many as a thousand were trained by the end of the war.[106] Like the Miliciens, PPF volunteers resented designation as German agents, arguing that they were accepting help from an ally in a joint crusade against communism.[107]

Since the PPF had left several underground groups in France, one of the tasks of the Beugras organisation was to re-establish contact with these formations. A number of party officials, including the general secretary and propaganda chief of its youth wing, had been ordered to remain in liberated Paris, where they were supposed to disperse propaganda, execute clandestine decrees and maintain communications with Germany. Several members of the former 'Radio Paris' staff had been given the same set of tasks, forming the so-called 'Équipe à Radio Paris'. Shortly after the Allies arrived in the capital, the PPF sent twenty men to reinforce these groups, although four of these parachutists, each carrying 500,000 francs, fell into the hands of the new authorities. Despite difficult conditions, the 'Équipe à Radio Paris' gradually developed some operational capabilities and allied itself with a remnant chapter of the 'Amis du Maréchal', which numbered seventy people. One fiery pamphlet, signed 'Danton', was written by insurance salesman Jean Amadéo, the group's leader and a 31-year-old regional secretary of the PPF. Amadéo was fond of revolutionary pseudonyms and also styled himself 'Voltaire'. As well as undertaking propaganda, the '*Équipe*' collected political intelligence and made preparations for armed attacks. With the assistance of an SD radio agent, Amadéo reported to Berlin on 8 January 1945: 'Personal Doriot. Much PPF activity in Paris. [A] clandestine press [has been] organised. Assassinations [have been] carried out. [We are] requesting directives and money. Voltaire.' Since the Germans suspected a trap, they hesitated in answering, although it was later reported that Amadéo succeeded in getting arms, money and radio equipment parachuted into the Paris region. By the spring of 1945, however, informers were keeping the *Direction de la Surveillance du Territoire* (DST) au courant with developments in the '*Équipe*', and in April thirty activists were arrested, including Amadéo.[108]

Outside Paris, Saint-Quin, the PPF chief in the Morbihan, was charged with running stay-behind operations in Brittany. Contact from Germany was supposed to be maintained by the former *Inspecteur Régional PPF de Bretagne*, Bolore, who was also responsible for Breton broadcasts on Radio Morgentheim.[109] In eastern France, a group of Corsicans, the '*Équipe à Francis*', was left behind in order to terrorise the Grenoble–Lyon region. Francis, the leader of this group, was a 35-year-old resident of Lyon. The parachute school at Mainau was devoted to supporting the '*Équipe à Francis*' and in late November 1944 seven men and one woman were training at Hersbach in order to reinforce this group. The PPF also set up several stations in south-western Germany from which to smuggle volunteers through the lines, sometimes by disguising them with FFI brassards. One PPF group, the '*Équipe à Thurotte*', sent a detachment into the Besançon area in November 1944, although this band was engaged by the French authorities and suffered heavy losses. Some individuals and small units were spirited through Switzerland.[110] The Allies suspected that such groups lay behind reports on a White *Maquis* in the region controlled by the US Seventh Army.[111] There were still PPF sabotage squads working in the Lyon region during the last days of the war, run by Jean Gregoire, '*Chef de Service d'Ordre du PPF*'. In mid-May 1945, French security forces arrested Gregoire after his location was revealed by FAK 313 parachutists who had been captured and 'turned' by the French.[112]

Beugras also set up several line-crossing organisations that were supposed to maintain communications with homeland groups of the PPF. Along the Western Front the main such detachment was '*Mission Marty*', which was run by an official who had led a special PPF police brigade in Tunisia and had then served as a police intendant in Lyon. 'Marty' was comprised of fifteen PPF men, mostly former policemen and gendarmes. The organisation was formed in Strasbourg during the autumn of 1944 and established a forward base at St Die, mainly with the help of the Baron de Barry. After Allied advances in Alsace, the headquarters were re-established in Baden-Baden. The purpose of 'Marty' was to establish a chain of safe-houses and hideouts spaced at 18-mile intervals between the Vosges and Paris, as well as gathering political intelligence on the French Communist Party (PCF) and taking retaliatory steps against PPF members who had remained in France without permission. Members of 'Marty' began crossing Allied lines on 10 October and were active in Remiremont, Bruyeres and Raon l'Étape.[113]

Another group of fourty-five volunteers was sent to northern Italy as part of Operation 'Tosca', which had the same objectives as 'Marty' and was run by the stocky Corsican

Victor Barthélémy, secretary general of the PPF. 'Tosca' was aimed at strengthening elements of the White *Maquis* in the French Alps. In late 1944, the Germans spent 20,000 lire attempting to buy the services of a smuggling gang that could get 'Tosca' saboteurs across the Alps and into French territory. The first PPF agent sent through enemy lines was a prominent Marseilles militant named Maurice Lachapelle, who was supposed to infiltrate the French *Résistance* and establish a drop-box in the Sospel region. Before Lachapelle could get through the frontier zone, he stepped on a mine and was killed. One source suggests that in early February 1945, a group under Noel Bailly, a Lyon industrialist, managed to get through the mountains and reinforce the White *Maquis*.

Faced with French patrols and minefields in the Alps, the Germans began to look for alternate means of facilitating the 'Tosca' enterprise. It is possible that some of the parachutists seen floating to the ground in south-eastern France had been dispatched by the PPF, but the main strategy was to move agents to the coast and get help from German naval forces in landing them on the French coast. Two initial volunteers, both recently liberated from an Italian jail, were moved into position by a rowing boat, but they never restored contact with German lines. One had been sent to reconnoitre safe routes to the Sospel region, the second was supposed to infiltrate the PCF. In early 1945, a dozen PPF volunteers, mostly *colons* from French North Africa, were moved to San Remo and prepared for dispatch by sea into southern France. This group was led by the ex-chief of the PPF chapter in Antibes and by *Obersturmführer* von Salewinski, a duelling-scarred *Junker* and former member of the Brandenburg unit. Shortly before the end of the war, two thirds of the San Remo group deserted to Italian anti-fascist Partisans, and although von Salewinski and three others subsequently left for the Côte d'Azur in a patrol boat, the vessel's motor was damaged by a shell burst, forcing it to return to Italy. Their mission had been to use plastic explosives to blow up the headquarters of the *Sécurité Militaire* in Nice.

While 'Tosca' sounded like a good idea, bureaucratic and personal rivalries made it difficult to implement. Shortly after 'Tosca' got underway, Section B sent *Obersturmführer* Hans Sommer to organise a centre for document forgery. Sommer was an old-time Austrian Nazi who had made so much trouble after the German arrival in Paris that he had been arrested by the SD and was then dispatched to the boondocks of Marseilles, where he was allowed to organise his own private network of Cagoulard informers. Since Sommer could not get along with PPF activists, he was joined at the end of 1944 by *Sturmbannführer* Gohl, who had once been stationed at an SD outpost in Nice and was officially designated as the German liaison officer with 'Tosca'. Gohl quickly won a reputation as a quarrelsome Nazi fanatic, and he made enemies in the Mil Amt by trying to control a 'play-back' operation based on the manipulation of several Allied agents whom the Germans had captured in January 1945. No one else connected with the 'Tosca' enterprise conducted themselves any better than Gohl or Sommer. FAK 211 officers cursed their SD counterparts for trying to re-conceptualise 'Tosca' as an experiment in radical politics. Barthélémy was ready to argue with all parties equally and von Salewinski spent much of his time drinking with his adjutant, although he cut through the alcoholic fog long enough to prepare an eventual flight to Switzerland. Given this atmosphere, it is hardly surprising that the PPF agents were demoralised and concerned mainly with finding a safe place to stash money that they had looted before leaving their homeland.[114]

Apart from the *Milice* and the PPF, a third category of French exiles included the various regional autonomist and separatist parties, some members of which had aligned themselves with the Germans in order to get leverage against French republican centralists. Chief amongst these groups was the *Parti National Breton* (PNB), which modelled its organisational structure on the IRA. The PNB's moderate wing wanted regional autonomy for Brittany, but the extremists, such as paramilitary leader Celestin Laîné, wanted complete independence and did not even loosely consider themselves French. Laîné had such a radical view of Breton self-determination that he denounced the leader of the ultras, Olivier Mordrel, when the latter adhered to Doriot's CLF in February 1945.[115]

Once the prospect of Allied landings in France became a concern, the die-hard faction of the PNB pledged help to the Germans and even promised to support a pro-German *Maquis* if the group could be supplied and reinforced by air. Matters on the German side were coordinated by Section B, particularly by Sipo intelligence chief Hermann Bickler, who recruited Guy Vissault de Coëtlogon to man a Breton stay-behind desk at the Parisian branch of the Sipo. Roland Nosek also played a major role in recruiting Breton saboteurs. Meetings were held at the end of 1943 and again in June 1944, the latter being attended by *Hauptmann* Gragert, representing FAK 210. Vissault collected an assemblage of young volunteers, nearly all from the districts of St Malo and Rennes, a few of whom were sent for sabotage training in Germany. Secret arsenals were laid at Rennes, Brest and Tréguier. Vissault volunteered to lead a stay-behind sabotage and intelligence group, but unfortunately for the Germans he was captured and executed, after telling the Allies much of what he knew about German sabotage programmes.[116] It is unlikely that Vissault's cells survived, although there were subsequent reports about a transmitter operating in Tréguier.[117]

With Vissault out of the picture, the SD fell back upon Laîné and a small company of PNB gunmen, which had been formed in 1943 as a counterweight to Breton elements of the Red *Maquis*. Many of these troops reached Germany under the leadership of their chief, who received a commission as an SS officer, although his following was then scattered amongst various special detachments and facilities. Several dozen Breton nationalists joined *Jagdeinsatz Nord*, which in February 1945 issued a call for volunteers willing to be parachuted into Brittany. About twenty-five men responded and were formed into the 'Commando Bretagne', which was moved to Tiefenthal for training. Some of Laîné's men also formed a '*Kommando*' in the SD's espionage organisation, codenamed 'Walter'. Yet another fifteen men remained with Laîné at Tübingen (and later Rottenburg). Two groups were dispatched to a pair of special schools, one at Ettmannsweiler, which trained spies and saboteurs, and a second at Stetten (near Lake Constance), where radio operators were prepared for deployment. One group of Laîné's men was left stranded in St Nazaire, and on 24 February 1945 the naval high command ordered the 'fortress commandant' to provide a list of local militants in order to reinforce sabotage operations in Brittany.

A detachment from the Ettmannsweiler facility was dispatched into Brittany near the end of the war. By late April, the sabotage school had been transferred to Fürstenfeldbruck, near Munich, where eight young men were split into three teams, equipped with 80,000 francs and phoney papers identifying them as forced labourers, then told to make their way to Brittany. Seven of the boys succeeded in reaching France, although the eighth was killed during an Allied bombing raid. Before their departure, the agents' handler, *Leutnant* Schumacher, told them to maintain liaison with their German controllers, although they were given emergency instructions in case the magnitude of German defeat was so great that it disrupted communications. In this case, team members were supposed to meet on the first Sunday of each month in a small village in the Ille-et-Vilaine; Schumacher would join them if possible. The infiltrators were also informed about the location of arms and supply dumps buried by the Germans before their hasty exit from Brittany, although two of the agents were eventually swept up in a French dragnet and revealed the locations of most of these dumps. Even after the end of the war, one of the operatives attempted to retrieve arms cached near Saint-Aubin du Cormier, but he was nearly spotted by two passing gendarmes and thereafter decided to abandon his mission.[118]

While the *Milice*, the PPF and the PNB were each spinning individual webs, Section S was also trying to undercut the liberation of France. Skorzeny's main ally was Gérard Litt, a black marketeer who controlled a group of ex-Cagoulards and gangsters called the 'National French'. Litt was something of a human toad, with a corpulent frame and an oversized head, and since he was a glutton, a coward and a bloodthirsty anti-Semite, his personality was as brutish as his physical composition. He had begun working for the Paris station of the *Abwehr* in 1942, assembling an intelligence and strong-arm unit and becoming one of the Germans' most trusted informers. In 1943, he was set to work on North Africa and in the course of this task he organised the '*Comité de Libération de l'Empire*'. This activity brought Litt into close contact with *Hauptsturmführer* Doering, chief of 'Parseval'. By the beginning of 1944, the 'National French' and the 'Imperial Liberation Committee' had begun working for the SD and Litt was recommended to Section S by Doering, who was a close associate of Besekow. The ubiquitous Roland Nosek also backed Litt. In May 1944, Doering and Besekow brought Litt to Berlin, where he met Skorzeny and agreed to form an 'anti-communist' movement that would fight leftist elements of the French *Résistance* and would make preparations to serve as a stay-behind network in case of an Allied invasion, a project for which Section S had already begun to train a volunteers at the special school near The Hague. On 10 May, a conference was held in Berlin to finalise arrangements. The project was codenamed 'Jeanne', perhaps after Litt's wife, although the name was also meant to suggest 'Jeanne d'Arc', whose image and legacy French right-wingers had attempted to expropriate.

In the late spring of 1944, Litt managed to recruit an important cadre of militants by striking up an old friendship with the mayor of Margency, a small, fat and vulgar man named Raymond Richard. Litt knew Richard from the pre-war nationalist milieu and he was also aware that since 1940, Richard had been organising a nationwide network of anti-communist activists, dubbed *l'Équipe*, largely at the behest of the personal physician and secretary to Marshal Pétain, Dr Menetral. Richard had enjoyed an audience with Pétain himself in 1943 and he had become the driving force behind the '*Amis du Maréchal*', as well as a number of 'free corps' that functioned against the Red *Maquis*, sometimes under the banner of the *Milice*. Richard liked to brag, however, that unlike the *Milice*, *l'Équipe* could distinguish between communist and anti-communist resisters and adjust its policies accordingly. In fact, *l'Équipe's* liaison officer, René Poncin, had made efforts to reach out to conservative elements of the French *Résistance* in an attempt to forge an anti-communist coalition and prevent an eventual take-over by the PCF. The SD was interested in these links. In two meetings in June 1944, Richard was introduced to Doering and Besekow – Litt did the translating – and Besekow asked if Richard's anti-communist contacts in the French *Résistance* would accept German weapons for a showdown with the PCF. Richard answered in the affirmative, although he added that such elements would have to be convinced that they were not controlled by the Germans. Litt and Besekow then left for Berlin and when they returned, some eighteen days later, Richard was asked to draw up a list of contacts, a job he assigned to Poncin. Most of the names came from the files of the '*Amis du Maréchal*' (although many of these potential recruits refused to cooperate). Richard was also assured by Litt that large amounts of money were available for the support of anti-communist coalitions. He henceforth became the joint leader, with Litt, of the French element of 'Jeanne'.

June 1944 also saw the arrival of *Obersturmführer* Charles Hagedorn, who was Skorzeny's plenipotentiary for 'Jeanne' and who set up shop on the Boulevard Flandrin in Paris. An *Auslandsdeutsche* born in Singapore in 1911, Hagedorn had spent much of his life in such exotic locales as Samoa and Mexico, and he was famous throughout the SD as a sporty and sociable *bon vivant*. Unfortunately for the Germans, he was also a heavy drinker and had already embarrassed himself while serving as Manfred Pechau's deputy, and briefly as his successor, at the Hague sabotage school.[119] Despite such foibles, Skorzeny believed that the French-speaking Hagedorn could handle sensitive work in Paris, where he had experience serving in the intelligence apparatus.

In truth, Hagedorn had been a contestant in a complicated fight for power within the German security regime in France, and his background in the country was not necessarily an asset. Shortly after his arrival, he presented his credentials to the security chief of the Sipo in Paris, whose I-*Netz* agents and radio operators had already been trained at The Hague and with whom 'Jeanne' personnel were supposed to work closely, although Hagedorn was careful to point out that his '*Sonderaktion*' was an independent initiative and that he answered solely to Skorzeny and Kaltenbrunner. To understand this chilly relationship we have to know something about the history of the Sipo and Section B in France. From 1942 to 1944, these organisations were rent by a struggle between two factions which disagreed about the SD-*Ausland's* purpose. One group, controlled by the Sipo commander in Paris, Helmut Knochen, and aligned with Kaltenbrunner, saw the SD apparatus as a security machine whose role was to fight the French *Résistance*, particularly its communist elements. Knochen's first two intelligence chiefs, Nosek and Hagedorn, both belonged to this faction, as did 'Parseval' boss Doering. The rival group, aligned with Schellenberg and led by the head of Section B, Eugen Steimle, regarded the SD-*Ausland* as an intelligence organisation designed to collect information and to counter the work of enemy espionage agencies. This clique included the head of Section B's bureau for France, Heinrich Bernhard, as well as the influential Alsatian lawyer and autonomist politician, Hermann Bickler, who succeeded Nosek and Hagedorn as the head of the Sipo intelligence bureau in Paris.[120] Since the Steimle-Bernhard-Bickler faction eventually won the struggle to control the Paris Sipo, the gravitation toward Litt and Richard by Doering, Nosek and Hagedorn constituted an attempt to work around the dominant powers in Section B and exploit the Johnny-come-lately Section S as an instrument for their own struggle against communist elements of the French *Résistance*.

By the time that Hagedorn and his French collaborators began to assemble 'Jeanne', the Allies had landed in Normandy and it was thought that the *Sonderkommando*'s primary function would be to organise resistance to communist guerrillas, perhaps with the help – or at least the connivance – of the Western Allies. Litt and Richard were equipped with a headquarters in a requisitioned hotel on the Avenue MacMahon and a camp was set up near Vitry to train both Parisian volunteers and recruits from the provinces. Hagedorn sent to Berlin two of his deputies, Ludwig Nebel and Hermann Valentin, who convinced senior echelons in the RSHA that the Paris Sipo should be ordered to support 'Jeanne' without reservation and to provide all necessary arms and ammunition. While a voluminous exchange of correspondence was still flying between Berlin and Paris, 'Jeanne' either begged or stole 720 automatic weapons, 220 pistols and three automobiles. Fuel was bought on the black market or bartered with German soldiers. Eventually, 150 weapons depots were laid at inconspicuous spots and a supply of guns and ammunition was distributed to willing collaborators, sometimes supposedly reliable elements in the French *Résistance*.

'*Noeuds de résistance*' were established in twenty-five towns in northern and western France, with 'Jeanne' organisers recommending that militants set up eighteen-man action groups run by 'troikas', an arrangement in which one leader was responsible for recruitment, one for intelligence and one for armament. Group leaders were sometimes graduates of the Section S programme at The Hague. Intelligence chiefs on the 'troikas' were told to reconnoitre suitable spots for future parachute drops and to hide weapons for stay-behind *Milicien* and German snipers. They were also instructed to make preparations in case right-wingers were forced to flee urban centres and form guerrilla bands, which Litt was already calling a prospective 'White *Maquis*'. Heavy woods in the Chalons-sur-Marne district, between Paris and Nancy, were projected as future points of retreat and 500 pounds of explosives were cached in an abandoned quarry in the Forest of Montmarency. According to Skorzeny and Radl, about 150 men were armed in Brittany and Normandy and another 400 in Paris; Nebel later claimed that Litt and Richard submitted a list of 4,000 'Jeanne' members and sympathisers. In August 1944, Skorzeny sent several million francs to Hagedorn – the last courier bearing funds arrived in Paris on 20 August – and Hagedorn distributed at least 150,000 francs to some of Litt's lieutenants. The 'Jeanne' network also had a supply of radio equipment, although as was the case in other German-stay-behind efforts, such devices were not available in adequate numbers, and it was regarded as a near-disaster when two Section S wireless specialists deserted on 12 August, taking with them radios, arms and grenades, all of which were subsequently given to members of the French *Résistance* at Ile de la Jatte.

Despite much frenetic activity, the 'Jeanne' programme was crippled by lack of adequate time to prepare for the Allied advance. Leaders could not fully activate the cells in Brittany before they were cut off, and a mission to eastern France was cancelled. This trip by Martin and Litt had been intended to cultivate support from the powerful regional chief of the *Milice*, Jacques de Bernonville. There were other problems too. Not all French anti-communists were willing to accept arms from the Germans, even indirectly. At Tours, for instance, the local president of the LVF, an intended recipient of 'Jeanne' supplies, refused delivery. The same thing happened at Rouen and Armentiers. Richard warned the Germans not to distribute arms themselves and not to meet directly with participants in the programme; he pressed this point in a tense meeting in early August with Hagedorn, Besekow and Litt. Richard was also dismayed to find Besekow trying to distribute sabotage equipment and he was mortified when Hagedorn gave his intelligence chief a number of pamphlets with information on how to identify Allied units and material, presumably so that intelligence could be provided to the Germans. Such actions strayed far from what Richard saw as the essential purpose of 'Jeanne': the distribution of arms in order to fight communism.

Not surprisingly, 'Jeanne' experienced a spectacular failure. Not one of the radio posts reported to its German controllers, nor did any of the assigned couriers return to German lines. When Hagedorn tried to assemble activists in Paris during mid-August, he could scrape together only a dozen die-hards. Many of the remaining recruits had deserted, taking with them their arms and money. Besekow was critical of the fact that German weapons and funds had been distributed to no apparent effect, but Hagedorn responded that he lacked an adequate radio network and that at crucial junctures there were no instructions from Berlin about how to deal with an extremely difficult situation.

On 12 August, the 'Jeanne' command structure began to evacuate Paris for Belfort, a process completed nine days later, when a final convoy of vehicles left the French capital. Hagedorn, Nebel, Valentin and Litt all fled as the Allies advanced, but Richard elected to remain, even though Litt encouraged him to come to Belfort. When it became clear that Richard would not move, Litt gave him 100,000 francs and promised to resume communications as soon as possible. Richard subsequently told his followers to go home and await orders, but even though he remained in touch with some of his lieutenants, he never restored contact with the Germans.[121]

The main 'Jeanne' officers spent much of the autumn in Belfort, where they established links with local *Wehrmacht* commanders and began making preparations to run agents into liberated France. In fact, Hagedorn is record on 15 September asking Besekow for 'an SS officer with tactical and technical army experience for liaison with Abwehr detachments in discovering gaps in the front'.[122] Hagedorn also told several officers to establish weapons caches for the use of future agents and German guerrillas in southern Alsace, and he laid demolition depots in order to destroy a Peugeot plant at Sochaux-Montbéliard and the Alsthom-*Werke*, an electric motor factory in Belfort. When he had trouble getting phoney identity papers for his infiltrators, he robbed an engraving works and set up his own forging office. Hagedorn and his lieutenants also spent much time interrogating prisoners and collecting front intelligence. Information gathered at Besançon aided in the deployment of three SS divisions that secured the retreat of German armies coming from central France. In one instance, while Hagedorn was engaged in 'scorched earth' demolitions near the front, he was obliged to take command of an infantry company whose captain had perished in battle. He spent three days in charge, successfully fending off a French attack, but he also left sensitive papers in the care of a battalion adjutant who was killed or captured by the French. As a result, he was called to RSHA headquarters in Berlin and given a sharp rebuke.

Much time was devoted to handling the stubborn Marshal Pétain, a vexing job to which Skorzeny had devoted himself in 1943. As early as August 1944, when the Germans were still in Paris, a 'Jeanne' force led by Richard, Litt and Valentin was assigned the task of travelling to Vichy and retrieving the aged *Maréchal*, only to be told on the eve of their departure that Pétain had already vacated the city for points unknown. By early September, the Germans had caught up to Pétain – he was in Belfort – but he was suspected of preparing a dash for the Swiss frontier. Hagedorn cabled Skorzeny on 10 September, alerting him to the latest news, and Skorzeny deployed 250 men from *Jagdverband Mitte* in order to reinforce German pickets along the Swiss border. Pétain was foiled again. Skorzeny did show, however, that he was not entirely without an understanding of Pétain's predicament, particularly when he later allowed one of his agents, the former vice-consul in Vichy's legation in Bern, Georges Herve Marachal, to go to Switzerland in order to arrange possible domiciles for Pétain and Pierre Laval. Marachal and a Swedish SS officer were driven to the Swiss frontier by Hagedorn's deputy, Ludwig Nebel, but both men were subsequently caught by the Swiss authorities.[123]

Meanwhile, Besekow told Hagedorn that 'Jeanne' would have to be reorganised. Instead of relying on the 'National French', very few of whom had withdrawn with the Germans, the new intention was to focus upon refugee *Miliciens*, PPF men and other collaborators, all of whom would be grouped under the umbrella of a new outfit called the '*Organisation Révolutionaire Intérieure Française*' (ORIF). Another brainchild of Gérard Litt, the ORIF was supposed to provide a new sense of organisational identity, and it was whispered that it might serve as the nucleus of a new regime carried to France in the baggage train of returning German armies. Litt and his colleagues even queried several recruits about their willingness to kill Pétain, Laval and Doriot, should the Germans ever seem on the cusp of retaking Paris. Hagedorn and Besekow apparently backed this plan. Despite such intrigues, few militants took the ORIF seriously.[124]

The most important measures in remodelling 'Jeanne' were taken at a level above Litt and Hagedorn. Worried about recruitment potential, Schellenberg and Skorzeny met with Darnand and Doriot in a conference hosted by Steimle at the infamous SS *Gästhaus* in Wannsee (scene of the 1942 meeting that had launched the Final Solution). Unlike his SS bosses, Skorzeny was more impressed by Darnand than by Doriot, particularly since the former claimed to have 5,000 followers still in France, situated in small cells of four to ten men and supposedly located in nearly every town and city. Darnand agreed to provide recruits to 'Jeanne' and other Skorzeny projects, as did Doriot, although the latter had more strings attached to his cooperation, wanting a continuing measure of say in the deployment of his men. The launch of an immediate sabotage campaign had to be postponed, given limitations of time and the lack of a training apparatus, and it was decided instead to organise '*points d'appui*' (support centres) in southern France. Skorzeny sensed that Doriot was unhappy about this change of course and he got the mistaken impression that the latter had a strictly military orientation, or as he later put it, that he 'preferred the role of an officer'. Skorzeny thought that the refitted 'Jeanne' enterprise should be based on a political foundation, so Darnand and Doriot were encouraged to visit their troops-in-training in order to maintain their influence and reinforce political indoctrination.[125]

As new recruits began to appear, Hagedorn organised a sabotage school at Badenweiler, near Freiburg-im-Breisgau. This facility was run by another veteran of the Sipo in Paris, Kurt Loba, and Gérard Litt was put in charge of anti-communist propaganda. Several groups of recruits from the *Milice* arrived in mid-October, after Hagedorn's second-in-command, Hermann Valentin, was sent to the *Milicien* collection centre at Ulm in order to raise volunteers. Unfortunately for 'Jeanne', the liquor-addled Hagedorn was not the sort of natural optimist who could build morale, and French recruits complained about his liberal attitude toward the training schedule – Hagedorn told one trainee that the course was being held 'to pass the time' – while on the other hand discipline was very strict. According to one Badenweiler graduate, German officers and administrative personnel 'treated the French as an inferior race'. In November 1944, much of the school was relocated to Skorzeny's *Jagdverband* facility in Neustrelitz.[126]

At the end of September 1944, Besekow called for the dispatch of new '*Zer-Gruppen*' through Allied lines and he launched Operation 'Charlie', which was intended to find Allied fuel pipelines running through northern France and to make contact with Richard and the Parisian remnants of the original 'Jeanne' network. The principal team assigned this task was led by Ludwig Nebel and consisted of three members, each of whom were individually infiltrated through Allied lines in late October and early November 1944. They were supposed to make use of existing arms dumps and await the arrival of explosives via parachute, although Nebel also carried a quantity of explosives, magnetic mines and fuses, which was packed in innocuous-looking meat tins. Nebel was also supplied with one million francs in currency. In addition to carrying out demolitions, Nebel and his cohorts had the task of setting up landing grounds for Fiesler Storch liaison aircraft and parachutists, all of which was supposed to be done on the country estate of Pierre Morand, a 'Jeanne' member who had fled Paris in August 1944. Hagedorn, ever the cynic, referred to the operation as 'a suicide mission' and told Nebel that he should have refused the assignment.

Other agents followed in the footsteps of Nebel's detachment. The first was the shrewish Benoite Ney, the wife of Hagedorn's French liaison officer, René Ney. Madame Ney had found it impossible to cooperate with anyone at Badenweiler and had repeatedly expressed her desire to return to France, so the Germans were more than happy to oblige, sending her through Switzerland in early November. She was told to locate the Allied pipeline near Paris, which she did, and then to await contact by Nebel. Ney was also joined by Charles Moreau, a stay-behind agent who was left in Belfort and who then travelled to Paris, as well as by three young women who were sent through Switzerland on 18 November and reached Paris two weeks later. This latter team, prosaically dubbed 'the three girls', consisted of two young members of the *Rassemblement Nationale Populaire* (RNP), plus an 18-year-old *Milicienne*. Their job was to locate stay-behind members of the RNP and the *Milice* and to make preparations for the establishment of a radio service in order to reconnect these elements to Germany. They were discouraged to find that a large number of their potential collaborators were either dead or under arrest, but they did contact RNP personnel who had coalesced under the banner of a new anti-communist group, the 'Union Française des Anciens Combattants de l'Intérieur'. 'The three girls' also met with Madame Ney, from whom they received funds.

'Charlie' might have born fruit except for the fact that Nebel switched sides at a crucial juncture, offering his services to the Allies. Nebel was a Swiss-German who spent much of 1942–1943 monitoring the activities of the small fascist parties in his homeland and had then become one of Skorzeny's early recruits. Madame Ney later described him as a vulgar and uncouth 'adventurer'; another acquaintance noted that his one master was money and his one passion was women. Several days after Nebel passed through Allied lines he was arrested by the CIC, and since he was caught armed and in civilian clothes, he was an obvious candidate for execution. In fact, the commander of the Seventh Army, General Alexander Patch, wanted to stand Nebel in front of a firing squad after a three-day interrogation in Paris. Sensing that his existence hung by a thread, Nebel provided information on the identities and passage routes of the remaining members of his team, which resulted in the capture of both men, and he also gave the French details about the activities of Raymond Richard, who was already under a degree of suspicion. Since he seemed willing to perform almost any service, Eisenhower's counter intelligence chief, Colonel Sheen, cancelled his return to the custody of the Seventh Army. Rather, he was recruited as a double agent, codenamed 'Ostrich', and was sent to Paris in order to trap Ney and Moreau, both of whom were captured in December. Information from these arrests and interrogations contributed to the apprehension of 'the three girls' at Delle, near the Swiss frontier, on 3 January 1945. The OSS also sat 'Ostrich' in the Café de la Paix for several days in late December, hoping that he could spot Skorzeny or other Jagdverband assassins supposedly sent to stalk Eisenhower.

By early 1945, the Allies were so sure of Nebel's reliability that they decided to send him back to Germany, where his job was to provide the SD with false information and keep tabs on 'Jeanne' leaders and training facilities. He was also supposed to ascertain the identities and whereabouts of three I-Netz radio operators who were still active in Paris.[127] Nebel reached German lines on 16 January and arrived at Friedenthal a week later. He claimed to have blown up two locomotives outside Paris and he said that 'his men' – Richard and company – had fired the shots directed at De Gaulle during August 1944 ceremonies celebrating the liberation of Paris. Skorzeny received 'Ostrich' cordially, feting him as a hero and proudly introducing him to an assemblage of one hundred SS officers. Nebel was then ordered to the Führer headquarters, where he personally reported to Hitler on events in France. He and Hitler reviewed a Swedish newsreel of the sniping attack upon De Gaulle. On 30 January, Nebel was promoted and awarded a First Class Iron Cross and the Deutscher Kreuz im Gold.

Not surprisingly, Nebel gave the Germans the picture of 'Jeanne' remnants that the Allies wanted them to have. According to Nebel, the efficiency of the Allies and the virulence of the French purge had left little of the Litt-Richard cells and none of the planned contact addresses were still intact. This was not entirely true. Although Parisian remnants of 'Jeanne' had been disabled by Allied repression, there were second-tier leaders who remained in touch with each other and were still trying to communicate with Germany. In the autumn of 1944, for instance, 'Jeanne' member Pierre Vernier was in continuing contact with several members of the organisation, which he described as an 'SS *Maquis*'. Naturally, the Germans would hear nothing of this from talking to Nebel. Although Nebel suggested that any activity behind Allied lines was difficult, it was possible, he claimed, to bribe French officials and to acquire phoney papers and funds needed for underground activity. He also told his controllers that he had established contact addresses along the southern outskirts of Paris and that he had also spotted a potential drop zone for *Luftwaffe*-borne supplies at La Rouillee. In reality, these locations were carefully watched by French authorities and several captured German agents had set up a bogus 'reception committee' at a farmhouse in La Rouillee. A month after Nebel's return to Germany, a German aircraft circled over the designated drop zone, but a mix up in signalling arrangements resulted in a failure to trick the *Luftwaffe* air crew.

Nebel's main aim was to lead a mission back to France, creating a trap at La Rouillee and luring in dozens of parachutists and a large amount of equipment and supplies. On 31 January, fresh from *Führer* headquarters, he got permission to draw a ton of weapons from Section S stocks, including a jeep, twelve anti-tank guns, explosives and automatic weapons. 'Ostrich' told Skorzeny that he hoped to organise a new *Maquis* in France, with Jacques Doriot playing the role of a French Tito. Skorzeny invited Doriot to Berlin and in early February, he, Doriot, Radl, Besekow and Nebel agreed upon a plan. Doriot was apparently ready to return to his homeland, although he then perished in the aerial strafing attack near Mengen. 'Ostrich', however, still intended to proceed, moving his equipment to a forward headquarters near Freiburg, where he came under the operational control of 18th SS Army Corps.

Disaster suddenly struck in early March 1945. Another German intelligence officer, Alois Tonin, had recently returned from France, bearing incriminating information. Tonin had been captured in Strasbourg, where he was told by his French interrogators that Nebel, who was an acquaintance, had also been captured and recruited by the Americans. The French offered Tonin a similar arrangement, to which he agreed, although unlike Nebel, he did not truly decide to join the winning side. Upon his return to German territory, he immediately revealed the story to his debriefers, including mention that Nebel had been 'turned' and dispatched as a double agent. When faced with this accusation, Nebel feigned outrage, assuming the role of the unjustly accused. His demeanour was convincing, but he was put under constant watch and several attempts were made to get him drunk, with the hope that this might loosen his tongue. Nonetheless, he adamantly denied Tonin's claims. Hagedorn asked Skorzeny to question 'Ostrich' personally, but Skorzeny once again displayed the lack of perspicacity that proved such a liability in underground work. He could not spare the time, he said, and in any case, he believed Nebel's denials, arguing that if Nebel was a double agent, he would have taken the opportunity to assassinate one of the senior officials whom he had recently met. It was thus left to Besekow to conduct the interrogation. After a preliminary discussion, Besekow gave Nebel a clean bill of health, although he was still under enough suspicion that he could no longer be trusted with a major mission to France. He subsequently had to keep a low profile. Nebel was finally overrun by Allied forces when Freiburg was occupied on 22 April 1945.[128]

Although Nebel helped stall efforts to revive 'Jeanne', Hagedorn was meanwhile urged by the *Wehrmacht* to get busy in sending newly recruited agents into France – the German Army needed a diversion for its offensive in the Ardennes. He was also encouraged by the report of a line-crosser who had visited Montbéliard and came back depicting the French as demoralised and in the throes of chaos. Besekow further pushed the pace by sending several teams into France straight from Friedenthal and Neustrelitz. One pair of SD radio agents were sent on a number of missions behind enemy lines, and in November 1944, Besekow's deputy, *Untersturmführer* Winter, led a group of ten Yugoslav mercenaries into Allied-held territory. Proudly introduced by Winter as 'my Serbs', members of this detachment had previously worked for Nebel. They were dressed in British, French and American uniforms and apparently performed well, committing sabotage and stealing sensitive documents.

Under heavy pressure, Hagedorn began to pitch his newly trained saboteurs into service, sending a number of sabotage parties into France. These units were equipped to attack Allied fuel pipelines and had special bombs designed to blow holes through pipe and incendiary charges meant to ignite petroleum. On 19 November, a small detachment was sent to blow up a bridge at Hericourt, although it made no effort to carry out its mission and was forced by the Allied advance to cross the Rhine and return to Badenweiler. Despite this failure, four three-man sabotage teams were formed in late November, when Besekow told members that a 'grand coup' was coming and that they would 'embarrass' the Allied transport system. On 15 December, the detachments were moved to the Alsatian Front at Ruffach and in the next several days they were sent across Allied lines, all members dressed in civilian clothes. Two teams were sent toward Nancy and Reims, where their task was to sabotage Allied fuel tankers. Both, however, got pinned down by American fire after crossing the lines at Labaroche and then attempting to hide in a forest. Dodging bullets, team members withdrew to German lines under cover of darkness. Two further units, under the command of Hermann Valentin, were sent toward Belfort and Dijon. They were supposed to destroy bridges near Colmar as well as blowing up Allied fuel dumps, but one group was unable to infiltrate the front and the other was captured on 18 December while attempting to cross enemy lines.[129]

Two heavily armed 'Jeanne' squads were parachuted into France from a German B-17. The first, an eight-man detachment comprised of *Miliciens* and French SS men, was dropped on 13 December near Blois. Codenamed '*Groupe Serpent*' and led by Charles Palmieri, the mission of this team was to blow holes in the Allied fuel pipeline, attack petroleum storage tanks and pumping facilities at Melun, and terrorise Parisians by leaving anti-personnel bombs in the Paris Metro. Fortunately, the engine noise of the *Luftwaffe* aircraft was reported by French peasants, and within twenty-four hours four of the saboteurs, including Palmieri, had been rounded up. The names and descriptions of the remaining parachutists were then circulated to virtually every police station in France, so that within several days three members of the surviving group had also been caught.[130]

On the day after the airdrop at Blois, a second detachment of parachutists floated to the ground in the Corrèze, although its intended landing zone had been in the neighbouring *département* of the Haute-Vienne. The latter location included the hometown of unit commander Paul Pasthier, who was supposed to contact with local sympathisers. A former Cagoulard, Pasthier had been captured by the Germans in 1940, while serving as an officer in the French Army. He and nine of his men were French POWs or civilian labourers who had been recruited by the SD in Austria and were then trained at

Friedenthal. Their mission was especially insidious. The region around Toulouse was felt by the Germans to be the most 'red' part of France and an area where the writ of the De Gaulle government did not run. Thus, Pasthier and his volunteers were instructed to form a movement with 'socialist tendencies' and to recruit local factory workers for assaults upon Allied lines of communication. Pasthier was also told to arrange the assassinations of French leaders such as André Marty. The parachutists were supplied with arms and explosives and Pasthier was carrying 500,000 francs when he was dropped. Like the Blois group, however, Pasthier's team quickly fell victim to a manhunt and the French police credited the aid of the population in facilitating some rapid arrests. One parachutist managed to bite a cyanide capsule after capture – a member of the Blois detachment had also managed this feat – while another hid with his family and friends in Lyon before giving himself up in January 1945.[131]

After the failure of the infiltration raids in north-eastern France, several of the 'Jeanne' commandos involved in that exercise told Hagedorn that they too would prefer to be dropped by air rather than again trying to cross the front. The most insistent of these volunteers was Paul François, an LVF veteran and convicted felon who was generally recognised as the most hard-bitten of the Badenweiler alumni. François explained that there was a clearing near his home in the Norman town of Guitry, which could serve as a perfect drop zone, and he also assured the Germans that his family and friends would help any parachutists who accompanied him back to France. This offer intrigued Hagedorn, who brought François to Berlin, where both men met with Besekow. François suggested that a squad of parachutists could bury explosives in a forest near his home and then use the cache as a starting point for missions by small teams, which could foray all over France, attacking Allied fuel pipelines and tankers, and also collecting intelligence, particularly on the strength of American and French forces around the Atlantic pockets. Like Hagedorn, Besekow thought that it was worth giving François charge of a team of Badenweiler volunteers, although he was reluctant to provide a radio operator, only agreeing to send such help a week after François's detachment had landed and established a base. Besekow also insisted that François personally track down and murder the two errant radio agents who had betrayed 'Jeanne' in August of the previous summer. In addition, the Germans later told François that before beginning any sabotage activities, he should travel to Guincamp and contact Monsieur Olivet, a prominent industrialist who was the reputed head of the White *Maquis* in Brittany.

In late December 1944, François's nine-man squad began looking for an available aircraft, a process which, in typical fashion, took a month to achieve. On 29 January, the paratroopers took off from an airport outside Frankfurt-am-Main, travelling in two aircraft bound for the Channel Islands. Although the mission of these *Luftwaffe* Heinkels was to deliver mail, the air crews had agreed to drop the saboteurs near Guitry. The agents were heavily armed, bearing ten automatic rifles and five machine pistols (with silencers), plus requisite ammunition. A separate box contained explosives. Although dressed in civilian garb, they had packed SD uniforms; they had been told by the Germans that if the *Wehrmacht* retook Paris, they would be expected to act as an advance guard and to secure electrical stations and telephone exchanges in the French capital. The parachutists were dropped in the early morning hours of 30 January, although one was injured upon landing and their presence was immediately detected by a hostile population. Thus, most members of the party, including François, were quickly arrested. A two-man reconnaissance team managed to make its way to Paris, but one of its members was spotted in Garenne Colombe, where he was recognised as a PPF man who had earlier played a role in the murder of newspaper editor Maurice Sarraut. Expecting no mercy, he tried to shoot his way out of trouble and was killed by members of a French dragnet.[132]

With defeat piled upon defeat, the 'Jeanne' *Sonderkommando* was starting to falter by March 1945. Except for some vials of poison and several luminescent watches, the 'Jeanne' allotment at the Section S supply depot in Munchberg was exhausted. Due to Hagedorn's heavy drinking, he was informally replaced as 'Jeanne' boss by *Sturmbannführer* Hans Duffner, who had earlier been stationed with the SD in Paris and Vichy.

In early April, Duffner ordered all remaining trainees at Badenweiler to join Nazi guerrilla bands preparing to deploy in the Black Forest, and he relocated his headquarters to a youth hostel near Lorrach. However, he was intent on sending a last few agents into France, mainly in order to buoy up pro-German networks and partisan bands already thought to be operating in the country. In mid-April, for instance, he dispatched a three-person team headed by Pierre Lagardere. This group had orders to join a radio-equipped unit that was functioning in Paris. Duffner also aimed to reinforce a White *Maquis* unit near the Swiss border with a small detachment led by Ernst Dunker, a veteran of the SD station in Marseilles who had been promised the leadership of all special units in France on the strength of his being the only *Reichsdeutsch* willing to run the risk of deployment in the country. In truth, Dunker was unenthusiastic about participating in such schemes, especially since he thought that military action was increasingly pointless, given the course of the war. Rather than joining a *Maquis* or even performing sabotage, he wanted to run a political terror campaign against leaders of the PCF. Secretly, his intention was to go to ground with his French mistress and lead a simple and quiet existence. On 19 April, he convinced five French volunteers at Badenweiler to join him in deserting. After commandeering a vehicle, they used their phoney identification papers to pass through Switzerland and then return to France, disguised as repatriated refugees.[133]

The leaders of 'Jeanne' did have a final card to play in Italy, although it proved no more effective than any other initiatives. The key figure in this operation was Werner Neisser, an expert skier and cultured polyglot who had served with the SD in France and had played an important role in the organisation of the I-*Netz*. Born in Klagenfurt, Neisser had been a school chum of Skorzeny and in late August 1944 he was invited to join Section S. It was also hoped that he would arrange the transfer of a number of his French agents who had fled to Alsace. During October, he was deployed in Budapest on Operation '*Panzerfaust*', but he was also plotting with his friend Hans Sommer in order to re-establish contact with a ring of pro-German 'friends' in France. After he and Sommer were told to launch operations from northern Italy, he travelled to Turin and began preparations with the help of a local gang of anti-communists led by a morphine-addicted physician named Bongiovanni. Turin, however, proved an inadequate base for such operations. The Alpine frontier district was so infested with anti-fascist Partisans that Neisser could hardly envision moving line-crossers into position, nor could he get help from local mountaineers or from the Republican Fascist secret police. To cap matters,

Neisser's main French lieutenant, the shaggy ex-Cagoulard Michel Harispe, was killed when Allied bombers raided Turin.

As a result of such difficulties, a squad of *Miliciens* whom Neisser had recruited were trained in a skiing course in the Tyrol, rather than in northern Italy, and when the group was finally brought across the Alps in February 1945, Neisser stationed them at San Remo, where he intended to work closely with Sommer and to get help from the Italian and German navies in moving personnel into France. Two such attempts were launched by boat crews of the Xth *Flottiglia* MAS in late February, each aimed at landing four *Miliciens* near Cannes, but heavy surf forced a return to base in each instance. On 5 April, the same four *Miliciens*, plus an additional recruit, were brought to the French Riviera by a German patrol boat, but again the landing was abortive, and it was only two days later that a German E-Boat finally succeeded in putting all five men ashore near Anthéor. Members of the group were then supposed to contact the 'Brown *Maquis*' and conduct 'political resistance', reconstituting the Cagoule. However, Neisser had informally advised the men that their best chance of staying alive was to keep quiet and go underground. Most of these agents were subsequently caught by the French police.

Shortly after this forlorn expedition, Neisser and Sommer tried to defy logic by going through France in order to reach Spain, hoping to get help along the way from a Giraudist intelligence officer in Nice. Sommer had a network of agents in Spain from which he expected a measure of assistance. On 23 April, the pair headed into the Alps, which they had crossed by early May, although Neisser could not locate his friend in Nice. Both men eventually surrendered to the French authorities.[134]

While Hagedorn dragged his charges through the long and ultimately fruitless 'Jeanne' saga, Skorzeny's Mil D units were also active in trying to destabilise liberated France.[135] Although the *Zweierorganisation* had long been active in cultivating a society of young Frenchmen supposedly willing to fight behind Allied lines, the so-called '*Coeur de France*',[136] when the hour of decision arrived in 1944, few of these volunteers showed up for duty and the *Abwehr*'s remnant, FAK 210, was left scrambling to mobilise pro-German elements. Without an existing network to leave behind, officers of FAK 210 turned to Alexandre Marceau, an LVF propagandist and recruiter who had made an impact in the northern French town of Hazebrouck by plastering its walls with anti-communist slogans and demolishing an effigy of the republic that still adorned its *Mairie*. Marceau was also the ringleader of the 'White *Maquis*' recruits trained at Thumeries, and in September 1944, after his flight to Germany, FAK officers explained that he was now wanted for a new assignment:

> As an LVF delegate you know most of the group's members as well as the members of the nationalist parties. You will return to France and make contact with all these people, aiding those who are in need and those who are hunted by the police. Eventually, we will send you money. You will regroup all these people so that when we return to France we will find armed clandestine groups similar to those that existed in France during our occupation. When these groups are formed, we will parachute officers and arms.

Marceau was further told to organise his prospective recruits in fourty-man '*centaines*', which would be subdivided into eleven-man '*dizaines*' and five-man '*mains*', and to do his best to ridicule Allied troops and cause clashes between these soldiers and the French population. He was also responsible for spotting terrain suitable for parachute drops, hopefully in time to divert attention from the forthcoming Ardennes Offensive. Finally, it was explained that Marceau's wife would be held by the Germans as a hostage, pending evidence of his good behaviour.

Over the next several weeks, Marceau was provided with the assistance of another Thumeries-trained 'White *Maquisard*', who agreed to accompany him to France, as well as being given 300,000 francs and identity papers that had been seized from French prisoners in Germany. In mid-October, Marceau and his deputy passed through enemy lines in the Vosges and succeeded in reaching Paris. They were picked up en route by American troops, but their cover stories held through questioning. Once in Paris, the pair did little to accomplish their mission, although Marceau made a fatal mistake by sending his assistant north to Hazebrouck, where he was recognised and arrested on 4 November 1944. The subsequent interrogation also brought to light Marceau's name and location, and he too was captured.[137]

FAK 210 also made a half-hearted attempt to start a resistance movement in Alsace, an area more suitable than northern France because it was not yet under enemy control. The key figure in this enterprise was a duelling-scarred Alsatian autonomist named Henri Klein, who had served as an interpreter with the German administration in Alsace-Lorraine. In early September 1944, Klein was recruited by Mil D because of his knowledge of Alsace, its people and its patois, and he was told to report to FAK 210, which was stationed at Gimmeldingen. He was also provided with a team of three Alsatian soldiers, each a fanatic Nazi. Klein's orders were to recruit Germanophile Alsatians for stay-behind teams, the job of which was to blow up railway locomotives with explosive coal.

Klein's detachment arrived in Strasbourg on 21 September, although its size was cut in half when two of Klein's men were immediately recalled to Germany. Klein was also denied use of a staff car. He and his remaining assistant thereafter dragged their heels, making little progress, and when Klein was told to finish his assignment by 1 November, he begged for an extra ten days. Despite getting an extension, his final report was reproved by the Germans for offering scant evidence of progress. Klein was subsequently ordered to report to St Ingbert, where a former LVF and *Milice* officer, Colonel Besson-Rapp, had assembled fifteen 'French nationalist *Maquisards*' who could be dropped by parachute in order to reinforce the Alsatian network. Unknown to the Germans, however, Klein had decided that it was an appropriate hour to switch sides – he had already given his report on the Alsatian Nazi underground to a friend of Gaullist sympathies – and when ordered to St Ingbert, he went to ground and awaited the arrival of Free French forces. As a result, the Alsatian sabotage organisation came to nothing,[138] although FAK 210 subsequently tried to run line-crossers behind the advancing Allied front, looking for opportunities for sabotage.[139]

FAK 213 also made a showing, at least in the extreme north of France, which was within its operational sphere. In 1942–1943, the sabotage bureau of the *Abwehr* had recruited, trained and armed a small network of saboteurs and pro-German sympathisers in the *département* of the Nord, a group that was inherited by FAK 213. In September 1944, one stay-behind saboteur from this organisation, a Belgian Rexist named Charles Bouchez, established radio contact from Lille. Although Bouchez refused to use his generous store of explosives, which he was supposed to employ three weeks after the departure of the Germans, he did supply information on Allied military traffic and on the damage caused by German V-weapons. He also contacted and tried to activate at least one other stay-behind saboteur, who had a supply of incendiary devices and blasting material. Since an active German radio agent in France was a relative rarity, FAK 130 officers tried to horn in on Bouchez's control, although they were waved away by Gerken, the commander of FAK 213. In any case, Bouchez eventually encountered difficulties in hearing his control station, and in late November 1944 he buried his radio set and abandoned his perilous existence as a spy.[140]

The most important function assigned to Mil D was to find, contact and supply the White *Maquis*. The Germans were in receipt of a steady stream of reports about 'white partisans', beginning with a dispatch from Spain on 24 September 1944, which suggested that 'violent coercion in France has led to a vigorous coalition of collaborators with Germany, who constitute a new Maquis'. This was good news, responded Mil Amt controllers, and they added that the high command was 'greatly interested in details... concerning place, time, organisation, persons, etc.'.[141] In November and December 1944, Mil D carried out Operation 'Charlemagne', which involved sending small groups to the Langres plateau, the Rhone valley, the Vichy region and other locales in France that were reported haunts of the White *Maquis*. 'Charlemagne' agents were drawn from the *Milice* and the PPF, and in January 1945 Skorzeny announced to Darnand and Doriot that he had already recruited enough of their men – about eighty – and that they should spend the next two months preparing 'a thorough political organisation among the White Maquis'. All further sabotage efforts, he explained, would be based on this framework.[142] Although the Germans eventually claimed to have 'coordinated' operations of the White *Maquis*, it is obvious that they did not succeed in finding all such groups because they continued to query radio agents on the whereabouts of guerrillas and they also kept sending fresh operatives into southern France in order to locate *Milicien* bands. As late as 11 April 1945, a unit of volunteers from the *Groupe* 'Collaboration' was landed near Anthéor in an attempt to locate a pro-German *Maquis* believed to be operating near Nice.[143]

Several Mil Amt officers also produced a fantastic scheme to use an abandoned French Air Force training field near Montpellier as a secret landing strip. The plan called for a French Air Force lieutenant, recruited from a POW camp and familiar with the southern Massif Central, to land by parachute and prepare the field for use. A radio operator would help this officer contact Germany and maintain communications with anti-Gaullist and anti-communist French elements, with whom the latter was already in contact. After the '*Vorkommando*' had groomed the field and set up landing lights, *Luftwaffe* aircraft would provide a shuttle service for the White *Maquis*, bringing in supplies and flying important people out of the country. This proposal was brought to the desk of P.W. Stahl, the commander of KG 200's western squadron, codenamed 'Olga', but he refused point blank: he wondered how the airfield could be hidden from the population in the area, however sparse, and he worried about betrayal from within the organisation using the field. A failure on either score could lead to the loss of a valuable aircraft and its crew. In addition, he could not understand why delivery of equipment by parachute was not adequate, since he was willing to organise this kind of supply system.[144]

Jagdverband Südwest's French resistance movement was codenamed '*Reichstadt*', and was intended to consist of separate underground clusters in the Massif Central ('Napoleon'), the Western Alps ('Hannibal') and Paris ('*Sacré Coeur*'). The initial goal was to facilitate the German reoccupation of France, a campaign for which the *Jagdverband* expected help from the large number of German soldiers thought to be hiding in the country. In fact, bands of bypassed troops had already been contacted by SS officers sent into France from Spain. Once the original aim of '*Reichstadt*' began to look unattainable, the programme dissolved into an attempt to conduct sabotage and political violence, hopefully with the result of bringing down the De Gaulle regime. A PPF official, Colonel Brun, was posted as liaison officer between *Südwest* and the CLF, with the responsibility of raising volunteers from French fascist parties, labour camps and the *Waffen*-SS, while *Südwest* agreed to train and arm these prospective guerrillas. As a result, in late 1944 and early 1945 fifty recruits were enrolled in six-week courses at Tiefenthal and a radio station was set up at the same location in order to provide a focal point for French guerrilla bands. After Tiefenthal was bombed by the Allies, the transmitter-receiver was moved to Fritzlar.

As Gerlach later described it, '*Reichstadt*' got closest to a point of activation in the Massif Central, so the codeword 'Napoleon' emerged as the main *Jagdverband* referent for underground work in France. Tiefenthal trainees were advised that a *Sonderkommando* of parachutists would distribute propaganda, weapons and supplies to sympathetic elements in the mountains. Darnand told Gerlach, as he had Skorzeny, that he had small groups of sympathisers who were ready to work with German organisers. Once a base was established, 'Napoleon' personnel would receive German specialists and advisors, and a nationwide resistance network would supposedly radiate from the Massif Central. Although Gerlach later told the Allies that little of this scheme advanced beyond the planning stage, one of his subordinates admitted that a platoon of thirty *Jagdverband* parachutists was actually dropped in the vicinity of Limoges, led by a 33-year-old Brandenburger named Harry Zimmacher. Other agents were landed in the Atlantic pockets and told to infiltrate into the interior.[145]

Despite the concentration on the Massif Central, *Südwest* did not ignore other locations. In January 1945, a small detachment was landed by Fiesler Storch in a field west of Paris, reportedly in order to conduct sabotage and help a band of *Miliciens* who had recently raided a prison and released thirty of their right-wing compatriots. The Tiefenthal radio station was also in contact with a White *Maquis* detachment operating near Paris under the command of a factory worker named Lagrange. In early February, a six-man team was assembled under the command of Lagrange's son, a PPF official who had recently graduated from the Tiefenthal programme. Members of this squad received false identity documents and were supplied with pistols and a radio transmitter. They were probably dropped near Paris, equipped with a mandate to harass Allied communications and reinforce local pro-German partisans.[146]

Initial work toward launching Operation 'Hannibal' was undertaken by *Jagdkommando* Stiegler, a constituent part of *Jagdeinsatz Italien*. 'Hannibal' ran parallel to 'Tosca' because it involved setting up a chain of middlemen in order to facilitate the entry of agents and commandos into southern France. SD officers hired specialists who knew the mountain footpaths, had influence with the local population and were familiar with French Savoy.

As far as Gerlach was concerned, a 'pitiful' amount of information on France had been provided by the SD, the Sigmaringen government and the Mil Amt, so his first priority was to use the chain to get radio operators into Haute-Savoie, where they would be met by agents in French and American uniforms and brought to their appointed destinations, forming a *'mosaïque de renseignements'*. At least a half-dozen of these agents were trained at Fritzlar during the spring of 1945. According to Gerlach, even the heavily armed commandos sent into southern France were essentially information gatherers, although their German handlers stressed their paramilitary functions in order to buoy up morale.

By early 1945, three groups of Stiegler commandos had been organised. Two of these were raised from the Marseilles wing of the PPF, with which *Jagdverband* officers Hans Pavel and Alfred Drescher had a good relationship. One platoon, *Gruppe* 'Vercingetorix', was a Corsican detachment formed in December 1944 and trained for several weeks at Tiefenthal. The unit was originally part of *Jagdeinsatz Nord*, but in February 1945 it was relocated to Turin and attached to *Jagdkommando* 'Stiegler'. The chief of 'Vercingetorix' was one of the PPF bosses from Marseilles, a beret-wearing SS sergeant named Pantalacci. He had reached Germany with *Streifkorps Nord Frankreich* and had been on several missions to Corsica and the Côte d'Azur. Prior to the group's deployment, whence it was intended to conduct sabotage in Marseilles, a French scout was sent to check local conditions. He returned two days later, reporting that it would be impossible to get through the lines. His apprehension proved correct when a subsequent infiltration attempt was checked by French military and security forces. Gerlach then suggested that it might be possible to get a KKV unit at San Remo to land the group by sea, and since German E-Boats did subsequently beach dozens of agents along the Mediterranean coasts of France and Monaco, it is possible that the unit was deployed in this fashion.

The two remaining commando units operated by Stiegler were *Gruppen* 'Sabiani' and 'Peggy'. The first was led by Joseph Sabiani, nephew of the PPF *Chef* of Marseilles. In the autumn of 1944, Sabiani was in south-west Germany, where he had already recruited sixty men who were awaiting deployment in France. Sabiani and his followers were trained at Tiefenthal in February and March 1945. *Gruppe* 'Peggy' was commanded by *Unterscharführer* Coletti and was recruited from the SS 'Charlemagne' Division, courtesy of Hans Schwinn, a member of Gerlach's staff, although it also included a female radio operator seconded from *Jagdeinsatz Süd*. Members of 'Peggy' were trained at Tiefenthal in December 1944 and moved to Turin in March 1945. Both groups were sent into France, apparently by land, although nothing is known about the outcome of these operations.[147]

As the staffs and combat forces of *Jagdverband Südwest* were pushed into Alsace, they made contact with elements of FAK 210 and prepared to launch a guerrilla war that was more intense than anything Mil D had been able to foster. In early January 1945, the Americans got their first indications of such activity, particularly when they captured a pigeon message released by a four-man commando unit that was stranded in Allied-held territory with a wounded French legionary. Several days later, the Allies apprehended the members of a two-man team deployed near Rooschwoog and both captives revealed detailed information about the nature of *Südwest* and its mission. Both of these French spotters had been skulking around no-man's land in generic camouflage smocks – they had passed themselves off as Romanian SS men to the *Volkssturm* and escaped Canadian POWs to Alsatian civilians – and they were terrified 'of being fired upon by [the] Volkssturm, [the] Wehrmacht and [the] Americans, separately or all together'. As a result, they surrendered to an enemy patrol.

Despite an increasing level of vigilance by the Allies – the First French Army warned of 'a tremendous reinforcement of the Fifth Column and the German intelligence service' – a number of aggressive young German officers succeeded in carrying out a programme of infiltration and raiding. Hans Pavel's *Jagdkommando* began reconnaissance operations in December 1944 and individual line-crossers returned from missions to Luxembourg and the Strasbourg district, although a French volunteer sent behind American lines near Wissembourg was either killed or captured. In January and February 1945, Pavel sent at least a dozen small units into Allied-held territory north of Strasbourg. His subordinate George Grossier, an ex-*Milicien* and fighter with the 'Charlemagne' Division, twice led detachments behind Allied lines in the Hagenau Forest. In the first instance, Grossier mined roads, disrupted Allied communications and captured a prisoner; in the second, he neutralised demolition charges on bridges and destroyed an American tank. A man after Pavel's own heart, Grossier was killed in April 1945 while on a mission near Strasbourg. Another of Pavel's task forces blocked Allied supply routes by felling trees in order to form a roadblock.

Another *Jagdkommando* leader, *Leutnant* Wissemberg, proved a similar bulldog. A bold and athletic ex-Brandenburger who had been badly burned in action, Wissemberg was a reluctant Nazi and only in late January sewed an SS escutcheon upon his uniform. His forty-man detachment ran its first mission in mid-December 1944, when a squad carried out reconnaissance near Bitche and wired plastic explosive to a railway track. On a subsequent occasion, he and a twenty-five-man shock troop ventured behind American lines and mined supply routes in the Bitche Forest. American accounts of the fighting in the Bitcherland confirm that German troops operated in Allied uniforms and that civilians were regarded with suspicion by the Allies. 'In one instance', an American soldier later recalled, 'a wholesale plan to sabotage our defensive position and routes of communication was discovered. Curfews were set and strictly enforced.'

In *Jagdeinsatz Süd*, the most active officer was *Obersturmführer* Hossfeld, a former Brandenburger with a philosophy doctorate, although Hossfeld's colleagues Träger and Schwinn handled many of the technical aspects of his *Jagdkommando*'s operations. Hossfeld started running reconnaissance forays in mid-November 1944, although his first idea for an attack, which aimed to blow up Allied munitions dumps and poison the wells and food supply of Belfort, was so shocking that it had to be abandoned. The French legionnaire chosen to lead the mission would not take possession of the poison. Nonetheless, a Flemish saboteur sent to Belfort managed to blow up a French armoured car, taking advantage of the fact that it was left unattended while crew members took their evening meal. A French infiltrator also laid mines near Montbéliard. On 19 December, a three-man team toppled an electrical power pylon near Ribeauville and cut communication wires in locations that were booby-trapped in order to kill or injure members of enemy repair crews. On 5 January 1945, twenty-two Spanish volunteers cut communication lines and attacked Allied forward posts, capturing four prisoners. Two members of the

Spanish platoon were caught behind enemy lines in civilian clothes, whence they were swiftly tried by the Americans and shot. Hossfeld also sent a Swedish *Jagdverband* trooper into Switzerland in order to reconnoitre railway lines that the Germans feared would be seized and exploited by the Allies.

After the bulk of German forces were driven across the Rhine, raiding parties from *Jagdeinsatz Süd* crossed the river and harassed Allied movements. One SS officer led a four-man team in destroying an electrical transformer; near Colmar, two reconnaissance patrols were carried out by *Unterscharführer* Rudy Rose and five Frenchmen clad in US uniforms; and several groups in American dress crossed the Rhine and ventured into southern Alsace. The intelligence officer of the 18th SS Army Corps, *Hauptsturmführer* Kubat, recruited *Jagdverband* agents who were ferried across the Rhine or sent into Alsace via Switzerland. Kubat worked closely with *Obersturmführer* Malzacher, an SD officer in Lorrach who had good relations with a Swiss customs official at Frenzacher Horn. Malzacher supplied his Swiss contact with information on fugitives in Switzerland, thus allowing the latter to get in the good graces of his superiors, while the official allowed Malzacher to send carloads of five or six men through Switzerland and on to Besançon or Montbéliard. These Germans posed as inspectors of French food supplies bound for Switzerland. The leader of the SS subversive propaganda organisation, *Skorpion-Rheingau*, spent a week in France in late March 1945, posing as an inspector of food stocks. Such reconnaissance troops were told to spot the location of Allied fuel dumps and investigate civilian sentiment, with special emphasis on signs of remaining fidelity to Germany. Indications of the latter were not always positive: 'We noted everywhere', said one agent, 'that the Alsatian population was indifferent to nationalities and that it was not always hostile to the German people, but only to the Nazi regime, which disturbs its bourgeois tranquillity.'[148]

After probing operations throughout the late winter and spring of 1945, Kubat began planning a major assault by 150 men, whom he envisioned crossing the Rhine and attacking the Dijon–Metz pipeline. The Alsatian *Unterscharführer* Lucien Hamm, a veteran of the Russian Front, undertook an extensive reconnaissance mission, in which he travelled as far north as Colmar and returned with valuable intelligence upon which a raid could be launched. Like many bold conceptions, however, Kubat's plan implied great risks. Unknown to Kubat, the French security services had inserted a spy, codenamed 'Queasy', into the ranks of *Jagdverband Südwest*, and it was not long before 'Queasy' was providing detailed information about the forthcoming operation. Understandably, the French saw a tempting opportunity to lay a snare. On 28 March they ambushed a six-man vanguard led by Hamm, which had slipped through Switzerland and was then lured to Colmar. Hamm and his cohorts were all killed 'attempting to escape', and a large quantity of Nipolit explosive fell into the hands of the enemy. The French then precipitately blew up a bridge over the Ill river in an attempt to trap a much larger raiding party expected in Hamm's wake, although that unit had not yet traversed the Rhine and, in view of the obvious commotion in Colmar, would never make that crossing. OSS observers concluded that the operation was spoiled by the French First Army's lack of discretion in setting the trap.[149]

Jagdverband Südwest also begged help from KG 200 and French reports suggest that there was air activity over Alsace by late December 1944: on Christmas Eve, there were numerous low passes over the Neihof–Plobsheim area, supposedly to drop supplies to German guerrillas, and on the night of 30/31 December German parachutists were dropped near Herlisheim. The French authorities captured two Skorzeny *Leute* in French uniforms, and after scouring the countryside, they discovered additional Germans as well. A military court was convened and several of these prisoners were executed. The Americans also promised 'immediate counter-measures' and Seventh Army CIC went on a state of alert: a radar detection system was organised in order to pinpoint parachutists, and special mobile squads were set up to track down saboteurs dropped by plane.

Late in January 1945, an airborne team fell into this net. Nine *Jagdverband* agents were dropped near Lunéville, but things immediately went awry. The parachutists' radio transmitter was smashed upon landing, and Allied radar tracked the progress of the aeroplane from which they had jumped, allowing the Americans to plot the likely drop zone. Shortly after the *Jagdverband* troopers floated to the ground, American mobile units converged upon the area and came upon the wreckage of the radio transmitter, which confirmed that Skorzeny personnel were in the area. The Americans fanned out and quickly discovered the nine *Jagdverband* saboteurs, all dressed in German military jumpsuits. Hopelessly trapped, only two of the parachutists elected to fight it out with their pursuers: one was killed and one wounded. The captives later admitted that they were an advance party for a *Sonderkommando* that was preparing to operate against Allied forces.[150]

Another airborne mission, Operation 'Greif', was supposed to unfold in the *département* of the Aisne, even further behind Allied forces. 'Greif' was the responsibility of *Unterscharführer* Frost, a former member of Panzer Brigade 150. His assignment was to land a glider near Laon and attack nearby enemy airfields, as well as sabotaging the Allied fuel pipeline. In January 1945, Frost and five other veterans of the Ardennes fighting had secured a glider, which was stored at the Degelsdorf airfield near Zelle, and they also asked the Mil Amt to provide them with phoney identification documents and papers. As was the case with all German projects by this stage of the war, the pace of preparations was slow, and only by mid-April had Frost wrangled the services of a towing plane. He teletyped Gerlach from Cottbus, claiming that he was about to start the operation, but the airfield near Zelle was already in Allied hands and the mission could hardly have proceeded without the glider.[151] Meanwhile, a party of German parachutists in Canadian uniforms was spotted near Laon by French and American military police, but this may have been a scouting expedition reconnoitring the area in advance of 'Greif'.[152]

While there was clearly no lack of German attempts to subvert liberated France, it is also obvious that many of these attempts were abortive and that the Germans faced myriad difficulties. Gerlach reported that not enough preparation had been made to support an anti-Allied movement and that German policy toward France 'had always been undecided and variable', which was apparently his way of admitting that the Germans had alienated the population.[153] As noted above, the Germans had little reliable information about France, aside from tidbits of tactical intelligence, and by the spring of 1945 the Allies suspected that the most valuable information from the country was being collected by the Spanish intelligence service and passed on to the Germans.[154]

In addition, once the front settled in place during the autumn of 1944, it became difficult for sabotage parties to cross the lines and there were not many opportunities for landing commandos by sea, unlike the case in Italy.[155] This meant that infiltration had to be accomplished by air, a problem in a period when the *Luftwaffe* was short of petrol. In fact, the Germans ran so low on fuel that not only did they restrict the flying of aircraft, but it was difficult to gather parachutists, jump equipment and PAGs at the airfields where they were needed in order to launch operations. Space on available flights was at a premium because espionage and counter-intelligence FAK units also depended on KG 200 to drop their spies into place. Perhaps worst of all, the Allied radar system and the lack of adequate weather forecasting forced German pilots to penetrate French airspace at a low altitude and without clear knowledge about flying conditions. The result was a distressing loss of aircraft and flight crews – and sometimes of agents – through crashes or enemy air activity. A KG 200 aircraft blew up after lifting off from Echterdingen airstrip, killing ten parachutists bound for the Pyrenees, and another machine disappeared after dropping agents near Rouen and Paris. Yet another plane failed during a trial flight, another crashed in southern France, and a German B-17 was shot down in Alsace by an American night-fighter. In the period from 31 December 1944 to 10 January 1945, 'Olga' lost three aircraft due to crashes, and sixteen personnel were killed in an American air raid. Special operations in France would have been crippled but for the help provided by *Transportgeschwader* 30, which was flying supplies to the Atlantic pockets and whose aircraft were used to drop commandos and agents.[156] In March 1945, 'Olga' warned that due to shortages of aircraft and PAGs, it could 'only transport undertakings with one man'.[157]

Neither did the French remain passive in the face of a virtual onslaught of German line-crossers and parachutists. Around the turn of 1944–1945, a panic gripped the nation, especially the eastern and southern *départements*, as word spread about '*parachutages*' and armed attacks by the Fifth Column.[158] It was in this alarmist atmosphere that a '*Services de Contre-Parachutages*' was organised by the army, which charged gendarmes, paramilitary groups and civilian look-outs with forwarding information on enemy parachute drops and with helping the authorities organise roadblocks and pickets. One prefect reported in late January that 'by the grace of this organisation and of individual initiatives, much parachuted material has been discovered'.

Despite the urgency, the civil and military organs of the new republic worried about handing out weapons to French *Résistance* veterans who typically manned the machinery of the anti-parachutist system. The question of whether surviving *Résistance* militias should be armed and authorised by the state divided France over the winter of 1944–1945 – the PCF only conceded the issue to the new authorities in late January – and in every location except the north-east, officials told the militants to use the weapons that they had already employed during the German occupation or to get out their hunting rifles.[159] In Alsace-Lorraine, the Americans armed a number of leftist militants who were deployed to track down parachutists or escaped German POWs; one such unit caught twenty-four German saboteurs and agents in the first two weeks of January 1945.[160]

One final difficulty for the Skorzeny programme was that the Germans and the French émigrés were not pursuing identical goals, a divergence of aims that had consequences. Although the Germans sometimes mused about political objectives, their main aim was to divert Allied attention. The PPF and the *Milice*, on the other hand, did have political goals, including wearing the shine off the reputation of the PCF, which was profiting from its central role in the French *Résistance*, and proving their own *bona fides* as anti-communist fighters. In fact, Jean Filliol explained to OT trainees that the *Milice* was letting the Germans think that parachutists were returning to France in order to commit sabotage, but that they actually had the political task of rallying an alliance of anti-communists. Indeed, while Sigmaringen's propaganda services continued to malign De Gaulle as a pro-communist 'dictator', it was becoming apparent by the winter of 1944–1945 that De Gaulle was no 'fellow traveller' and that his military officer corps was still inspired by many of the conservative and anti-communist traditions of the French Army.[161]

Joseph Darnand was aware that the right-wing and officer-dominated elements of the French *Résistance* had long been opposed to 'brigandage' by communist guerrillas and he probably also knew of a report in September 1944 that nationalist elements of the *Résistance* had 'started fighting against the Allies'.[162] After the reconstruction of the French Army had begun in earnest, the generals of the new force were rumoured to be weighing the creation of a military dictatorship.[163] Some of these senior figures, including Henri Giraud and Jean Lattre de Tassigny, had served Vichy before belatedly mending fences with the Western Allies in 1942–1943. In late 1944, the Sigmaringen regime claimed that there were still numerous partisans 'of the old French military spirit' and that such elements were being rallied by De Gaulle's arch-rival, Giraud, particularly in an attempt to block entry into the army by veterans of the French *Résistance*.

Darnand and other ex-Cagoulards sensed a particular community of interest with Giraud, who was rumoured to have supported the Cagoule. In 1944, former members of the Cagoule aligned with the Germans, such as Michel Harispe, tried to contact ex-Cagoulards in Giraud's entourage, especially Jacques Lemaigre-Dubreuil and Jean Rigaud, manoeuvres that were carried out with the blessing of Hans Sommer and Werner Neisser. The Giraudists, it was believed, would provide a handy conduit to the Americans, whom conservative Frenchmen thought were worried about the prospect of France's communisation and who were imagined to be still backing Giraud. Darnard sent emissaries to meet with Giraud in Portugal. Most of these projects failed: two of the principal Vichyites who attempted to dicker with Giraud were arrested by the Gestapo, while on the other side Giraud refused to receive Darnand's representatives. However, one semi-successful initiative involved Lemaigre-Dubreuil. In July 1944, Neisser flew to Madrid and met with Lemaigre-Dubreuil in a discussion about possible means to check De Gaulle. Five months later, Lemaigre-Dubreuil and Rigaud secretly returned to France. The Mil Amt suspected that the pair was attempting to create a US-backed White *Maquis* and much the same kind of speculation was expressed in the corridors of power in Paris, where arrest warrants for Lemaigre-Dubreuil and Rigaud were reactivated. The Mil Amt sent agents to make contact with Lemaigre-Dubreuil and Rigaud, but the two conspirators were quickly picked up by the French police.[164]

Rightly or wrongly, such incidents made an impression on Darnand, who believed that despite earlier rebuffs, he could still cosy up to Giraud. Minor bureaucratic rivalries got in the way of some approaches. In northern Italy, three *Miliciens* were detached from a White *Maquis* unit, *Sonderkommando* Berger, and they were deployed in an effort to contact the Giraudists, although these agents quickly fell afoul of Jean Filliol, who accused them of stealing from *Milicien* coffers and prevented their dispatch into France. Darnand also had no inkling of how badly he had soiled his reputation, even among republican conservatives. In early 1945, he ordered a Sigmaringen official named Heyraud to travel to Switzerland and meet with Giraud's representatives, although nothing came of these contacts. One German officer who discussed political matters with Darnand later suggested that '[he] still believed he could go back to France on a fight-communism basis... Darnand failed in these efforts because even the French who didn't like De Gaulle refused to listen to him.'[165]

Doriot, meanwhile, had begun to court Lattre de Tassigny, a manoeuvre backed by certain Germans. Besekow, Kubat and the head of *Skorpion-Rheingau*, *Oberleutnant* Derksen, were all interested in Lattre and considered him 'the only man with whom it would be possible to have dealings'. Lattre was felt to be conceited and open to flattery, especially of a nature that honoured his importance and promised a role commensurate with his elevated view of himself. He was also thought to be a strident anti-communist and receptive to a 'Europe-for-the-Europeans' argument. In crafting an image potentially acceptable to Lattre and other French generals, the PPF began to portray itself as an anti-communist bulwark for which alliance with Germany had been a tactical necessity. In fact, *Radio Patrie* appealed to ex-resisters who had been drawn into the French *Résistance* only because of their hatred of the Germans, and in January 1945 the station broadcast a number of appeals to officers of the First French Army in Alsace. Many of these officers, Doriot reminded them, had been hostile to the Popular Front, sympathetic to the Cagoule, and loyal to Pétain, but their understanding of the war as a Franco-German conflict was blinding them to the dangers of communism. 'If I believed', said Doriot, 'that this war was worthwhile for my country and that you were truly defending its existence, I would be on your side, among the ranks as an infantry officer.'

Amazingly, this tripe had some appeal for listeners on the other side of the line, and Lattre's *Deuxième Bureau*, with the complicity of right-wing Lyonnais elements of the French *Résistance*, sent emissaries to Lorrach in order to feel out Doriot and discuss the possibility of an anti-communist alliance. Doriot was apparently not sure that the main agent, Louise Delbreil, the wife of a PPF militant, was really a representative of Lattre, and he feared that his fellow collaborationists' desire to unite with sympathetic republican conservatives tended to cloud their judgement in such cases. According to Dieter Wolf, Doriot expressed some willingness to cooperate with Delbreil, although Jacques Delperrié de Bayac suggests that he smelled a trap and showed Delbreil the door, after which she was arrested and interrogated by the SD. The German handling of the emissaries was run by the Section B overlords, Steimle and Bickler, although Schellenberg flew into a rage because his two subordinates managed the case without his knowledge. In fact, the only reason Schellenberg learned of the affair was because he saw a *Waffen*-SS report mentioning the presence of French couriers along the Western Front.

Several accounts suggest that because Darnand and Doriot had extended feelers to the French generals, their willingness to send agents into France diminished. In fact, Delbreil is supposed to have told Doriot that the price of alliance with Lattre was cessation of all '*parachutages*'. Thus, one of the theories about Doriot's death is that he was on the cusp of cancelling parachute and infiltration operations, thereby making dangerous enemies in the SS, who arranged to have him neutralised.[166] Another argument along the same lines contends that Doriot had suspended '*parachutages*' and line-crossing because German remittances for such activities had fallen behind expenditures and that the Germans resented this demonstration of contrariness.[167] Henri Amouroux dismisses all such conjectures, arguing that they were later offered as palliatives by PPF members hoping to diminish the severity of post-war punishments.[168]

One final surprise involved the ultimate disposition of SD and Mil D agents still in training at the end of the war. Instead of releasing all such operatives, the Germans provided them with money and phoney cover as forced labourers, whence they were expected to return to France amidst the more than two million French prisoners and workers who were liberated as the Third Reich was overrun.[169] This scheme was the brainchild of Hans Schwinn, a multilingual Palatine-German who had once been based in Nice, where he served with *Streifkorps Süd Frankreich* and organised the infiltration of agents into the French *Résistance*. After the autumn of 1944, Schwinn was charged with planning *Jagdverband* operations in France, and even as he was being chased into Bavaria near the end of the war, he selected fifty French trainees and ordered them to return to France in order to 'form a resistance nucleus'. These agents were then passed through the lines by *Jagdkommando* 'Perner'.[170] Naturally, the French authorities soon became aware that there were German agents hidden among the repatriation convoys reaching France by the late spring of 1945.[171] In Paris, a captured Doriotiste admitted that the PPF was attempting to reorganise its combat groups and that it was laying arms depots for the use of militants.[172] Not coincidentally, there were a number of cases of sabotage in May and June 1945, and the director of the French Electricity Works warned that infiltrators among returning POWs and deportees were a danger to the country's infrastructure. 'Severe measures' were appropriate, he maintained, 'with a view toward ensuring the protection of production installations, transport and the electric power grid against attacks that appear to have been executed by these agents'.[173] The worst such acts of sabotage were two explosions at the 'Gnome and Rhône' aircraft engine works at Gennevilliers; thirteen labourers died and forty were injured in these blasts.[174]

What are we left to think about the effectiveness of German special operations in liberated Western Europe? Obviously, the absence of the Red Army and its capacity to prod anti-communist activism had a neutralising effect. Nonetheless, there were on hand some pro-communist Partisan movements that were sufficiently active to upset right-wingers and native fascists, particularly when the latter found themselves suffering because of purges, and had Skorzeny been able to lure the French and Italian communists into precipitate action – had operations to suppress the 'Fifth Column' mutated into open attempts to seize power – then the Germans would have been dealt the chance to play a winning hand. That option was eliminated by the prudent leaderships of the French and Italian communist parties, whose primary concern was to win the war and who abjured the need for a revolution in order to reign in the Fifth Column, although they were only too happy to exploit its existence in political manoeuvring. As a result, these parties willingly condoned a round of summary punishments of fascists and collaborators, but they then grudgingly accepted the fact that their own resistance militias would have to be disarmed and that the maintenance of order was the ultimate prerogative of the state.

The stakes were high in other ways too. A France wracked by disorder and sabotage would have been threatened with the establishment of an Allied military government, much like the one that had been imposed upon Italy, and the country's re-emergence as a great power would have been threatened. French police believed that the German special forces were deliberately trying to provoke an Allied clampdown and thereby hinder France's ability to put forward its claims at an anticipated post-war peace conference.[175] While there is no evidence that Skorzeny was ever this devious or far-sighted, there is no doubt that the fears he prompted were real.

Italy's claims to respect and to the integrity of its borders and its empire were even more balanced on a tightrope. Having jumped into the war as Germany's ally, anything that re-emphasised the influence of Italian Fascism was bound to weaken Italy's position and to encourage its erstwhile enemies to impose a tough peace treaty. Even some Italians admitted that Fascism was a 'collective responsibility' and that Italy had to earn its 'return ticket',[176] so one can imagine how the standing of the nation would have suffered had the favourable impression created by the growth of an anti-fascist resistance movement been balanced by the emergence of an equally powerful analogue backed by Germany and the Fascist Republic.

Finally, as was the case in Eastern Europe, the real impact of Skorzeny's activities was to increase the scale of pain, suffering and humiliation that had already afflicted so many beleaguered Europeans. Although there was no Red Army on hand to impose reprisals and collective punishments, communist vigilantes did their best to perform this function. Thus, while one could have expected a wave of summary executions and hostage-takings to have petered out in southern France over the winter of 1944–1945, as the initial zeal of the *épuration* cooled, in reality such outrages continued, partly because parachutists, Fifth Columnists and White *Maquisards* kept former *Résistance* militants on edge. Vigilante punishments and the seizure of hostages never entirely ceased until the war was over and the threat from Sigmaringen and Mainau was gone.[177]

A special degree of repressive damage was inflicted upon regional autonomy and separatist movements, whose radicals worked either directly or indirectly for the Germans, but whose moderates paid the price of such collaboration. Several writers have noted how the Breton nationalist movement was suffocated under maladroit measures from 1944 to 1947, even to the extent that Bretons eventually emerged to demonstrate in such towns as Folgoët. Observers in Ireland and Wales were outraged by such heavy-handedness.[178] Similar conclusions apply to the Flemish and Corsican movements in France, or to the Sicilian and Sardinian autonomists in Italy. Once the cudgels of state oppression began to swing, guilty and innocent alike were battered.

5
North by North-West

Jagdverband Nordwest faced special challenges compared to the other three '*Territorialen Jagdverbände*'. Since the unit covered the Low Countries and Scandinavia, many of its operational zones were never taken by the enemy and there was little need for various parts of the organisation to evolve beyond an embryonic stage of development. It is true that Belgium was liberated by the Western Allies in September 1944 – it thereafter became *Nordwest's* main theatre of operations – but only the fringes of the Netherlands and Norway were overrun by Germany's foes. Finland, one of the Third Reich's hesitant allies, remained unoccupied by any of the major belligerents, a peculiar situation that both facilitated and stymied German efforts at subversion. Neither the Western Allies nor the Soviets were able to move forces into Denmark, at least before the final German capitulation in north-western Europe, although Skorzeny established a presence in that country because of his efforts to terrorise the Danish patriot resistance movement.

It was this relative lack of battlefield commitment that limited the number of *Nordwest* personnel, although one also has to take into consideration that no Brandenburg contingents were allotted to *Nordwest*. Plans had been made in the summer of 1944 for *Leutnant* Pavel to field an '*Einsatzgruppe Flandern*' under the auspices of '*Streifkorps Nord Frankreich*', but this process was little advanced before the mobilisation of the *Jagdverbände*.[1] This left *Jagdverband Nordwest* as something of an orphan. The Germans addressed this problem by recruiting 130 volunteers at the *Waffen*-SS training grounds at Sennheim, mostly Belgians and Dutchmen, but also a handful of Danes, and they augmented this group with a trickle of manpower from the SS 'Langemarck' and '*Niederlande*' brigades, some of whom passed through a parachute training course at Papa, Hungary. Belgian and Dutch policemen and SD agents were also signed up, including fifty men from the SD school at Drogen, and later recruitment efforts focussed upon foreign 'volunteers' from German factories or Hitler Youth training camps. A few additional troops were attracted from the *Luftwaffe*.[2]

Himmler ordered *Nordwest* organisers to meet with the leaders of the Belgian fascist parties and to draw recruits from their ranks, particularly since 2,000 to 3,000 Belgians had fled to Germany, settling in the Lüneburg Heath and the Alfeld district of Hanover. Ironically, the largest fascist movement, the *Vlaamsch National Verbond* (VNV), was not invited to participate in destabilising Belgium, mainly because its strident Catholicism and support for Flanders's union with the Netherlands, rather than Germany, alienated it from the SS. Indeed, Himmler restricted the movements of senior VNV leaders in Germany and he limited their political activity.[3] Having thus forsaken the help of a party with a legitimate mass base in western and northern Belgium, Himmler was forced to depend on its two more minor counterparts, the Flemish *DeVlag*, under Jef van de Weile, and the Wallonian Rex, which was led by Léon Degrelle. Both *DeVlag* and the

Rex insisted that a pro-German resistance movement be built solely from their cadres, although the results of recruitment actions yielded only mixed results. Van de Weile helped *Jagdverband* recruiters who roamed the Lüneburg Heath in autumn of 1944, although the Germans were unhappy with the outcome and suspected that Van de Weile's relative lack of popularity had hindered their efforts. In fact, the chiefs of the *Jagdverbände* decided to keep a close watch on Van de Weile, even though he was favourably treated in German propaganda. The Rexists offered even more disappointments. Although the Rex had once been a major political force, its brand of all-Belgian nationalism was betrayed, rather than augmented, by association with an occupying power that wanted to dismember the country. As a result, Rexist support diminished during the time of the German occupation,[4] and its ability to provide a base for pro-German guerrilla warfare was limited. In addition, Degrelle forwarded most of his men to his *Waffen*-SS unit on the Eastern Front, and few volunteers were available to *Nordwest*. In fact, Degrelle pulled personnel out of the *Jagdverbände* and reassigned them elsewhere.[5]

Total numbers of *Jagdverband Nordwest* personnel have been estimated at between 60 and 120 soldiers, which was Radl's characteristically low approximation, and 400 effectives, which was the figure provided by Skorzeny. Evidence from veterans of *Nordwest* suggest that Skorzeny's estimate was closer to the mark.[6] One *Nordwest* volunteer who was schooled at the unit's main training camp from September 1944 to February 1945 later recalled that there were 800 people who undertook sabotage instruction at the facility (although some of these were Werewolves and trainees from other *Jagdverbände*).[7]

The commander of *Nordwest* was 34-year-old Heinrich Hoyer, a natural choice because he had been born in the Dutch East Indies and was comfortable in the culture of the Low Countries. He was also a close friend of Skorzeny. Subordinates regarded Hoyer as the most outstanding personality in the *Jagdverbände*, and he was a talented linguist, an expert saboteur and a skilled shot with a pistol, although he was also indiscreet and overly trusting. Hoyer, interestingly, was an enthusiastic Nazi, although his straight black hair and dark complexion led to whispers about an Indo-Malayan element in his ancestry, a delicate issue in the SS. It was his activism that got *Nordwest* involved in the fighting at Schwedt, where he was severely wounded in the body and face, the skin around his eye sockets being shredded by shell splinters. The eventual result was a series of scars that contributed to what one contemporary described as his 'quiet yet violent appearance'. In any case, his injuries earned him a stay in a Prague military hospital, where he was visited by Skorzeny, although he had to cede command of the *Nordwest* battalion. When released from hospital, he was reassigned to *Werwolf* matters.[8]

Hoyer was replaced by *Hauptsturmführer* Willy Dethier, a ruddy-faced and pot-bellied Rhinelander who was an '*Alte Kämpfer*' – he looked the part – and had good connections in the senior echelon of the Nazi Party. Dethier had a long history in the *Waffen*-SS and had served with the 'Langemarck' brigade in heavy fighting on the Eastern Front. He was an expert in anti-tank warfare and Flak gunnery.[9]

Like the other *Jagdverbände*, *Nordwest* was divided into a number of geographically defined companies, all of which were led by a cadre of young SS officers who had trained together at the Bad Tölz '*Junkerschule*'. *Jagdeinsatz Flandern* was the largest of the constituent companies, consisting of more than 200 men, plus an auxiliary of forty

Flemish and Dutch women being trained as radio operators. Some of the men in the unit had been recruited with the assurance that they would prevent Allied demolitions during a prospective German reconquest of Belgium, only to later learn that they were actually expected to wage anti-Allied partisan warfare and infiltrate the ranks of the Belgian Communist Party. The women were promised that they would serve in a non-combat role as '*Nachrichtenhelferinnen*' (communications assistants). Volunteers were guaranteed plum posts in any future regime to be established by the Germans in Belgium.[10] The assemblage was led by a small and vicious Antwerp adventurer named Josef Bachot, who was one of the Bad Tölz cohort. Bachot already had hundreds of lives on his conscience, having led repressive operations against Jews and patriot resisters in German-occupied Antwerp. Despite such crimes, he participated in several behind-the-lines missions that carried him back into his home country. In March 1945, for instance, he was spotted in the eastern Belgian town of Eupen, where the *Jagdverbände* hoped to induce local German-speaking inhabitants to carry out guerrilla warfare. Bachot's two main lieutenants were *Unterscharführer* Pasques and a former member of the Belgian judiciary police named Peters, who had once helped to smuggle downed Allied fliers through the front and was now selling his line-crossing services to the *Jagdverbände*.[11]

On 28 December 1944, Bachot sent an advance party to Giessen, where he established a base for operations against Belgium; an additional 140 troops arrived on 10 January. He eventually determined that half of these men were unsuitable for guerrilla warfare and he dispatched that group to the Eastern Front, a course of action that contributed to his general unpopularity. The remaining unit members were trained as tank hunters and informed that they would work in civilian clothes. Bachot formed special detachments to operate inside Belgium. He had told an acquaintance that he had a mandate to assassinate senior Belgian political figures, including the Prince Regent, Premier Hubert Pierlot and Auditor General Ganshof van der Mersch.[12] While Bachot was unable to murder such men, he did send parachutists into Belgium and he infiltrated line-crossers by overland routes. He tried and failed to slip two SS men from Antwerp across the front, but another of his volunteers, a German South African named Sturm, accomplished several missions in the company of three female agents. On 12 April, *Unterscharführer* Pasques was sent on a 'special mission' with an eight-man team.[13]

Jagdeinsatz Niederlande originally consisted of forty Dutch recruits and was built up to a level of several hundred men, although it was severely during heavy fighting at the Schwedt bridgehead from 10 to 13 February 1945. According to one account, the company attracted unwanted attention from superiors when a number of Dutch trainees, resenting the miserable state of their rations, were caught selling equipment to German civilians in exchange for food. *Nordwest*'s judicial officer, *Untersturmführer* Egner, brought this situation to Skorzeny's attention, whence the entire company was stood before a court martial and tried. Five men were sentenced to penal servitude and dismissed from the SS; a further 100, judged too unreliable for deployment behind Allied lines, were posted to *Jagdverband Mitte* and sent to Schwedt. As for the rest, most were dispatched on missions to Holland or sent to Hoogeveen, the training ground of the Dutch SS '*Landstorm*' Division. The leadership staff was put under the command of *Obersturmführer* Stielau, the bespectacled English speaker who had led the 'jeep teams' in the Battle of the

Bulge. The unit headquarters were moved to Bad Bentheim, near the Dutch frontier, and communications with Friedenthal were maintained via Skorzeny's powerful short-wave station at Schloss Inselhof, which became operational in early 1945.[14]

Nordic Scandinavia was covered by three small units that barely advanced beyond the planning stage. *Jagdeinsatz Dänemark* was one of *Nordwest's* original companies, although in September 1944 it only had seventeen men on its roster. It was eventually built up to a level of forty volunteers, who were commanded by Kurt Rathje, a Copenhagen-born SS officer and veteran of the Bad Tölz programme. Most members of *Dänemark* were eventually marched to a forward base at Glücksberg, Schleswig, where they were housed in 'Elin' cottage and kitted in navy dress. Willy Dethier used his contacts in the *Kriegsmarine* to lay his hands on a supply of such uniforms, which were of interest because there was a fear in *Jagdverband* ranks that sabotage troops would be shot if captured. It thus seemed good sense to immerse *Jagdverband* elements among the blue-clad masses of sailors in northern Germany and Denmark.

Nordwest also included a minuscule *Jagdeinsatz Schweden*, which represented an attempt to cover a country that had not been evacuated by German troops and was thus not part of its mandate. Nonetheless, the establishment of a *Jagdverband* presence in Sweden was vital to operations in Finland and Norway, and by December 1944 a handful of Swedish volunteers had been gathered under the leadership of *Obersturmführer* Erich Eklöf, yet another alumnus of Bad Tölz. Eklöf was a 22-year-old Swede from Ragunda.

The preparation of an anti-Allied resistance movement in Norway was the responsibility of *Jagdeinsatz Norwegen*, which was commanded by *Untersturmführer* Schneider, a 25-year-old Norwegian national who had served in the *Waffen*-SS as a tank commander. Codenamed 'Silberfuchs', the Norwegian company initially consisted of ten men, although it was reinforced in the early months of 1945. Four guerrilla organisers were dispatched to Oslo in late January and by March they had established 'Meldekopf Nordland', which maintained wireless contact with *Jagdverband Nordwest*, probably via Inselhof. Schneider himself headed to Norway in the spring of 1945, reportedly in order to recruit personnel for an 'Einsatz'.[15]

Skorzeny also engaged an advisor on Nordic affairs, a post occupied by Carl Edquist, a highly strung Scandinavian fascist. Edquist was a Swedish businessman who defected to the Germans in September 1944 by sailing to Norway in a small boat. According to Edquist, there were plans to detach the Scandinavian elements of *Nordwest* and create a distinctive 'Jagdverband Nord', with Edquist himself in charge, although in considering the validity of this claim, it should be noted that Edquist was a megalomaniac and was legally declared insane in 1946. Such was the condition of Skorzeny's main 'expert' on Scandinavian issues. In any case, 'Jagdverband Nord' never materialised and Edquist was arrested by the Gestapo on 2 February 1945, allegedly for making remarks 'insulting to the *Führer*'.[16]

Finland was a special case. Like the other Scandinavian companies, *Jagdeinsatz Finnland* was a small outfit, comprised largely of prisoners of war captured after Germany's violent breach with Finland and gathered from the Kongsvinger POW camp in Norway. Since relations with Finland were delicate – the Soviets did not militarily occupy the defeated state and the Germans continued to have contact with senior figures in the Finnish Army – Schellenberg prohibited active operations. As a result, *Jagdeinsatz Finnland* was employed largely as a collecting and training centre for men eventually passed on to Section D, which had direct contact with the anti-communist resistance movement. In fact, the chief of Section D's Finnish bureau, Alarich Brohs, was given control of all RSHA operations in Finland, including activity of the *Jagdverbände*. Brohs, a level-headed officer born in 1904, had a poor opinion of Skorzeny and of *Jagdeinsatz Finnland's* commanding officer, *Obersturmführer* Kotkas, both of whom he feared were headstrong fanatics. Kotkas, who had been a cadet at Bad Tölz and was a veteran of SS Mountain Division 'Nord', was indeed a romantic hothead and ardent fascist/Germanophile (he spoke the German language without trace of an accent). Most worryingly, he was rumoured to be contemplating a Finnish '*Einsatz*' with a '*Sprengboot*' (exploding boat), despite Schellenberg's prohibition of such operations.

In March 1945, the Finns were preparing for deployment when a small quantity of plastic explosive used in training accidentally detonated, badly injuring an instructor. Shortly after this event, they were moved to Glücksburg, where they were housed together with the Danes in 'Elin' cottage and spent their days in a programme of demolition training run by *Unterscharführer* Tamm. Like the Danes, the Finns were disguised in German Navy uniforms.[17]

The leaders of *Jagdverband Nordwest* also attempted to field an English-speaking company, potentially for use along the Western Front, but also intended for the launching of small-scale expeditions to Britain or America. Although one account suggests that this 'English' unit existed only on paper, another contemporary witness thought that it was built up to a level of 200 to 300 men by the late autumn of 1944, but was then depleted through the transfer of 'volunteers' to *Panzer* Brigade 150. One commando who was assigned to the unit in February–March 1945 recalled that the Germans were busy building the detachment back up to strength, and that its members had been issued with American automatic pistols. The commanding officer was *Obersturmführer* Wolf, a young German national who spoke excellent English and was scheduled for a trip to Britain in the company of his deputy, *Hauptscharführer* Rosbach, although Rosbach was badly wounded in the fighting at Schwedt.[18]

In mid-December 1944, several *Nordwest* officers, including Hoyer, Bachot and Henri Morael, attended a send-off party for *Unterstürmführer* Langhe, who was called the '*Einsatzführer für England*' and was about to depart for Britain with a small detachment.[19] This is a significant snippet of information because it has long been rumoured that Skorzeny helped plan a rebellion of German POWs in Britain, an outbreak that was supposed to begin at the time of the Ardennes Offensive and which would have exercised a diversionary effect. Indeed, in early December 1944 the British pre-empted a mass break-out of POWs from the Devizes camp in the west of England, and there was also a rash of unrest and escape activity at other camps. Historians are divided about whether the German prisoners were in contact with the SD and about whether their escape attempts were coordinated, although Skorzeny later insisted that he had never undertaken operations in Britain, mainly because he was aware of the tight security measures on the island.[20] Nonetheless, knowledge of the Langhe affair gives reason for pause, and one *Nordwest* member who worked in the *Führungsstab* later claimed that '*Einsätze*' were carried out in England and Ireland.[21]

Skorzeny is also on record negotiating with the Mil Amt's naval specialist, *Kapitän zur See* Bechtolsheim, in order to reserve spaces on a U-Boat bound for North America. The initial discussions about this operation occurred in the autumn of 1944, although arrangements were momentarily put on hold as the operatives finished their training. Several officers who were present at Friedenthal through the winter of 1944–1945 later claimed that the chief of this team was naval lieutenant Mollitor, an English speaker who had been recruited from *Panzer* Brigade 150 and was in the midst of his training in December 1944. According to Bechtolsheim, two agents eventually departed from Kiel and their submarine called at a port in Norway before heading into the North Atlantic.[22] The ultimate outcome of the mission is unknown.

In addition to the various companies of *Nordwest*, the battalion formed a battle school, which was situated in the Mecklenburg town of Neustrelitz, sixty miles north of Berlin. Flemish and Dutch trainees at Friedenthal were sent to Neustrelitz in late October and scores of incoming recruits were directed to the same location. Since the Brandenburgers had bequeathed little of value to *Nordwest*, Hoyer had to build his own training apparatus by redeploying the personnel and supplies of the old Section S facility near The Hague, which closed its doors in June 1944. The Neustrelitz school was run by *Hauptsturmführer* Heinz Winter, a grey and balding veteran of the Brandenburg Division who had extensive experience in fighting partisans and knew a great deal about the technical aspects of guerrilla warfare. Classes started in the late autumn of 1944 and Winter organised an effective curriculum, showing students how to blow up vehicles and demolish railway tracks with British explosives. Agent reports from Belgium were used to whip up the sentiments of Flemish trainees, particularly gloomy descriptions of the treatment of former collaborators, and if the potential treatment meted out by the enemy did not scare recruits, they were led to believe that their own side could pose an even greater threat to their existence. Recently arrived attendees were warned that if they deserted or divulged any secrets, avengers would deliver a bullet to their brains, even if they were behind enemy lines and even if the war was over.[23]

As was the case in other theatres of operation, Skorzeny was partially dependent upon fragments of the *Abwehr* that he was able to draw to his banner. The Mil D staff behind the Western Front was run by *Hauptmann* Hellmers, a veteran of *Abwehr* work in Spain, and it was located first at Bad Ems and then at Bad Orb (near Fulda). This staff ran a number of programmes, particularly in a facility at Kehlbach, which trained Belgian saboteurs and parachutists, and in a radio/Morse school at Pension Wilhelma, Bad Ems. Several *Jagdverband* sergeants helped organise the training at Kehlbach, and recruits were told that their leader was the man who had rescued Mussolini. Graduates were called 'F und S Männer' ('Funk' and 'Sabotage' men).

FAK 213 was Mil D's main operational element in north-western Europe and ran missions in the Low Countries and western Scandinavia. The unit was based in a Capuchin monastery in Münster, which was convenient since the monks performed domestic duties, and it trained agents at Quentz and at half a dozen camps run by reconnaissance units in Belgium, the Netherlands and Denmark. The commander was a stodgy, bull-necked and dyspeptic Hanoverian named Richard Gerken, who was a professional policeman. Although ambitious and ruthless, Gerken was also a moralist who hated the Nazi Party. At FAK 213, he fought an ongoing battle with *Hauptmann* Uhrmann, a Viennese chum of Skorzeny who had been sent to Münster as an SD spy. In fact, FAK 213 was wracked by tensions between anti-Nazi veterans of the *Abwehr* and a new breed of Nazified officers who sympathised with the *Jagdverbände*.[24]

Several Belgian sabotage missions were also undertaken by units of FAK 307, especially since this detachment's counter-intelligence functions diminished after the German retreat from the Low Countries. FAK 307's commander was the brilliant Hermann Giskes, the man who had masterminded the *Abwehr*'s infiltration of the Dutch patriot underground, but Giskes had a low opinion of Skorzeny — 'big, bold, brave, but not all too bright' was his assessment — and he preferred to run his operations independently. One of his officers later recalled that cooperation with the *Jagdverbände* was 'nonexistent', although one of *Nordwest*'s female radio operators did find her way into Giskes's organisation. At least one of Giskes's units, *Trupp* 363, deployed a five-man Belgian demolition group, which had orders to attack Allied fuel pipelines.[25]

Finally, Skorzeny was supposed to cooperate with the remnants of the former *Abwehr* station in Helsinki, which was reassembled at Heringsdorf and called *Sonderkommando* '*Nord*'. This formation remained under the control of the *Abwehr*'s ex-liaison officer with the Finnish General Staff, *Fregatten Kapitän* Alexander Cellarius.[26] Unfortunately for the SD, both Cellarius and his boss, Werner Ohletz, were old-time *Abwehr* officers who despised the *arriviste* Skorzeny, a fact ensuring that their relationship with the *Jagdverbände* remained tense.

A WINTER OF DISCONTENT

As soon as the Allies reached Belgium in September 1944, they noticed that enemy agents were 'far more numerous… than in any part of France'. Partly this owed to the fact that the Germans had long expected an Allied invasion of the Low Countries and had made early preparations; partly it was the result of Flemish ethnic kinship with the Germans, which the latter were quick to exploit and which provided the base for a doctrine of Nordic racial superiority. Canadian Field Security noted that Flemish separatism and Germanic ethnic affinity resulted 'in a somewhat more fanatical devotion to the Nazi ideal even — or perhaps by preference — in a lost cause'.[27] On the other hand, the vigilance of the Belgian patriot resistance was more severe even than that of its French counterpart, and the Canadians noted that 'practically all the most dangerous suspects who had not already escaped were locked up before we arrived'.[28]

Skorzeny controlled three stay-behind rings in Belgium, each of which failed miserably. His most important organisation was launched in early 1944 as the 'Henriette' *Zerstörergruppe*. 'Henriette' was run from a headquarters at 18 rue Émile Claus in Brussels, mainly by *Hauptsturmführer* Lawrenz, a 35-year-old SD officer who was fond of wine, women and double-breasted suits. Lawrenz's authority, however, was frequently superseded by Arno Besekow, who took a personal interest in 'Henriette', and Lawrenz was also reputed to be highly dependent upon his staff. Most actual work was done by Lawrenz's executive officer, a slender Flemish spy named Joseph Verstraeten. Lawrenz 'borrowed' Verstraeten from the Sipo police commander in Brussels, who had used him as an operative and was willing to contribute manpower because he felt that preparation of anti-Allied resistance was a task of unsurpassed importance.

Verstraeten was a colourful character. Although he enjoyed speeding around Belgium in his automobile or atop his Ariel motorbike, he was hardly a dashing figure. Due to his poor driving skills, he was constantly damaging his vehicles, and although in his mid-thirties, he was still living at home. Family life consisted of a constant stream of arguments between Verstraeten junior and senior, the latter of whom was sympathetic to the Allies and made a practice of listening to the BBC. Verstraeten also walked a romantic tightrope between two mistresses, Delphine Lagrou and Adrienne Volcke, both of whom he recruited as 'Henriette' agents, despite the fact that they were each highly strung women given to fits of temper. The resultant contact between the two rivals led to a series of violent quarrels that terminated in an incident on 28 August 1944, when Lagrou and Verstraeten drew pistols on each other. Lagrou's increasing alienation was a serious matter because she was supposed to serve as the future liaison agent between 'Henriette' cells, and the wisdom of such romantic entanglements was the cause of a major row between Verstraeten and Besekow.

According to Skorzeny, Verstraeten developed 'Henriette' into an organisation of twenty-five members, stationed mainly along the Belgian coast and in Brussels. Volunteers were mainly Flemish and were drawn from the Belgian fascist parties, Nazi auxiliaries and the *Waffen*-SS. Ten of the recruits were run through an eighteen-day course at Skorzeny's training facility near The Hague. Once at the school, pupils signed a pledge of secrecy and were forced to remain on the grounds, which were patrolled by Dutch SS sentries. Training focused on techniques for damaging industrial machinery, blowing up ships and interfering with rail traffic. In fact, agents were brought on a tour of the Belgian Railway Technical Museum and the Amsterdam docks, where they were given on-site instructions for spotting sabotage targets and priming them for destruction. After completing the course, the agents spent the summer of 1944 laying sabotage dumps, a priority since an Allied invasion of Belgium was imminent. Supplies came via a lorry-load of equipment from Berlin, which arrived in June 1944, plus captured British material provided by the Brussels Sipo. Arms caches were established at a dozen locations in Belgium, plus several spots in the extreme north of France (St Omer, Dunkirk). Radio outposts were established at Brussels and Antwerp.

Verstraeten found it hard to motivate the personnel of the *Zerstörergruppe*, although he hardly inspired loyalty through his practice of stealing from the unit's payroll, or by his more general management of 'Henriette' like a scheme for his own enrichment. One of the members of 'Henriette' suggested that the operation was shaped by Verstraeten's need to pay for the upkeep of two mistresses, which he was able to do only at German expense. For instance, he convinced Besekow that he needed 250,000 francs for the purchase of an Antwerp hotel/casino as a 'Henriette' 'meeting spot' – Volcke would preside as proprietress – although he then squandered the money before it could be invested in the property. Verstraeten did secure the evacuation of his volunteers' families, who were escorted to Germany by his deputy, Jan Huygens, but his rosy picture of ample rations and a fraternal reception was belied by poor treatment of the evacuees – one family had all its possessions stolen – and such news naturally reached the ears of the stay-behind agents. Whatever Verstraeten's intentions, this effort brought him little credit.

As a result of such dampers, as well as recognition of the overall course of the war, 'Henriette' personnel rarely discussed their sabotage assignments nor did they seem ready to carry out their missions. In fact, since many had criminal backgrounds, they were not the type of idealists likely to sacrifice for a greater cause. Besekow had two of the agents shot after he discovered, around August 1944, that they were involved in a plan to kill a prominent Brussels dowager and then avail themselves of the woman's cash and jewellery. Both men were professional thieves and cardsharps. Another volunteer from the *Waffen-SS* was returned to his unit after he was caught stealing from the canteen at the Hague sabotage school. Yet another volunteer also proved a murderer and a thief, although he was tolerated because his victims were anti-German patriots and because he procured a steady supply of petrol that was stolen from the garage of the National Socialist Transport Corps (NSKK). Verstraeten was aware of the source of this fuel, but the thief was allowed to split the profits with a partner working in the NSKK motor pool.

There are thus grounds for doubting the potential eagerness of 'Henriette' agents, even under optimal operational conditions, and such an environment never developed. Quite to the contrary, when Belgium was liberated in September 1944, a summary purge swept through the land and the main strike force of the Belgian patriotic resistance, the *Brigade Blanche*, sprang into action. Most of the Belgian fascists and collaborators who comprised 'Henriette' were bagged immediately and many of their supply caches were uncovered, particularly since Verstraeten had disobeyed Besekow's instructions and had allowed the agents to hide their own dumps. One woman was caught red-handed as she was attempting to rebury boxes and drums of sabotage material that had already been situated in her garden in Drogenbosch.

Rather than go down with a sinking ship, Verstraeten and Volcke joined a Sipo convoy that left Brussels on the evening of 30 August 1944, vowing to return by Christmas in the company of '5,000 German-trained parachutists'. Section S, of course, could hardly rally such legions of agents, although the Germans did eventually brag of having 1,000 Belgian parachutists in training and they were willing to devote further resources in order to revive 'Henriette'.[29] In fact, as was the case with the 'Jeanne' enterprise in France, Besekow could not bear to write off the work already put into 'Henriette', and he thus cast about Section S and the *Jagdverbände*, looking for even more manpower and material to throw at the operation. Verstraeten was an obvious starting point. Initially, he was sent to the Lüneburg Heath in order to recruit new volunteers, but in late September he was recalled to Friedenthal. He was no longer the young enthusiast – in fact, he was arrested and briefly detained by Hoyer, perhaps for undercutting morale among female radio trainees at Friedenthal – but in late October Besekow offered him a chance to 'atone for his… sins' by heading back to Belgium. Verstraeten got drunk at his departure party, not a positive indicator about his state of mind, but he was infiltrated successfully through enemy lines. Heavily armed, he may have had access to a radio transmitter because Skorzeny later recalled receiving signals suggesting that the original 'Henriette' *Zerstörergruppe* had been wiped out, but that Verstraeten was willing to lay a new foundation, provided he could be supplied with airborne manpower and supplies.

A day after Verstraeten's departure, reinforcements were sent in the form of Dutch SS man Hugo LaHaye and his Belgian girlfriend Simone Desirant, both of whom had been trained at Friedenthal and were smuggled across the lines near Roermond, posing as Belgian refugees. The LaHaye-Desirant mission was to contact Verstraeten and then track down the remainder of the original 'Henriette' agents and arms dumps. The pair was also supposed to reconnoitre landing sites for airdrops of supplies, blow up railways and power lines, use poison to contaminate water reservoirs, and act as *agents provocateurs*, throwing hand grenades and firing rifles whenever Belgian communists gathered for a demonstration. The fact that German agents had such instructions is significant given the near-revolutionary levels of communist agitation that had developed in Belgium by the late autumn of 1944.

LaHaye and Desirant were unable to carry out their mission because they were captured after slipping across the Nederweert–Wessen Canal and penetrating Allied lines. LaHaye had been disgusted by what he had seen of German atrocities on the Eastern Front and he also had a personal axe to grind, since he discovered that his wife had been impregnated by a German soldier stationed in Belgium. As a result, he had no objection when he stopped at a farm for directions and the occupant asked whether he would mind having an American officer called in order to check his credentials. Once in Allied hands, LaHaye revealed a great deal in interrogation and he also agreed to act under Allied control, with the intention of capturing Verstraeten and trapping Jan Huygens, who was being trained as a radio operator and was due to follow LaHaye into Belgium. LaHaye did not complete either of these assignments, although he did lead the Allies to several arms dumps and he also revealed the identities of 'Henriette' members who had already been arrested as collaborators but had succeeded in hiding the full range of their activities. Delphine Lagrou, who had been twice arrested in September 1944 but had charmed her way out of captivity, was now apprehended again and forced to admit her central role in the 'Henriette' undertaking. The Allies considered using Desirant as a hostage and sending LaHaye back to Germany – Section S had scheduled him to return by 15 December – but they eventually decided against such a risky gambit.[30] In any case, the Germans suspected that LaHaye and Desirant had been captured.[31]

The reason that LaHaye was unable to trap Huygens was that the latter found it impossible to get a functioning radio and his trip to Belgium was thus postponed. After puttering around Friedenthal for three months, Huygens, by late February 1945, was struggling with his fourth wireless apparatus, another lemon that still did not function properly. Besekow nonetheless decided that it was time to send him on his way, arguing that it was the responsibility of either Lawrenz or Skorzeny to find a working radio. Huygens was attached to a team of four Belgian saboteurs, all *Jagdverband* recruits whom the Germans had tried to infiltrate through the front but had eventually decided to airdrop. Led by Henri Morael, this group had the usual demolition tasks, although members were advised to avoid high-profile targets in favour of fuel pipelines. They were also instructed to contact remnants of 'Henriette' and to reconnoitre canals and aerodromes, particularly in order to check on the effectiveness of earlier demolitions. The Germans also wanted to know about the extent of damage caused by V-1 strikes in Brussels. Anyone who got in the way of the parachutists was to be eliminated, and they also had instructions to kill their own comrades if the latter were wounded. In addition, Besekow ordered Huygens to murder Paul Laroche, a captain in the *Brigade Blanche*.

In a typical KG 200 fiasco, the 'Henriette' reinforcements were mistakenly airdropped *not* into the Limburg province of Belgium, which was their intended destination, but into northern France, nearly 150 miles off-target. Plunged into this unfamiliar environment, Morael and his fellow team member, Annita Prelogar, were arrested by local civilians, who quickly found their parachutes and took note of Flemish-speaking strangers in their midst. The group's arms and wireless transmission equipment also fell into enemy hands. Two other team members posed as Belgian refugees and succeeded in getting frontier-crossing passes from the Belgian consul in St Quentin, although their ruse was not sufficient to get passed Belgian customs officials. Huygens did somewhat better. He managed to sneak across the frontier and reach Brussels, where he learned that he was being hunted by the *Brigade Blanche*. He then made several attempts to contact LaHaye, but he was arrested on 20 March 1945 after he had approached a fellow *Jagdverband* operative whom he met on the street. Unfortunately for him, this acquaintance had already been arrested and 'turned' by the Belgian authorities, and he gave up Huygens to the *Deuxième Direction Belge*. Since several of the 'Henriette' parachutists had once played a brutal role in the suppression of the Belgian patriot resistance, their captures were of juridical value, particularly that of Morael, who had once been a section leader in both the Flemish fascist militia and the Belgian SS, and had bragged of sniping at pro-Allied crowds that had gathered during Belgium's liberation.[32]

Around the time that Huygens was attached to the Morael *Gruppe*, Besekow also decided to deploy yet another 'Henriette' agent who would remain unknown to both Huygens and Morael. This individual was *Oberscharführer* Leo Poppe, a bearded Antwerp adventurer who had been flirting with the German espionage service since the 1930s and had once inspected Belgian troops while disguised as a foreign dignitary, a hoax for which he was imprisoned. After tours of duty in the French Foreign Legion and the *Waffen*-SS, he was picked by Skorzeny as a recruiter for *Jagdverband Nordwest*, a job he performed while also serving as a propagandist for Jef van der Weile's exile 'regime'. At Friedenthal, he became the talk of the camp through his wild exploits, particularly his practice of firing a pistol while in bed, lodging bullets inches above the bedstead of his roommate. His real mistake, however, was to indulge his loquaciousness during recruitment tours, particularly since he doubted Skorzeny's genius as a commando leader. In February 1945, Besekow called him to his office and gave him a dangerous assignment: he would, said Besekow, enter Switzerland posing as a Belgian refugee. After his arrest by Swiss border guards, he would demand to see the Belgian consul and request repatriation. Upon reaching his homeland, he would track down the remaining manpower and material of 'Henriette', reconnoitre parachute drop zones, rent safe-houses and procure Belgian currency, identity papers and ration cards. If he had the chance, he could commit impromptu acts of sabotage.

Poppe dutifully headed for southern Baden, where Karl Hagedorn's line-crossing organisation helped him cross the Swiss frontier near Basel. He hid his gun and reported to the Swiss authorities. It was then that he apparently had a change of heart. Upon presenting himself to the Belgian consul, he admitted that he was a German agent and revealed the details of his mission. The Belgians extradited him and found that he proved helpful in interrogations. While on a conditional release, it was Poppe who was recognised by Huygens, who knew him from Friedenthal, and who then betrayed his fellow agent. The Huygens affair greatly impressed the Belgians, who decided to employ Poppe as a double agent. The British were not so sure about the wisdom of this strategy. They wondered why one of the most enthusiastic Flemish collaborators at Friedenthal had rushed to give himself up as soon as he was outside of Germany, even despite his apparent breach of faith with *Jagdverband* leaders. They suspected an attempt to penetrate the Allied intelligence services, although officers at 21st Army Group admitted that it would be impossible to talk the Belgians out of deploying Poppe. There the matter stood for the last several weeks of the war.[33]

While Section S squandered its time with 'Henriette', Mil D organised two equivalent networks. As early as 1941, the *Zweierorganisation* had been recruiting Flemish volunteers for service in Britain, where they were supposed to pose as Belgian refugees. Due to transport and camouflage problems, only one of these agents was dispatched to England, while the remainder were eventually rolled into a stay-behind organisation for West Flanders. Recruits from the Flemish fascist parties, the Belgian SS and the gendarmerie were also inveigled into joining this network, sometimes without a clear recognition of its nature. Others were enticed by the promise of an easy salary or by an assurance that sabotage duty would protect them from drafts of compulsory labour in Germany. At the time, the chance of an Allied invasion seemed remote.

The boss of the West Flanders network was Dr Marschall, chief of the *Zweierorganisation* in Belgium, although the executive officer was a curly-headed German-Fleming named Martens. As early as the autumn of 1942, Martens was running Flemish recruits through a series of sabotage courses at several locations in Antwerp, particularly Fort Schooten, on the outskirts of the city. Agents were acquainted with an array of British sabotage equipment that had been taken from the patriot underground. They were also trained in the use of British weapons, mainly with the rationale that they might someday have to operate with equipment captured from the enemy. The eventual aim of Martens's sabotage programme was to prepare agents for 'individual actions', such as wire cutting, which would take place in the immediate wake of any Allied invasion of Belgium, plus subsequent participation in more elaborate attacks against airfields and railways. These latter operations would depend on the airborne deployment of 'ringleaders' five to six weeks after the enemy's arrival. Communications would be the responsibility of couriers and a radio specialist, Armand de Coort, who would maintain contact with *Abwehr* controllers.

In the autumn of 1943, the Germans concluded that there would be no invasion of the Low Countries that year and Martens promptly disappeared, perhaps because he was transferred to another *Abwehr* unit. Martens's departure caused the elevation of his second-in-command, Jules van Beek, a paunchy, chain-smoking Antwerp journalist who had fought on Franco's side in the Spanish Civil War. Van Beek ran the West Flanders ring for the last year of its existence and spent most of his time hiding copious amounts of demolition material, as well as trying to maintain the focus of the organisation's agents, who were scattered throughout a dozen Belgian and French towns.

Despite Van Beek's efforts, most of the network collapsed upon the arrival of the Allies. Saboteurs in Ypres and Courtrai immediately reported to the *Brigade Blanche*, tattling on their fellow agents and revealing the location of supply dumps. In Wervik, one saboteur was so upset by his initial interrogation by the *Brigade Blanche* that upon his conditional release, he dug up his sabotage equipment and threw it into a local stream. The team leader in Courtrai tried to flee to Germany but could get no further than Maaseyck, whence he eventually returned to his hometown and gave himself up to Belgian police. The Antwerp chief, René Lagrou, craftily planted a story in the newspaper *La Libre Belgique* suggesting that he had already been arrested, a subterfuge that gave him the chance to escape to Germany, where he subsequently served with Van de Weile's exile 'government'.[34] One agent in Le Panne was suspected of sabotage and another was spotted lurking around Allied bivouacs in the Bruges district, but Canadian Field Security reported on 12 October that the West Flanders ring had 'been effectively dealt with. All but one Leader of the group have been caught and about ten of their agents. Large quantities of their material has also been found... Their effectiveness has greatly been depleted and their taste for their work has turned slightly "brown".'[35]

As the position of the *Abwehr* began to weaken in 1944, one of the agency's autonomous sabotage units, FAK 213, moved to fill the void in Brussels. As early as 1943, FAK 213's chief, *Hauptmann* Gerken, was working on the establishment of a stay-behind resistance network, codenamed '*Parti*'. In the late spring and summer of 1944, engineers from *Trupp* 260 laid sixty-five sabotage caches, mostly near targets such as traffic arteries, power lines and harbour facilities. In June 1944, Gerken sent to Brussels an advance '*Parti*' unit charged with recruiting agents and laying sabotage dumps. The idea was to set up *Sonderkommandos* of pro-German Belgians and Frenchmen, using captured Allied equipment and supplies. These *Sonderkommandos* would each be organised in a different district and members would be trained in isolation and deprived of knowledge about the identities of members in other groups. The leader of each cell would be equipped with a wireless transmitter and would remain in direct contact with Mil D controllers.

Initial preparations were undertaken by *Oberleutnant* von Winterfeld, a young and unkempt German officer. Winterfeld's Belgian recruiter and paymaster was Achille Mareel, a shady publisher who had married into wealth. Throughout the summer of 1944, '*Parti*' organisers interviewed potential recruits at a number of sites in Brussels, and some of the entrants were run through a one-month training programme at the Château Linkebeek, near Hal. Given the state of Axis fortunes, von Winterfeld and Mareel found it difficult to gather recruits, and the *Wehrmacht* denied access to twenty-two Flemish factory guards who were under army command. Nonetheless, a number of right-wing Belgians were recruited at Assche, between Brussels and Ghent, and some volunteers stepped forward in northern France, mainly thanks to the intervention of Blaise Agostini, Secretary General of the LVF.

By the time the Allies reached Belgium, the Germans had hardly done more than to lay a skeletal foundation for '*Parti*'. Von Winterfeld fled Brussels on 2 September, shortly after he had buried a wireless transmitter and transferred 400,000 francs to Mareel. Many of the '*Parti*' saboteurs were caught in the post-liberation purge and Mareel was arrested on 4 September as a result of denunciation by one of his employees. On the other hand, FAK 213 was still in contact with radio agent 'Charles' as late as November 1944, and a number of '*Parti*' agents escaped to Germany. As was the case in similar situations, the Germans could not bear to write off the '*Parti*' undertaking, and throughout the autumn of 1944 they continued to train and deploy agents who were supposed to reactivate '*Parti*' cells.[36]

In addition to Skorzeny's mediocre efforts, the Belgian fascist parties made attempts to strand stay-behind nets in Belgian territory, aided in this endeavour by the Mil Amt and the Brussels Sipo. The Rexists got the help of the SS-Police bureau in Brussels in organising a guerrilla training school at Hotel des Postes, in Dinant, a facility that opened its doors in the summer of 1944. Recruits were taught map reading, field craft and reconnaissance techniques and were assured that prospective White *Maquis* bands would be supplied with airborne German material and equipment. The course lasted a fortnight and was conducted by German officers under *Obersturmführer* Graff. Former members of the '*Légion Wallonie*' were required to take the course and were run through the curriculum in groups of ten. Veterans of the Dinant school were left to await the Allies, particularly in the districts around Liège and Namur. In the hilly region of the Hautes Fagnes, two graduates of the course, Jean Pirmollin and Jean Peeters, had already developed a network to fight the patriot resistance and in September 1944 this circle was reoriented toward supporting the embryonic White *Maquis*. Pirmollin and Peeters even convinced the mayor of Spa that they represented a band of 150 pro-Allied resisters, supplies for which were promised by local merchants. Matters proceeded smoothly until Pirmollin was wounded by a sub-machine gun burst. He was evacuated to a field hospital in Germany, although both he and Peeters subsequently re-entered Belgium in order to contact the White *Maquis*.

In order to support Rexist operatives, a six-week course was organised in Eickampf, Grunewald, focussed upon members of SS Division 'Wallonien' interested in returning to Belgium by parachute. The job of such volunteers was to pay Rexist agents and lead them into greater levels of pro-German resistance, blocking transportation routes and killing members of the *Brigade Blanche*. It is likely that this programme produced a dozen Wallonian SS men, led by *Oberscharführer* Maurice Slangen, who were scheduled for descent near Brussels on 10 October 1944. This detachment was equipped with several radio transmitters. A similar formation, led by *Feldwebel* Mesmacher, was slated for a drop near Namur on 15 January 1945.[37] Rexist infiltrators also took advantage of the Ardennes Offensive, during which residents of Stavelot noticed members of the 'Wallonian Legion' mixing with the population and acting as fifth columnists.[38]

De Vlag stay-behind efforts were centred upon the shadowy figure of Robert Verbelen, the head of the *De Vlag* security service and the chief of a Brussels death squad that had killed dozens of Jews and patriot resisters. When Verbelen fled Belgium on 5 September 1944, he left several '*équipes*' in place, particularly in Limburg province, where some activists were supplied with false papers. The country town of Notre Dame au Bois, for instance, served as a base for two agents, one a fanatic Rexist whose son was in the *Waffen*-SS, the other a member of the *Allgemeine* SS who was married to a German woman. After Verbelen's arrival in Germany, he was posted as 'police minister' in Van de Weile's 'exile government' and he formed a special formation that was intended to provide security in Belgium after its prospective reconquest by the *Wehrmacht*. At the height of the Ardennes Offensive, Verbelen moved this police battalion to St Vith and infiltrated a few of its members through the front, whence they were supposed to head for Flanders. These men were bilingual and had been prepared for deployment by *Jagdverband Nordwest*. One, a former officer of the *Brigade Blanche*, had been specially trained in Friedenthal and Neustrelitz.[39]

The VNV also contributed volunteers toward such initiatives, despite getting limited help from the SS. Most of these efforts were undertaken by the *Stabsführer* of the '*Zwarte Brigade*', Bert Meuris, and by the chief of the VNV propaganda service, Karl Lambrechts, both of whom raised recruits from the ranks of the *Vlaamsche Wacht*, the Factory Guard and the *Vlaamsche Jongeren Corps* (VJC). Hundreds of activists were trained at the Casteel Moretus, near Putte, where sabotage courses were run by Belgian civilians and members of SS Legion '*Flandern*'. In fact, the exiled leaders of the VNV had ordered the party's lower echelon to remain in Belgium and they dared to hope that tens of thousands of former members of the paramilitaries – perhaps 70,000 people in the Low Countries – would serve as the base for an anti-Allied resistance movement. The ultimate aim was to prepare a campaign, due to begin in the summer of 1945, which would aim at sabotaging airfields, railways and bridges and would supposedly lay the groundwork for a German reoccupation. Meuris even claimed that if Germany lost the war, the VNV would still return: 'We are going to clean up Belgium until the last pro-British sympathiser has given in; we shall not be so patient as the Germans.' Help for such efforts was provided mainly by Mil D: it contributed the services of a line-crossing expert, *Leutnant* Farber, who passed individuals and small groups through the front, and propaganda boss Lambrechts was spotted touring the Mil D training school at Pension Wilhelmina.[40]

Given this degree of preparation, and of help from Germany, it is hardly surprising that there were occasional flare-ups of violent resistance in newly liberated Belgium. Several cars, occupied by 'Gestapo personnel in Allied battledress', roared around the countryside, reportedly killing fifteen Belgians and precipitating a shoot-out at the gates of an ammunition depot at Oostakker. One of these cars was shot up by troops of the 1st Polish Armoured Division, resulting in the deaths of three agents.[41] In Ghent, there was much gunplay after the fall of the city, possibly involving fifth column snipers, and several Canadian troops were stabbed while visiting the community on leave.[42] There were also reports of illicit radio transmissions and wire cutting, several cases of the latter being blamed on a 15-year-old graduate of the JVC course at Casteel Moretus.[43] Sabotage incidents ranged from the destruction of a Canadian tank by landmines to the dynamiting of a headquarters of the Belgian patriot resistance, which was destroyed on 20 October 1944.[44] Canadian Field Security noted 'a general and probably well-founded impression of considerable covert activity… [although] reports of interrogation of agents captured do not give the impression that this mass activity is part of an organised plan'.[45] One minister in the Belgian Government admitted that 'a powerful German fifth column is flourishing',[46] and the Germans received reports about a Flemish White *Maquis*, which was supposedly based in Limburg and Antwerp provinces.[47]

Aside from reports about sabotage, there was also news of political resistance. Although ninety per cent of the Belgian population was sympathetic to the Allies, there were pockets of pro-German sentiment, such as the town of Maldegem, where the Allies worried about the security of local military installations and called for large numbers of townsfolk to be interned or evacuated. There were reports about underground VNV meetings, particularly in St Nicholas, Dixmude and Turnhout, and similar allusions to Rexist activity in Liège. Pro-German elements maintained escape lines that spirited *Wehrmacht* stragglers and escaped POWs to their homeland, and they extended their influence into internment camps, promising detainees that they could build a powerful anti-communist movement, mainly of Flemish character. There were several uprisings in the detention camp at St Kruis.[48] During the Battle of the Bulge, the Allies were disconcerted to learn that an escaped internee who was recaptured, Jean Beauwin, had received 'orders', while still in detention, to contact German parachutists and rendezvous with a man in Liège who would lead him to hidden arms dumps. Beauwin was one of several hundred detainees who escaped during the panicky evacuation of 2,000 political prisoners from holding camps around Liège, on around 29–30 December 1944.[49]

Not only was the pilot light of Belgian fascism never completely extinguished, but the nation's political and military situation went from bad to worse during the last months of 1944. In no country in Western Europe did conditions more resemble the inflammable situation in liberated Greece. The government of Hubert Pierlot was built upon a core of émigré politicians who had fled the country in 1940, although this flight had prompted the scorn of Belgium's stand-pat king, Leopold III, and it was unpopular among domestic resisters. With the support of neither right nor left, the restored government struggled with the severe problems of feeding and heating the population, as well as trying to both legalise and mitigate the anti-fascist purge. Conscious of its vulnerability, the government in November 1944 tried to disarm the major patriot resistance groups, a challenge that exasperated labour tension and caused violent clashes between gendarmes and demonstrators.[50] Allied forces backed Pierlot, although they worried that a strike of railway workers was preventing war material from reaching the front and they noted that there were occasional instances of rail sabotage.[51]

Watching events from vantage points in western Germany, the Nazis and their Belgian friends could barely believe their good fortune. The disturbances in Belgium seemed to prove the validity of Nazi propaganda – the retraction of German authority yields chaos – while at the same time the Germans did everything in their power to encourage such unrest. On 18 November, the German liaison officer with the Belgian exiles, Roland Krug von Nidda, noted that 'the situation in Belgium merits particular attention in view of the numerous indications of a crisis', and he pointed out that it was time for the Germans to make full use of Wallonian and Flemish personalities employed in their service. Within two weeks, the *Reichsfunk* was beaming out the voice of Léon Degrelle, who congratulated the striking miners of Hainault, and in early 1945 the Germans launched a 'fake proletarian station' that described the British and Americans as occupiers and urged workers to murder Allied troops. Naturally, Belgian workers were furious at the Nazi appropriation of their cause, but the Allies were concerned that some rioters were armed with German weapons and that at least one detainee was a German national.[52] Both Eisenhower's headquarters and the British Embassy in Brussels believed that German agents and sympathisers were actively exploiting the troubles in Belgium.[53]

Belgians were further shocked by the violence and suddenness of the Ardennes Offensive, which involved heavy fighting in eastern Belgium. In Belgium's German-speaking townships, there was never much sympathy for the Allies, and the children of Nazi collaborators had already been caught participating in Hitler Youth activity or attempts to revive the *Heimattreue Front*.[54] More disturbingly, even Walloons in Liège, Namur and Luxembourg provinces showed a distinct lack of enthusiasm for the Allies by late December 1944, and the French Fifth Bureau reported that inhabitants of Beauvrains and Ciney had become actively hostile. When the US First Army evacuated Spa on 21 December, the town mayor immediately released twenty collaborators from confinement and American flags were torn down.[55]

Not surprisingly, such events provided a fertile field for the German intelligence services, which literally showered parachutists upon Belgium; according to one German officer, forty airborne agents descended upon the country in the single month of November 1944. German planes were spotted buzzing over wooded regions and on 1 February 1945, a twin-propeller aircraft landed in a field near Mons, spending several minutes on the ground while protected by a circling fighter. Matters got so bad that the Belgian *Sûreté* assembled a mobile anti-parachutist company, which was fielded in early 1945.[56]

Skorzeny took full advantage, dispatching wave after wave of parachutists and infiltrators, although few of these missions yielded significant dividends. Initial reconnaissance missions involved sending out individuals and small teams. In the autumn of 1944, two female radio operators completed a task in Belgium and then return to Friedenthal. Around the same time, the former mayor of Berlaar, Jules Croonen, was sent on a reconnaissance mission in the company of a *Waffen*-SS trooper named Persyn. Croonen and Persyn crossed the Albert Canal and spotted the location of Allied units in Antwerp, even being thrown cigarettes from soldiers atop British tanks. They repaid this bonhomie by calling in German artillery fire upon the British armour. A former policeman and official of the *De Vlag* security corps also flew into Belgium by plane, and shortly before the key month of December 1944, a three-man 'Vorkommando' was dispatched by Bachot on a 'special mission'. Although the fate of these elements is unknown, Bachot later bragged that teams in Antwerp had established radio contact, signalling 'Alles in Ordnung' and 'Befehl ausgeführt'.

Naturally, activity accelerated at the time of the Ardennes Offensive. A group led by Henri Morael penetrated Allied lines around the 22 December, although it is not clear if it was deployed by air or infiltrated near St Vith, nor if it succeeded in its mission. Morael had served as Robert Verbelen's security chief in South Limburg and his efforts were connected with Verbelen's intrigues. Another group of three Wallonian agents was sent to Liège, where their task, at the insistence of the chief of Section B, was to assassinate two of the city's industrialists who had run afoul of the Germans. *Jagdverband Südwest* also contributed by sending three Belgian-Germans to the Eupen–Malmedy district, where the sympathetic population was expected to back Nazi guerrillas. These agents were supposed to form a framework organisation, but the German failure to penetrate as far north as expected meant that the team could not bury the arms needed to support future efforts. The material allotted to Eupen–Malmedy was eventually redirected to the Eifel district, where it was hidden in February 1945 in order to provide for the Werewolves. Finally, several of Skorzeny's 'Stielau' jeep teams were engaged in Operation 'Währung', a scheme to carry 25 million francs worth of forged Belgian and French currency notes across the front. The main idea was to bribe strike-prone Belgian dockworkers and railwaymen into staying home for a week, thus hampering Allied movement at the height of the German Offensive. Despite high hopes, the plan fizzled and only half the teams charged with '*Währung*' activity were able to struggle back to German lines.[57]

Regardless of the failure of the German counter-strike in Belgium, Mil D joined the fray in February 1945, deploying the first of numerous sabotage teams that it was preparing for service. Members of the initial detachment were trained at Bad Ems and then moved to an airfield near Stuttgart shortly before departure on the night of 3 February. Their mission was to find suitable drop zones for fellow teams and to sabotage railway lines near Antwerp, as well as murdering the minister of justice and the Burgomaster of Antwerp. Although they reached the ground safely in a PAG, all three men were quickly apprehended by the Belgian authorities, their leader, Joseph de Mesmacker, having voluntarily surrendered. Mesmacker was subsequently run by the Belgians as a double agent, and he had some success in ascertaining the dispatch time and drop zone of a party of eight agents due to arrive near Mechelen on 17 March. The Mil D also moved an additional team to a Stuttgart airstrip in the wake of Mesmacker's departure, but this unit was held up by bad weather until it was forced by the Allied advance to relocate to Furstenfeldbruck airfield, in southern Bavaria. Its deployment was further prevented by lack of aviation fuel and bomb damage to the runway; on 27 April, members of the team were told to lie low in local villages until the Americans had passed and then to return to Belgium individually, posing as refugees. Their task, interestingly, was to recover material from sabotage caches and attack Allied supply routes while disguised as communists. They were also supposed to kill senior American and Belgian authorities and murder members of the Belgian nobility, the latter task reflecting the faux 'proletarian' theme.

In March 1945, the Germans launched Operation 'Waterloo', which involved the dispatch of a six-man group charged with contacting the White *Maquis*. After abandoning the idea of a '*parachutage*' in the Waterloo district, the Germans planned to have the unit bypassed in the Rhineland, where members would perform reconnaissance behind Allied lines and then move on to their primary mission in Belgium. The team was overtaken by American forces at Kalenborn, near Bonn, but members then buried their arms and radio equipment and released their carrier pigeons. All six men were rounded up by the Allies before reaching Belgium. This operation was organised by a detachment of the German counter-espionage service, *Trupp* 363, but team leader Joseph Covent made an arrangement with a *Jagdverband* representative, Martin Peters, in order to carry *Jagdverband* codes and wireless frequencies and to contact Skorzeny's headquarters by radio.

Even as the Third Reich collapsed, *Nordwest* continued its flailing efforts. In April 1945, a group of fourteen *Jagdverband* troopers, led by *Untersturmführer* Verlinden, left Neustrelitz for destinations in their homeland. They reached Emden in late April and were moved by motor launch to Amsterdam and Rotterdam, although they were recalled to The Hague, which they reached on 5 May. They then learned that the war was over and that their original mission had been cancelled, although this termination was not regarded as the final word on the matter. Members of the Verlinden *Gruppe* were now instructed to journey to Belgium by whatever means available, making use of their phoney Belgian and Dutch identity papers, and to go underground until they were contacted by Verlinden or his deputy. During this quiet period, they were supposed 'to join a communist group and if possible spread discontent within the group'. One team member was charged with getting work at his uncle's cafe in Brussels, where his companions could gather on 31 May–1 June 1945, but this trooper surrendered to Dutch police before this scheme could unfold.[58]

Political cover for Skorzeny's efforts was provided by 'liberation committees', which were organised with help from the Foreign Office. During the troubles in November 1944, Krug von Nidda argued that Belgium was ripe for subversion and that the Foreign Office ought to exploit the situation:

> In order to cause difficulties for the former exile government of Pierlot, and in order to accelerate the subversion of the Belgian state, it seems necessary to strengthen the position of both *Volkssturm* leaders [Van de Weile and Degrelle] by allowing the establishment of liberation committees... We have a great political and military interest in causing unrest in Belgium, in disrupting the Allied zone of communications and armaments production, in organising resistance movements against the Pierlot government, and in stirring up discontent about prevailing conditions, so it seems urgently necessary that [such] work be consolidated under the control of the Foreign Office.

Throughout the late autumn of 1944, the Germans debated the name and composition of the committee, focusing particularly on whether the Walloons and Flemings ought to form separate panels or be united in a single body. By early December, Ribbentrop had decided in favour of a unitary 'Flemish-Wallonian Liberation Committee', although the two halves of the body were allowed to function autonomously. During the height of the fighting in the Ardennes, Ribbentrop used the committee as a rationale for firing off instructions to Kaltenbrunner and Berger regarding Belgian resistance groups – one can imagine how such directives were received in the senior echelon of the SS – but the committee proved an ineffective mechanism for supporting the pro-German cause. Since Degrelle devoted most of his time to the Eastern Front, the Wallonian half of the committee was dominated by his weak-kneed deputy, Victor Matthys, and by Matthys's ruthless secretary, Louis Collard, who exploited the laziness of his boss in order to magnify his own importance. The Flemish side of the committee saw direct involvement by Van de Weile, who gathered an able staff led by René Lagrou. After the failure of the Ardennes Offensive, a sense of demoralisation descended upon both sides of the structure and it languished.[59]

The 'liberation committees' did cooperate with the SS Main Office and the German Government in the management of the 'Flemish Freedom Station' and the 'Revolutionary Radio of Socialist Wallonia', both of which were based at Wipperfürth. These stations encouraged discontent in the Belgian patriot resistance and launched wild calls for anti-Allied guerrilla warfare and industrial sabotage. The impact was negligible, particularly since the Rexists and the Flemish nationalists supplying copy could not agree about whether the stations should be camouflaged as clandestine transmitters or openly acknowledged as instruments beaming from Germany. Since no compromise was reached on this essential matter, French- and Flemish-language broadcasts differed considerably.[60]

As was the case in Nazi plans for a number of countries, Hitler's imperialist obsessions prevented the implementation of a truly effective policy. Because Hitler dreamed of converting Flanders and Wallonia into 'Reichsgaue' attached to the Third Reich, German bureaucrats and military officers were prohibited from expressing support for the 'Belgian concept' or even using the word 'Belgian' to designate the exile committees. Had the Foreign Office and SD not been constrained by such strictures, they could have openly acknowledged Belgium's sovereignty and returned the country to its king, Leopold III, rather than having Kaltenbrunner haul the hapless monarch back to Germany as a hostage. Given Leopold's *attentisme* and pro-fascist sympathies, his early repatriation might have brought the royal question to a head, and Belgian Foreign Minister Paul-Henri Spaak admitted the likelihood of 'a political crisis'.[61] In the post-war period, the threat of Leopold's homecoming did indeed push Belgium to the brink of civil war. Such a situation in 1944–1945 would have suited German purposes admirably, but neither Himmler, Kaltenbrunner nor Skorzeny were willing to risk a gambit that flew so directly in the face of the *Führer's* ideological objectives.

AT THE FRINGE OF 'FORTRESS HOLLAND'

Organising anti-Allied resistance in the Netherlands provided Skorzeny with a mixed bag of challenges and opportunities. The flat and cultivated terrain of the country was inappropriate for guerrilla warfare, but the lowland of Holland proper – the coastal stretch between the Wadden See and the Waal and Maas estuaries – posed potential difficulties for the Allies because it could be flooded through the demolition of dykes and pumping facilities. After the Allies failed to grab Arnhem in an airborne assault, and then struggled to clear the Scheldt estuary, they decided that the geopolitical insignificance of the central and northern Netherlands meant that these territories would have to be bypassed and only the southern fringe of the country could be freed, at least in the short term. The eastern Netherlands was belatedly liberated in March and April 1945, but the coastal regions remained in German hands until the end of the war.

Like the landscape, the nature of the population cut both ways. In the first place, the Dutch capacity for any type of sustained action was undercut by the overwhelming power of hunger. Because of the collapse of the German provisioning system, the population of occupied Holland was starving by the turn of 1944–1945, the height of the 'Hunger Winter', and nearly 1,000 people died from lack of food. This situation resulted in a well-deserved hatred of the occupying power, but in the liberated zone of the country, the Allies too struggled with the food problem, which hardly won them any acclaim.[62] Contrary to popular mythology, there were cool relations between Allied troops and the population of North Brabant, the Netherlands' southernmost province, and Canadian troops sometimes accused civilians of spotting for German artillery or harbouring Nazi operatives. Several towns in the vicinity of 's-Hertogenbosch were placed under severe curfews or partially evacuated.[63] Only when Allied troops reached the territories north of the River Maas did they find a more uniformly friendly reception.

Before the 'Hunger Winter', the Dutch had engaged in a degree of anti-German resistance and had supported several large-scale labour disruptions, despite the fact that the

Nazis had expected a more cooperative attitude from a fellow 'Germanic' nation. On the other hand, the Dutch patriot resistance had been infiltrated by the counter-intelligence wing of the *Abwehr*, which had led to the capture of a large amount of British sabotage material, and the advancing Canadians found that Dutch resistance groups were more poorly manned, armed and organised than their French and Belgian counterparts.[64] The Dutch had also volunteered 50,000 men to the ranks of the *Waffen*-SS and other German military forces, proportionally the largest contribution in any German-occupied country. In addition, the Netherlands had provided the base for a fascist party of considerable size and influence. In 1943, this group, the *National-Socialistische Beweging* (NSB), was given control of a 'consultative council' – a sort of advisory cabinet – but the NSB did not have as much value to the Germans as one might imagine. By 1944, its strength had waned badly and more than 30,000 NSB members fled to Germany in a blind panic during the first days of September 1944, when it seemed as if the Allied advance might sweep through the entire Netherlands.[65] NSB chief Anton Mussert did not have close relations with either the *Jagdverbände*, Section S or Mil D.[66]

Skorzeny thus enjoyed a less-than-overwhelming set of advantages, although it was assumed in Berlin 'that there was a lot of sympathy for Germany in Holland'[67] and that carrying out agitation propaganda could lay the groundwork for a large-scale anti-Allied resistance campaign. In fact, the Germans paid more attention to this aspect of their guerrilla programme than in any other country along the Western Front. The Dutch component of the SS subversive propaganda unit, *Skorpion-West*, was highly active, particularly in leaflet spreading and in operating the 'Voice of the Free South' from a transmitter in Hilversum. One of the main messages of these organs consisted of an appeal for southerners to hang on to their arms and resist being drafted into the revived Dutch Army. *Gruppe Skorpion* also prepared several of its own sabotage-subversion units, which were armed from a dump in Utrecht that had belonged to the patriot underground but had been discovered by the Germans.[68]

The Sassen family of Veghel played a large role in these operations. Willem (Wim) Sassen was the Dutch head of *Skorpion-West* and he formed a stay-behind detachment, the 'Neurop' Group, which included his sister, his girlfriend and several of his cohorts in the Dutch-SS. This outfit was active until June 1945, when its chief figures were arrested by Canadian Field Security. Sassen also convinced his father, the ex-Burgomaster of Veghel, to make broadcasts over Hilversum Radio, using his folksy North Brabant dialect to full effect, and Sassen senior was involved in a series of covert attempts to return to Veghel, mainly with the intent of organising a rallying centre for disaffected members of the patriot resistance. A reconnaissance agent was captured by the Allies while trying to sound out the local population about a prospective return of Sassen to the region.[69]

FAK 213 was also active in the propaganda sphere. FAK officers under Hans Dreves had prepared a number of anti-Allied leaflets for distribution in France, but the unit was chased out of that country before its agents and propagandists had a chance to spread this material. Once the front bogged down in the Netherlands, FAK 213's 'Z' ('*Zersetzungs-propaganda*') elements had an opportunity to approach the problem of subversion in a more systematic fashion. Working from an office in Amersfoort, they produced anti-communist circulars warning about 'Bolshevik'-induced chaos in Greece, France and

Belgium. 'It can also be pointed out', said a 'Z' directive, '[that] food conditions in the liberated countries have in no way improved since the time of the German occupation.' Running parallel to this effort was a programme to publish pseudo-communist pamphlets with the aim of creating distrust between Limburg miners and the Allies, as well as convincing 'Anglo-American troops' of Stalin's perfidy. The 'Z' Section also made use of the transmitter at Hilversum.[70]

There is no doubt that German propaganda had some impact on Dutch popular opinion. Canadian analysis of the situation in the liberated town of Oss, south of the Maas, suggested that German propaganda was being disseminated and was dominating local discourse. Reports from the spring of 1945 make repeated mention of a pervasive Dutch interest in the 'Russian Bogey' and of rumours about East-West tension, which the Canadians attributed to German influence and to the impact of the Dutch churches.[71] The spread of such ideas, however, did not have the desired effect. In mid-February 1945, the *Reichskommissar* in The Hague, Arthur Seyss-Inquart, informed Goebbels that even conservative Dutchmen could not be brought around to a belatedly pro-German attitude because they felt that the Soviets would, at best, conquer Germany's eastern provinces, leaving the western half of the country – and the continent – in the hands of the Allies.[72]

Such observations meant little to Skorzeny, whose inclination was simply to lean into the headwind and persevere. Heedless of the starvation in the Netherlands, he began operations by setting up six-man 'provisioning parties', which lurked around The Hague, Zwolle and Utrecht, pilfering anything of value and searching for gin and other potables. In most theatres such units attracted little attention, but conditions in the Netherlands were so desperate that there was little fat to gnaw upon. Four Dutch SS men in one such party were arrested by the German *Feldgendarmerie* and charged with looting, and in early 1945 even the Gestapo warned that these detachments were a burden in a country so short of food. One *Jagdverband* team was curtly informed that it could not be fed from local stocks and that the food situation demanded that all special units justify their presence in the country.

Next came sabotage teams, starting with *Jagdkommando* 'Holland', which was sent north by *Hauptsturmführer* Gerlach. The chief of this unit, it will be recalled, was a Dutch-speaking officer named Golombiefski, who was a former Brandenburger. He was transferred to the SS in October 1944 and quickly assembled a group of Dutchmen at Herschbach, in the Unterwesterwald, telling them that they would be used as anti-insurgency troops. For several weeks members of the group were lodged in a school house and trained in sabotage, infantry tactics and cross-country marching. Part of the detachment was then posted at Castle Hulcrath, a *Werwolf* training camp, and the entire group was eventually reassembled at Maarsbergen, where they occupied a villa called the Andersteen House.

Golombiefski's second-in-command, Hendrik Slot, immediately began operations against the Dutch patriot underground, but the troops were shocked to learn that their main task was to disguise themselves in civilian clothes and conduct missions behind enemy lines. Golombiefski mounted a successful two-man reconnaissance expedition in November 1944, but the next three operations were disasters. On the evening of 30

November, he got the help of *Luftwaffe* ground troops in providing a rubber raft and an armed escort for three men sent across the River Maas at Bokhoven. Led by Anton Doorewaard, members of this team had been briefed only for a vague mission, which involved wandering around Allied-held territory and spotting enemy formations. They lacked maps and cover stories and had never been trained for unit identification tasks. After tramping through fields ankle-deep in floodwaters, the agents rested in a barn for the night. On 1 December, they approached several farmers, looking for information, but they were immediately reported to the *Marechaussee* (Dutch gendarmerie) and arrested. In a sequel several days later, two additional agents were ferried across the Maas at Willemstad, but they were apprehended almost as rapidly as their predecessors. The members of this team were equally poorly trained for reconnaissance. Persevering in the face of failure, Golombiefski tried to put a third detachment across the river at Geertruidenberg, on around 3 December, but owing to bad weather the boat was unable to land on the south bank and the team was forced to return to Maarsbergen.[73] 'It would be optimistic', sneered an SIS officer, to suppose that such endeavours were 'the worst of which Skorzeny's new Jaeger Battalion is capable.' Seeking to set a precedent, a Dutch military court at Eindhoven sentenced three of the captured saboteurs to death and two others to lengthy terms of confinement.[74]

Not only was Golombiefski incompetent, but he was also widely disliked. His imperious manner created enemies in the Sipo, where officers resented the way that he sported about German-occupied territory, flashing mysterious letters of authorisation from Skorzeny, and he was no more popular among the intelligence officers of Army Group H, who had encouraged him to send spies behind Allied lines, but eventually agreed that he was incapable of any organised action. Worst of all, the bosses of *Jagdverband Nordwest* looked on in horror as Golombiefski fouled the ground upon which their own formations would soon have to function. The fact that Golombiefski was formally under *Nordwest's* oversight from October 1944 to March 1945 did not help matters. In late December, Heinrich Hoyer sent his unit 'snitch', Louis de Roo, to conduct an investigation of goings-on at Andersteen House, although Golombiefski soon learned of De Roo's snooping and briefly arrested the interloper before he was able to establish his *bona fides*.[75] Although Golombiefski subsequently worked together with elements of *Nordwest*, it was agreed that he should stay away from the front, concentrating instead on laying sabotage dumps and setting up a stay-behind network. In March 1945, Gerlach recalled him to the headquarters of *Jagdverband Südwest*, but he refused to appear.[76]

After the failure of *Jagdkommando* 'Holland', *Nordwest* deployed two Dutch *Sonderkommandos*, 'Zeppelin' and 'Benno', both of which were carved out of *Jagdeinsatz Niederlande*. Hoyer arranged radio communications for these detachments, with contact relayed through the forward command post of *Niederlande* in western Germany, although the cessation of regular communications in late March meant that 'Zeppelin' and 'Benno' both came under the functional control of the SS-Police headquarters in The Hague.

Sonderkommando 'Zeppelin' was commanded by *Untersturmführer* Pieterson, who was personally codenamed 'Zeppelin', and the detachment consisted of 100 men stationed at Nordhorn and then at Groningen. Pieterson was an unmilitary figure who knew nothing about the technical aspects of sabotage, but whose expertise was political agitation.

Although little is known about the operation of the Dutch version of 'Zeppelin', it apparently had moved radio operators behind Allied lines by the end of March 1945, probably into North Brabant.

Sonderkommando 'Benno' was also endowed with the nickname of its chief, Alfred Hakkenberg van Gaasbeek, and was half the size of its sister detachment. Although Hakkenberg was a dedicated Nazi and an aspirant 'political soldier', even SS officers realised that he had an impetuous temperament and required constant supervision, a combination of factors that did not promise success in guerrilla activity. Hakkenberg operated from Apeldoorn, although Allied advances meant that in mid-April he had to debouch for the western Netherlands, where he eventually ended up in The Hague. As was the case in the Golombiefski Affair, the intelligence officers at Army Group H encouraged Hakkenberg to carry out reconnaissance and they made clear that their cooperation – that is, the provision of fuel, oil and operating funds – was dependent on Hakkenberg's achievement of rapid results. Hakkenberg got around this problem by providing fallacious reports about the locations of Allied food and petroleum dumps, airfields and command posts, which he claimed to get from spies already inserted into North Brabant, but which he actually invented after scrutinising maps for the likely locations of such targets.

Despite the success of this swindle, Hakkenberg knew that he had to extend real tentacles into the south. On 19 March 1945, he sent a three-man team, led by *Rottenführer* Cornelius de Jonghe, on a mission to Amsterdam, where members were supposed to pose as escaped slave labourers and join the patriot resistance, thereby gaining access to valuable passes and letters of introduction that might facilitate eventual infiltration of Allied lines. This operation failed and the De Jonghe team was recalled, although Hakkenberg was still intent on passing men through the lines as soon as possible. Hakkenberg then formed a seven-man detachment, again led by De Jonghe, and this unit was sent to Zutphen on 2 April, where members were provided with civilian clothes and ordered to seep through the front. Only three of the party had phoney papers, but they were all told to present themselves as escaped deportees in flight from Germany. Their mission was to scatter throughout the towns around Tilburg, gathering information on the state of civilian morale and Allied military dispositions. In particular, they were supposed to ascertain the strength of the guard at an internment camp in Vught – the Germans were planning to organise a break-out – and to verify the locations of Allied food and munitions dumps around Oss. They were also interested in the condition of bridges across the Maas, the Waal and the Rhine. Couriers would run information back to German lines and reinforcements, perhaps the remaining forty men of *Sonderkommando* 'Benno', would be landed by submarine in order to seize any opportunities that had become available.

On the night of 3/4 April, De Jonghe and two members of his team were passed through the front at Warnsveld, crossing the Rhine in a rowboat. They were followed by four other members of the unit, who themselves split up into two separate parties. De Jonghe's entourage was uncovered at a refugee screening centre in Nijmegen when one of its members admitted that he was a German agent; a similar fate befell another of the parties when one of its members voluntarily reported to the Dutch authorities. With the information gleaned from the interrogation of the initial captives, the Allies were able to pluck the final two saboteurs from a stream of refugees near Nijmegen. Within a week, all the members of De Jonghe's detachment had been apprehended.

In mid-April, Hakkenberg sent out another agent in order to find out what had happened to De Jonghe's unit. While awaiting the reappearance of this operative – in fact, he never returned – Hakkenberg also prepared the dispatch of two more agents to Tilburg, although this operation was vetoed by his new boss, SS-Police *Obersturmbannführer* Ispert, who considered it too dangerous. A four-man '*Einsatz*' to Hakkenberg's old base of Apeldoorn was also cancelled, and it is unlikely that a ten-man tank destroyer detachment, *Gruppe* Schumann, saw action either.[77]

While none of the *Jagdverbände*'s probes had direct results, they did cause a minor diversion of Allied resources. After Canadian Field Security discovered that there were SS *Sonderkommandos* prowling around the Allied communications zone, they doubled the guard on ammunition dumps and railway lines, and they also increased mobile patrols along dykes. On 18 April 1945, trains on one line were held up for five hours while engineers checked the rails for mines. A company of Canadian military policemen was still searching for saboteurs in 's-Hertogenbosch as late as May 1945.[78] However, there was a limited number of men whose attention was drawn away from the front and the military effect was negligible.

Mil D units also organised a number of line-crossing expeditions. As early as 1942, the *Zweierorganisation* had begun training Dutchmen in a demolitions programme in Antwerp, although this experiment ended when all ten trainees went on strike and were sent home. Thereafter, initiatives aimed at preparing Dutch saboteurs and anti-Allied resisters were sporadic,[79] although by the time of the *Abwehr*'s reorganisation in the mid-summer of 1944, efforts were again underway, this time based at the Andersteen villa that was later turned over to *Jagdkommando* 'Holland'. Courses at this school concentrated on map reading, small arms training and work with sabotage material of British make. Interestingly, the students were told that they were the mirror image of the anti-German resisters active throughout Europe. Their specific task was to carry explosives across the front and either use these materials to blast British tanks and vehicles or cache them for the use of later line-crossing groups. The initial missions were carried out in the autumn of 1944; one three-man group was captured by the *Marechaussee* in Lith.[80]

By the autumn of 1944, FAK 213 was also assembling forces in the Netherlands, first at Doorn and then at sabotage schools in Zwolle and Gramsbergen. Trainees at these schools were told to commit desultory acts of sabotage and to launch an attack upon Camp 030, the chief Allied interrogation centre for captured German agents. In early 1945, FAK 213 carried out several parachute drops of saboteurs, codenamed '*Nordwind*' and '*Brausewind*'. Although the Allies received reports of parachutists floating to the ground on Dutch soil, none of whom they could locate, one three-man team was caught when it was dropped off target in northern France. Led by Ludzerd Lautenbach, this unit was supposed to attack objectives in Breda and Tilburg, particularly the Kromhoute Barracks, which was an Allied command and intelligence headquarters. Since team-members did not have enough explosives to demolish the entire building, they were expected to bribe their way passed the guards and then locate a file room within the structure, blowing it up with explosives. This fanciful operation was never executed because of faulty map work by the navigator of a German B-17, part of the same crew that had dumped the 'Henriette' *Gruppe* into the wrong country. On the morning after the group's descent, a French farmer offered them coffee, but found it odd that three bewildered Dutchmen and Germans should be wandering around the French countryside. He called the gendarmerie, who promptly arrested all three men, bringing a quick end to this inglorious adventure.

One of FAK 213's forward units, *Trupp* 260, launched a number of raids into enemy-held territory, although like the *Jagdverband* elements in the Netherlands, they were pushed by the German Army to carry out reconnaissance, reserving sabotage as a secondary objective. In January 1945, *Leutnant* Walter Schlemmer led two patrols across the Hollandsch Diep, the second of which resulted in a heavy firefight and the destruction of an Allied machine gun post, although Schlemmer's squad suffered six casualties. These missions were followed by a prolonged debate between Mil D officers, who defended the functional right of the *Zweierorganisation* to focus on sabotage, and the intelligence officers of 30th Corps, to which *Trupp* 260 was subordinate, who insisted that efforts on sabotage caused barely a ripple in the pattern of Allied strategy, while reconnaissance was the real need of the hour. In late March, *Trupp* 260 was transferred to the oversight of the 34th Dutch SS Division, which was happy to indulge its penchant for direct action. As a result, Schlemmer set out on 9 April in the company of four comrades (plus three Dutch SS men manning the boats used to cross the Waal). After penetrating Allied lines near Alem, they hid in the woods for a day and then crept out on the night of 10/11 April, mining railway tracks. Supplementary charges were laid in order to disable relief trains. According to a Canadian report, Allied ammunition dumps were raided in this same area. In the final analysis, the railway was blown in five spots, bringing an eastbound train to a halt and forcing the closure of the line for twenty-four hours, although some of the supplementary charges were discovered and neutralised before they could detonate. Two Dutch guards were killed and one was wounded.

Another group, led by *Leutnant* Weber, staged a parallel raid that was scheduled to last six days and make use of supplies that had previously been cached in the southern Netherlands. This operation, which was also launched on 9 April, resulted in the mining of a road near Empel, which forced the Allies to close the effected district to traffic. Members of Weber's unit were ordered to again blast the rail line near 's-Hertogenbosch, which could be done on their return march to German lines, and they were probably responsible for an explosion that ripped up the tracks at Rosmalen around the 15 April.[81]

In late April, *Trupp* 260 was devoted entirely to an expansion of 'patrol activity' demanded by *Generaloberst* Blaskowitz, who had received instructions in this vein from OKH. Assembling a camp at Zeist, FAK officers sent out a request for volunteers from units in 30th and 88th Corps (excepting the 34th Dutch SS '*Landstorm*' Division, whose 'volunteers' would likely be hapless Dutch inductees looking for a quick passage to Allied-held territory, and which was instead instructed to send the names of 'reliable personnel'). By late April more than 100 recruits had appeared at Zeist, although the level of instruction provided by FAK officers was intentionally poor. Strategically, the handwriting on the wall had become legible even to the most myopic of Nazis. Nonetheless, several seven-man infiltration groups were organised on 25 April, being armed mainly with British explosives taken from the patriot underground. On 27 April, one of these squads was sent to the headquarters of the 762nd Grenadier Regiment at Woudenberg, whence it was ordered to cross the front and destroy enemy vehicles at its discretion. Two scouts attached to this unit got lost and were immediately captured by the enemy; the remaining members were caught on 2 May, after their Dutch SS guide had deserted. They had no chance to lay their demolition charges, although they became involved in a skirmish with Canadian troops. The prospect for such gunplay worried their FAK controllers because shortly after the unit's dispatch the Germans negotiated a regional truce, ostensibly as a means of getting food into the starving Netherlands. This meant that actions of the group could be regarded as a violation of the armistice. Other teams awaiting deployment were disbanded after the cease-fire went into effect on 28 April.[82]

Despite intermittent successes by Skorzeny's units, the real story of sabotage in the Netherlands involves frontline *Waffen*-SS units. Some of these formations took advantage of the stasis along the Dutch front in order to field their own sabotage line-crossers, mainly with the hope of causing nuisance damage to the enemy. On 23 January 1945, for instance, three uniformed infiltrators were captured by the Allies on their way to spot traffic on the 's-Hertogenbosch–Grave highway and then blow up a length of railway. These men were caught in possession of ten pounds of high explosive.[83]

A special degree of activity was undertaken by the Dutch SS 'Landstorm' Division, which was originally fielded as a home guard but was refashioned in 1944–1945 into an SS combat unit, mainly by recruiting young Dutchmen who wanted rations or were seeking to escape labour drafts, although the formation also had a small core of NSB enthusiasts. By the autumn of 1944, the Germans were recruiting 'Landstorm' members for low-grade sabotage tasks. Sixty trainees were schooled at the Venlo air base in the eastern Netherlands, and one of these men, Martinus Hendriks, admitted cutting Allied signal cables and blowing up a munitions dump near Lussen (although he later claimed that these confessions were extracted by torture). 'Landstorm' men were also sent to *Jagdeinsatz Niederlande*, which at one time hoped to incorporate a platoon of 'Landstorm' troopers stationed at Hoogeveen, home of the division's replacement battalion. Hakkenberg eyed these men as a possible source of reinforcements for his *Sonderkommando* enterprises in North Brabant.

In late February 1945, the headquarters of SS Division 'Landstorm' assigned one of its intelligence officers, *Obersturmführer* Ludwig Fuchs, to train a platoon of volunteers in sabotage and reconnaissance tasks. In order to get a secure supply of equipment and arms, Fuchs offered his new unit to SS-Police boss Ispert, who was engaged in a complex effort to win over anti-communist elements of the Dutch patriot resistance and required political intelligence from the southern Netherlands. With Ispert's support, Fuchs organised a training camp at Apeldoorn and laid stay-behind depots of rations and ammunition. In March and April 1945, he sent a number of small teams into the Apeldoorn–Barneveld–Zwolle triangle, most of which returned, although two Dutch SS men, Van Vliet and Van Zanten, were captured and summarily shot by patriot resisters. After the Van Vliet/Van Zanten expedition, Fuchs dispatched teams only in the company of *Waffen*-SS shock units that protected personnel during ingress and egress.[84]

Although German sabotage efforts failed to yield a strategic or even tactical impact, Canadian and British soldiers felt harassed, especially at the front along the Maas. Wire cutting was more extensive than in France or Belgium and in late November 1944 an Allied intelligence summary noted that 'for the first time since the start of the campaign widely dispersed incidents of suspected sabotage in First Cdn Army area have been reported'. In the troubled town of Oss, a former NSB Burgomaster was suspected of leading a band of young saboteurs and there were instances of wire cutting, rail sabotage and mine laying; in January 1945, the Allies evacuated nearly 300 'undesirables' from this community. On the night of 20/21 November, two men disguised in Canadian battledress were suspected of blowing up a bridge-building barge on the River Waal. Two months later, German commandos demolished a water tower and several buildings in Philipsland. There were also cases of shooting by snipers in civilian clothes, particularly in Zutphen, where one *franc-tireur* had to be burned out of a house with a flame-thrower. A few Canadian soldiers were killed in such incidents, particularly several men who were pushed into the canals that cut across the landscape. At Goor, two trucks and a jeep were destroyed when a bridge blew up after Canadian troops had taken the town. Three Canadian soldiers died in the blast.[85] In a similar incident, two members of the Polish 1st Armoured Division were killed in the Westerwolde when their vehicle detonated a mine on an approach to a bridge that had been in use for five days.[86]

Apart from conducting sabotage in the southern and eastern Netherlands, Mil D and the *Jagdverbände* also organised stay-behind groups in the core of Fortress 'Holland'. Once the Allies arrived in May 1945, a FAK 213 'R-*Netz*', which had been organised by Rolf Steneberg, quickly collapsed, as did a fifteen-man stay-behind unit in Leeuwarden, Friesland. Ten members of the latter detachment were captured by the Canadians on 21–22 April 1945, along with their explosives and equipment, although their chief, Rudolf Meesters, managed to elude pursuers.[87]

The *Jagdverbände*, it will be recalled, left stay-behind matters to the oversight of *Jagdkommando* 'Holland', although Golombiefski showed scarcely more competence in this task than in his infiltration efforts. He buried at least five sabotage kits in German-occupied Holland, all of which were marked by *Werwolf* insignia and contained French rifles and ammunition, plus boxes of German and British explosives. In order to coordinate these operations, Golombiefski's mentor, a Cologne industrialist and Nazi organiser named Tillmann, was conscripted into *Jagdkommando* 'Holland' and given SS rank. Golombiefski also organised stay-behind networks in various Dutch cities. In Amsterdam, the cell was controlled by the De Jonghe brothers, who set up a supply dump through black market purchases of food and equipment. In Driebergen, Golombiefski established a '*Werwolf*' formation in a local convalescent home. In The Hague, he tried to get permission from the Gestapo for one of his agents, a petty criminal named Van Drunen, to operate a gaming parlour, which was intended to serve as a prospective meeting point for agents. This matter ended badly when Van Drunen shot one of his patrons in March 1945, prompting Dutch police to close the establishment. In April, the core of *Jagdkommando* 'Holland' was ordered to retreat into the Alpine Redoubt, but Golombiefski left his second-in-command, *Unterscharführer* Slot, in charge of a stay-behind squad. This team functioned under the oversight of *Obersturmführer* Ispert.[88]

The advancing Allies got a lucky break in this case when Friedrich Tillmann was captured in the German town of Settrupp, on around 15 April 1945, carrying several thick files of documents on *Jagdkommando* 'Holland'.[89] Nonetheless, it was not until after the war that Slot and the stay-behind team fell into Allied hands, and as late as June–July 1945, Canadian Field Security was still breaking up surviving sabotage rings. Twenty-five people were arrested on 15 June.[90] The post-war Netherlands was plagued by rumours about a '*Werwolf*' organisation, which is of some significance given Golombiefski's use of '*Werwolf*' iconography. This network was supposed to contain hundreds of NSB members and Dutch policemen, and to have ties to its sister movement in Germany, but Canadian investigations suggested that such stories were either a canard or the product of over-active imaginations.[91] A few elements of the Dutch SS continued to hold out beyond 8 May, causing casualties amongst Canadian troops and anti-Nazi resisters, but there is little evidence that this was part of a planned effort.[92]

THE LAST GASP OF NORDIC FASCISM

The two nations of western Scandinavia, Denmark and Norway, were the most northerly countries under Hitler's thumb. They shared much in common. The languages of the countries were almost identical and they had similar political cultures, both having established traditions as liberal democracies. While there was little basis for fascism in either country, neither was there much foundation for anti-German resistance. Neither country had been occupied during the First World War and at the outset of the Second World War both had sought to retain neutrality. Despite such efforts, both nations were overrun early in the conflict, and since the Germans were still in place at the end of the war, they were occupied longer than any other countries except Poland and Bohemia-Moravia. Local Nazi administrators and troops realised that this familiarity did not work to the benefit of their cause, although this realisation had not sunk in at the highest echelon of the SS, where everything was seen through a racial prism and the two countries, along with the Netherlands, were regarded as highly favoured Nordic dependencies. Gottlob Berger told Himmler in September 1944 that 'our work in the Germanic lands is not in vain', and that in any forthcoming showdowns with the enemy, Scandinavians would share a common sense of purpose with Germany.[93]

The chief difference between Denmark and Norway was that the Danish king dickered with the Germans and accepted the fact of Nazi occupation (however reluctantly); in Norway, the monarch followed the more standard practice of fleeing to Britain and organising an exile government. These contrasting courses of action did much to shape the wartime histories of the two countries and deeply influenced the environment in which Skorzeny could undertake preparations for stay-behind operations. Since the Danes initially showed some heart for collaboration, the Germans allowed Denmark a degree of political autonomy and did not impose a military government or a Nazi civil commissioner, rather continuing to view the country as a formally sovereign state. This meant that the ultimate representative of Nazi authority was the German ambassador, who was styled, after 1942, as 'Reich Plenipotentiary'. Denmark's status as the so-called 'Model Protectorate' was eroded in 1942–1943 by a rising tide of anti-German sabotage, which the occupiers found difficult to address because of the semi-independence of the Danish administrative apparatus, police and courts. For the Germans, the only bright spot was the formation of the 'Schalburg Corps', a counter-insurgency force comprised of Danish volunteers back from the Eastern Front and named after an officer who had fallen in Russia. In Copenhagen, the Sipo forged a close relationship with the intelligence service of the 'Schalberg Corps', the *Efterretnings-Tjensten* (ET).

It was the deteriorating security situation in Denmark that first enmeshed Skorzeny in the country's affairs. As anti-German sabotage proliferated, Nazi hard-liners contended that they could depend neither upon the Danish police nor upon their own 'plenipotentiary', Werner Best, in crafting a policy of merciless repression. On 30 December 1943, Hitler hosted a staff conference attended by Himmler, Kaltenbrunner and Best, all of whom were subjected to a tongue lashing because of their supposed negligence in allowing Danish sabotage to reach serious proportions. Hitler's response, as was the case in similar situations, was one of violence. The *Führer* claimed to have learned early in his career that the only answer to brute force was to respond in kind, and he also argued that the best way to avoid making martyrs of Danish patriots, particularly the intellectual architects of the resistance movement, was to liquidate them without benefit of trial. Henceforth, for every Danish collaborator killed by the patriot resistance, a Danish opponent of the Nazis would be killed in turn; for every case of sabotage in a Danish factory working for German purposes, a facility supplying Danish civilian needs would be destroyed in turn. Best's methods of conciliation, Hitler averred, were ineffective.

The local SS-Police commander in Copenhagen lacked the manpower to carry out this mandate. In addition, he pointed out that his men had little expertise in explosives and that they were so well known in Denmark that they would quickly be recognised as the force behind anti-resistance terrorism. The answer, according to Himmler, was to send a joint SD-Gestapo band to Denmark and have its members inflict the desired mayhem. Matters on the SD side were assigned to Skorzeny, who was told to assemble a team from the staff at Oranienburg. Von Fölkersam picked six men led by Otto Schwerdt, a 28-year-old officer and veteran of the Mussolini rescue. The infamous Ludwig Nebel was part of the original complement. Section F supplied the unit, codenamed 'Peter', with pistols and silencers, while the SS-Police commander in Copenhagen provided phoney identification papers, which suggested that Schwerdt and his accomplices were 'commercial travellers'. For its side of the project, the Gestapo contributed only a translator from Flensburg, Karstensen, plus the notorious SS officer Alfred Naujocks, who had once been the top commando in the Third Reich but had since quarrelled with Reinhard Heydrich and been degraded. Naujocks was transferred to Denmark from the Netherlands, where he had been employed in suppressing the black market. Although *Gruppe* 'Peter' was originally German in composition, it soon integrated Danish volunteers from the 'Schalburg Corps' and was built up to strength of thirty men. Nebel was told that his job was to instruct Danish Nazis in the intricacies of sabotage with high explosives.

Schwerdt's party left Berlin in late December 1943. After a brief stop in Flensburg, the local *Abwehr* chief brought the men across the Danish frontier and put them on a train to Copenhagen. Once in the Danish capital, Schwerdt met with German police officials in order to draw up a list of targets; such liaison was maintained until the end of the war. All the names on the black list were discussed with Best, who had near-veto authority and used his influence to save a number of persons, including prominent Social Democrats. On the other hand, Best occasionally added names to the list, particularly those of businesses that were reluctant to supply German needs. As the *Führer* had indicated, journalists and writers were primary targets, and Schwerdt's first operation was to break into the office of newsman Christian Damm, who was shot twice, once through the temple. Although Damm survived, this attack marked the beginning of a reign of terror that eventually amounted to 226 acts of violence, mostly assassinations of figures in the Danish opposition. The most famous victim was Denmark's top dramatist, Pastor Kai Munk, whom Schwerdt, Nebel and Karstensen kidnapped from his home in Odensee on 3 January 1944. On the road to Aarhus, Munk was told to get out of his assailants' vehicle, whence he was shot in the back and killed. Munk subsequently became a national martyr-hero and his killing was regarded as the most outrageous act of German terrorism in Denmark. *Gruppe* 'Peter' also specialised in demolitions: Nebel, for instance, was assigned to blow up the Danish Student Union Building, the Student Boathouse and several cinemas that were used as gathering points for Danish oppositionists. Despite half-hearted efforts at dissimulation, it did not take the Danish police long to figure out who was behind such events. In one case, a car lent to Schwerdt by the SS-Police commander in Copenhagen was spotted leaving the scene of a shooting; Danish police subsequently used the licence plate number to prove that the vehicle belonged to the German authorities.

Berlin kept tabs on *Unternehmen* 'Peter' through bi-monthly reports that were sent to Radl (and then forwarded to Schellenberg), but a crisis occurred in July 1944, when the Gestapo delivered to *Führer* headquarters a highly critical assessment of counter-terror measures in Denmark. Still largely free of involvement in the 'Peter' enterprise, Gestapo officials charged that 'acts of terror' by the patriot resistance were outnumbering the 'Peter' *Gruppe*'s attacks by an eight to one ratio. Since Radl was sure that this claim would cause an uproar, he quickly gathered his own statistics, which showed Schwerdt and company in a more positive light (at least from a Nazi point of view). According to Radl, murders by the patriot underground outnumbered Schwerdt's killings thirty-five to ten; oppositional attacks on industry outweighed the 'Peter' *Gruppe*'s similar instances of sabotage ninety-five to eighteen; assaults on public gatherings showed the German special forces in the lead, with thirty-five cases compared to twenty-five. A report to this effect was sent to Hitler, but the sceptical *Führer* demanded photographic evidence of attacks, which was then assembled and included in a re-submission of the report.

Unternehmen 'Peter' was not a popular operation and it was the source of a constant stream of remonstrations from Best, who complained through Foreign Office channels. For their part, neither Skorzeny nor Radl were enthusiastic − 'Peter' comprised an outrageous breach of the rules of war and also seemed a waste of highly trained sabotage specialists − so they took advantage of the Gestapo's negative report to argue that the secret police, rather than complaining, should supply its own personnel to the 'Peter' enterprise. Prospectively, such a dispatch of manpower could serve as an opportunity to relieve the 'Peter' personnel from Section S. In August 1944, the Gestapo agreed to provide a ten-man party, which was trained at Friedenthal and then sent to Denmark. This band was commanded by *Hauptsturmführer* Issel. In September, Skorzeny's contingent to 'Peter' was released from service and returned to Berlin.

According to post-war claims by Skorzeny and Radl, Schwerdt's recall marked the end of Section S involvement in Danish counter-terrorism, a convenient coincidence since *Gruppe* 'Peter' engaged in its most vicious phase of activity over the last eight months of the war. In reality, the demarcation line between the two phases of *Unternehmen* 'Peter' was not as clear as Skorzeny and Radl later liked to contend. Friedenthal continued to provide sabotage material to the Gestapo, although Skorzeny knew that this material was finding its way to Denmark, and Section S trained reinforcements for Issel's detachment.[94] A German police official who served in Copenhagen during 1945 claimed that it was Skorzeny, rather than Gestapo chief Müller, who was still selecting personnel for 'Peter' and was directly responsible for much villainy.[95] It is also apparent that even though Schwerdt was reassigned to *Jagdverband Mitte* and carried out various tasks in France and Eastern Europe, he frequently returned to Copenhagen and never divorced himself from the ongoing operations of *Gruppe* 'Peter'.[96] Even after the end of the war, Schwerdt continued to linger around Flensburg, making preparations to re-enter Denmark, and one acquaintance heard him remark in September 1945 that operations 'were about to start up again'.[97]

Apart from worries about internal enemies, the Germans fretted about external threats to their 'Model Protectorate', particularly the possibility of an Allied amphibious invasion of Jutland, which was the main strategic concern until the end of 1944. Naturally, such worries prompted planning for a post-occupation resistance network. An opportunity to split the patriot underground movement also cropped up unexpectedly. In January 1944, *Kapitän* Berndt, a Danish representative from the 'nationalist' faction of the patriot resistance, reported to the Sipo that there were increasing fears in conservative circles about the underground growth of the Danish Communist Party and its potential to seize power upon the evacuation of German forces. Berndt claimed that he was authorised to ask the Germans for the provision of secret supply and weapons stores, which the 'nationalists' could use to fight communism in the wake of a prospective German retreat.[98]

With such factors in mind, *Hauptsturmführer* Daufeld, a representative of Section S, launched efforts in May–June 1944 to create a '*Nachrichten- und Sabotagedienst*' that would operate after the arrival of the Allies. 'Reliable' Danish collaborators were chosen for 'special training', especially members of the ET, whose leader, Erik Petersen, was inducted into the conspiracy, as was his deputy, Oktavius Noreen, who took over control of the ET after Petersen was assassinated. Nearly forty agents were trained at two German sabotage schools, one in the Harz Mountains and the other in Fürstenwalde. Trainees learned how to collect information and transmit radio messages, and how to blow up Allied ammunition dumps and disable power stations. Weapons and supplies were drawn from equipment that the RAF had dropped for the patriot underground but had fallen into the hands of the Germans. Dumps of such material were laid throughout Jutland, with technical assistance provided by FAK 213.

In September 1944, Himmler officially charged the RSHA with the organisation of a Danish resistance movement, and Daufeld was replaced by *Hauptsturmführer* Issel, which further suggests a continuing relationship between *Gruppe* 'Peter' and Skorzeny's headquarters in Friedenthal. The SS-Police command in Copenhagen complained that Issel was now receiving double pay from two separate channels of command and that he was increasingly difficult to control, since he took orders directly from Berlin and refused to consult with the local Sipo about stay-behind matters. Protests to Schellenberg brought no response. By the end of the war, Issel had managed to submerge one ET detachment and he had additional units preparing for deployment of a like nature, perhaps by posing as members of the patriot resistance. When Danish police officers in Brønderslev uncovered five hidden supply dumps in June 1945, they found amongst the cached material British military uniforms and brassards of the type worn by pro-Allied freedom fighters. Issel also established a wireless station in Oldburg and there were plans for basing similar transmitters in Copenhagen, Oldensee and Aahuis.

The '*Nachrichten- und Sabotagedienst*' was supposed to function in the presence of a continuing centre of resistance in Germany, which was absent after 8–9 May 1945. Nonetheless, when Issel made his final stop at the Copenhagen Sipo headquarters on 7 May, begging money, he still had plans to flee to Jutland and meet with a group of prospective Danish collaborators. The SS police commander, Otto Bovensiepen, tried to persuade him to report first to Flensburg, where Schellenberg was sure to prohibit any outlandish behaviour, but it is not clear what course Issel subsequently followed.[99]

As the British surged into north-western Germany, threatening Denmark from the south, Skorzeny drew a *Jagdkommando* from *Jagdeinsatz Dänemark*, on 1 April 1945 moving this detachment to the 'Berghof', a house adjacent to the Danish frontier that was used as a barracks by the German Border Guard. This unit was commanded by a cadre of young lieutenants, Lange, Iringsen, Fink and Anderse, who spent much time shuttling between the 'Berghof' and a local *Nordwest* headquarters in the Flensburg firemen's school. The Danish platoon was originally comprised of a handful of men, but reinforcements – mostly recruits from the ET and the 'Schalburg Corps' propaganda unit – brought the level of strength up to thirty troops. Germans were also added to the unit. While at the 'Berghof', Anderse did little except provide members of the *Jagdkommando* with occasional instruction in Morse signalling, although a few teams snuck across the Danish frontier, where they reconnoitred the terrain and begged food and coffee from ethnic German farmers living in North Schleswig. Plans for a course in explosives never materialised.

On 3 May 1945, members of the *Jagdkommando* were ordered to don civilian clothing and cross into Denmark at Pattburg, even though they had previously been assured that they would become operational only in case of a Soviet occupation of their homeland. At least one team carried weapons and explosives across the border and buried this material in the barnyard of a farmer who had previously shown them sympathy. Their transport situation was so desperate that they had to borrow a farmer's horse cart in order to carry their box of supplies to its designated position. Some of the infiltrators yearned for the war to be over so that they could return home; at least two deserted before they could be deployed. The few personnel remaining at the 'Berghof' then buried their weapons and scattered throughout northern Germany, although they were warned that the *Jagdverband* would yet call upon their services, probably after one or two months. One native Hamburger, who had been trained in Skorzeny's programme for 'human torpedoes', was sent back to his home town in order to learn about the attitude of British troops toward the civilian population.[100] There is no evidence that any of these elements undertook the demolitions for which they had been trained, although it is possible that a few participated in post-war skirmishing. In July 1945, the British Military Mission in Copenhagen reported that all Danish members of *Jagdverband Nordwest* had been arrested.[101]

Several other special detachments made preparations to go underground, even while simultaneously undertaking counter-resistance activities. One such formation was the 'Schiøler Group', which in November 1944 became the fourth department of the ET.[102] This detachment was originally formed by a member of the 'Schalburg Corps', Ib Ibsen, who in the spring of 1944 was recruited as an agent by FAK 213. In June 1944, Ibsen and sixteen colleagues were sent to FAK 213's sabotage school at Thumeries, France, where they were enrolled in a five-week course consisting of fieldcraft and work with high explosives. Upon their return to Denmark, most of the men were stationed near Viborg, on Jutland, mainly because an Allied seaborne assault on the western coast of the peninsula was the most likely enemy action. A small staff, including Ibsen, was also sent to Copenhagen, and the size of this group increased as the Germans began to worry about a possible Soviet invasion of Zealand. Both of these groups established weapons dumps, which numbered eighty on Jutland and fifty-five on Zealand, some of this material being British explosives provided by *Hauptsturmführer* Issel. Both groups also participated in '*Bulldoggenaktion*', that is, the tracing and capture of supplies dropped by the RAF, and toward the end of the war they engaged in a number of nefarious operations, codenamed 'Hydra', 'Seehund' and 'Guiscard', some of which involved using fishing smacks for '*S und Z Unternehmen*' ('Sabotage and Destruction Undertakings'). To maintain communications, volunteers from the sabotage groups ran their own motorboat, the 'Condor', which was on loan from the *Kriegsmarine*, and Ibsen also helped the Germans recruit a radio operator, who was trained at Bad Ems and whose task was to preserve contact between the two wings of the organisation.

After the Copenhagen group was reinforced and transferred to the oversight of the ET, its members received cover names and became active in what the Germans euphemistically called 'police work'. Even at the time of the demolitions course in France, Ibsen was already concocting a plan to send mail bombs to thirty prominent Danes, including several senior police officers and princes of the royal family. His German training officer approved this plan and promised to provide the requisite explosives. When Ibsen later decided to launch direct assaults upon political opponents, the Germans again promised to provide him with the necessary pistols and silencers. Along with members of the 'Peter *Gruppe*' and the uniformed ET '*Hilfspolizei*' (Hipo), members of the 'Schiøler Group' participated in the infamous '*Schalburgtage*' of 1944–1945, a reign of summary killing, looting and destruction inflicted upon enemies of the new order. Ibsen personally shot at least one member of the patriot resistance and he also rewarded one of his overly talkative followers by killing him and then dumping the body in a woods outside Copenhagen. In addition, Ibsen firebombed the 'Luna' Cafe, which he believed was the site of communist gatherings, and in April 1945 he stole a fuel tanker and pilfered 8,000 litres of petrol from an Esso depot in Hillerød.

The Jutland half of the sabotage organisation, unlike the 'Schiøler Detachment', remained under the full control of FAK 213 and was thus convinced to maintain a lower profile, abjuring activities that could have 'blown' its agents' cover. Numbering ten operatives, these men were encouraged to seek regular work and then attempt infiltration of the patriot resistance, particularly so that they could lay their hands on stocks of weapons and explosives supplied by the British. In March 1945, the Germans reinforced the Jutland detachment by recruiting new volunteers in Århus, mainly with the help of Lieutenant Petersen, a Danish Nazi Party organiser. Scouring the ranks of the local 'Schalburg Corps', Petersen found eight willing activists, who were given a brief explosives and weapons course near Viborg and then stationed in their hometown.

As British forces neared the Danish border, FAK officers decided to stand down their forces, particularly since the capitulation of the Third Reich seemed imminent. In addition, the Danish guerrillas had signed a contract promising to fight any opponent who appeared on Danish soil, but they had been assured that their main potential foes were the Soviets, and that in such a task they would be able to join forces with conservative factions in the patriot resistance. As matters turned out, the Soviets occupied only the eastern Danish island of Bornholm. The men of the 'Schiøler Detachment' were already well known to Danish police and most, including Ibsen, were picked up by British security forces, although two were killed in desultory fighting. Under interrogation, these captives revealed the locations of their secret supply dumps. The militants of the Århus Group, on the other hand, were enthusiastic about their deployment, even against the British, and most were still on the run in the summer of 1945.[103]

Given the violent background of German stay-behind preparations, it is hardly a surprise that outrages by Danish paramilitary fascists continued for several months after the end of the war, constituting a sort of post-liberation '*Schalburgtage*'. On 12 May, two German-trained saboteurs came within a hair's breadth of attacking Field Marshal Montgomery as he drove from Copenhagen's airport to the centre of the capital. The would-be assassins rented a flat overlooking the likely route of Montgomery's passage, but at the last moment the initiator of the plot, a 23-year-old Dane named Ibsen, lost his nerve and failed to throw a grenade that he had intended to lob into Montgomery's vehicle.[104] Despite this botch, a number of terrorist attacks continued to occur as ET hold-outs fired at their political enemies. On the evening of 19 May, two attempts were made on the life of Frode Jacobsen, a member of the Danish Freedom Council, and later in 1945 fascist gunmen killed Colonel Riis Lassen, a former leader of the patriot resistance. A 'gunpowder plot' in late May resulted in the round-up of seventeen terrorists who tried to blow up a British depot, and a month later five bomb blasts in Copenhagen damaged shops and injured several people. Despite 4,000 arrests in the first three days after liberation, Danish authorities suspected that a gang of 150 Hipo resisters was still at large, even as late as the autumn of 1945. Post-liberation skirmishes resulted in the deaths of approximately eighty people and the wounding of 450, mostly in the period 5–7 May 1945.[105] It is a little known fact, and one not usually brought up in polite company, but more Danes were killed and wounded resisting the liberation of Denmark than the number who suffered while opposing the original German invasion of the country in 1940.

Norway was absent many of the ambiguities of the 'Model Protectorate', particularly in the sense that there was no doubt about the country's status. Although the *Wehrmacht* had arrived in Oslo in 1940 bearing the same message that it had brought to Copenhagen – 'we come as protectors' – the Norwegians would have none of it. They offered staunch military resistance, a process in which they were aided by the Allies, and after fleeing to a northern redoubt, their king and government escaped into exile. As a replacement for the conventional forces of order, the Germans eventually (and reluctantly) hoisted into power the much-maligned Vidkun Quisling, archetype of the twentieth-century traitor, and they also built up Quisling's miniscule Norwegian fascist party, the *Nasjonal Samling* (NS).

Although the RSHA was ordered in September 1944 to prepare an anti-Allied Norwegian underground, the peripheral location of Norway did not suggest that the construction of such a movement should have priority.[106] By the winter of 1944–1945, *Wehrmacht* signals intelligence suggested that the Western Allies did not intend to invade German-occupied Scandinavia, and the Germans began to transfer forces from Norway to the German homeland, which seemed in worse danger of being overrun.[107] Nonetheless, Skorzeny instructed Section S to start work on an 'I-*Netz*', at least for safety's sake. Three non-commissioned officers were sent from *Jagdverband Nordwest*, and some forty Norwegians were recruited and trained as the requisite manpower for this system, although it never became fully operative. In particular, the different cells were never able to establish reliable radio contact.

After the German retreat from Finland, Skorzeny also set to work on building a full-scale Norwegian resistance movement, codenamed 'Lorelei'. It was intended to organise 'strong points' (bunkers) that would be manned by 'reliable' Norwegians and stocked with sabotage equipment. It was also suggested that the movement should lie low and only launch operations several months after any prospective Allied occupation. The original efforts to establish this network were unsuccessful. Skorzeny sent a *Nordwest* officer to Norway, but this individual failed to even start in building a cohesive organisation. Skorzeny and Radl then asked the RSHA to supply them with someone familiar with Norwegian culture and they were provided with *Haupsturmführer* Hellmuth Romeick, who had been in the SD since 1935 and had been stationed at Kiel. Romeick was sent to Friedenthal for training and was then dispatched to Oslo, where he was subordinated to the local Sipo commander and instructed to disguise his headquarters as part of the German labour corps or as a private construction firm. Over the winter of 1944–1945, Romeick conducted Operation '*Silberfuchs*', in which a platoon of Norwegians was sent to Neustrelitz and Friedenthal for training. As was the case with the Section S programme, 'Lorelei' was not ready to operate at the time of the final German surrender, nor was it meant to function after the collapse of the Third Reich.[108] On the other hand, at least one *Jagdverband* squad was left in the northern province of Finnmark, which was liberated by the Red Army over the late autumn and winter of 1944–1945. In February 1945, German navy officers complained about this detachment, which was operating under control of the 270th Infantry Division and had been left in the Alte Fjord, where its presence was hindering the mining of the waterway.[109]

As it dawned on Skorzeny that Norwegians seemed more willing to perform sabotage for the Allies than for the Germans, he decided to host a conference devoted entirely to 'Norwegian questions'. This roundtable was held in Berlin on 8 January 1945, after which Skorzeny directed his advisor on Scandinavian affairs, Carl Edquist, to draw up a memorandum. Edquist had already recommended the deposition of Quisling, whom he deemed more of a burden than an asset, and he advised that the Germans free Norwegian concentration camp inmates (although Edquist had himself helped to put several Norwegians into Sachsenhausen concentration camp). The release of Scandinavian prisoners was concurrently being sought by the Swedish Red Cross and was subsequently arranged between Himmler and Count Folke Bernadotte, the nephew of King Gustav of Sweden. SD officer Rudolf Danziger was put in charge of the transports.[110]

Aside from Section S and the *Jagdverbände*, a few other German units in Norway also developed plans for resistance activity. Section S work was aided by several FAK officers, probably members of *Trupp 261*, which had personnel in Norway in order to engage in '*Bulldoggenaktion*'. Members of the FAK '*Teilgruppe Norwegen*' were withdrawn from the country after learning that *Jagdverband Nordwest* was already busy with 'Lorelei', and they probably left without laying any sabotage supply caches.[111] FAK 144 helped organise a sixty-man detachment of Germans (*Streifkorps*), which was supposed to engage in reconnaissance and sabotage in northern Norway or Sweden, particularly if the latter country jumped into the war against Germany. Once again, however, it was a matter of too little, too late – the *Streifkorps* training course was about to begin when the capitulation was announced – and there was no coordination between this effort and 'Lorelei'. In fact, Romeick was not even aware of the *Streifkorps'* existence.[112] Naval Special Detachment 30 also planned raids against the coast of Soviet-occupied Finnmark, mainly in order to destroy supply posts and shipping. One such attack was scheduled for 1 May 1945, when it was intended to put thirty men ashore from a U-Boat, but it is unclear whether this raid was actually staged.[113]

The NS also had plans to launch its own guerrilla movement. Originally, it was hoped to establish an anti-Soviet underground in the Arctic region of Finnmark, where there were many Lapps and Finns who bore no animosity to the *Wehrmacht* – local German garrisons were comprised largely of well-behaved Austrians – and where the Quislingites had enjoyed success in stirring up the anti-establishment resentments of the northerners. Despite such advantages, the Germans opted for a policy of civilian deportation and 'scorched earth' destruction, rather than supporting a campaign of sub rosa resistance, and Jonas Lie, the NS 'Ruler of Finnmark', was cajoled into cooperating. Thus, the *Wehrmacht* forced 45,000 people to leave their homes and then systematically wrecked Finnmark's infrastructure and means of production, a process that obviously did nothing to encourage pro-German feelings among the Finnmarkinger who evaded deportation and remained in the province.[114]

After this episode, NS efforts were refocused on preparing underground resistance throughout the remainder of the country. Henrik Rogstad, the chief of the NS paramilitary, the Hird, favoured die-hard resistance, as did Jonas Lie, the number two man in the Quisling regime. 'Volunteers' were inducted into a covert NS organisation called the 'ZBF', and these militants were sent for training in Elverum and Trondelag.[115] It all came to nothing. After striking some brave poses, Quisling lost heart, announcing in early May 1945 that the NS sought Norwegian 'neutrality' in case of an Allied landing, and that the Hird would not run the risk of civil war. After adopting this stance, Quisling surrendered to the patriot resistance on 9 May 1945. Rogstad and Lie put up a fight, encouraging NS ultras to struggle 'so that our culture may survive'. Lie published a belligerent declaration in the journal *Germanen* on 5 May, the same day that local German forces decided to capitulate, and he encouraged a round of shootings that disturbed the peace of Oslo and Trondheim for several weeks after the liberation, although the scale of the skirmishing did not equal that of the similar outbreaks in Denmark. Lie and Rogstad also gathered two hundred of their followers and fled to Skavgum Castle outside Oslo, where they were promptly penned in by Norwegian patriots. Hopelessly surrounded, they both committed suicide on 11 May.[116] For the remainder of 1945, a few Norwegian 'Werewolves' spread underground propaganda and issued threats, and a handful of *Ostfront* veterans took refuge in the mountains, where they hunted reindeer and occasionally forayed forth to ambush convoys of trucks.[117] Nonetheless, by the time the dust settled, Norway – save Finnmark – had enjoyed an easier process of liberation than any other country in Europe.

A NATION IN LIMBO

The other combatant country in Scandinavia, Finland, was part of a genus of pro-German nations – also including Hungary, Bulgaria, Albania and Denmark – that had spent much of the war in a shadow land between neutrality and belligerence. Historically, Finland had been friendly to Germany because the *Kaiserreich* had supported Finland's separation from Russia in 1917. In fact, a 2,000-man unit of Finnish volunteers (*Jäger*) had served in the German Army during the First World War, and the Germans had sent a small expeditionary force in order to help the Finns establish an anti-Bolshevik state. The Finns were disappointed that Germany had not come to their aid during an abortive Soviet invasion of the country over the winter of 1939–1940, although even without such help the Finns outfought the Red Army and had ended up losing only some frontier regions of the country. Naturally, the Finns took advantage of 'Barbarossa' to reoccupy the lost borderland territories and also to grab part of Outer Karelia, but they never formally joined the Axis alliance system nor did they drive deeply into the USSR, instead satisfying a narrow range of aims and then holding their lines and demobilising much of their army. The Germans contemptuously described this modest effort as the '*Sitzkrieg*',[118] and although they urged the Finnish Army to cut the crucial Soviet supply route between Murmansk and Moscow, the most the Finns would do was to carry out long-range raids against this rail line, using Finnish volunteers, German Brandenburgers and Russian Vlasovites as manpower.[119] The Finnish Army also supported the operations of small anti-Soviet partisan groups in eastern Karelia.[120]

Despite the limited Finnish contribution to the Axis effort, the Germans wanted to keep their ally engaged in the conflict and they worried about periodic rumours of peace feelers between Helsinki and Moscow. After a Soviet offensive in June 1944 pushed back Finnish forces all along the front, the Finns were put on notice: if they did not quickly withdraw from the conflict, they would be trounced militarily and overrun. In August 1944, Finland's founding father, Marshal Gustav Mannerheim, assumed the presidency with a mandate to seek peace with the USSR. A cease-fire was declared on 4/5 September and two weeks later, Finland signed an armistice with Moscow. This agreement included stiff terms, but unlike the arrangements negotiated by Romania, Bulgaria and Hungary, it did not provide for Soviet military occupation. Why the Soviets passed up the opportunity to occupy Finland is a matter of some speculation. Part of the reason involved Finland's lack of participation in the Axis alliance, although it is also true that the country's peripheral location meant that it was not a route that potential invaders could use to reach the Soviet heartland.[121] More important was the fact that Finland was well situated for guerrilla warfare and would have been a difficult morsel to digest. Finland has much forested and heavily watered terrain, including 60,000 lakes, a fact that typically channels invaders along narrow passageways and exposes assault columns to partisan warfare and flanking attacks. The Finns have traditionally been adept at such tactics because of a sports-oriented culture that has produced many fine skiers and marksmen; military patrols recruited from such elements had produced endless difficulties for Soviet units during the Winter War and they had again proven their worth in long-range operations against the Murmansk railway.[122] After suffering a bloody nose in such confrontations, Stalin had little desire to encourage a Finnish guerrilla movement that could have tied down Soviet forces.

The lack of Soviet occupation created a peculiar situation for the Finnish anti-communist resistance movement. With Soviet forces only present in the extreme north of the country, which the Soviets claimed as their own, and in the neighbourhood of a Soviet naval base at Porkkala, there was not much of a bullseye upon which Finnish resisters could focus their efforts. In fact, the only outstanding act of violence was the assassination of a Russian naval officer in Helsinki, which occurred on 7 November 1944.[123] The German ambassador had noted in early September that an open rebellion against Mannerheim's peace policy was contingent upon a Soviet occupation of the country, and another diplomat had pointed out that direct action against the limited targets in the country would be unproductive, since they would work to precipitate the very Soviet occupation that the Finns dreaded.[124] On the other hand, there is no doubt that the absence of the Soviets allowed for the development of a significant resistance movement, which faced direct opposition only from the Finnish Communist Party.

In structure, the Finnish nationalist underground consisted of a number of overlapping military and civilian cliques, some of which included powerful and prestigious activists. Most were advocates of 'Greater Finland', which meant that they favoured expansion into the Soviet Union, or they were believers in the 'Finno-Ugrish idea', that is, the notion that Finns had a racial affinity with Estonians, Hungarians and Turks, and ought rightly to be the ally of those nations. A few were members of the influential Finno-Swedish minority and were thus advocates of Scandinavian union.

The central organiser of the Finnish resistance movement was Karl Jansen, the chief spokesman for Colonel Lindh, an ex-*Jäger* and pulp-and-paper magnate who was the head of the Finnish veteran's league. With Lindh's blessing, Jansen met in the summer of 1944 with the SD station chief in Helsinki, Alarich Brohs. Jansen agreed to form a '*Bodenorganisation*' ('ground organisation') that would attempt to coordinate the various anti-Soviet cliques, although there was never any question of the movement being structured on a centralised basis. The Finns also agreed to prepare a number of country houses in central Finland and the Pori–Vaasa–Oulu coastal region as potential bases for the resistance movement. They committed themselves to organising a boat service to maintain contact with the rocky islets between Helsinki and the Åland Islands and to meeting German submarines that could surface in these waters. Similar arrangements were made for finding parachute drop zones and for locating remote lakes where seaplanes could alight. KG 200 had a small unit with two Leo H-246 flying boats that had been evacuated from Finland and were now based on the Baltic island of Rügen. As a final measure, Jansen and his cohorts promised to organise a maritime courier service to Sweden, with one route running directly across the Gulf of Bothnia and another via the Åland Islands, and to set up a parallel channel across the Torne river.

Even as early as January 1945, Jansen could report progress in attending to these tasks. He told the Germans that decentralised staffs had been put in place all over Finland and that an intelligence service had been organised in order to deflect the hostile attention of the Finnish communists. Powerful figures in the movement insisted, however, that the time for direct action was not yet propitious, and that Finland would have to comply with Soviet demands, at least superficially, until the Western Allies could be convinced to come to the country's aid.

The military segment of the resistance movement included the most famous generals in the country, particularly Hugo Österman, the former commander-in-chief of the Finnish Army; Paavo Talvela, the Finnish equivalent of George Patton; and Ruben Lagus, the country's foremost authority on armoured warfare. Interestingly, all of these men had been honoured by Mannerheim, but they had, on occasion, run afoul of the grand patriarch. Also fitting in the same category was Lauri Malmberg, a veteran *Jäger* who had served since 1921 as chief of the Civic Guard, a militia descended from the White forces that had won the Finnish Civil War of 1918.[125] Actually, the Germans had hoped that such men would flee to the *Wehrmacht* element in Finland, the 20th Mountain Army, and would stick with their ally. Hitler talked about 60,000 Finns aligning themselves with the German Army and the SS. By the late summer of 1944, the commander of 20th Mountain Army was the Nazi hard-liner Lothar Rendulic, whose idea of a resistance movement was to have Talvela and his loyalists hold a redoubt in southern Finland with the help of a German infantry division and an assault gun brigade.

Mannerheim's prestige and force of personality prevented such elements from going astray and the German cause was also hurt by the fact that Finno-German fighting broke out in Lapland.[126] The Soviets cleverly arranged for the armistice terms to allow only two weeks for the 20th Mountain Army to withdraw from Finland, an impossibly short schedule that the Soviets knew would cause trouble. Although the Germans and Finns had secretly planned a bogus war, meant solely to satisfy the requirements of the Russians, real clashes occurred at the start of October 1944, particularly as Soviet liaison officers showed up at Finnish military headquarters, demanding action from their new colleagues.[127] At the same time, Rendulic sent two insulting notes to officers at the Finnish high command, in which he questioned the honour of his former 'brothers in arms' and implied that they were no longer free agents. The Foreign Office complained that Rendulic's lack of tact 'antagonises parts of the Finnish armed forces still sympathetic', and it warned that such actions 'do not help our attempts to organise a partisan war against the Russians or to win Finnish soldiers to [a policy of] collaboration'.[128]

The most important initiative of the military resistance movement was the caching of weapons, food and medicine, an operation run by Lieutenant-Colonel Sakari Haahti. Inspired by the example of the German *Reichswehr*, Finnish officers discussed a nationwide dump-laying campaign as early as the spring of 1944, and they began making specific arrangements several months later. At this point, the project had an anti-German as well as anti-Soviet animus, since it was intended to support a fight against any power likely to threaten the country's freedom of action. After the Finno-Soviet armistice, the Soviets began to loom as the chief potential menace, despite the fighting in Lapland, particularly because Finnish conservatives feared that the Russians would break their pledge not to occupy the country or that the Soviets would support internal subversion. Haahti eventually rallied between 5,000 and 10,000 activists, mostly soldiers but also demobilised troops, who were legion because of Soviet demands to cut the size of the Finnish Army from half a million men to 37,000. Militiamen from the Civil Guard also played a key role, at least until that organisation was denounced by the Russians as 'fascist' and dissolved by fiat. Despite such problems, Haahti organised an elaborate network of provincial caching circles that functioned independently, but which together filled the barns and cellars of the nation with enough supplies to equip 35,000 guerrilla fighters.[129] By the end of 1944, preparations had been completed and this success was reported to the Germans,[130] who began to realise that among their ex-friends in Eastern Europe, the Finns rivalled the Romanians in anti-Soviet pugnaciousness.

On the civilian side of the Finnish resistance movement, the chief figure of note was the banker and municipal politician J.A. Norrmén, who was famous in local political lore for having arranged a chilly reception when Tsar Nicholas visited Helsinki in 1915. Long before the Finnish armistice, Norrmén had told German officers that he was willing to keep fighting the Soviets even should his country drop out of the war, and he claimed to represent an echelon of senior business leaders possessed by similar sentiments. Shortly before the armistice, Norrmén told Brohs that a coterie of Finnish business magnates was willing to fund a Finnish anti-communist underground as long as the movement served solely Finnish interests and as long as direct action awaited the development of favourable circumstances. Norrmén was especially valuable to the Germans because he served as a link to other tycoons and policy-makers with whom the Germans had no direct contact. These people included Hjalmar Procopé, an ex-foreign minister who saw the resistance movement as a counterweight to the Finnish Communist Party; Petter Forsström, the owner of the nation's largest lime and cement works; Esko Riekki, the former chief of the Finnish State Police and a figure who still exerted much influence in the Interior Ministry; and Bruno Salmiala, a university professor of Finno-Ugrish tendencies and the leader of the Finnish fascist party, the *Isänmaallinen Kansanliike* (IKL).

Another key contact was Dr Helanen, the chief of the Academic Karelian League (AKS) and another authority on Finno-Ugrish ethnicity and its supposed implications. As a young student, Helanen had been in the original nationalist resistance movement, which had targeted the Romanov Tsar as Finland's ultimate enemy, and he thereafter became an advocate of Finnish expansion into Karelia and Estonia. During the Continuation War, he had been entrusted with resettling the Ingermanlanders, who had lived in the Leningrad region and were presumed to be a surviving fragment of the Finnish 'race'. While engaged in this project, Helanen had worked closely with the SD's local 'expert' on nationality matters, *Obersturmführer* Wassermann, and the two men had struck up a close friendship. After the Finno-Soviet armistice, Helanen contacted Wassermann in order to alert the Germans to the existence of a Finnish underground, which he said was in need of material support. According to Helanen, the movement aimed to resist an occupation of Finland by the Red Army, which he felt was inevitable. Realising that Helanen had considerable influence, the Germans took his initiative seriously and Wassermann was transferred to Brohs's staff, after which he served as the latter's deputy and as his liaison officer with *Jagdverband Nordwest*, although his main task was to cultivate Helanen.[131]

Although the leaders of the Finnish underground disclaimed any immediate intention of building a mass movement, there was a considerable pool of sympathisers. This reserve included the veterans' association (40,000 members and rapidly getting larger because of the demobilisation of the Finnish Army), the AKS (8,000 active and passive cardholders), the IKL (100,000 supporters), the Civic Guard (140,000 participants) and veterans of the *Waffen*-SS (1,000 cadres, including 120 ex-officers). All of these groups had been officially dissolved under the terms of the armistice agreement, but the Soviet political delegate in Helsinki, Andrei Zhdanov, complained that this stipulation was the part of the armistice he had the most difficulty in impressing upon the Finns and that the banned organisations were still functioning underground. The Finnish resisters, on the other hand, complained to the Germans that the dissolution of the 'patriotic organisations' had hindered their efforts. During the summer of 1944, the German minister in Helsinki had noted that pro-German elements only comprised three per cent of the Finnish population, and that they were bereft of charismatic leaders, but even such a limited constituency formed a sufficient basis for a network of sympathisers. Helanen also believed that if Finnish peasants were organised 'under responsible leadership', they would rise *en masse*, a conclusion inspired by memory of the anti-communist 'Lapua' movement, which had reached its peak in the early 1930s and had provided the precursor to the IKL.[132]

Obviously, the Germans tried to encourage their Finnish friends and to remain in contact with anti-Soviet leaders. Following Bulgarian and Romanian precedents, the Foreign Office formed a 'Finnish National Committee', which was based in Berlin. At first, the Germans had hoped to land a major catch for their committee, namely Toivo Kivimäki, a former prime minister and the Finnish envoy in Berlin. Kivimäki was known to be 'extremely bitter over the Finnish defeat', but ever the loyal patriot, he returned home when recalled. As a second choice, the Germans picked *Graf* von Ungern-Sternberg, although it was embarrassing that von Ungern-Sternberg was not a Finn but a Baltic German nobleman. Like all the 'national committees', the Finnish version was supposed to support active resistance in the home country, and in December 1944 the German diplomatic agent assigned to the body, Johannes Metzger, was ordered to submit a report on the measures necessary to encourage partisan warfare. Metzger, who considered the mere organisation of the committee as 'sheer folly', could hardly believe that his political masters would now encourage violent resistance. Such a policy, he marvelled, '[plumbed] the depths of crass idiocy'. In his subsequent report, he stressed that only decisive successes on the Eastern Front could rally pro-German forces, and that failing such a shift in fortunes, the Finnish resistance movement would refuse to cooperate in waging guerrilla warfare. Metzger also reiterated that the project afforded the USSR the official excuse it needed to occupy Finland.[133]

The main instrument of the 'national committee' was 'Finnish Freedom Radio', which the committee ran jointly with the SD, the SS Main Office and the Propaganda Ministry. Broadcasting from Berlin's 'Concordia' transmitter, 'Finnish Freedom Radio' was managed by a highly energetic and ambitious SS officer named Purjo, although it seemed unable to exercise significant influence in Finland. Part of the problem was that the output, which was designed by Finns and was intended to suit a Finnish sensibility, was undercut by the clumsy Finnish-language broadcasts of Radio Königsberg, which simply re-broadcast German programmes translated into the Finnish language. 'Free Finland' propaganda was also weakened by the wild claims that the Germans put forth in September and October 1944, when they contended that 'OGPU executioners' were stalking Finland, that preparations were underway for mass deportations to Siberia, and that the country's 'real' leaders were fleeing abroad, including a number of generals who had supposedly approached the 'national committee'.

German contact with the Finnish resistance movement was maintained via several radio transmitters that were set up before the breach in Finno-German relations. As early as December 1943, Brohs had been ordered by his SD boss, Theodor Päffgen, to organise wireless stations for a prospective I-*Netz* in Finland. In March 1944, Brohs recruited a Danish radio engineer, Thoralf Kyrre, in order to man such a transmitter, and Kyrre proved a quick learner when provided with technical instruction. He was then given a wireless transmitter and located this equipment at his place of employment, a radio engineering plant that provided perfect cover because it continually produced transmission signals as technicians tested newly finished radio sets. Thus was established radio post '*Invasionsnetz* (Ida) 101'.

After 8 September 1944, Kyrre maintained links between Brohs and the Finnish *Bodenorganisation*, and from late October he also handled the message flow between Helanen and Wassermann. In November 1944, Kyrre also began cultivating 'friends' among Russian officers with the Control Commission and he may have been able to tap the Soviet telephone cable in the Helsinki suburb of Mullungsby, a task for which Brohs had supplied necessary technical equipment. Ida 101 proved an intelligence gold mine and for five months Kyrre sent a seemingly endless supply of information about the Finnish communists, Soviet oversight measures, the composition of the government and the seizure of Porkkala. Some of this intelligence was used to inform the broadcasts of the 'Finnish Freedom Station'. Kyrre was arrested on 31 January 1945, which was a blow to both the Germans and the Finnish underground, although he escaped after several weeks in confinement, probably with the assistance of sympathisers in the Finnish police.[134]

An even more important line of communication was arranged by Alexander Cellarius, the brilliant but neurotic spy master whose high-level contacts throughout Scandinavia and the Baltic States made him the most important *Abwehr* figure in the region. Before Cellarius was evacuated from Helsinki, he extracted a promise of ongoing cooperation from Colonel Reino Hallamaa, a Finnish secret service officer whom Cellarius considered the real leader of the anti-Soviet resistance movement. Hallamaa was also head of the Reconnaissance Department of the Finnish General Staff and the creator of 'Headquarters Patrols', the staff that had run the infiltration units so dreaded by the Red Army. Thus, Hallamaa's participation was crucial in any credible effort to launch a guerrilla war. In addition, Hallamaa was a cypher expert and a superb source of information on the Russian armed forces. Shortly before Cellarius left Finland, he agreed to supply Hallamaa with German information about the USSR in return for a continuing flow of intelligence. Two channels for communications were suggested: a secret cable running from Finland to Estonia, and a radio link between Helsinki and Cellarius's new headquarters at Tallinn. The Finns were squeamish about using the cable, though, cutting it before the Soviets could find it, and radio contact was disrupted by the rapid German retreat from Estonia. The Hallamaa–Cellarius radio link was re-established by December, only to be subsequently abandoned by the Finns due to jitters about security.

By 1945, two new arrangements were being developed. By sending pouches to the Finnish Embassy in Sweden, Hallamaa was able to funnel information to Makato Onodera, the Japanese military attaché in Stockholm. A personal friend of Hallamaa and Cellarius, Onodera shared much of this intelligence with the Germans. With the collapse of Ida 101, Berlin asked Onodera to get Hallamaa's assistance in re-establishing radio contact with the Finnish underground. Hallamaa was in a natural position to help because his deputy, Lieutenant Juho Kallio, had already begun to set up a radio network for the resisters. Hallamaa agreed to attend a meeting in Stockholm in order to discuss linking Kallio's web to the Germans, but the war ended before this conclave could be held.

Hallamaa also developed a courier route by sending a Finnish line-crossing expert named Paatsalo to northern Sweden, where he was responsible for a range of special duties, including sharing information with SMT and the organisation of an illegal traffic service between Finnish Lapland and northern Sweden. As part of this enterprise, Paatsalo was supposed to send runners to the German garrison at Narvik, Norway, which became a crucial channel of contact after the retreat of the 20th Mountain Army.

From the German side, this system was run by Edmund Salla, an intelligence officer with 20th Mountain Army, and Hans Scheidt, who had been deputy chief of the SS liaison staff in Finland. Salla and Scheidt collected a team of Finnish prisoners of war from a camp at Kongsvinger, to which they added the ubiquitous Swedish traitor, Carl Goran Edquist. Operating under the banner of the 'Free Finland' movement, this unit established return routes to Finland and cooperated with Paatsalo's couriers. Once *Jagdverband Nordwest* was strong enough, it was supposed to inherit this operation.[135]

Over the winter of 1944–1945, the Germans sent several U-Boat missions to Finland, although the story of these trips reveals a degree of internal intrigue and rivalry that nearly crippled the German programme of assistance for the *Bodenorganisation*. The first of these voyages was organised by the Foreign Office, which had long been interested in establishing a resistance movement in Finland.[136] In early November, one of the former members of the German legation in Helsinki, Johannes Metzger, learned from a Swedish agent that a number of escaped German POWs were being hidden by peasants in western Finland and that they desired conveyance back to Germany. Metzger's Swedish friend, while visiting Helsinki, had been recommended by a member of General Talvela's staff to Jansen, who was described as the chief organiser of the Finnish underground. Jansen suggested sending a U-Boat to gather the desperados and he mentioned that a coastal inlet near Vaasa might serve as an appropriate pick-up point. Upon his return to Stockholm, the Swedish agent brought this suggestion to Metzger, who was then being serving with the German Embassy in Sweden. Metzger and the German naval attaché in Stockholm brought up the matter with *Grossadmiral* Dönitz, who agreed to supply a submarine.

The operation was soon underway. Details concerning the dates of approach and recognition signals reached Stockholm on 15 November and were sent on to Jansen, who said that a small craft would come out to meet the U-Boat when it surfaced at the lightship Storkallegrund, near the Finnish coast. The German submarine reached Storkallegrund in early December and cruised for four days in the vicinity, although the Finns did not succeed in contacting the vessel. Stormy weather and icy conditions prevented the resisters from launching their motorboat. Obviously, none of the escaped German prisoners were rescued, although several naval officers were later extracted by KKV vessels.

The abortive U-Boat mission was the cause of a subsequent row between the Foreign Office and the SD, whose relations descended from frosty to glacial. In truth, Brohs had learned of the plight of the German POWs before Metzger, since Kyrre had reported about the situation through Ida 101. Acting in his capacity as German liaison for the Finns, Brohs had decided that the situation did not merit the dispatch of a U-Boat, and instead he advised Jansen to smuggle the men into Sweden, whence they could be returned to Germany. When Metzger's agent reached Helsinki, Jansen assumed (wrongly) that he was working for Brohs and that the latter had changed his mind and was now willing to send a submarine to fetch the escaped POWs. Finnish cooperation with the project proceeded on this basis.

Brohs hit the proverbial ceiling when he discovered that his contacts in Finland had been used to attempt contact with a U-Boat, particularly since he only learned about the submarine mission after the fact. As was typical, the right hand was ignorant of what the left hand was doing. Despite the fact that the Finnish resisters did not discover the clumsiness of their German allies, Brohs never revealed to Jansen that the voyage had lacked his sanction or foreknowledge, although he was forced to impress upon the *Bodenorganisation* that all future enterprises should be confirmed personally by him. Brohs and Metzger then met in Berlin in order to prevent further mishaps, and although Brohs accepted Metzger's plea that the affair arose from a misunderstanding, his SS bosses were not so easily placated. Päffgen complained to Kaltenbrunner, whose worst impressions of the Foreign Office seemed confirmed. Kaltenbrunner subsequently wrote a scathing letter to Ribbentrop's deputy, Gustav von Steengracht, charging that Metzger had 'horned in' on an SD network and that he had tried to use information gleaned from the incident for his own private ends. Steengracht repudiated these allegations, although Kaltenbrunner then switched tactics and charged that Metzger had a Swedish mother, an accident of descent that transgressed the *Führer's* order that all persons of alien extraction be dismissed from the Foreign Service. As a result, Metzger was fired in February

1945, although by this juncture he had been posted as envoy to the 'Finnish National Committee', a position from which he was only too happy to retire.

Meanwhile, Brohs was planning further German expeditions, although this time he intended to play a central role. Although Brohs was reluctant to dispatch a submarine to pick up fugitive German soldiers, his interest was piqued by a new proposal from Dr Helanen, who suggested in early November that he was prepared to visit Germany in the company of eight demobilised Finnish officers, all of whom were willing to undertake *Jagdverband* training. In order to facilitate this exchange, Brohs approached the commander of the KG 200 squadron on Rügen, but an early frost in Finland prevented the landing of a seaplane on a lake in the south-western part of the country. Helanen, Lindh and Forsström then suggested sending another U-Boat to the Finnish coast, a proposal to which Brohs agreed and for which he obtained the approval of Cellarius. In fact, it was suggested that not only could the boat pick up Helanen and his Finns, but that new radio sets and codes could be delivered to Ida 101 and that one of Cellarius's collaborators, Lieutenant Heikkilä, could bring wireless transmitters and codes to Hallamaa. In addition, funds amounting to a million Finnish marks and 8,000 Swedish kronor could be supplied to the resistance movement, along with stores of small arms, petrol and copper wire. The allocation of another U-Boat was obtained from the navy, although the head of the German submarine service, *Admiral* Godt, began to complain that his precious vessels were being sent to Finland dependent only on the good faith of foreigners and that such plans should not be arranged by radio, just in case the enemy had deciphered the code. Godt may have been a chauvinist, but he had a well-deserved suspicion of the integrity of wireless codes.

On 9 January 1945, U-242 left Danzig on an operation that the *Kriegsmarine* dubbed *Unternehmen* 'Nord'. On board were Brohs, Cellarius, two of their Finnish hirelings, Heikkilä and Runolinna, plus a fifty-man crew. Newly equipped with a *Schnorchel*, U-242 was well suited for 'Nord' because her commander and crew had recently completed several months of operations in the Baltic and were familiar with the waters around southern Finland. After sailing through a mine-ridden passage north of the Åland Islands, U-242 reached the lightship Storkallegrund, the same contact point used during the earlier U-Boat mission. The vessel spent the day cruising at periscope depth and taking bearings on coastal landmarks, although representatives of the *Bodenorganisation* failed to show up at the appointed place and time. Godt had ordered the U-Boat captain, *Oberleutnant zur See* Panke, to wait six days for contact and then return home. From 13 to 19 January, U-242 lay on the bottom, occasionally rising to periscope depth and surfacing at night to recharge her accumulators. Radio signals from Ida 101 suggested that a party of Finnish resisters was based in a nearby fishing village and was trying to make contact, but that wind and ice were preventing their motorboat from putting to sea. On the evening of 19 January, Godt ordered Panke to sail back to Danzig, but several hours later, near midnight, crewmen spotted a light signal from the Finnish resisters, who had managed to launch a small boat belonging to the Finnish veterans' association. The U-Boat responded with its own signalling apparatus, and after the Finns drew within hailing distance, code phrases were exchanged and the Finns, led by Jansen, were invited onboard U-242.

In the subsequent meeting, Brohs, Cellarius and Jansen attended to several matters. Jansen reported that Helanen had been prevented from making the rendezvous. Since Helanen had once been charged with removing the Ingermanlanders from northern Russia, Mannerheim felt it was fitting to make him responsible for bringing those unfortunate people back to their place of origin, as demanded by the Soviets. This act of deliberate irony limited Helanen's freedom of action, and he now found it impossible to leave Helsinki, even for a short period. The eight demobilised Finnish officers whom he had promised also failed to arrive, although Jansen said that two of the men in his boarding party, the young officers Törni and Korpela, both wished to go to Germany, where they could be trained for special operations. Törni, in particular, had been one of Hallamaa's deputies in Headquarters Patrols and had much experience behind Soviet lines, which led the Finns to think that he was suited for advanced training in guerrilla warfare. The fourth Finn in the group, Lieutenant-Colonel Johan Christian Fabritius, was a strident Nazi sympathiser and one-time fortifications expert with the Finnish General Staff. He was being sent to Germany as the liaison officer of the Finnish resistance movement, a task for which he had been personally picked by Österman and Forsström. Fabritius's real job was to observe the internal situation in Germany and determine what value, if any, the Germans still had for the Finnish underground.

Jansen also reported on the state of the Finnish resistance movement, which he depicted as vigorous, although he confided that the Finns were worried by further Soviet advances along the southern coast of the Baltic, which they felt could hardly fail to effect the position of Finland. Despite these concerns, Jansen assured Brohs and Cellarius that the *Bodenorganisation* was anxious for even closer cooperation, and that the preparation of secret landing sites and meeting places would be completed within several months. Brohs and Cellarius told Jansen, in turn, that they wanted German radios to be used for expanding the network of underground wireless stations reporting to Germany and also for augmenting an internal Finnish web, the Kallio network, which could feed information to a central hub in Helsinki. They also agreed to start a regular U-Boat shuttle that could stash supplies for pick-up among rocky islets along the Finnish coast and they provided a short wave radio for further local communications with German submarines (light signalling had proved cumbersome). In addition, the Germans introduced Jansen to his new liaison agent, Heikkilä, and they promised that in June 1945 a squad of highly trained Finns, who were currently being prepared in Germany, would be sent to Finland and put at the disposal of the underground. After an hour in conference, Jansen, accompanied by Heikkilä, set off with their newly acquired equipment and supplies, and U-242 departed for its return cruise to Germany, using the same course as on the outbound journey.

Fabritius's mission to Germany is of some interest. Unlike Törni and Korpela, who were still in Germany during the Battle of Berlin, Fabritius had a one month deadline. He had left Helsinki on the pretext of going to central Finland in a search for clay and marl deposits suitable for Forsström's cement works, and thus could not dally. On 30 January, Brohs asked Fabritius for a memorandum that could be shown to senior RSHA leaders, such as Schellenberg and Kaltenbrunner. In the resulting paper, Fabritius claimed that anti-Soviet sentiment was increasing in Finland, particularly as the Russians offered support to the Finnish communists and hoisted their own friends into government, although the Soviets were careful to undertake such measures covertly. Barring any opposition, he claimed, thirty to forty per cent of the working class would soon be won over to the Communist Party and, in the long run, Finland would cease to exist as a nation state. Although Fabritius admitted that the Finnish resistance movement was weakened by the break up of 'patriotic institutions', it could supposedly claim the loyalty of the Finnish Army, and he even suggested that 'if foreign military units' could effect an airborne landing and occupy the Tampere–Hämeenlina–Riihimäki–Lahti region, the Finnish Army could secure this pocket's flanks until a solid beachhead was established. When Brohs read the phrase 'foreign military units', he immediately thought of the *Wehrmacht* – although Fabritius may not necessarily have been signalling such a hope – but the SD officer's heart sank, since he knew that the German armed forces no longer had such capabilities. He also believed that Fabritius knew as much, but that the proposal had earlier been drafted by Finnish military leaders and that Fabritius felt that it was still his responsibility to bring it to the table. The best that Fabritius could do, suggested Brohs, was to encourage the accelerated development of an underground wireless network and prepare for further U-Boat contact.

On 9 February, Brohs and Cellarius brought Fabritius to meet Ernst Kaltenbrunner and provide the gist of his memorandum. Playing the gracious host, Kaltenbrunner said that he greatly admired Finnish stubbornness, as evinced by the country's resistance movement, and he promised that in spite of the Third Reich's difficulties, the Germans would do their utmost to 'help' the Finns. Päffgen, who was also present, assured Kaltenbrunner of ongoing contact and support for the resistance movement.

After arranging courier and mail contact, Fabritius returned to Finland on 19 February 1945. He travelled to Stolp, in Pomerania, and from there flew out in a KG 200 aircraft, jumping eighty miles south-east of Rauma and safely floating to ground by parachute. He then reported to Lohja, where he told Forsström about the results of his discussions, and he subsequently returned to Helsinki, where no one had reason to doubt the reasons for his absence. Fabritius subsequently operated for over a year, until the Finnish police caught up to him in July 1946. During this time, he built up the internal radio network desired by the Germans and established new contact stations in Vaasa and Helsinki, both of which were necessary after Kyrre's arrest. Officers at the Havel Institute noted that there were initial difficulties with these stations, particularly in use of codes, but that the establishment of smooth communications was anticipated by mid-May 1945.[137]

While emissaries such as Fabritius shuttled back and forth across the Baltic, Brohs and Cellarius spent the winter and spring of 1945 training the Finnish volunteers whom they had promised to send to Finland. It is in connection with this task that Skorzeny and his Finnish platoon commander, Kotkas, come into the story most directly. It will be recalled that Skorzeny and Kotkas were held at arm's length by the Brohs/Cellarius duo, who feared their impetuosity and requested that Schellenberg prevent the planning or execution of any 'independent operation'. Nonetheless, Brohs and Cellarius maintained contact with *Jagdeinsatz Finnland*, which they used as a resource upon which to build their own detachment, as well as exploiting its training facilities and stores of supplies. The Brohs-Cellarius squad, called the 'Finnish Collaboration Group', was assembled partly by drawing volunteers from *Jagdverband Nordwest*, partly by recruiting Finnish fishermen who had been interned as enemy nationals and whom Cellarius found languishing in a concentration camp near Danzig. The first chief of the 'Collaboration Group', *Obersturmführer* Aaltonen, was sent to Neustrelitz for special training, and eventually all fifteen members of the group were run through a two-week weapons course at the *Nordwest* battle school. The arms and ammunition sent to Finland via U-242 were drawn from *Nordwest* stocks.

In addition to getting technical help from Skorzeny, Brohs and Cellarius organised a radio training programme run by the Havel Institute, plus a parachute course conducted by KG 200 officers. Fabritius took part in this parachute training, which was conducted on the island of Rügen in early February 1945. Cellarius probably also used these facilities to train two Estonian agents who were supposed to contact the Estonian émigré community in Finland and stir up trouble. One of these men was dropped by parachute near Rauma in late February 1945; the other was sent through Sweden a month later.

While it had been intended to deploy the 'Finnish Collaboration Group' by June 1945, before the bright nights made covert activity more difficult, the rapid collapse of German arms forced Brohs and Cellarius to scramble. In March 1945, they shifted their base from Heringsdorf, near Swinemünde, to Twedterholz, near Flensburg, a move calculated to put distance between the Finnish trainees and the advancing Red Army. By this time, Aaltonen's personal conduct had proven him 'unsuitable for independent operational employment', and he was replaced by a young SS veteran and graduate of Bad Tölz, Kai Laurell. With the end of the war in sight, Laurell was charged with bringing the 'Collaboration Group' through Denmark to Norway, where he was supposed to ask the Sipo commander in Oslo for help. Members of the group were charged with using the existing channels through northern Norway and Sweden in order to reach Finland, where they were then supposed to coalesce in the Vaasa area and contact Jansen's *Bodenorganisation*. Whether they managed this feat is unclear, although the fact that Laurell and company debouched from Twedterholz on 30 April suggests that there was not much time for such an endeavour. Cellarius later suggested that members of the *Sonderkommando* were too young and inexperienced to be effective, and that their main intention was to get home by the shortest route available. As for Cellarius's fishermen, he equipped them with a yawl, the 'Wotrum', with which he hoped to move them and their radios to a forward base in Sweden, although the rapid retraction of German lines forced him to release the men on 2 May. He then advised them to make their way home individually.[138]

While the Third Reich hurtled toward final collapse, the Finnish resistance movement also fared poorly. Police investigations of the underground had been launched as early as January 1945, but these early efforts were superficial; in one case, the investigating inspector sympathised with suspects who had been hiding an arms cache. In March 1945, however, a sea change occurred when the Finnish communists, or 'People's Democrats', performed well in national elections and one of their leaders, Yrjö Leino, was appointed interior minister in a coalition government. Police controlled by Leino pursued investigations more aggressively that had previously been the case, particularly since the communists worried that they were the potential objects of nationalist resistance activity. A disaster also befell the movement when Lauri Kumpulainen, a Finnish soldier and black marketeer, attempted to extort 500,000 Finnish marks from Haahti in return for keeping quiet about covert arms stores. Haahti refused, believing that he could move the material to new locations, but Kumpulainen's subsequent complaint exposed much of the caching operation in Oulu province and began the collapse of the national network. Haahti was arrested in June 1945 and, after a direct appeal from Mannerheim, revealed all that he knew. Eventually, over 1,300 secret dumps were uncovered, resulting in the recovery of 22,000 rifles, forty-two anti-tank guns and over 40,000 pounds of explosive. More than 2,000 people were arrested and brought to trial, although many were acquitted and those who were found guilty were given lenient sentences.[139] Finnish communists cried foul, but the Soviets passed up a superb excuse to intervene in the country's affairs. Perhaps they felt that with more strategically located countries still only half pacified – Poland and Romania were outstanding examples – they had enough to occupy their energies without challenging the Finns.

All factors considered, *Jagdverband Nordwest* cannot be rated as one of the most successful of Skorzeny's units. The acid test for any sabotage/guerrilla movement is whether it draws enemy troops away from the front, thus functioning as a diversion, but even in Belgium and the southern Netherlands, where the Allies feared the outbreak of wide-scale partisan warfare led by Skorzeny,[140] there is scant evidence of such success. In fact, certain leitmotifs already familiar in the history of *Jagdverband Südwest* again appear in the chronicle of its northern counterpart: agents often received insufficient training; their belief in German victory faded with each passing day and they often used their deployments to disappear back into the populations of their homelands; they worried that their families in Germany were not being properly supported; there were not enough German aircraft or crews to guarantee parachutings or to keep operatives supplied by air; and as even Skorzeny eventually admitted, the saboteurs lacked the support of local civilians in their operational zones. 'A resistance movement without the cooperation of a great part of the population', he conceded, 'is a stillborn child.'[141] It is no wonder that the Skorzeny *Leute* usually wilted when confronted with the enormity of their tasks, particularly once they became aware of the heavy odds pitted against them.

Skorzeny's units in Scandinavia faced a different set of problems and challenges. Since the Germans eventually determined that Denmark and Norway were not immediate targets of Allied interest, Skorzeny's efforts in these two countries were tentative, although he was heavily involved in Denmark because of Operation 'Peter'. In Finland, there was an environment favouring the growth of a powerful resistance movement, but that network did not evolve beyond the preparatory stage because of the reluctance of the Soviets to occupy the country and thus provide the negative force against which an underground could exert itself. In such a delicate situation, Skorzeny was discouraged from thrashing around directly, and instead was instructed to support the more discriminating efforts of Brohs and Cellarius. A resistance movement could hardly flourish in a country where there was no antagonist to resist, and in a situation where there were no bullets flying, Skorzeny was left waiting in the wings.

6
The Time of the Wolf

The intention in setting up Skorzeny's special units was that they would function in areas outside Germany, whereas responsibility for guerrilla warfare within the Third Reich would be assumed by an SS directorate led by *Oberstgruppenführer* Hans Prützmann. Skorzeny later claimed to have suggested this division of labour. Despite this arrangement, the Skorzeny *Leute* were deeply involved in the sponsorship of German partisan warfare, the so-called '*Werwolf*' programme, and from the start they served as advisors, trainers and procurers of material. After *Jagdverband* and FAK units were pushed back into German territory, the operational and organisational boundary between such groups and the *Werwolf* began to blur at the same time that the definition of '*Werwolf*' was being expanded to include all categories of Nazi guerrilla fighters and vigilantes. Skorzeny's units eventually became one of the driving forces behind '*Werwolf*' resistance, at least during March and April 1945, and the *Jagdverbände* also reinforced the so-called 'Alpine Redoubt'. Significantly, the desperate events that inspired these last-minute changes turned Skorzeny into an extremely ugly character, even in the eyes of fellow members in his 'Vienna clique'.

HELPING THE WEREWOLVES

Although it was widely presumed in 1944–1945 that Skorzeny was running the *Werwolf*,[1] the SS segment of the movement was actually controlled by regional Sipo inspectors operating under Himmler's command. As early as the spring of 1944, Prützmann, then an SS-Police commander, had suggested setting up a network of eastern German guerrillas, and he was later given the job of supervising these elements, serving as Himmler's direct representative. He then '[began] wildly to organise', according to Schellenberg, although he was crippled by a shortage of manpower, supplies and fuel. Prützmann told Skorzeny that his plan was to build up the movement as a collection of small *Gruppen*, each led by a '*Gruppenführer*' and operating in both the eastern and western frontier provinces. Every *Gruppe* would have a radio and would receive sixty days' rations. Each individual volunteer would be issued with fifteen to twenty pounds of explosives, plus two small arms, and they would have access to underground bunkers where extra material would be stored. Prützmann declared that he would form as many *Gruppen* as possible, depending on the time available, and in each borderland *Gau* he would appoint a representative, hopefully a military man, in order to deal with recruitment and organisational issues.[2] Not only were *Werwolf Gruppen* supposed to harass the enemy, but they were also authorised to kill 'collaborators' and carry out 'scorched earth' measures, thereby helping prevent 'another November 1918'.

Although these arrangements were in SS-*Werwolf* hands, Himmler ordered other elements of the RSHA 'to instruct and support this organisation through all manner of human, personnel and material difficulties',[3] and Skorzeny was told to aid Prützmann in this 'Sonderauftrag' ('special task'). Prützmann called on Skorzeny in late September, and over the course of the next four months the two met on half a dozen occasions. During these conferences, Skorzeny provided a few words of counsel, telling Prützmann that the digging of underground depots would prove problematic in areas that were not heavily forested, and pointing him toward local factories as a source for explosives, since hauling anything over a distance had become a nightmare in bomb-battered Germany.[4]

In principle, Skorzeny backed the Werwolf idea – he thought it a natural response by a country in peril[5] – and he agreed to provide Prützmann and Hitler Youth leader Axmann, who was also involved, with three kinds of help. First, he ordered his supply officer, Reinhardt Gerhardt, to provide Prützmann's quartermaster with material aid, although he warned Gerhardt not to make extravagant promises and not to jeopardise the needs of the Jagdverbände, which meant never handing out more than ten to twenty per cent of available stocks. All requests for special weapons (complex fuses, pistols with silencers) were to come to Skorzeny's desk. A similar order was teletyped to Mil D, where Major Ehrmann was in charge of supplies. The Territorialen Jagdverbände were told to expect the arrival of Prützmann's representatives but to forward all requests for equipment to the Führungsstab, where the indents would be evaluated and handled centrally. Each Jagdverband subsequently complained about excessive demands by their SS-Werwolf counterparts, which Skorzeny ordered them to refuse. Nevertheless, some aid was forthcoming: the Führungsstab, for instance, supplied the Werewolves with 150 captured British Sten guns, and Jagdverband Südwest gave the graduates of a Werwolf course at Tiefenthal a kit containing fifteen kilograms of explosive, a pistol and ammunition.

Second, Skorzeny agreed that he would help recruit personnel for the SS-Werwolf and that he would train these volunteers. Jagdverband Ost had little to do with such matters – Skorzeny had his hands full simply reconstituting that unit after the Hohensalza disaster – while Ernst Benesch and the leaders of Jagdverband Südost bickered so much with their Werwolf liaison officers that they had little to offer.[6] The most that Skorzeny could arrange for the Eastern Front was the training of a few Hitler Youth-Werewolves at Friedenthal, plus the parachuting of these boys behind Russian lines.[7] Otherwise, aid for the Werwolf came largely from Jagdverbände Nordwest and Südwest. Skorzeny helped raise volunteers behind the Western Front and in the Italian theatre,[8] and in October 1944 there was a three-day conference between Südwest, Hitler Youth and Nazi Party officials, the main point of which was to launch the Werwolf. In the same month, the training camps at Neustrelitz and Tiefenthal were opened to Werwolf Gruppenführer-in-training. Standards for the length and curricula of Werwolf courses at the two camps were determined locally, although both regimes focussed on map reading, small arms instruction and demolitions. At Neustrelitz, students worked in two- or three-man groups, which were meant to simulate Werwolf field units. Courses at Neustrelitz lasted from five to ten days, while those at Tiefenthal lasted three weeks. Students from the initial classes were also run through a six-day refresher course in January 1945, mainly in order to familiarise personnel with a new form of explosive called Nipolit. As a result of the rapid rate of turnover, Neustrelitz was able to graduate 300 to 400 trainees, plus another 200 to 400 from Killeschowitz, while Tiefenthal produced only a fraction of that number before it was demolished by Allied bombing. Of the entire programme, thirty per cent of the graduates were women and ten per cent were boys from the Hitler Youth. Finally, it should be noted that Skorzeny ordered *Südwest* to send two officers to a Hitler Youth-*Werwolf* camp north of Stuttgart, plus one other – *Leutnant* Brandt – to the SS-*Werwolf* school at Hülcrath, and that he wrote a training memorandum on 'cold sabotage', that is, destruction techniques without the use of special weapons or devices. This document was jointly published by Mil D and the technical bureau of the SD-*Ausland*.[9]

Mil D was expected to contribute as well, particularly by helping along the Eastern Front. In July 1944, Naumann ordered Gotthard Gambke to visit Königsberg and provide technical advice for the organisation of *Werwolf* detachments in East Prussia. Gambke was also supposed to provide weapons and sabotage material, since the East Prussian organisers were short of supplies. Mil D organised Operation 'Vera', which involved the dispatch of a special instructor, *Hauptmann* Kutschke, although Kutschke returned after a week in Königsberg because there were no training facilities available. Mil D also agreed to provide FAK 212 as a scaffolding structure for the East Prussian *Werwolf*, but this did not suit the Königsberg '*Zentrale*', and FAK 212 was sent to Silesia instead. Privately, Gambke and other Mil D officers considered the situation in East Prussia nearly hopeless. The *Werwolf* coordinator, *Sturmbannführer* Schmitz, had no instructions from Prützmann and made arrangements for guerrilla operations only in heavily wooded or unpopulated areas, although even in such regions the presence of refugees and *Wehrmacht* 'scratch units' made it impossible to camouflage preparations. *Werwolf* recruits were drawn heavily from the ranks of the Nazi Party, the only people Schmitz regarded as reliable, although such men were sure to attract the interest of the Soviets.[10]

Third, Skorzeny was ordered to coordinate operations by mobile *Jagdverband* squads and FAK-mounted *Streifkorps* with *Werwolf Gruppen*, which, unlike the Skorzeny *Leute*, were stationary and based in bunkers behind enemy lines.[11] This cooperation was supposed to be facilitated by military intelligence officers and *Jagdverband-Werwolf* liaisons. There is little evidence of such collaboration in practice, although on 8 April, FAK 213 provided a radio operator to a Hitler Youth-*Werwolf* unit that was running sabotage forays near Gummersbach, and the guerrillas were urged to contact *Trupp* 262 if they required explosives or other equipment. Several *Südwest* troopers captured by the Americans claimed that their unit was coordinating *Werwolf* activity, with Gerlach's liaison with the *Werwolf*, Haas, playing the key role.[12]

Along the Eastern Front, the locations of FAK detachments were passed on to Prützmann's staff, which shared this information with relevant *Werwolf* headquarters, and there was some cooperation in Silesia. The key Mil D unit was FAK 212, the formation whose assistance had been refused by the East Prussians, while the local *Werwolf* was run by the infamous *Obersturmbannführer* Müller-Altenau, a figure who had played a role in the 1934 Blood Purge and was regarded as 'a cunning, dangerous and unprincipled man'. In August 1944, Naumann and Prützmann met to delineate the respective tasks of their Silesian units, and Naumann was shocked to learn that Prützmann saw the potential surrender of Upper Silesia, eastern Germany's main industrial region, as an event tantamount to the loss of the war. Understandably, given this view, the *Werwolf* was allotted responsibility only for a few narrow bands of frontier territory, while FAK 212 assumed control of Operations 'Sixtus' and 'Wachholder', which involved burying caches of sabotage material throughout Upper Silesia, as well as training volunteers to make use of these supplies. After the Soviets stormed into the region in January 1945, the FAK 212 dumps and personnel were transferred to Müller-Altenau's control, as were caches and men in the Glatzer district, which had been prepared on direct orders from General Schörner.[13] Mil D claimed that these Werewolves were responsible for the demolition of a Red Army billet in the town of Hindenburg, one of the most publicised sabotage acts along the Eastern Front. Although German media suggested that a Hitler Youth group had carried out this attack, Ernst zu Eikern noted that FAK 212 had left well-equipped personnel in Hindenburg and that 'in all likelihood these men are the cause of the blast'.[14]

In general, Skorzeny was sceptical of the *Werwolf*. Himmler had once suggested that the project rightly fell into Skorzeny's sphere but that he was already overburdened, a proposition to which Skorzeny agreed,[15] although he never escaped the impression that Prützmann was botching the job. Skorzeny had little regard for the capabilities of the *Werwolf* trainees at Neustrelitz and Tiefenthal, and he thought that the only regions where the *Werwolf* had established a presence were the Rhineland and East Prussia.[16] In fact, Skorzeny regarded the Prützmann programme as an unnecessary duplication of the *Jagdverbände*, since he assumed that the latter would eventually be called upon to engage in '*Werwolf*' activities. Skorzeny, Schellenberg and Kaltenbrunner worked from an early date to sabotage the SS-*Werwolf* effort, pleading ignorance or being evasive when requests from Prützmann came through their offices.[17] Skorzeny rationalised such responses by arguing that the activation of the *Jagdverbände* was still underway and that he had to give priority to his own units' interests.[18]

The personality clashes typical of the Nazi administrative system also played a role in minimising *Jagdverband-Werwolf* cooperation. Prützmann quickly gravitated toward *Waffen*-SS recruitment boss Gottlob Berger, an enemy of the 'Vienna clique', and he appointed as his chief of staff Karl Tschiersky, a personal foe of Skorzeny, who called him an 'intriguer'. Tschiersky was an SD officer who had briefly served as chief of *Unternehmen* 'Zeppelin', but Schellenberg considered him incompetent and after having tried to unload him upon Section S, where Skorzeny refused to have him, he was dumped upon Prützmann.

By March 1945, Kaltenbrunner and Prützmann had begun to clash openly, and in April Schellenberg reproached Himmler about the *Werwolf* programme, calling it 'criminal and stupid'.[19] Two weeks before the end of the war, Kaltenbrunner made plans for Skorzeny to infiltrate the *Werwolf* and acquire as much power as possible within the organisation, a venture for which he allotted several million Reichsmarks. In order to launch this operation, Skorzeny was supposed to cooperate with two other members of the 'Vienna clique', Wilhelm Höttl and Werner Göttsch, who were given control of the operating funds. Göttsch was also supposed to act as Skorzeny's project liaison with Kaltenbrunner. It is likely that this brainstorm was linked to a cynical attempt by Höttl to penetrate the *Werwolf* and then trade information with the advancing Americans, thus hopefully winning concessions for himself. Whatever the case, the project was launched too late to be of practical significance.[20]

THE 'R'-*AUFGABEN*

Although Skorzeny failed to subjugate the SS-*Werwolf*, by 1945 his own units were being ordered to undertake 'R'-*Aufgaben*, stay-behind tasks on German soil that replicated the functions of the Prützmann programme and for which the '*Werwolf*' codeword was often employed. In fact, nearly all elements of the Mil Amt were eventually involved in such operations. In early 1945, an experiment in Army Group Upper Rhine melded together units of the *Zweierorganisation* with intelligence and counter-intelligence FAK detachments, thus yielding a '*Leitkommando*' designed to support raiding operations and guerrilla warfare. Several of this formation's *Trupps* operated in Alsace.[21] By March 1945, general orders for such activity were issued by Schellenberg and his deputy Sandberger, and although some FAK units failed to respond, many dutifully buried supplies or prepared false papers in order to disguise the identities of officers. On 15 April, 'remaining elements' of FAK 130, *Trupp* 262 and FAK 307 were ordered, 'in view of [the] changed situation', to destroy Allied supply columns and launch ambush attacks against enemy staffs, and there is evidence that *Trupp* 262 carried out such activities from a base in the Ruhr Pocket. FAK 120 was told to parachute a squad of wireless personnel and guides in order to contact cut-off SS troops fighting a guerrilla war in the Spessert region, although these agents were never able to re-establish contact with German lines. Along the Eastern Front, Army Group Vistula used FAK 104 to support the dispatch of raiding groups – *Streifkorps* – into Soviet held-territory, and FAK 102 was built up with a cadre of Hitler Youth boys and *Volkssturm* personnel in order to fight a guerrilla campaign, which it was supposed to do in concert with Polish nationalist guerrillas and Vlasovites. In the latter case, Skorzeny, ever the parochialist, insisted that a unit with such functions should properly come under the control of Mil D and Mil F.[22]

In a mind-boggling lack of foresight, Skorzeny failed to anticipate 'a rapid collapse of the fronts', believing that 'wonder weapons' would get Germany out of a tough spot, or trusting in Himmler's assurance that the Red Army was bled white. Nonetheless, by March 1945 the scales had fallen from his eyes and he ordered *Jagdverband* personnel to prepare '*Werwolf*' activity.[23] Unit staffs were supposed to allow themselves to be overrun by the enemy. At least one of the territorial *Jagdverbände* had already begun such preparations. In February 1945, the chief of *Jagdverband Südost*, Ernst Benesch, convened a conference of *Jagdeinsatz* commanders and instructed these officers to locate hideouts in eastern Austria, to prepare local supply dumps and – despite their disdain – to cooperate with the SS-*Werwolf*. *Jagdeinsatz Ungarn* was told to prepare for '*Überrollung*' in the Leitha Mountains and the eastern part of the Vienna Forest; *Rumanien* was assigned the northern part of the Vienna Forest and the mountains south of Melk; and *Slovakie* was alloted to the Bohemian-Moravian Heights.[24]

Along stretches of the Eastern Front, such preparations led to considerable spates of guerrilla fighting. On 8 April 1945, Skorzeny visited *Jagdverband Ost* II at Janske Lazne, Bohemia, probably in order to alert the unit to its imminent deployment in Silesia. Two days later, Skorzeny met with the commander of Army Group Centre, the fanatic Ferdinand Schörner, and he approved Schörner's plans for two behind-the-lines attacks against Soviet-controlled bridges, one near the Nazi-held citadel of Breslau. Within a short period, two *Ost*

Sonderkommandos were dispatched and the designated bridges were destroyed.[25] The formation sent to Breslau was still in enemy-held territory when the war ended on 9 May 1945. It reportedly guided a column of refugees westwards and did not cease fighting until a week after the formal termination of hostilities.[26] Another small *Kommando*, consisting of an officer and six men, was carried by a He III to the vicinity of a Soviet-occupied airfield on the outskirts of Breslau. This team parachuted into place and over the next three nights received supplies dropped by KG 200, although its radio operator soon reported that he was the unit's sole survivor, all five of his comrades having been killed in clashes with the enemy.[27]

In February 1945, the reconnaissance element of Army Group Vistula, FAK 204, started the training of *Streifkorps*, which were platoon-sized raiding detachments manned by volunteer soldiers. The term was adopted from the word '*Freikorps*', but with the adjectival component '*Streif*', meaning 'patrol' or 'scout', replacing '*Frei*'. Such units were consciously intended to serve as Mil D equivalents of the *Jagdverbände*, which originally upset Skorzeny since he interpreted them as a slight on his own competence. Skorzeny also resented the fact that such units were operationally subordinate to regional army commands rather than to Mil D. *Streifkorps* troops were armed with machine pistols, anti-tank weapons and explosives and they were usually in radio contact with controllers behind German lines. They were ordered to harass enemy lines of communication, gather intelligence and stiffen the backbone of German civilians in enemy-held territory. Each fighter was told to 'comport yourself in a manner worthy of a member of the German *Wehrmacht*. Strengthen the trust of the remaining population in coming German victory and reinforce their hope in approaching liberation.'

FAK 204's *Streifkorps* was run by *Hauptmann* Thomsen, who was seconded by the headquarters of the Second Army, and it consisted of 200 combat troops, combined with a cadre of anti-communist Poles and Russians recruited from POW camps. One *Streifkorps* unit was infiltrated into the district around Hohensalza, but was ambushed by a Polish police formation. Only a few survivors were able to regain German lines. Another squad under *Leutnant* von Staden operated in West Prussia and was able to glean some tidbits of intelligence. Once the Red Army bore down upon Danzig, the *Streifkorps* was thrown into the line as an infantry unit.

The first *Streifkorps* was formed by FAK 202, which in the autumn of 1944 set up training unit 'Schill', so named for a German *Freikorps* officer who had died in a patriotic flash of glory in 1809. Based near Cracow, *Einheit* 'Schill' was led by *Leutnant* Moritz, who had participated in the *Kleinkrieg* in the Caucasus. In the first several months of 1945, at least fifteen 'Schill' squads were sent into Silesia, which was newly conquered by the Red Army. Groups were comprised of approximately ten men each. Polish and Soviet records provide descriptions of clashes with bands that resemble FAK or *Streifkorps* squads. For instance, German paratroopers landed in gliders in the Soviet-occupied neighbourhood of Hundsfeld, near Breslau, and then helped the defenders of the besieged 'fortress town'. On 2 March, an off-course Ju 52 ditched on the ground behind Soviet lines, disgorging its crew and passenger-saboteurs, nineteen men in total. The survivors attempted to conceal the fuselage and then fled the scene of the crash, although a Soviet patrol tracked them down and wiped out the entire party. Two days later, a guerrilla detachment of nineteen Vlasovites and three German nationals was ambushed by an NKGB platoon near

Striegau, an action that resulted in the death of fourteen 'diversionists' and the capture of the remaining eight. The platoon commander, *Feldwebel* Rob, was amongst those killed. This unit had infiltrated through Soviet lines in late February. For their part, the Germans acknowledged that the Silesian *Streifkorps* bore heavy casualties, especially because of exposure to the elements, and they admitted that whole teams deserted to the Soviets. Despite the intention of improving civilian morale, they typically had poor relations with a population that was terrified of Soviet reprisals and sometimes threatened to turn over *Streifkorps* troops to the occupying power. In addition, the Germans conceded that *Streifkorps* intelligence data was often 'full of gaps'. Nonetheless, they spoke of 'numerous results' and Schörner made a fuss of several returnees, holding decoration ceremonies.

After the start of the Soviet Winter Offensive, the headquarters of *Einheit* 'Schill' were evacuated to Beuthen and Glatz, and eventually to Bergland. 'Schill' continued to prepare infiltration squads, of which another dozen were ready for service by April 1945. Although many of these forces may not have been deployed, by the end of the war one such unit was functioning in the Ukrainian district near Maszina.[28]

FAK 202's commander, Dietrich Witzel, attended the Skorzeny-Schörner planning session on 10 April, and according to one of the unit's non-commissioned officers, he was given an important assignment. His new job was to create a post-occupation network of FAK and SD personnel who would maintain close contact with the UPA and with the Polish Brigade, and is probably significant that Witzel's *Jagdverband Ost* counterpart, Alexander Auch, lodged a request in mid-April for six million Reichsmarks, which was intended for '[the] special undertaking discussed with the *Reichsführer*-SS'. It was suggested that a new German-Ukrainian-Polish underground would engage in espionage, carry out sabotage and maintain a readiness to participate in an 'impending' Soviet-American clash. In fact, the Poles were supposed to help precipitate this conflict. The Polish Brigade was moved from Kosseck to the western Bohemian town of Pilsen, the anticipated point of contact between converging Soviet and American forces. The Poles were broken up into small groups, disguised as 'displaced persons' and equipped with sabotage material and wireless sets. Their mission was to pose as 'Soviet agents', thus provoking direct clashes between Soviet and American forces.[29]

Many members of the Polish Brigade surrendered when the Americans approached Pilsen,[30] but a remnant of 1,500 men was still holding out in the summer of 1945. Members of the unit survived by looting Czech peasants, although the Czechoslovak authorities also uncovered supply and arms dumps, and shooting affrays in late July resulted in the deaths of two Czechoslovak soldiers and seven Polish irregulars. The Czechoslovaks charged that the guerrillas were working with Sudeten-German Werewolves and the Soviets further alleged that they were doing exactly what they had been trained to do, that is, sowing dissension between the great powers. In early August 1945, the US Third Army promised to wipe out Polish underground nests in Bohemia, a job that it reported completing by mid-August, although many of the Poles were simply absorbed by American forces and were subsequently employed as auxiliary guard battalions.[31]

In south-eastern Europe, *Jagdverband Südost* could not hold the 'Überrollung' territories designated at the February 1945 planning session, thus losing many of the supplies cached in those locations. Parts of *Jagdeinsätze Rumanien* and *Slowakei* were deployed with *Wehrmacht* combat commands along the eastern edge of the Bohemian-Moravian Protectorate, but the remainder of *Südost* was withdrawn to Austria, where a new headquarters was set up at Admont. *Rumänien* organised bases in the region west of the Vienna Forest, *Ungarn* in the Rax Mountains, *Bulgarien* in the vicinity of Semmering, and *Kroatien* in St Veit *Kreis*. *Jagdeinsatz Donau* also began sending squads and individuals to the north German ports, where their demolitions skills might be put to use. For instance, Arno Besekow ordered Ernst Heckel, a specialist on ship sabotage, to return to his hometown of Hamburg and blow up Allied shipping.

Südost's different companies established radio communications and hastily prepared caches of food, ammunition and dynamite, although these measures were undertaken so late and in such cursory fashion that nothing seemed secure. Thus, wireless contact was often sporadic and some of the supply dumps were looted by civilians or destroyed by retreating German troops. Lack of civilian support was demoralising and Austrians seemed particularly hostile toward the Hungarians serving with *Südost*. By early May 1945, all radio communications had ceased and the stay-behind detachments began to disintegrate. Many members headed for American lines, where they expected relatively comfortable conditions of confinement.[32]

The example of *Jagdeinsatz Kroatien* is illustrative. In mid-April, lieutenants Gerhard Dowe and Viktor Sokolow were ordered to report to *Kroatien's* unit adjutant, a Nazi fanatic named Krüger. Dowe and Sokolow were told that *Kroatien* had been instructed to organise resistance to the Titoist Yugoslavs in the Austrian province of Carinthia, where there was a Slovenian minority that the Titoists had talked of 'liberating'. On 23 April, Dowe and Sokolow were ordered to evacuate Zagreb and lead twenty men to the village of Glödnitz, a centre of dense support for National Socialism. Dowe and Sokolow were also supposed to evacuate the stores of *Jagdeinsatz Kroatien*, which would be transported by rail. After a difficult journey punctuated by Allied air attacks and stops at demolished rail lines and bridges, Sokolov left most of the unit's supplies at Radmannsdorf. He was caught by the British on 11 May, along with fifteen men, but Dowe and his contingent succeeded in reaching Glödnitz, where they cached a large number of arms, 20,000 rounds of ammunition and several pieces of radio equipment, all of which was buried near the hamlet of Deutsch-Griffin. One of Dowe's non-commissioned officers was provided with information on the location of nearby *Werwolf* groups and was expected to liaise with these units. On 4 May, *Jagdverband* personnel helped the *Volkssturm* suppress a revolt of Russian slave labourers at Flattnitz, and during the same period they were visited several times by Krüger, who instructed the unit to move ahead with plans to resist advancing Titoist forces. It soon became clear, however, that the British Fifth Corps had beaten the Titoists in the race to occupy the major cities and towns of Carinthia, and that the British were in no mood to countenance a long-term presence by their rivals. In fact, the Yugoslavs were made to feel unwelcome and on 18 May they withdrew their forces. With *Kroatien's* assignment now redundant, Krüger said that further resistance was impractical and he ordered unit members to disperse and either head home or find work on local farms.

Kroatien's story, however, does not yet come to a full stop. Instead of leaving the Glödnitz region, Krüger, Dowe, radio operator Burgfeldt and several other men remained with local sympathisers, where they comprised a threat to regional security. On 28/29

May, 150 SS troopers escaped from a POW compound near Glödnitz and were suspected of receiving aid from 'a considerable hostile band', perhaps a reference to *Jagdverband* remnants. On 1 June, Krüger and Dowe attempted to get false identification documents from the Austrian gendarmerie in Glödnitz, but their presence was soon reported by a German deserter and attracted the interest of British Field Security. Fifteen *Jagdverband* members and Austrian civilians were arrested, including Dowe on 5 June and Burgfeldt on 11 August. Only Krüger escaped the dragnet. The British also uncovered and dismantled caches of supplies and sabotage equipment.[33]

Remnants of *Jagdverband Südwest* functioned in a similar fashion. Units of *Jagdeinsatz Italien* were ordered to withdraw to the southern slopes of the Alps, where they hid supply dumps and prepared hideouts. They were well equipped with radios and were part of a wireless net that was reputably the best German system still in operation. By the end of the war, one *Jagdverband* party, probably part of *Jagdkommando* 'Stiegler', was spotted skulking around the Aosta region, where French-Italian frontier tensions offered opportunities for stirring up trouble and there were active Republican Fascist bands.

Two hundred miles to the east, in the South Tyrol, 186 members of *Jagdkommando* 'Solder' were ensconced in the rugged Ortler Massif. They were barricaded in the Hotel Paradis-Cevedale, halfway up the Zufritt-Spitze, a superb defensive position that could be held with only a few defenders. Arms and equipment had been stockpiled in local barns, whose owners provided the guerrillas with supplies and intelligence, and aid stations had been prepared in alpine huts hidden behind the Cevedale glacier and situated at a height of over 10,000 feet. Vehicles could reach the hotel only along a single road, and the *Jagdverband* resisters had stationed lookout posts throughout the valley and along the highway between Meran and Schlanders. As of 21 May 1945, Allied occupiers were contemplating a difficult encircling action,[34] but there is no report of a subsequent battle and it is likely that Solder's men, mostly native South Tyroleans, filtered out of their stronghold and went home.

The three *Jagdkommandos* of *Jagdeinsatz Süd*, 'Haase', 'Perner' and 'Hossfeld', each went to ground in the Black Forest, as did Hans Pavel's platoon, which was part of *Jagdeinsatz Nord*. Cooperating closely with the SS-*Werwolf*, Section S and the staff of 18th SS Army *Korps*, these *Jagdverband* groups laid secret supply stores and were reinforced by hundreds of young trainees from the *Junkerschule* in Bad Tölz, who were organised in groups of ten. In late April, these units received '*Werwolf*' orders and allowed themselves to be overrun. Elements of *Jagdkommando* 'Hossfeld' were deployed north-east of the Black Forest, in the Heilbronn-Neckarsulm area, where they destroyed Allied jeeps. Detachments operating around Oberroth disabled three enemy trucks and one of these bands regained German lines. Although part of *Jagdkommando* 'Hossfeld' withdrew to Oberstdorf,[35] most personnel remained in local hideouts and were active well into May 1945, when French estimates of their number ranged between sixty and 190 men. A French-paid infiltrator reported that the 'Haase'-'Hossfeld'-'Perner' organisation was deployed in six-man guerrilla teams that were supposed to attack French convoys between Badenweiler and Neuenweg. They were well armed with Sten and Thompson guns, grenades and anti-tank rockets, and they had enough food to last for sixty days. Another group of fifty Germans and Frenchmen was led by *Hauptsturmführer* Kubat and situated in an isolated chalet near Obermünsterthal.

The main problem with such efforts was that neighbourhood civilians had become alienated from the Nazi Party and offered little support. On 16 April, Kubat reported that the *Volkssturm* was deserting to the enemy in whole companies and that German women had been spotted clearing road blocks for the Allies. Although a few local folk agreed to provide contact points for *Jagdverband* fugitives, the *Deuxième Bureau* soon managed to penetrate these networks.[36] When Ludwig Nebel crossed Allied lines in late April, he brought information on the Black Forest *Maquis* and he also arranged the surrender of two highly trained guerrillas, one a veteran of the Mussolini rescue, whom he recommended to *Sécurité Militaire* as informers. By early June, French soldiers reported that they had uncovered *Milicien* supply dumps in Baden, although German-French resistance bands were still perpetrating a limited programme of sabotage and soldiers of the French First Army remained on a state of alert, particularly at night.[37] Despite signs of persistence, the guerrillas, lacking public support, soon melted away.

The staff of the *Südwest* battle school, now under the command of Hans Schwinn, retreated into the Swabian Alps, where they cached weapons and supplies. One seven-man squad, under *Untersturmführer* Robert Schnorr, was instructed to go to ground between Ulm and Freiburg and then attack Allied supply lines, as well as avenging German civilians against 'undisciplined soldiers'. The Germans had received reports that marauding American troops had plundered houses and raped women, a problem that, ever conscious of race, they blamed on black enlisted men. Schnorr performed reconnaissance around Honan and took up a defensive position near Stetten, although it was the French, rather than the Americans, who appeared in the area. Schnorr hid most of his equipment in a tunnel, although in blasting the entrance he alerted the civilian population of Stetten, who informed the French about the location of the explosion. On 24 April, Schnorr realised that the French had avoided running astride his strong point, using alternate routes in their march forward. After ten days of prowling around the French communications zone, he was disheartened by news of the German capitulation in northern Italy and disbanded his unit.[38]

In Hessen, the southern Rhineland and Franconia, units of *Jagdeinsatz Nord* fought a brief but bitter guerrilla war against the advancing Allied forces. In early March, *Jagdkommando* 'Wissemberg' mined Allied supply routes near Trier, and several weeks later, the unit was bypassed in the Palatine Forest, west of Neustadt, where it spent nearly two weeks behind Allied lines, mining roads and destroying Allied trucks. On 5 April, the surviving members of the unit tried to build a raft in order to cross the Rhine, but at the moment of launching their craft they were attacked by an enemy patrol. Several men still managed to steer the raft across the river, but others, including Wissemberg, jumped into the frigid water and swam across. Six men failed to make the crossing and were captured by a French patrol. *Untersturmführer* Heppen, the deputy commander of the platoon and an old Brandenburger, was listed as missing in action.[39] Remnants of the detachment fled into the Allgau, accompanying the staff of *Jagdeinsatz Nord*.

Another unit, *Jagdkommando* 'Berndt', was divided in the middle of March 1945, apparently because its commander, Ernst Berndt, owed his posting more to his friendship with Hans Gerlach than to any special affinity for the French. In fact, Berndt, although a former Brandenburger and an excellent sportsman, lacked knowledge of the French language. Feeling uncomfortable in his new job, Berndt asked for a change of assignment. As a result, his deputy, a French-speaking medical student named Kahlenberg, was given control of Berndt's legionaries and sent to Gemünden-Wohra, where several *Jagdverband* groups were organising for operations. Kahlenberg also got control of two companies of Belgian and Dutch SS men who had received parachute training and were awaiting a commitment in American uniforms. This French-Belgian-Dutch agglomeration received five captured American jeeps and was sent to the rugged Spessert Hills, where they had success in harassing American military traffic. At least two armoured cars were destroyed with anti-tank weapons.

Meanwhile, Berndt was given command of forty recruits who had recently been inducted into the *Waffen*-SS or transferred from the *Luftwaffe*. The latter were the remains of a much larger group of signalmen who had volunteered for the *Jagdverbände* and had been run through an eight-day sabotage course at Tiefenthal. Berndt discovered at Marburg that his 'green' recruits were tactically clumsy, which would limit their ability to attack American supply lines or flanks. Faced with American armour, and with his own increasing doubts, Berndt retreated south-eastward, bypassing Alsfeld and Fulda and eventually reaching the German-held town of Hammelburg. After this fiasco, he was told to reinforce Kahlenberg's tank-hunters in the Spessert. Berndt's men subsequently reached the area and took up positions, but the truck carrying their anti-tank weapons was strafed by Allied aircraft and destroyed, so the group retreated toward a bridge at Marktbeidenfeld, which was still believed to be held by the *Wehrmacht*. When it was discovered that the bridge was destroyed, Berndt and his guerrillas hid in the woods near Würzburg. Berndt sent out four small patrols, only two of which returned, and he then broke up his force into small squads and told them to infiltrate back to German-held territory and reassemble at Aschfeld, north-west of Karlstadt. Twenty survivors reached the collection point, whence Berndt sent them to Nuremberg while he travelled to Stuttgart in order to get new orders.

Gerlach told Berndt to deploy the *Jagdkommando* near Nuremberg, where it would reunite with Kahlenberg's group, attach itself to the 13th SS Army *Korps*, and allow rampaging Allied forces to sweep by. When Berndt and Kahlenberg met on 10 April, Berndt was dismayed to learn that Kahlenberg had sustained disastrous losses of men and material, particularly in fighting near Bamberg, and that he had only twenty men left. After 15 April, Berndt moved the detachment to Nuremberg and reported to the SS 'Götz von Berlichingen' Division, which was defending the city. On 20 April, troops of the *Jagdkommando* engaged an American armoured column, but they were soon forced to retreat to the woods, where they went into hiding. Two men deserted and Berndt again began to despair, thinking that his unit had no further combat capabilities. From this point onward, the *Jagdkommando* was steadily withdrawn through southern Bavaria and into the Alps, only once more coming into contact with the enemy when it was attacked by an American patrol near Augsburg. When Germany surrendered on 8 May 1945, Berndt demobilised the small squad that was still left, recommending that the men either go home or place themselves under Allied care as POWs.

A sister unit of *Jagdkommando* 'Berndt', *Jagdkommando* 'Stein', organised guerrilla attacks in the Westerwald, the Hunsrück and the Taunus, and it laid arms dumps on both sides of the River Rhine. Led by *Untersturmführer* Stein, a *Jagdverband* instructor with knowledge of the French language, this sixty-five-member *Kommando* included sixteen French parachutists who were training at Tiefenthal until that facility was destroyed. It was initially deployed by the

Seventh Army near Kochem, where it tried to destroy American tanks and gather operational intelligence, albeit without success. This mission was run by *Untersturmführer* Woyters, who was later transferred to Kahlenberg's company and killed in the Spessert hills. Another group, under *Untersturmführer* Neumann, ambushed a convoy in the Hunsrück Forest, destroying an American jeep and two trucks. When the platoon's command post at Morsdorf was shelled, it withdrew through the Hunsrück and the Bingerwald to the Rhine, which was crossed at St Goar, although a deserter stayed behind and then provided the Americans with intelligence on guerrilla supply caches. Parachute drops of men and equipment were also planned for the Eifel and the Westerwald. In the former case, two German-speaking Belgians had been instructed to lay the groundwork for guerrilla activity and recruit local manpower.

In the *Jagdkommando*'s largest mission, twenty-five French legionaries and German troops were infiltrated through Allied lines near Wirges on the night of 24 March 1945. This party was led by *Leutnant* Walter Lenz, an ex-Brandenburger and former instructor at Tiefenthal. The task of Lenz's personnel, as decided in conference with officers of the 272nd Infantry Division, was to locate six American tanks and thirty soldiers reported to be billeted in a village near the front. The group was supposed to knock out the armour with anti-tank grenades, capture or kill the enemy troops, plant mines, and then return to German-held territory. Unfortunately for the commandos, civilians in the area refused to give them support – they were terrified by the threat of Allied reprisals – and they unexpectedly encountered masses of American troops, who had launched an attack in the same sector. The detachment was surrounded and fifteen of its members captured, including Lenz, who was badly wounded. Ten men were killed.

The main goal of *Jagdkommando* 'Stein' was to infiltrate Allied lines, mainly by disguising personnel as American or Free French soldiers, and then to conduct guerrilla warfare. Ultimately, the infiltrators were expected to change into civilian clothes and return to France, where they were supposed to reinforce the PPF and *Milicien* underground. In March 1945, the company launched preparations while it was stationed in Wirges. Local police were told to prepare phoney papers for the French members of the unit, identifying them as forced labourers, and on the evening of 23 March a truckload of fifty American uniforms and captured weapons arrived at Stein's headquarters. The original scheme was to infiltrate the entire company, disguised as a formation of '*Armée* Leclerc' that had lost its way while on patrol, but the rapid American advance threw matters into flux, particularly when nearly the half the unit's men were lost over the night of 24 March. Stein then ordered the remainder of the detachment to switch to civilian garb and hide in the forests around Wirges, waiting to be overrun, although he changed his mind on 26 March, ordering all remaining personnel to head for Gemünden-Wohra, where one of his officers had already led a contingent on 13 March. Gemünden-Wohra was supposed to serve as a new base for the infiltration of Allied lines, but it is likely that there were no further operations, at least before the end of the war, and members of *Jagdkommando* 'Stein' had no intention of carrying on after the final defeat of the *Wehrmacht*. In such a situation, Lenz later suggested, the German population would become even more hostile to guerrillas, and 'against the population, no partisan warfare is possible'.[40]

Staffs and subunits of *Jagdverband Nordwest* were deployed in a similar fashion, although some of them were willing to entertain missions of a potentially post-war character.

Willy Dethier reinforced the Belgian *Kampfgruppe* stationed at Giessen, especially with partisan warfare specialists. One of these stay-behind detachments was assembled at Neustrelitz by Dethier's adjutant, Kurt Jarond. On 1 April, Jarond gave instructions to the eight hand-picked members of this squad, plus their guide, Lidia Keller, a young women from Giessen who had earlier enjoyed close company with some of Bachot's men. Keller and the group's radio operator, an SS trooper named Wieland, were supposed to reside in Giessen while the other seven members of the group scattered throughout the adjacent region. The agents were then issued with civilian clothes, plus a supply of pistols, plastic explosive and anti-personnel mines. Their job was to form a focus for guerrilla warfare projects, and Keller was supposed to recruit members for Prützmann's *Werwolf* organisation and to report names and addresses via wireless transmissions.

After travelling to Hessen, the group was overrun by the Americans in the neighbourhood of Langen-Leiten, although three of the guerrillas became detached from their comrades and were probably killed in a skirmish. The remaining six members of the unit hid in the woods and worked their way to Kothen, although Keller fell into a foxhole and injured her knee. As a result, she was left to recuperate with local villagers. The five men, led by *Oberscharführer* Dumahn, travelled to Nidda, where they established a bivouac and launched sabotage actions. They also operated Wieland's radio set, through which they contacted Jarond and perhaps shared operational intelligence with similar *Nordwest* groups that had been dispatched to Heidelberg and Saarbrücken. Disaster struck on 24 April, when Keller was arrested in Rodheim, near Giessen, and immediately provided the CIC with full details about her guerrilla companions. Keller's revelations precipitated an intense search of the forest near Nidda by one hundred US troops, although it is not clear that the Dumahn-Wieland band was swept up in this net. At the very least, their range of operational opportunities was narrowed.

As the Belgian *Sonderkommando* retreated in the face of the American advance, it continually shed stay-behind elements – a Nazi serpent moulting its skin. At Schreiersgrün, Joseph Bachot tried to slip a German volunteer, Hans Seeger, through enemy lines. Seeger was given orders to report to a safe-house in Düsseldorf, although the attempt to infiltrate him through the front was unsuccessful and he had to wait to be bypassed in a small village near Auerbach. Interestingly, Seeger reported to the address in Düsseldorf nearly three months after the end of the war and was surprised to find a skeletal *Jagdverband* structure still intact. In Schilberg and Moosbach, Bachot detached Belgian '*Überrollung*' teams whose members were clothed in civilian gear and equipped with papers identifying them as forced labourers. It was an open secret that many members of such groups were no longer interested in fighting the Allies, but simply wanted to trudge home and live ordinary lives, albeit under assumed identities. Bachot increasingly seemed to regard such intentions as understandable. The last of these stay-behind detachments were left in the Vogtland, the south-western corner of Saxony. The forty men still with Bachot then abandoned an intention to reach Berlin and instead turned south, retreating along the line Hof–Regensburg–Freising–Munich–Bad Aibling.[41] The unit finished the war manning the defences of the Alpine Redoubt.

While *Kommando* 'Bachot' was southward bound, *Jagdeinsatz Niederlande* was instructed to supplement *Werwolf* activity in northern Germany. Once this unit's forward headquarters in Bentheim were threatened by the Allied advance, its commander, *Obersturmführer* Stielau, pulled his staff back to heavily wooded and watered terrain in the old duchy of Lauenburg, along the boundary between Schleswig-Holstein and Mecklenburg. Equipment and supplies were hidden in the bush and members of the unit scattered to a number remote farm houses and forest wardens' cottages. Near Mölln, a bunker was stocked with a wireless set, a machine gun, light arms and food. A forest lodge near Roseburg became the main contact point for agents, who were supposed to use the codeword 'Alma' in order to get reach Stielau, and a Dutch operative was told to gather an ongoing supply of food. Yet another agent, a Romanian *Volksdeutsch* named Ernst, was ordered to tend a boat used to ferry Stielau's guerrillas across the Elbe–Lübeck Canal. Ernst was disguised as an agricultural labourer and was supplied with explosives in order to blow up a bridge over the canal.

As was often the case with such enterprises, not everything went according to plan. *Niederlande*'s disciplinary officer, a former Gestapo man named Ksiwan, was sent from Neustrelitz with a truckload of explosives for Stielau, but the idea of riding atop this dangerous cargo so rattled him that he abandoned the vehicle and showed up in Roseburg empty-handed. He was sent back to pick up his truck and subsequently disappeared. In another incident, one of the detachment's message-runners was intercepted and killed near Haselüne.

Stielau sent out several patrols and long-range forays, but to little avail. His deputy, Erich Odey, was dispatched with a number of Hitler Youth boys who had orders to report on the British advance, but Odey was captured in Lüneburg, on around 20 April 1945. Two Dutch operatives were sent on perilous journeys across northern Germany in order to restore contact with *Jagdverband* groups in the Netherlands and disperse funds, but at least one of these missions ended in disaster when the agent voluntarily surrendered to the Americans and provided detailed information on Stielau's hideouts near Lauenberg.[42]

The central staff of *Jagdverband Nordwest* also made preparations for resistance activity, particularly its former commander Heinrich Hoyer, who was discharged from hospital in March 1945 and then collaborated closely with *Nordwest*'s training officer, Heinz Winter, in an acceleration of *Werwolf* and *Volkssturm* training. Hoyer was also reputed to be working on projects in the Netherlands and Great Britain. Post-war rumours suggested that leaders of *Nordwest* had made plans to remain quiet for a year after the capitulation and then to unfold various schemes.[43] Certainly, contact points were established throughout Germany, many of which were maintained by relatives of *Nordwest* officers. Willi Dethier's wife and father, for instance, both served as facilitators for underground operations, and the password for activating the contact network was simply 'Dethier'. Key agents, such as *Kapitän zur See* Lipp in Flensburg, were equipped with radio transmitters.[44]

Dethier also sent a unit to Nordhausen, in the Harz Mountains. These men had orders to reinforce *Werwolf* packs, particularly Fritz Harstang, who had originally been assigned to organise Werewolves in the Ruhr. A team under Dr Ludwig, the 'handler' for French trainees at Tiefenthal, was also sent to the mountains. Several of these operatives went into hiding around Mount Brocken and in Torfhaus. Others, feeling their mission was pointless, deserted and fled to the Sudetenland. Bachot's operations officer, Walter Jakobs, was last seen by his comrades in early April, while on a mission between Hanover and the Harz hills. Some members of his *Sonderkommando* spoke English and two were able to converse with an American lilt.[45]

Dethier was still at Neustrelitz as late as 11 April,[46] but he then moved his staff and battle school to Hof, where Skorzeny had located a temporary headquarters. From there, he pushed on to the Czech town of Killeschowitz, another way station on the road to a final base in the Alpine Redoubt, where Dethier planned to hide in the mountains and control his units through a radio transmitter. Killeschowitz was chosen as the site, however, for the *Nordwest* battle school, and sixty boys from local Hitler Youth training camps were ordered to attend this facility. These adolescents underwent an eight-day training course focussed on demolitions, pistol shooting and 'cold sabotage', although many were already secretly planning to desert once deployed behind Allied lines. Interestingly, the boys were told that they were *not* part of the *Werwolf*, which was scorned at Killeschowitz; rather, they belonged to *Jagdverband Nordwest* and were under the command of Otto Skorzeny.

In late April, the battle school, including its complement of Hitler Youth trainees, was broken up into small units, each consisting of an SS man and three to four boys. All team members received civilian clothes and the officers travelled with phoney papers, although the boys had only their genuine Hitler Youth *Ausweis* and were supposed to tell Allied patrols, if encountered, that they were returning home from Hitler Youth training camps. Group leaders also had an order, signed by Himmler, identifying them as Skorzeny *Leute*. The intention of these teams was to slip behind Allied lines and attack airfields, factories, bridges and railway stations. To accomplish these feats, team members were armed with pistols, plastic explosive and Nipolit, which the *Jagdverband* workshop in Killeschowitz had worked into various forms and devices, including tyre-busters. After exhausting their explosives, team members were supposed to return home, seek employment with enemy forces and continue to sabotage the occupation of the country. A group of thirty men left Killeschowitz on 27 April 1945, followed two days later by a second unit. These formations radiated toward their operational zones, some of which were situated as far away as Cologne and Munich. One detachment, directly under Heinz Winter, left in a limousine on 30 April, accompanied by five SS men. Its mission was to undertake sabotage in the north German ports.

Although the *Nordwest* sabotage squads were ordered to avoid direct clashes with Allied troops, there was at least one skirmish near Hof. In this case, two Hitler Youth boys, Schuster and Röderer, and a 23-year-old officer cadet named Kästner, were headed for Bayreuth, where they were supposed to destroy an airfield and a power plant, as well as knocking down the main radio tower and blowing up railway lines. Schuster and Röderer were eager to desert, although Kästner kept them in line by threatening to shoot them. The group had a large amount of explosives contained in luggage – so much that they had to employ a cart to move it and to recruit several waifs in order to help bear the burden – but Kästner relied on the laxity of American patrols and pickets in order to reach his area of operations. For several days, his expectations bore fruit: on one evening, an American lieutenant billeted the group in a building opposite a US command post, without thinking to give the party's baggage a cursory check. On 2 May, the detachment's luck ran out. When challenged by CIC officers at a checkpoint near Rehau, Kästner tried to shoot his way out of trouble and was killed in an exchange of fire. Five German boys were captured, including three who had no idea that they had been hired to push along a mass of sabotage equipment.[47]

Skorzeny also encouraged Mil D units to involve themselves in 'Werwolf' matters, although they were less enthusiastic than Jagdverband forces. One unit that did respond was Trupp 249. In the spring of 1945, the men of this unit smuggled plastic explosives into the enemy hinterland in order to blow up bridges and railway tracks, a project run by Unteroffizier Martens. A sabotage party infiltrated through the lines near Karlsruhe destroyed railway lines and signal boxes, as well as blasting several locomotives that had been left intact after the German retreat. A truckload of high explosives was driven behind the enemy front and the raiders used this material in order to carry out operations. Before retreating from its base at Hochst, Trupp 249 also provided plastic explosives used by Skorzeny's swimming saboteurs in the attempt against the Allied-held bridge at Remagen.

After American tanks broke through to Hanau, Trupp 249's explosives and weapons were loaded into trucks and sent to the Harz Mountains, along with the unit's personnel. After two days in Wernigerode, the detachment's commander, Oberleutnant von Winterfeld, called together the formation and announced that they were about to undertake innovative operations that could cause a shift in the tide of events, at least in their sector of the front. Von Winterfeld said that he needed volunteers. The large assembly before him was then broken up into smaller groups, which he addressed individually. The new plan, he related, was focussed upon launching 'Einsätze' along enemy supply lines. Only the young and eager were needed, particularly men who had experience as shock troops or scouts along the Eastern Front. Von Winterfeld explained that older men and 'green' recruits could step back and that this would not reflect upon 'their honour as soldiers'. Fifteen men volunteered for special operations, including a number of non-commissioned officers.

After the volunteers were assembled, they were instructed about their tasks and equipped with compasses, pistols and four days' rations, which they were instructed not to touch until they were in the field. Placed on twenty-four-hour call, they were mobilised and sent behind American lines on 15 April 1945. A day later, American tanks approached Wernigerode and the remaining members of the Trupp reloaded their trucks and debouched for the Sudetenland, although most of the vehicles were overrun or destroyed by Allied fighter-bombers. With their support base gone, the Harz guerrillas were cut off and surrounded by the Americans, although they managed to establish radio communications with a surviving fragment of Trupp 249. Their first message was brief and explained that the guerrillas had 'contacted enemy tanks'. Then came a desperate appeal for help; the volunteers had been chased up the slopes of Mount Brocken, the highest peak in the Harz, and they were hopelessly encircled. By 22 April, the wireless had fallen silent and officers of Trupp 249 assumed that their comrades had been either killed or captured.[48] Both German and American accounts suggest, however, that SS men in the Brocken area changed into civilian clothes and that there were instances of sabotage and underground activity long after 22 April.[49]

UPON THE NEXT TREE SHALT THOU HANG

One of the most disturbing aspects of the 'Werwolf' programme was its animus against civilians who either doubted the victory of the Third Reich or were ready to work with the occupying powers. *Jagdverband* personnel were ordered to eliminate Germans who cooperated with the Allies or Soviets, and the Hitler Youth boys trained at Killeschowitz were told that they would have to kill even their parents if the latter merited such punishment.[50] Such actions typically fell into one of two categories: behind-the-lines assassinations of Germans sympathetic to the Allies, which were usually undertaken by special teams; or vigilante killings of supposed 'enemies' still residing in Nazi-held territory. This latter type of outrage often occurred spontaneously.

Several Germans in Allied-occupied territory were slated for special handling. In February 1945, Skorzeny was visited at Schwedt by Emil Stürtz, the *Gauleiter* of Brandenburg, and Werner Neumann, Goebbels's right-hand man at the Propaganda Ministry. Neumann had come directly from Hitler's headquarters and bore an order indicating that the American-appointed mayor of Aachen, Franz Oppenhoff, had been sentenced to death 'in contumacia' and that the *Führer* wanted this command executed by any means possible, even assassination. Oppenhoff had become an embarrassment because he was cooperating with the Americans in the administration of the largest German city yet to fall into Allied hands. Skorzeny protested that he had no personnel for such a task and that it was best left to the SS-Werewolves, but Neumann replied that the order had already been given to the *Werwolf* and that both that organisation and the *Jagdverbände* were supposed to work on the task concurrently. After the departure of Naumann and Stürtz, Skorzeny cleared the operation with Schellenberg, who was already aware of the plot, and he asked Schellenberg to add Mil D to the list of agencies assigned to the job. Skorzeny then sent a teletype to Gerlach, noting that 'it is the view of Dr Goebbels and of the public that this man [Oppenhoff] must be liquidated'. Gerlach all but refused the assignment, saying that he had no men available, that Aachen was outside his operational zone and that it was properly a matter for the *Werwolf*.[51] Meanwhile, Prützmann's people were already in the advanced stages of an operation against Oppenhoff, and it was a *Werwolf* parachute squad that actually tracked down and murdered the unfortunate mayor on 25 March 1945.

The Kästner–Schuster–Röderer team assembled in late April 1945 was also charged with killing an 'enemy' who had let down the Nazi cause, namely *Gauleiter* Fritz Wächtler of Bayreuth. Through 1944 and early 1945, Wächtler had slid into a 'defeatist' funk, a condition aggravated by alcoholism. He had ignored the defence of his *Gau* and made himself unpopular by hindering the evacuation of top Gestapo and SD-*Ausland* staffs into his district. Before *Jagdverband* avengers could bring him to account, however, he was shot by SS personnel, probably at the instigation of his own deputy and rival, Ludwig Ruckdeschel. Members of the *Jagdverband* team learned after being sent behind Allied lines that Wächtler was already dead – they were not sure by whose hand – and that they were free of this responsibility. In any case, as will be recalled, Kästner, Schuster and Röderer were intercepted before they reached Bayreuth.[52]

A similar incident involved plans to kill two Rhenish businessmen named Kost and von Korte, both of whom were accused of undercutting German defence efforts (Kost had supposedly hidden two million litres of petrol from the retreating *Wehrmacht*). By the spring of 1945, both men were staying at a residence at Agnetenhof, near Mörs, where they assumed that they were safely ensconced behind Allied lines. On 12 March, two instructors at the

Werwolf school in Hulcrath were ordered to report to *Obergruppenführer* Karl Gutenberger, the SS-Police chief in North Rhineland and local boss of the Werewolves. These two SS sergeants, Friedrich Lehmann and Wolfgang Herfurth, were tough customers – both were former members of the *Leibstandarte* 'Adolf Hitler' and had joined *Jagdverband Nordwest* before being seconded to the Werewolves – so Gutenberger assumed that they were prepared to act without compunction. During their meeting, Gutenberger described the various 'crimes' of Kost and von Korte and the two assassins were then sent to the office of Gutenberger's deputy, *Standartenführer* Raddatz, who supplied them with civilian clothes and provided a guide from the Hitler Youth, Gustav Hegermann. Pistols, a silencer and explosives were furnished by the Nazi Party *Gauleitung* in Essen, which also gave Lehmann and Herfurth details on the location of their prey and provided written authorisation for the killings.

On the night of 13 March, the two SS men and their teenage scout crossed the Rhine at Wesel and then walked to Ossenberg, where they found an abandoned house and settled down for the night. *Wehrmacht* stragglers reported that the Americans were nearby, a claim substantiated by the onset of heavy shelling. By this point, Lehmann had decided that he had no heart for killing Kost and von Korte, particularly since he felt that Skorzeny had recommended him to Gutenberger as an act of malice and that the commando chief wanted to expose him to peril. After some persuasion, Lehmann convinced Herfurth and Hegermann to throw away their arms and abandon the operation. They crumpled their written orders and tossed them on a coal pile. On the morning of 14 March, when Ossenberg was captured by the Americans, all three gunmen surrendered to US troops, claiming to be innocent civilians.[53]

While most such missions were unsuccessful, several violent incidents do bear the mark of *Jagdverband* involvement. In one instance, a two-man *Werwolf* team, led by a Belgian SS officer, crept behind enemy lines and shot a German physician who was working with the American authorities. A card left at the scene bore the term 'collaborator'. This outrage occurred in late March 1945, during the first hours after the Allied occupation of Giessen.[54] As will be recalled, Giessen had been the headquarters of *Sonderkommando* 'Bachot' and *Jagdverband Nordwest* had inserted Belgian agents into this district.

A similar incident occurred near the end of the war. In this case, a *Werwolf* infiltrator, Heinrich von Beddington, was arrested by the British on 13 May 1945 and was charged with complicity in the murder of the mayor of Mehlbeck, a small town on the Lüneburg Heath. The mayor had been killed several days previously. Beddington also admitted, at least to his colleagues, that he had painted a *Werwolf* symbol on the mayor's door. An enthusiastic Nazi, Beddington was one of a number of 'Werewolves' who had been recruited by National Socialist Leadership Officers (NSFOs) in the *Luftwaffe's* paratroop divisions, and who were then formed into guerrilla teams and sent into the Allied-occupied parts of the Altmark and the Lüneburg Heath. The main mission of these units was to carry out demolitions, collect political intelligence and locate a small battle group under the command of Wilhelm Kuhlwilm, a paratroop officer who had voluntarily stayed in enemy-occupied terrain, together with fifteen of his men. Several bits of evidence, including the final location of the NSFO's headquarters in a village near Neustrelitz, plus the fact that *Jagdverband Nordwest* was known to have aggressively recruited paratroopers as 'Werewolves', suggests that this operation was backed by the *Jagdverbände*.[55]

While killing opponents in enemy-held territory was a risky business for which *Jagdverband* personnel showed little enthusiasm, the violent bullying and abuse of 'opponents' behind German lines was a safer proposition. In fact, such activity was supported by the connivance of the regime, particularly as Hitler's conventional authority eroded and German society faced an increasing spate of Nazi vigilantism. Skorzeny showed great heart for such quasi-police actions, arguing that 'total war' implied 'total responsibility', and that no one – high or low alike – should be immune to summary forms of punishment. During the last year of the war, he frequently complained to Kaltenbrunner about the prevalence of anti-Nazi resistance activities in their home town of Vienna, claiming that the local Gestapo was not doing enough to quash opposition elements.[56]

It was at Schwedt, however, that Skorzeny provided his most savage example of how to deal with 'defeatists'. He executed four of his own soldiers on charges of cowardice and desertion, and he also insisted that the *Luftwaffe* try an airfield commander who had fled his post, supposedly without making adequate arrangements to destroy aircraft, equipment and radios. In addition, he terrorised the town, presiding over a summary court that hanged at least ten people. On Skorzeny's order, inhabitants were prohibited from cutting down the bodies that adorned their lampposts and bridge beams. The most senior of these victims was Kurt Flöter, an '*Alte Kämpfer*' who was executed on 5 February 1945 because he had fled his post as mayor of Königsberg-in-der-Neumark. Bormann subsequently complained about 'encroachment' upon the sphere of the party, although Skorzeny argued that he had treated the mayor in his capacity as a *Volkssturm* officer. The impact of this killing, along with concurrent death penalties inflicted upon the police chief of Bromberg and the Deputy *Gauleiter* of Breslau, forced the Nazi Party to systematise such procedures. Thus, a decree of 16 February 1945 provided for the creation of special courts martial 'in the Reich Defence Districts threatened by the enemy'. Henceforth, the *Gauleiter* were given authority to deal 'with anyone who tries to escape his duties towards the community, especially if he does so out of cowardice or selfishness', and they had the power to manage such cases 'with the necessary rigour'.[57]

With the chief having brought down a mailed fist, the Skorzeny *Leute* showed a similar desire to impose lethal doses of punishment, regardless of legal niceties. Near the end of March 1945, *Untersturmführer* Wolf killed a French woman serving with the Neustrelitz battle school because she was rumoured to be spying for the Allies, and troopers of *Jagdverband Nordwest* stomped to death a German sailor who they accused of lacking faith in victory.[58] In Baden, a *Südwest* sergeant killed two *Wehrmacht* deserters, whom he caught sleeping in a barn, and a *Jagdverband* patrol also arrested a farmer who had supposedly made an anti-war remark.[59]

One of the chiefs of *Jagdeinsatz Dänemark*, naval *Leutnant* Iringsen, was responsible for an especially gruesome slaying. On 29 April 1945, Iringsen was given custody of a captured SS deserter at the police presidium in Flensburg, after which he drove his charge to the villa 'Berghof'. Several days later, Iringsen called together his Danish guerrillas and made a violent speech, describing how his prisoner had attempted to abandon their 'sacred cause' at the very hour when 'the Führer had just died at the head of his troops'. He then dealt his victim a fearsome blow and encouraged the Danes to fall upon him with their truncheons. After the deserter was beaten into unconsciousness, Iringsen drew his pistol and dispatched him with a shot through the head.

Two days later, Iringsen caught another two deserters hiding in the yard of the 'Berghof', and the men in his platoon feared once again having to participate in a savage beating. In this instance, however, Iringsen forced the two men to dig their own graves, but then suggested that unless they wanted to topple into the holes that they had just prepared, they should take advantage of his offer to join *Jagdverband Nordwest*. Both men wisely accepted and wound up having to contribute only four days of service before they were released at the time of the Third Reich's final capitulation.[60]

Two cases in late April involve priests and thereby illustrate the inherent friction between Nazism and the Roman Catholic Church, which got worse as the war drew to a conclusion. Heinrich Perner, a former French Foreign Legionary who commanded the Skorzeny *Jagdkommando* in southern Baden, was the instigator of one of these incidents. Although not a member of the Nazi Party, Perner was a staunch supporter of Hitler who assumed, like other militant Nazis, that the Catholic faith was incompatible with true devotion to the Third Reich. In fact, he observed that the Münster Valley, where his unit was based, 'needs to throw off these black fetters'. Ominously, Perner had already played a role in the large-scale massacre of Jews in Russia, so he was no stranger to killing or to the manhandling of perceived opponents. After spending the day of 21 April terrorising Münsterhalden – forcing townsfolk to put Nazi symbols back on display and arresting the district *Volkssturm* chief – Perner decided to strike at the supposed heart of the problem by eliminating 68-year-old Willi Strohmeyer, abbot of the St Trudpert Monastery. Perner had already daydreamed about hanging Strohmeyer in the town square and positioning snipers to shoot anyone who tried to cut him down, but he decided upon a less public means of dispatching the pastor. On the following morning, he burst into St Trudpert Monastery and snatched Strohmeyer, who was bundled into a staff car and whisked away. After driving to Münsterhalden, Perner left Strohmeyer in the custody of his deputy, Horst Waver, and four French legionaries, who were subsequently instructed to drive the pastor to the heights near Haldenhof and there to shoot him. Waver and the Frenchmen did as they were told. After escorting Strohmeyer to a remote spot, the unfortunate priest was shot through the neck and his body stripped of his clothes, including his gold watch, which was pocketed by legionary Delotter. He was buried in an unmarked grave. The team then reported success in its nefarious task, although Perner was careful to treat the matter as a secret. When asked by the Nazi *Kreisleiter* what had happened to Strohmeyer – the abbot, ironically, was not unpopular among local Nazi Party officials – Perner claimed that he was being held in custody. The reason for seizing Strohmeyer, Perner claimed, was that he had been convincing young people to sabotage the launch of the *Werwolf*.[61]

A similar incident was the handiwork of *Kommando* 'Bachot', which by this stage of the war was retreating from southern Bavaria into Austria. Bachot's rearguard was in the small village of Götting, where powerful feelings were aroused by a Bavarian autonomist revolt. On the morning of 28 April, when anti-Nazis briefly grabbed control of radio stations in Munich and Laibach, claiming to have seized power, the pastor of Götting arranged, with the help of a local labourer, to haul down the swastika flag above his church tower and replace it with the Bavarian provincial colours. This prelate, Josef Grimm, also suggested sabotaging a *Jagdverband* vehicle, although this comment was overheard by some of Bachot's men. When Bachot learned of Grimm's behaviour, he rushed to the village presbytery and arrested the insubordinate priest. After questioning Grimm, Bachot pushed him into a staff car, slapped handcuffs on his wrists and drove him to the outskirts of Götting, where Bachot and a Flemish SS man led him into the woods and shot him through the neck. As was the case in Münsterhalden, the murderers stole the victim's watch, although in this instance the body was left unburied and was discovered on the following day, shortly after the last elements of Bachot's unit had departed.[62]

Such cases are important because they highlight severe tensions between German civilians and foreign *Jagdverband* personnel, the latter of whom often remained more devoted to the Nazi cause than the Germans around them. By this late date in the war, ideology and sentiment for or against the conflict had come to dominate Nazi thinking, even superseding more familiar themes, such as nationality and race. Indeed, by the spring of 1945, the SS and the Nazi Party, supposedly the most fanatic defenders of Germandom, had empowered *Jagdverband* foreigners to do the same thing that their liberated countrymen in the Allied forces were doing – that is, kill Germans.

The last act of such savagery took place on the final day of the war. The perpetrator was *Hauptscharführer* Thomas Krafft, a 23-year-old weapons instructor at the Section S camp in Mürz Zuschlag. On 20 April 1945, Krafft led a group of twenty-five SD instructors and trainees – an assemblage of men from various Eastern European countries – on a south-westward march designed to evade the Red Army. After a week-long trek, *Gruppe* 'Krafft', weighed down by weapons and sabotage equipment, came to rest in the Austrian village of Radenthein, near the Millsätter See, although the motley band was hardly welcomed by the population. Radenthein was a one-industry town built around the magnesium works, and civilians feared that their plant would be damaged if the Americans were forced to advance against opposition or if Krafft chose to carry out 'scorched earth' demolitions. To make matters worse, Krafft was charged by local Nazis with handling 'politically unreliable elements', and the bullet-ridden body of a former communist soon turned up in the forest.

After several weeks of increasing tension, a shooting affray broke out on the morning of 8 May, pitting SS guerrillas against factory guards at the magnesium works, and on the same morning Krafft marched into the gendarmerie headquarters and hauled down an Austrian flag that had been hoisted from the building, trampling the banner in front of a crowd of onlookers. In order to defuse this explosive situation, the district *Volkssturm* commander organised a meeting between Krafft and the managers of the magnesium works, the latter delegation being led by the firm's executive officer, Dr Carmen. At this conclave, Krafft agreed to leave Radenthein if the magnesium works would provide him with a heavy goods truck, a driver and a supply of food and alcohol from the plant's canteen. To speed matters along, one of the plant's chief engineers, Geistler, agreed to guarantee the firm's good faith by staying in Krafft's company, particularly since the latter promised to have him home by the afternoon. During the meeting, Krafft learned of the Third Reich's unconditional surrender, which did little to improve his grim mood. Like many Skorzeny *Leute*, he had believed that the Nazi regime would find a way to avoid defeat, and it came as a tremendous shock to learn of the movement's bankruptcy. A heavy drinker, Krafft eased the pain by working his way through a steady flow of schnapps and rum, showing signs of inebriation by midday.

Meanwhile, Krafft led his troops on an organised looting of the magnesium works' canteen. When Carmen protested, Krafft ordered him to climb aboard his newly acquired truck, firing several shots at his feet in order to emphasise the command. Krafft also told one the plant's engineers to get in the truck, thus joining Carmen and Geistler as a hostage, and when Carmen's deputy attempted to intervene, Krafft struck out and knocked him to the ground. As the truck pulled out of Radenthein, Krafft picked up his girlfriend and he also kidnapped three additional hostages, two women and yet another engineer, obviously with the intent of using these people in order to ensure an undisturbed retreat to Spittal.

Given such considerations, when *Gruppe* 'Krafft' left the Radenthein district, the hostages lost their value. Unfortunately, this occurred at the same time as drink and the pressure of the day's events were worsening Krafft's already dark mood. Krafft released one of the engineers, but as the group approached the hamlet of Dellach, he ordered the driver to stop and he lurched from the cab, ordering Carmen, the two remaining engineers and one of the women out of the truck. These three men had supposedly shown their true colours by trying to foil Krafft's purposes, while the woman had displayed kindness to British POWs, an infraction of the Nazi code of conduct for which she would now pay a heavy price. Krafft ordered all three men to lie down on the slope of a nearby pasture, after which he sprayed the victims with fire from his machine pistol. He then turned to the woman, who was standing next to him, and shot her as well. He was about to leave the killing grounds when his troopers pointed out that several of the victims were trying to get up, whence he whirled around and fired another hail of bullets. Geistler and the female hostage were killed instantly, but even after the second round of shooting Carmen and the remaining engineer were merely wounded: they both died subsequently while under care in a village hospital. Having thus achieved a level of besotted satisfaction, Krafft remounted his vehicle and sped away from the scene. Both the lorry driver and the surviving female hostage later escaped the clutches of their tormenter, but not before Krafft had warned the woman never – on pain of death – to talk about the events she had witnessed. *Gruppe* 'Krafft' subsequently fled into American-occupied territory, hoping to avoid a fight with the Soviets, and Krafft went into hiding, disguised as a Baltic German refugee.[63]

Such incidents attest to the fact that there was a wide spectrum of motives behind *Jagdverband* terrorism, ranging from xenophobic patriotism to Nazi anti-clericalism to drunken feelings of spite. As the historian Vico once noted, the satisfaction of passions and minor aims is often the mainspring of individual action, however difficult this makes it to read a sense of coherence into human history.

THE '*SCHUTZKORPS ALPENLAND*'

While elements of the *Territorialen Jagdverbände* were transmogrifying into Werewolves, Skorzeny decided to relocate the core of his special forces in the fabled Alpine Redoubt. In late 1944, RSHA offices began a southward shift from Berlin, moving first to Central Germany and then to the Austrian Alps, a passage that was naturally attractive to homesick Austrians and Bavarians.[64] The *Jagdverband Führungsstab* joined this exodus in February and March 1945, as did the control structures of Section S and Mil D, plus as many sabotage troops as Skorzeny could withdraw from Schwedt and other points along the front. Skorzeny even evacuated slave labour from the Sachsenhausen concentration camp, a manpower pool that he was using to make initiators for plastic explosives. These prisoners were transferred as far as Hof.

In early March, Skorzeny rented a 'lodging train' from the *Reichsbahn*, mainly so that his headquarters could become mobile and seek cover along various rail sidings. With this new means of transport at his disposal, Skorzeny withdrew his staff, led by Walter, Besekow and Hunke, plus his mistress, the Berlin film actress Marianne Simson, along the line Hof–Teisendorf–Puch–Pongau–Klammstein–Radstadt. At Puch, Skorzeny reduced the size of his entourage, releasing his female secretaries; at Radstadt he handed his train over to the army so that it could be used to move troops to the Eastern Front.[65] According to one witness, Skorzeny spent time in late March and early April at the Bad Tölz *Junkerschule*, supervising the training of frogmen and aviator/parachutists seconded from the *Luftwaffe*, who were said to be preparing a special mission.[66] Radio intercepts suggest that his headquarters were at Pottenstein on 5 April and Traunstein twelve days later.[67] By 24 April, his staff was based at Achtal, where one observer described the organisation as consisting of twenty officers and 170 men, many of them bearers of the *Blutorden* and the Golden Combat Badge and all bristling with armament. Radl remained in Friedenthal until 20 April, organising supplies for southward-bound troops, and then he too joined Skorzeny in Austria.[68]

Although Skorzeny later suggested that he was 'ordered' into the Alps,[69] there is no record of any senior echelon either devising or controlling such a shift of forces, and Radl later claimed that Skorzeny simply decided, on his own initiative, to leave Friedenthal, mainly with the intention of escaping the enemy advance. The final decision was made after the Allies had crossed the Rhine.[70] There was certainly no question of Schellenberg providing orders to his nominal subordinate; rather, Skorzeny laid down the law for his chief, telling him 'in a rather condescending manner' that the *Jagdverbände* were coalescing in the Alps. In fact, Schellenberg complained to Ohletz that 'Skorzeny now has full powers from the Führer and the Reichsführer such as no other man in Germany has'. Neither does it appear that Kaltenbrunner provided Skorzeny with relevant instructions, although Skorzeny advised Schellenberg that he and Kaltenbrunner were 'absolutely agreed' on the move into the mountains, and Höttl later recalled that Skorzeny 'reported to Kaltenbrunner on the progress of preparations'.[71]

After Skorzeny had rallied 400 to 500 men under his banner, he formed a '*Schutzkorps Alpenland*' ('Alpine Guard Corps', SKA), probably hoping that this assemblage could be expanded into a much larger force. According to Radl, Skorzeny believed that he could eventually gather several thousand men, who would form substantial bodies of skirmishers throughout western, southern and central Austria. By late April, Skorzeny's chief of staff, a former Brandenburger named Walter, had begun negotiating with officers of a Brandenburg unit in northern Yugoslavia, hoping to get much-needed reinforcements for the SKA, and it was also hoped that the SKA could recruit from the local civilian population. Skorzeny attended to matters of supply too. In February 1945 he had begun laying a huge weapons depot in a copper mine at Mitterberghütten, a dump that eventually contained 2,100 boxes of explosives and sabotage equipment, including tons of Nipolit and 750,000 rounds of ammunition and grenades. Karl Hagedorn sent several gazogene trucks lumbering into the mountains, carrying sub-machine guns, pistols and ammunition, most of which was deposited at Achtal, where the *Jagdverbände* assembled ten tons of supplies. Rations for three months duration were distributed to the troops. It was enough to supply a small guerrilla army.

To provide a sense of structure for his new creation, Skorzeny organised a SKA *Führungsgruppe* at Annaberg and he set up platoon-sized units of troops at Hochkönig (under Fucker), Lofer (under Girg), Alt Aussee (under Schürmann), Mitterndorf (under Winter and Besekow), Altenmarkt (under Streckfuss), Bischofshofen (under Wilscher), Kitzbühel (under Bihrer) and Maishofen-Saalbach (under Ludwig). Each unit received a seventy-watt wireless transmitter that was linked to a central station codenamed '*Brieftaube*'. The regional formations were typically comprised of a hodgepodge of various commando elements, thrown together at the last minute. *Einheit* 'Schürmann', for instance, consisted of men from *Jagdverbände Südost* and *Mitte*, veterans of *Kampfgruppe* 'Schwedt', plus half a dozen combat swimmers. By the second half of April, Skorzeny was busy preparing SKA defence positions, supply depots and medical aid stations, threatening death to 'traitors' who refused to cooperate. Eventually, the platoons were broken up into twelve-man detachments and ordered to move their stores to hiding places in the mountains. One platoon built an elaborate base in the woods, complete with electric power outlets and a subterranean bunker. This same unit also recruited servants from amongst the ranks of the Nazi girl guides (the *Bund deutscher Mädel*, BdM) and made arrangements with local farmers for laundry.[72]

Kaltenbrunner also provided resources beyond the limited range supplied by the *Jagdverband* quartermaster section. In late March 1945, he ordered his RSHA supply specialist, Josef Spacil, to organise food and medical dumps in the Innsbruck area and to make these facilities available to the *Jagdverbände*. When Skorzeny approached Kaltenbrunner, begging funds for his troops, Kaltenbrunner forwarded him to Spacil. On 27 April, Spacil met with Radl and transferred nearly $10,000,000 worth of gold, securities and cash, most it recently snatched at gunpoint from the *Reichsbank*. Radl and Skorzeny then fled to the Tyrolean and Upper Austrian Alps, where they buried this loot. One Mil D officer later recalled helping to carry £12,000 in gold bars, plus piles of foreign exchange, to a depot at Brandach-Wiesen-Alm. These assets, he later claimed, were earmarked for Nazi propaganda and *Werwolf* activities.[73]

Several interpretations of the SKA's purpose have been advanced, none of which are mutually exclusive. Skorzeny and Radl later claimed that the situation in the Alps was so desperate that there was need for a strong hand, which the SKA was meant to bring to bear. German armies in the Balkans, northern Italy and southern Germany had begun retreating into the mountains as a tangled mass of stragglers and military refugees, and if a coherent defence of the Alps was to be mounted, a field patrol service was necessary in order to prevent desertions and reorganise dissolving units. At the urging of *Gauleiter* Eigruber, a Nazi stalwart, Skorzeny got Kaltenbrunner's sanction in forming SS-*Sicherheitspolizei-Grenadier Bataillon* 2. The final authorisation probably came during a meeting between Eigruber, Kaltenbrunner and Skorzeny on 12 April, and Walter Girg later claimed that the name 'SKA' was first used three days later. Radl contended that in the broadest sense, the SKA was supposed to prevent 'Bolshevisation' and 'preserve law and order'. Considering the brutal Nazi understanding of these functions, such operations were almost bound to increase a propensity for terrorism that had already begun to manifest itself. Various accounts describe Skorzeny's storm troopers roughly searching the homes of Austrian civilians in an attempt to flush out deserters, and a number of summary executions were carried out. At the same time, the usual heavy-handed methods were used to force Alpine farmers and their wives and daughters into building defence works.[74] Even according to Wilhelm Höttl, 'Skorzeny developed into an unpleasant type in the last stages of the war and immediately afterwards. His pretensions to greatness had increased enormously... [and] he became obsessed with a boundless ambition.'[75] Several army officers later charged that Skorzeny abused his powers by dealing out quick vengeance to old antagonists (and also eliminating potential rivals should he ever wish to trade *Ostfront* intelligence with the Allies).[76] Georg Buntrock, the head of Mil F, was sentenced to death but managed to elude his pursuers and hide in the Salzburg Mountains.[77]

Although Skorzeny and Radl were later loath to admit it, there is no doubt that they intended to convert the SKA into an Alpine guerrilla force, and that the intention to proceed in this direction accelerated as they realised how few provisions had been made for a conventional defence of the National Redoubt. This lack of preparation left partisan warfare as the only viable option. Contact with Prützmann had convinced Skorzeny that the SS-*Werwolf* was hardly ready for guerrilla fighting in the Alps, and that if the task was to be performed adequately, he would have to assume the burden. Höttl noted that 'Skorzeny undoubtedly flattered himself that he was the commander-in-chief of the coming German guerrilla war', although Kaltenbrunner was quizzical and nicknamed Skorzeny 'the Partisan Napoleon'.[78] Skorzeny told Schellenberg that his troops would fight in the Alps 'as Maquis. All who would join would have to place themselves under his orders, everything else was rubbish.'[79] Skorzeny also informed Göttsch that he planned to retire into the mountains with 3,000 to 4,000 followers and wait out the situation as it matured.[80] In addition, the SKA's chief of staff, Wilhelm Walter, admitted that the Skorzeny *Leute* were intending to act as a sabotage force, making extensive use of civilian clothes and Allied uniforms, and Girg claimed that they were meant to offer substantial resistance, if only to the Russians.[81]

To fully understand the implications of this strategy, it is necessary to note that normal channels of control in the SD had begun to collapse by late April 1945, and that as subsections of the organisation began to coalesce into a composite mass, Skorzeny's power and influence increased correspondingly (at least within the shrinking bounds of the Nazi state). On 26 April, Skorzeny and Waneck managed to convince Kaltenbrunner to fire Schellenberg as chief of SD-*Ausland* and to scrap the organisation's long-standing lines of division into Sections B, C, D, E, S and G. This decision was made on the spur of the moment during a meeting in the Hotel Österreichischer Hof, apparently upon receipt of news that Schellenberg's deputy, Sandberger, was shopping for Austrian accommodations for the SD-*Ausland* headquarters. Skorzeny complained that it was too late to revive the old outfit, particularly given the collapse of telephone communications, and he sneered that some of Schellenberg's section chiefs had already fled from an SD hideout in Burg Lauenstein when American tanks had drawn near. Kaltenbrunner groused that Schellenberg had 'double-crossed' him and thrown in his lot with Himmler and Berger, who were trying to mediate a cease-fire through Sweden. Waneck and Skorzeny then drafted an order that remoulded the SD-*Ausland* to include only a Skorzeny-controlled sabotage wing, the '*Geheimer Zerstörungs Dienst*', into which Mil D was fused, and a Waneck-dominated intelligence component, the '*Geheime Meldedienst*', which included the espionage elements of the SD-*Ausland*, plus the intelligence bureaux of the Mil Amt. Kaltenbrunner signed the decree. Schellenberg, upon hearing the news, shrugged his shoulders: 'At five minutes to twelve', he observed, 'they take time out for a thing like that!'[82]

At a more general level, the distinction between the SD's external and internal halves also began to collapse. In fact, the SD-*Inland*'s southern plenipotentiary, *Sturmbannführer* Dr Spengler, had a mandate to organise an intelligence network for Nazi terrorists in Bavaria and Austria, and to work closely with Skorzeny in training the functionaries involved. Indeed, Spengler, Skorzeny and Kaltenbrunner met on a number of occasions in April, mostly at locations in Linz and Salzburg. Skorzeny had already provided the SD-*Inland* headquarters with infantry weapons and explosives, and upon Spengler's request he handed over a store of mountain equipment and winter survival supplies for a unit of fifty men.

A crucial part of this amalgamation process involved a proposal to merge the SD-*Ausland*'s foreign guerrilla and intelligence networks with parallel groups set up by SD-*Inland* (and which drew heavily from the foreign labour and pro-German refugee communities that were supervised by the domestic SD). This combined operation was codenamed '*Regenbogen*' and on 23 April Spengler ordered *Sturmbannführer* Franz Pacher to contact Skorzeny's headquarters and introduce himself as the SD-*Inland* liaison officer for '*Regenbogen*' matters. Pacher spent three days in conversations with Walter. The ultimate intention was to organise a system through which '*Regenbogen*' intelligence agents and scouts could operate throughout Europe, spotting sabotage targets and gathering weapons, while SKA and *Werwolf* groups would stand ready in their mountain fastness, occasionally sallying forth to attack objectives suggested by the reconnaissance network. Eventually a great offensive would be launched out of the mountains, sweeping Germany clean of its foes.

'*Regenbogen*' offered advantages to Skorzeny because it promised to add extra agents and contact points to his foreign networks and because SD-*Inland* personnel had distributed considerable funds abroad, particularly in Argentina, and they had also set up financial dispersing centres in Switzerland and Spain. By the end of the war, for instance, the PPF underground in France was controlled largely from Spain and one of the leaders of the Breton nationalist movement, Olivier Mordrel, was ordered to go to Spain in order to exploit the funds and agent networks already established in that country. Although most aspects of '*Regenbogen*' never got beyond the planning stage, by late April section leaders had been appointed for various nations, agents were being assembled for repatriation to their home countries (suitably disguised as returning slave labourers), and pamphlets were being published – signed by 'the Peoples of Europe' – that called for 'nationalists' to protect 'European civilisation'.[83] Several '*Regenbogen*' agents were captured by the Allies, including one who had orders to reactivate the fascist underground in Belgium and then travel to Venezuela, where he was supposed to make contact with pro-German elements.[84]

As the SKA took shape, Kaltenbrunner and his cronies debated the formation's merits. In late March 1945, Himmler had ordered Kaltenbrunner to organise security in the

Alpine Redoubt, after which Kaltenbrunner set up police patrols (such as the SKA) and developed a plan to blow up key passes in order to block Allied ingress. He also collected huge amounts of treasure from the *Reichsbank* and the financial office of the RSHA, moving much of this wealth to hidden locations in the mountains. Several weeks later, Himmler appointed Kaltenbrunner as his Alpine plenipotentiary and the Germans informed their Japanese ally that they planned to hold the Alps as a 'last stronghold', conducting partisan warfare 'separately in every area'. As the weeks wore on, however, Kaltenbrunner increasingly realised that a conventional defence of the Redoubt was impossible. By 26 April he had 'lost hope', and it is possible that he cancelled full-scale defence measures after a meeting with *Feldmarschal* Kesselring and Hermann Neubacher, although preparations to fight the Soviets continued apace. In a message to Berlin on 1 May, he was still talking about readying the Redoubt for a fight.

Kaltenbrunner's increasing sense of uncertainty meant that he was willing to entertain a 'back-up' plan for Austria, which gradually assumed a more central role in his thinking. In 1943, the RSHA chief had tasked Werner Göttsch to penetrate the anti-Nazi underground in Vienna, a process in which Göttsch made contact with various Social Democratic, conservative and monarchist groups. By December 1944, Göttsch had decided that the 'Vienna clique' might be able to extract its homeland from a lost war by reviving an Austrian free state and forming an anti-communist coalition government from amongst the opposition elements with whom he had come into contact. 'Reform' Nazis would supposedly form a loyal opposition. Although Höttl, Waneck and Neubacher all backed this plan, codenamed 'Herzog', Kaltenbrunner long remained cool, preferring to organise a stolid defence for the Redoubt. However, he did allow Höttl to elicit a response from OSS officers in Switzerland, letting slip that he and other pro-Western leaders were willing to lead a Tauroggen-type movement and to move troops to the side of the Allies as *Freikorps*. Kaltenbrunner also authorised Höttl to offer the SD's anti-Soviet resistance networks as a sweetener, should the Allies appear ready to dicker, and he pointed out that the Germans had left substantial forces in western Hungary and Croatia in order to encourage these movements. The anti-communist undergrounds in Romania and Yugoslavia were particularly dangled as a lure. When the organisation of a credible Redoubt began to seem impossible, Kaltenbrunner grew more interested in 'Herzog', especially when he noticed that the Western Allies refused to recognise a Soviet-backed government organised by Karl Renner on 27 April. He finally approved the operation in late April–early May 1945, although by this time it was too late to launch a practical alternative to Renner. Kaltenbrunner hoped, however, that should 'Herzog' succeed, despite the odds, he would be permitted to fade comfortably into the background. At this stage, his intention was to retire to the mountains and lead a shadowy anti-Bolshevik movement, which would have lines of contact all over Central and Eastern Europe and would cooperate with his proposed Austrian government, perhaps even being tolerated by the British and Americans.[85]

For a while, it was unclear how the SKA would fit into this new arrangement (if at all). Advocates of 'Herzog' worried that Skorzeny favoured defence of the Redoubt, perhaps to the exclusion of all other options. Given this expectation, Höttl, Göttsch and Waneck all set to work on their headstrong friend, soliciting his views and sounding out the capability for a conventional defence of the mountains. Conversations with Skorzeny suggested, however, that he was no longer spoiling for a fight and he proved to be uncharacteristically modest, explaining that his role was relatively unimportant and that his goal was to retreat into the hills with several companies of men. Göttsch and his colleagues were also concerned about the SS-*Werwolf*, but in this regard too they were happy to learn that Skorzeny had provided a limited degree of weapons and training to the Werewolves and that he knew the identities of only a few of the movement's regional commanders. In fact, Skorzeny did not seem enthusiastic about the Werewolves, although he appeared favourably disposed toward the 'Herzog'. In late April he told Waneck that he agreed with Kaltenbrunner's halt of operations against the Western Allies.

Once the 'Herzog' plotters had assured themselves that Skorzeny was not a threat, they began exploring the best means of co-opting the SKA. Göttsch believed that remnants of the *Jagdverbände* could be recruited as a 'palace guard' for Kaltenbrunner's prospective Austrian regime, especially since it was thought that the new government might have to fight for control with the local *Gauleiter* and Nazi Party machinery, some of which was loyal to Kaltenbrunner's deadly enemy, Martin Bormann. Kaltenbrunner was in contact with two Austrian *Gauleiter*, Franz Hofer and August Eigruber, both of whom was trying to win over to the 'Herzog' scheme, although only the former was sympathetic.

Since Göttsch had an incorrigibly conspiratorial nature, he never told Skorzeny or Kaltenbrunner how he planned to exploit the SKA in service of 'Herzog', even after he no longer had reason to fear that the two men would fight to defend the Redoubt. Instead, he embarked on a number of underhanded schemes designed to place a trusty in Skorzeny's vicinity and then penetrate the commando chief's organisation so that he could gradually turn it toward his own purposes. The first of these enterprises involved *Oberleutnant* Krautzberger, an old Brandenburger who had served as Zervas's liaison officer and had since withdrawn to the Alps, where he became deeply enmeshed in 'Herzog'. Krautzberger controlled a fifty-man FAK detachment in Schloss Thalheim, and when he offered this unit for any mission that Goettsch might propose, the latter decided to use Krautzberger and his men as go-betweens with Skorzeny. Krautzberger was already nominally under Skorzeny's command and Göttsch thought that his credentials would impress the commando chief. Göttsch's intention was to introduce Krautzberger's men as couriers for the *Jagdverband* bands scattered throughout Austria, although he eventually realised that Skorzeny would recognise this as a blatant attempt to spy on the SKA. In any case, Krautzberger became absorbed in the manipulation of four British parachutists whom the Germans captured near Judenberg and wanted to use as contacts with the Allies. As matters turned out, the busy Krautzberger never met Skorzeny.

Göttsch's next brainstorm was to try the same approach with ten men from Section E, who had gathered at Alt Aussee in late April and were looking for an assignment. Since Section E already had a close relationship with the *Jagdverbände*, Göttsch felt that it might seem proper to offer these personnel to Skorzeny as a means of maintaining liaison between scattered SKA detachments. All ten men were competent mountaineers and were qualified to act as couriers. The chosen instrument for the implementation of this scheme was Viktor Zeischka, the liaison officer between Section E and the Balkan 'national governments'. Although Göttsch began working on this project about 20 April, explaining to Zeischka why it was necessary to keep track of Skorzeny and his guerrillas, he never managed to insert the agents into a SKA communications network, mainly because Skorzeny was hesitant about accepting such help. Apparently, Skorzeny was not confident that the Zeischka group would be loyal to the SKA rather than to some outside authority. Eventually, the ten men were withdrawn to a mountain cabin near Alt Ausee, and Waneck then attempted to curry last minute favour with the enemy by reporting their location to the Americans.[86]

ENTER EICHMANN, EXIT SKORZENY

By late April 1945, it was clear that the Allies had breached the outer defences of the Alpine Redoubt and that they were driving for Berchtesgaden, Innsbruck and Salzburg. A conventional defence of the region had already failed, but the rough outline of a 'back-up' plan was obvious: Skorzeny, Kaltenbrunner and Waneck would retreat to the hills and the SKA would support the 'Regenbogen' concept, the main animus of which was the Red Army, but which was also aimed at the Western Powers. If Kaltenbrunner's projected Austrian regime could still be formed, it would provide cover for these activities.

Unfortunately for the Nazis, Waneck was left to map out the structure of this prospective 'anti-Bolshevik' movement, and the Section E chief had made a career out of concocting half-baked notions. When Höttl visited Waneck in late April, he found that the latter had already put elaborate plans on paper and that he had drawn up a chart showing the location of the key mountain hide-outs and channels of communication between each location. Most importantly, Waneck felt that three principal groups – under himself, Kaltenbrunner and Skorzeny – needed an independent agency to maintain liaison and provide couriers. This idea probably reflected the thinking of Göttsch, who was still toying with the idea of infiltrating Skorzeny's contingent by controlling of the means of communication between its scattered fragments.

Of the large number of RSHA personnel gathered in southern Germany, the man whom Waneck and Göttsch picked for this delicate assignment was the notorious Adolf Eichmann, chief organiser of the Final Solution. Although both men knew about Eichmann's background – Göttsch called him 'a swine and a gangster' – they nonetheless displayed a stunning degree of myopia in thinking that Eichmann could be of value. The main arguments in Eichmann's favour were that he knew the region around Alt Aussee, having grown up in the area, and that he had nothing left to lose, since he and his men had such an atrocious record that they could hardly afford to let themselves fall into the hands of the enemy. This argument was expected to appeal to Skorzeny, who was known to be concerned about the reliability of anyone posted to his service as a courier. What Waneck and Göttsch did not realise, of course, was that Eichmann's radioactive reputation would outweigh all other factors surrounding his prospective deployment.

In late April 1945, Eichmann and a small number of his personnel showed up in Alt Aussee, probably because they had been called by Waneck and told to report to Kaltenbrunner. Zeischka, on orders from Waneck, procured billets for the party, and once Eichmann had a sense of the situation, he telephoned his headquarters in Prague and called up thirty-five reinforcements, who arrived in two separate trucks. They bore treasure that had been looted from murdered European Jews and was now earmarked for the Nazi guerrilla movement. Eichmann was enraged that the Sipo security chief in Prague, Weinmann, had sent him disabled and superannuated personnel, but he was even more upset by the reception accorded him by Waneck and Göttsch, who wanted to employ his men but also had an obvious desire to keep him at arm's length. Eichmann seized supplies from a Section E depot, *sans* authorisation, and he was displeased with the adjunct personnel sent to him by Waneck, many of whom looked like redundant functionaries who had no other purpose to fulfil.

Despite the fact that Eichmann was treated like a contagious disease, complaints about his presence in Alt Aussee soon grew deafening, and SS leaders were still mindful of the old German saying '*Mitgegangen, mitgefangen, mitgehangen*' ('grouped together, caught together, hanged together'). The Section E personnel assigned to Eichmann's command were unhappy, and neither Höttl nor Skorzeny wanted anything to do with their colleague, despite his vaunted willingness to fight to the death. In particular, Eichmann's presence brought dismay to people in Kaltenbrunner's entourage, especially the RSHA chief's mistress, Gisela von Westarp, as well as Iris Scheidler, the wife of his adjutant. Frau Scheidler roundly denounced Eichmann and convinced the garrison commander in Alt Aussee to ask Eichmann's cut-throats to vacate their billets in the Park Hotel, mainly on the pretext that Alt Aussee was a hospital town and had to be cleared of armed personnel. Kaltenbrunner himself grew concerned. On 6 May, he told Höttl that Waneck's plan was 'insane' – not a ringing endorsement – and in a subsequent meeting with the Section E boss, he asked what detailed preparations Waneck had made toward launching a flight to the mountains. This question flummoxed Waneck, who was in his usual state of organisational disarray, and Kaltenbrunner responded by saying that plans to conduct a coordinated retreat into the mountains should be officially discarded. Eichmann had helped poison the atmosphere necessary for such an operation. The RSHA chief also told Waneck to order Eichmann out of Alt Aussee immediately.

Kaltenbrunner met directly with Eichmann and was equally curt. When Eichmann told Kaltenbrunner that he still planned to carry out last ditch resistance in the Totesgebirge, the latter, dripping with sarcasm, said that Himmler could now enjoy renewed confidence in talks with General Eisenhower, knowing that he had such an asset. 'It's all a lot of crap', he finally barked, 'The game is up'. Soon afterwards, Höttl saw Eichmann, who complained loudly about the 'disloyalty' of the SD-*Ausland*. Nonetheless, he (Eichmann) was still willing to lead his men into the hills and to burn all his bridges behind him, which is exactly the course that he pursued. He was lucky to encounter Horia Sima's Iron Guardists, who were in the Alps in order to provide an external centre of direction for the Romanian resistance movement. Sima's Legionaries had much experience living as hunted men, and during the first weeks after the end of the war, it was through their assistance that Eichmann was able to escape the Allied dragnet, at least until he could assume a false identity and go underground.[87]

Meanwhile, the collapse of the Waneck scheme left Kaltenbrunner and Skorzeny to their own devices. Kaltenbrunner had been working closely with Skorzeny, who on 5 May handled some of the RSHA chief's baggage and later shared a hut with him for several days. In the final analysis, however, Kaltenbrunner's desire to flee to the mountains had become half-hearted, at best, and he feared that Skorzeny's gung-ho activism would draw the unwanted attention of the enemy. As a result, he refused a mountain cabin that Skorzeny had offered, instead preferring to occupy his own hut in the Totesgebirge, taking with him only a few men and hoping to use radio gear provided by Skorzeny and Höttl in order to stay in touch with remnants of the SD. Kaltenbrunner craftily shaved off his moustache and started using the identity of a dead acquaintance, although going mufti was a difficult prospect for a man who stood six foot four inches in height and had a duelling scar slashed across his face. He also displayed a misplaced trust in the population of the Ausserland, since local anti-Nazi freedom fighters almost immediately reported his presence to advancing American forces. He was arrested in an Allied raid on the morning of 12 May 1945.[88]

Skorzeny, in truth, seemed scarcely more eager to play out his hand. Following Kaltenbrunner's orders, he instructed SKA detachments to cease operations against the Western Allies. Rather, he advised, they should 'prevent the formation of Bolshevik groups', protect the population against rebellious foreign labourers, and help farmers with agricultural work. Despite this retreat from confrontation, SKA fighters were informed that they remained at Skorzeny's disposal and many still expected some final combat, perhaps against the Soviets. Over the next few days, however, bad news descended like rain. Local cease-fires were arranged with the Allies in northern Italy and along the Alpine Front, and on 6 May it was learned that the German Government was arranging a general armistice. Worst of all, reports began to circulate about the death of Hitler, perhaps by his own hand, a scenario that was 'incomprehensible' to stalwarts of the Skorzeny stripe, particularly since part of the reason for maintaining the National Redoubt had been to provide the *Führer* with a point of refuge. Hitler, they cried, 'had left us in the lurch'. Members of one SKA platoon, on learning the news, drank themselves into a stupor. One young recruit had a fit of hysterics and slashed apart a wall hanging.

As these storm clouds gathered, Skorzeny toyed with the notion of suicide or of a getaway, perhaps via a Ju 88 based on one of the airfields still in German hands. He later claimed that senior German bankers and officials offered him the opportunity to fly several long-range aircraft to Argentina, along with $14,000,000 worth of gold, but that he refused, believing his future was in Germany. He also thought about going underground, which was discussed on 7–8 May during a staff conference in the Theodor Körner Hütte near Annaberg. It was concluded, however, that Skorzeny's height and distinctive appearance would make this option difficult, particularly since the Allies had plastered Western Europe with 'Skorzeny wanted' posters, and that the only practical option was to surrender the SKA as a group. It was assumed that the Western Allies were on the verge of fighting the Soviets and might accept the SKA with open arms. This was Skorzeny's final mistake as a unit commander, but it suggests that he never abandoned the anti-Soviet objectives of his brief. He merely concluded that the best chance of carrying forward the mission was to obtain sanction from former enemies in the West.

The decision to approach the Allies set in motion a comedy of errors and suggested that Skorzeny might not have enjoyed as much cachet as he imagined. He heard that the Americans were searching for him, but when he finally presented himself to the enemy, no one seemed to notice. On 10 May, while American and French officers reconnoitred

Annaberg, Skorzeny showed up in person, offering to gather his SKA detachments and have them join *Obergruppenführer* Gille's Sixth SS *Panzer* Corps. He feared that the spatial disposition of his troops would suggest that they had been deployed as guerrillas, and he was probably also scared that some of the groups would engage in unauthorised action or that they might disband spontaneously unless they were integrated into a larger mass. The Allied officers showed no interest in this proposal and they left town without issuing any instructions.

By 12 May, a company of American troops had arrived at Annaberg and Skorzeny decided to try again. He sent a messenger to the town, graciously informing the garrison commander not to bother looking for him and his men; he would present himself voluntarily in a few days and at that time he would appreciate the use of an American jeep so that he could travel to the headquarters of the US Third Infantry Division in Salzburg, where he would arrange the surrender of his men. On 16 May, Skorzeny, Radl, Hunke and their interpreter, a former *Luftwaffe* parachutist named Herbert Petter, strode into town, still bearing their sidearms, and they were provided with a US jeep that carried them to Salzburg. It was humbling that no one at the US divisional headquarters had any idea who Skorzeny was. To the US officer handling the case, his opposite number was an obscure lieutenant-colonel who wanted a pass to go back into the mountains and gather up stragglers. Since Skorzeny's request had not set off alarm bells, a US junior officer, Lieutenant McLean, was attached to Skorzeny's party and the group was sent to St Johann im Pongau in order to get passes from the German *Ortskommandant*. These documents would give the commando chief official access to the hills. It was only in the course of this drive that it finally dawned on McLean that he was sitting beside the infamous 'prince of saboteurs', stalker of Eisenhower and general menace to the peace and security of Europe. McLean then left the group in order to return to Salzburg, telling Skorzeny to proceed to Werfen, where his passes would be countersigned by US personnel. It is not clear whether McLean alerted the authorities at Werfen about his charge's identity, but Skorzeny was certainly recognised when he arrived to get his passes verified. In an excited phone call to divisional headquarters, staff officers of the 15th Infantry Regiment claimed that they had 'intercepted' Skorzeny.

Much to Skorzeney's chagrin, his US captors ordered him disarmed, arrested and handcuffed, and his watch was stolen. This seemed unsporting. On the following day, he was brought to the headquarters of the local CIC detachment and paraded like a lion in chains. By the time he appeared before a gaggle of reporters, he was clenching his jaw and glowering at his guards. 'You treat me', he carped, 'as if I were a common criminal.' Apparently, the Americans were not interesting in cultivating him as an ally against the Red Army.

Shortly before his capture, Skorzeny had detached Werner Hunke from his party. Hunke was told that if Skorzeny and Radl had not returned within three hours, he should report to a nearby SKA detachment at Radstadt and order the group to dissolve, giving individual personnel the option of either surrendering or returning home.[89] It is possible that Hunke subsequently obeyed this injunction, although he was captured at Salzburg on 22 May and it is clear that not all the widely scattered SKA detachments received a stand-down order. An eyewitness account of the experiences of one such squad depicts this post-surrender period as both romantic and sordid. Members of this group occupied a draughty tool shed in the hills near Innsbruck, where they lived the lives of Neolithic tribesmen, cooking on an improvised hearth and huddling together at night for warmth. Sometimes they would have their BdM attendant read passages by Hölderlin and Weinheber, but they also spent much time in an alcoholic haze, since they had been careful to stash nearby supplies of brandy and champagne. As time passed, members of the detachment grew more mercenary and when the local SKA commander showed them a cache of jewels that had been looted from Hungary, supposedly in order to fund future operations, they began to entertain thoughts more befitting bandits than military men. More than once they considered forcing their chief to divide the valuables between the men of the band, using their pistols to enforce the demand. Most members of the group eventually left for home or they attempted to hide amidst surrendering columns of German troops, although they were still organised enough in early June 1945 to establish a field hospital in a winter sports hostel. This facility was intended to serve several squads, which suggests that other detachments were still in the field and that these groups remained in contact.[90]

Eventually, the Americans tracked down the surviving SKA detachments. One advantage derived from the arrest of Skorzeny was that they recovered ten passes that had been issued at St Johann and indicated the identity of SKA platoon commanders and the rough whereabouts of their retinues.[91] The Americans organised aerial reconnaissance of the mountains, sent out patrols and burned watch fires at night. In June 1945, an undercover agent provided information about the SKA supply dump at Achtal. Austrian freedom fighters also helped by arresting suspected SKA members, including several men who had begged help from Alpine dairywomen and had begun living as their tenants.[92] The US 80th Division also employed a senior German officer, *General* Fabriunke, chief of Third Corps, in order to scour the mountains and negotiate the surrender of isolated SS groups. After several days of work, Fabriunke brought in Hubert Schürmann, chief of the SKA's *Sturmzug* 'Schürmann', and the young SS lieutenant agreed to lead his entire unit – forty-four soldiers and four women – to Alt Aussee. This capitulation was important because Schürmann's baggage, which was seized by the Americans, contained a map outlining the location of several SKA huts. In addition, one of the detachment's members, sabotage expert Hans Manderschied, revealed the existence of the huge arms and ammunition depot in Mitterberghütten. Manderschied, who had fought on the Eastern Front and lost a brother in combat, had returned home on furlough to find that the Nazi authorities had sterilised his father. He was only too happy to help the Americans, even volunteering to personally defuse booby traps around *Jagdverband* weapons caches. The dump at Mitterberghütten was subsequently overrun by American troops and its material confiscated, along with a log book detailing the dates that weapons and explosives had been charged out of the facility and the names of *Jagdverband* and *Werwolf* officers to whom this equipment had been entrusted.

The comportment of Schürmann and his officers is a story in itself. Allied interrogation reports suggest that the troops 'were in an arrogant frame of mind', that Schürmann was 'still an arrogant Nazi' and that he was hesitant to reveal information. On 12 May, when Schürmann first met with an American delegate in order to discuss his surrender, he pointed out that his unit was supposed to fight the Soviets and that it wanted to undertake this mission in coordination with Anglo-American forces. When the American negotiator, Major Ralph Pearson, pointed out that Schürmann had been ordered to capitulate by his own chain of command, Schürmann retorted that 'the high command is not always right', a heresy that caused Fabriunke to blush. 'We had quite a conference', Pearson later noted in his diary.[93]

Toward the end of his life, Skorzeny claimed that he had often been asked why he had resisted so long, a question he answered by saying that survivors of a shipwreck will swim as long as they can.[94] The real issue, however, is *not* why Skorzeny stayed in the field until 16 May 1945, but why he did not persevere even longer, leading the SKA to fulfil its ultimate rationale as a guerrilla force. Karl Patel suggests that Skorzeny was a robot – a professional soldier rather than a National Socialist fanatic – and that he ceased to function once there were no more orders to follow.[95] This seems a misinterpretation. In truth, Skorzeny was a Nazi militant and terrorist, and he was hardly hesitant about making decisions without reference to the chain of command. Even before the end of the war, he had begun to will the independent deployment and positioning of his forces.

On the other hand, Skorzeny was not a mercenary nor, as Schellenberg claimed, a '*Landsknecht* who would probably cause a great deal of mischief while the German people would have to foot the bill'.[96] To get a true sense of his decision to surrender, we must have the full measure of Skorzeny as an ideologue. Despite occasional flourishes of Jungerian existentialism – he adopted Nietzsche's motto, '*Lebe gefährlich*', and announced in late March 1945 that since the war was lost, it was time 'to die in splendour'[97] – Skorzeny was not a nihilist. In fact, he did not see war as an end in itself but as an instrument of revolutionary politics. This was what it meant to be a 'political soldier'. As a result, once Hitler was dead and the Nazi movement was in abeyance, the need for violent resistance correspondingly diminished.

Two other factors also entered into this equation. First, Skorzeny realised that he had little public support in the Alps. In fact, an SS report on 1 May 1945 noted that any attempt to fight in the Alps lent importance to 'the political attitude of the local population', but that the indicators were unfavourable: 'Everything that helps to prolong the war is rejected. Slogans of the Viennese opposition government and of the clergy are being followed.'[98] Skorzeny himself had contributed to the development of this mood by manhandling the population, and the popular attitude toward guerrilla operations grew even more hostile after the war was over.[99] Partisan warfare is problematic without some degree of public support. Second, as noted above, Skorzeny hoped that he might find new patrons in the shape of the Western Allies (although he was soon disabused of this notion).

In the final analysis, Skorzeny refused to wage guerrilla warfare *or* to end his existence *or* to take flight. Rather, having shot the last arrow in his quiver, he performed one of the few laudable acts of his career and attempted to surrender his forces as a coherent whole.

Epilogue and Conclusion

With Skorzeny in custody after 16 May 1945, the occupying powers let down their guard and Skorzeny began spinning the innocuous narrative that he would continue to relate until his death in 1975. He was a simple soldier, he explained, *not* a Nazi true believer; moreover, his career should be considered in light of several high profile commando missions that he had carried out, *not* as a pattern of consistent support for subversion and terrorism. By July 1945, the British, at least, were becoming convinced that the one-time scourge of Europe was no longer a threat: 'Skorzeny personally has been somewhat overestimated. A "man of action" with a penchant for the dramatic, it is considered unlikely that he could have organised any effective measures for post-occupational underground work.'[1]

This contention was overly optimistic. Although Skorzeny had lambasted Schellenberg in February 1945 because the latter was already talking about the need for post-war preparations, within several weeks the pressure of events had forced Skorzeny himself to undertake such planning. In March 1945, he met with Hitler Youth leaders in order to discuss the training and deployment of boys on post-war missions, and Besekow admitted as early as January that Germany had lost the war and that preparations were increasingly focussed on the post-war period. *Jagdverband* agents would supposedly lie low until receiving a general signal, after which they would rise up in a campaign of assassination, sabotage and insurrection.[2]

Skorzeny particularly fixed his attention on *Jagdverband Nordwest*, the relatively most intact of his units and the formation most heavily manned by Nordic specimens who were supposed to have a racial bond of affinity to the Third Reich. It is likely that *Nordwest's* training of Hitler Youth boys at Killeschowitz resulted from Skorzeny's talks with the Reich Youth Leadership Staff, the latter having laid plans for a far-reaching post-war resistance movement. In addition, *Nordwest* developed a network of safe-houses, contact points and Alpine hideouts, some of which were still operating after the end of the war, and the unit also established relationships with bankers and businessmen who could provide funding long after the paymasters of the Third Reich had ceased functioning. Skorzeny *Leute* spied on German communists and one ex-*Jagdverband* officer, Walter Peters, murdered a socialist youth organiser in north-western Germany. A *Nordwest* '*Einsatzgruppe*' was still operating in Hamburg in 1948 and one veteran of the formation later recalled running missions as late as 1962![3] The Americans got a glimpse of this organisation when three former *Jagdverband* troopers, including chief of staff Wilhelm Walter, were captured while searching for valuables that had been cached near Annaberg during the last days of the war. One of these prisoners turned informer and told the US authorities about an evolving organisation of former *Jagdverband* and Brandenburg personnel who were maintaining contact and helping their fellows evade capture. The Americans made further arrests, but most of the detainees held up well under interrogation, denying any wrongdoing. The CIC felt that some of these men knew far more than they were willing to admit, but failure to pry them open eventually prompted senior echelons to order their release. Thus terminated Operation 'Brandy', the only formal Allied investigation of the post-war Skorzeny network.[4]

During the early phase of the *Jagdverbände's* afterlife, Skorzeny was still under lock and key. He spent much of 1946–1947 defending himself from a war crimes indictment – the Americans considered his Ardennes jeep units to have operated outside the rules of war – but this challenge was not enough to keep him out of trouble, particularly since he reckoned that he might need to escape should he be faced with a sentence of capital punishment. By August 1946, Skorzeny had established contact with an elaborate underground railway, some members of which were holding his personal belongings, weapons and treasure. The Polish guard detail at the Dachau Holding Camp, Skorzeny's place of internment, was made up partly of right-wing anti-communists who aided such contact, at least for a price, and were willing to act as couriers. In addition, Skorzeny, ever the rogue, charmed a number of female camp secretaries and interpreters and he maintained secret communications with women outside camp wire, particularly his wife and mistresses. Although Skorzeny could have availed himself of this network's services, he decided to forego escaping because he felt that the Allies would devote endless resources to tracking a target of his stature. In any case, once the US authorities discovered the breadth of his contacts, they isolated him in solitary confinement, doubled his guard and inserted more informers into his vicinity, especially amidst his Polish guard detail.[5]

On 9 February 1947, Skorzeny was acquitted of war crimes by an American military tribunal in Dachau, although he was still detained on the basis of his membership in the SS, which after the Nuremberg verdicts was defined as an illegal organisation. He also faced a denazification hearing.[6] Nonetheless, Skorzeny's relationship with the Western Allies began to warm. Many Allied officers and enlisted men were already sympathetic, having bought his 'I-was-only-a-soldier' line.[7] The Americans allowed Skorzeny to reunite with his aide, Karl Radl, and in March 1948 both men were transferred to German custody and moved to the Darmstadt Civilian Internment Enclosure, where the circumstances of their confinement became more pleasant. On at least one occasion, Skorzeny was released on furlough and travelled into the Alps without CIC surveillance. Although Skorzeny had earlier asked the Americans to relocate him in Austria, he now professed a reluctance to return to his homeland, claiming that he had heard about aggressive local operations by the MGB and that he feared being snatched by Soviets. He also began to complain about 'communists' spying on him. As a result, he escaped from the Darmstadt Camp on 26 July 1948, leaving Radl to explain that he had grown weary of repeated postponements of his denazification hearing and that he feared 'outside elements' were intervening to prevent him from getting a fair trial. Security at the Darmstadt Camp was so poor that the door was open to anyone intent on leaving.[8] In fact, the camp commandant simply let Skorzeny walk through the gate, and even lent the commando chief a car and driver so that he could catch his train on time.[9]

After Skorzeny's getaway, he re-entered the shadowy world of the Nazi underground and the contours of the story become blurred. There were 'Skorzeny sightings' at many locations, and it is almost certain that he visited Argentina, even if he did not live there.[10] He later told a gathering of German neo-fascists that he had hidden in the home of a German right-wing politician and then spent eight months in Paris, where he was protected by a sympathetic *Sûreté* officer.[11] At one point, he was staying in a pension in Saint-Germain-en-Laye under the alias 'Rolf Steiner', but in a famous incident he was snapped by a news photographer while strolling along the Champs Élysées, arm in arm with a female escort.[12] He then beat a hasty retreat from Paris and his protector was dismissed from his post. In the autumn of 1949 it came to light that Skorzeny had been making periodic visits to the remote Bavarian hamlet of Sutten, where he let a room and was occasionally seen studying Spanish or addressing a huge volume of correspondence from Iberia and Latin America. An exposé in a Bavarian newspaper suggested that he had already used this base in order to hold meetings with a network of active Nazis calling themselves '*Organisation Spinne*' ('Spider').[13]

In 1950, Skorzeny established a permanent residence in Madrid, where he rented a flat and became a social lion. At the same time, he left his faithful wife Emmi – he no longer needed her participation in maintaining an escape line – and he entered into a common-law relationship with a Bavarian countess, Ilsa Ludwig Finkenstein, the niece of financial tycoon Hjalmar Schacht. Skorzeny and Finkenstein wed in March 1954. Skorzeny's financial circumstances were initially poor and he was visibly happy if offered a bottle of scotch or a carton of American cigarettes, but the favour of the Franco regime and the increasingly cosy relationship with Schacht soon paid handsome dividends. In fact, he soon came to earn a good living through engineering and real estate, particularly through commissions for selling equipment to the Spanish national rail corporation. By 1954, he was living in a villa, where he entertained lavishly, and he was also operating an office with a small staff. Most importantly, however, he emerged as an 'arms merchant' and recruiter of mercenaries, a line of work that fit comfortably with his ongoing role as '*Spinne*' mastermind.[14]

After settling in Spain, Skorzeny established a complicated set of relationships with the espionage services of the major powers. In the late 1940s, he had been protected by the *Service de Documentation Extérieure et de Contre Espionage* (SDECE), but he later claimed that he had broken all ties to the French and that the separation had not been amicable.[15] He then had contact with a number of American officers and agents, particularly the air attaché in Madrid, and he was held in high esteem by some of his former captors in the CIC, although he regarded that organisation as being riddled with 'communists'. Skorzeny admired J. Edgar Hoover and wanted to work with the FBI, which briefly considered his offer, but he was scorned by the CIA, the new centre of power in the American intelligence community. The CIA judged him too famous and too vocal, the Berlin station noting that '[he] has never been taken seriously except by American journalists'. The 'agency' favoured the more low-key Reinhard Gehlen, who became the chosen instrument of US anti-communist intrigues in Central and Eastern Europe, and in 1951 Skorzeny embarrassed himself by trying to sell faulty intelligence about Soviet penetration of the West German Government. The affair suggested either that he had been defrauded by his contacts in Germany or that he was consciously attempting to deceive the Americans. The Gehlen Organisation, originally a dependency of the CIA, shared the low opinion of Skorzeny and had little contact with him.

Even more unsettling, Skorzeny was rumoured to have been recruited in 1944 by Viktor Abakumov, chief of Soviet military counter-intelligence (SMERSH), and Abakumov had supposedly used him to penetrate Nazi stay-behind networks. Indeed, Gottlob Berger told American interrogators in 1945 that Skorzeny had betrayed German projects in Slovakia and Romania. The fact that the Soviets held Skorzeny's brother, Alfred, until 1955 suggests that they had some means of exercising leverage. Skorzeny did not help his cause by maintaining relationships with a number of friends and former comrades-in-arms who were suspected of working for the Soviets. In addition, he occasionally warned that the anti-communist zeal of German officers could sour, were their needs not served, and despite his anti-Soviet rhetoric, by the mid-1950s he was parroting the 'neutralisation' theme then popular among German nationalists.[16]

By the early 1950s, Skorzeny was predicting an imminent East–West war, precipitated either by a direct Soviet onslaught or by uprisings of German, French and Italian communists. In either case, NATO forces would be forced into a headlong retreat to Britain or Iberia. Given this expectation, he offered to train German military cadres in Spain, creating a structure that could absorb the mass of a retreating German Army, and to form a commando corps to support guerrilla warfare by stay-behind networks throughout Europe, even in countries already behind the Iron Curtain. He claimed to have contact with exiles, such as Romanian Legionaries, who could support such a project. In other words, he wanted to re-establish the *Jagdverbände*. The Spanish General Staff expressed interest in the scheme, but asked for evidence of American support, which was lacking. In order to organise a project of such a scale, Skorzeny also needed good relations with non-Nazi officers who were planning to rebuild German military capacity, but he instead aligned himself with General Heinz Guderian and a surviving cabal of Nazi hardliners. These two groups were at odds over the legacy of the July 20th Conspiracy.[17] In January 1951, the West German chancellor, Konrad Adenauer, complained about apparent American support for Skorzeny and warned that the ex-commando chief was working to revive National Socialism.[18]

As part of his scheme for a Spanish redoubt, Skorzeny established close relations with German neo-Nazis, some of whom were maintaining youth groups that could play a role in stay-behind operations. Skorzeny saw the Federal Republic as an unstable entity, similar to its Weimar predecessor, and he believed that former soldiers were especially bitter. Indeed, he wanted to build a right-wing bloc of parties potentially capable of toppling the new structure, and he confided to a friend that he thought it his destiny to one day lead a revived German state. In the meantime, he had connections with the Socialist Reich Party (SRP), which was making electoral progress in the northern part of West Germany, although he worried about the SRP's lack of clandestine nature. His preference was to support Goebbels's former deputy Werner Naumann, whose circle of neo-Nazi conspirators was attempting to infiltrate centrist parties, such as the Free Democrats. Both these forces were dealt a blow in 1952–1953 when the SRP was banned by the West German authorities and Naumann and his chief collaborators were arrested by the British.[19] The Federal Republic had proven more durable than anticipated.

With prospects in Europe looking increasingly dim, Skorzeny shifted attention to the Arab world, where there were fresh opportunities to support a brand of 'national socialism' and radical anti-Semitism. After receiving a request from the Egyptian military attaché in Madrid, he began recruiting former German officers to train the Egyptian Army, an activity in which, for once, he was supported by the CIA and the Gehlen Organisation. In 1953, Skorzeny started visiting Egypt on a regular basis, being entertained by General Naguib and Colonel Nasser. While his main concern was to flog Spanish weapons, he also provided advice on anti-British guerrilla warfare in the Suez Canal Zone and he apparently reconnoitred the terrain. It is possible that he procured trainers for the Palestinian *Fedayeen*, and Ilsa Skorzeny later claimed that her husband was on good terms with Yasser Arafat.[20] By 1954, there were rumours that he had been approached by the Arab League in order to rescue Morocco's ex-Sultan, Sidi Muhammad ben Youssef, who had been deposed by the French and detained in exile.[21] In the same year, French newspapers charged that Skorzeny was smuggling guns to Algerian rebels and that his Egyptian commandos were training guerrillas for service in French North Africa. He was lucky not to have been killed by the SDECE, which launched a counter-terror campaign against anyone connected with the insurgents. One of his gun-running associates, Wilhelm Beisner, was badly injured by a car bomb.[22]

If Skorzeny was ever involved in such intrigues, by the late 1950s and early 1960s he had decided to change sides. Convinced by the argument that a right-wing recoil against decolonisation could be exploited to revive European fascism, he linked '*die Spinne*' to white supremacist advocates of French Algeria and Belgian neo-colonialists supporting the Congo's breakaway province of Katanga. Skorzeny had long been interested in central and southern Africa, and he helped train thirty Katangan commandos at a base in Spain. He often visited South Africa, which had a political system much to his liking and where he had friendships with senior apartheidists and fascist leaders. In 1963 he also helped the Mossad, introducing two of their agents to a rocket scientist working for the Egyptians and promising to help convince German technical experts to withdraw from the country. In this case, however, Skorzeny may have been fooled by a 'false flag' deception, since the Mossad operatives had introduced themselves as 'NATO officials'.

By the early 1960s, the maniacal pace at which Skorzeny had led his life was starting to wane. Now in his fifties, he increasingly spent time at his estate in Ireland. The snatching of Adolf Eichmann scared him and there were more legal problems, as the Jewish community in Vienna accused him of having killed Sachsenhausen concentration camp inmates in order to test poison bullets. There were also new questions about his participation in the murder of Austrian civilians near the end of the war. The Austrian regime, which consistently worked to obscure the country's record during World War Two, refused to extradite Skorzeny and hoped that he would keep a low profile, although he then held a press conference to deny all charges. By the late 1960s, he was ill. In 1970, he survived a six-hour operation to remove a cancerous growth at the top of his spinal column, although his recovery was long and painful and he never recovered his full vigour. After a lifetime of tumultuous villainy, he died *not* in a hail of bullets, but in a quiet Madrid hospital ward, spitting up blood from cancerous lungs. He was sixty-seven years of age.[23]

As for Skorzeny's fighters, they scattered across Europe and the Americas. Some prospered, others struggled; some remained right-wing radicals, even founding new fascist parties,[24] others drifted ideologically. Karl Radl followed Skorzeny's lead by escaping from the Darmstadt Civilian Enclosure. After attempting to mediate between Skorzeny and the CIC, he was recaptured in 1949 and was eventually hired by SDECE. This service estranged him from Skorzeny (along with the fact that he cast doubt on some of his former chief's more fantastic stories).[25] Robert Verbelen and Walter Girg worked for the CIC, as did Ludwig Nebel, although the Americans gave up Nebel to the Danes, who wanted to try him for participation in the *Schalburgtage*, particularly the assassination of Kai Munk. In 1949, he was sentenced to a twelve-year term of imprisonment.[26] Ladislav Niznansky was recruited by Radio Free Europe. In 2004, he was tried for his crimes with the 'Edelweiss' unit, but he was released by a German court due to lapses of memory by a key witness. Károly Ney also moved to West Germany and began smuggling arms into Eastern Europe. At the time of the 1956 Hungarian Uprising, he tried to recruit Hungarian refugees for guerrilla warfare.[27] In Sweden, Carl Edquist continued his career as a fascist rabble-rouser and one of his anti-Social Democratic screeds was found by Swedish police in the home of Christer Pettersson, who was suspected of complicity in the murder of Prime Minister Olaf Palme.[28] Otto Begus gravitated to the opposite pole, apparently labouring on contract for the Soviet intelligence service.[29] Xhafer Deva retreated to private life, moving to California and becoming an administrator at Stanford University.[30]

Sixty years after the events described in this volume, and thirty years after Skorzeny's passing, one must wonder if any of it still matters. Can the experience of SS special forces tell us anything significant about our contemporary understanding of war and peace? Did the lives of Skorzeny and his fighters make the world any different than would have been the case had they never existed? What were the historical consequences of the Skorzeny units and how should their legacy fit into our culture? The question of questions, as one historian put it, is what parts of the 'exploded past' will gravitate into the present. After some consideration, there are three factors that spring to mind.

First, the Skorzeny *Leute* had limited success in encouraging anti-communist guerrilla warfare, mainly in Central and Eastern Europe. The fact that significant partisan groups eventually worked their way to the Germans – or, like the AK, they considered doing so – definitely wears the shine off the reputation of such movements. The pro-Allied mythology originally surrounding groups like the Chetniks and the UPA has already eroded, particularly because of work done by historians during the 1960s and 1970s; it is now time to face facts even more openly. On the other hand, such turns toward the Germans do not suggest affection for the Third Reich or its principles, but signify only a measure of desperate expediency. In addition, Skorzeny and his colleagues never controlled nationalist guerrilla groups, but tried to exploit whatever elements seemed willing to collaborate, even if only in the loosest fashion. Stewart Menzies noted in December 1944 'that… the [German] penetration of resistance movements is more likely to consist of joining in trouble and converting [it] into a shooting affair than of actual participation in the councils of the resistance movements'.[31] It will also be recalled that the German special services were not averse to infiltrating communist partisan groups and militias if they thought such a strategy could serve their purposes.

What was the final result of such policies? – extra death, destruction and loss of property added to the great tide of such malaise that had already engulfed Europe since

1939. In the east, the advancing Soviets met guerrilla threats with violent reprisals and deportations, especially in West Ukraine, the Baltic States, Poland and Romania, while in Yugoslavia Tito's forces dealt with domestic enemies through large-scale massacres and 'death marches'. Even in Western Europe, the perception of a continuing fascist peril encouraged a severe round of purges, the initial phases of which were carried through in extra-legal form. In France and Italy, a combined total of 20,000 to 25,000 people died through such means, some as late as 1946 or 1947.[32] In exchange for prompting such outrages, the Germans obtained minimal strategic or even tactical benefits.

It is easy to see the tragic consequences of guerrilla warfare if we focus upon the forms sponsored by Skorzeny, particularly since we are accustomed to seeing all things Nazi from a critical perspective. The bitter truth, however, is that such criticisms apply to nearly all forms of guerrilla warfare and violent resistance, even the sort undertaken by the pro-Allied movements that proliferated during the Second World War. In any situation short of genocide, deportation or massive social dislocation, one must think long and hard about the moral rectitude of individually raising the cudgel against conquering armies or occupation garrisons. Unless the invaders are in an extraordinarily weak position, little of military value is gained, while on the other hand, individuals and small groups – at most militant minorities – have assumed the state's monopoly of violence and have done so without benefit of the social contract or any other form of legitimating authority, although they are hardly alone in bearing the cost. Innocents are typically killed in the crossfire or, worse yet, the occupying power reacts with collective reprisals that are predictable (and sometimes anticipated). After the Second World War, resistance existentialists argued that the importance of an insurgent act lay in its symbolic and ethical value rather than in its consequences, but this is sophistry in a world of flesh-and-blood human beings. As time passes, a new breed of historians, such as Claudio Pavone, Rab Bennett and Tzvetan Todorov, are gradually unwrapping the Second World War resistance groups from the romantic gauze that has so long cocooned them, and we are developing an understanding of such movements that is more critical than past appreciations, but also more balanced.[33]

A second reason that we should consider the importance of Skorzeny's forces involves the Cold War, which certainly must rate as the dominant geopolitical phenomenon of the late twentieth century. Of course, 'realists' will assert that the Cold War arose from the structural nature of international relations, and that it would have occurred with or without the activity of Skorzeny's units. This contention may be true, although it smacks of determinism and it has often been pointed out, most famously by A.J.P. Taylor, that it is the responsibility of historians to identify the particular causes of events as well as the more general reasons why they occur.[34] Certainly there is no doubt that the *Jagdverbände*, the *Zweierorganisation* and their guerrilla allies helped affect the timing and nature of the Cold War. Skorzeny stood at a suspicious proximity to some of the key incidents of the early Cold War, including the downfall of the Radescu regime in Romania, the weapons-stashing affair in Finland and the secret civil war in Poland. In Soviet Russia, the vigorous reassertion of Communist Party prerogatives in 1945–1946 was linked to nationalist underground resistance along the western fringe of the Soviet state, and in Slovakia remnants of an underground once supported by Skorzeny provided an excuse for the Czechoslovak coup d'état of February 1948, which destroyed Eastern Europe's last surviving democracy. In France and Italy, fifth column attacks caused national crises and led to fears of retaliatory communist vigilantism. All of these episodes heightened the level of tension within the Anglo–American–Soviet coalition and created a pattern of mutual distrust.

Lest we conclude that such events only served German interests in a coincidental and unanticipated fashion, it is worth noting that in September 1944 Hitler cast a pox on the houses of both his enemies (east and west): 'From the political point of view', he advised, 'it is hoped that wherever we withdraw we can kindle and fan strife between communist and nationalist forces.' *Generaloberst* Jodl added that such a coming to blows would hopefully draw in the 'Anglo-Saxons' and the 'Bolsheviks', each on opposite sides.[35] As an essential part of this strategy, Skorzeny was ordered to make use of *agents provocateurs* in trying to cause clashes between Germany's foes. Thus, near the end of the war we find the 'Polish Brigade' ordered to masquerade as 'pro-Soviet agents' in Bohemia, thereby to annoy the Americans, while the same strategy was also used against the Soviets by dropping *Jagdverband* parachutists behind Russian lines in American uniforms.[36] Near Trieste, Ustashe bands were assembled with the intent of embroiling the Western Allies in clashes with the Titoists.[37]

There is a great book waiting to be written about how the Germans systematically began efforts in 1943 to crack the Allied-Soviet alliance and about the degree to which this policy aggravated Cold War animosities. Such a volume would fit admirably into a strain of Cold War historiography that has been termed 'pericentric' and which refuses to privilege the bipolar nature of power characteristically emphasised by earlier literature. Rather, the new focus is upon the impact of local events and regional actors.[38] There is no doubt that Nazi Germany qualified as such a 'third force' and that it was desperate to see a violent unravelling of the Allied-Soviet entente.

Use of Skorzeny's forces was only one device in a larger Nazi repertoire of tactics designed to bring about the desired effect. The Germans spread rumours and disinformation, suggesting (and half-believing) that many British and American POWs in eastern Germany would fight advancing Soviet forces if armed to do so.[39] The Gestapo attempted to use its infiltration of Soviet spy networks in order to stir up East-West animosities, warning the British of sinister Soviet plots.[40] Press and radio propaganda was exploited in an artful fashion, particularly to alert British and Commonwealth opinion to the dangers of a 'Bolshevised' Germany,[41] and to convince such constituencies that a powerful and independent Reich would prevent an 'Iron Curtain' from descending across the European continent. Winston Churchill's celebrated employment of this exact terminology, which was used by Joseph Goebbels and Count Schwerin von Krosigk in 1945,[42] suggests the way in which Nazi thinking came to permeate a wider Western discourse about Soviet power, almost by osmosis. The intelligence section of the Canadian First Army warned, for instance, that a Nazi-created 'Bolshevik Bogey' had caused consternation among Canadian troops in north-western Europe.[43] In the last weeks of the war, the Foreign Office and Propaganda Ministry tried to organise 'high level' radio broadcasts 'for the English governing class, with the object of exhibiting the critical situation of Europe, and in particular of England, in consequence of subservience to Bolshevism'.[44]

Beginning in September 1944, the Germans also began floating a number of cease-fire proposals involving belligerent forces in Italy and the Balkans and specifically designed to lure the Western Allies away from the Soviets. The underlying theme in all such initiatives was that the Germans should be allowed to disengage troops so that they could redeploy these forces along the Eastern Front and thus perform a service to all of 'Western Civilisation'. Supplementary propaganda appealed to the West not to 'stab Germany in the back'. In fact, there was a disruption of Soviet-American relations when Stalin eventually charged that the Germans were exploiting negotiations in Italy in order to send troops eastwards, supposedly with the tacit connivance of the Americans, although this ugly affair was not sufficient to destroy the Grand Alliance.[45] There is no doubt that the Third Reich tossed countless coins into this wishing well, but the major yield was post-mortem.

There was also one final way in which Skorzeny and his men added to the general insecurity of the modern world. The *Jagdverbände* and its sister agencies provided the network of contacts behind '*die Spinne*', which by 1949 was developing as one of the main Nazi escape lines and self-help agencies. Skorzeny had '*Spinne*' ties with Prince Valerio Borghese, his Italian counterpart and an officer with whom he had worked during the war. Borghese had long impressed Skorzeny with his 'European' outlook and was an important contact because he helped lead the MSI, which carried considerable electoral weight in post-war Italy. In fact, ex-*Sturmbannführer* Hass, one of Skorzeny's troubleshooters in wartime Italy, served as '*die Spinne*' liaison officer with Borghese. After Borghese launched a failed coup against the Italian Government, Skorzeny welcomed him into exile in Madrid.[46] During the war, Skorzeny had also made the acquaintance of Belgian fascist chief Léon Degrelle, and he too became an important crony in Madrid. As early as 1947, Degrelle was organising armed Nazis who smuggled former SS personnel through Switzerland and into Spain.[47] Degrelle also set up skeletal partisan networks south of the Pyrenees, with the hope that 'legionaries' manning this system could be activated in case of the outbreak of a new European war.[48] With the formation of '*die Spinne*', Degrelle became Skorzeny's collaborator, a crucial relationship because he still had a following among a small fringe of Belgian and French fascists. Skorzeny had a similar rapport with Horia Sima, leader-in-exile of the Iron Guard. Sima arrived in Madrid in 1951 and began begging arms, money and medicine for guerrillas that he claimed were still holding out in the mountains of his homeland.[49]

As suggested by these lines of contact, Skorzeny subscribed to a brand of post-war fascism that had pan-European tendencies and reflected the internationalist trends that had emerged in the SS during the Second World War. In 1951, Skorzeny brought neo-fascist organiser Jean Beauverd to Madrid, where he secured him a job as a journalist. Beauverd's 'European Social Movement' organised one of the first post-war gatherings of international fascists, which was held at the Alcázar. Skorzeny and Degrelle were both in attendance.[50] Such inclinations were further signalled by Skorzeny's association with the 'New European Order', another umbrella group of neo-fascist movements, and by his vague ties with neo-fascist organiser Otto Karl Düpow, whose aim was to inspire a right-wing Atlanticism broad enough to include Charles de Gaulle and Barry Goldwater. Skorzeny also had contact with Jean-François Thiriart, a Belgian veteran of his special forces and leader of the '*Jeune Europe*' movement. Thiriart was originally a strident opponent of decolonisation, although he then swung to the left and attempted to link his group to the Romanians, the Chinese and the Iraqis, seeking support for a guerrilla war to liberate Western Europe from American domination. Skorzeny sympathised, but even he realised that this scheme was unworkable.[51]

'*Die Spinne*' thus helped Eurofascism get off to a running start and it even managed to cultivate the participation of young people born after the war, who comprised a new generation of activists. It is significant that at the time of Skorzeny's interment in 1975, be-medalled greybeards (like Hans-Ulrich Rudel) stood in attendance side-by-side with young neo-Nazis and uniformed students.[52] Initiatives to mobilise a fresh crop of fascist militants had a marginal yield, although as Paul Wilkinson notes, it was amazing that fascism – with its blood-drenched history and odour of defeat – survived at all.[53] Skorzeny and Degrelle tutored violent young activists such as Michael Kühnen and Stefano delle Chiaie, who launched the 'black terrorism' of the late twentieth century. One of the Skorzeny *Leute*, Herbert Schweiger, provided counsel for the *Nationalistische Front*, a neo-Nazi organisation implicated in the round of attacks on foreigners and Jews that plagued post-reunification Germany.[54]

It was this effort, grounded in the *Jagdverbände* and resuscitated in '*die Spinne*', that formed the essential link between the 'old' fascism of the interwar era and the neo-fascism that is currently a nasty element in the political systems of many European states. Skorzeny and his collaborators attended the demise of the old movement, but they were also present at the creation of its successor.

In the end, the Skorzeny *Leute* had a limited impact, particularly if we measure their intentions against what they actually accomplished. There is no doubt, however, that through a range of nefarious means – right-wing guerrilla warfare, terrorism, provocation, the provision of escape routes, support for neo-fascism – they played a consistently negative role in modern European affairs. Their legacy is clear: although the German Nazis and their satellites were defeated in open battle in 1944–1945, their advocates would attempt to perpetuate the fight by any means available.

Glossary of Foreign Terms and Names

Abwehr	defence; German military intelligence
'Alles in Ordnung'	'Everything is okay'
Allgemeine	general
Alte Kämpfer	old fighter; Nazi Party activist from the pre-1933 period
Amis du Maréchal	Friends of the Marshal
andartes	Greek guerrilla bands
Anschluss	union; specifically, the German annexation of Austria
Arditi	Italian Army shock troops
Armija Krajowa	Home Army
Aufgabe (pl. *Aufgaben*)	task
Ausland	foreign
Auslandsdeutsche	'foreign' Germans
Ausweis	identity card
Balli Kombetar	National Front
Basmachi	Central Asian guerrilla bands
'Befehl ausgeführt'	'Orders carried out'
Bodenorganisation	ground organisation
Brigade Blanche	White Brigade
Bulldoggenaktion	bulldog action
Bund deutscher Mädel	Federation of German Girls
bundnisfähig	cooperative
Cagoule	'hooded ones'
Carabinieri	Italian gendarmerie
Chef	chief
chetas	Albanian guerrilla groups
Coeur de France	'Heart of France'
Comité de Libération de l'Empire	Liberation Committee for the Empire
Comité de Libération Française	French Liberation Committee
Comités Départementaux de la Libération	Departmental Committees of Liberation
compartimento	Italian administrative district
département	French administrative district
Deutschesnachrichtenbüro	German News Bureau
Deuxième Bureau	Second Bureau; French military intelligence
Deuxième Direction Belge	Belgian military intelligence
De Vlag (*Deutsch-Vlämische Arbeitsgemeinschaft*)	The Flag (German-Flemish Association)
Dienststelle (pl. *Dienststellen*)	office
Direction de la Surveillance du Territoire	Directorate for Territorial Surveillance
Efterretnings-Tjensten (ET)	intelligence service of the Schalburg Corps
Einheit	unit
Einsatz	action
Einsatzführer	operation chief
Einsatzstaffel	action staff
Einsatztruppe	action squads
épuration	cleansing; purges
Équipe	team, group
Federale	Republican Fascist Party district leaders
Feldgendarmerie	German military police
Feldjägerdienst	Weimar-era borderland guerrilla service

Fliegerkorps	Air Corps
Flottiglia	flotilla
franchi tiratori	civilian snipers
Freikorps	free corps
Frontaufklärung	front reconnaissance
Führung	leadership
Führungsgruppe	leadership group
Führungsstab	leadership staff
Funk und Sabotage Männer	radio and sabotage men
Gästhaus	guesthouse
Gau	Nazi Party region
Gauleiter	Nazi Party regional chief
Gauleitung	Nazi Party regional leadership
Geheimer Meldedienst	Secret Intelligence Service
Geheimer Zerstörungs Dienst	Secret Demolition Service
Gerarchi	hierarchs
Gruppe (pl. *Gruppen*)	group
Gruppenleiter	group leader
Gruppi d'Azioni Giovanile	Youth Action Groups
Guardie ai Labari	Guards of the Gonfalon
Guardia di Finanza	Department of Finance police
Guardia Nazionale Repubblicana	Republican National Guard
Hilfspolizei (Hipo)	Auxiliary Police
Hird	party militia of the *Nasjonal Samling*
Inland	domestic
Insurgierungsunternehmen	insurgency operation
Isänmaallinen Kansanliike	Patriotic People's Movement
Heimattreue Front	Homeland Patriot Front
Jagdeinsatz	*Jagdverband* company
Jagdkommando	*Jagdverband* platoon
Jagdschloss	hunting lodge
Jagdverbände (sing. *Jagdverband*)	SS Hunter Detachments; the four territorial *Jagdverbände* (with mainly foreign personnel) were *Ost* (East), *Südost* (South-East), *Südwest* (South-West) and *Nordwest* (North-West); *Jagdverband Mitte* (Centre) was comprised largely of German nationals
Jäger	hunter; rifleman
Jägerbatallion 502	Hunter Battalion 502
Jägerbatallion 600	Hunter Battalion 600
Jeune Europe	Young Europe
Judenfrei	'free of Jews'; euphemism for the condition after having purged or killed all Jews
Junkerschule	elite Nazi training academy
Kaiserreich	imperial Germany
Kampfgeschwader 200	*Luftwaffe* special formation; comprised of units 'Olga', 'Toska', 'Carmen' and 'Klara'
Kampfgruppe	battle group
Klein Kampf Verbände	German Navy special units
Kleinkrieg	small unit warfare
Kolkhozy	collective farms
Komitadji	committees; Macedonian guerrilla bands
Komitet Osvobozhdyeniya Narodov Rossi	Committee for the Liberation of the Peoples of Russia
Kopjás	pikemen
Kreisleiter	Nazi Party district chief
Kriegsmarine	German Navy
Kristallnacht	Nazi anti-Semitic pogrom (November 1938)
Lager	camp
Länder Beauftragter	area commissioners
Landsknecht	knight for hire; a mercenary
Légion des Volontaires Français	Legion of French Volunteers

Légion Wallonie	Wallonian Legion
Leute	people; personnel
Luftflotte	Air Fleet
Luftwaffe	German Air Force
Mairie	town hall
Maquis	bush; guerrilla bands
Maquisards	guerrillas
Marcia su Roma	March on Rome (October 1922)
Marechaussee	Dutch gendarmerie
Meldekopf	communications centre
Milice	Militia; members called *Miliciens*
Militärisches Amt	Military Office of the Reich Security Main Office
Mileter Tgänst	Military Intelligence Service
Ministersvo Gosudarstvennoye Bezopasnosti	Ministry of State Security
mosaïque de renseignements	mosaic of information
Movimento dei Giovani Italiani Repubblicani	Movement of Young Italian Republicans
Movimento Sociale Italiano	Italian Social Movement
Nachrichtenhelferinnen	female radio operators
Nachrichten- und Sabotagedienst	Communications and Sabotage Service
Nachschub	supply
nach Westen	'to the West'
Narodny Kommissariat Gosudarstvennoye Bezopasnosti	People's Commissariat for State Security
Narodowe Siły Zbrojne	National Armed Forces
Nasjonal Samling	National Gathering
National-Socialistische Beweging	National Socialist Movement
Netz	net; network
noeuds de résistance	resistance knots
nuclei di fascisti repubblicani	Republican Fascist nuclei
Oberkommando des Heeres	Army High Command
Oberkommando der Wehrmacht	Armed Forces High Command
Obrana	Croatian defence force
Oel Sabotage Abwehr Organisation	Oil Sabotage Defence Organisation
Orden	order
Organisation Révolutionaire Intérieure Française	Revolutionary Organisation of the French Interior
Organisation Technique	Technical Organisation
organizzazione V	Organisation V
Ostfront	Eastern Front
Ostheer	German Army on the Eastern Front
Odeljenje za Zaštitu Naroda	Department for the Protection of the People
Panzer	tank; armour
parachutage	parachutings
Parti National Breton	Breton National Party
Parti Populaire Français	French Popular Party
Parti Social Français	French Social Party
Partito Fascista Repubblicano	Republican Fascist Party
Personenabwurfgerät	three-man parachute drop container
Platzkommandant	Town Major
points d'appui	support centres
Rassemblement Nationale Populaire	National Popular Rally
Ratnitsi Napreduka na Bulgarshtinata	Guardians of the Advancement of the Bulgarian National Spirit
Referat	department
Reichsbahn	German railways
Reichsbank	German central bank
Reichsdeutsche	German nationals
Reichsführer-SS	head of the SS
Reichsgau	imperial territory
Reichskommissar	German civil commissar in an occupied country

Reichsrundfunk, Reichsfunk, Rundfunk	German radio
Reichssicherheitshauptamt	Reich Security Main Office
Reichswehr	Weimar-era German Army
Schutzkorps Alpenland	Alpine Guard Corps
Schutzstaffel	Guard Corps
segreto	secret
Service de Documentation Extérieur et de Contre Espionage	External Intelligence and Counter Espionage Service
Services de Contre-Parachutages	Counter-Parachutist Service
Services de Sécurité Militaire	Military Security Service
Sicherheitsdienst	SS Security Service
Sigurantza	Security Service
Skorpion	Scorpion; SS propaganda organisation; regional sections called *Ost* (East), *West* (West) and *Rheingau* (Rhine District)
Sonderauftrag	special task
Sonderabteilung, Sonderkommando, Sonderregiment	special unit
Sonderaktion, Sondereinsatz, Sonderunternehmen	special action
Sonderstab	special staff
Sotnia	100-man companies of Ukrainian nationalist guerrillas
Spinne	Spider
Sprengboot	exploding boat
Squadrismo	violent activism of Italian Blackshirt squads
Stavka	Red Army high command
Stelle	office
Streifkorps, Streifkommandos	scouting units
Sturmgeschutz	Storm Guard
Sturmzug	storm platoon
Südstern	South Star
S und Z Unternehmen	Sabotage and Demolition Undertakings
Sûreté	police
technische Hochschule	technical academy
Teilgruppe	subsidiary group
Tiszti Különítmény	'white terror' squads
Totaleinsatz (pl. *Totaleinsätze*)	near-suicide mission
Totenkopf	Death's Head; SS concentration camp guard units
Trupp	troop; a small unit
Überrollung	stay-behind advancing enemy troops
Untermenschen	subhumans
Unternehmen	operation
Vlaamsche Jongeren Corps	Flemish Youth Corps
Vlaamsch National Verbond	Flemish National Union
Vlaamsche Wacht	Flemish Watch
Volksdeutsche	ethnic Germans living outside the boundaries of the Third Reich
Volkssturm	People's Storm; Nazi mass militia
Vorkommando	vanguard commando unit
Waffen	armed; weapons
Wehrmacht	Armed Forces
Werwolf	Werewolf; Nazi guerrilla movement
Zentralbüro	Central Bureau
Zentrale	main office
Zer-Gruppen	demolition groups
Zernetz	demolition network
Zersetzungsunternehmen	propaganda operation
Zerstörergruppe	demolition group
Zwarte Brigade	Black Brigade
Zweierorganisation	Second Section of the *Abwehr*, later the *Militärisches Amt* Section D

Table of Ranks

German Army	SS	British Army	US Army
Reichsmarschall			
Generalfeldmarschall	Reichsführer-SS	Field Marshal	General of the Army
Generaloberst	Oberstgruppenführer	General	General
General	Obergruppenführer	Lieutenant-General	Lieutenant-General
Generalleutnant	Gruppenführer	Major-General	Major-General
Generalmajor	Brigadeführer	Brigadier	Brigadier-General
	Oberführer		
Oberst	Standartenführer	Colonel	Colonel
Oberstleutnant	Obersturmbannführer	Lieutenant-Colonel	Lieutenant-Colonel
Major	Sturmbannführer	Major	Major
Hauptmann	Hauptsturmführer	Captain	Captain
Oberleutnant	Obersturmführer	Lieutenant	1st Lieutenant
Leutnant	Untersturmführer	2nd Lieutenant	2nd Lieutenant
Stabsoberfeldwebel	Sturmscharführer	Regt. Sergeant-Major	Sergeant-Major
Oberfähnrich			
Oberfeldwebel	Hauptscharführer	Sergeant-Major	Master-Sergeant
Feldwebel	Oberscharführer	Quartermaster-Sergeant	Technical Sergeant
Fähnrich			
Unterfeldwebel	Scharführer	Staff Sergeant	Staff Sergeant
Unteroffizier	Unterscharführer	Sergeant	Sergeant
Stabsgefreiter			
Obergefreiter			
Gefreiter	Rottenführer	Corporal	Corporal
Obersoldat	Sturmmann	Lance-Corporal	
Soldat	Oberschütze	Senior Private	Private 1st Class

List of Illustrations

All illustrations from the author's collection unless otherwise stated.

Endnotes

ABBREVIATIONS

ACS	Archivio Centrale dello Stato
ADAHP	Archives Départmentales des Alpes-de-Haute-Provence
AdAP	*Akten zur deutschen Auswärtigen Politik*
AN	Archives Nationales
app.	appendix
AS	Archives de la Savoie
BA	Bundesarchiv
BC	Bramstedt Collection
BMA	Bundesmilitärchiv
c.	circa
CI	Counter Intelligence
CIANF	CIA Name Files
CIR	Consolidated Interrogation Report
DDRJNSV	*DDR-Justiz und NS-Verbrechen*
FO	Foreign Office
FOWPIS	*Foreign Office Weekly Political Intelligence Summaries*
fr.	frame(s)
FRUS	*Foreign Relations of the United States*
'GPG'	'German Propaganda and the German'
HCIC	*History of the Counter Intelligence Corps*
int.	interrogation
IRR	Investigative Records Repository
IWM	Imperial War Museum
JNSV	*Justiz und NS-Verbrechen*
LA–BA	Lastenausgleichsarchiv des Bundesarchivs
NA	US National Archives
NAC	National Archives of Canada
NAUK	National Archives of the United Kingdom
'ND'	'News Digest'
OD	Ost Dokumente
r.	reel
RG	Record Group
SAPMO	Stiftung Parteien und Massenorganisationen der DDR
SHAT	Service Historique de l'Armée de Terre
UPASND	*UPA v Svitli Nimetskykh Dokumentiv*
vol.	volume
WO	War Office
WWIIGMS	*World War II German Military Studies*
UMC	Ultra Microfilm Collection.

INTRODUCTION

1   *The New York Times*, 31/12/50; *The Washington Star*, 31/12/50; Baynton to Hoover, 15/5/51; E.P. Dutton and Co. to Baynton, 30/4/51; Acheson to Hicog, 16/5/51; 'SS Colonel Otto Skorzeny', 28/6/51; and Gernand to Commanding Officer, USAREUR CR (Prov), 13/5/63, all in CIANF, Entry 86, RG 263, NA.

2   Charles Foley, *Commando Extraordinary* (London, 1954), chapter 1; and *New York Herald Tribune*, 20/10/54.

3   *The New York Times*, 27/10/60; and 'Controversy between Otto Skorzeny and General Hans Doerr', 27/3/51, CIANF, Entry 86, RG 263, NA.

4   For Skorzeny's exaggerated account of the battle he supposedly waged while snatching Nicholas Horthy Jr, see C.A. McCartney, *October Fifteenth* (Edinburgh, 1957), 400. For Skorzeny's fallacious account of the Mussolini rescue, see SRGG 1290, 13/5/45, WO 208/4170, NAUK; and 'Factual Report Concerning Mussolini's Liberation', CIANF, Entry 86, RG 263, NA. Wilhelm Höttl suggests that 'but for the success of the enterprise [Skorzeny] would have been court-martialled', mainly because he ordered a glider pilot to crash land on a rock-strewn meadow. Wilhelm Höttl, *The Secret Front* (New York, 1954), 312. In his memoirs, Skorzeny repeatedly bragged of an operation to resupply a body of German troops cut off in Byelorussia, although his account of this action was challenged as early as 1952. Eyewitness testimony suggested that Skorzeny had been the victim of a Soviet ruse designed to get supplies and divert German attention, but the most he would admit was that the affair *might* have been a Soviet trap. Other German officers admitted, however reluctantly, that they had been duped. Otto Skorzeny, *Wir Kämpften – Wir Verloren* (Königswinter, 1973), 63–64; *Die Zeit*, 19/6/52; and Günther Gellermann, *Moskau ruft Heeresgruppe Mitte...* (Koblenz, 1988), 165, 169.

5   *The Times*, 6/4/50; 20/4/50; *The New York Times*, 6/4/50; 11/4/50; 19/4/50; 29/12/50; and *The Washington Star*, 31/12/50.

6   Aside from Foley's *Commando Extraordinary*, see Charles Whiting, *Skorzeny* (New York, 1972). Even Glenn Infield's more critical *Skorzeny: Hitler's Commando* (New York, 1981) accepts much of Skorzeny's chronology, narrative and inclination toward high-profile stunts. For a brief literature review, see Christopher Simpson, *Blowback* (London, 1988), 347–48.

7   P.W. Stahl, 'Geheimgeschwader' *KG 200* (Stuttgart, 1980), 115; Gellermann, 97; 'CIR 4 – The German Sabotage Service', 23/7/45, IRR File XE 070687, RG 319, NA; and *The Stars and Stripes*, 9/2/47. For the large number of *Jagdverband* and FAK operations behind Soviet lines around the turn of 1944–1945, see Otto Skorzeny, *La Guerre Inconnue* (Paris, 1975), 364; Arno Rose, *Werwolf* (Stuttgart, 1980), 205; Gerhard Boldt, *Die letzten Tage der Reichskanzlei* (Hamburg, 1964), 27; and 'Zusammenfassung der Frontaufklärungsmeldungen', 10/1/45, RH 2/2127, BMA.

8   Nicholas Horthy, *Memoirs* (New York, 1957), 206.

9   Adolf Hitler, *Mein Kampf* (Munich, 1927), 744–49.

10   Michael Burleigh, *The Third Reich* (New York, 2000), 425–28.

11   For Hitler's radical foreign policy versus more traditionalist objectives, see Ian Kershaw, *Hitler, 1936–1945* (London, 2001), 67–68; *Germany and the Second World War* (Oxford, 1990, 1998, 2000), i, 553–55; iv, 39–42, 488–49; and v, part i, 152–66. For a comparison of different Nazi plans for Eastern Europe, see Roman Ilnytzki, *Deutschland und die Ukraine* (Munich, 1955), 2–51.

12   'Interrogation Report' 10, 21/6/45, IRR File XE 000440, RG 319, NA.

13   'ND' 1675, 5/2/45; 1681, 12/2/45; and 1688, 20/2/45, all in BC, Robbins Library.

14   Helmut Heiber, *Reichsführer!* (Stuttgart, 1968), 272–73; and Alexander Dallin, *German Rule in Russia* (London, 1957), 616, 646–47.

15   'GPG', 6/11/44, FO 898/187, NAUK.

16   Gerhard Weinberg, 'German Plans for Victory, 1944–45', *Central European History* 26, (1993), 225–27; David Yelton, '"Ein Volk Steht auf"', *The Journal of Military History* 64 (2000), 1061–64, 1067–75; Heiber, 289–90; and 'Enemy Expectations, Intentions and Sources of Information (16 March 1945)', WO 208/3616, NAUK.

17   Krallert int., app. 'D', Entry 119A, RG 226, NA.

18   Willem C.M. Meyers, 'La "Vlaamse Landsleiding"', *Cahiers d'Histoire de la Seconde Guerre Mondiale* no. 2 (1972), 265.

19   Tony Judt, 'The Past Is another Country', in *The Politics of Retribution in Europe* (Princeton, 2000), 306.

20   Alan Milward, 'The Economic and Strategic Effectiveness of Resistance', in *Resistance in Europe* (London, 1975), 186–203; Werner Rings, *Life with the Enemy* (New York, 1982), 265–76; and Douglas Porch, *The French Secret Services* (New York, 1995), 260–61.

CHAPTER ONE: THE SKORZENY *LEUTE*

1   Fritz Fischer, *Germany's War Aims in the First World War* (New York, 1967), 35, 84, 114–15, 126–27, 129, 135, 137, 153, 389; Percy Sykes, *A History of Persia* (London, 1951), 442–47, 449–50, 453–54, 455–56, 460–61, 475–76; F.J. Moberly, *Operations in Persia* (London, 1987); Peter Hopkirk, *On Secret Service East of Constantinople* (Oxford, 1994); William Olson, *Anglo-Iranian Relations during World War I* (London, 1984), 51–52, 71–75, 79–80, 88–90, 93–96, 97–99, 103–04, 118, 153, 156, 162; Hans-Ulrich Seidt, 'From Palestine to the Caucasus: Oskar Niedermayer and Germany's Middle Eastern Strategy in 1918', *German Studies Review* 24, no. 1 (2001), 1–13; Edmund Burke, 'Moroccan Resistance, Pan-Islam and German War Strategy, 1914–1918', *Francia* 3 (1975), 439–57; Antony Polonsky, 'The German Occupation of Poland during the First and Second

World Wars', in *Armies of Occupation* (Waterloo, 1984), 115; Waclaw Jedrzejewicz, *Pilsudski* (New York, 1982), 57; and Olen Fedyshyn, 'The Germans and the Union for the Liberation of the Ukraine', in *The Ukraine, 1917–1921* (Cambridge, 1977), 311, 314.

2   'Auslandsarbeit', 31/3/28, RH 2/418, BMA.

3   Donald McKale, *The Swastika outside Germany* (Kent, 1977), 78–79, 159–160; Kurt Schuschnigg, *The Brutal Takeover* (London, 1971), 48–49, 92–93, 112–15, 156–57; Ernst Rudiger Prince Starhemberg, *Between Hitler and Mussolini* (London, 1942), 136–38, 152–72; Gottfried-Karl Kindermann, *Hitler's Defeat in Austria* (Boulder, 1988), 35, 91–131; Radomir Luza, *Austro-German Relations in the Anschluss Era* (Princeton, 1975), 24–25; Jurgen Gehl, *Austria, Germany and the Anschluss* (London, 1963), 58, 62, 89–91, 97–100; Bruce Pauley, *Hitler and the Forgotten Nazis* (Chapel Hill, 1981), 105–07, 125–33; Vaclav Kral, 'Odsun Nemcov z Ceskosloven-ska', in *Nemecka Otazka a Ceskoslovensko* (Bratislava, 1962), 27–28; Martin Broszat, 'Das Sudetendeutsche Freikorps', *Vierteljahrshefte für Zeitgeschichte* 9 (1961), 30–49; Zdenek Liška, 'Vznik tvz. Sudetonemeckéno Freikorpsu a Jeho Akce na Ašsku v Zárí', *Historia a Vojenství* 34, (1985), 56–68; Gerald Reitlinger, *The SS* (London, 1981), 117–18; Anthony Komjathy and Rebecca Stockwell, *German Minorities and the Third Reich* (New York, 1980), 40–41, 93–96, 141–42, 159, 161, 178, 191, 199; Ernst von Salomon, *Das Buch vom deutschen Freikorpskämpfer* (Berlin, 1938), 38–42; MacAlister Brown, 'The Third Reich's Mobilization of the German Fifth Column in Eastern Europe', *The Journal for Central European Affairs* 19 (1959), 134; Julius Mader, *Hitlers Spionagegenerale sagen aus* (Berlin, 1971), 13–14, 115–121, 154–57, 309, 315, 318–19, 346, 349, 399; Karol Marian Pospieszalski, *Sprawa 58,000 'Volksdeutschow'* (Poznan, 1959), 47–52; Eric Lefebvre, *La Division Brandenbourg* (Paris, 1984), 16–25; Edmund Zarzycki, 'La Diversion Allemande le 3 Septembre 1939 à Bydgoszcz'; Tadeuz Jasowski, 'La Diversion Hitlerienne le 3 Septembre 1939 à Bydgoszcz', both in *Polish Western Affairs/La Pologne et les Affaires Occidentales* 22 (1981), 279–308; Edward Wynot, 'The Polish Germans, 1919–1939', *Polish Review* 27 (1972), 61–62; Peter Aurich, *Der Deutsch-polnische September 1939* (Munich, 1969), 10–11, 108–125; Gert Buchheit, *Der deutsche Geheimdienst* (Munich, 1966), 310–12; Louis de Jong, *The German Fifth Column in the Second World War* (Chicago, 1956), 43–45, 150–51, 153–56, 197–98, 230, 232–33, 245–46; Heinz Höhne, *Canaris* (London, 1979), 336–38, 345, 349–51, 354; Herbert Kriegsheim, *Getarnt, Getäuscht und doch Getrue* (Berlin, 1958), 293–95; Helmuth Spaeter, *Die Brandenburger* (Munich, 1978), 13–18, 65–66; Elizabeth Wiskemann, *Germany's Eastern Neighbours* (London, 1956), 43–46; Paul Leverkeuhn, *German Military Intelligence* (London, 1954), 44–45; Karol Marian Pospieszalski, 'O Znaczeniu Zamachu Bombowego w Tarnowie in Innych Prowokacjach Nazistowskich z Sierpnia i Wrzesnia 1939 r. dla Polityki Okupacyjnej Trzeciej Rzeszy Wobec Polski', *Przeglad Zachodni* 41 (1985), 97–109; and Wlodzimierz Jastrzebski, 'Tzw. Bydgoska Krwawa Niedziela w Swietle Zachodnioniemieckiej Literatury Historycznej', *Przeglad Zachodni* 39 (1983), 255–62.

4   Ingeborg Fleischauer, '"Operation Barbarossa" and the Deportation', in *The Soviet Germans* (London, 1986), 80–81; Fred Koch, *The Volga Germans* (University Park, 1977), 284–85, 290–91; De Jong, 130–32, 239–40; and D.M. Smirnov, *Zapiski Chekista* (Minsk, 1972), 180–92.

5   Buchheit, 308–10, 312–14; Oscar Reile, *Geheime Ostfront* (Munich, 1963), 366; *German Military Intelligence, 1939–1945* (Frederick, 1984), 306; Leverkeuhn, 44–45; De Jong, 287; Lauren Paine, *German Military Intelligence in World War II* (New York, 1984), 155–56; Lefebvre, 26–31; Walter Görlitz, *Der zweite Weltkrieg* (Stuttgart, 1952), 75; Johannes Steinhoff, Peter Pechel, Dennis Showalter, *Voices from the Third Reich* (Washington, 1989), 112–13; André Brissaud, *Canaris* (London, 1973), 31–32; and Höhne, *Canaris*, 288–89, 376–77.

6   Spaeter, 308–10; Buchheit, 307–08; Kriegsheim, 59–60, 288–89, 305, 311, 314; Peter Hoffmann, *The History of the German Resistance* (Montreal, 1996), 31–32; Görlitz, 75; von Pfuhlstein int., 20/4/45, IRR File ZF 011666, RG 319, NA; Gambke/Raupach/Peters int., 15/8/45; and Kuehlwein int., both in Entry 119A, RG 226, NA.

7   'Auslandsarbeit', 31/3/28, RH 2/418, BMA; and Haller int., ETO MIS-Y-Sect. CSDIC/WEA Final Inter-rogation Reports 1945–47, RG 338, NA.

8   Buchheit, 319–21; Reile, 234–35, 245–47, 366–67; Spaeter, 168–70; Nicholas Bethel, *The War Hitler Won, September 1939* (London, 1972), 135–36; Alexander Dallin, *German Rule in Russia* (London, 1957), 114–20; John Armstrong, *Ukrainian Nationalism* (New York, 1955), 42–43, 53–62, 73–74, 76–77, 82–83, 86, 153; Reitlinger, *The SS*, 203–04; Paul Robert Magocsi, *Galicia* (Toronto, 1983), 211–12; Mader, *Hitlers Spionagegenerale sagen aus*, 122–24, 147–48, 184–85, 275, 311–13, 324, 355, 400; John Erickson, *The Road to Stalingrad* (London, 1975), 166; De Jong, 153, 155; Ilnytzki, 76, 92, 241, 269–79; Malkov to Burgess, 9/10/46, IRR File XE 020651, RG 319, NA; Abwehrstelle Breslau negotiations, T-77, r. 1499, fr. 722–25, NA; Nosske int., 11/5/46; Haller int., 7/8/46, app. 'A', both in ETO MIS-Y-Sect. CSDIC/WEA Final Interrogation Reports 1945–47, RG 338, NA; 'Ukrainian Political Groups', 31/8/45, XL 27108, Entry 19, RG 226, NA; 'Organization of and Appoint-ments in the German Military Abwehr against Espionage and Sabotage', 20/6/45; Gambke/Raupach/Peters int., 15/8/45, both in Entry 119A, RG 226, NA; and 'Die OUN-UPA', 17/11/44, R6/150, BA.

9   Mader, *Hitlers Spionagegenerale sagen aus*, 185, 334, 347, 354; Sol Littman, *War Criminal on Trial* (Toronto, 1983), 41–45; Zenonas Ivinskis, 'Lithuania during the War: Resistance against the Soviet and Nazi Occupants', in *Lithuania under the Soviets* (New York, 1965), 64–68; Visvaldis Mangulis, *Latvia in the Wars of the 20th Century*

(Princeton, 1983), 93–97; August Jurs, *Estonian Freedom Fighters in World War Two* (1990), 20–29; Leverkuehn, 167–71; De Jong, 238; Reile, 296, 368–71; Evald Uustalu, *For Freedom Only* (Toronto, 1977), 26–27; OSS Report, 18/4/44, 75716, Entry 16, RG 226, NA; 'Bureau (Büro) Cellarius', 27/4/45, Entry 171, RG 226, NA; and Cellarius int., 23/6/45, Entry 119A, RG 226, NA.

10 Mader, *Hitlers Spionagegenerale sagen aus*, 184–85.

11 Leverkuehn, 161–62; Hans von Herwarth, *Against Two Evils* (New York, 1981), 200–01; David Thomas, 'Foreign Armies East and German Military Intelligence in Russia', *Journal of Contemporary History* 22 (1987), 265, 272; and H.W. Posdnjakoff, 'German Counter-Intelligence in Occupied Soviet Union', 145–47, in *WWIIGMS* (New York, 1979), ixx.

12 Perry Biddiscombe, 'Unternehmen Zeppelin', *Europe-Asia Studies* 52 (2000), 1115–42.

13 ULTRA/ZIP/ISOSICLE 9206, 31/12/43, HW 19/241, NAUK.

14 For operations by two 'Zeppelin' detachments in the Rybinsk district, see ULTRA/ZIP/ISOSICLE 12683, 10/7/44; 12684, 21/11/44; 12685, 29/2/44; 12686, 29/2/44; 12690, 26/6/44; 12698, 2/10/44; 12701, 17/1/45; 12707, 28/11/43; 12708, 9/1/44; 12711, 28/2/44; 12735, 1/6/44; 12740, 26/7/44; 12741, 22/10/44; 12745, 17/5/44; 12751, 4/3/44; 12752, 1/4/43; 12865, 1/10/43; 12866, 31/10/44; 12879, 9/5/44; and 12881, 12/6/44, all in HW 19/248, NAUK. For operation '*Nordbahn*', which was aimed against the railway around Kirov, see ZIP/ISOSICLE 7687, 16/10/43; 7795, 22/10/43, both in HW 19/238, NAUK; 8012, 27/10/43; 8125, 11/10/43, both in HW 19/239, NAUK; ULTRA/ZIP/ISOSICLE 9656, 30/1/44; 9759, 5/2/44; and 9597, 27/1/44, all in HW 19/242, NAUK.

15 Timothy Patrick Mulligan, *The Politics of Illusion and Empire* (New York, 1988), 47; and Robert Stephen, 'Smersh', *Journal of Contemporary History* 27 (1987), 603.

16 Spaeter, 194–97; Kriegsheim, 312; A. Voronin, 'Chekisty v Oborone Stalingrada', in *Front bez Linii Fronta* (Moscow, 1970), 155; 'Erfolgsmeldungen – S-Ferneinsatz des Abw. Kdos. 202 vom 1.4 bis 31.10.42'; Amt Ausland/Abwehr, Abw II/JON to W Pr, 26/10/42; 'Merkblatt für Führer und Ausbilder der K-Trupps im Osten', all in T-77, r. 1499, fr. 767–69, 856, 896–907, NA; and Gambke/Raupach/Peters int., 15/8/45, Entry 119A, RG 226, NA.

17 Sven Steenberg, *Vlasov* (New York, 1970), 76; 'Einsatzbericht', 10/7/42; 7/9/42; 'Unternehmen Posaune', 28/4/43; 'Einsatz-Bericht', 6/4/43; Wiemann, report, 12/9/43; 'Einsatzbericht nr. 67/43', 20/9/43; 'Unternehmen Quinta', 1/10/43; and 'Einsatz-Bericht', 6/11/43, all in T-77, r. 1499, fr. 908–09, 912–13, 930, 963–70, NA.

18 'Jahresübersicht über Abwehr II-Arbeit der Abw. Kommandos und Trupps. 1942', 28/6/43, T-77, r. R1502, fr. 51, NA.

19 Mader, *Hitlers Spionagegenerale sagen aus*, 369, 375–76, 380; F.L. Carsten, 'A Bolshevik Conspiracy in the Wehrmacht', *Slavonic and East European Review* 47 (1969), 483–509; Erickson, *The Road to Stalingrad*, 378–79; Alexander Werth, *Russia at War* (New York, 1964), 578–81; Hélène Carrère d'Encausse, *Stalin* (London, 1981), ii, 103; John Armstrong, *Soviet Partisans in World War II* (Madison, 1964), 582; *Stalin and His Generals* (New York, 1969), 452; Khadzhi-Murat Ibragimbeili, 'To Tell the Truth about the Tragedy of Peoples', *Soviet Studies in History* 29 (1990–91), 72–80; Aleksandr Nekrich, *The Punished Peoples* (New York, 1978), 52–55, 58–59; Sebastian Smith, *Allah's Mountains* (London, 1998), 58–65; Sonderverband Bergmann reports, 16/2/43, T-311, r. 151, fr. 7198701–03, NA; 'Auszug aus Kgf.-Vernehmung (IIb-#4364)', 6/11/44; and Leitstelle I Ost für FAK to OKH Gen. St. d. Heeres/FHO, 21/12/44, both in RH2/2337, BMA.

20 Mader, *Hitlers Spionagegenerale sagen aus*, 191, 193, 329, 333, 342, 361, 364, 365, 370, 377–78, 383, 388; Görlitz, 76; Patrik von zur Mühlen, *Zwischen Hakenkreuz und Sowjetstern* (Düsseldorf, 1971), 208–09, 213, 214–15; *Study of German Intelligence Activities in the Near East and Related Areas Prior to and during World War II*, 15–16, IRR File ZA 022138, RG 319, NA; ULTRA/ZIP/ISOSICLE 12020, 16/9/1944, HW 19/247, NAUK; 'Antibolschewistische Widerstandsbewegungen und Banden in der Sowjetunion', 15/8/44, T-78, r. 493, fr. 6480053–54, 6480060–64, NA; and 'Zusammenstellung von Meldungen über sowjetfeindliche Banden im rückwärtigen Gebiet', 2/44, T-78, r. 497, fr. 6485201–03, NA.

21 Mader, *Hitlers Spionagegenerale sagen aus*, 343, 350, 352, 357–58, 359, 362–63, 364, 367, 368, 369, 374; Buchheit, 268; Leverkuehn, 185–89; Görlitz, 76; *Study of German Intelligence Activities in the Near East and Related Areas Prior to and during World War II*, 49–56, IRR File ZA 022138, RG 319, NA; 'Witzel', 31/7/45, Entry 119A, RG 226, NA; Brandt int., 5/12/44, HS 5/98, NAUK; 'Miscellaneous', 27/4/45, WO 208/3617, NAUK; 'Ind Inf Regt. 950', 16/3/45, WO 208/3615, PRO; and Murad int., 18/1/46, in *Covert Warfare* (New York, 1989), xiii.

22 Leverkuehn, 9–10; David Kahn, *Hitler's Spies* (New York, 1978), 297; Mader, *Hitlers Spionagegenerale sagen aus*, 324–25, 348–49, 351–52, 353–54, 360- 361, 363, 369, 370–71, 373, 380–81, 387, 388, 391; John Eppler, *Operation Condor* (London, 1977), 79, 105, 151, 163–66; Buchheit, 280; Görlitz, 76; T.H.Vail Motter, *The Persian Corridor and Aid to Russia* (Washington, 1952), 238, 362; ULTRA/ZIP/ISOSICLE 9793, 23/8/43, HW 19/242, NAUK; 'Notes on Mil Amt C and Other Departments of RSHA', 11/9/45, WO 208/3620, NAUK; 'Weekly Report', 9/5/43; 22/5/43, both in Entry 92, RG 226, NA; 'Note on the Franz Meyer documents',

Entry 172, RG 226, NA; MID miliary attaché report, 7/7/43, 40955, Entry 16, RG 226, NA; 'Extracts from Defence Security Office, CICI Persia CI Summary no. 11, Dated 20th September 1943', Entry 119A, RG 226, NA; *Study of German Intelligence Activities in the Near East and Related Areas prior to and during World War II*, 97–98, IRR File ZA 022138, RG 319, NA; and Schüler int., 28/1/46, ETO MIS-Y-Sect. CSDIC/WEA Final Interrogation Reports 1945–47, RG 338, NA. For the memoirs of the main German agent in Iran, see *Daybreak in Iran* (London, 1954).

23   Leverkuehn, 61; and *Study of German Intelligence Activities in the Near East and Related Areas prior to and during World War II*, 133, IRR File ZA 022138, RG 319, NA.

24   Simon Kitson, *Vichy et la chasse aux espions nazis 1940–1942* (Paris, 2005), 31.

25   Anthony de Luca, 'Der "Grossmufti" in Berlin', *International Journal of Middle East Studies* 10 (1979), 128–29; Mader, *Hitlers Spionagegenerale sagen aus*, 341, 345, 346, 347, 348, 352–53, 360, 365, 366–67, 376, 377, 384; Eppler, 179–83; Gellermann, 23–27, 92–95; Kempner, 274–75; Hellmuth Felmy and Walter Warlimont, 'German Exploitation of Arab Nationalist Movements in World War II', *WWIIGMS* (New York, 1979), xiii; 'Enterhung Dschadde (or Jadde)', 4/9/43, Entry 196, RG 226, NA; 'Tel Afar Parachute Expedition', 9/12/44, XL 5487, Entry 19, RG 226, NA; 19/12/44, XL 5709, Entry 19, RG 226, NA; 'German Use of Poison for Assassination Purposes', 25/4/45, CAD 014 Germany, RG 165, NA; Murad int., 18/1/46, in *Covert Warfare*, xiii; *Study of German Intelligence Activities in the Near East and Related Areas prior to and during World War II*, 107–08, 145, 154–55, IRR File ZA 022138, RG 319, NA; and 'Eisenberg, Werner, Case 3516', 28/5/45, Entry 119A, RG 226, NA.

26   Eppler, 203–40; Kriegsheim, 309–10; Gellermann, 96; Mader, *Hitlers Spionagegenerale sagen aus*, 372; Spaeter, 188, 197–202; *Study of German Intelligence Activities in the Near East and Related Areas prior to and during World War II*, 34–37, 134–35, IRR File ZA 022138, RG 319, NA; *Le Patriote*, 1/5/44; ZIP/ISOSICLE 6410, 17/8/43; 6288, 27/8/43; 5324, 1/9/43; and 6279, 13/9/43, all in HW 19/237, NAUK.

27   Buchheit, 323–24; Kriegsheim, 167–83; Mader, *Hitlers Spionagegenerale sagen aus*, 371, 374, 379, 380, 383, 386; Spaeter, 295–98; Felmy and Warlimont, 'German Exploitation of Arab Nationalist Movements in World War II', *WWIIGMS*, xiii; Clissman int., ETO MIS-Y-Sect. CSDIC/WEA Interim Reports, Special Interrogation Reports 1945–46, RG 338, NA; and ZIP/ISOSICLE 6296, 31/7/43, HW 19/237, NAUK.

28   ULTRA/ZIP/ISOSICLE 12350, 10/12/42, HW 19/247, NAUK; and 'Amt VI of the RSHA, Gruppe VI B', 17/10/45, Entry 119A, RG 226, NA.

29   Gellermann, 27–32, 75–76, 85–86; and Stahl, 116–23.

30   Sean O'Callaghan, *The Jackboot in Ireland* (London, 1958), 29–30, 61, 76–79, 82–111, 114–115, 124–35, 151–53; Mader, *Hitlers Spionagegenerale sagen aus*, pp. 316–17, 325–26, 329–30, 333–35, 338, 340, 356, 362–63, 345; Leverkuehn, 102–06; Karl Heinz Absagen, *Canaris* (Stuttgart, 1949), 273–80; Carolle Carter, 'The Spy Who Brought His Lunch', *Éire-Ireland* 10 (1975), 3–13; Robert Fisk, *In Time of War* (Brandon, 1983), 237, 322; 'Referat VI D 2 of Amt VI RSHA', 1/10/45, WO 208/3620, NAUK; Haller int., 7/8/46; Clissmann int., 7/11/45, both in ETO MIS-Y-Sect. CSDIC/WEA Final Interrogation Reports 1945–47, RG 338, NA; Pieter van Vessem, r. A3343 SSOK-204B, fr. 1290, RG 242, NA; 'Note on AA File Ireland (Veesenmayer)'; 'Note on Helmuth Clissmann'; note on Veesenmayer, 3/9/44; 'Amt VI S', 1/5/45; note on Schüddekopf, 24/7/45; and Schoeneich int., 31/10/45, all in Entry 119A, RG 226, NA.

31   Otto Skorzeny, *Lebe gefährlich* (Königswinter, 1973), 174–76; Foley, 37; Öbsger/Röder int., 29/7/46; 'Ludwig or Louis Nebel', both in CIANF, Entry 86, RG 263, NA; Van Cranenbroeck int., 17/4/45; 'Supplement to "Operational Units of Amt VI S" of 9.4.45', 24/4/45; Radl int., 4/6/45; WRC2 to 1st US Army, 28/6/45, 'Extract from Camp 020 Interim Report dated 21.11.44 re Arthur Garritt, SD agent', all in Entry 119A, RG 226, NA; Clissmann int., ETO MIS-Y-Sect. CSDIC/WEA Final Interrogation Reports 1945–47, RG 338, NA; '6a Delbruchstrasse, Grunswald (Amt VI F) 54-general-4', IRR File XE 001063, RG 319, NA; 'CIR 4 – The German Sabotage Service', 23/7/45, IRR File XE 070687, RG 319, NA; 'German Intelligence', 26/12/44, IRR File XE 000417, RG 319, NA; and 'Ostrich' int., 2/11/44, KV 2/1327, NAUK.

32   Skorzeny, *Lebe gefährlich*, chapters 1–8; Foley, chapter 2; Höttl, 311; Martin Lee, *The Beast Reawakens* (Boston, 1997), 15–16; Otto Skorzeny (fr. 1113); 'Lebenslauf des SS-Sturmbannführers Otto Skorzeny' (fr. 1130); RF-SS Personalamt to Generalinspekteur der verst. SS-Totenkopfstandarten, 1/12/39 (fr. 1222); SS-Oberabschnitt Donau to SS-Personalamt, 4/12/39 (fr. 1221); SS-Personalamt to SS-Oberabschnitt Donau, 4/12/39 (fr. 1223); Neblich to Kommandeur SS Division 'Reich', 16/2/41 (fr. 1189); sig. illegible, SS Artillerie Regiment, SS Verfugungstruppe, 17/2/41 (frame 1182); SS- und Polizeigericht III to SS Personalhauptamt, 4/7/42 (fr. 1176–77); SS-Führungshauptamt to SS Personalhauptamt, 25/7/42 (fr. 1179); von Herff to Skorzeny, 6/5/43 (fr. 1168); 'Betr.: Beförderung des SS-Ostuf. Skorzeny zum SS-Hauptsturmführer', 30/6/43 (fr. 1162); SS Kraftfahr-Ausbildungs- und Ersatz-Abteilung Gerichts-SS-Führer to the Reichssicherheitshauptamt, 21/5/43 (fr. 1182); 'Begrundung' (fr. 1169), all in r. A3343 SSO 139B, RG 242, NA; 'Skorzeny zum Sturmbannführer befördert', 16/9/43, WO 208/4505, NAUK; AFHQ 'Extract from "Revision Notes no. 1 on The German Intelligence Services" dated 6 Dec. 44', WO 204/11839, NAUK; Skorzeny int., 23/5/45; 'German Intelligence',

26/12/44; 'Excerpts from an article by SS War Reporter Robert Kroetz in "Der deutsche Polizei," XI, no. 19 (1/10/1943), p. 395f'; Interpress-Hamburg, 29/7/47, all in IRR File XE 000417, RG 319, NA; 'Possible Underground Organization of Former Members of Skorzeny's Jagdverbaende and SS', IRR File ZF 011666, RG 319, NA; Radl int., 28/5/45; Morael int., 30/3/45; 'Amt VI S', 1/5/45; 'Exploitation de l'Affaire Neisser', 26/5/45, all in Entry 119A, RG 226, NA; and Berger int., 8/6/45, IRR File XE 000440, RG 319, NA.

33   Foley, 18–20; Skorzeny, *Lebe gefährlich*, pp. 45–54; 'A Character Sketch of Schellenberg, chief of Germany's Espionage Service', 12/7/45; 'Progress Report on the Case of Schellenberg', 17/7/45, both in IRR File XE 001752, RG 319, NA; 'Possible Underground Organization of Former Members of Skorzeny's Jagdverbaende and SS', IRR File ZF 011666, RG 319, NA; and Hügel int., 28/5/46, ETO MIS-Y-Sect. CSDIC/WEA Final Interrogation Reports 1945–47, RG 338, NA. For Gregor Strasser's definition of a 'political soldier', see Claudia Koonz, *Mothers in the Fatherland* (New York, 1987), 89, 446.

34   Foley, 128–29; Eugenio Dollmann, *Roma Nazista* (Milan, 1949), 193; Höttl, 311; LaHaye int., 22/11/44; Morael int., 30/3/45; Olmes int.; Radl int., 28/5/45; Radl int., 4/10/45; 'Note de Renseignements'; 'Olmes', 18/6/45, all in Entry 119A, RG 226, NA; Edquist int., 17/7/45, supplement, Entry 125A, RG 226, NA; Karl Radl, r. A3343 SSOK-002B, RG 242, NA; Arno Besekow, r. A3343 SSo-064, fr. 934, RG 242, NA; and 'PF: 601, 603', KV 2/1327, NAUK. For von Fölkersam's background, see Mader, *Hitlers Spionagegenerale sagen aus*, 375; and Leverkuehn, 166.

35   Skorzeny, *Wir Kämpften – Wir Verloren*, 10, 171; and Hunke int., 17/1/46, Entry 119A, RG 226, NA.

36   Foley, 130.

37   Ibid., 130; *JNSV* (Amsterdam, 1969), ii, 577; memo by SS-O/Gruf. Jüttner, 5/8/43, R 58/862, BA; 'Extracts from CSDIC(UK) SIR 1124 Report'; 'S.S. Jägerbatallion 502', 11/8/44; 'Supplement to "Operational Units of Amt VI S" of 9.4.45', 24/4/45; De Roos int., 12/2/45; Obladen int., 1/6/45; Hunke int., 17/1/46, all in Entry 119A, RG 226, NA; Kaltenbrunner to Himmler, 13/3/44 (fr. 1246–47); Chef of Hauptamt SS-Gericht to SS-Richter beim RFSS, 22/4/44 (fr. 1233–45); Bender to Hauptamt SS-Gericht (fr. 1230); 'Vermerk für SS-Sturmbannführer Grothmann', 12/5/44 (fr. 1232); Bender to RSHA, 13/5/44 (fr. 1231), all in r. A3343 SSO 139B, RG 242, NA; 'Total-Einsatz Skorzeny', 12/4/45, IRR File XE 000417, RG 319, NA; Girg int., 22/1/46, XL 41372, Entry 19, RG 226, NA; 'CIR 4 – The German Sabotage Service', 23/7/45, IRR File XE 070687, RG 319, NA; 'German Sabotage Organizations', c. 2/45, Entry 92, RG 226, NA; DEG 3303, 10/6/44, HW 19/275, NAUK; and Wandel int., 23/1/46, ETO MIS-Y-Sect. CSDIC/WEA Final Interrogation Reports 1945–47, RG 338, NA. For general evaluations of military elitism, see Eliot Cohen, *Commandos and Politicians* (Cambridge, 1978); and Roger Beaumont, *Military Elites* (Indianapolis, 1974).

38   'CIR 4 – The German Sabotage System', 23/7/45, IRR File XE 070687, RG 319, NA; Girg int., 22/1/46, XL 41372, Entry 19, RG 226, NA; and 'Ostrich & the S.D.', 12/1/45, CIANF, Entry 86, RG 263, NA.

39   Skorzeny, *Wir Kämpften – Wir Verloren*, 40–43; Foley, 67–70; Skorzeny, *Le Guerre Inconnue*, 193–95; John Erickson, *The Road to Berlin* (London, 1983), 150–54, 679; Keith Eubank, *Summit at Teheran* (New York, 1985), 188–97; Michael Reilly, *Reilly of the White House* (New York, 1947), 168–88; Aleksandr Lukin, 'Operatsiya "Dalnyi Prizhok"', *Ogonek* no. 33, 1990 (15/8/65), 25; no. 34, 1991 (22/8/65), 25–27; Pavel Sudaplatov, *Special Tasks* (Boston, 1994), 130–31; Viktor Egorov, *Evriki protiv 'Evriki'* (Moscow, 1968); Gerhard int., 24/4/45; SHAEF CI War Room G-2 to 12th AG, 5/6/45; Radl int., 4/6/45; 12th AG AMZON to War Room, 7/7/45, all in Entry 119A, RG 226, NA; memo, 20/9/46; 'German Intelligence', 26/12/44, both in IRR File XE 000417, RG 319, NA; 'CIR 4 – The German Sabotage Service', 23/7/45, IRR File XE 070687, RG 319, NA; 'Ludwig or Louis Nebel', CIANF, Entry 86, RG 263, NA; 'PF: 601, 603', 15/9/45; 'Ostrich' int., 2/11/44, both in KV 2/1327, NAUK; and DEG 3270, 29/5/44, HW 19/275, NAUK.

40   K. Kociková and K. Beran, 'Sonderunternehmen "Anzio"', R 58/471, BA; and 'German Terrorist Methods', 2/4/45, Entry 119A, RG 226, NA.

41   Walter Schellenberg, *Memoiren* (Cologne, 1956), 300–02; Dollmann, 190–98, 216, 287, 343, 349; Foley, 40–62; report on the rescue of Mussolini, 12/9/43, r. A 3343 SSO 139B, fr. 1252, RG 242, NA; Kappler int., 8/6/45, Entry 174, RG 226, NA; Hügel int., 28/5/46, ETO MIS-Y-Sect. CSDIC/WEA Final Interrogation Reports 1945–47, RG 338, NA; SRGG 1290, 13/5/45, WO 208/4170, PRO; 'Excerpts from an Article by SS War Reporter Robert Kroetz in "Die deutsche Polizei" XI, no. 19 (1/10/1943), p. 395f'; memo re 'Eiche', 20/5/49, both in IRR File XE 000417, RG 319, NA; Radl int., 28/5/45; 'The Sicherheitsdienst (Security Service) in Italy', 13/9/45, both in Entry 119A, RG 226, NA; ZIP/ISOSICLE 5328, 14/8/43; 5387, 31/8/43; 5467, 1/9/43; 5470, 1/9/43; 5475, 7/9/43; 5486, 1/9/43; 5492, 8/9/43; 5497, 8/9/43; 5498, 89/43; 2/9/43; 5544, 29/8/43; 5545, 29/8/43; 5546, 29/8/43; 5565, 21/8/43; 5628, 10/9/43; 5631, 10/9/43; 5690, 25/8/43; 5696, 10/9/43; 5706, 11/8/43; 5726, 10/8/43; 5759, 11/8/43; 5731, 11/8/43; 5763, 12/9/43; 5764, 12/9/43; 5770, 11/9/43; 5779, 12/9/43; 5781, 12/9/43; 5782, 12/9/43; 5783, 12/9/43; 5797, 12/9/43; 5837, 12/9/43; 5839, 13/9/43; 5981, 15/8/43; 5984, 15/8/43; 5993, 5/9/43; 6037, 15/8/43; 6074, 8/8/43; 6085, 12/8/43; 6190, 4/8/43, all in HW 19/237, NAUK; and 8032, 29/8/43, HW 19/239, NAUK.

42   Berger int., 8/6/45, IRR File XE 000440, RG 319, NA; 'Factual Report Concerning Mussolini's Lib-

eration', CIANF, Entry 86, RG 263, NA; 'Daily Digest of World Broadcasts', 3–4/10/43, WO 208/4505, NAUK; ZIP/ISOSICLE 5787, 19/9/43, HW 19/237, NAUK; and 7804, 23/10/43, HW 19/238, NAUK.

43   ZIP/ISOSICLE 5785, 12/9/43; 6204, 17/9/43; and 6431, 20/9/43, all in HW 19/237, NAUK.

44   ZIP/ISOSICLE 7804, 23/10/43, HW 19/239, NAUK.

45   Dollmann, 198, 400–04; Kappler int., 8/6/45, Entry 174, RG 226, NA; 'Miscellaneous', 21/3/45, WO 208/3615, NAUK; and ZIP/ISOSICLE 6217, 18/9/43, HW 19/237, NAUK.

46   Das Schwarze Korps, 16/11/44; Heinz Höhne, The Order of the Death's Head (London, 1969), 502–03; George Stein, The Waffen-SS (London, 1966), pp. 147–48; and Bernd Wegner, The Waffen-SS (Oxford, 1990), 3–4, 327–30, 338, 350–59.

47   Wegner, 336–39; and Höhne, The Order of the Death's Head, 499–500.

48   Matthias Schröder, Deutschbaltische SS-Führer und Andrej Vlasov (Paderborn, 2001), 135–63, 189–93; Sven Steenberg, Vlasov (New York, 1970), chapter 5; Wilfred Strik-Strikfeldt, Against Stalin and Hitler (London, 1970), chapters 15–18; George Fischer, Soviet Opposition to Stalin (Cambridge, 1952), chapter 2; Catherine Andreyev, Vlasov and the Russian Liberation Movement (Cambridge, 1987), 57–61; Gerald Reitlinger, The House Built on Sand (London, 1960), 351–70; Wolf-Dietrich Heike, Sie wollten die Freiheit: Die Geschichte der Ukrainischen Division (Dorheim/H., 1973), 70; Höhne, The Order of the Death's Head, 504–08; and Dallin, 592–607, 611–20, 628–29, 631–36.

49   Krallert int., app. 'D', Entry 119A, RG 226, NA.

50   Wegner, 329.

51   'GPG', 25/9/44, FO 898/187, PRO.

52   'CIR 4 – The German Sabotage Service', 23/7/45, IRR File XE 070687, RG 319, NA; Tostain int., 21/2/45; Gouillard to the Direction de la Surveillance du Territoire, 4/1/45; 'Jagd Verband Mitte (and the Fuehrungs Stab of the Jagd Verbaende)'; and 'Collated Report on the SS Sonderkommando at the Jagdverband Kampfschule in Tiefenthal', 12/5/45, all in Entry 119A, RG 226, NA.

53   12th AG to SHAEF CI War Room, 7/7/45, Entry 119A, RG 226, NA.

54   Himmler to Kaltenbrunner, 16/9/44, T-175, r. 122, fr. 2648214, NA; HP 7004, 18/11/44, UMC, r. 50, NAUK; and DEG 3759, 19/11/44, HW 19/276, NAUK.

55   'Kampf in Rücken des Feindes', 21/11/44, RH 2/1929, BMA.

56   'Notes on SS, SD and RSHA/Mil Amt', 10/4/45, WO 208/3616, NAUK.

57   Lefebvre, 261; Kriegsheim, 273, 305–06, 315; Spaeter, 482–501; 'CIR 4 – The German Sabotage Service', 23/7/45, IRR File XE 070687, RG 319, NA; 'Intelligence Notes' 47, 17/2/45, XL 6103, Entry 19, RG 226, NA; Tostain int., 21/2/45; Kuehlwein int.; 'Operational Units of Amt VI S', 9/4/45; and 'Concealment of Arms, Ammunition and Explosives by the Streifkorps for the use of Wehrwolf', 30/7/45, all in Entry 119A, RG 226, NA.

58   Karen Hagermann, 'Of "Manly Valor" and "German Honor"', Central European History 30 (1997), 213–14; Körners sämtliche Werke (Stuttgart, 1893), 73; and Gambke/Raupach/Peters int., 15/8/45, Entry 119A, RG 226, NA.

59   Desirent int., 2/1/45, Entry 119A, RG 226, NA.

60   Skorzeny, Wir Kämpften – Wir Verloren, 55, 166; 'CIR 4 – The German Sabotage Service', 23/7/45, IRR File XE 070687, RG 319, NA; Vanhoeke int.; Gambke/Raupach/Peters int., 15/8/45; 'SS Jagd Verband Mitte (and the Fuehrungs Stab of the Jagd Verbaende)'; 'Internal Memorandum – Sandberger', 22/8/45, all in Entry 119A, RG 226, NA; 'German Sabotage Organizations', Entry 92, RG 226, NA; and DEG 3662, 8/10/44, HW 19/276, NAUK.

61   Bird to Noble, 12/12/44; Huygens int., 30/3/45; Morael/Prelogar/Claes/Maggen int.; Claes int., 13/4/45; Mackert int., 11/5/45; and Hakkenberg van Gaasbeek int., 4/7/45, all in Entry 119A, RG 226, NA.

62   Prelogar, int., 1/4/45, Entry 119A, RG 226, NA.

63   'Extract from "Revision Notes no. 1 on The German Intelligence Services" dated 6 Dec 44', WO 204/11839, NAUK; and DEG 3759, 19/11/44, HW 19/276, NAUK.

64   'German Intelligence', 26/12/44, IRR File XE 000417, RG 319, NA; Huegel int.; 'Amt VI of the RSHA, Gruppe VI G'; Olmes int.; Radl int., 4/6/45, all in Entry 119A, RG 226, NA; and 'CIR 4 – The German Sabotage Service', 23/7/45, IRR File XE 070687, RG 319, NA.

65   'Referat VI D2 of Amt VI RSHA', 1/10/45, WO 208/3620, NAUK; 'Translation of Statement handed in by Sandberger on 2.8.45', 13/8/45; War Room to USFET, 13/8/45; and 'Internal Memo – Sandberger', 2/8/45, all in Entry 119A, RG 226, NA. For a description of Schoen (and mention of his connection with Rapp), see Leyer int., app. 'B', 7/45; 'Sandberger', 2/8/45; Krallert int., 17/8/45, all in Entry 119A, RG 226, NA; and 'Translation of a Statement handed in by Schellenberg on 28.8.45', Entry 81, RG 263, NA.

66   Kahn, 267–70; and Skorzeny, Wir Kämpften – Wir Verloren, pp. 24–25.

67   Gambke/Raupach/Peters int., 15/8/45, Entry 119A, RG 226, NA.

68   German Military Intelligence, 44–45; Mader, Hitlers Spionagegenerale sagen aus, 40; Skorzeny, Wir Kämpften – Wir

Verloren, 54, 171–72; 'Progress Report in the Case of Schellenberg', 17/7/45, IRR File XE 001752, RG 319, NA; 'CIR 4 – The German Sabotage Service', 23/7/45, IRR File XE 070687, RG 319, NA; Kaltenbrunner int., 28/6/45, IRR File 000440, RG 319, NA; 'Monthly Summary' 2, 16/5/45; Sandberger int., 29/5/45; Kurrer int., 2/6/45; 'Case History of Georg Duesterberg', 14/5/45; 'Sandberger', 22/8/45; 'Leitstelle II Sud Ost'; Huegel int., 14/6/45; Radl int., 19/5/45; Eisenberg int., 28/5/45; Koch int., 15/6/45; Bertolsheim int., 1/7/45; Buntrock int., 7/8/45; Gambke/Raupach/Peters int., 15/8/45; Naumann int., 29/8/45; Loos int., 19/8/45; Radl int., 4/6/45, all in Entry 119A, RG 226, NA; 'Notes on Leitstelle III West für Frontaufklärung', 29/8/45, WO 208/3620, NAUK; 'CI-IIR/11 KdM Prague', 10/1/46; and Murad int., 18/1/46, both in *Covert Warfare*, xiii.

69 'Notes on Mil Amt C and other Departments of RSHA', 11/9/45, WO 208/3620, NAUK.

70 *UPASND* (Toronto, 1983), vi, 97.

71 E.H. Cookridge, *Gehlen* (New York, 1971), 93; 'Fremde Heere Ost', 5/6/45, WO 208/3617, NAUK; and 'Notes on Mil Amt C and other Departments of RSHA', 11/9/45, WO 208/3620, NAUK.

72 Oliver Radkey, *The Unknown Civil War in Soviet Russia* (Stanford, 1976); Micheal Malet, *Nestor Makhno in the Russian Civil War* (London, 1982), 150–56; and Nicholas Vakar, *Byelorussia* (Cambridge, 1956), 139. For the re-emergence of 'Green' bands in the Soviet rear during World War Two, see 'Frontaufklärungsmeldungen', 13/1/45, RH 2/2127, BMA; Joachim Hoffmann, *Deutsche und Kalmyken* (Freiburg, 1974), 91–2; Vakar, *Byelorussia*, 196; *UPASND*, vi, 84; and vii, 87. For 'green cadres' in Yugoslavia, see Brian Jeffrey Street, *The Parachute Ward* (Toronto, 1987), 38–39.

73 'Vortragsnotiz über zur Aktivierung der Frontaufklärung', 25/2/45, RH 2/1930, BMA.

74 *UPASND*, vi, 126–27; vii, 204; 'Comments by D/H61 on GCA/308 of July 15th from E. Med. Grp.', 26/7/44, HS 5/241, NAUK; and 'Precis of Message from Jugoslavs of Gen. Mihailovich to the Greeks', 23/6/44, HS 5/626, NAUK.

75 *UPASND*, vii, 91; and ULTRA/ZIP/ISOSICLE 10858, 31/3/44, HW 19/244, NAUK.

76 'Amt VI of the RSHA Gruppe VI G', Entry 119A, RG 226, NA.

77 Gellermann, 33–35; Stahl, 82–91; Kahn, 285–86; Skorzeny, *Wir Kämpften – Wir Verloren*, 15; James Lucas, *Kommando* (New York, 1985), 281–304; 'CIR 4 – The German Sabotage Service', 23/7/45, IRR File XE 070687, RG 319, NA; and 'Interrogation Report on Survivors of a German Crew', 6/3/45, 120249, Entry 16, RG 226, NA. For a strength report in February 1945, see BT 4583, 11/2/45, UMC, r. 61, NAUK.

78 Lucas, *Kommando*, 216, 246–47; Skorzeny, *Wir Kämpften – Wir Verloren*, 10–15; 'MEK zbV (Training Depot for MEKs), MEK 40 (Naval Combat Group)', 28/1/45, WO 208/3611, NAUK; SRX 2136, 16/4/45, WO 208/4164, NAUK; Post int., 4/5/45; Hoppe int., 19/5/45; Obladen int., 1/6/45; Radl int., 28/5/45; 'Extracts from CSDIC(UK) SIR 1124 Report', all in Entry 119A, RG 226, NA; and 'CIR 4 – The German Sabotage Service', 23/7/45, IRR File XE 070687, RG 319, NA.

79 von zur Mühlen, 82–138; Hoffmann, 137; Fischer, *Soviet Opposition to Stalin*, 21, 90–91; Heike, 158–59; Nekrich, 73; Armstrong, *Ukrainian Nationalism*, 168; Dallin, 135, 136–37, 556–65, 568, 573, 574–77, 609–12, 622, 628–36, 637–38, 651, 654; Carrère d'Encausse, *Stalin*, 103; Werth, 579; Mulligan, 166–74; Steenberg, *Vlasov*, 49–52, 83, 153–54, 157–61; 'Vorschläge für ein vorläufiges Organisationsschema des Russischen Nationalkomitees (RNK)'; 'Russisches Nationalkomitee', both in R 6/72, BA; 'Grundthesen für Besprechungen zur Bildung eines RNK'; 'Ukrainisches Nationalkomitee', 6/5/43, R 6/141, BA; 'Bericht: Organisation des Ukrainischen Komitees', 25/5/43; 'Besprechung mit der Vertretern der kaukasischen Verbindungsstäbe am 4.10.1944'; 'Vertretungen der baltischen Länder im deutschen Reich', 23/11/44; 'Schaffung eines lettischen Nationalkomitees', 29/11/44; memorandum by Rosenberg, 30/11/44; 'Lettisches Nationalkomitee', 5/12/44, all in R 6/141, BA; Brandt to Berger, 9/2/45; Berger to Himmler, 9/2/45, both in NS 19/3836, BA; and Rosenberg to the Georgian Liaison Staff, 17/3/45, R 6/74, BA.

80 Manfred Rauchensteiner, *Der Krieg in Österreich 1945* (Vienna, 1984), 24; John Lukacs, *The Great Powers and Eastern Europe* (New York, 1953), 641–42, 667; Wagner to Berger and Kaltenbrunner, 21/3/45, NS 19/3969, BA; Kaltenbrunner int., 23/5/45, Entry 119A, RG 226, NA; Schüler int., 28/1/46, ETO MIS-Y-Sect. CSDIC/WEA Final Interrogation Reports 1945–47, RG 338, NA; 'CIR 3 – Amt VI-E of the RSHA', 21/6/45, IRR File XE 000440, RG 319, NA; 'GPG', 2/10/44; 9/10/44, both in FO 898/187, PRO; and *The New York Times*, 10/1/45.

81 von zur Mühlen, 91.

82 Dallin, 609.

83 Metzger int., app. 'E', 14/2/46, ETO MIS-Y-Sect. CSDIC/WEA Interim Reports, Special Interrogation Reports 1945–46, RG 338, NA.

84 Huegel int., 14/6/45, Entry 119A, RG 226, NA; and 'Progress Report in the Case of Schellenberg', 17/7/45, IRR File XE 001752, RG 319, NA.

85 Hermann Neubacher, *Sonderauftrag Südost* (Göttingen, 1956), 14, 64, 91, 105, 123, 133, 191; 'CIR 3 – Amt VI-E of the RSHA', 21/6/45, IRR File XE 000440, RG 319, NA; 'Statement handed in by Kaltenbrunner on 8.8.45 with translation by Ledebur – Minister Dr. Neubacher', Entry 119A, RG 226, NA; and 'Progress

Report in the Case of Schellenberg', 17/7/45, IRR File 001752, RG 319, NA.

86   Olmes int.; and 'SS Jagd Verband Mitte (and the Fuehrungs Stab of the Jagd Verbaende)', both in Entry 119A, RG 226, NA.

87   Nicholas Kállay, *Hungarian Premier* (Westport, 1970), 463; Skorzeny, *Wir Kämpften – Wir Verloren*, 70–89; Thomas Sakmyster, *Hungary's Admiral on Horseback* (New York, 1994), 369–79; McCartney, ii, 356–435; Mario Fenyo, *Hitler, Horthy and Hungary* (New Haven, 1972), 230–31, 236; Horthy, 229–38; 'Begründung und Stellung nahmen der Zwischenvorgesetzten', r. A3343 SSO 139B, fr. 1116, RG 242, NA; 'CIR 4 – The German Sabotage Service', 23/7/45, IRR File XE 070687, RG 319, NA; 'Information from: Huhn – Re: Karl Radl', IRR File XE 000417, RG 319, NA; 'CIR 3 – Amt VI-E of the RSHA', 21/6/45, IRR File XE 000440, RG 319, NA; Huegel int., 14/6/45; Schnorr int., 30/5/45; Schnorr int., 11/10/45, all in Entry 119A, RG 226, NA; 'Progress Report in the Case of Schellenberg', 17/7/45, IRR File XE 001752, RG 319, NA; and DEG 3713, 31/10/44, HW 19/276, NAUK.

88   Sakmyster, *Hungary's Admiral on Horseback*, 370.

89   Biddiscombe, 'Unternehmen Zeppelin', 1129; 'Kak Gitler Planiroval Ubiistvo Stalina', *Lubyanka* no. 2 (Moscow, 1999), 256; and 'PF: 601, 603', 15/9/45, KV 2/1327, NAUK.

90   P.L. Thyraud de Vosjoli, *Lamia* (Boston, 1970), 120; *l'Aurore*, 12/4/45; 'Agent ennemi envoyé en Belgique par la Suisse', 23/3/45; Tostain int., 14/1/45; 12th AG AMZON to War Room, 7/7/45, all in Entry 119A, RG 226, NA; report on 'Ostrich', 30/4/45, CIANF, Entry 86, RG 263, NA; and 'Connection with GIS – PF: 601, 603 Besekow', KV 2/1327, NAUK.

91   Kraizizek int., 10/45, Entry 119A, RG 226, NA.

92   Harry Butcher, *My Three Years with Eisenhower* (New York, 1946), 727–28; Skorzeny, *Wir Kämpften – Wir Verloren*, 147–51; Infield, 78, 87–88, 93; Charles Whiting, *Decision at St. Vith* (New York, 1969), 95–96; William Breuer, *The Secret War with Germany* (Novato, 1988), 286–88; *HCIC* (Baltimore, 1959), xxviii, 12–13, 23, NA; Radl int., 4/6/45, Entry 119A, RG 226, NA; Normandy Base Section Com Z ETOUSA to Normandy, Brittany, Oise, Seine, Channel Base Sections, Advance Section and Solon, 23/12/44; 25/12/44; 'Alleged Plot to Assassinate General Eisenhower', 30/8/45, all in IRR File XE 000417, RG 319, NA; 'German Agents Operating behind the Allied Lines at the Time of the German Offensive and Wearing American Uniforms', Entry 171, RG 226, NA; 'Summary' 10, 31/12/44, WO 204/11839, NAUK; and *Christian Science Monitor*, 22/5/45.

93   Teja Fiedler, 'Zweiter Weltkrieg: Operation Eisenhower', <http://www.stern.de/politik/historie/?id=522962&nv=ma_ct>, as of 6/5/04.

94   Kraizizek int., 8/7/45; and Kraizizek int., 10/45, both in Entry 119A, RG 226, NA.

95   'Supplement to "Operational Units of Amt VI S," of 9.4.45', 24/4/45; Tostain int., 14/1/45; Tostain int., 21/2/45, all in Entry 119A, RG 226, NA; and 'Scheuern Training Center', 31/1/45, IRR File XE 001063, RG 319, NA.

96   Gehlen to Stecher, 31/3/45, T-78, r. 488, fr. 6473229–30, NA.

97   Gehlen to RSHA/Mil F (Copy to SS-Jagdverband Ost), 28/3/45, T-78, r. 488, fr. 6473241, NA; and Reinhard Gehlen, *The Service* (New York, 1972), 105–06.

98   Skorzeny, *Wir Kämpften – Wir Verloren*, 167–68.

99   BT 7122, 13/3/45, HW 1/3599, NAUK. For attacks by 'Special Detachment Rübezahl', see DEG 4035, 12/3/45, HW 19/277, NAUK.

100 Skorzeny, *Wir Kämpften – Wir Verloren*, 195–96; *Fuehrer Conferences on Naval Affairs, 1939–1945* (London, 1990), 450; 'Attack on Nijmegen Br. – 29 Sep', 8/11/44, vol. 10811, RG 24, Series 90, NAC; BT 7122, 13/3/45, HW 1/3599, NAUK; 'GPG', 20/11/44, FO 898/187, NAUK; 'Countersabotage Bulletin' 2, 17/4/45, IRR File XE 070687, RG 319, NA; and Vogt int., annex 1, 18/7/45, Entry 119A, RG 226, NA.

101 Skorzeny, *Wir Kämpften – Wir Verloren*, 57; 'Future Operations of Flusskämpfer', 1/5/45, WO 208/3617, NAUK; and SRX 2138, 22/4/45, WO 208/4164, NAUK.

102 VAR/4909/ER, War Room, outgoing telegram, 28/3/45, Entry 119A, RG 226, NA.

103 Skorzeny, *Wir Kämpften – Wir Verloren*, 162; 'CIR 4 – The German Sabotage Service', 23/7/45, IRR File XE 070687, RG 319, NA; and Heckel int., 28/5/45, Entry 119A, RG 226, NA.

104 Skorzeny, *Wir Kämpften – Wir Verloren*, 168–69; Skorzeny, *La Guerre Inconnue*, 364–67; Foley, 139–40; *JNSV* (Amsterdam, 1981), xxii, 286; 'Intelligence Notes' 47, 17/2/45, XL 6103, Entry 19, RG 226, NA; *HCIC*, xx, 14, NA; 'SS Jagd Verband Mitte (and the Fuerungsstab of the Jagd Verbaende)'; Tostain int., 14/1/45; 'Olmes', 18/6/45, all in Entry 119A, RG 226, NA; Girg int., 22/1/46, XL 41372, Entry 19, RG 226, NA; Walter Girg (fr. 864); 'Antrag auf Verleihung des Eichenlaubes zum Ritterkreuz des Eisernen Kreuzes' (fr. 873–75), 31/3/45, both in r. A3343 SSO-014A, RG 242, NA; and ULTRA/ZIP/ISOSICLE 11000, 20/4/44, HW 19/244, NAUK.

105 'Einsatzbericht', 31/12/44, T-77, fr. 836–45, r. 1499, NA; Murad int. 18/1/46, in *Covert Warfare*, xiii; Forras int., 10/12/45, app. 'A', ETO MIS-Y Sect. CSDIC/WEA Final Interrogation Records 1945–1947, RG 338, NA; 'FAT 213', 21/11/45; Gambke/Raupach/Peters int., 15/8/45, both in Entry 119A, RG 226, NA; and

ULTRA/ZIP/ISK 139543, 22/3/45, HW 19/233, NAUK.

106 Gotti Laurent, 'Skorzeny à Malmedy', *Malmedy-Folklore* 57 (1997/98), 255–71; Skorzeny, *Wir Kämpften – Wir Verloren*, 100–05, 113–46, 151–61, 165–66; John S. D. Eisenhower, *The Bitter Woods* (New York, 1969), 122–24, 137–39, 165–66, 171, 213, 241; *German Military Intelligence*, 200; Whiting, *Decision at St. Vith*, 94–95; John Strawson, *The Battle of the Ardennes* (New York, 1972), 94; Hugh Cole, *The Ardennes* (Washington, 1970), 269–70, 360–63; Butcher, 728; Breuer, 279–86; Robert Merriam, *Dark December*, (Chicago, 1947), 127–8, 131–2, 135; James Weingartner, 'Otto Skorzeny and the Law of War', *The Journal of Military History* 55 (1991), 209–15; Infield, 78–88, 93; Kenneth Koyen, *The Fourth Armoured Division* (Munich, 1946), 66; Jeremy Taylor, *Record of a Reconnaissance Regiment* (Bristol, 1950), 150; Percy Schramm, 'Preparations for the German Offensive in the Ardennes (Sept.–16 Dec. 1944)', 97–100, in *WWIIGMS*, ccx; 'Intelligence Summary' 120, 23/1/45, vol. 10889, RG 24, Series 90, NAC; 'Progress Report in the Case of Schellenberg', 17/7/45, IRR File XE 001752, RG 319, NA; Berger int., 8/6/45, IRR File XE 000440, RG 319, NA; Lang int., 7/3/46; USFET G-2 to Theatre JAGD (War Crimes Branch), 25/3/46, both in IRR File XE 000417, RG 319, NA; Wollgarten int., 9/2/45; Schnorr int., 30/5/45; Korbitz int., 7/6/45; 'Interrogation report on 1 officer and 15 EM of Jagdeinsatz Nord FPN 40478', 6/4/45, all in Entry 119A, RG 226, NA; Oberbefehlshaber des Ersatzheeres to Verteiler, 26/1/45, RH 15/124, BMA; HP 5274, 1/11/44; HP 5461, 3/11/44 (both in r. 48); BT 3821, 31/1/45 (r. 60); BT 6054, 2/3/45; BT 6094, 2/3/45 (both in r. 64); BT 7166, 14/3/45 (r. 65), all in UMC, NAUK; 'CIR 4 – the German Sabotage Service', 23/7/45, IRR File XE 070687, RG 319, NA; 'German Agents Operating Behind Allied Lines at the Time of the German Offensive and wearing American Uniforms', Entry 171, RG 226, NA; 'Panzer Brigade 150', 18/7/45, ETO MIS-Y-Sect. CSDIC(UK) Special Interrogation Reports 1943–45, RG 332, NA; Skorzeny Trial Transcripts, 1947, 506–657, *Covert Warfare*, xvii; Albert Praun, 'German Radio Intelligence' MS #R038, 3/50, in *Covert Warfare*, xvi; 'Summary 710 – Georg Reinhold Gerhardt', IWM; 'Summary' 10, app. 'F', 31/12/44, WO 204/11839, NAUK; DEG 3702, 28/10/44, HW 19/276, NAUK; *HCIC*, xxviii, 12–13, 23, NA; *The Washington Post*, 19/5/45; 22/5/45; and *Christian Science Monitor*, 22/5/45.

107 DEG 3999, 2/3/45, HW 19/277, NAUK.

108 Olmes int.; and Schnorr int., 11/10/44, both in Entry 119A, RG 226, NA.

109 Gellermann, 56–58; Stahl, 151–67; Werner Baumbach, *Zu Spät?* (Munich, 1949), 268–71; Skorzeny, *Wir Kämpften – Wir Verloren*, 15–24; Beeger int., 21/1/46, ETO MIS-Y-Sect. CSDIC/WEA Final Interrogation Reports 1945–47, RG 338, NA; 'Extracts from CSDIC(UK) SIR 1124 Report', 17/12/44; Radl int., 4/6/45; and Olmes, all in Entry 119A, RG 226, NA.

110 Gellermann, 47–49, 63–72; Stahl, 178–90; Görlitz, 76; Skorzeny, *La Guerre Inconnue*, 195–96; Skorzeny, *Wir Kämpften – Wir Verloren*, 188–89; Baumbach, *Zu Spät?*, 97–98; 'CIR 4 – German Sabotage Service', 23/7/45, IRR File XE 070687, RG 319, NA; Teich int., 21/1/46; Beeger int., 21/1/46, both in ETO MIS-Y-Sect. CSDIC/WEA Final Interrogation Reports 1945–47, RG 338, NA; 'Skorzeny, Otto', 19/5/45; Kaltenbrunner int., 29/5/45; Radl int., 4/6/45, all in Entry 119A, RG 226, NA; ZIP/ISOSICLE 5666, 10/8/43; 5747, 18/8/43; 5752, 9/9/43; 5755, 10/9/43; 5869, 7/9/43; 6333, 1/9/43; 6340, 30/7/43, all in HW 19/237, NAUK; ULTRA/ZIP/ISOSICLE 9220, 1/1/44; 9221, 2/1/44; 9369, 12/1/44; 9512, 22/1/44, all in HW 19/241, NAUK; 9605, 28/1/44; 9636, 2/2/44; 9642, 2/2/44; 9655, 2/2/44; 9681, 3/2/44; 9682, 3/2/44; 9763, 5/2/44; 9765, 7/2/44; 9786, 6/2/44; 9907, 9/2/44; 9917, 11/2/44; 9956, 12/2/44; 10081, 14/2/44, all in HW 19/242, NAUK; DEG 4028, 10/3/45; 4044, 13/3/45; 4045, 15/3/45; 4058, 16/3/45, all in HW 19/277, NAUK; BT 7012, 12/3/45; and BT 7114, 13/3/45, both in r. 65, UMC, NAUK.

111 'Support to a USAFE Operation', 27/10/47; and 'Offiziersverein', 7/1/48, both in IRR File XE 002221, RG 319, NA.

112 'CIR 4 – The German Sabotage Service', 23/7/45, IRR File 070687, RG 319, NA.

113 Skorzeny, *Wir Kämpften – Wir Verloren*, 170–94, 186–87, 197; Foley, 139–49; *Hitler Directs His War* (New York, 1950), 134; Lucas, *Kommando*, 207; *DDRJNSV* (Amsterdam, 2002), ii, 765; *Berliner Illustrierte Zeitung*, 22/2/45; Blumenfurth int., 20/9/45, IRR File XE 000417, RG 319, NA; Corby int., 25/4/45; De Roo int., 28/5/45; Radl int., 4/6/45; Post int.; Schuermann int.; 'Interrogation of Subject by 307th CIC Det, 19 May 45', all in Entry 119A, RG 226, NA; Karl Fucker, A3343 SSO-228, fr. 1073, RG 242, NA; and 'Comments on the Political and Military Situation and the Consequences Thereof', app. 1 and 2a, CIANF, Entry 86, RG 263, NA.

114 Obladen int., 1/6/45, Entry 119A, RG 226, NA.

CHAPTER TWO: EAST IS EAST

1 *German Military Intelligence*, 290; Foley, 28–29; Spaeter, 490, 495; 'CIR 4 – The German Sabotage Service', 23/7/45, IRR File XE 070687, RG 319, NA; Gambke/Raupach/Peters int., 15/8/45; Van Weile int., 2/45; De Roos int., 22/3/45; De Ridder int., 16/4/45; Kuehlwein int.; and 'Otto Skorzeny', 19/5/45, all in Entry 119A, RG 226, NA; Manfred Pechau (fr. 203); and 'Lebenslauf', 18/3/40 (fr. 207–08), both in r. A3343 SSO-638A, RG 242, NA. For estimates on numbers of guerrillas, see Hengelhaupt to Gehlen, 12/4/44, T-78, r. 566, fr. 893, NA; and 'Aufgaben und Gliederung der polnischen Landesarmee und die Entwicklung der

Aufstandspläne des Polnischen Generalstabes', 1/12/44, T-78, r. 576, fr. 20, NA.

2   Foley, 129–30; W. Friedrich 'Fragebogen A', 3/2/56; G. Methner 'Zu Fragebogen A', 17/11/52, both in OD 1/99, LA-BA; E. Heinzmann 'Bericht über meine Tätigkeit als Sachbearbeiter an der Regierung-Festellungsbehörde in Hohensalza (Wartheland) und über Ereignisse vor und nach der Winteroffensive 1945', OD 8/477, LA-BA; 'CIR – The German Sabotage Service', 23/7/45, IRR File XE 070687, RG 319, NA; Radl int., 4/6/45; Sowers int.; and Gambke/Raupach/Peters int., 15/8/45 all in Entry 119A, RG 226, NA.

3   Ints Vanadzins, *Starp Sarkano un Melno* (Riga, 2001), 65; Gambke/Raupach/Peters int., 15/8/45; Olmes int., both in Entry 119A, RG 226, NA; ULTRA/ZIP/ISOSICLE 12796, 14/3/45; 12813, 14/3/45; 12828, 5/3/45; 12829, 9/3/45; 12840, 24/2/45, all in HW 19/248, NAUK; Alexander Auch, r. A3343 SSO-019, RG 242, NA; Adolf Engelmann, r. A3343 SSO-188, frame 549, RG 242, NA; Gerlach int., annex, 11/8/45, XL 13744, Entry 19, RG 226, NA; and 'CIR 4 – The German Sabotage Service', 23/7/45, IRR File XE 070687, RG 319, NA.

4   Skorzeny, *Wir Kämpften – Wir Verloren*, 168; Percy Schramm, 'The Wehrmacht in the Last Days of the War (1 January-7 May 1945)', in *WWIIGMS* (New York, 1979), ii; 'Summary 710 – Gerhardt', IWM; and 'CIR 4 – The German Sabotage Service', 23/7/45, IRR File XE 070687, RG 319, NA. For the destruction of German bands in the Łódz area, see *Pogranichnye Voiska SSSR v Velikoi Otechestvennoi Voine*, 505–06.

5   Bower, *The Red Web* (London, 1989), 38–41, 45, 59, 61; 'CIR 4 – The German Sabotage Service', 23/7/45, IRR File XE 070687, RG 319, NA; Horn int., 18/6/45; Radl int., 4/6/45, both in Entry 119A, RG 226, NA; 'Baltic States: Evacuation of Baltic Nationals to Sweden', WO 208/2076, NAUK; and 'Einsatzbericht' 2, 15/2/45, T-580, r. 78, NA.

6   Stahl, 113–15; A. Gornitskii, *Sredi Vragov i Druzei* (Uzhgorod, 1965), 286; Haley to MFIU, 22/6/45, IRR File XE 000417, RG 319, NA; 'CIR 4 – The German Sabotage Service', 23/7/45, IRR File XE 070687, RG 319, NA; Radl int., 4/6/45; War Room to 12th AG, 4/6/45; 12th AG AMZON to War Room (London), 11/6/45; and 'Extract from USFET Weekly Counter-Intelligence Summary for Week ending 10th July, 1945', all in Entry 119A, RG 226, NA.

7   Gambke/Raupach/Peters int., 15/8/45, Entry 119A, RG 226, NA.

8   For evidence of sharing of personnel between Skorzeny's units and 'Zeppelin', see ZIP/ISOSICLE 5378, 1/9/43; 5388, 3/9/43, both in HW 19/237, NAUK; 8060, 30/10/43; and 8097, 1/11/43, both in HW 19/239, NAUK.

9   Huegel int., 14/6/45; Gambke/Raupach/Peters int., 15/8/45; 'Internal Memorandum: Sandberger', 22/8/45, all in Entry 119A, RG 226, NA; and 'Vlassov Army or ROA', 16/9/46, IRR File ZF 015110, RG 319, NA.

10 'Kampf in Rücken des Feindes', 12/11/44, RH 2/1929, BMA.

11 ZIP/ISOSICLE 9208, 31/12/43, HW 19/241, NAUK; and ULTRA/ZIP/ISOSICLE 11962, 3/10/44, HW 19/247, NAUK.

12 Hengelhaupt to Gehlen, 12/5/44, T-78, r. 566, fr. 892–93, 896–97, NA; 'Antibolschewistische Widerstandsbewegungen und Banden in der Sowjetunion', 15/8/44, T-78, r. 493, fr. 6480051–67, NA; 'Zusammenstellung von Meldungen über sowjetfeindliche Banden im rückwärtigen Feindgebiet', 2/44, T-78, r. 497, fr. 6485191–204, NA; 'Nachrichten über Bandenkrieg', 3/5/43, T-78, r. 493, NA; 'Russland – Ernährungswirtschaft', 10/44, T-78, r. 488, fr. 6473582, NA; 'Zusammenfassung der Frontaufklärungsmeldungen', 20/11/44, RH 2/2126, BMA; 'Frontaufklärungsmeldungen', 13/1/45, RH 2/2127, BMA; 'Sowj. Nachr. Agent Wyspakow, M.P. (Raum Stanislaw)', 7/7/44, RH 2/2123, BMA; 'Auszug aus Kgf.Vern Leitstelle II Ost Nr. 202/1.45', 8/2/45; 'Auszug aus Ic Tagesmeldung v. 2.11.44', both in RH 2/2337, BMA; 'Auszug aus Abwehrmeldungen FHO IIa Nr. 372/45 geh. v. 13.1.45', T-78, r. 566, fr. 421, NA; and Gambke/Raupach/Peters int., 15/8/45, Entry 119A, RG 226, NA.

13 Andreyev, 209; Mark Elliot, 'Andrei Vlassov', *Military Affairs* 16 (1982), 86; Ilya Dzhirkvelov, *Secret Servant* (New York, 1987), 34–35; 'Zusammenstellung von Meldungen über sowjetfeindliche Banden im rückwärtigen Feindgebiet', 2/44, T-78, r. 497, fr. 6485195, NA; 'GPG', 20/11/44, FO 898/187, PRO; 'Vlassov Army or ROA', 16/9/46, IRR File ZF 015110, RG 319, NA; and Gambke/Raupach/Peters int., 15/8/45, Entry 119A, RG 226, NA.

14 'Der V-Mann: Ratschläge zu seiner Ausbildung im Rahmen eines Einsatzlagers', enclosure 1–2, T-77, r. 1453, fr. 974–75, NA.

15 ZIP/ISOSICLE 1328, 28/7/43; and 6868, 7/9/43, all in HW 19/237, NAUK.

16 ZIP/ISOSICLE 6231, 10/9/43; and 6396, 10/9/43, both in HW 19/237, NAUK.

17 Nekrich, 69–83; Conquest, 47–48, 100–05; Hoffmann, 43, 91–92, 95–96; 181, 192–93; Gellermann, 81–82; Öbsger/Röder int., 26/7/46, CIANF, Entry 86, RG 263, NA; 'Zusammenstellung von Meldungen über sowjetfeindliche Banden im rückwärtigen Feindgebiet', 2/44, T-78, r. 497, fr. 6485199–200, NA; Johannsohn int., 26/7/45, XL 13274, Entry 19, RG 226, NA; 'Die Innere Lage in der UdSSR', 22/4/44, T-78, r. 583, fr. 402–03, NA; 'Zusammenstellung von Meldungen über sowjetfeindliche Banden im rückwärtigen Feindgebiet', 2/44, T-78, r. 497, fr. 6485200, NA; 'Antibolschewistische Widerstandsbewegungen und Banden in

der Sowjetunion', 15/8/44, T-78, r. 493, fr. 6480064–65, NA; Gambke/Raupach/Peters int., 15/8/45, Entry 119A, RG 226, NA; ZIP/ISOSICLE 7862, 24/10/43; 8174, 4/11/43; 7881, 25/10/43; 7882, 25/10/43, all in HW 19/238, NAUK; 7932, 26/10/43; 8036, 30/10/43; 8045, 29/10/43; 8083, 30/10/43; 8084, 31/10/43; all in HW 19/239, NAUK; and ULTRA/ZIP/ISOSICLE 12055, 8/9/44, HW 19/247, NAUK.

18   'Auszug Leitst II Ost Nr. D 11117/44g (A/Ausw. 486) v. 22.11.44 Reg. Nr. 11885/44g-II/4528' (fr. 452–453); and 'Auszug aus Kgf.Vern. Frd. H. Ost (IIIa) Nr. 1267 v. 17.1.45' (fr. 400), both in T-78, r. 566, NA.

19   'Die Innere Lage in der UdSSR', 22/4/44, T-78, r. 583, fr. 391–92, 395, 406, 408–09, NA; Hengelhaupt to Gehlen, 12/5/44 (fr. 896–97); 'Feststellungen zur Feindlage', 1/2/45 (fr. 394), both in T-78, r. 566, NA; 'Antibolschewistische Widerstandsbewegungen und Banden in der Sowjetunion', 15/8/44, T-78, r. 493, fr. 6480052, 6480056–57, NA; 'Zusammenstellung von Meldungen über sowjetfeindliche Banden im rückwärtigen Feindgebiet', 2/44, T-78, r. 497, fr. 6485191–93, NA; and Gambke/Raupach/Peters int., 15/8/45, Entry 119A, RG 226, NA.

20   Gambke/Raupach/Peters int., 15/8/45, Entry 119A, RG 226, NA.

21   Steenberg, 76–80.

22   'Auszug aus Übersetzung Nachrichten v. 16.4.44 (III f Nr. 107/44 v. 17.4.44', T-78, r. 583, fr. 653–54, NA; Hengelhaupt to Gehlen, 12/5/44 (fr. 893); and 'Auszug aus Obkdo d. Luftw. Führ. St. Ic Nr. 25/45 geh. V. 25.1.45: Kgf.Vern.' (fr. 363), both in T-78, r. 566, NA.

23   DEG 3433, 17/7/44, HW 19/276, NAUK; ULTRA/ZIP/ISOSICLE 12774, 27/10/44; 12775, 4/11/44; 12776, 12/11/44; 12777, 13/11/44; 12778, 17/11/44; 12779, 27/11/44; 12780, 23/12/44; 12781, 23/12/44; 12782, 24/1/45; 12783, 29/1/45; 12784, 31/1/45; 12786, 30/10/44; 12787, 13/11/44; 12788, 16/11/44; 12789, 27/11/44; 12792, 2/11/44; 12793, 27/1/45; 12794, 20/10/44; 12801, 7/9/44; 12802, 28/9/44; 12803, 16/10/44; 12806, 23/8/44; 12807, 28/8/44; 12815, 21/8/44; 12816, 21/9/44; 12817, 4/10/44; 12822, 30/8/44; 12823, 1/9/44; and 12826, 30/8/44, all in HW 19/248, NAUK.

24   Gellermann, 77–78, 95; Simpson, 220–21; and Gambke/Raupach/Peters int., 15/8/45, Entry 119A, RG 226, NA.

25   'Interview of White Russian Leaders', 25/5/46, IRR File ZF 015110, RG 319, NA.

26   'Der V-Mann: Ratschläge zu seiner Ausbildung im Rahmen eines Einsatzlagers', T-77, r. 1453, fr. 968–69, NA; and Gambke/Raupach/Peters int., 15/8/45, Entry 119A, RG 226, NA.

27   Gellermann, 81, 187.

28   V.V. Korovin and V.I. Shibalin, 'Gitlerovskii Abwehr Terpit Porazhenie', Novaia i Noveishaia Istoriya 12 (1968), 104; Gellermann, 186; Hilz int., 9/8/45, in Covert Warfare, xiii; Hilz int., 7/5/45; Gambke/Raupach/Peters int., 15/8/45, both in Entry 119A, RG 226, NA; 'Interrogation Report on Survivors of a German Crew', 6/3/45, 120249, Entry 16, RG 226, NA; Dudarov to the Kommanduer der Osttruppen zbV. 741 b. Obkdo. H. Gr. A, 5/9/43; and 'Protokoll über den Beschluss des Kabardinischen Nationalauschusses den 6. September 1943', both in R 6/145, BA.

29   Steenberg, 124; and JNSV (Amsterdam, 1978), ixx, 44–46.

30   Gellermann, 187; Gambke/Raupach/Peters int., 15/8/45, Entry 119A, RG 226, NA; and 'CIR 4 – The German Sabotage Service', 23/7/45, IRR File XE 070687, RG 319, NA.

31   Deutsche Allgemeine Zeitung, 22/10/44; Berliner Illustrierte Nachtausgabe, 25/11/44; 'GPG', 23/10/44; 30/10/44; 20/11/44; 4/12/44, all in FO 898/187, NAUK; and 'ND' 1597, 6/11/44, BC, Robbins Library.

32   'GPG', 22/1/45; and 18/2/45, both in FO 898/187, NAUK.

33   Vakar, 190, 195–196, 203–06, 220; and Lester Eckman and Chaim Lazar, The Jewish Resistance (New York, 1977), 220–221.

34   'Zusammenstellung von Meldungen über sowjetfeindliche Banden im rückwärtigen Feindgebiet', 2/1944, T-78, r. 497, fr. 6485192, NA; 'IIb Auszug aus Übersetzung Nachrichten v. 16.4.44 (III f Nr. 107/44 v. 17.4.44', 18/4/44, T-78, r. 583, fr. 653–54, NA; and 'Zusammenfassung der Frontaufklärungsmeldungen', 20/11/44, RH 2/2126, BMA.

35   Smirnov, 217–19; Pogranichnye Voiska SSSR v Velikoi Otechestvennoi Voine, 416–18, 491; Vladimir Pozniakov, 'Commoners, Commissars, and Spies', in Victory in Europe, 1945 (Lawrence, 2000), 186; 'Antibolschewistische Widerstandsbewegungen und Banden in der Sowjetunion', 15/8/44, T-78, r. 493, fr. 6480055, NA; 'Frontaufklärungsmeldungen', 19/12/44, RH 2/2126, BMA; Weisel, report, 4/10/44, RH 15/297, BMA; and 'Bericht über Gefechtshandlungen des Gren. Rgt. 487 (267 ID) von 22.6 bis 6.7.44 und anschliessendes Durchschlagen der Kampfgruppe "Blechwenn"', 28/9/44, RH 15/380, BMA; 'Auszug aus Kgf.-Aussagen (II b-Nr. 4382) – AOK 9 Ic/AO v. 7.11.44' (fr. 465); and 'Aufstellung von polnischen und weissrussischen nationalen Banden', 7/11/44 (fr. 462), T-78, r. 566, NA.

36   Smirnov, 261; John Loftus, The Belarus Secret (New York, 1982), 42–43; Pozniakov, 186–87; Vakar, Belorussia, 196, 221–22, 278; 'Funkspruch' 45, 3/11/44, RH 19/300, BMA; 'Frontaufklärungs-meldungen', 16/12/44, RH 2/2126, BMA; 'Übersicht über die Bandenlage in der Zeit vom 1.12–13.12.1944', 6/1/45, RH 2/2130, BMA; 'The Situation in East Prussia', 9/1/45, L 52395, Entry 21, RG 226, NA; 'Auszug aus LNA (III)/Chef

HNW v. 1.12.44' (fr. 452); 'Auszug aus Gen. D. Nachr. Aufkl. Nr. 97/45 g. Kdos. v. 22.3.45' (fr. 342), both in T-78, r. 566, NA; and Gambke/Raupach/Peters int., 15/8/45, Entry 119A, RG 226, NA.

37 Hans Becher, *Devil on My Shoulder* (London, 1955), 59–73; Paul Carell, *Scorched Earth* (Boston, 1966), 510–13; Weisel, report, 4/10/44; 'Rückkämpferbericht zu den Ereignissen vom 30.6.44 nachmittags', 24/12/44, both in RH 15/297, BMA; 'Bericht über die Gefechtshandlung des Gren. Regt. 487 (267ID) vom 22.6 bis 6.7.44 und anschliessendes Durchschlagen der Kampfgruppe "Blechwenn"', 28/9/44, RH 15/380, BMA; 'Abschrift der Anlage zu Schreiben Wehrkreiskommando XXI Ic Az. Allg. vom 6.8.1944', RH 2/2129, BMA; 'Auszug aus Auswertung von Kgf.-Aussagen (IIb-Nr. 4259) – Pz. AOK 3 Ic/AO Dolm. Nr. 01900/44 geh. vom 19.10.44', T-78, r. 566, fr. 471, NA; 'Stimmen von der Front und aus der Heimat' 21, 4/8/44, NY 4034/577, SAPMO-BA; and *UPASND*, vii, 130.

38 Foley, 170–75; Skorzeny, *La Guerre Inconnue*, 349–55; Skorzeny, *Wir Kämpften – Wir Verloren*, 58–64; Gellermann, 112–41, 168; Stahl, 139–50; *Krasnaya Zvezda*, 23/9/95; 'Unternehmen Scherhorn', c. 31/12/44, RH 2/2152, BMA; 'Vortragsnotiz', 25/2/45; Bahrenbruch, FAK 103 to Gen. St. d. Heeres/FHO, 12/2/45; Skorzeny to Gehlen, 6/3/45; 'Vortragsnotiz', 6/3/45; Scherhorn to Abt. FHO(Ib), 8/3/45; FHO(Ib) to Scherhorn, 9/3/45; 'Vortragsnotiz', 9/3/45; 'Vortragsnotiz', 10/3/45; 'Unternehmen Scherhorn', 11/3/45; 'Unternehmen Scherhorn', 17/3/45; 'Geheime Kommandosache, ' 10/4/45, all in RH 2/2153, BMA; 'Notes on SS, SD and RSHA Mil Amt', 10/4/45, WO 208/3616, NAUK; and 'CIR 4 – The German Sabotage Service', 23/7/45, IRR File XE 070687, RG 319, NA.

39 *Pogranichnye Voiska SSSR v Velikoi Otechestvennoi Voine*, 400–16, 422–24; 'Stimmen von der Front und aus der Heimat' 20, 15/7/44; and 21, 4/8/44, both in NY 4034/577, SAPMO-BA.

40 Gellermann, 142–69; Stephen, *Stalin's Secret War*, 175–82; Dieter Sevin, 'Operation Scherhorn', *Military Review* 46 (1966), 42–43; Pavel Sudaplatov, *Special Tasks* (Boston, 1994), 152–60, 167–69; *Krasnaya Zvezda*, 23/9/95; and *Die Zeit*, 19/6/52.

41 Armstrong, *Ukrainian Nationalism*, 99–100, 148–49, 152–54, 177–78, 184; Peter Potichnyj, 'The Ukrainian Insurgent Army (UPA) and the German Authorities', in *German-Ukrainian Relations in Historical Perspective* (Edmonton, 1994), 164–65; Reuben Ainsztein, *Jewish Resistance in Nazi-Occupied Europe* (London, 1974), 253, 358–60, 446; Görlitz, 103, 109; Eckman and Lazar, 10–11; SID 4th SVC Report, 26/7/45, OSS XL 13274, Entry 19, RG 226, NA; Gambke/Raupach/Peters int., 15/8/45, Entry 119A, RG 226, NA; 'Vortragsnotiz', 19/5/43, RH 2/2089, BA; *UPASND*, vi, 79–81, 92, 97–98, 144–45; vii, 124, 132, 140, 141, 142; 'Vortragsnotiz', 15/1/44, T-78, r. 556, fr. 701, NA; and E. Köstring and F. Halder, 'The Peoples of the Soviet Union', in *WWIIGMS*, ixx. For brief mention of Borovets's special services unit, see Pavlo Shandruk, *Arms of Valor* (New York, 1959), 254.

42 Leonid Grenkevich, *The Soviet Partisan Movement, 1941–1944* (London, 1999), 139; and Potichnyj, 169.

43 'Vortragsnotiz', 15/1/44, T-78, r. 556, fr. 701–02, NA. For the term 'Green Cadre', see Heike, 24.

44 Heike, 53–54, 64–65, 68, 105, 111, 133, 137; Armstrong, *Ukrainian Nationalism*, 169–74; Myroslav Yurkevich, 'Galician Ukrainians in German Military Formations and the German Administration', in *The Ukraine during World War II* (Edmonton, 1986), 77–78; Erich Kern, *Der Grosse Rausch* (Zurich, 1948), 150–51; Bohdan Panchuk, *Heroes of their Day* (Toronto, 1983), 154; *UPASND*, vi, 138, 169; vii, 127; 'Auszug aus Bandenlagebericht, 24.5.44', RH 2/2090, BMA; 'Die OUN-UPA', 17/11/44, R 6/150, BA; and 'Politische Informationen', 15/10/44, T-78, r. 493, NA; 'Auszug aus Pz AOK 3 Nr. 1/45 v. 1.1.: Überl.- v. Gef. Auss.' 22/3/45, T-78, r. 566, fr. 341, NA; Gambke/Raupach/Peters int., 15/8/45; and Heinze int., 7/9/45, both in Entry 119A, RG 226, NA.

45 *UPASND*, vi, 112–15, 117, 119, 155–56; V.F. Nekrasov, 'Vnutrennie Voiska na Zavarshaiushchem etape Velikoi Otechestvennoi Voiny', *Voprosy Istorii* 5 (1985), 98; and Malkov to Burress, 9/10/46, IRR File XE 020651, RG 319, NA.

46 *UPASND*, vi, 112–13, 114, 115, 117–18, 125–26, 139, 142, 143–44, 155–56, 158, 168–70, 178–79, 180–81, 182, 196; vii, 11, 36, 164, 196–97; Potichnyj, 169, 176; 'Auszug aus Bandenlage für die Monat April der 4. Panzerarmee', 5/5/44, RH 2/2090, BMA; 'Monatsbericht für Mai 1944'; 'Auszug aus Monatsbericht der GFP Mai 1944', 29/6/44, both in RH 2/2129, BMA; 'Bandennachrichtenbericht' 17, 20/7/44, RH 19II/243, BMA; 'Die OUN-UPA', 17/11/44, R 6/150, BA; interview with Yetven Shtendera, 25/10/88; 'Interrogation Report' 26, 2/8/45, XL 15457, Entry 19, RG 226, NA; 'CIR 4 – The German Sabotage Service', 23/7/45, IRR File XE 070687, RG 319, NA; Malkov to Burress, 9/10/46, IRR File XE 020651, RG 319, NA; 'FAK 205', 28/1/46; Gambke/Raupach/Peters int., 15/8/45, both in Entry 119A, RG 226, NA; Murad int., 18/1/46, in *Covert Warfare*, xiii; 'Politische Informationen', 15/10/44, T-78, r. 493, NA; ULTRA/ZIP/ISO-SICLE 12539, 20/2/45; 12519, 22/2/45; and 12769, 17/3/45, all in HW 19/248, NAUK.

47 *UPASND*, vi, 158, 181; and vii, 28, 69; and Potichnyj, 170.

48 *UPASND*, vii, 15, 32, 69, 119, 131; Dallin, 605; John Armstrong, *Ukrainian Nationalism* (Littleton, 1980), p. 292; Gellermann, 95, 176–77; N. Sokolenko, 'Serdtse Chekista', in *Front bez Linii Fronta* (Moscow, 1970), 378–81; Heike, 156; Stephen Khrin, 'Battle at Lishchava Horishnya', in *The Ukrainian Insurgent Army in Fight*

for Freedom (New York, 1954), 189–90, 195, 198–99, 201–02, 205; 'FAK 202', 23/11/45, IRR File XE 020651, RG 319, NA; 'II b Auszug aus Pz-AOK 3 Nr. 1/45 v. 1.1.: Überl.V. Gef. Auss.' (fr. 341); RSHA/Amt Mil to FHO (I Bd.) and Mil D (über V.O.), 7/3/45 (fr. 357); 'Auszug aus Gef.Vern. Nr. 314–78 Volks-Sturmdivision v. 11.2.45' (fr. 390), all in T-78, r. 566, NA; 'Skorzeny, Otto', 19/5/45; and Gambke/Raupach/Peters int., 15/8/45, Entry 119A, RG 226, NA.

49   *UPASND*, vi, 181; vii, 13, 30, 37, 69, 106–09, 122, 123, 130–31, 135, 164, 181, 188, 189, 190, 191, 194, 196, 202, 205; Skorzeny, *La Guerre Inconnue*, 336–38; Skorzeny, *Wir Kämpften – Wir Verloren*, 112–13; Gellermann, 177–80; Potichnyj, 169–70; 'CIR 4 – The German Sabotage Service', 23/7/45, IRR File 070687, RG 319, NA; Murad int., 18/1/46, in *Covert Warfare*, xiii; Malkov to Burress, 9/10/46, IRR File XE 020651, RG 319, NA; Gambke/Raupach/Peters int., 15/8/45, Entry 119A, RG 226, NA; '15 Tage Meldung über UPA Einheiten in Feindgebiet', 1/12/44, RH 2/2126, BMA; 'Auszug aus Kgf.–Vernehmung (IIb – Nr. 4242) – 371 I.D. Ic vom 30.9.44' (fr. 470); 'IIb Auszug aus Kgf.-Vernehmung Nr. 69 (IIb-Nr. 4380) – 544 Gren. Div. Ic v. 22.10.44' (fr. 440); 'Auszug aus Kgf.-Vernehmung (IIb – Nr. 4327) – 544. Gren. Div. Ic v. 23.10.44' (fr. 452); 'Anlage zu Schrb. Frontaufkl.Trupp 150/2 (Rü/T) über A. Gr.Wöhler Ic/AO (Abw.) Nr. 471/44 off v. 5.12.44' (fr. 437); '15 Tage-Meldung über UPA-Einheiten im Feindgebiet', 1/4/45 (fr. 330, 334); 'Auszug aus Obkdo. D. Luftw. Führ St. Ic Nr. 25/45 geh.V. 25.1.45: Kgf.Vern.' (fr. 363), all in T-78, r. 566, NA; and *The New York Times*, 18/4/46.

50   *History of the Great Patriotic War of the Soviet Union, 1941–1945* (Moscow), iv, 424; Pozniakov, 186; *UPASND*, vii, 32, 90, 122–43, 163, 165; 'Die OUN-UPA', 17/11/44, R 6/150, BA; 'Übersicht über die Bandenlage in der Zeit vom 5.10–31.10.1944', 4/11/44; '1.11–30.11.1944', 5/12/44, both in RH 2/2130, BMA; 'Übersicht über das im Monat Oktober beim Referat IIb eingegangen Material', 14/11/44, T-78, r. 497, fr. 6485408, NA; 'Auszug aus Kgf.-Vernehmung (Iib-Nr. 4250) – Gen. Kdo. LIX A.K. Ic vom 7.10.1944' (fr. 480); 'Auszug aus Kgf.-Vernehmung (IIb-Nr. 4327) – 544. Gren Div.V. 23.10.44' (fr. 452); Rf-SS to Abt. FHO, RSHA/Mil D/SO, RSHA/Amt VI C, 17/11/44 (fr. 456); 'Auszug aus Information SS-Standarte "Kurt Eggers" SS Jagdverband Befehlstelle Ost Ic v. 3.1.45' (fr. 416), all in T-78, r. 566, NA; ULTRA/ZIP/ISOS 94058, 8/1/45, HW 19/79, NAUK; Berger int., IRR File XE 000417, RG 319, NA; and Gambke/Raupach/Peters int., 15/8/45, Entry 119A, RG 226, NA.

51   *UPASND*, vii, 125, 135, 143, 163, 164, 192, 202, 203; 'IIb Auszug aus Kgf.-Vernehmung Nr. 69 (IIb-nr. 4380) – 544 Gren. Div. Ic v. 22.10.44' (fr. 440); 'Auszug aus Gefangenenvernehmung Nr. 85 und 86 v. 31.10.44, 544. Volks-Gren. Div., Abt. Ic (IIb-Nr. 4441)' (fr. 428); and '15-Tage-Meldung über UPA-Einheiten im Feindgebiet', 1/4/45, all in T-78, r. 566, NA.

52   David Marples, *Stalinism in the Ukraine in the 1940s* (New York, 1992), 90–91.

53   'CIR 4 – The German Sabotage Service', 23/7/45, IRR File XE 070687, RG 319, NA; 'FAK 202', 23/11/45, IRR File 020651, RG 319, NA; Dörner to OKH/FHO, 7/3/45, RH 2/2006, BMA; RSHA/Amt Mil to FHO (I Bd.) and Mil D (über V.O.), 7/3/45, T-78, r. 566, fr. 357, NA; and *UPASND*, vii, 201.

54   'CIR 4 – The German Sabotage Service', 23/7/45, IRR File XE 070687, RG 319, NA; and 'FAK 202', 23/11/45, IRR File 020651, RG 319, NA.

55   Potichnyj, 169.

56   *UPASND*, vii, 109–10; and Gambke/Raupach/Peters int., 15/8/45, Entry 119A, RG 226, NA.

57   Rings, 267.

58   Bower, 23, 54, 120–21, 133; Fischer, *Soviet Opposition to Stalin*, 81; Shandruk, 195–213, 218–39, 247–48, 257–59; Jeffrey Burds, 'The Early Cold War in Soviet West Ukraine, 1944–1948', Carl Beck Papers No. 1505 (Pittsburgh, 2001), 20–23, 60; Potichnyj, 169–70, 176; Jürgen Thorwald, *The Illusion* (New York, 1974), 187–92, 234; Armstrong, *Ukrainian Nationalism*, 178–80, 185; Skorzeny, *La Guerre Inconnue*, 336–38; W. Kosyk, 'Le Mouvement National Ukrainien de Résistance 1941–1944', in *Revue d'histoire de la deuxième guerre mondiale et des conflits contemporains* 141 (1986), 74; Steenberg, 163–64; Dallin, 621–25, 646; *UPASND*, vi, 154, 155, 172, 181; vii, 12, 13, 27–28, 32, 37, 119–20, 152–53, 154, 157, 181; 'Aufzeichnung-Gegenwärtiger Stand der ukrainischen Frage', 28/9/44, R 6/141, BA; Berger to Himmler, 6/10/44, NS 19/1513, BA; 'Die OUN-UPA', 17/11/44, R 6/150, BA; Sperber to Lindeiner, 27/3/45, RH 2/2008, BMA; Böhrsch to Einsatzkommandos mit FS-Verbindung, 18/12/44, T-175, r. 640, fr. 621, NA; RSHA/Amt Mil to FHO (I Bd.) and Mil D (über V.O.), 7/3/45, T-78, r. 566, fr. 358, NA; SSU report, 31/8/45, XL 27108, Entry 19, RG 226, NA; 'CIR 4 – The German Sabotage Service', 23/7/45, IRR File XE 070687, RG 319, NA; Gambke/Raupach/Peters int., 15/8/45, Entry 119A, RG 226, NA; and interview with Yetvhen Shtendera, 25/10/88.

59   'CIR 4 – The German Sabotage Service', 23/7/45, IRR File 070687, RG 319, NA.

60   Reitlinger, 205; and Dallin, 182–85.

61   Visvaldis Mangulis, *Latvia in the Wars of the 20th Century* (Princeton, 1983), 136, 145–46; Vanadzins, 63, 65; Dallin, 648; Rosenburg to Lammers, 11/44; 'Vertretungen der baltischen Länder im deutschen Reich', 23/11/44; 'Schaffung eines lettischen Nationalkomitee', 5/12/44, all in R 6/141, BA; Brandt to Berger, 9/2/45; Berger to Himmler, 9/2/45, both in NS 19/3836, BA; 'ND' 1691, 23/2/45, BC, Robbins Library; and *Völkischer Beobachter*, 23/2/45. For Berger's support of Pechau's company, see 'Summary 710 – Gerhardt', IWM.

62   'Mežakaki (SS mednieku savieniba - Austrumzeme)', *Latvijas Vesture Interneta*, <http://www.historia.lv/alfabets/M/Me/mezakaki/mezakaki.htm>, as of 3/1/05.

63   Mangulis, 145–46, 151; Müller to Dönitz, 5/5/45, T-77, r. 864, fr. 5611862, NA; and Hilpart to Keitel, 6/5/45, R 62/18, BA.

64   'CIR 4 – The German Sabotage Service', 23/7/45, IRR File XE 070687, RG 319, NA.

65   Evald Uustalu, *For Freedom Only* (Toronto, 1977), 27, 84, 89–90, 104.

66   Neumann int., 15/9/45, ETO MIS-Y-Sect. CSDIC/WEA Interim Reports, Special Interrogation Reports 1945–46, RG 338, NA; and 'Auszug aus Stbs. Offz. B. Obkdo. H. Gr. Kurland Nr. 400/45 geh. v. 8.2.45', T-78, r. 566, fr. 391, NA.

67   Gambke/Raupach/Peters int., 15/8/45, Entry 119A, RG 226, NA.

68   'CIR 4 – The German Sabotage Service', 23/7/45, IRR File XE 070687, RG 319, NA; Le Haye int., 22/11/44; Pott int., 20/5/45, both in Entry 119A, RG 226, NA; ULTRA/ZIP/ISOSICLE 12799, 20/3/45; 12810, 3/3/45; 12825, 6/3/45; and 12833, 4/3/45, all in HW 19/248, NAUK.

69   Seppo Myllyniemi, *Die Neuordnung der baltischen Länder 1941–1944* (Helsinki, 1973), 277–80; Thomas Remeikis, *Opposition to Soviet Rule in Lithuania* (Chicago, 1980), 180–82; Bower, 41–42; Juozos Daumantis, *Fighters for Freedom* (New York, 1975), 68; Clarence Manning, *The Forgotten Republic* (Westport, 1971), 227; and report by Lithuanian refugees, 25/8/44, 103435, Entry 16, RG 226, NA.

70   'Bericht über Gefechtshandlungen des Gren. Rgt. 487 (267 ID) vom 22.6 bis 6.7.44 und anschliessendes Durchschlagen der Kampfgruppe "Blechwenn"', 28/9/44, RH 15/380, BMA; and Becker, report, 30/9/44, RH 15/297, BMA. A seventy-man Lithuanian guerrilla group overrun by the Soviets west of Alitus in the spring of 1945 contained several German soldiers and was commanded by a German officer. *Pogranichnye Voiska SSSR* (Moscow, 1975), 67.

71   Remeikis, 183; and 'Einsatz' 1485, 14/9/44, RH 19II/300, BMA.

72   'Kampf in Rücken des Feindes', 1211/44, RH 2/1929, BMA; 'CIR 4 – The German Sabotage Service', 23/7/45, IRR File XE 070687, RG 319, NA; Huygens int., 30/3/45; Gambke/Raupach/Peters int., 15/8/45, both in Entry 119A, RG 226, NA; ULTRA/ZIP/ISOSICLE 12811, 8/3/45; 12834, 9/3/45; 12843, 12/3/45; and 12845, 11/3/45, all in HW 19/248, NAUK.

73   Daumantis, 79; Stephen Dorril, *MI-6* (New York, 2002), 273; Remeikas, 59–60; Stanley Vardys, 'The Partisan Movement in Postwar Lithuania', in *Lithuania under the Soviets: Portrait of a Nation* (New York, 1965), 94–95; FAK 103 to Ic/AO, 19/8/44; 'Anlage nr. 1 zu Nr. 166', 28/8/44, both in RH 19II/300, BMA; and Gambke/Raupach/Peters int., 15/8/45, Entry 119A, RG 226, NA.

74   Remeikis, 60, 178–79.

75   Bower, 46–47; Barbara Armonas, *Leave Your Tears in Moscow* (Philadelphia, 1961), 27–34, 37; Daumantis, 79–80; Vardys, 85–107; 'Auszug aus V-Mann Meldung Leitst. II Ost Nr. 190/1.45 v. 9.1.45', T-78, r. 566, fr. 421, NA; and 'Zusammenfassung der Frontaufklärungsmeldungen', 4/1/45, RH 2/2127, BMA.

76   Anatole Lieven, *The Baltic Revolution* (New Haven, 1993), 10, 35, 46, 51, 57, 58, 59; and Fischer, *Germany's War Aims*, 108, 117, 239, 241, 273–77, 348, 353–54, 456–62, 480–81, 489–90, 494–95, 503, 598–607.

77   Vanadzins, 43, 46–47; Adolf Blodenieks, *The Undefeated Nation* (New York, 1960), 260–61; Bower, 44–45; Dorril, 272–73; Mangulis, 131, 136–37; 'Lage-bericht', 23/11/44, RH 2/2129, BMA; Johnson to the Secretary of State, 3/2/45, Enclosure 1, 188090, Entry 16, RG 226, NA; 'Auszug aus Auswertung von Kgf.-Aussagen (IIIb-Nr. 4225) – AOK/Nr. 3422/44 geh. Vom 18.9.1944', T-78, r. 566, fr. 464, NA; 'Interrogation Report' 22, 19/7/45, IRR File XE 002693, RG 319, NA; Gambke/Raupach/Peters int., 15/8/45, Entry 119A, RG 226, NA; and 'Mežakaki (SS mednieku savieniba - Austrumzeme)', <http://www.historia.lv/alfabets/M/Me/mezakaki/mezakaki.htm>, as of 3/1/05. For the recruitment and training of Latvians by the 'Zeppelin' apparatus in Germany, see Sowers int., Entry 119A, RG 226, NA. For the character assessment of Jeckeln, see 'I. Notes on Police Organisation of Duisberg, Hamborn incl. General Notes on Police; II. SD, SS and Schupo Personalities', 18/1/45, WO 208/3611, NAUK.

78   'Übersicht über die Bandenlage in der Zeit vom 1.11–30.11.1944', 5/12/44, RH 2/2130, BMA.

79   Vanadzins, 46; and 'Lage-bericht', 23/11/44, RH 2/2129, BMA.

80   'Mežakaki (SS mednieku savieniba - Austrumzeme)', <http://www.historia.lv/alfabets/M/Me/mezakaki/mezakaki.htm>, as of 3/1/05.

81   Vanadzins, 49; 'Lage-bericht', 23/11/44, RH 2/2129, BMA; and Gambke/Raupach/Peters int., 15/8/45, Entry 119A, RG 226, NA.

82   Vanadzins, 47–48, 75; *Borba Latyshkogo Naroda v gody Velikoi Otechestvennoi Voiny* (Riga, 1970), 903–04; and Bower, 46.

83   Vanadzins, 58, 63, 64–66; Sowers int.; 12th AG to War Room (London), 11/6/45; War Room to 12th AG, 14/6/45; 'Minute Sheet', 18/6/45, all in Entry 119A, RG 226, NA; 'CIR 4 – The German Sabotage Service', 23/7/45, IRR File XE 070687, RG 319, NA; ULTRA/ZIP/ISISICLE 12882, 15/3/45, HW 19/248, NAUK; and Gunars Grapmanis, r. A3343 SSO-028A, fr. 1008, RG 242, NA.

84   Vanadzins, 65; DEG 3860, 22/12/44, HW 19/277, NAUK; ULTRA/ZIP/ISOSICLE 12800, 20/3/45;

12882, 15/3/45, both in HW 19/248, NAUK; 'CIR 4 – The German Sabotage Service', 23/7/45, IRR File XE 070687, RG 319, NA; Olmes int., Entry 119A, RG 226, NA; and 'Mežakaki (SS mednieku savieniba - Austrumzeme)', <http://www.historia.lv/alfabets/M/Me/mezakaki/mezakaki.htm>, as of 3/1/05.

85   'Kampf in Rücken des Feindes', 12/11/44, RH 2/1929, BMA.

86   Documents on Polish-German Relations (London, 1967), ii, 331. See also 69, 84, 123, 317, 319, 374, 531.

87   Richard Lukas, The Forgotten Holocaust (Lexington, 1986), 48, 50, 52–53, 63–64, 74.

88   Zbigniew Siemaszko, Norodowe Siły Zbrojne (London, 1982), 93.

89   Lukas, 73, 110, 113–14; Documents on Polish-Soviet Relations, ii, 1–3, 7, 696–702; John Fox, 'Der Fall Katyn und die Propaganda des NS-Regimes', Vierteljahrshefte für Zeitgeschichte 30 (1982), 496–97; and Report 62067, 24/2/44, Entry 16, RG 226, NA.

90   Krakauer Zeitung, 26 Oct. 1944; Lukas, 115–16; and 'Final Report on the Case of Walter Friedrich Schellenberg', in Covert Warfare, xiii.

91   Stanislaw Piotrowski, Hans Frank Tagebuch (Warsaw, 1963), 198; Werner Maser, Nuremberg (New York, 1979), 46–47; 'ND' 1686, 17/2/45, BC, Robbins Library; 'Interrogation Report' 10, 21/6/45, IRR File XE 000440, RG 319, NA; and 'Intelligence Summary' 146, 22/3/45, vol. 16396, RG 24, Series 90, NAC.

92   'Bericht', 14/1/44, T-175, r. 642, fr. 2, NA; 'Die Widerstandsbewegung im Gebeit des Ehem. Polen', 9/2/44, T-78, r. 497, fr. 6485337, NA; and 'Übersicht über die Banden in der Zeit vom 21.7–31.8.1944', 7/9/44, RH 2/2130, BMA.

93   Witold Sagajllo, Man in the Middle (London, 1984), 23, 44–46, 66–67, 72, 77, 79–80, 112–13, 121; Lukas, 116; Z.S. Siemaszko, 'Rozmowy z Wehrmachtem w Wilnie, Luty 1944', Zeszyty Historyczne 69 (1984), 87–107; Jozef Swida, 'Wyjasnienie Dotyczace Okresu 1943/1944', Zeszyty Historyczne 73 (1985), 76–79; Z.S. Siemaszko, 'Płk Prawdzic-Szlaski Organizator AK na Nowagródczyznie', Zeszyty Historyczne 67 (1984), 20, 22; Johnson to Secretary of State, Enclosed Report, 7/6/44, 86928, Entry 16, RG 226, NA; 'Vortragsnotiz: Weisspolnische Banden (Walli III-Meldung)', 19/3/44, T-78, r. 556, fr. 672, NA; 'Weiss polnische Banden', 18/1/44; 'Aktennotiz – Rücksprache mit Major Christiansen von OKW-Verbindungsstelle', 18/1/44; and memo, all in R 6/369, BA.

94   'Politische Ausrichtung der AK', 17/9/44, T-78, r. 576, fr. 129–34, NA.

95   Leitstelle II Ost für Frontaufklärung to Gehlen, 23/9/44, T-78, r. 576, fr. 127, NA; and 'Report on the British Observer Mission Despatched to German Occupied Poland', HS 4/249, NAUK .

96   Sagajllo, 124; Janusz Prawdzic-Szlaski, Nowogródczyzna w walce (London, 1976), 214–15; Swida, 79; Siemaszko, 'Rozmowy z Wehrmachem w Wilnie', 104–07; Schröder, 111; Norman Davies, Rising '44 (London, 2004), 425–27, 438; J.K. Zawodney, Nothing but Honour (Stanford, 1978), 97–99; Erickson, The Road to Berlin, 495; Tadeusz Bor-Komorowski, The Secret Army (London, 1951), 366–84; Documents on Polish-Soviet Relations, ii, 68–71, 88–89, 214–15, 272–77, 281, 465–66, 475, 790; Krakauer Zeitung, 26/10/44; 'Bandenlage in Bereich der Heeresgruppe Mitte', 5/10/44, RH 19II/243, BMA; Schneider to Thiel, 3/10/44, R 70/197Polen, BA; 'Politische Informationen', 15/9/44, T-78, r. 493, NA; 'Vermark – Neuordnung der Polenpolitik, hier: Auflockerung innerhalb des GG', 17/10/44, T-175, r. 575, fr. 832, NA; and 'Report on the British Observer Mission Despatched to German Occupied Poland', HS 4/249, NAUK. For German boasts of 'generosity' to captured AK fighters, see Danziger Vorposten, 29/9/44; and Ostdeutscher Beobachter, 29/9/44.

97   Hanns von Krannhals, Der Warschauer Aufstand (Frankfurt a.M., 1962), 52, 211; 'Übersicht über die Bandenlage in der Zeit vom 5.10–31.10.1944', 4/11/44, RH 2/2130, BMA; and 'Aufgaben und Gleiderung der polnischen Landesarmee und die Enwicklung der Aufstandspläne des Polnischen Generalstabes', 1/12/44, T-78, r. 576, fr. 41–42, NA. For Thomson, see Harro Thomson, fr. 260, reel A3343 SSO-181B, RG 242, NA.

98   Stefan Korbonski, The Polish Underground State (New York, 1978), 211–12; Alexander Werth, Russia at War (New York, 1964), 1009–14; Geoffrey and Nigel Swain, Eastern Europe since 1945 (London, 1978), 37; Documents on Polish-Soviet Relations, ii, 465–66, 491, 501–03, 543–44, 550–51, 553–55, 556–58, 573–74, 579, 580–82, 585, 587–94, 600, 601–05, 607–11, 612–16, 623, 637–38, 807–08, 810, 812–13, 815; Pogranichnye Voiska SSSR v Velikoi Otechestvennoi Voine, 489; FRUS: The Conferences at Malta and Yalta (Washington, 1955), 221–22; UPASND, vii, 137; Moscow to Foreign Office, 22/12/44, HS 4/145, NAUK; 'Übersicht über die Bandenlage in der Zeit vom 1.12–31.12.1944', 6/1/45; '1.1–31.1.1945', 8/2/45; '1.2–28.2.1945', 6/3/45, all in RH 2/2130, BMA; 'Tagesmeldung', 23/8/44, RH 15/380, BMA; 'Zusammenfassung der Frontaufklärungsmeldungen', 2/11/44; 23/12/44, both in RH 2/2126, BMA; 'Prop.-Unterlagen Truppenmeldungen vom 1.11–30.11.1944', T-78, r. 564, fr. 366, NA; 'Auszug aus Kgf.-Aussagen (IIb-Nr. 4382) – AOK 9 Ic/AO v. 7.11.44' (fr. 465); 'Auszug aus Gefangenenvornehmungen Nr. 42 (IIb-Nr. 4527)' (fr. 413), both in T-78, r. 566, NA; Witiska to Müller and Bierkamp, 18/12/44, T-175, r. 640, fr. 412, NA; and 'German Wireless Security Service (Funküberwachung)', 17/9/45, WO 208/3620, NAUK.

99   'Feststellungen zur Feindlage', 13/2/45, T-78, r. 566, fr. 388, NA.

100 John Coutouvidas and Jaime Reynolds, Poland (New York, 1986), 153–68.

101 Józef Garlinski, Poland, SOE and the Allies (London, 1969), 215–19; Roberts to Perkins, 8/12/44; Memo,

5/12/44; Selborne to Churchill, 14/12/44; Sargent to the Polish Ambassador, 23/12/44; MPP to MP.1 and OC Freston, 26/12/44; Perkins to Siudak, 27/12/44; Eden to O'Malley, 4/1/45; 'Review of the Polish Situation', 17/1/45; Warner to Sporborg, 18/1/45; Bromley to CD, 22/2/45; MPP to A/DH, 10/5/45; Foreign Office to Moscow, 19/6/45, all in HS 4/145, NAUK; Threlfall to AOC Balkan AF, 27/11/44; Speedwell to Maryland for Punch, 14/12/44, both in HS 4/159, NAUK; and PA/CSS Minute Sheet, 22/12/44, HW 47/4, NAUK. Britain resumed provision of airborne supplies to the AK on 23 December 1944, but the last flight was flown only five days later.

102 Bor-Komorowski, 385–87; The Times, 21/4/45; Documents on Polish-Soviet Relations, ii, 521; and 'Amt VI of the RSHA Gruppe VI C', 28/2/46, Entry 119A, RG 226, NA. For Benninghaus, see Karl-Otto Benninghaus, r. A3343 SSO-056, RG 242, NA.

103 Teich int., 21/1/46, ETO MIS-Y-Sect. CSDIC/WEA Final Interrogation Reports 1945–47, RG 338, NA. For charges by the 'Lublin Poles' against Bor-Komorowski, see Davies, 440–41.

104 'Report on the British Observer Mission Dispatched to German Occupied Poland', HS 4/249, NAUK.

105 'C/Auswertung 101: Neujahrsrede Niedwietzkis (Niedzviadek)', 13/2/45, T-78, r. 566, fr. 389, NA.

106 'Vortragsnotiz über zur Aktivierung der Frontaufklärung', 25/2/45, RH 2/1930, BMA. For offers of 'anti-communist collaboration' by the Polish legation in Lisbon, see ULTRA/ZIP/ISK 131826, 17/1/45, HW 19/222, NAUK.

107 Swains, 37; and Anna Cienciala, 'The View from Poland', in Victory in Europe, 1945 (Lawrence, 2000), 60, 62–63.

108 See, for instance, ULTRA/ZIP/ISOS 96699, 18/4/45, HW 19/84, NAUK.

109 'Interrogation Report' 26, 2/8/45, XL 15457, Entry 19, RG 226, NA; de Mulder int.; 'Appendix A: Personal Statements by de Mulder', both in Entry 119A, RG 226, NA; and Tarbuk int., 19/1/46, in Covert Warfare, xiii.

110 Pape to Hoyer, 15/3/45, T-175, r. 640, fr. 387–92, NA.

111 DEG 4009, 4/3/45, HW 19/277, NAUK; 'Erfolgsmeldungen zur Einsatz Nr. 114(S) "Blutfink" vom 28.12.1944', 3/3/45 (fr. 343); 'Vernehmung', 18/2/45 (fr. 344–45), both in T-78, r. 566, NA; Notzny int., 10/6/45; and Gambke/Raupach/Peters int., 15/8/45, both in Entry 119A, RG 226, NA.

112 Lev Kopelev, No Jail for Thought (London, 1977), 95–97.

113 'Gefechtsbericht über der Einsatz vom 18.1–25.1.1945 in Grünkirch, Südostwarts Bromberg', 4/2/45, OD 8/245, BA-LA.

114 Pogranichnye Voiska SSSR v Velikoi Otechestvennoi Voine, 554–55; HCIC, xx, 4, NA; 'FAT 206'; Weissweiler int.; Weissweiler int., 15/3/45; Weissweiler int., 5/5/45; report on KDM Breslau, 16/11/45, all in Entry 119A, RG 226, NA; Skorzeny int., 19/5/45, IRR File XE 000417, RG 319, NA; and 'Intelligence Summary' 146, 22/3/45, vol. 16396, RG 24, Series 90, NAC.

115 Korbonski, 104–07, 178; Lukas, 44–45, 53–58, 83, 92–93, 113, 249; Michael Radziwill, One of the Radziwills (London, 1971), 165–66; Siemaszko, Narodowe Siły Zbrojne, 8, 32, 35–36, 47–50, 105–08, 112, 137–38; Krannhals, 51; Erickson, The Road to Berlin, 259; untitled testimony, T-175, r. R642, fr. 83, NA; 'Übersicht über die Bandenlage in der Zeit vom 1.11–30.11.1944', 5/12/44; '1.12–31.12.1944', 6/1/45, both in RH 2/2130, BMA; note for the Kommandeur der Sipo und des SD für den Dist. Radom, Aussendienststelle Tomaschow, 11/1/45, R 70Polen/134, BA; and Gambke/Raupach/Peters int., 15/8/45, Entry 119A, RG 226, NA.

116 Siemaszko, Narodowe Siły Zbrojne, 106–09, 136–38, 151; Sagajllo, 121–22; RIS SNN/IR to Keller, 2/12/44; Gambke/Raupach/Peters int., 15/8/45, both in Entry 119A, RG 226, NA; Fernspruch to the Kommandeur der Sipo und des SD für den Distrikt Radom, 11/4/44 (fr. 100); IV N to Illmer, 22/5/44 (fr. 127–28), both in T-175, r. R642, NA; 'Vermark – Neuordnung der Polenpolitik, hier: Auflockerung innerhalb des GG', 17/10/44, T-175, r. 575, fr. 832, NA; 'Bandenlagebericht für die Zeit vom 21.11–20.12.1944', 23/12/44, R 70Polen/156, BA; untitled reports from Tomoszów Camp re Polish deserters, 14/1/45; 15/1/45, both in R 70/134, BA; and 'Report on the British Observer Mission Despatched to German Occupied Poland', HS 4/249, NAUK.

117 Siemaszko, Narodowe Siły Zbrojne, 153–58, 171; Georges Mond, 'La fin de la deuxième guerre mondiale en Pologne', Guerres Mondiales et Conflits Contemporains no. 147 (1988), 17; Pogranichnye Voiska SSSR v Velikoi Otechestvennoi Voine, 557; and Gambke/Raupach/Peters int., 15/8/45, Entry 119A, RG 226, NA.

118 Siemaszko, Narodowe Siły Zbrojne, 158–61; KO 1122, 22/4/45, UMC, r. 72, NAUK; and 'General Situation Report' 2, 15/7–1/9/45, OMGUS AG Security-Classified Decimal File 1945–49, 350.09 (Intelligence General), RG 260, NA.

119 UPASND, vi, 125–26.

120 Vakar, 121.

121 'Zusammenstellungen von Meldungen über national-ukrainische (UPA), national-polnische und sowjet-feindliche Banden im rückwaertigen Feindgebiet', T-78, fr. 494–1109, r. 675, NA; and 'Memorandum of Conference with Marshal Stalin, 15th January, 1945', Papers Relating to the Allied High Command, r. 4.

122 Alfred Rieber, 'The Crack in the Plaster: Crisis in Romania and the Origins of the Cold War', Journal of

Modern History 76, no. 1 (2004), 92.

123   Dzhirkvelov, 34–35.

124   'SS Colonel Otto Skorzeny', 28/6/51, Entry 81, RG 263, NA.

125   Erickson, *The Road to Berlin*, 447.

126   John Armstrong, *Ukrainian Nationalism* (New York, 1963), 296–300; Egil Levits, 'Lettland unter der Sow-
      jetherrschaft und auf dem Wege zur Unabhängigkeit', in *Die Baltischen Nationen* (Cologne, 1991), 145; and
      Lieven, 87–90.

127   Hugh Thomas, *The Armed Truce* (London, 1986), 240–241; Werth, 1016–20; and R.J. Crampton, *Eastern
      Europe in the Twentieth Century* (London, 1994), 219–20.

128   Coutouvidis and Reynolds, 220–21, 293.

129   Burds, 36–40, 52; and Pozniakov, 184.

CHAPTER THREE: THE BALKAN COCKPIT

1   Skorzeny, *Wir Kämpften – Wir Verloren*, 41; E.D. Smith, *Victory of a Sort* (London, 1988), 147; Michael Jung,
    Sabotage unter Wasser (Hamburg, 2004), 126; Spaeter, 495; *AdAP*, series E, viii; 'CIR 4 – The German Sabo-
    tage Service', 23/7/45; 'Countersabotage Bulletin' 7, 21/6/45, both in IRR File XE 070687, RG 319, NA;
    'Progress Report on the Case of Schellenberg', 17/7/45, IRR File XE 001752, RG 319, NA; Gambke/
    Raupach/Peters int., 15/8/45; Radl int., 4/6/45; Waneck int., 29/6/45; Waneck int., 11/8/45; Dowe and
    Sokolov int., 8/8/45; 'Collated Report on the SS Sonderkommando at the Jagdverband Kampfschule in
    Tiefenthal', 12/5/45; 'Special Brief – Twelfth Army Group, SCI Det., Munich – dated 8 July 1945'; 'State-
    ment handed in by Kaltenbrunner on 8.8.45 with translation by Ledebur – Minister Dr. Neubacher'; 'Sect.
    VI E 7 of RSHA and Funds of Sect. VI E 7', all in Entry 119A, RG 226, NA; 'Interrogation Report' 10,
    21/6/45; 'CIR 3 – Amt VI-E of the RSHA', 21/6/45, both in IRR File XE 000440, RG 319, NA; Kirchner
    int., 3/1/46, XL 40257, Entry 19, RG 226, NA; Wilhelm Waneck (fr. 606); 'Dienstzeitbestätigung', 21/1/37
    (fr. 632), both in r. A3343 SSO-220B, RG 242, NA; 'PF: 601, 603', 15/9/45, KV 2/1327, NAUK; SRX 2138,
    22/4/45, WO 208/4164, NAUK; 'Skorzeny's Biography', WO 204/11839, NAUK; and ULTRA/ZIP/ISO-
    SICLE 12647, 8/3/45, HW 19/248, NAUK.

2   Koch int., 15/6/45; Modriniak int., 15/7/45; 'Leitstelle II Sued Ost', all in Entry 119A, RG 226, NA; Murad
    int., 21/12/45; Murad int., 18/1/46, both in *Covert Warfare*, xiii; and 'Interim Report on: F.H. Brandt',
    5/12/44, HS 5/98, NAUK.

3   Spaeter; Kuehlwein int., Entry 119A, RG 226, NA; and 'PF: 601, 603', 15/9/45, KV 2/1327, NAUK.

4   12th AG to War Room, 2/6/45; 'FAT 223'; and 'FAK 205', 28/1/46, all in Entry 119A, RG 226, NA.

5   Weissweiler int.; and 'PWI Report' 11, 15/3/45, both Entry 119A, RG 226, NA.

6   <http://www.sueddeutsche.de/muenchen/schwerpunkt/250/25225/index.html/muenchen/artikel/250/
    43207/article.html>, as of 18/11/04; Eugen Steiner, *The Slovak Dilemma* (Cambridge, 1973), chapter 7; M.R.
    Myant, *Socialism and Democracy in Czechoslovakia* (Cambridge, 1981), 40–46; Yeshayahu Jelenik, *The Lust for
    Power* (New York, 1983), 68–76; Erickson, *The Road to Berlin*, 291–307; Gustáv Husák, *Der Slowakische Nation-
    alaufstand* (Berlin, 1972), part two; Ceteka, 12/11/62; 'Niznansky, Ladislaus Milan', CIANF, Entry 86, RG
    263, NA; Bari to Resident Minister Central Mediterranean, Caserta, 20/9/44; 'Report by Maj. J. Sehmer',
    both in HS 4/27, NAUK; Murad int., 21/12/45; Murad int., 18/1/46, both in *Covert Warfare*, xiii; Gambke/
    Raupach/Peters int., 15/8/45; Girg int., 15/9/45; 'FAK 206', 24/1/46, all in Entry 119A, RG 226, NA; Forras
    int., 10/12/45, ETO MIS-Y-Sect. CSDIC/WEA Final Interrogation Reports 1945–47, RG 338, NA.

7   Husák, *Der Slowakische Nationalaufstand*, 612; Kaltenbrunner int., 28/6/45; and 'CIR 3 – Amt VI-E of the
    RSHA', 21/6/45, both in IRR File XE 000440, RG 319, NA.

8   '4. Flüchtlinge aus Preschau', 12/2/45, T-175, r. R641, fr. 42, NA.

9   *Völkischer Beobachter*, 27/3/45; 'PF: 601, 603', 15/9/45, KV 2/1327, NAUK; and 'Fortnightly Directive for
    BBC Czechoslovak Services, April 12–25 1945', FO 371/46790, NAUK.

10 Hoffmann to Witiska, 3/3/45, T-175, r. R641, fr. 44, NA; 'Vermark – Propagandabesprechung am 6.3.1945
    um 16,00 Uhr im Dienstzimmer von Hauptsturmführer Dr. Böhrsch', 9/3/45; 'Vermark – Flugblatt-
    Propaganda zum 14.3.45', 10/3/45; 'Slowakische Volk!'; 'Slowakische Brüder!'; and 'Flugblattpropaganda in
    slowakische Orten, die von deutschen Truppen geräumt werden', 11/3/45, all T-175, r. R653, NA.

11 *The New York Times*, 24/3/46; 25/3/46; and 'Digest' 21, 9/2/46, FO 1007/289, NAUK.

12 Josef Kalvoda, 'Czechoslovak-Ukrainian Relations', *The Ukrainian Quarterly* xliv (1988), 66–68; Report
    LC-322/LC-323, 12/10/45, XL 21059, Entry 19, RG 226, NA; 'Weekly Intelligence Summary' 32, 21/2/46,
    State Dept. Decimal File 1945–49, 740.00119 Control (Germany), RG 59, NA; 'Joint Fortnightly Intelli-
    gence Summary' 44, 1/11/47; and 45, 15/11/47, both in FO 1007/302, NAUK.

13 Mark Aarons and John Loftus, *Ratlines* (London, 1991), 217–19; 'Vermark – Verlagerung eines Schwarzsend-
    ers ins Reich', 14/3/45; Hoffmann to Höfle, 16/3/45, both in T-175, r. R653, NA; 'Niznansky, Ladislaus
    Milan'; 'Dr. Ferdinand Durcansky; His Political Activities; Political Trials of Slovak Democratic Party Offi-

cials (Ursiny, Kempny, Bugar) and their Affiliation with the Durcansky Movement', 23/7/52; 'The Slovak Liberation Committee (SOV)'; 'Information from Biographic Intelligence Division Files, Department of State, as of September 1954'; 'Durcansky, Ferdinand (Dr.) (State/BID, Sep. 54)', 2/11/54, all in CIANF, Entry 86, RG 263, NA.

14   Nicholas Nagy-Talavera, *The Green Shirts and the Others* (Stanford, 1970), chapter 3; and McCartney, *October Fifteenth*, chapter 18.

15   'CIR 4 – The German Sabotage Service', 23/7/45, IRR File XE 070687, RG 319, NA; Kirchner int., 3/1/46, XL 40257, Entry 19, RG 226, NA; 'The Neu-Strelitz Sabotage Training School', 13/3/45, IRR File XE 001063, RG 319, NA; and François int. 10/2/45, Entry 119A, RG 226, NA.

16   Nagy-Talavera, 121–22, 127–28, 137–38, 141–42, 153–54, 194–95, 232, 235.

17   'Resistance Organisation SOWA', 18/12/46, IRR File XE 081544, RG 319, NA.

18   *The Times*, 9/3/45.

19   Skorzeny, *Wir Kämpften – Wir Verloren*, 162–63; 'CIR 4 – The German Sabotage Service', 23/7/45, IRR File XE 070687, RG 319, NA; and Kirchner int., 3/1/46, XL 40257, Entry 19, RG 226, NA.

20   'Organisation of the Abwehr I Wirtschaft in Hungary', 13–14/9/44; Report LS-188, 26/6/45; 'Hungarian Military Organisation', 6/12/48; 'Rom-Reise Dr. Karl Neys', 25/1/49; 'Major Dr. Karl Ney', 8/2/49; cable re Karoly Ney, 15/2/49; 'Ney, Karoly', 24/2/49; 'Rome Activity of Dr. Carl Ney', 11/5/49; 'Dr. Carlo Ney', 5/8/49; 'Dr. Karl Ney', 25/8/49; 'Rome Activity of Carlo Ney', 13/9/49; S4 (34/7/III/Z) to SO, 13/10/49; 'General – ODEUM; Specific – Ney, Karoly', 13/10/49; 'ODI Records on Willi Hoettl', 26/4/55, all in CIANF, Entry 86, RG 263, NA.

21   Murad int., 18/1/46, in *Covert Warfare*, xiii; and Forras int., 4/12/45, ETO MIS-Y-Sect. CSDIC/WEA Final Interrogation Reports 1945–47, RG 338, NA.

22   ULTRA/ZIP/ISK 128773, 28/11/44; 128775, 29/11/44, both in HW 19/218, NAUK; 129285, 29/11/44, HW 19/219, NAUK; and 130623, 1/12/44, HW 19/221, NAUK.

23   'News Sheet' 25, 13/7/45, WO 205/997, NAUK; ULTRA/ZIP/ISK 130565, 4/12/44, HW 19/221, NAUK; Murad int., 21/12/45, in *Covert Warfare*, xiii; 'FAK 202', 23/11/45, IRR File XE 020651, RG 319, NA; Koch int.; Gambke/Raupach/Peters int., 15/8/45; 'FAT 215', 24/10/45; and 'FAK 205', 28/1/46, all in Entry 119A, RG 226, NA.

24   Report S-44, 12/12/44, XL 2690, Entry 19, RG 226, NA; ULTRA/ZIP/ISOSICLE 12657, 7/3/45; 12672, 10/3/45; 12899, 9/4/45, all in HW 19/248, NAUK; and 'ND' 1597, 6/11/44, BC, Robbins Library.

25   Kirchner int., 3/1/46, XL 40257, Entry 19, RG 226, NA; 'Leading Personalities in the Kopjas "Arrow Cross" Organization', 18/6/48, CIANF, Entry 86, RG 263, NA; and Forras int., 10/12/45, ETO MIS-Y-Sect. CSDIC/WEA Final Interrogation Reports 1945–47, RG 338, NA. For Záko and the ABI, see McCartney, 293, 358, 423.

26   *Pogranichnye Voiska SSSR v Velikoi Otechestvennoi Voine*, 523–26; Schramm, 'The Wehrmacht in the Last Days of the War (1 January–7 May 1945)', in *WWIIGMS*, ii; *Völkischer Beobachter*, 13/1/45; ULTRA/ZIP/ISK 129285, 29/11/44, HW 19/219, NAUK; ULTRA/ZIP/ISOS 96233, 5/4/45, HW 19/83, NAUK; Kirchner int., 3/1/46, XL 40257, Entry 19, RG 226, NA; 'Zusammenfassung der Frontaufklärungsmeldungen', 11/1/45; 11/2/45, both in RH 2/2127, BMA; Geschke to Winkelmann, 19/11/44, R 58/538, BA; 'Übersicht über die Bandenlage in der Zeit vom 1.1.-31.1.1945', 8/2/45, T-78, r. 497, fr. 6485181, NA; 'Übersicht über die Bandenlage in der Zeit vom 1.2.-28.2.1945', T-78, r. 576, fr. 195, NA; 'Vermark – Propagandabesprechung am 2.2.45 um 17 Uhr im Dienstzimmer des L III beim BdS Slowakei in Pressburg', 3/2/45, T-175, r. R653, fr. 776, NA; and 'ND' 1687, 19/2/45, BC, Robbins Library.

27   Leverkuehn, 63; Kirchner int., 3/1/46, XL 40257, Entry 19, RG 226, NA; and Forras int., 10/12/45, ETO MIS-Y-Sect. CSDIC/WEA Final Interrogation Reports 1945–1947, RG 338, NA.

28   CI War Room to Noakes, GSI(b) BOAR, 9/10/45; 'Brief for the Interrogation of E. Forras'; War Room to GSI(S), BAOR, 26/2/46; 8/3/46, all in Entry 119A, RT 226, NA; 'Intelligence Diary for Hungary', entry for 23/6/45; and entry for 28/8/46, both in WO 208/4522, NAUK.

29   Peter Gosztony, *Endkampf an der Donau* (Vienna, 1969), 192–93; and 'Anlage zu VI Wi Wiesbaden, no. 708/45', T-78, fr. 6474435, r. 488, NA.

30   *The Manchester Guardian*, 5/7/45; *The New York Times*, 9/8/45; Adrian Webb, *Central and Eastern Europe since 1919* (London, 2002), 141–42; George Schöpflin, 'Hungary', in *Communist Power in Europe, 1944–1945* (London, 1977), 100; Swains, 45–46; Vladislav Zubok and Constantine Pleshkov, *Inside the Kremlin's Cold War* (Cambridge, 1999), 99; 'Brief for the Interrogation of E. Forras', Entry 119A, RG 226, NA; 'Intelligence Diary for Hungary', entry for 28/1/46, WO 208/4522, NAUK; and 'Leading Personalities in the Kopjas "Arrow Cross" Organization', 18/6/48, CIANF, Entry 86, RG 263, NA.

31   Komjathy and Stockwell, *German Minorities and the Third Reich*, 111–14; Joseph Schechtman, 'The Elimination of German Minorities in Southeastern Europe', *Journal of Central European Affairs* 6 (1946), 155; and Schmidt to Berger, 28/8/44, T-175, fr. 2580254, r. 64, NA.

32 Himmler to Kaltenbrunner, 16/9/44, T-175, r. 122, fr. 2648215, NA.

33 Karl Reinerth and Fritz Cloos, *Zur Geschichte der Deutschen in Rumänien* (Bad Tölz, 1988), 162–63, 207, 209; Reitlinger, *The SS*, 197; Hans Hartl, *Das Schicksal des Deutschtums in Rumänien* (Würzburg, 1958), 94–96; and *AdAP*, series E, viii, 398.

34 Reinerth and Cloos, 227–28; Gambke/Raupach/Peters int., 15/8/45, Entry 119A, RG 226, NA; Report GR-150, 13/1/45, L 51507, Entry 21, RG 226, NA; Report GR-291, 3/3/45, L 55146, Entry 21, RG 226, NA; and 'Intelligence Diary for Roumania', entries for 20/3/44; 21/4/44, both in WO 208/4561, NAUK; ULTRA/ZIP/ISOSICLE 12632, 4/3/45, HW 19/248, NAUK. For the relationship between Romanian *Volksdeutsche* and German troops gone to ground, see Hans Sänger, *Die 79. Infanterie Division* (Friedberg, 1979), 241, 243–44; Albert Seaton, *The Russo-German War* (New York, 1970), 483; M. Knorr 'Protokoll', 20/6/52, OD 2/348, LA-BA; R. Fleps 'Protokoll', 12/11/52; E. Schenker 'Protokoll', 15/11/52, both in OD 2/352, LA-BA; and B. Mayer 'Protokoll', 8/3/53, OD 2/357, LA-BA.

35 Reinerth and Cloos, 215–16, 225–27; 'CIR 3 – Amt VI of the RSHA', 21/6/45, Entry 119A, RG 226, NA; and ULTRA/ZIP/ISOSICLE 12556, 17/2/45, HW 19/248, NAUK.

36 Reinerth and Cloos, 164–165, 209–12, 222; Hartl, 96–111; *Documents on the Expulsion of the Germans from Eastern Central Europe* (Bonn, 1954), ii/iii, 69–77; and H. Kastenhuber 'Protokoll', 20/9/52, OD 2/347, LA-BA.

37 Reinerth and Cloos, 216, 218–19.

38 Reitlinger, *The SS*, 200; Erich Kern, *Der Grosse Rausch* (Zurich, 1948), 160, 162; Hartl, 111; Skorzeny, *Wir Kämpften – Wir Verloren*, 64–65; 'Vorschlag no. 3783 für Verleihung des Ritterkreuzes des Eisernen Kreuzes', 1/10/44, r. A 3343 SSO-014A, fr. 887–80, RG 242, NA; 'Summary 2955 – Kurt Heermann', IWM; H. Kastenhuber 'Protokoll', 20/9/52, OD 2/347, LA-BA; and Gambke/Raupach/Peters int., 15/8/45, Entry 119A, RG 226, NA.

39 H. Hoerth 'Protokoll', 26/7/52, OD 2/344, LA-BA; M. David 'Protokoll', 14/10/52, OD 2/346, LA-BA; O. Liess 'Die deutsche Volksgruppe in Rumänien unter der Führung von Andreas Schmidt', OD 16 Rum./8, LA-BA; 'Summary 137 – Dr. Kaltenbrunner', IWM; Ehlich int., 9/11/45, ETO MIS-Y-Sect. CSDIC(WEA) Interim Interrogation Reports 1945–46, RG 338, NA; 'Volksdeutsche Mittelstelle (VOMI)', 7/45, Intelligence Division Captured Personnel and Material Branch Enemy POW Interrogation File (MIS-Y) 1943–45, RG 165, NA; and Krallert int., Entry 119A, RG 226, NA.

40 Reinerth and Cloos, 205–06; H. Hoerth 'Protokoll', 26/7/52, OD 2/344, LA-BA; H. Ehrmann 'Protokoll', 17/10/52, OD 2/346, LA-BA; and R. Sonntag 'Protokoll', 15/10/52, OD 2/347, LA-BA.

41 H. Kastenhuber 'Protokoll', 20/9/52, OD 2/347, LA-BA.

42 Hartl, 84; Reinerth and Cloos, 206; Höhne, *The Order of the Death's Head*, 480; Schmidt to Berger, 28/8/44 (fr. 2580245–55); Schmidt to Wanner (fr. 2580236–38); Himmler to Phlepps, 31/8/44 (fr. 2580250); Brandt to Berger, 1/9/44 (fr. 2580251); Berger to Himmler, 30/8/44 (fr. 2580252), all in T-175, r. 64, NA; and M. Petri 'Protokoll', 20/9/53, OD 2/357, LA-BA. Schmidt and Phleps eventually launched counter-propaganda through radio and leafleting. See Reinerth and Cloos, 165, 214.

43 Rimann to Himmler, 26/9/44, T-175, r. 64, fr. 2580230, NA.

44 Hartl, 116–19; Reinerth and Cloos, 166–67, 228–30, 237; *AdAPolitik*, series E, iii, 485–86; Mathias Liebhard, r. A3343 SS-260A, fr. 533; Christian Bloser, r. A3343 SSO-077, fr. 694; Hans Kastenhuber, r. A3343 SSO-156A, fr. 1487; Erich Müller, r. A3343 SSO-328A, fr. 249, all in RG 242, NA; H. Hoerth 'Protokoll', 26/7/52, OD 2/344, LA-BA; H. Kastenhuber 'Protokoll', 20/9/52; R. Sonntag 'Protokoll', 15/10/52, both in OD 2/347, LA-BA; H. Scheiner 'Erlebnisbericht', 10/1/52, OD 2/355, LA-BA; O. Liess 'Die deutsche Volksgruppe in Rumänien unter der Führung von Andreas Schmidt', OD 16 Rum./8, LA-BA; Berger to Himmler, 6/1/45; Brandt, memo, 8/1/45; Brandt to Berger, 13/1/45; Brandt, memo, 19/1/45; 'Aktenvermark', 23/1/45, all in NS 19/3825, BA; Berger to Brandt, 4/11/44 (fr. 2609789–90); Brandt to Berger, 13/11/44 (fr. 2609788); Müller to Himmler, 29/12/44 (fr. 260987); Brandt to Müller, 31/12/44 (fr. 2609783); Berger to Lorenz, 8/1/45 (fr. 2609780); Brandt to Berger, 19/1/45 (fr. 2609780), all in T-175, r. 84, NA; and ULTRA/ZIP/ISOSICLE 12593, 25/1/45, HW 19/248, NAUK.

45 H. Scheiner 'Erlebnisbericht', 10/1/52, OD 2/355, LA-BA.

46 Hartl, 119; Reinerth and Cloos, 167, 234–37, 241; ULTRA/ZIP/ISOSICLE 12515, 22/2/45; 12522, 3/3/45; 12523, 8/2/45; 12524, 8/2/45; 12528, 12/2/45; 12532, 15/2/45; 12545, 24/1/45; 12554, 14/2/45; 12588, 1/2/45; 12589, 1/2/45; 12590, 1/2/45; 12624, 28/2/45; 12680, 10/3/45; 12681, 10/3/45, all in HW 19/248, NAUK; Berger to Himmler, 23/1/45, NS 19/3825, BA; O. Liess 'Die Deutsche Volksgruppe in Rumänien unter der Führung von Andreas Schmidt', OD 16 Rum./8, LA-BA; R. Sonntag 'Protokoll', 15/10/52, OD 2/347, LA-BA; H. Scheiner 'Erlebnisbericht', 10/1/52, OD 2/355, LA-BA; and Berger int., IRR File XE 000440, RG 319, NA.

47 Reinerth and Cloos, 230, 240; H. Kastenhuber 'Protokoll', 15/12/52, OD 2/346, LA-BA; H. Kastenhuber 'Protokoll', 20/9/52, OD 2/347, LA-BA; H. Scheiner 'Erlebnisbericht', 10/1/52, OD 2/355, LA-BA; and ULTRA/ZIP/ISOSICLE 12549, 8/2/45, HW 19/248, NAUK.

48   Report GR-291, 3/3/45, L 55146, Entry 21, RG 226, NA; and 'CIR 4 – The German Sabotage Service',
      23/7/45, IRR File XE 070687, RG 319, NA.
49   ULTRA/ZIP/ISOSICLE 12546, 2/2/45; 12524, 8/2/45; 12533, 15/2/45; 12541, 21/2/45; 12514, 22/2/45;
      12560, 23/2/45; 12603, 28/2/45; 12664, 8/3/45; 12635, 4/3/45; 12668, 9/3/45; 12674, 9/3/45; 12755,
      21/3/45; 12909, 13/4/45; 12954, 19/4/45, all in HW 19/248, NAUK.
50   ULTRA/ZIP/ISOSICLE 12523, 8/2/45; 12513, 21/2/45; 12606, 16/2/45; 12591, 8/2/45; 12592, 7/2/45;
      12548, 8/2/45; 12562, 23/2/45; 12597, 25/2/45; 12614, 28/2/45; 12654, 1/3/45; 12636, 4/3/45; 12544, 5/3/45;
      12646, 6/3/45; 12649, 5/3/45; 12755, 21/3/45; 12791, 23/3/45; 12911, 13/4/45, all in HW 19/248, NAUK;
      'Sect.VI E 7 of RSHA and Funds of Sect.VI E 7', 23/5/45; and 'CIR 3 – AmtVI-E of the RSHA', 21/6/45,
      both in Entry 119A, RG 226, NA.
51   ULTRA/ZIP/ISOSICLE 12583, 30/1/45; and 12768, 17/3/45, both in HW 19/248, NAUK.
52   Gellermann, 180–83.
53   H. Scheiner 'Erlebnisbericht', 10/1/52; and Scheiner to Scheider, 17/3/56, both in OD 2/355, LA-BA.
54   Reinerth and Cloos, 166, 235.
55   Perry Biddiscombe, 'Prodding the Russian Bear', European History Quarterly 23 (1993), 213; Report GR-292,
      3/3/45, L 53658, Entry 21, RG 226, NA; and Report GR-291, 3/3/45, L 55146, Entry 21, RG 226, NA.
56   H. Kastenhuber 'Protokoll', 15/12/52, OD 2/346, LA-BA; B. Mayer 'Protokoll', 8/3/53, OD 2/357, LA-BA;
      and ULTRA/ZIP/ISOSICLE 12627, 4/3/45, HW 19/248, NAUK.
57   ULTRA/ZIP/ISOSICLE 12549, 8/2/45; 12543, 22/2/45; 12562, 23/2/45; and 12619, 27/2/45, all in HW
      19/248, NAUK.
58   ULTRA/ZIP/ISOSICLE 12531, 15/2/45, HW 19/248, NAUK.
59   Report GR-219, 7/2/45, L 53621, Entry 21, RG 226, NA.
60   Reinerth and Cloos, 240; and H. Kastenhuber 'Protokoll', 20/9/52, OD 2/347, LA-BA.
61   Spaeter, 528; Gellermann, 185; and B. Mayer 'Protokoll', 8/3/53, OD 2/357, LA-BA.
62   Elmér Illyés, National Minorities in Rumania: Change in Transylvania (New York, 1982), 100–01; Rieber, 93;
      Hartl, 120–23; Documents on the Expulsion of the Germans, ii/iii, 79–82; Biddiscombe, 'Prodding the Russian
      Bear', 210–11; 'Report on Political Situation in Rumania 9th-31st January 1945', FO 371/48549, NAUK;
      R. Crutzescu 'Memorandum', 24/1/45, HS 5/800, NAUK; Report GR-139, 14/1/45, L 51509, Entry 21,
      RG 226, NA; Report GR-150, 13/1/45, L 51507, Entry 21, RG 226, NA; Report GR-157, 14/1/45, L
      51637, Entry 21, RG 226, NA; Report GR-160, 16/1/45, L 51646, Entry 21, RG 226, NA; Report GR-161,
      17/1/45, Entry 21, RG 226, NA; Report GR-175, 23/1/45, L 51960, Entry 21, RG 226, NA; and 'ACC
      Field Trip through Oltenia, Banat and northern Transylvania, March 27 to April 8', 127242, Entry 16, RG
      226, NA.
63   ULTRA/ZIP/ISOSICLE 12550, 9/2/45, HW 19/248, NAUK.
64   R. Fleps 'Protokoll', 12/11/52, OD 2/352, LA-BA; and Report GR-152, 13/1/45, L 51501, Entry 21, RG
      226, NA.
65   AdAP, Series E, viii, 642–43; and Berger to Himmler, 23/1/45, NS 19/3825, BA.
66   ULTRA/ZIP/ISOSICLE 12555, 17/2/45; and 12620, 27/2/45, both in HW 19/248, NAUK.
67   See, for instance, 'Gefechtsbericht', 4/12/44, T-78, r. 139, fr. 6067868, NA.
68   Documents on the Expulsion of the Germans, ii/iii, 70–74, 76–77; and Reinerth and Cloos, 165.
69   'ACC Field Trip through Oltenia, Banat and northern Transylvania, March 27 to April 8', 127242, Entry 16,
      RG 226, NA.
70   FRUS, 1944 (Washington, 1966), iv, 270, 279; Illyés, 101–02; Bela Vago, 'Romania', in Communist Power in
      Europe, 1944–1945 (London, 1977), 115; John Cadzow, Andrew Ludonyi, Louis Elteto, Transylvania (Kent,
      1983), 203; Rieber, 72, 84; Hugh Seton-Watson, The East European Revolution (London, 1961), 203; N.I.
      Lebedev, Padenie Diktatury Antonesku (Moscow, 1966), 380–81, 423–24; Gasztony, 170, 320; Report GR-116,
      29/12/44, L 52134, Entry 21, RG 226, NA; 'Balkan Political Review' 4, 27/9/44; 22, 30/1/45, app. 'F', both
      in WO 201/1628, NAUK; 'Intelligence Diary for Rumania', entry for 13/11/44, WO 208/4561, NAUK;
      Le Rougetel to FO, 1/5/45; 3/5/45, both in FO 371/48554, NAUK; Marjoribanks to FO, 3/2/45, FO
      371/48577, NAUK; 'Report – Tour of Northern Transylvania (Ardeal), Feb. 27th-March 7th 1945'; 'Report
      on a Visit to Cluj from 9th-13th July 1945', both in FO 371/48578, NAUK; and 'Prime Minister Groza's
      Address at "ARLUS" meeting yesterday (10th March 1945)', Entry 92, RG 226, NA.
71   R. Crutzescu 'Memorandum', 24/1/45, HS 5/800, NAUK.
72   Report GR-195, 28/1/45, L 52214, Entry 21, RG 226, NA; Report GR-291, 3/3/45, L 55146, Entry 21,
      RG 226, NA; BMM to WO, 16/2/45, FO 371/48573, NAUK; and Gambke/Raupach/Peters int., 15/8/45,
      Entry 119A, RG 226, NA.
73   'Vice Commissar Vishinski's reply to the Rumanian deputation headed by Prime Minister Groza', Entry
      92, RG 226, NA; ULTRA/ZIP/ISOSICLE 12762, 17/3/45; 12855, 27/3/45, both in HW 19/248, NAUK;
      and transcript of a discussion, Schuyler-Susaikov, 19/4/45, FO 371/48575, NAUK.
74   Yvi Yavetzi, 'An Eyewitness Note: Reflections on the Rumanian Iron Guard', in The Impact of Western

Nationalisms (London, 1992), 250–51; and Henry Roberts, *Political Problems of an Agrarian State* (New Haven, 1951), 91.

75   Komjathy and Stockwell, *German Minorities and the Third Reich*, 117; Armin Heinen, *Die Legion 'Erzengel Michael' in Rumänien* (Munich, 1986), 460–461; Robert Lee Wolff, *The Balkans in Our Time* (Cambridge, 1956), 237; Michel Sturdza, *The Suicide of Europe: Memoirs of Prince Michel Sturdza* (Boston, 1968), 243; Mihai Fatu and Ion Spaletelu, *Garda de Fier: Organizatie Terorista de Tip Fascist* (Bucharest, 1971), 389–90; Höttl, 175–78; *AdAP*, series E, v, 146–47; 'Underground – Rumania 6.22.1944', Entry 92, RG 226, NA; 'Legionary Movement, 1919 to Present', 30/12/49, CIANF, Entry 86, RG 263, NA; Noske int., 11/5/46, ETO MIS-Y-Sect. CSDIC/WEA Final Interrogation Reports 1945–47, RG 338, NA; Schmidt to Himmler, 5/8/43, T-175, r. 62, fr. 2578242, NA; and 'Intelligence Diary for Roumania', entries for 7/1/43; 12/43–1/44; 29/3/44, all in WO 208/4561, NAUK.

76   Heinen, 461–62; Ghita Ionescu, *Communism in Rumania* (London, 1964), 87; Sturdza, 257, 260; A. Simion, *Regimul Politic din România în Perioada Septembrie 1940–Januarie 1941* (Cluj, 1976), 308–09; Reinerth and Cloos, 207, 218, 235–36; Andreas Hillgruber, *Hitler, König Carol and Marschall Antonescu* (Wiesbaden, 1965), 227–28; Florin Constantiniu, 'Victoria Insurectiei din August 1944 si Falimentul Politic Definitiv al Garzii de Fier', *Revista de Istorie* 32 (1979), 1497; Nagy-Talavera, 338; Fatu and Spaletelu, 397–401; *AdAP*, series E, viii, 381–82, 410; Schmidt to Berger, 28/8/44, T-175, r. 64, fr. 2580253, NA; Sima to Ribbentrop, 29/10/44; von Leeson to Himmler, 3/11/44; Kaltenbrunner to Himmler, 11/12/44; 'General Gheorge'; von Leeson to Brandt, all in NS 19/3268, BA; 'Rumanian Iron Guard Activity in Germany', 10/1/45; 'Sima, Horia'; 'Legionary Movement, 1919 tp Present', all in CIANF, Entry 86, RG 263, NA; 'Balkan Political Review' 1, 6/9/44, WO 201/1628, NAUK; and 'GPG', 28/8/44, FO 898/187, NAUK.

77   Reinerth and Cloos, 224; 'Organisationstand der Nationalen Rumänischen Regierung nach 6 wöchiger Tätigkeit', NS 19/2155, BA; and Sima to Himmler, 8/9/44, NS 19neu/2789, BA.

78   *AdAP*, series E, viii, 502; Himmler to Kaltenbrunner, 16/9/44, T-175, r. 122, fr. 2648215, NA; and 'Rumanian Collaboration with the Germans', CIANF, Entry 86, RG 263, NA.

79   Spaeter, 490; SS-Führungshauptamt IIa to the Reichssicherheitshauptamt, 26/5/44; 'Beförderung des SS-Obersturmführers Roland Gunne zum SS-Hauptsturmführer', 15/8/44, both in r. A3343 SSO-043A, fr. 161, 174–76, RG 242, NA; 'CIR 4 – The German Sabotage Service', 23/7/45, IRR File XE 070687, RG 319, NA; and 'CIR 3 – Amt VI-E of the RSHA', 21/6/45, Entry 119A, RG 226, NA.

80   Reinerth and Cloos, 204; and 'SS-Hauptsturmführer Roland Gunne, SS-Nr. 456 012(V)', 1/12/44, r. A3343 SSO-043A, fr. 144, RG 242, NA.

81   Constantiniu, 1496–97; Sturdza, 260, 321; Fatu and Spalatelu, 401, 403–05; Hilz int., 9/8/45, in *Covert Warfare*, xiii; Report GR-219, 7/2/45, L 53621; Report GR-291, 3/3/45, L 55146, both in Entry 21, RG 226, NA; Forras int., 10/12/45, ETO MIS-Y-Sect. CSDIC/WEA Final Interrogation Reports 1945–47, RG 338, NA; Wanek int., 11/8/45; 'Sect. VI E 7 of RSHA and Funds of Sect. VI E 7', 23/5/45; De Roos int., 22/3/45, all in Entry 119A, RG 226, NA; and 'CIR 4 – The German Sabotage Service', 23/8/45, IRR XE 070687, RG 319, NA.

82   Fatu and Spalatelu, 405; *AdAP*, series E, viii, 381–82; and H. Kastenhuber, 'Protokoll', 20/9/52, OD 2/347, LA-BA.

83   Waneck int., 11/8/45, Entry 119A, RG 226, NA; 'CIR 4 – The German Sabotage Service', 23/8/45, IRR File XE 070687, RG 319, NA; and Murad int., 18/1/46, in *Covert Warfare*, xiii.

84   Reinerth and Cloos, 237; Gellermann, 182; Report GR-283, 28/2/45, L 54862; Report GR-219, 7/2/45, L 53621, both in Entry 21, RG 226, NA; 'Leitstelle II Sud Ost', 8/10/45, Entry 119A, RG 226, NA; 'Legionnaire Activities'; Piff int., 27/10/53, both in CIANF, Entry 86, RG 263, NA; and ULTRA/ZIP/ISOSICLE 12594, 28/1/45, HW 19/248, NAUK. SD officers working with the Romanians in Vienna suspected that a Soviet agent had penetrated their ranks. 'Sect VI E 7 of RSHA and Funds of VI E 7', 23/5/45, Entry 119A, RG 226, NA.

85   Report RB-9557, 31/3/45, L 54831, Entry 21, RG 226, NA; ULTRA/ZIP/ISOSICLE 12533, 15/2/45; 24/3/45; 12870, 26/3/45; 12854, 27/3/45; 12860, 27/3/45; 12867, 27/3/45; 12902, 12/4/45; 12909, 13/4/45; and 12954, 19/4/45, all in HW 19/248, NAUK.

86   ULTRA/ZIP/ISOSICLE 12901, 9/4/45; and 12904, 9/4/45, both in HW 19/248, NAUK.

87   'Monthly Summary' 1, 15/4/45, Entry 119A, RG 226, NA.

88   'Sect. VI E 7 of RSHA and Funds of Sect. VI E 7', 23/5/45, Entry 119A, RG 226, NA.

89   Waneck int., 11/8/45, Entry 119A, RG 226, NA; 'Leitstelle II Sud Ost', 8/10/45, Entry 119A, RG 226, NA; ULTRA/ZIP/ISOSICLE 12934, 23/4/45; 12937, 24/4/45; 12946, 23/4/45; 12952, 3/5/45, all in HW 19/248, NAUK.

90   'Operation Gill'; 'Mouet Operation', 9/11/53, both in CIANF, Entry 86, RG 263, NA; and 'Leitstelle II Sud Ost', 8/10/45, Entry 119A, RG 226, NA.

91   ULTRA/ZIP/ISOSICLE 12669, 9/3/45, HW 19/248, NAUK. On 6 March 1945, the resisters told Vienna

that false reports on Radio Danube were 'lose[ing] all confidence of our listeners'. ULTRA/ZIP/ISOSI-CLE 12645, 6/3/45, HW 19/248, NAUK.

92   Rieber, 71–72; and 'Rumanian Collaboration with the Germans', Entry 81, RG 263, NA.

93   Fatu and Spalatelu, 404–05; 'Memorandum on Visit to Galatz', c. 11/44, FO 371/44033, NAUK; and 'Auswertung von Aussagen rumänischer Kriegsgefangener', 1/2/45, T-175, r. R641, fr. 49, NA. For the mission to rescue Ionescu, see ULTRA/ZIP/ISOSICLE 12441, 5/1/45; 12516, 22/2/45; 12561, 23/2/45; and 12613, 28/2/45, all in HW 19/248, NAUK.

94   Graiul Nou, 7/1/45.

95   Kaltenbrunner int., 22/5/45, Entry 119A, RG 226, NA; 'Auswertung von Aussagen rumänischer Kriegsgefangener', 1/2/45, T-175, r. R641, fr. 49, NA; and 'Legionary Movement, 1919 to Present', 30/12/49, CIANF, Entry 86, RG 263, NA.

96   ULTRA/ZIP/ISOSICLE 12612, 27/2/45; and 6/3/45, both in HW 19/248, NAUK.

97   ULTRA/ZIP/ISOSICLE 12647, 8/3/45, HW 19/248, NAUK.

98   ULTRA/ZIP/ISOSICLE 12671, 10/3/45, HW 19/248, NAUK.

99   ULTRA/ZIP/ISOSICLE 12900, 11/4/45, HW 19/248, NAUK.

100   Gellermann, 182; and Reinerth and Cloos, p. 229.

101   Vojtech Mastny, Russia's Road to the Cold War (New York, 1979), 198–99.

102   Rieber, 69, 87; Radu Ioanid, The Sword of the Archangel (Boulder, 1990), 101; and '36 Wochenbericht über Aussen- und Innenpolitik der SU', 10/3/45, RH 2/2330, BMA.

103   Rieber, 73; Le Rougetel to FO, 1/10/44, FO 371/44009, NAUK; and 27/10/44, FO 371/43988, NAUK.

104   'Truppenmeldungen vom 1.11–30.11.1944', T-78, r. 564, fr. 376, NA; and 'Intelligence Diary for Roumania', entry for 1/12/44, WO 208/4561, NAUK.

105   Gosztony, 171; FRUS, 1944, iv, 282–83, 286; Curierul, 1/1/45; and Timpul, 1/1/45.

106   Libertatea, 31/12/44; Semnalul, 2/1/45; and Graiul Nou, 5/1/45.

107   Ionescu, 98; Biddiscombe, 'Prodding the Russian Bear', 203–04; 'Memorandum on Visit to Galatz', c. 11/44, FO 371/44033, NAUK; and 'Communists and Legionaires', 28/11/45, FO 371/59095, NAUK.

108   'Mouet Operation', 9/11/53, CIANF, Entry 86, RG 263, NA.

109   Fatu and Spalatelu, 408; Lebedev, 373–74; Emil Dorian, The Quality of Witness (Philadelphia, 1982), 348; 'Legionary Movement, 1919 to Present', 30/12/49, CIANF, Entry 86, RG 263, NA; and Le Rougetel to Eden, 23/11/44, FO 371/43989, NAUK.

110   Constantiniu, 1496; and Sima to Ribbentrop, 29/10/44, NS 19/2155, BA.

111   Kaltenbrunner int., 22/5/45, Entry 119A, RG 226, NA; Kaltenbrunner int., 28/6/45, IRR File 000440, RG 319, NA; 'Anti-Russian Activities in Rumania'; 'Legionary Movement, 1919 to Present', 30/12/49, both in CIANF, Entry 86, RG 263, NA; and Berger to Himmler, 23/1/45, NS 19/3825, BA.

112   ULTRA/ZIP/ISOSICLE 12584, 31/1/45, HW 19/248, NAUK.

113   'Intelligence Diary for Roumania', entry for 2/2/45; entry for 5/2/45, both in WO 208/4561, NAUK.

114   ULTRA/ZIP/ISOSICLE 12899, 9/4/45, HW 19/248, PRO.

115   Kaltenbrunner int., 22/5/45, Entry 119A, RG 226, NA.

116   Fatu and Spalatelu, 407–08; and 'Legionary Movement, 1919 to Present', 30/12/49, CIANF, Entry 86, RG 263, NA.

117   'Auswertung von Aussagen rumänischer Kriegsgefangener', 1/2/45, T-175, r. R641, fr. 46–47, NA.

118   ULTRA/ZIP/ISOSICLE 12682, 11/3/45; and 12671, 10/3/45, both in HW 19/248, NAUK.

119   Nagy-Talavera, 339; and 'CIR 4 – The German Sabotage Service', 23/7/45, IRR File XE 070687, RG 319, NA.

120   'Auswertung von Aussagen rumänischer Kriegsgefangener', 1/2/45, T-175, r. R641, fr. 49, 51–52, NA; and Report GR-219, 7/2/45, L 53621, Entry 21, RG 226, NA.

121   Heinen, 462; and ULTRA/ZIP/ISOSICLE 12660, 5/3/45, HW 19/248, NAUK.

122   Reinerth and Cloos, 227; and ULTRA/ZIP/ISOSICLE 12553, 11/2/45, HW 19/248, NAUK.

123   ULTRA/ZIP/ISOSICLE 12558, 18/2/45; 12559, 21/2/45, both in HW 19/248, NAUK; and 'Intelligence Diary for Roumania', entry for 2/2/45, WO 208/4561, NAUK.

124   Reinerth and Cloos, 235; ULTRA/ZIP/ISOSICLE 12554, 14/2/45, HW 19/248, NAUK; 'Rumanian Collaboration with the Germans'; 'Horia Sima's Visit to the German Front'; 'Avramescu's Plans for Seeking Refuge for His Family with the Germans', 2/11/53; 'Avramescu's Projected Desertion to the Germans with the 4th Army', all in CIANF, Entry 86, RG 263, NA; and R. Sonntag 'Protokoll', 15/10/52, OD 2/347, LA-BA.

125   Maurice Pearton and Dennis Deletant, 'The Soviet Takeover in Romania', in The End of the War in Europe, 1945 (London, 1995), 216; Reinerth and Cloos, 236–37; Sturdza, 274; and ULTRA/ZIP/ISOSICLE 12532, 15/2/45, HW 19/248, NAUK.

126   Erickson, The Road to Berlin, 371; and Rieber, 92.

127   FRUS, 1945 (Washington, 1967), v, 488–89, 493; BMM to WO, 16/2/45, FO 371/48573, NAUK; 1/3/45; and

2/3/45, both in FO 371/48549, NAUK.

128 ULTRA/ZIP/ISOSICLE 12757, 7/3/45, HW 19/248, NAUK.

129 Rieber, 102; *FRUS, 1945*, v, 497; *FRUS, 1946* (Washington, 1969), vi, 559; Clark-Kerr to FO, 7/3/45, FO 371/48549, NAUK; and ULTRA/ZIP/ISOSICLE 12615, 1/3/45, HW 19/248, NAUK.

130 ULTRA/ZIP/ISOSICLE 12702, 12/3/45; 14/3/45; 12769, 17/3/45; 12949, 19/4/45, all in HW 19/248, NAUK; *Krasnaya Zvezda*, 3/4/45; 'Zusammenstellung von Chi-Nachrichten' 1021, 3/4/45, T-78, r. 496, fr. 6484383, NA; Clark-Kerr to FO, 6/4/45; memo on ms R6699, 15/4/45, both in FO 371/48608, NAUK; 'Mouet Operation', 9/11/53, CIANF, Entry 86, RG 263, NA; and transcript of a discussion, Schuyler-Susaikov, 19/4/45, FO 371/48575, NAUK.

131 Seton-Watson, 202–06; Ionescu, 88–109; Hélène Carrère d'Encausse, *Big Brother* (New York, 1987), 53–54; Keith Hutchins, *Rumania* (Oxford, 1994), 512–16; and Pearton and Deletant, 'The Soviet Takeover in Romania', 204–13. For Stalinist 'intentionalism', see Seton-Watson, 168–71; Carrère d'Encausse, *Big Brother*, 37–50; and John Campbell, 'Soviet Policy in Eastern Europe: An Overview', in *Soviet Policy in Eastern Europe* (New Haven, 1984), 5–6. For a view of Soviet intentions informed by documents from the Russian archives, see Rieber, 63–64, 104–05.

132 ULTRA/ZIP/ISOSICLE 12533, 15/2/45; and 12633, 5/3/45, both in HW 19/248, NAUK.

133 ULTRA/ZIP/ISOSICLE 12616, 1/3/45, HW 19/248, NAUK.

134 *The Goebbels Diaries – The Last Days* (London, 1978), 50.

135 Waneck int., 11/8/45, Entry 119A, RG 226, NA; ULTRA/ZIP/ISOSICLE 12580, 28/1/45; 12581, 28/1/45; 12595, 29/1/45; 12596, 2/2/45; 12602, 31/1/45; 12651, 6/3/45; and 12900, 11/4/45, all in HW 19/248, NAUK.

136 Heinen, 462; Höttl, 178; and 'Legionary Movement, 1919 to Present', 30/12/49, CIANF, Entry 86, RG 263, NA.

137 'Legionary Movement, 1919 to Present', 30/12/49, CIANF, Entry 86, RG 263, NA; and ULTRA/ZIP/ISOSICLE 12999, 27/4/45, HW 19/248, NAUK.

138 Sturdza, 268; Gosztony, 276–77; Spearhead to Warroom, 3/6/45, IRR File XE 000440, RG 319, NA; ULTRA/ZIP/ISOSICLE 12943, 24/4/45, HW 19/248, NAUK; 'Further Information on Jewish Persecutions in Hungary'; and 'Sima, Horia', both in CIANF, Entry 86, RG 263, NA.

139 ULTRA/ZIP/ISOSICLE 12951, 3/5/45; 12953, 3/5/45, both in HW 19/248, NAUK; and 'German W/T station in Pilsen Area', 7/5/45, Entry 171A, RG 226, NA.

140 'Legionary Movement, 1919 to Present', 30 Dec. 1949, 30/12/49; and 'Mouet Operation', 9/11/53, both in CIANF, Entry 86, RG 263, NA.

141 Sturdza, 274–75; Fatu and Spalatelu, 406, 413–16; 'Italy – Report on the "Iron Guard"', 1/6/49; 'Legionary Movement, 1919 to Present', 30/12/49; 'Eugen Teodorescu', 17/9/53; 'Sima, Horia', 5/12/53, all in CIANF, Entry 86, RG 263, NA.

142 Nissan Oren, *Revolution Administered* (Baltimore, 1973), 29–33, 48, 51, 53; J.R. Crampton, *A Concise History of Bulgaria* (Cambridge 1997), 129–32; Lukacs, 741; and Naum Kajcev and Ivanka Nedeva, 'A Minor Affair or an Important Factor?', *Bulgarian Historical Review* 26 (1998), 103.

143 Marshall Lee Miller, *Bulgaria during the Second World War* (Stanford, 1975), 73–75, 117–18; 'Notes on World War II', 12/10/45, WO 208/3148, NAUK; Kaltenbrunner int., 28/6/45; and 'CIR 3 – Amt VI-E of the RSHA', 21/6/45, both in IRR File 000440, RG 319, NA.

144 Schellenberg, 304; Kajcev and Nedeva, 103–04; Miller, 126; Georgi Daskalov, 'Bulgarskite Aktsionni Komitet v Vardarska Makedoniia (April-Avgust 1941 G.)', *Istoricheski Pregled* 47 (1991), 58–74; J. Matl, et al., 'Zwischen Kollaboration und Resistenz', in *Das Dritte Reich und Europe* (Munich, 1957), 156, 161; 'The Sicherheitsdienst in Sofia'; Kaltenbrunner int., 22/5/45, both in Entry 119A, RG 226, NA; Kaltenbrunner int., 28/6/45; 'CIR 3 – Amt VI-E of the RSHA', 21/6/45, both in IRR File XE 000440, RG 319, NA; and 'Final Report on the Case of Walter Friedrich Schellenberg', IRR File XE 001752, RG 319, NA.

145 Kajcev and Nedeva, 104; 'CIR 3 – Amt VI-E of the RSHA', 21/6/45, IRR File 000440, RG 319, NA; 'Final Report on the Case of Walter Schellenberg', XE 001752, RG 319, NA; 'A. Schule Sudost (SD) 54-general-4', IRR File, XE 001063, RG 319, NA; Rexroth int., 27/5/45; 'Leitstelle II Sud Ost', 8/9/45, both in Entry 119A, RG 226, NA; ULTRA/ZIP/ISK 115105, 7/9/44, HW 19/197, NAUK; 116118, 12/9/44, HW 19/199, NAUK; and 120374, 25/9/44, HW 19/206, NAUK.

146 ULTRA/ZIP/ISK 114518, 3/9/44; 114519, 3/9/44, HW 19/197, NAUK.

147 Schellenberg, 304; Hans-Joachim Hoppe, *Bulgarien – Hitlers eigenwilliger Verbündeter* (Stuttgart, 1979), 174–75, 179, 181–82; *AdAP*, series E, viii, 379, 404, 414; 'A History of Germany's Campaigns in World War II by Genobst (Col Gen) Heinz Guderian', 26/7/45, WO 208/3148, NAUK; 'Final Report on the Case of Walter Friedrich Schellenberg', IRR File XE 001752, RG 319, NA; ULTRA/ZIP/ISK 114294, HW 19/196, NAUK; 11896, 2/9/44; 11798, 10/9/44, both in HW 19/246, NAUK; 'Daily Sitrep' 380, 4/9/44; and 'Daily Sitrep' 381, 5/9/44, both in WO 208/113B, NAUK.

148 Hoppe, 176–80, 182, 183–84; Miller, 209–10; *AdAP*, series E, viii, 411; and ULTRA/ZIP/ISK 115307, 12/9/44, HW 19/198, NAUK.

149 Kajcev and Nedeva, 104–07.

150 Walter Warlimont, *Inside Hitler's Headquarters* (London, 1964), 471; Murad int., 21/12/45, in *Covert Warfare*, xiii; and 'Daily Sitrep' 377, 1/9/44, WO 208/113B, NAUK.

151 Crampton, 181; Hoppe, 176–78; *AdAP*, series E, viii, 411–12; ULTRA/ZIP/ISK 114519, 3/9/44, HW 19/197, NAUK; 'Notes on World War II', 12/10/45, WO 208/3148, NAUK; and 'Daily Sitrep' 389, 14/9/44, WO 208/113B, NAUK.

152 Miller, 191; Hoppe, 181; *AdAP*, Series E, viii, 379–80, 403–04, 413–14; and ULTRA/ZIP/ISK 114518, 3/9/44, HW 19/197, NAUK.

153 Hoppe, 380, 404–05; *The New York Times*, 10/9/44; Scheidler int., 11/7/45, IRR File XE 000440, RG 319, NA; 'Intelligence Diary for Bulgaria', entry for 9/9/44, WO 208/4391, NAUK; and ULTRA/ZIP/ISK 116162, 12/9/44, HW 19/199, NAUK.

154 Untitled note; 'Information received from our Missions who were S. of Plovdiv', 10/9/44; and D.R. to Terence, 20/9/44, all in WO 208/113B, NAUK.

155 'ND' 1672, 1/2/45; and 1674, 3/2/45, both in BC, Robbins Library.

156 D. Kossev, H. Hristov and D. Angelov, *A Short History of Bulgaria* (Sofia, 1963), 401; and Report G-5669, 23/9/44, HS 5/248, NAUK.

157 'ND' 1567, 2/10/44; 1569, 4/10/44; 1572, 7/10/44; 1573, 9/1044, all in BC, Robbins Library; and *La France*, 28–29/10/44.

158 For the example of a *Ratnitsi* cohort from Veles, see ULTRA/ZIP/ISK 116162, 12/9/44, HW 19/119, NAUK.

159 'CIR 3 – Amt VI-E of the RSHA', 21/6/45, IRR File XE 000440, RG 319, NA; ULTRA/ZIP/ISOS 87408, 9/10/44; 87667, 1/10/44, both in HW 19/75, NAUK; 'ND' 1672, 1/2/45; and 1674, 3/2/45, both in BC, Robbins Library.

160 Murad int., 21/12/45, in *Covert Warfare*, xiii.

161 Von Herz int., 29/10/45, ETO MIS-Y-Sect. CSDIC/WEA Interim Reports, Special Interrogation Reports 1945–46, RG 338, NA; ULTRA/ZIP/ISK 127326, 5/1/45, HW 19/216, NAUK; 127770, 22/12/44, HW 19/217, NAUK; 128664, 1/1/45, HW 19/218, NAUK; and 136833, 23/2/45, HW 19/229, NAUK.

162 ULTRA/ZIP/ISK 139746, 15/3/45, HW 19/233, NAUK; and Murad int., 18/1/46, in *Covert Warfare*, xiii.

163 Gellermann, 96; Murad int., 18/1/46, in *Covert Warfare*, xiii; 'ND' 1672, 1/2/45, BC, Robbins Library; 'CIR 3 – Amt VI-E of the RSHA', 21/6/45, IRR File XE 000440, RG 319, NA; 'Leitstelle II Sud Ost', 8/10/45, Entry 119A, RG 226, NA; 'Intelligence Diary for Bulgaria', entry for 26/4/45, WO 208/4391, NAUK; ULTRA/ZIP/ISK 135944, 20/2/45, HW 19/228, NAUK; 138313, 25/3/45; 138342, 25/3/45, both in HW 19/231, NAUK; 139328, 28/3/45, HW 19/232, NAUK; 139726, 5/3/45; and 139793, 3/3/45, both in HW 19/233, NAUK. For the connection between the Bulgarian fascists and the creation of a communist-led militia, see Michael Ball, *Cold War in the Balkans* (Lexington, 1984), 66, 73, 85.

164 Crampton, 184–86; Wilfried Loth, *The Division of the World* (London, 1988), 83; Edward Judge and John Langdon, *A Hard and Bitter Peace* (Upper Saddle River, 1996), 44; Irwin Sanders, *Balkan Village* (Lexington, 1949), 196–97, 209; and 'Intelligence Diary for Bulgaria', entry for 30/8/45, WO 208/4391, NAUK. For initial Soviet reluctance to intervene in Bulgaria, see Mastny, 200–02.

165 *FRUS, 1945*, iv, 174; and 'ND' 1752, 5/5/45, BC, Robbins Library.

166 'ND' 1640, 26/12/44; 1675, 5/2/45; 1686, 17/2/45; and 1691, 23/2/45, all in BC, Robbins Library.

167 Miller, 191, 217; Lukacs, 667; *The New York Times*, 20/4/46; Spearhead to War Room, 3/6/45; and 'CIR 3 – Amt VI-E of the RSHA', 21/6/45, both in IRR File XE 000440, RG 319, NA.

168 Mark Mazower, *Inside Hitler's Greece* (New Haven, 1993), 349; Dominique Eudes, *The Kapetanios* (New York, 1972), 108, 156; Nicholas Hammond, *Venture into Greece* (London, 1983), 86, 89, 92, 97; 'Political Humpty Dumpties', 16/5/43; 'Athens', 9/8/43; 'Political – Royalist Activity', 4/9/43; 'Information from G. Kastanakis, a Cretan Doctor and Member of EKKA'; PAO memo, all in HS 5/238, NAUK; 'PIC Memoranda on Greek Resistance Organisations', PIC/272/21, 15/12/43; 'Report by Colonel (Inf.) Panayotis Goulas, representative of PAO to M. Tsouderos, dated 23 December 1943'; 'Proposal for reforming the Panhellenic Liberating Organisation (PAO)'; 'CSDIC Allied Source, Interrogation Report "F" Series – Security Political, Secret Organisations, Guerrilla Activities', 20/5/44, all in HS 5/239, NAUK; sig. illegible to Larden, 14/2/44; sig. illegible to Warner, 12/3/44, both in HS 5/240, NAUK; Tsouderos, memo, 17/7/43; 'Memorandum on Activities in Greece', 29/7/43, both in HS 5/423, NAUK; 'Greek Security Battalions', HS 5/249, NAUK; 'Paper on PAO Bands in Central Macedonia, August–December 1943', 9/12/43; 'Information on PAO and the Different Categories of Armed Peasants in Macedonia'; 'Present Situation of PAO'; SOE, note by acting head, 16/11/43; 'Comments by Major Micklethwaite'; and 'PAO', 28/10/44, all in HS 5/627, NAUK.

169 C.M. Woodhouse, *The Struggle for Greece* (London, 1983), 58–59, 60, 91–92, 147; Mazower, 327, 329; E.D. Smith, *Victory of a Sort* (London, 1988), 129–30; Eudes, 108–09; Nigel Clive, *A Greek Experience* (Salisbury,

1985), 60–61, 75–77, 82; Leeper to FO, 2/12/43, HS 5/220, NAUK; 'Reports of Collaboration between Epirus EDES and the Germans', 8/12/43; Cairo to Shepshed, 11/12/43; Shepshed to Cairo, 12/12/43; 14/12/43; Discus to Cairo, 18/12/43, all in HS 5/638, NAUK; 'PIC Memoranda on Greek Resistance Organisations', 15/12/43; 'Greece: Political' 0125/0121, 6/11/43; Bovington to Cairo, 5/12/43; Shepshed to Cairo, 6/12/43; 'Recent Developments in Athens'; Budge to Warner, 21/12/43, all in HS 5/239, NAUK; 'Recent Developments in Greece'; 'Report of the position of Military Organisations in Greece and the creation of a Military Staff', 15/12/43; Kreon, memo, 20/1/44; Yvonne to Cairo, 30/3/44; Force 133 to Renovation, 18/5/44, all in HS 5/240, NAUK; Int. 654/43/MI3b to MO5c, 6/11/43; 'Recent Developments in Athens', 24/11/43; D/HV to OD through AD, 26/11/43; D/HV to OD through AD, 10/12/43; 'Recent Crisis in Free Greece', 19/10/43, all in HS 5/423, NAUK; 'The Problem of the Security Battalions', 15/5/44; 'Post-Liberation Problems of the Allied Military Mission in Greece, Crete & the Aegean', 19/6/44, both in HS 5/224, NAUK; 'Security, Political, Secret Organisations, Guerrilla Activities', 5/3/44, HS 5/247, NAUK; 'Greek Security Battalions', HS 5/249, NAUK; 'Notes on World War II', 12/10/43, WO 208/3148, NAUK; Yvonne to Force 133, 11/7/44, both in HS 5/241, NAUK; Koch int., 15/6/45, Entry 119A, RG 226, NA; and ULTRA/ZIP/ISK 116127, 7/9/44, HW 19/199, NAUK.

170 Mazower, 328–30; 'Arrests of Security Battalion Leaders and Govt. Crisis', 28/6/44, HS 5/248, NAUK; 'Greek Security Battalions', HS 5/249, NAUK; and D/HV to OD through AD, 1/12/43, HS 5/423, NAUK.

171 Clive, 119–21; Smith, 147; Woodhouse, p. 91; 'FAT 377', Entry 119A, RG 226, NA; Report G-5670, 23/9/44, HS 5/638, NAUK; ULTRA/ZIP/ISK 114466, 25/8/44, HW 19/197, NAUK; ULTRA/ZIP/ISOSICLE 11801, 10/9/44, HW 19/246, NAUK; 'Intelligence Diary for Greece', entry for 18/2/45, WO 208/4519, NAUK; and Force 133 to Renovation, 14/7/44, HS 5/241, NAUK.

172 Mazower, 352–53; 'Suggested Plan for the Prevention of the Seizure of Power by EAM/ELAS in Greece at the Termination of the Axis Occupation', 18/7/44; 'German Military Mission to the Seventh Army', 7/6/45, both in Entry 119A, RG 226, NA; 'Intelligence Diary for Greece', entry for 1/6/45, WO 208/4519, NAUK; and Report GA-187, 188, 9/12/44, XL 2687, Entry 19, RG 226, NA.

173 ZIP/ISOSICLE 8063, 1/11/43, HW 19/239, NAUK.

174 For the 'chaos thesis', see Mazower, 232–33, 344–45.

175 Ibid., 238, 336–39, 357; Hammond, 75; Tsimbas int., 6/8/46; Report LWX-42, 23/7/45, both in Entry 119A, RG 226, NA; ULTRA/ZIP/ISK 115765, 11/9/44, HW 19/198, NAUK; ZIP/ISOSICLE 7908, 26/10/43, HW 19/238, NAUK; ULTRA/ZIP/ISOSICLE 11045, 22/5/44; 11090, 27/5/44; 11096, 27/5/44, all in HW 19/244, NAUK; 11630, 27/7/44, HW 19/246, NAUK; 11922, 2/10/44; 11929, 8/10/44; 11930, 11/10/44, all in HW 19/247, NAUK; 'Information on PAO and the Different Categories of Armed Peasants in Macedonia', HS 5/627, NAUK; 'EASAD and EEE', 17/5/44; 'Report by an AMM Interpreter, Thessaly', 19/5/44; 'Statements by 54th Regiment', 5/44, all in HS 5/248, NAUK; and 'Greek Security Battalions', HS 5/249, NAUK.

176 Otto Begus, A3343 SSO-052, RG 242, NA; 'The "Bertram" Group'; 'Extracts from C.I.S. Summaries nos. 1, 2 and 3, dated October 26th, November 8th and 23rd'; 'C' to Cavendish-Bentinck, 16/12/44; 'S.I.M.E. Report' 4, 7/12/44; 'CIR 4 – The German Sabotage Service', 23/7/45, IRR File XE 070687, RG 319, NA; Kaltenbrunner int., 28/6/45, IRR File 000440, RG 319, NA; 'Greece: O.E.D.E.', 21/5/44, HS 5/248, NAUK; Morael int., 30/3/45; Claes int., 13/4/45; 'Look-up Summaries – MI-5 Sources: Tsimbas', 19/4/45; Uzicanin int., 31/5/45; 'CIR 3 – AmtVI-E of the RSHA', 21/6/45; X-2 London Near East Desk to Monigan, 8/6/45; 'Papadopulos, Panajotis', 23/7/45; untitled notes on Papadopulos, Ludewig and Kronberger; Tsimbas int., 6/8/45, all in Entry 119A, RG 226, NA; ULTRA/ZIP/ISOSICLE 10383, 17/3/44; 10678, 8/4/44, both in HW 19/243, NAUK; 11045, 22/5/44; 11090, 27/5/44; 11069, 27/5/44, all in HW 19/244, NAUK; 11621, 26/7/44; 11796, 9/9/44; 11630, 27/7/44; 11818, 16/9/44; 11855, 23/2/44, all in HW 19/246, NAUK; 11920, 28/9/44; 11921, 28/9/44; 11922, 2/10/44; 11925, 6/10/44; 11926, 7/10/44; 11927, 7/10/44; 11928, 8/10/44; 11929, 8/10/44; 11930, 11/10/44, all in HW 19/247, NAUK; 'Notes on CI in Italy' 6, 8/2/45, WO 204/822, NAUK; and 'Extract from "Revision Notes no. 1 on the German Intelligence Services" dated 6 Dec. 44', WO 204/11839, NAUK.

177 Anthony Cave Brown, *The Secret Servant* (London, 1988), 652; Uzicanin int., 31/5/45; 'C' to Cavendish-Bentinck, 16/12/44; 'Observations on the fighting in Greece, December 3rd to 9th, 1944', 109701, Entry 16, RG 226, NA; 'The "Bertram" Group'; 'Extracts from C.I.S. Summaries nos. 1, 2 and 3, dated October 26th, November 8th and 23rd', all in Entry 119A, RG 226, NA; 'CIR 4 – The German Sabotage Service', 23/7/45, IRR File XE 070687, RG 319, NA; and 'Intelligence Diary for Greece', entry for 18/2/45, WO 208/4519, NAUK. For the Germans in ELAS, see Hammond, 165, 196; Smith, 174; Henry Maule, *Scobie: Hero of Greece* (London, 1975), 9, 55, 73; Heinz Kühnrich, *Der Partisanenkrieg in Europa* (Berlin, 1968), 401–02; *Manchester Guardian*, 8/1/45; *The New York Times*, 17/12/44; 'Intelligence Diary for Greece', entries for 6/11/44; 2/1/45, both in WO 208/4519, NAUK; and Dragoumis to Greek Embassy, 8/12/44, HW 1/3370, NAUK.

178   Spearhead to Warroom, 3/6/45, IRR File XE 000440, RG 319, NA; Huygens int., 30/3/45; Claes int., 13/4/45; and SHAEF CI War Room to 12th AG, 5/6/45, all in Entry 119A, RG 226, NA.

179   Neubacher, 193; Mazower, 357; DEG 3903, 15/1/45, HW 19/277, NAUK; and 'Intelligence Diary for Greece', entry for 8/1/45, WO 208/4519, NAUK.

180   Murad int., 21/12/45, in *Covert Warfare*, xiii; CI War Room 'FAT 250', 6/12/45, Entry 119A, RG 226, NA; 'Greece', 21/2/45, 117451, Entry 16, RG 226, NA; Koch int., 15/6/45; 'Kino Operation'; CI War Room to Harry, 29/10/45; 'FAT 219', all in Entry 119A, RG 226, NA; 'Intelligence Report', 8/3/45, 119698, Entry 16, RG 226, NA; 10/3/45, 120820, Entry 16, RG 226, NA; 'Memoranda on Greek Resistance Organisations', 15/12/43, HS 5/239, NAUK; 'Intelligence Diary for Greece', entry for 22/2/45, WO 208/4519, NAUK; 'Albano-Greek Relations 1944', WO 204/9428, NAUK; ULTRA/ZIP/ISOS 94363, 20/12/44, HW 19/80, NAUK; ULTRA/ZIP/ISK 113899, 10/8/44, HW 19/196, NAUK; 116322, 5/9/44; 116034, 10/9/44; and 116035, 10/9/44, all in HW 19/199, NAUK.

181   Kermit Roosevelt, *The Overseas Targets* (New York, 1976), 330; and 'Intelligence Report', 16/5/45, 130765, Entry 16, RG 226, NA. For reference to reports from 'Greek VAR', see ULTRA/ZIP/ISK 138327, 7/3/45, HW 19/231, NAUK.

182   Julian Amery, *Sons of the Eagle* (London, 1948), 64–65; Neubacher, 105–10; 113, 116; Buchheit, 355–56; M.R.D. Foot, *Resistance* (London, 1976), 184; Matl, et al., 159–61; 'Report on Albania', HS 5/4, NAUK; ZIP/ISOSICLE 6125, 16/9/43, HW 19/237, NAUK; and 'Brief Notes on Conversation 1/(Stevens)', WO 204/9428, NAUK.

183   Neubacher, 108; Spaeter, 390–91; David Smiley, *Albanian Assignment* (London, 1984) 60–63, 77, 143, 145; Amery, 65–66, 188–90, 252–53, 287–88; Christoph Stamm, 'Zur deutschen Besatzung Albaniens 1943–1944', *Militärgeschichtliche Mitteilungen* 30 (2/1981), 109–10; 'Trotsky' Davies, *Illyrian Adventure* (London, 1952), 116, 119–20, 148, 156; Elizabeth Barker, *British Policy in South-East Europe in the Second World War* (London, 1976), 177–79; *AdAP*, series E, viii, 229–30; 'Report on Albania'; 'Albania: Review for Week Ended 9 July 44'; 'Albania: Review for the Week Ended 23 July 44', all in HS 5/4, NAUK; 'Albania'; Cipher Telegram to Cairo, 29/12/43; D/HT to A/DH, 17/1/44; AD/H to CD, V/CD, K/POL, D/PLANS, 25/2/44; 'Albania: Appreciation of the general situation', all in HS 5/11, NAUK; 'Albania: Daily Situation Report no. 209 of 17th March 1944'; 'Attitude of the Population to King Zog'; 'Note on the Two Frasheris'; 'Comments by Col. Wheeler on Report by Capt. Amery', 9/6/44; 'The Mitrovica Government and Balli Kombetar Forces', 15/6/44, all in HS 5/68, NAUK; 'Proposed Co-Operation with Balli Kombetar', 22/2/44, HS 5/85, NAUK; ULTRA/ZIP/ISOSICLE 10917, 6/4/44, HW 19/244, NAUK; 11823, 16/9/44, HW 19/246, NAUK; and 11914, 17/8/44, HW 19/247, NAUK.

184   Frasheri & Muftija to Molotov, 7/1/45, HS 5/1, NAUK; 'Valona', 20/11/44; Report SO/248, 13/4/45; 'Armed Opposition – Scutari Area', 3/2/45, all in HS 5/4, NAUK; 'Brief Note on Conversation 1/(Stevens)'; and 'Political Review for Period ending February 4th', both in WO 204/9428, NAUK.

185   Koch int.; and 'Kino Operation', both in Entry 119A, RG 226, NA.

186   Amery, 169; and 'Report by Lt. Col. MacLean, dated 18th June (Consensus 4 of 18 June)', HS 5/68, NAUK.

187   ULTRA/ZIP/ISOS 85151, 23/8/44, HW 19/72, PRO.

188   Amery, 66–67, 120, 144, 162, 164, 218–21, 223, 241, 244–45, 248–49, 256–58, 260, 262–64, 278–86, 288, 291, 295, 297–99, 301, 307–08; Noel Malcolm, *Kosovo* (New York, 1998), 306–09; Barker, 179–81; Smiley, 140–45; Stamm, 113; 'Information from Albania'; 'Albania: Review for Week Ended 25 June 44' through to 'Albania: Review for Fortnight Ending 20 Aug 44', all in HS 5/4, NAUK; MacLean to Eden, 24/5/44; 'Recommendation of Policy to be followed in connection with the "Movement of Legality" in Northern Albania', 1/6/44; Maclean telegram, 5/6/44; 'Memorandum by S.O.E.', 7 June 1944; 'Comments on Telegram 3094 dated 7.6.44 from Bari'; MacLean telegram, 10/6/44; 21/6/44; 24/6/44; 'Copy of telegram received from Bari dated 4.7.44'; D/Ht to AD/H, 14/7/44, all in HS 5/11, NAUK; 'Copy of a telegram received from Bari dated 8.9.44', HS 5/16, NAUK; L/B.2 to D/H 109, 4/5/44; 'Attitude of the Population to King Zog', 4/5/44; 'Cipher Tel from Force 266', 29/5/44; D/HJ to D/H 109, 9/5/44; B8 Section, Force 399 to D/H 109, 26/5/44; D/H 109 to D/HT, 2/6/44; AMSSO to AFHQ, 8/6/44; AFHQ to AMSSO, 16/6/44; 'Albania: Report by Lt. Col. MacLean, dated 18th June 1944 (Consensus 4 of 18 June)'; B8 Section, Force 399 to D/H 109, 19/6/44, all in HS 5/68, NAUK; ULTRA/ZIP/ISOSICLE 10975, 16/4/44; 10977, 15/4/44; 11087, 24/4/44; 11103, 26/4/44, all in HW 19/244, NAUK; 11116, 27/4/44, HW 19/245, NAUK; 11482, 5/7/44; 11428, 29/6/44; 11510, 8/7/44; 11530, 11/7/44; 11561, 14/7/44; 11868, 13/8/44; 11819, 17/9/44; 11871, 31/8/44; 11872, 26/8/44; 11887, 22/9/44, all in HW 19/246, NAUK.

189   Murad int., 21/12/45, in *Covert Warfare*, xiii; ULTRA/ZIP/ISOS 85151, 23/8/44; 85187, 23/8/44; 85222, 24/8/44, all in HW 19/72, NAUK; 86543, 24/9/44, HW 19/74, NAUK; 87226, 7/10/44; 87227, 5/10/44; 87408, 9/10/44; 87666, 1/10/44; 87668, 3/10/44; 87670, 5/10/44; 87680, 6/9/44; 87686, 2/10/44; 87688, 5/10/44; 87689, 16/10/44; 87701, 3/10/44; 87708, 2/10/44; 87718, 14/10/44; 88000, 26/8/44; 88013, 25/9/44; 88042, 4/9/44; 88589, 30/10/44; 88590, 30/10/44; 88793, 2/11/44, all in HW 19/75, NAUK; 90284,

21/11/44; HW 19/76, NAUK; and ULTRA/ZIP/ISK 120239, 26/9/44, HW 19/205, NAUK.

190 Koch int., 15/6/45, Entry 119A, RG 226, NA.

191 ULTRA/ZIP/ISOSICLE 11889, 4/9/44, HW 19/246, NAUK.

192 Amery, 302, 308, 310–11; Neubacher, 120–21; *The New York Times*, 1/11/44; ULTRA/ZIP/ISOS 88979, 5/11/44, HW 19/75, NAUK; ULTRA/ZIP/ISOSICLE 11392, 25/6/44, HW 19/245, NAUK; 11804, 10/9/44, HW 19/246, NAUK; 11913, 30/9/44, HW 19/247, NAUK; and 'ND' 1591, 30/10/44, BC, Robbins Library.

193 'Armed Opposition – Scutari Area', 3/2/45, HS 5/4, NAUK; and 'Political Review for Period ending February 4th', WO 204/9428, NAUK.

194 Neubacher, 190; Kaltenbrunner int., 28/6/45, IRR File 000440, RG 319, NA; Modriniak int., 15/7/45; 'FAK 201', 23/10/45, both in Entry 119A, RG 226, NA; and ULTRA/ZIP/ISK 136444, 28/2/45, HW 19/228, NAUK. For the evacuation of Albanian students and noblemen, see ULTRA/ZIP/ISOSICLE 10844, 9/3/44; 10908, 7/5/44; 10956, 14/5/44, all in HW 19/244, NAUK; 11803, 9/9/44; 11828, 27/8/44; 11840, 1/9/44; 11876, 21/9/44; 11894, 8/9/44, all in HW 19/246, NAUK; and 11973, 17/10/44, HW 19/247, NAUK.

195 Neubacher, 193; and Grosspaetsch int., 26/6/44, Entry 119A, RG 226, NA.

196 HP 5649, 5/11/44, UMC, r. 48, NAUK; ULTRA/ZIP/ISOS 88904, 3/11/44, HW 19/75, NAUK; 90259, 21/11/44; 90284, 21/11/44; 90637, 10/12/44, all in HW 19/76, NAUK.

197 ULTRA/ZIP/ISOS 89016, 5/11/44, HW 19/75, NAUK; and 90066, 30/11/44, HW 19/76, NAUK.

198 *FRUS, 1945*, iv, 37; 'Albania: Political Review for the Week ending 31 Dec. 1944'; 'Armed Opposition – Scutari Area', 3/2/45, both in HS 5/4, NAUK; 'Report on Present Administration of Albania', 30/4/45; BMM Albania to GHQ, CMF, 21/2/46, both in WO 204/374, NAUK; 'Political Review for Period ending February 4th', WO 204/9428, NAUK; and 'ND' 1672, 1/2/45; 1695, 28/2/45, both in BC, Robbins Library.

199 Amery, 340; Smiley, 159; Gordon Shepherd, *Russia's Danubian Empire* (New York, 1954), 232; *The Memoirs of Enver Hoxha* (London, 1986), 81–83; Dorril, chapter 19; Nicholas Bethell, *The Great Betrayal* (London, 1984); and DEG 3892, 28/12/44, HW 19/277, NAUK.

200 Stamm, 103; Malcolm, 292–93; and Buchheit, 355–56.

201 Kaltenbrunner int., 28/6/45, IRR File 000440, RG 319, NA.

202 Malcolm, 305–06; Miranda Vickers, *Between Serb and Albanian* (New York, 1998), 133–34; Spaeter, 391–401; Lefébvre, 247–56; 'Information from Albania'; 'Albania: Review for the Week ending 11 June 44' through to 'Albania: Review for the Fortnight ending 20 Aug 44', all in HS 5/4, NAUK; 'Kosovar Albanians', 28/3/44; 'Note on the Military Significance of Albania', 5/6/44, both in HS 5/68, NAUK; 'Interim Report on: F.H. Brandt', 5/12/44; 'Supplementary Report by W/Cmdr. P.A.B. Neel on Fred Hermann Brandt,' both in HS 5/98, NAUK; and ULTRA/ZIP/ISOS 85320, 24/8/44, HW 19/72, NAUK.

203 Neubacher, 117, 119; Murad int., 21/12/45, in *Covert Warfare*, xiii; ULTRA/ZIP/ISOS 87701, 3/10/44, HW 19/75, NAUK; ULTRA/ZIP/ISOSICLE 10933, 11/4/44, HW 19/244, NAUK; 11285, 13/6/44; 11400, 28/6/44, both in HW 19/245, NAUK; 11886, 4/9/44, HW 19/246, NAUK; and 11936, 6/8/44, HW 19/247, NAUK.

204 Malcolm, 311–12, 320–21; Vickers, 141–43; Mark Wheeler, 'White Eagles and White Guards', *Slavonic and East European Review* 66 (1988), 452–54; Michelle Lee, 'Kosovo between Yugoslavia and Albania', *New Left Review* 140 (July-Aug. 1983), 84; 'ND' 1597, 6/11/44, BC, Robbins Library; Lasky, memo, 19/5/45; Howard to Ramanos, 22/5/45; Hodgkinson to Howard, 25/5/45, all in FO 371/48817, NAUK; ULTRA/ZIP/ISOS 89016, 5/11/44, HW 19/75, NAUK; 89655, 23/11/44, HW 19/76, NAUK; ULTRA/ZIP/ISOSICLE 10105, 14/9/44, HW 19/242, NAUK; 'Balkan Radio Monitoring Report – Albania', 14/12/44; Bethesda 265, 24/12/44; and PRIMUS 51, 21/1/45, all in WO 202/300, NAUK.

205 Neubacher, 119.

206 Vjekoslav Luburic, 'The End of the Croatian Army', in *Operation Slaughterhouse*, (Philadelphia, 1970), 53, 68.

207 Murad int., 18/1/46, in *Covert Warfare*, xiii; 'CIR 3 – Amt VI-E of the RSHA', 21/6/45, IRR File XE 000440, RG 319, NA; 'Deva, Djafer', 12/7/45, CIANF, Entry 86, RG 263, NA; 'Leitstelle II Sud Ost', 8/10/45, Entry 119A, RG 226, NA; ULTRA/ZIP/ISK 139736, 10/3/45, HW 19/233, NAUK; and *The New York Times*, 1/11/44. For Brüggeboes, see Koch int., 15/6/45, Entry 119A, RG 226, NA.

208 'Xhafer Deva'; note, 21/4/50; 'Meeting with Xhafer Deva', 4/12/50; 'Intelligence Summary', 1/1/51; American Embassy, Belgrade to State Department, 5/4/51; 'Xhaffer Deva'; CIA Security Information to Special Operations, FDP (1–2), 31/1/52; 'Political Comments of Xhafer Deva', 14/2/52; 'Deva Proposal for Settling His Responsibility Regarding Current AIS Use of ex-Agents', 5/3/52; and 'Activities of Albanian Refugees, Athens', all in CIANF, Entry 86, RG 263, NA.

209 Neubacher, 146–49, 151–63; Hoettl, 154–55; Murad int., 21/12/45, in *Covert Warfare*, xiii; Camp 020 'Statement handed in by Kaltenbrunner on 8.8.45 with translation by Lebedour – Minister Dr. Neubacher'; Kaltenbrunner int., 22/5/45; 'Kaltenbrunner', 31/8/45, all in RG 119A, RG 226, NA; and 'Nazi Under-

ground in Austria and American Zone of Germany', 23/6/48, IRR File ZF 011665, RG 319, NA.

210   Ivan Avakumovic, 'Yugoslavia's Fascist Movements', in *Native Fascism in the Successor States* (Santa Barbara, 1971), 138.

211   Jozo Tomasevich, *The Chetniks* (Stanford, 1975), 201; Neubacher, 154, 188, 190; Murad int., 21/12/45, in *Covert Warfare*, xiii; 'CIR 3 – Amt VI-E of the RSHA', 21/6/45, IRR File XE 000440, Rg 319, NA; 'Kaltenbrunner', 31/8/44; Kaltenbrunner int., 22/5/45; 'Statements of four officers of the Leitstelle II Sud Ost, Kommandomeldegebeit, Vienna', all in Entry 119A, RG 226, NA; ULTRA/ZIP/ISOS 12/2/44, HW 19/73, NAUK; 89766, 25/11/44, HW 19/76, NAUK; OKW WfSt/Qu. 2 (Süd/Südost) to Ritter, 3/10/44 (fr. 1230); and 'Entlassung jugoslawischer kriegsgefangener Offiziere', 18/12/44 (fr. 1223–24), both in T-77, r. 1423, NA.

212   OKW WFSt/Qu. 2(I) to Himmler, 9/2/45 (fr. 1218–19); and Grothmann to Wagner, 17/2/45 (fr. 1217), both in T-77, r. 1423, NA.

213   Karl Hkinka, *Das Ende auf dem Balkan* (Göttingen, 1970), 314–15; Neubacher, 182, 188; *Trial of the Major War Criminals before the International Military Tribunal* (Nuremberg, 1948), 540; Haller int., 7/8/46, app. 'A', ETO MIS-Y-Sect. CSDIC/WEA Final Interrogation Reports 1945–47, RG 338, NA; ULTRA/ZIP/ISOS 95815, 24/3/45, HW 19/82, NAUK; ULTRA/ZIP/ISK 128034, 19/12/44; and 128313, 29/12/44, both in HW 19/217, NAUK.

214   'Serbien', 22/11/44, T-77, r. 1423, fr. 1169–70, NA.

215   'GPG', 15/1/45, FO 989/187, NAUK; 'ND' 1672, 1/2/45; 1674, 3/2/45; 1680, 10/2/45; 1681, 12/2/45; 1683, 14/2/45; 1688, 20/2/45; 1689, 21/2/45; 1690, 22/2/45; 1692, 24/2/45; 1693, 26/2/45; 1694, 27/2/45, all in BC, Robbins Library.

216   Tomasevich, 134–40, 148–50, 196–201, 206–09, 226–31, 247, 252–55, 341–42, 344–45, 348–58, 407–09; Matteo Milazzo, *The Chetnik Movement & the Yugoslav Resistance* (Baltimore, 1975), 35–38, 132–35, 162–66, 169–71; Mark Wheeler, *Britain and the War for Yugoslavia* (Boulder, 1980), 103–07; Walter Roberts, *Tito, Mihailovic and the Allies* (New Brunswick, 1973), 40–41, 56, 67–69, 72–73, 90, 92, 157, 199, 225–26; Hoettl, 163–67; Matl, et al., 157–58; David Martin, *Ally Betrayed* (New York, 1946), 154–57; Hlinka, 51, 53; Kriegsheim, 238–64, 312–13; Buchheit, 325–36; Neubacher, 147, 165–66; Murad int., 21/12/45, in *Covert Warfare*, xiii; 'Summary 2006 – Lt. Col. Rudolf Kogard', IWM; 'The Personal Responsibility of General Mihailovic', 5/1/44; 'Minute Regarding Collaboration of the Mihailovic Forces with the Enemy'; 'Chetnik Collaboration with the Axis in Serbia', 1/8/44, all in HS 5/959, NAUK; DEG 2965, 22/2/44, HW 19/275, NAUK; ULTRA/ZIP/ISOS 90462, 25/3/44; 91641, 31/3/44; 91669, 16/3/44, all in HW 19/77, NAUK; ZIP/ISOSICLE 6863, 9/9/43, HW 19/237, NAUK; 7669, 1/9/43, HW 19/238, NAUK; ULTRA/ZIP/ISOSICLE 9519, 26/1/44; 9539, 27/1/44; 9598, 31/1/44; 9898, 12/2/44, all in HW 19/241, NAUK; and Berndt int., 6/11/44, IRR File 011666, RG 319, NA.

217   Höttl, 154–56; 'Final Report on the Case of Walter Schellenberg', IRR File XE 001752, RG 319, NA; 'Kaltenbrunner', 31/8/45, Entry 119A, RG 226, NA; and ULTRA/ZIP/ISOS 90980, 17/2/44, HW 19/76, NAUK.

218   'The Germans and Mihailovic', 10/5/44, L 49640, Entry 21, RG 226, NA.

219   Wheeler, *Britain and the War for Yugoslavia*, 220–21; Roberts, 70, 93–94, 211–12; *British Policy towards Wartime Resistance in Yugoslavia and Greece* (London, 1975), 210; 'Daily Sitrep on Withdrawal of BLOs with MVIC', 59, 30/5/44; and 60, 31/5/44, both in HS 5/899, NAUK.

220   Hlinka, 51.53; Roberts, 258–59, 261; Tomasevich, 391–96, 433–34; 'Yugoslavia pp Cetnik Strength in Serbia', 11/8/44, HS 5/959, NAUK; ULTRA/ZIP/ISOS 86234, 16/9/44; 86382, 21/9/44, both in HW 19/74, NAUK; 86833, 25/9/44; 87366, 8/10/44; 87455, 6/10/44; 87737, 16/9/44; 87769, 27/9/44; 87930, 6/10/44, all in HW 19/75, NAUK; 89370, 21/9/44; 89386, 21/9/44; 89531, 15/9/44, all in HW 19/76, NAUK; and ULTRA/ZIP/ISK 120373, 26/9/44, HW 19/206, NAUK.

221   Neubacher, 157, 163–68; Tomasevich, 342–43; Milazzo, 369–71; *Trial of Dragoljub-Draza Mihailovic* (Belgrade, 1946), 84–85, 265–68, 270–71, 395–98; Jodl to von Weichs, 29/8/44, T-77, r. 1423, fr. 1171, NA; 'CIR 3 – Amt VI-E of the RSHA', 21/6/45, IRR File XE 000440, RG 319, NA; 'Source RI/AR, 4 December 1944', CIANF, Entry 86, RG 263, NA; ULTRA/ZIP/ISK 115307, 12/9/44, HW 19/198, NAUK; 137606, 18/3/45; 138183, 8/3/45, both in HW 19/230, NAUK; and ULTRA/ZIP/ISOS 95970, 21/2/45, HW 19/82, NAUK.

222   Walter Warlimont, *Inside Hitler's Headquarters* (London, 1964), p. 469; Neubacher, 170; Tomasevich, 346; *AdAP*, series E, viii, 393; 'Final Report in the Case of Walter Schellenberg', IRR File XE 001752, RG 319, NA; 'Notes on World War II', 12/10/45, WO 208/3148, NAUK; ULTRA/ZIP/ISOS 91677, 28/9/44, HW 19/77, NAUK; 93193, 26/1/45, HW 19/78, PRO; 93266, 16/1/45, HW 19/79, NAUK; ULTRA/ZIP/ISK 115891, 10/9/44, HW 19/198, NAUK; 13/12/44, HW 19/217, NAUK; DEG 3694, 29/9/44; 3695, 23/10/44, both in HW 19/276, NAUK; and 'Summary no. 381 – Col. Gen. Lothar Rendulic', IWM.

223   Tomasevich, 344–45; *AdAP*, series E, viii, 325, 327, 336–37, 371; ULTRA/ZIP/ISOS, 13/9/44, HW 19/73, NAUK; ULTRA/ZIP/ISK 115307, 12/9/44, HW 19/98, NAUK; and 'Final Report on the Case of Walter

Schellenberg', IRR File XE 001752, RG 319, NA.

224 Milazzo, 178–79; Schramm, 'The German Wehrmacht in the Last Days of the War (1 January–7 May 1945)', 362, 371, 377, 379–80, in *WWIIGMS* (New York, 1979), ii; HP 5483, 4/11/44 (r. 48); BT 2029, 12/1/45 (r. 58); BT 4801, 14/2/45 (r. 62); KO 939, 20/4/45 (r. 71), all in UMC, NAUK; ULTRA/ZIP/ISOS 89101, 7/11/44; HW 19/75, NAUK; 90109, 28/11/44; 90984, 27/10/44; 91424, 16/12/44, all in HW 19/76, NAUK; 92983, 11/12/44; 93044, 23/12/44; 93078, 3/1/45, all in HW 19/78, NAUK; 93466, 31/1/45, HW 19/79, NAUK; 94211, 1/1/45, HW 19/ 80, NAUK; 94745, 27/10/44, HW 19/81, NAUK; 95780, 3/3/45; 95807, 2/3/45, both in HW 19/82, NAUK; 95848, 24/3/45, HW 19/82, NAUK; ULTRA/ZIP/ISK 125827, 16/11/44, HW 19/214, NAUK; 128025, 24/12/44; 128034, 19/12/44; 128036, 26/12/44; 128074, 4/1/45, all in HW 19/217, NAUK; 128460, 23/12/44; 128556, 30/12/44; 128557, 30/12/44, all in HW 19/218, NAUK; 129302, 29/11/44, HW 19/219, NAUK; 131269, 28/11/44, HW 19/221, NAUK; 134938, 13/2/45, HW 19/226, NAUK; 135226, 5/2/45, HW 19/227, NAUK; and 136083, 6/3/45, HW 19/228, NAUK.

225 For attempts by Chetniks near Ozren to reach Zvornik, see ULTRA/ZIP/ISOS 92626, 12/12/44, HW 19/78, NAUK.

226 *AdAP*, series E, viii, 561.

227 ULTRA/ZIP/ISOS 94211, 1/1/45, HW 19/80, NAUK.

228 Tomasevich, 198; *The Trial of Dragoljub-Draza Mihailovic*, 46–47; Murad int., 21/12/45, in *Covert Warfare*, xiii; Modriniak int., 15/7/45, Entry 119A, RG 226, NA; BT 2029, 12/1/45, UMC, r. 58, NAUK; DEG 2965, 22/2/44, HW 19/275, NAUK; and ULTRA/ZIP/ISK 136446, 28/2/45, HW 19/228, NAUK.

229 Milazzo, 87–88; *The Trial of Dragoljub-Draza Mihailovic*, 48; Toplak int., 6/6/45, Entry 119A, RG 226, NA; ULTRA/ZIP/ISK 127381, 31/12/44; HW 19/216, NAUK; 129919, 7/12/44; 127930, 24/12/44, both in HW 19/217, NAUK; 130341, 10/12/44, HW 19/220, NAUK; 136142, 24/2/45, HW 19/228, NAUK; and 138314, 25/3/45, HW 19/231, NAUK.

230 The New York Times, 15/5/45.

231 *AdAP*, series E, viii, 561; and 'Serbien', 22/11/44, T-77, r. 1423, fr. 1170, NA.

232 ULTRA/ZIP/ISOS 91854, 20/1/44, HW 19/77, NAUK; 93092, 8/11/44, HW 19/78, NAUK; 95048, 7/3/45, HW 19/81, NAUK; 95827, 15/3/45, HW 19/82, NAUK; ULTRA/ZIP/ISK 137298, 20/3/45; 137453, 17/3/45; and 137823, 14/3/45, all in HW 19/230, NAUK.

233 '35 Wochenbericht der Innen- und Aussenpolitik der UdSSR', 3/3/45, RH 2/2330, BMA.

234 *AdAP*, series E, viii, 610; Neubacher, 192; and *The Trial of Dragoljub-Draza Mihailovic*, p. 280.

235 Street, 141–43, 151, 169, 221.

236 *The Trial of Dragoljub-Draza Mihailovic*, 276–77, 281–82; *Borba*, 31/3/45; ULTRA/ZIP/ISOS 95807, 2/3/45; 96898, 31/3/45, both in HW 19/82, NAUK; 96901, 31/3/45, HW 19/84, NAUK; ULTRA/ZIP/ISK 125827, 16/11/44; and 128037, 3/1/45, both in HW 19/217, NAUK.

237 ULTRA/ZIP/ISK 140555, 25/2/45, HW 19/234, NAUK; and 'ND' 1684, 15/2/45, BC, Robbins Library.

238 Neubacher, 193; Gellermann, 96; *Borba*, 31/3/45; Murad int., 18/1/46, in *Covert Warfare*, xiii; 'Leitstelle II Sud Ost', 8/10/45; 'FAK 201', 23/10/45, both in Entry 119A, RG 226, NA; ULTRA/ZIP/ISOS 96577, 16/3/45; 96723, 14/1/45; 97162, 8/4/45, all in HW 19/84, NAUK; ULTRA/ZIP/ISK 130308, HW 19/222, NAUK; 133740, 10/2/45, HW 19/224, NAUK; 138182, 8/3/45, HW 19/230, NAUK; and 139993, 25/3/45, HW 19/233, NAUK.

239 Murad int., 18/1/46, in *Covert Warfare*, xiii; and ULTRA/ZIP/ISOS 89565, 20/11/44, HW 19/76, NAUK.

240 'CIR 4 – The German Sabotage Service', 23/7/45, IRR File 070687, RG 319, NA; 'Notes Extracted from Lord Rothschild's Interrogation of Bebel@Niedermayer', 6/12/44; 'Descriptions of Students and Personnel of Radio and Sabotage School at 9. Adriaan Goerroplaan, The Hague', 2/9/44, Entry 119A, RG 226, NA; and 'CIR 3 – Amt VI-E of the RSHA', 21/6/45, IRR File XE 000440, RG 319, NA.

241 *AdAP*, series E, viii, 605; 'CIR 4 – German Sabotage Service', 23/7/45, IRR File XE 070687, RG 319, NA; ULTRA/ZIP/ISK 127655, 20/12/44; and 128223, 21/12/44, both in HW 19/217, NAUK.

242 *The Trial of Dragoljub-Draza Mihailovic*, 52, 85, 271–81, 550; and ULTRA/ZIP/ISK 139993, 25/3/45, HW 19/233, PRO.

243 Milovan Djilas, *Wartime* (New York, 1977), 447; and Tomasevich, 434–35, 439.

244 Neubacher, 168–69, 185, 192–93; *The Trial of Dragoljub-Draza Mihailovic*, 499; Milija Lašic-Vasojevic, *Enemies on all Sides* (Washington, 1976), 159, 165–66, 168–71; James Lucas, *Last Days of the Reich* (Toronto, 1986), 137; Milazzo, 179–81; Luburic, 53; 'Concerning Serbian Emigrants', CIANF, Entry 86, RG 263, NA; Dreher and Artholde int., 11/7/45; Kops int., 24/7/45; Kops int., 8/8/45; Kops int., 7/9/45, all in Entry 119A, RG 226, NA; BT 9476, 4/4/45, UMC, r. 68, NAUK; ULTRA/ZIP/ISOS 94813, 3/2/45, HW 19/81, NAUK; 97065, 10/3/45, HW 19/84, NAUK; ULTRA/ZIP/ISK 128074, 4/1/45, HW 19/217, NAUK; 138382, 27/3/45, HW 19/231, NAUK; 139997, 25/3/45, HW 19/233, NAUK; and DEG 3928, 21/1/45, HW 19/277, NAUK.

245 Mihailovic quoted in John Keegan, *The Second World War* (New York, 1989), 494.

246 Dimitrije Djordjevic, 'Fascism in Yugoslavia', in *Native Fascism in the Successor States* (Santa Barbara, 1971),

132; J.B. Hoptner, *Yugoslavia in Crisis* (New York, 1962), 136–38, 288; and Tomasevich, 78–79. See also James
      Sadkovich, *Italian Support for Croatian Separatism* (New York, 1987).

247   Luburic, 52.

248   Charles Thayer, *Guerrilla* (London, 1963), 152; *Operation Slaughterhouse*, 501; ULTRA/ZIP/ISOS 93284,
      26/1/45, HW 19/79, NAUK; and ULTRA/ZIP/ISK 140546, 24/2/45, HW 19/234, NAUK.

249   ULTRA/ZIP/ISOS 95573, 18/3/45, HW 19/82, NAUK.

250   Luburic, 52–54, 57–58, 61–64; and Lucas, *Last Days of the Reich*, 138. For reports about British encourage-
      ment and support for the Ustashe, see ULTRA/ZIP/ISOS 93369, 26/12/44, HW 19/79, NAUK; 94103,
      14/2/45; 94568, 7/2/45, both in HW 19/80, NAUK; ULTRA/ZIP/ISK 127341, 5/1/45, HW 19/216,
      NAUK; and 128927, 3/1/45, HW 19/218, NAUK.

251   Murad int., 21/12/45, in *Covert Warfare*, xiii.

252   'CIR 3 – AmtVI-E of the RSHA', 21/6/45, IRR File 000440, RG 319, NA; Dowe and Sokolov int., Entry
      119A, RG 226, NA; ULTRA/ZIP/ISOS 95573, 18/3/45, HW 19/82, NAUK; and DEG 3770, 22/11/44,
      HW 19/277, NAUK.

253   Tomasevich, 71, 78–79; Milazzo, 5–6; 'Kaltenbrunner', 31/8/45; 'SD and German Agents in Slovakia and
      Jugoslavia 1939 to 1943', 28/8/44, both in Entry 119A, RG 226, NA.

254   ULTRA/ZIP/ISOS 86220, 17/9/44, HW 19/74, NAUK; 95231, 11/3/45, HW 19/81, NAUK; ULTRA/
      ZIP/ISK 114197, 20/8/44, HW 19/196, NAUK; 128087, 31/12/44, HW 19/217, NAUK; 130866, 12/12/44,
      HW 19/221, NAUK; DEG 2951, 18/2/44, HW 19/275, NAUK. For 'white partisans', see Mark Wheeler,
      'White Eagles and White Guards', 459.

255   'Kaltenbrunner', 31/8/45; 'FAT 208', both in Entry 119A, RG 226, NA; and Modriniak int., 15/7/45, Entry
      119A, RG 226, NA.

256   ALP/JY 127 NIG/JY 124 PK 116 CO 38, 11/4/44, Entry 119A, RG 226, NA.

257   Report 6049, 11/11/44, L 49165, Entry 21, RG 226, NA; ULTRA/ZIP/ISOS 86050, 17/9/44, HW 19/73,
      NAUK; 88737, 30/9/44, HW 19/75, NAUK; 90586, 4/12/44, HW 19/76, NAUK; 92803, 22/1/45, HW
      19/78, NAUK; 93289, 29/1/45; 93295, 29/1/45, both in HW 19/79, NAUK; 94813, 3/2/45, HW 19/81,
      NAUK; 95896, 27/3/45, HW 19/82, NAUK; 96228, 3/4/45, HW 19/83, NAUK; and 96861, 21/4/45, HW
      19/84, NAUK.

258   ULTRA/ZIP/ISOS 92535, 11/12/44; 93045, 23/12/44; 93079, 3/1/45, all in HW 19/78, NAUK; 93295,
      29/1/45, HW 19/79, NAUK; 94813, 3/2/45, HW 19/81, NAUK; 96228, 3/4/45, HW 19/83, NAUK;
      ULTRA/ZIP/ISK 133083, 7/2/45, HW 19/224, NAUK; and KO 939, 20/4/45, UMC, r. 71, NAUK.

259   DEG 3947, 9/2/45, HW 19/277, NAUK; ULTRA/ZIP/ISOS 90586, 4/12/44, HW 19/76, NAUK; 92713,
      17/1/45; 92823, 19/1/45; 92829, 22/1/45, all in HW 19/78, NAUK; 93289, 29/1/45; and 93691, 27/1/45,
      both in HW 19/79, NAUK.

260   ULTRA/ZIP/ISOS 92535, 11/12/44, HW 19/78, NAUK; 93295, 29/1/45; 93691, 27/1/45; 93784, 7/2/45,
      all in HW 19/79, NAUK; 94621, 24/2/45, HW 19/80, NAUK; ULTRA/ZIP/ISK 130926, 2/12/44, HW
      19/221, NAUK; and 135818, 19/2/45, HW 19/227, NAUK.

261   ULTRA/ZIP/ISOS 95896, 27/3/45; 95907, 27/3/45, both in HW 19/82, NAUK; and 96005, 27/3/45, HW
      19/83, NAUK.

262   De Roos int., 22/3/45, Entry 119A, RG 226, NA; ZIP/ISOSICLE 5865, 9/9/43; 5888, 5/9/43, both in HW
      19/237, NAUK; 9270, 7/1/44, HW 19/241, NAUK; ALP/JY 127 NIG/JY 124 PK 116 CO 38, 11/4/44;
      ALP/JY 167 NIG/JY 159 PK 149, 26/4/44; and ALP/JY 179 NIG/JY 171 PK 161, 2/5/44, all in Entry
      119A, RG 226, NA.

263   'CIR 4 – The German Sabotage Service', 23/7/45, IRR File 070687, RG 319, NA; Dowe and Sokolov int.,
      8/8/45, Entry 119A, RG 226, NA; and 'Miscellaneous', 27/4/45, WO 208/3617, NAUK.

264   'Joint Fortnightly Intelligence Summary' 3, 23/3/46, FO 1007/301, NAUK; Rexroth int., 27/5/45; Dowe
      and Sokolov int., 8/8/45, both in Entry 119A, RG 226, NA; ULTRA/ZIP/ISOS 95573, 18/3/45, HW
      19/82, NAUK; BT 7979, 22/3/45, UMC, r. 66, NAUK; and 'PF: 601, 603', 15/9/45, KV 2/1327, NAUK.

265   BT 7461, 17/3/45, UMC, r. 65, NAUK.

266   'Weekly Intelligence Summary' 3, 25/7/45, FO 1007/299, NAUK; and 'Joint Weekly Intelligence Summary'
      4, 27/7/45, FO 371/46611, NAUK.

267   BT 2300, 14/1/45 (r. 58); BT 3032, 22/1/45 (r. 59); BT 4550, 11/2/45 (r. 61); BT 4777, 14/2/45; BT 5076,
      18/2/45 (both in r. 62); BT 5929, 28/2/45; BT 5952, 28/2/45 (both in r. 63); BT 6002, 1/3/45; BT 6088,
      2/3/45; BT 6280, 4/3/45 (all in r. 64); BT 7461, 17/3/45 (r. 65); all in UMC, NAUK; DEG 3905, 15/1/45;
      3918, 25/1/45; 4000, 2/3/45; 4010, 5/3/45; and 4078, 19/3/45, all in HW 19/277, NAUK.

268   Modriniak int., 15/7/45, Entry 119A, RG 226, NA; and ULTRA/ZIP/ISOS 94317, 16/12/44, HW 19/80,
      NAUK.

269   'FAK 201', 23/10/45; 'FAT 208', 24/10/45, both in Entry 119A, RG 226, NA; ULTRA/ZIP/ISOS 93673,
      5/2/45; 93961, 17/1/45; 94060, 10/1/45, all in HW 19/79, NAUK; 94771, 23/12/44; 94931, 31/1/45; 94932,

14/1/45; 94933, 14/1/45; 94934, 14/1/45, all in 19/81, NAUK; 95526, 17/3/45; 95730, 15/3/45, both in HW 19/82, NAUK; 96784, and 3/4/45, HW 19/84, NAUK.

270   ULTRA/ZIP/ISOS 92472, 26/11/44; 92551, 19/11/44; 92552, 9/12/44; and 92561, 19/11/44, all in HW 19/78, NAUK.

271   Murad int., 21/12/45, in *Covert Warfare*, xiii.

272   ULTRA/ZIP/ISOS 94271, 30/11/44, HW 19/80, NAUK; ULTRA/ZIP/ISK 130634, 1/12/44; and 130668, 1/12/44, both in HW 19/221, NAUK.

273   ULTRA/ZIP/ISOS 95413, HW 19/82, NAUK.

274   Rexroth int., 27/5/45; Redlein int., 11/6/45, both in Entry 119A, RG 226, NA; and ULTRA/ZIP/ISK 137061, 15/3/45, HW 19/229, NAUK.

275   Modriniak int. 15/7/45, Entry 119A, RG 226, NA.

276   Djilas, 442; Lucas, *Last Days of the Reich*, 138–40; *Operation Slaughterhouse*, 69–70, 78-79, 162, 209–11, 220, 225, 344–45, 347, 411, 483–84, 501–03, 533–34; Aarons and Loftus, chapter 6; Wheeler, 'White Eagles and White Guards', 449–51, 460; Stevenson to FO, 10/12/45; British Embassy, Belgrade to Southern Dept., FO, 11/12/45, all in FO 371/48876, NAUK; and 'Consolidated Intelligence Report' 15, 31/10/45, FO 1007/297, NAUK. H.M. Embassy in Belgrade thought that the figure of 35,000 '*Križari*' guerrillas was an overestimate.

277   Albert Speer, *Inside the Third Reich* (New York, 1970), 434; and *AdAP*, series E, viii, 589.

278   Loth, 42, 82, 100–01; Zubok and Pleshakov, 28–34; Mastny, 97, 142–44, 212–17, 223–24, 249–53, 260–61, 308–10; Judge and Langdon, 37–39; Crampton, 211–14, 222; Jukka Nevakivi, 'The Soviet Union and Finland after the War, 1944–53', in *The Soviet Union and Europe in the Cold War* (New York, 1996), 92–93; William McCagg, *Stalin Embattled* (Detroit, 1978), 50; and Swains, 7–8, 28–29, 47.

279   ULTRA/ZIP/ISOSICLE 12941, 23/4/45, HW 19/248, NAUK.

280   *FRUS: The Conferences at Malta and Yalta*, 453.

281   Stefan Karner, *Im Archipel GUPVI* (Munich, 1995), 25–31; Alexander von Plato, 'Zur Geschichte des sowjetischen Speziallagersystems in Deutschland. Einführung'; and Vladimir Kozlov, 'Die Operationen des NKVD in Deutschland während des Vormarsches der Roten Armee (Januar bis April 1945)', both in *Sowjetische Speziallager in Deutschland 1945 bis 1950. Studien und Berichte* (Berlin, 1998), i, 51–53, 136–37.

282   'Memorandum of Conference with Marshal Stalin, 15th January, 1945', Papers Relating to the Allied High Command, r. 4.

CHAPTER FOUR: SOUTH OF THE ALPS AND WEST OF THE RHINE

1   *Kölnische Zeitung*, 8/12/44; *La France*, 4/12/44; 29/1/45; *Le Petit Parisien*, 23/2/45; *Völkischer Beobachter*, 9/1/45; 17/1/45; 20/1/45; 6/2/45; 8/2/45; 14/2/45; 23/3/45; 25/3/45; 27/3/45; 29/3/45; 30/3/45; 1/4/45; 16/4/45; 26/4/45; 'GPG', 11/9/44; 6/11/44; 8/1/45, all in FO 898/187, NAUK; 'ND' 1569, 4/10/44; 1673, 2/2/45; 1676, 6/2/45; 1692, 24/2/45, all in BC, Robbins Library; and DEG 3943, 6/2/45, HW 19/277, NAUK.

2   'ND' 1686, 17/2/45; and 1678, 8/2/45, both in BC, Robbins Library.

3   Dollmann, 379; *Bodensee Rundschau*, 31/10/44; *Völkischer Beobachter*, 24/2/45; 'Security Intelligence Summary' 5, 6/6/44; 'Security Summary' 21, 15/1/45, both in WO 204/831, NAUK; Bruno int., Entry 174, RG 226, NA; 'Situation Summary, Feb. 1945', 1/3/45, XL 7485, Entry 19, RG 226, NA; 'War Diary', 11/44, vol. 16388, RG 24, Series 90, NAC; and Wallner, memo, 30/6/45, State Dept. Decimal File 1945–49, 740.00119 Control (Germany), RG 59, NA.

4   Skorzeny, *Wir Kämpften – Wir Verloren*, 105, 112; 'Notes on Brandenburg Division and SS Jagdverbände der Waffen SS', 1/4/45, WO 208/3615, NAUK; 'Notes on the SS Jagdverbaende', 8/4/45; 'The Maquis Blanc in France', 8/4/45, both in Entry 119A, RG 226, NA; Gerlach int., 11/8/45, XL 13744, Entry 19; RG 226, NA; and HP 3194, 13/10/44, UMC, r. 45, NAUK.

5   'Jacques Labes', Entry 119A, RG 226, NA.

6   'Rapporto Situazione del Mese di Gennaio 1945', XL 8290, Entry 19, RG 226, NA.

7   Claudio Pavone, *Alle origini della Repubblica* (Torino, 1995), chapter 1; and 'Appunto per il Duce', 28/10/44, RSI Segretaria Particolare del Duce – Carteggio Riservato, busta 61, fasc. 630/4, ACS.

8   Paul Farmer, *Vichy* (New York, 1955), 314; Kahn, 396; *German Military Intelligence*, 290; 'The Activities of the German Intelligence Service in France and Belgium', 7/3/45, WO 219/1700, PRO; and 'Notes on Abwehr IH in France and Germany', 15/6/45, WO 208/3618, NAUK.

9   Andrew Cowan, 'The Guerrilla War against Franco', *European History Quarterly* 20 (1990), 230–33, 242; Spaeter, 415, 489; Wayne Bowen, 'The Ghost Battalion', *The Historian* 63 (2001), 381; Gerlach int., 11/8/45, XL 13744, Entry 19, RG 226, NA; 'Unternehmen W', 12/6/45, IRR File XE 049888, RG 319, NA; Dumbo to Bliss, 8/2/45; Schwarts int., 3/12/44; Smits int., 2/12/44; Doorewaard int., 4/12/44; Michels int., 14/3/45; 'Note de Renseignement', 7/5/45; Schnorr int., 30/5/45; 'Concealment of Arms, Ammunition and

Explosives by the Streifkorps for the Use of Wehrwolf', 30/7/45; Schreider int.; Kettler int., 30/8/45; 'Collated Report on the SS Sonderkommando at the Jagdverband Kampfschule in Tiefenthal', all in Entry 119A,
RG 226, NA; 'Notes on Brandenburg Division and SS Jagdverbände der Waffen SS', 1/4/45, WO 208/3515,
NAUK; ULTRA/ZIP/ISK 116460, 20/9/44, HW 19/199, NAUK; 120806, 23/10/44, HW 19/206, NAUK;
125661, 2/10/44, HW 19/214, NAUK; and 139282, 8/10/44, HW 19/232, NAUK.

10   Spaeter, 415–16; *JNSV*, ii, 576–77; 'German Intelligence, W/T and Sabotage Schools', 13/3/45, IRR File
XE 001063, RG 319, NA; Gerlach int., 11/8/45, XL 13744, Entry 19, RG 226, NA; 'Intelligence Notes' 47,
17/2/45, XL 6103, Entry 19, RG 226, NA; 'CIR 4 – The German Sabotage Service', 23/7/45, IRR File
XE 070687, RG 319, NA; Tostain int., 14/1/45; Olmos int., 2/2/45; Tostain int., 21/2/45; 'Renseignements
sur la 6ème Compagnie de la Division Brandenburg', 1/3/45; Carl int., 6/3/45; Michels int., 14/3/45;
'The Maquis Blanc in France', 8/4/45; Lamblin int., 4/4/45; 'Operational Units of Amt VI S', 9/4/45;
Renoue int., 7/5/45; Schnorr int., 30/5/45; Radl int., 4/6/45; Kuehlwein int., all in Entry 119A, RG 226,
NA; Pfuhlstein int., 20/4/45; Berndt int., 6/11/45, both in IRR File ZF 011666, RG 319, NA; SRX 2138,
22/4/45, WO 208/4164, NAUK; and 'Notes on Brandenburg Division and SS Jagdverbände der Waffen
SS', 1/4/45, WO 208/3615, NAUK. For the development of the PAG, see Jean Chastrusse, Rene Garnier
and Louis Vaux, *Le dernier sursaut nazi en Corrèze* (Tulle, 1990), 62–63; Stahl, 34–35; *HCIC*, xix, 54, NA;
Weissweiler int., 18/1/45, Entry 119A, RG 262, NA; 'Parachutists Landing Container', 26/2/45, IRR File
XE 070687, RG 319, NA; and ULTRA/ZIP/ISK 125692, 12/10/44, HW 19/214, NAUK. For sniping and
sabotage in Normandy, see 'War Diary', 6/44, vol. 16391, RG 24, Series 90, NAC; 'Censorship Report',
30/6/45, vol. 10738, RG 24, Series 90, NAC; 'Counter Int Report' 1, 24/7/44; 'War Diary', 31/8/44, both
in vol. 12176, RG 24, Series 90, NAC; 'War Diary', 31/8/44, vol. 16397, RG 24, Series 90, NAC; 'CI Report'
6, 27/8/44, vol. 10706, RG 24, Series 90, NAC; and 'Counter Intelligence Report' 3, 25/8/44, vol. 10811,
RG 24, Series 90, NAC.

11   ULTRA/ZIP/ISOS 89052, 1/11/44; 86305, 16/9/44, both in HW 19/74, NAUK; 89031, 2/11/44, HW
19/75, NAUK; ULTRA/ZIP/ISK 114904, 9/9/44, HW 19/197, NAUK; 115900, 17/9/44, HW 19/198,
NAUK; 126063, 1/12/44; 126086, 1/12/44, both in HW 19/215, NAUK; 131339, 10/2/45, HW 19/222,
NAUK; 134512, 3/3/45, HW 19/226, NAUK; 140295, 21/4/45, HW 19/234, NAUK; Ruzy to Paris,
13/2/45; 'Extract from OSS X-2 Paris Report dated 22.5.45 on Edmond Grosskopf', both in Entry 119A,
RG 226, NA; and Wollert and Stange int., 2/10/45, WO 208/4212, NAUK.

12   ULTRA/ZIP/ISK 139133, 6/4/45, HW 19/232, NAUK; and SRX 2138, 22/4/45, WO 208/4164, NAUK.

13   *L'Aurore*, 6/4/45; 'Notes on Leitstelle III West für Frontaufklärung', 29/8/45, WO 208/3620, NAUK;
and 'Frontaufklärungskommando 313 and Miscellaneous Abwehr Personalities', 20/5/45, WO 208/3617,
NAUK.

14   Pennors int., 7/1/45; Zebra to Bliss, Crusade, 18/3/45; and Moglia int., 30/4/45, all in Entry 119A, RG 226,
NA.

15   'Report' 1135, 21/6/45, XL 11790, Entry 19, RG 226, NA; Reme int., 27/5/45; Keilholz int., 14/6/45, both
in Entry 119A, RG 226, NA; and ULTRA/ZIP/ISK 115652, 13/9/44, 19/198, NAUK.

16   'Operation Easter Egg', *Intelligence Bulletin*, March 1946, <http://www.lonesentry.com/articles/easteregg/>,
as of 21/10/05; Roosevelt, 251; Paul Paillole, *Services Spéciaux* (Paris, 1975), 557; 'Sabotage Depot in France',
Entry 92, RG 226, NA; 'Organization of a Group of German Intelligence Service Agents Known as the
"Maquis Blanc"', 13/4/45, Entry 171, RG 226, NA; 'German Sabotage School near Terrascon', 27/11/44,
IRR File XE 001063, RG 319, NA; Clissmann int., 7/11/45, ETO MIS-Y-Sect. CSDIC/WEA Interim
Reports, Special Interrogation Reports 1945–46, RG 338, NA; Lambert int., 11/10/44; Clep int., 11/10/44;
Decousser int., 11/10/44; Schramme int., 10/11/44; Lentremy int., 26/11/44; Schramme int., 5/12/44;
'Source Sheet: C.E.A. Darius (Main Report)', 17/1/45; 'Personalities of FAT 251 and 250', 27/1/45; Den-
jean/Massia int.; Deanjean/Massia int., 17/1/45; Lentremy int., 7/2/45; 'Student from Thumeries', 30/3/45;
'Mil Amt D – Leitstelle II West fuer Frontaufklaerung – II-Kommandos and Trupps in the West', 17/4/45;
'Summary of Traces: Lamour, Michel', 23/4/45; Schoeneich int., 2/6/45; Presse int., 11/6/45; Vogt int.,
10/7/45; Bergner int., 8/8/45; Schlemmer int., 11/8/45; Spiess int.; 'FAT 251'; 'FAT 252'; Schuler int.; 'FAT
249', 2/10/45, all in Entry 119A, RG 226, NA; 'Counter Intelligence in the Present Campaign in the West';
'Counter-Intelligence Report' 14, 11/1/45; 15, 26/1/45, all in vol. 10704, RG 24, Series 90, NAC; and 'Note
sur la Sabotage', 24/11/44, 132–67 CAB K, AS.

17   *German Military Intelligence*, 290; Gerlach int., 11/8/45, XL 13744, Entry 19, RG 226, NA; Berndt int.,
6/11/45, IRR File ZF 011666, RG 319, NA; Michels int., 14/3/45, Entry 119A, RG 226, NA; 'Report' 1135,
21/6/45, XL 11790, Entry 19, RG 226, NA; and 'Notes on the Brandenburg Div.', 3/5/45, WO 208/3617,
NAUK.

18   Leverkuehn, 62; 'Amt VI of the RSHA Gruppe VI B', Entry 119A, RG 226, NA; Kappler int., 8/6/45, Entry
174, RG 226, NA; and Ilariucci int., Entry 174, RG 226, NA.

19   ZIP/ISOSICLE 7718, 19/10/43, HW 1/238, NAUK.

20 'Rapporto Situazione del Mese di Gennaio 1945', XL 8290, Entry 19, RG 226, NA.

21 ZIP/ISOSICLE 5365, 28/8/43; 5380, 3/9/43; 5521, 26/8/43; 5522, 26/8/43; 5531, 26/8/43; 5721, 10/8/43; 5803, 13/8/43; 5836, 28/8/43; 5881, 24/8/43; 6021, 10/8/43; 6041, 19/8/43; 6064, 15/9/43; 6143, 7/8/43; 6197, 5/8/43; 6198, 5/8/43; and 6218, 5/8/43, all in HW 19/237, NAUK.

22 Willi Schubernig, r. A3343 SSO 103B, fr. 1251, RG 242, NA; 'CIR 4 – The German Sabotage Service', 23/7/45, IRR File XE 070687, RG 319, NA; 'Belgrade Sabotage Course', 22/7/44, IRR File XE 001063, RG 319, NA; report on German saboteurs; 'Ferruccio Furlani – Sabotage Considerations', 5/44; report on Schubernig, 31/7/45; De Roos int., 27/3/45, all in Entry 119A, RG 226, NA; 'Security Instruction' 67, 21/5/44, WO 204/831, NAUK; ZIP/ISOSICLE 5337, 14/8/43; 5416, 4/9/43; 5757, 11/8/43; 5998, 14/9/43; 6154, 17/9/43; 6343, 19/9/43, all in HW 19/237, NAUK; 7634, 16/10/43; 7718, 19/10/43; 7789, 22/10/43; 7936, 27/10/43; 8082, 28/10/43; 8091, 1/11/43; 8112, 2/11/43; 8142, 3/11/44, all in HW 19/239, NAUK; ULTRA/ZIP/ISO-SICLE 9260, 7/1/44; 9283, 3/1/44; 9333, 11/1/44; 9336, 11/1/44; 9383, 15/1/44; 9391, 17/1/44; 9418, 18/1/44; 9428, 19/1/44; 9433, 19/1/44; 9469, 7/12/43; 9533, 22/1/44; 9550, 28/1/44, all in HW 19/241, NAUK; 9683, 4/2/44; 9760, 7/2/44; 9836, 8/2/44; 10000, 16/2/44; 10007, 16/2/44; 10029, 17/2/44; 10086, 19/2/44; 10099, 21/2/44; 10160, 25/2/44; 10162, 26/2/44, all in HW 19/242, NAUK; 10820, 31/3/44, HW 19/244, NAUK; 'Counter-Espionage and Counter Sabotage Measures in the North African and Italian Campaign', vol. 12337, RG 24, Series 90, NAC; 'Notes on CI in Italy', 29/9/44, vol. 10946, RG 24, Series 90, NAC; 'War Diary', 3/44, vol. 16394, RG 24, Series 90, NAC; and Kaltenbrunner memo, 8/2/44, R58/471, BA.

23 Reme int., 6/6/45; 'FAK 212', 22/11/45, both in Entry 119A, RG 226, NA; 'Security Summary' 15, 17/7/44; 17, 15/9/44; 19, 15/11/44; 'Notes on CI in Italy', 28/11/44, all in WO 204/831, NAUK.

24 Giuseppe Conti, 'La RSI e l'attività del fascismo clandestino nell'Italia liberata', Storia Contemporanea 10 (1979), 983–84; Georgio Pisanò, Storia della Guerra Civile in Italia (Milan, 1965), ii, 704; Ceccacci int., 5/5/45; Padovano int., 12/5/45; Piscia int., 22/12/44, all in Entry 174, RG 226, NA; 'Security Intelligence Summary' 15, 31/5/44, WO 204/ 831, NAUK; and 'Enemy Intelligence Services and Activities in Italy', 16/7/44, vol. 16496, RG 24, Series 90, NAC.

25 Reme int., 6/6/45; 'FAK 212', 22/11/45, both in Entry 119A, RG 226, NA; ULTRA/ZIP/ISOS 87917, 28/8/44; and 88122, 11/8/44, both in HW 19/75, NAUK.

26 Roosevelt, 93; C.R.S. Harris, Allied Military Administration of Italy (London, 1957), 370–71; Stars and Stripes Weekly, 8/7/44, p. 2; 'Counter Espionage and Counter Sabotage Measures in the North African and Italian Campaign', vol. 12337, RG 24, Series 90, NAC; 'Enemy Intelligence Services and Activities in Italy', 16/7/44, vol. 16496, RG 24, Series 90, NAC; report on German saboteurs; Kappler int., 8/6/45, Entry 174, RG 226, NA; 'Amt VI of the RSHA Gruppe VI B'; Huegel int., 6/5/45; Huegel int., 10/6/45, all in Entry 119A, RG 226, NA; 'Security Summary' 15, 17/7/44; 16, 15/8/44, both in WO 204/831, NAUK; ULTRA/ZIP/ISOSICLE 9383, 15/1/44; 9550, 28/1/44, both in HW 19/241, NAUK; 9632, 1/2/44; and 9850, 9/2/44, both in HW 19/242, NAUK.

27 ULTRA/ZIP/ISOSICLE 10007, 16/2/44, HW 19/242, NAUK.

28 'CI News Sheet' 8, 19/10/44, WO 205/997, NAUK; and 'Rapporto Situazione del Mese di Gennaio 1945', XL 8290, Entry 19, RG 226, NA.

29 Harris, Allied Military Administration of Italy, 48, 102–03; Conti, 942–50, 956–60, 963–64, 984, 987; The Stars and Stripes, 25/12/43; 'Report on Slovene Prison Camps in Sardinia (Jan. 2nd to Jan. 27th 1944)', app., 28/1/44, Entry 154, RG 226, NA; 'War Diary', 12/43; 4/44; 5/44, all in vol. 16393, RG 24 , Series 90, NAC; 'War Diary', 5/44; 7/44, both in vol. 16394, RG 24, Series 90, NAC; 'Monthly Police Report', 6/44, vol. 10735, RG 24, Series 90, NAC; 'War Diary', 12/43–1/44; 2/44; 3/44; 4/44; 5/44; 'Security Report', all in vol. 16395, RG 24, Series 90, NAC; 'War Diary', 8/44, vol. 16388, RG 24, Series 90, NAC; 'Counter Espionage and Counter Sabotage Measures in the North African and Italian Campaigns', vol. 12337, RG 24, Series 90, NAC; 'Security Intelligence Summary' 14, 30/4/44; 15, 31/5/44; 'Security (CI) Report' 8, 31/5/44; 'Security Intelligence Summary' 5, 6/6/44; 'Security Intelligence Summary' 10, 15/6/44; 'Security Summary' 15, 17/7/44; 16, 15/8/44; 17, 15/9/44; 'Security Report', 5/3/44, all in WO 204/831, NAUK; and 'Republican Fascist Organisation at Lecce', 20/4/44, Entry 171A, RG 226, NA.

30 Dollmann, 378–80; Pisanò, ii, 702; Conti, 954–55, 960–63; and Luigi Villari, The Liberation of Italy, 1943–1947 (Appleton, 1959), 159.

31 Kappler int., 8/6/45, Entry 174, RG 226, NA.

32 Huegel int., 6/5/45; Harster int., 20/5/45, both in Entry 119A, RG 226, NA; 'Rapporto Situazione del Mese di Gennaio 1945', XL 8290, Entry 19, RG 226, NA; Bruno int., 17/1/45; Alessi int., 12–13/2/45, both in Entry 174, RG 226, NA; 'Security Summary' 17, 15/9/44, WO 204/831, NAUK; and 'Notes on CI in Italy' 6, 8/2/45, WO 204/822, NAUK.

33 Conti, 1002–03; ULTRA/ZIP/ISOS 94901, 3/3/45, HW 19/81, NAUK; 'Notes on CI in Italy', 26/12/44; 6, 8/2/45; 8, 10/4/45, all in WO 204/822, NAUK; Alessi and Boselli int., 23/2/45; Cesario int., 5/1/45; Bruno int., 17/1/45, all in Entry 174, RG 226, NA; Reme int., 27/5/45; Keilholz int., 14/6/45; and Huegel int., 3/9/45, all in Entry 119A, RG 226, NA.

34 *History and Mission of the Counter Intelligence Corps in World War II* (Fort Holabird, 1951), 32–33; Gellermann, 79;'War Diary', 11/44; 1/45, both in vol. 16395, RG 24, Series 90, NAC;'Security Summary' 18, 15/10/44; 20, 15/12/44;'Notes on CI in Italy', 28/11/44, all in WO 204/831, NAUK; 6, 8/2/45, WO 204/822, NAUK; and Bucovini and Ovan int., 19/11/44, Entry 174, RG 226, NA.

35 Conti, 988, 990, 1004–1017; *The New York Times*, 2/1/45; *Daily Express*, 7/2/45; *Völkischer Beobachter*, 27/3/45; 26/4/45;'Security Summary' 17, 15/9/44; 18, 15/10/44; 19, 15/11/44; 20, 15/12/44; 21, 15/1/45; 22, 15/2/45; 23, 15/3/45; 24, 15/4/45; 'General Security Report', 9/5/45, all in WO 204/831, NAUK; 'Notes on CI in Italy', 29/12/44; 6, 8/2/45, both in WO 204/822, NAUK; 'Background Notes', 15/3/45, FO 371/46790, NAUK;'Situation Summary, Feb. 1945', 1/3/45, XL 7485, Entry 19, RG 226, NA;'Monthly Police Report', 10/44; 11/44; 12/44, all in vol. 10735, RG 24, Series 90, NAC;'War Diary', 10/44, vol. 16394, RG 24, Series 90, NAC;'War Diary', 11/44; 1/45;'War Diary', app., 12/44, all in vol. 16395, RG 24, Series 90, NAC;'War Diary', 11/44; 12/44; 1/45; 2/45;'Security Report for Period ending 17 Jan 45';'War Diary', 1/45, all in vol. 16388, RG 24, Series 90, NAC;'War Diary' 1–31/12/44;'Security Report for period ending 17 Jan 45', both in vol. 12176, RG 24, Series 90, NAC;'War Diary', 2/45;'Security Intelligence Report' 49, 15/2/45, both in vol. 16389, RG 24, Series 90, NAC; 'Security Report for period ending 12 Feb 45', vol. 12176, RG 24, Series 90, NAC.

36 *The New York Times*, 6/3/45; 11/3/45; 14/3/45; 24 Aug. 1945; and *The Manchester Guardian*, 10/3/45. For criminal gangs and private armies in Rome's southern suburbs, see *The New York Times*, 19/1/45; 29/1/45; 6/2/45; and *The Glasgow Herald*, 29/1/45.

37 Renato int., 16/1/45, Entry 174, RG 226, NA.

38 'Rapporto Situazione del Mese di Gennaio 1945', XL 8290, Entry 19, RG 226, NA.

39 Roosevelt, 92–93; ULTRA/ZIP/ISOSICLE 9622, 31/1/44, HW 19/242, NAUK; and 'Notes on CI in Italy', 28/11/44, WO 204/831, NAUK.

40 Keilholz int., 14/6/45, Entry 119A, RG 226, NA; and 'Notes on CI in Italy' 8, 10/4/45, WO 204/822, NAUK.

41 Renzo de Felice, *Mussolini l'alleato 1940–1945: II. La guerra civile* (Turin, 1997), iv, 505–10; Felice Bellotti, *La Repubblica di Mussolini* (Milan, 1947), 166–67;'Ancora della Situazione Generale e Politica', 30/10/44, PCM Segreterie Burroca (1943–45), busta 1, fasc. 26, ACS; 'The Zimmer Note-books'; Bellotti int., 18/11/52, both in CIANF, Entry 86, RG 263, NA; 'Report' 1135, 21/6/45, XL 11790, Entry 19, RG 226, NA; Calascibetta di Altamirano int.; Cesario int., 5/1/45; Cesario int., 12/12/44; Cesario int., 21/2/45, all in Entry 174, RG 226, NA; Reme int., 27/5/45; Huegel int., 10/6/45, both in Entry 119A, RG 226, NA; 'Security Summary' 17, 15/9/44; and 'Notes on CI in Italy', 29/4/45, app. 'A', both in WO 204/831, NAUK.

42 'War Diary', 1/45, vol. 16394, RG 24, Series 90, NAC; 'Security Summary' 18, 15/10/44, WO 204/831, NAUK;'Notes on CI in Italy', 26/12/44; 7, 8/3/45; 8, 10/4/45, all in WO 204/822, NAUK; and 'Monthly Information Report', 1/5/45, WO 204/805, NAUK.

43 F.H. Hinsley, *British Intelligence in the Second World War* (London, 1988), iii, part ii, 881–83; *German Military Intelligence*, 290–91; ULTRA/ZIP/ISOS 92432, HW 19/77, NAUK; BT 4588, 11/2/45 (r. 61); BT 4501, 10/2/45 (r. 62); BT 6176, 3/3/45 (r. 63); BT 6246, 4/3/45 (r. 63); BT 6088, 2/3/45; BT 6454, 6/3/45; BT 6948, 12/3/45 (all in r. 64); BT 7454, 17/3/45; BT 7468, 17/3/45 (both in r. 65); BT 7553, 18/4/45 (r. 66); BT 8186, 24/3/45 (r. 67); BT 9065, 1/4/45; 9084, 1/4/45; BT 9113, 1/4/45; BT 9409, 4/4/45; BT 9500, 5/4/45 (all in r. 68); BT 9945, 9/4/45 (r. 69); KO 398, 14/4/45 (r. 70); KO 656, 17/4/45; KO 984, 21/4/45 (both in r. 71), all in UMC, NAUK; DEG 4003, 3/3/45; 4040, 12/3/45; 4063, 17/3/45, all in HW/277, NAUK;'Rapporto Situazione del Mese di Gennaio 1945', XL 8290, Entry 19, RG 226, NA; Keilholz int., 14/6/45, Entry 119A, RG 226, NA; Ceccacci int., 5/5/45, Entry 174, RG 226, NA;'Countersabotage Bulletin' 5, 28/5/45, IRR File XE 070687, RG 319, NA;'CI News Sheet' 24, 27/6/45, WO 205/997, NAUK;'Notes on CI in Italy', 27/10/44;'Security Summary' 19, 15/11/44;'Notes on CI in Italy', 28/11/44;'Security Summary' 21, 15/1/45, all in WO 204/831, NAUK;'Notes on CI in Italy', 29/12/44; 6, 8/2/45; 8, 10/4/45, all in WO 204/822, NAUK;'Security Intelligence Report' 42, 15/10/44, vol. 16389, RG 24, Series 90, NAC;'War Diary', 12/44;'Summary for Period 10 Dec.–17 Dec. 1944', both in vol. 12176, RG 24, Series 90, NAC;'War Diary', 12/44, vol. 16388, RG 24, Series 90, NAC;'War Diary', 12/44, vol. 16338, RG 24, Series 90, NAC; and 'Intrep' 19, 27/12/44, vol. 10889, RG 24, Series 90, NAC. For the guarding of railway bridges, see Hill-Dillon to DMRS (Rep.), 3/10/44; Hill-Dillon to G-3, 27/11/44; and Noce to 3rd District, all in WO 204/794, NAUK.

44 BT 6088, 2/3/45, r. 61, UMC, NAUK.

45 BT 7546, 18/3/45, r. 66, UMC, NAUK; and 'Notes on CI in Italy' 8, 10/4/45, WO 204/822, NAUK.

46 Hinsley, iii, part ii, 882; DEG 4062, 17/3/45; 4071, 18/3/45; 4107, 26/3/45, all in HW 19/277, NAUK;'Italy – Limpet Mine attack at Leghorn, Report of', 1/12/44, XL 2831, Entry 19, RG 226, NA; 'Information obtained from captured enemy agents', 21/11/44; and Padovano/Ossi/Pettoni int., 20/4/45, Entry 174, RG 226, NA.

47 Jack Greene and Allesandro Massignani, *The Black Prince and the Sea Devils* (Cambridge, 2004), 151–157, 163–64, 169–73; Piscia int., 22/12/44, Entry 174, RG 226, NA; Reme int., 27/5/45, Entry 119A, RG 226,

NA; and Borghese and Rossi int., 23/9/45, WO 208/4212, NAUK.

48   Conti, 967–71; Reme int., 27/5/45, Entry 119A, RG 226, NA; Posta da Campo 713 to Commissario Soc.
      An. 'San Marco'; Direttore Generale, Ente Nazionale to Presidenza del Consiglio dei Ministri, 14 March
      1944, both in PCM Segreterie Burroca (1943–45), busta 15, fasc. 350, ACS; and Dietrich to Presidenza del
      Consiglio dei Ministri, Sottosegretario di Stato, 2 April 1944, PCM Segreterie Burroca (1943–45), busta 8,
      fasc. 144, ACS.

49   'War Diary', 2/44, vol. 16394, RG 24, NAC; and 'War Diary', 2/44, vol. 16395, RG 24, Series 90, NAC.

50   Conti, 974–75; 'Appunto per il Col. Collu', PCM Segreterie Burroca (1943–45), busta 2, fasc. 102, ACS; and
      Pasqualucci to Segretario del PFR, 4 July 1944, RSI Segreteria Particolare del Duce – Carteggio Ordinario,
      busta 65, fasc. 5697, ACS.

51   'Notizie Fiduciarie della Situazione a Roma', 19 June 1944, PCM Segreterie Burroca (1943–45), busta 3,
      fasc. 358, ACS.

52   Conti, 973–78; and Pavolini to Mussolini, 19 June 1944, RSI Segreteria Particolare del Duce – Carteggio
      Riservato, busta 62, fasc. 631/2, ACS.

53   Pavolini to Mussolini, 24 June 1944, RSI Segreteria Particolare del Duce – Carteggio Riservato, busta 62,
      fasc. 631/2, ACS.

54   Conti, 978; Pisanò, ii, 702–03, 732–39; F.S.V. Donnison, *Civil Affairs and Military Government Central Organi-
      zation and Planning* (London, 1966), 282; and 'Herewith Report on Political Situation in Florence during
      the period of the Fight for its Liberation', 27/8/44, vol. 10991, RG 24, Series 90, NAC.

55   'War Diary', 7/44, vol. 16388, RG 24, Series 90, NAC; and 'Security Intelligence Report' 39, 31/8/44, vol.
      16389, RG 24, Series 90, NA.

56   *Daily Express*, 1/2/45.

57   Donnison, 280; 'Weekly Security Report', app. 2, 26/8/44, vol. 16395, RG 24, Series 90, NAC; and 'War
      Diary', 9/44, vol. 16395, RG 24, Series 90, NAC.

58   'Ettore Muti salito tra i geni tutelari della Patria', RSI Segreteria Particolare del Duce – Carteggio Ris-
      ervato, busta 42, fasc. 389, ACS.

59   'Notes on CI in Italy' 8, 10/4/45, WO 204/822, NAUK.

60   *FOWPIS* (Millwood, 1983), 11, Summary 288, 11/4/45; and 'Security Summary', 16/6/45, WO 204/831,
      NAUK.

61   'Xth Flotilla MAS: Personalities Apprehended', 18/10/44, Entry 174, RG 226, NA.

62   Reme int., 27/5/45, Entry 119A, RG 226, NA.

63   Conti, 1001–02.

64   'Notes on CI in Italy', 27/10/44, WO 204/831, NAUK; 8, 10/4/45, WO 204/822, NAUK; and 'Rapporto
      Situazione del Mese di Gennaio 1945', XL 8290, Entry 19, RG 226, NA.

65   'Notes on CI in Italy' 8, 10/4/45, WO 204/822, NAUK.

66   Harris, 48; and Bruno int., 17/1/45, WO 204/822, NAUK.

67   Conti, 949–51; 'Security Report', 13/10/43; 16/11/43; 'Security Summary' 16, 15/8/44; 17, 15/9/44, all
      in WO 204/831, NAUK; 'Canadian Operations in Sicily, July-August 1943', vol. 10735, RG 24, Series 90,
      NAC; 'War Diary', 11/43; 12/43, both in vol. 16394, RG 24, Series 90, NAC; and 'Subversive Activity, Fas-
      cist', 6/1/44, Entry 92, RG 226, NA.

68   Harris, 213, 221; Conti, 997, 999; David Elwood, *Italy* (Leicester, 1985), 61; *The New York Times*, 10/1/45;
      1/2/45; and 'Rapporto Situazione del Mese di Gennaio, 1945', XL 8290, Entry 19, RG 226, NA.

69   Conti, 950–52, 995–99; Harris, 221; *The New York Times*, 21/10/44; 16/12/44; 7/1/45; 10/1/45; 17/1/45;
      1/2/45; Rie, report; 'Riots in Catania', 21/12/44, 108709, both in Entry 16, RG 226, NA.

70   Huegel int., 6/5/45; and Caesar int., 22/6/45, both in Entry 119A, RG 226, NA.

71   Harris, 323; Greene and Massignani, 162–63, 164–65, 170–72, 175; Jean Hérold-Paquis, *Des Illusions… Désil-
      lusions!* (Paris, 1948), 140; *The New York Times*, 31/5/45; 'Minutes of a Meeting held on 11 April 1945 in the
      office of G-3 Ops AFHQ', 12/4/45, Entry 92, RG 226, NA; and 'The Zimmer Note-books', CIANF, Entry
      86, RG 263, NA.

72   Otto Begus, r. A3343 SSO-052, RG 242, NA; 'CIR 4 – The German Sabotage Service', 23/7/45, IRR File
      XE 070687, RG 319, NA; Gerlach int., 11/8/45, XL 13744, Entry 19, RG 226, NA; Kappler int., 8/6/45;
      Cesario int., 5/1/45, both in Entry 174, RG 226, NA; AFHQ to War Room, 24/5/45; Huegel int., 6/5/45;
      Huegel int., 10/6/45; Benveduti int., 12/8/45; Olmes int.; 'Amt VI of the RSHA Gruppe VI B', all in Entry
      119A, RG 226, NA; and 'The Zimmer Note-books', CIANF, Entry 86, RG 263, NA.

73   Otto Begus, r. A3343 SSO-052, RG 242, NA; 'CIR 4 – The German Sabotage Service', 23/7/45, IRR File
      XE 070687, RG 319, NA; Gerlach int., 11/8/45, XL 13744, Entry 19, RG 226, NA; Kappler int., 8/6/45;
      Cesario int., 5/1/45, both in Entry 174, RG 226, NA; AFHQ to War Room, 24/5/45; Huegel int., 10/6/45;
      Benveduti int., 12/8/45; Olmes int.; 'Amt VI of the RSHA Gruppe VI B'; Huegel int., 6/5/45, all in Entry
      119A, RG 226, NA; and 'The Zimmer Note-books', CIANF, Entry 86, RG 263, NA.

74　Huegel int., 6/5/45; 'Amt VI of the RSHA Gruppe VI B', both in Entry 119A, RG 226, NA; and Sartorio int., 20/5/45, Entry 174, RG 226, NA.

75　F.W. Deakin, *The Brutal Friendship* (London, 1962), 728–29, 787–89, 792, 808, 815–16; Max Gallo, *Mussolini's Italy* (New York, 1973), 409, 414, 421–24; and 'Situazione Presumibile', PCM Segreterie Burroca (1943–45), busta 1, fasc. 3, ACS.

76　Greene and Massignani, 168, 200–01; 'Notes on CI in Italy' 8, 10/4/45, WO 204/822, NAUK; Borghese and Rossi int., 23/9/45, WO 208/4212, NAUK; 'Security Summary', 16/6/45, WO 204/831, NAUK; Ceccacci int., 25/5/45; '10th Flottiglia MAS', 2/6/45; '10th MAS Flotilla Stay-Behind Network', 4/6/45; Cuchiara int., 11/6/45; 'Report of Roundup of X Flotilla MAS Underground Movement in Bologna and Modena by Fifth Army CIC', 16/6/45; SCI Unit Z 'Report by Fernando Pellegatta on the Activities of the 5th Column organized in the 10th MAS (Vega Bn.)', 16/6/45; and Mambelli int., 16/6/45, all in Entry 174, RG 226, NA.

77　Harris, 304; and *Christian Science Monitor*, 22/9/45.

78　'Weekly Intelligence Summary' 35, 14/3/46, State Dept. Decimal Files 1945–49, 740.00119 (Germany), RG 59, NA; and 'Joint Fortnightly Intelligence Summary' 50, 24/1/48, OMGUS ODI Miscellaneous Reports (ACA Austria), RG 260, NA.

79　Greene and Massignani, 182–94.

80　'CI Report' 6, 27/8/44; and 7, 10/9/44, both in vol. 10706, RG 24, Series 90, NAC.

81　*FRUS, 1945*, iv, 661–62.

82　Ibid, iv, 662–63; *La Croix*, 17/3/45; *L'Éclair des Pyrénées*, 19–20/11/44; 21/12/44; 9/1/45; *La France*, 6/12/44; 1/3/45; 2/3/45; 'Période du 16 au 28 Février 1945', F/1a/2041, AN; 'Rapport Mensuel pour le période du 16 Février au 15 Mars 1945', i, F/1cIII/1211, AN; 'Période du 15 Mars au 15 Avril 1945', i, F/1cIII/1229, AN; Report R 1460pt, 5/11/44, L 49057, Entry 21, RG 226, NA; ULTRA/ZIP/ISOS 91167, 20/12/44, HW 19/76, NAUK; 96118, 18/12/44, HW 19/83, NAUK; 'HQ L of C Periodical Counter-Intelligence Report' 15, 27/1/45; 16, 11/2/45; and 17, 27/2/45, all in vol. 10704, RG 24, Series 90, NAC.

83　*FRUS, 1945*, iv, 662–65; *The Age*, 27/3/45; 'HQ L of C Periodical Counter-Intelligence Report' 17, 27/2/45, vol. 10704, RG 24, Series 90, NAC; and 'Rapport Mensuel', 1/2/45, i, F/1cIII/1225, AN.

84　Sybil Hepburn, *Wingless Victory* (London, 1969), 188; *Le Patriote*, 4/1/45; *The Times*, 28/12/44; and Préfecture des Basses-Alpes, Cabinet du Préfet to mayors of the department, 5/9/44, 0011 W0002, ADAHP.

85　Robert Paxton, *Vichy France* (New York, 1972), 293.

86　Perry Biddiscombe, 'The Last White Terror', *Journal of Modern History* 73 (2001), 813, 826, 836, 839; Megan Koreman, *The Expectation of Justice* (Durham, 1999), 50–51; *L'Humanité*, 17/12/44; 'Activities and Organizations controlled by Sturmbannfuhrer Skorzeny'; Chavannes int., both in Entry 119A, RG 226, NA; 'HQ L of C Periodical Counter-Intelligence Report' 15, 27/1/45, vol. 10704, RG 24, Series 90, NAC; and ULTRA/ZIP/ISK 131573, 11/2/45, HW 19/222, NAUK.

87　*L'Étendard*, 7/10/44.

88　*Ouest-France*, 16/11/44; *La France*, 17/11/44; and 20/11/44.

89　*En Avant!*, 23/9/44; *La Nouvelle République des Pyrénées*, 20/10/44; 21/10/44; 2–4/12/44; 12/12/44; 13/12/44; 19/12/44; 23/12/44; *Les Allobroges*, 23/11/44; 27/11/44; 4/12/44; 12/12/44; 16/12/44; 28/12/44; 8–9–10/2/45; *La Patriote de Provence*, 25/11/44; *La Croix*, 26/12/44; *L'Humanité*, 28/11/44; 30/11/44; 3–4/12/44; 16/12/44; 21/12/44; 22/12/44; 26/12/44; 6/1/45; 24/1/45; 9/2/45; *Libération*, 26–27/11/44; 28/11/44; 10–11/12/44; *Le Figaro*, 2/12/44; 22/12/44; *L'Aube*, 26–27/11/44; 28/11/44; 29/11/44; 2/12/44; 3–4/12/44; 26/12/44; *Le Provençal*, 26–27/11/44; 28/11/44; 3/12/44; 12/12/44; 28/12/44; 29/12/44; *L'Éclair des Pyrénées*, 5/12/44; *L'Aurore du Sud-est*, 18/12/44; and *The New York Times*, 27/11/44.

90　*Le Méridional*, 22/10/44; 20/1/45; *L'Humanité*, 5/12/44; 17/12/44; 20/1/45; 30/1/45; *Avant-Garde*, 22/12/44; *Les Allobroges*, 6/1/45; *L'Aube*, 7–8/1/45; *Le Figaro*, 20/1/44; *L'Aurore*, 20/1/45; and *La Croix*, 9/3/45.

91　'CI Report', 4/5/44; and 2/6/44, both in WO 204/803, PRO.

92　Le Commissaire des Renseignements Généraux à Albertville to the Commisaire Principal, Chef du Service Départemental des Renseignements Généraux à Chambéry, 21/10/44; and 'A/S d'émissions de signaux optiques à Villeroger', 16/2/45, both in 109–67 CAB K, AS.

93　*Fuehrer Conferences on Naval Affairs* 461; *Daily Express*, 10/3/45; *L'Aurore*, 10/3/45; 'German Pockets around Bordeaux: Military and Political Situation', 22/11/44, XL 2835, Entry 19, RG 226, NA; 'Monthly Information Report', 31/3/45, IRR File ZF 015109, RG 319, NA; 'Dielette Sabotage Party', 14/4/45; CTG 122.2 to CTF 122, 11/4/45, both in Entry 119A, RG 226, NA; and BA 6745, 9/3/45, UMC, r. 64, NAUK. For raids from La Rochelle upon surrounding districts, see 'Rapport Mensuel', 10/2/45, F/1cIII/1213, AN; and BT 4816, 14/2/45, UMC, r. 62, NAUK.

94　Roosevelt, 253–55; Alain Le Grand and Georges-Michel Thomas, *39–45: Finistère* (Brest, 1987), 375, 379; Stockmann int., 29/1/46, in *Covert Warfare*, xiii; *The New York Times*, 31/12/44; *Daily Herald*, 26/4/45; 'Monthly Summary' 1, 15/4/45, Entry 119A, RG 226, NA; War Room to Paris X-2, 25/4/45; War Room to Paris, 28/4/45; Godet-la-Loi int.; 'Notes on Fish', 11/5/45, all in Entry 119A, RG 226, NA; 'Jacques

Ramet', 16/1/46, Entry 171, RG 226, NA; ULTRA/ZIP/ISK 127156, 4/1/45, HW 19/216, NAUK; 127914, 11/1/45; 127915, 12/1/45; 127931, 7/1/45; 127987, 7/1/45, all in HW 19/217, NAUK; 129068, 24/1/45; 129082, 25/1/45, both in HW 19/219, NAUK; 130503, 3/2/45, HW 19/220, NAUK; 130649, 3/2/45; 130669, 5/2/45; 130670, 3/2/45; 130689, 6/2/45; 130727, 6/2/45; 130782, 5/2/45; 130816, 7/2/45; 130844, 4/2/45; 130935, 7/2/45; 131020, 8/2/45; 131052, 8/2/45; 131113, 7/2/45, all in HW 19/221, NAUK; and DEG 3742, 13/11/44, HW 19/276, NAUK.

95   Paquis, 50–53, 100–01; *The Stars and Stripes*, 3/11/44; *La France*, 23/1/45; *Combat*, 7/6/45; and 6/7/45.

96   'Rapport Bi-mensuel de 30 Novembre 1944', viii, F/1cIII/1220, AN.

97   Christian de la Mazière, *Ashes of Honour* (London, 1975), 52–54; Kurrer int., 17/8/45; Kurrer int., 30/5/45; 'Organisation Technique (OT)', 15/2/45; 'Agissements de Miliciens Actuellement en Allemagne à Sigmaringen', 2/12/44; 'Parachutage de miliciens dans la région de Seilhac (Corrèze)', 9/1/45; 11/1/45; Muchery int., 27/2/45; 'Organisation Technique', 28/2/45; 'Organisation Technique or OT', 19/3/45; 'CEA Sully', 22/3/45; 'C/Poinsot', 3/5/45; Herrlitz int., 20/2/46, all in Entry 119A, RG 226, NA; 'German Intelligence, W/T and Sabotage Schools', 13/3/45, IRR File XE 001063, RG 319, NA; Himmler to Kaltenbrunner, 16/9/44, T-175, r. 122, fr. 2648214, NA; 'Renseigements sur l'Allemagne', 13/1/45; and 'Renseignements', 15/8/45, both in 7P 125, SHAT.

98   'Besprechung mit dem Generalsekretär der franz. Miliz Bouisson am 15.12.44'; and Herrlitz int., 20/2/46, both in Entry 119A, RG 226, NA.

99   Sevin int., 9/1/45; 'Parachutages de miliciens dans la région de Seilhac (Corrèze)', 9/1/45; 11/1/45; 'Renseignements d'Archives', 14/1/45; 'Compte-Rendu d'Arrestation', 26/1/45; 'Information Bulletins nos. 23 to 26', 24/2/45; 'Organisation Technique', 28/2/45; Sevin int., 2/3/45; 'Organisation Technique or OT', 19/3/45; 'CEA "Oaf"', 7/4/45; 'Weekly Progress Report no. 22 for week ending 7.4.45', 12/4/45; and 'C/Poinsot', 3/5/45, all in Entry 119A, RG 226, NA.

100   Pierre Giolitto, *Volontaires Français sous l'Uniforme Allemand* (Paris, 1999), 318; Dieter Wolf, *Die Doriot-Bewegung* (Stuttgart, 1967), 290–93, 297–99; Otto Abetz, *Das Offene Problem* (Cologne, 1951), 300; Paquis, 56–58, 100, 102–04; Robert Aron, *The Vichy Regime* (London, 1958), 510–11; *Völkischer Beobachter*, 9/1/45; *Le Petit Parisien*, 8/1/45; 9/1/45; 23/2/45; *La France*, 8/1/45; Himmler to Kaltenbrunner, 16/9/44, T-175, r. 122, fr. 2648214, NA; 'Vermerk über die Französische Waffen-SS', 10/12/44; Berger to Himmler, 16/12/44, both in NS 19/1569, BA; 'Vermerk für Amtschef II', 18/12/44, R 58/1007, BA; 'The Maquis Blanc in France', 8/4/45; Mordrelle int., 14/6/45, both in Entry 119A, RG 226, NA; BT 6560, 7/3/45, UMC, r. 64, NAUK; DEG 3602, 2/9/44, HW 19/276, NAUK; and 4012, 6/3/45, HW 19/277, NAUK.

101   Milton Dank, *The French against the French* (Philadelphia, 1974), 282–83; Paquis, 57, 105–110; Wolf, 299–300; Giolitto, 318–20; *La France*, 24–25/2/45; *Le Petit Parisien*, 24/2/45; *Völkischer Beobachter*, 25/2/45; *L'Aurore*, 12/6/45; and *Les Allobroges*, 21/6/45.

102   'The Maquis Blanc in France', 8/4/45, Entry 119A, RG 226, NA.

103   Paquis, 58, 71–75, 77–78, 80–86, 88–90, 93–97, 117–18; Wolf, 294; Lucien Rebatet, *Les Mémoires d'un Fasciste* (Paris, 1976), ii, 200, 214; *Le Petit Parisien*, 6/1/45; *Combat*, 13/7/45; and Delioux int., 7/7/45, Entry 119A, RG 226, NA.

104   Wolf, 274–75; 'Summary of Traces: Mattei, Paul', 27/2/45; Corregi int., 13/2/45; and 'Rauff – SS Sabotage Commando, North Africa', 20/2/43, all in Entry 119A, RG 226, NA. For the history of the PPF in Algeria, see Francis Arzalier, *Les Perdants* (Paris, 1990), 138–44.

105   Arzalier, 121–26; Roland Nosek, r. A3343 SSO-353A, fr. 297, RG 242, NA; 'Notes on Leitstelle III West für Frontaufklärung', 29/8/45, WO 208/3620, NAUK; Bernhard int., 4/12/45, in *Covert Warfare*, xiii; and 'Connection with GIS', 20/2/45, Entry 119A, RG 226, NA.

106   Paquis, 70; Wolf, 296; Paul Jankowski, *Communism and Collaboration* (New Haven, 1989), 138–40; 'Schools, training, etc.'; 'German Intelligence, W/T and Sabotage Schools', 13/3/45; Tostain int., 14/1/45; and Herrlitz int., 20/2/46, both in Entry 119A, RG 226, NA

107   'Notes on Leitstelle III West für Frontaufklärung', 29/8/45, WO 208/3620, NAUK.

108   Wolf, 296; *L'Aube*, 5/4/45; *Libération*, 5/4/45; 6/4/45; 10/4/45; *Le Figaro*, 6/4/45; *Combat*, 6/4/45; *L'Aurore*, 6/4/45; *L'Humanité*, 6/4/45; 7/4/45; *La Croix*, 7/4/45; *La Bataille*, 12/4/45; *Manchester Guardian*, 6/4/45; *The New York Times*, 6/4/45; Georges int., 3/10/44; 'Pair', 18/11/44; CX 22638/27/S Case Officer VB1, Paris, 18/1/45; 19/1/45; 13/2/45; Georges int., 13/2/45; 'Extract from ALP/SH 183 dated 19 Feb 45'; 'Information Bulletins nos. 23 to 26', 24/2/45; Andre int., 4/3/45; WR/C3 to 105 SCI, Bliss, Paris, 10/3/45; Marcaud int., 18/3/45; 'Notice Individuelle', 7/4/45; 'The Maquis Blanc in France', 8/4/45; Paris SP for WR Var 5103 refers, 14/4/45; 'Renoue, Edouard Joseph', 7/5/45, all in Entry 119A, RG 226, NA.

109   'Renoue, Edouard Joseph', 7/5/45, Entry 119A, RG 226, NA.

110   'The Maquis Blanc in France', 8/4/45; 'C/Poinsot', 3/5/45; 'Note de Renseignement', 7/5/45, all in Entry 119A, RG 226, NA.

111   'Weekly Summary no. 13 for White', 15/1/45, CIANF, Entry 86, RG 263, NA.

112 55 SCI Lyons to Paris X-2, 2/5/45; 3/5/45; 9/5/45; 15/5/45; 20/5/45, all in Entry 119A, RG 226, NA.

113 Piotr int., 14/11/44; and Chavannes int., 17/1/45, both in Entry 119A, RG 226, NA.

114 Jankowski, 139; 'Report' 1135, 21/6/45, XL 11790, Entry 19, RG 226, NA; 'Amt VI of the RSHA Gruppe VI B'; 'Monthly Summary' 1, 15/4/45; Zuang int., 18/6/45; Jacobs int., 12/4/45; Dodon int., 14/4/45; 'Exploitation de l'Affaire Sommer', 20/5/45; Delioux int., 7/7/45; Sessler int., 3/10/45, all in Entry 119A, RG 226, NA. For reports of parachute drops in southern France, see 'Rapport du 10 Janvier 1945', annex 1, F/1cIII/1207, AN; 'Rapport Bi-mensuel du 16 Décembre 1944', iv, F/1cIII/1208, AN; and 'Rapport du 10 Janvier 1945', xiv, F/1cIII/1230, AN.

115 Hervé le Buterf, *La Bretagne dans la Guerre* (Paris, 1971), iii, 663–68; *Le Petit Parisien*, 23/2/45; Haller int., 7/8/46, ETO MIS-Y-Sect. CSDIC/WEA Final Interrogation Reports 1945–47, RG 338, NA; and Mordrelle int., 14/6/45, Entry 119A, RG 226, NA.

116 Arzalier, 120, 210; 'SIPO and SD Station Organization etc.', 28/11/44; Zuang int., 18/6/45; 'Connection with GIS', 20/2/45, all in Entry 119A, RG 226, NA; and DEG 3396, 10/7/44, HW 19/276, NAUK.

117 *L'Humanité*, 17/12/44.

118 Le Buterf, 618–19, 668–70, 686; Arzalier, 203–04; Alain Déniel, *Le mouvement breton* (Paris, 1976), 309; Bernhard int., 4/12/45, in *Covert Warfare*, xiii; Tostain int., 14/1/45; 'Renseignements sur la 6ème Compagnie de la Division Brandenburg', 1/3/45; 'The Maquis Blanc in France', 8/4/45; 'Renseignements recueillis sur la RSHA (Mars–Début avril 1945)'; Zuang int., 18/6/45, all in Entry 119A, RG 226, NA; and DEG 3994, 27/2/45, HW 19/277, NAUK.

119 'Ludwig or Louis Nebel', CIANF, Entry 86, RG 263, NA; 'CIR 4 – The German Sabotage Service', IRR File XE 070687, RG 319, NA; 'Revision Notes no. 5 on the German Intelligence Services', IRR File XE 013764, RG 319, NA; 'Notes extracted from Lord Rothschild's interrogation of Nebel', 6/12/44; Kautz int.; 'Summary of Traces for Hans Kautz', 20/1/45; 'Statement of Rene Poncin', 21/12/44; 'Hagedorn – Traces'; 'Summary of Traces – De Bernonville', 23/12/44; Richard int., 4/1/45; Gouillard to DST, Paris, 4/1/45; Ponchelet int., 19/1/45; Van Weile int., 2/45, all in Entry 119A, RG 226, NA; 'Ostrich' int., 2/11/44; 'PF: 601, 603', 4/1/45, both in KV 2/1327, NAUK; and Charles Hagedorn', r. A3343 SSO-051A, fr. 094, RG 242, NA.

120 For the background of SD operations in France, as well as descriptions of key personalities, see Philip Charles Farwell Bankwitz, *Alsatian Autonomist Leaders* (Lawrence, 1978), 52–57, 90–92; Bernhard int., 4/12/45, in *Covert Warfare*, xiii; Zuang int., 18/6/45; and 'Amt VI of the RSHA Gruppe VIB', both in Entry 119A, RG 226, NA.

121 'Ludwig or Louis Nebel', CIANF, Entry 86, RG 263, NA; 'CIR 4 – The German Sabotage Service', 23/7/45, IRR File XE 070687, RG 319, NA; 'Note des Renseignements: Hans Kautz'; Bliss to Crusade, 25/11/44; Cable from Case Officer V48B5M, Paris, 27/11/44; 'Rene Poncin', 21/12/44; 'Gouillaud, Rene', 4/1/45; Ponchelet int., 19/1/45; 'Henri Cathelain', 9/3/45; 'Roger Charles Henri Lambic', 10/3/45; Richard int., 21/6/45, all in Entry 119A, RG 226, NA; 'Ostrich' int., 2/11/44; and 'PF: 601, 603', 4/1/45, both in KV 2/1327, NAUK.

122 HP 3194, 13/10/44, UMC, r. 45, NAUK.

123 'Ludwig or Louis Nebel', CIANF, Entry 86, RG 263, NA; 'The Badenweiler Sabotage Training School', 7/2/45; Nebel int., 28/1/45; Cable by Case Officer V48B5M, Paris, 3/1/45; 'Renseignement', 16/7/45, all in Entry 119A, RG 226, NA; and 'Ostrich' int., 2/11/44, KV 2/1327, NAUK.

124 Guyot int., 6/2/45; 'François gave the following information about the O.R.I.F.', 5/3/45; 'Organisation Revolutionaire Interieure Française', all in Entry 119A, RG 226, NA; and 'Periodical Counter Intelligence Report' 17, 27/2/45, vol. 10704, RG 24, Series 90, NAC.

125 'CIR 4 – The German Sabotage Service', 23/7/45, IRR File XE 070687, RG 319, NA; and 'Exploitation de l'Affaire Neisser', 26/5/45, Entry 119A, RG 226, NA.

126 'Ludwig or Louis Nebel', CIANF, Entry 86, RG 263, NA; 'The Badenweiler Sabotage Training School', 4/1/45; 'German Intelligence, W/T and Sabotage Schools', 13/3/45, both in IRR File XE 001063, RG 319, NA; Raillard int., 27/12/44; Guyot int., 6/2/45; 'The Badenweiler Sabotage Training School', 7/2/45; and Nebel int., 20/6/45, all in Entry 119A, RG 226, NA.

127 'Ludwig or Louis Nebel'; Nebel int., 3/11/44; 'Custody of Nebel, Ludwig and Zeller, Maurice by SCI Paris', 10/11/44; Lt. Michaelis to Chief, SCI, 6/12/44; 28/12/44, all in CIANF, Entry 86, RG 263, NA; 'Zeller, Maurice'; 'Maurice Charles Zeller'; Paris to Saint-London, 14/11/44; Rothschild to Theresa, 20/11/44; Cable from Case Officer V48B5M, Paris, 27/11/44; Raillard int., 27/12/44; Belle int., 29/12/44; Ney int., 1/1/45; Allix int., 9/1/45; Clerget int., 10/1/45; 'The Ney Network', 11/1/45; 'Gull', 18/1/45; Courbis int., 20/1/45; 'Charles Auguste Moreau', 31/1/45; 'The Three Girls', 20/2/45; 'Odette Jeanne Louise Broust', 23/2/45; 'The Three Girls', 6/3/45; 'Reginald Manach', 16/3/45; 'Personalities of the Amt VI S of RSHA', 6/4/45, all in Entry 119A, RG 226, NA; and 'Ostrich' int., 2/11/44, KV 2/1327, NAUK.

128 DSO, Hut 3 to Section F, 5/2/45; DSO Hut 3 to Sec. V Ryder Street, 15/3/45; Bliss to Crusade and Spearhead, 15/3/45; 'Der Leo', 18/3/45; Morael int., 30/3/45; Andre int.; Michaelis to Paris X-2, 19/4/45; 'Synthese des Activités de l'Oberstleutnant Hans Johann Philipp Freund, Amt Ausland Abwehr III F3

– RSHA VI/Z', 1/5/45; 'Renseignements', 16/7/45, all in Entry 119A, RG 226, NA; 'SCI Weekly Report', 29/11/44; note on Nebel, 31/12/44; 'Counter-Sabotage Measures vs. Amt VI (Besekow) Organization', 22/1/45; Michaelis to Chief, SCI, 25/1/45; Holcomb to Ahalt, 11/2/45; Crusade to Bliss, 26/4/45; 'Ostrich' int., 26/4/45; Michaelis to Holcomb, 28/4/45; 'Source FPX698', 30/4/45, all in CIANF, Entry 86, RG 263, NA; and 'CIR 4 – The German Sabotage Service', 23/7/45, IRR File XE 070687, RG 319, NA.

129   Raillard int., 27/12/44; Guyot int., 6/2/45; 'Jacques Labes', 16/3/45; Morael/Prelogar/Claes/Maggen int., 20/3/45; Prelogar int., 1/4/45; 'Daily Report in the Case of Prelogar', 5/4/45; 'Organisation Revolutionaire Interieure Française'; 'Renseignement', 16/7/45, all in Entry 119A, RG 226, NA; and 'The Badenweiler Sabotage School', 4/1/45, IRR File XE 001063, RG 226, NA.

130   Report on parachutists dropped near Blois, 20/12/45; 'Compte-rendu du Service Anti-Parachutistes au 26 Decembre 1944', both in Entry 119A, RG 226, NA; Ministère Intérieur, DST (Paris) to all Prefects, 225 and 266, 15/12/44; and CTA Commissaire Divisionnaire Police Judiciaire, Lyon to various Commissaires Principaux Police Judiciaire, 187, 17/12/44, both in 132–67, CAB K, AS.

131   Chastrusse, Garnier and Vaux, 13–14, 18–19, 62–63, 64–97, 122–24; Henri Amouroux La page n'est pas encore tournée (Paris, 1993), 344–45; 103 SCI Unit HQ (Main) 21 AG 'La Haye, Hugo Henri Hubert', 22/11/44; 'French saboteurs parachuted in Dept. Correze, 14–15/12/44', 'Paul Louis André Maire Pasthier'; 'Compte-rendu du Services Anti-Parachutistes au 26 Decembre 1944'; 'Compte-rendu d'arrestation d'une équipe d'agents SRA parachutés en France', 27/12/44; Fonfriede int., 10/1/45; Pasthier int., 21/1/45, all in Entry 119A, RG 226, NA.

132   DSO, Hut 3 to Section V, 3/2/45; 5/2/45; VAR/4307/SH CX 12727/239, 6/2/45; Dupertuis int., 5/2/45; 'Paul Lucien François', 11/2/45; François int., 10/2/45; 'The Guitry Party'; 'Jacques Labes'; and 'Weekly Progress Report no. 25 for week ending 28.4.45', all in Entry 119A, RG 226, NA.

133   Mackert int., 11/5/45; and Dunker int., 25/5/45, both in Entry 119A, RG 226, NA.

134   Jacques-Augustin Bailly, La Libération Confisquée (Paris, 1993), 386–87; Werner Neisser, r. A3343 SSO-345A, fr. 1188, RG 242, NA; 'Ludwig or Louis Nebel', CIANF, Entry 86, RG 263, NA; 'Maurice Charles Zeller'; Raillard int., 28/12/44; 'Compte Rendu de Mission à Geneve, le 22 Février 1945: CEA "Quid"'; 'Paul Lucien François', 11/2/45; 'The Badenweiler Sabotage School', 28/2/45; Michaelis to Paris X-2, 19/4/45; Jacobs int., 12/4/45; Dodon int., 14/4/45; Mackert int., 11/5/45; Dunker int., 25/5/45; 'Exploitation de l'Affaire Neisser', 26/5/45; Sessler int., 28/5/45; Delioux int., 7/7/45, all in Entry 119A, RG 226, NA; and 'Ostrich' int., 2/11/44, KV 2/1327, NAUK.

135   Skorzeny, Wir Kämpften – Wir Verloren, 126.

136   Vogt int., 10/7/45, Entry 119A, RG 226, NA.

137   'Alexandre, Marceau, Torrez, Francis', 13/12/44; 'CEA Darius', 28/12/44; 'Source Sheet: France, CE, CEA "Darius" (Main Report)', 17/1/45; 'CEA Darius', 17/1/45; WRE (Stuart) to WRC 2, 10/4/45; and 'FAT 252', all in Entry 119A, RG 226, NA.

138   'Renseignement – Source: Legrand', 14/12/44; 'Henri Maria Joseph Klein', 20/3/45; Paris X-2 to Forsythe, 20/4/45; Saint, Paris to Saint, London and Commanding Officer, 6th AG SCI Detachment, 14/5/45; 'FAK 210'; and 'FAT 251', all in Entry 119A, RG 226, NA.

139   'Denjean-Massia, Joël Robert Marcel', 9/3/45, Entry 119A, RG 226, NA.

140   Noulet int., 1/5/45; Bouchez int., 3/5/45; 'Gruppe II, Ast Belgien', 14/5/45; and 'Compte Rendu d'Arrestation' 45, 25/5/45, all in Entry 119A, RG 226, NA.

141   ULTRA/ZIP/ISOS 86787, 24/9/44, HW 19/74, NAUK; and 96546, 14/11/44, HW 19/82, NAUK. See also ULTRA/ZIP/ISOSICLE 12885, 3/11/44; and 12886, 4/12/44, both in HW 19/248, NAUK. For reports about White Maquis and 'Pétain Militia' operating as far north as Paris, see ULTRA/ZIP/ISK 131638, 15/1/45; 131339, 10/2/45, both in HW 19/222, NAUK; and 139574, 7/1/45, HW 19/233, NAUK.

142   'CIR 4 – The German Sabotage Service', 23/7/45, IRR File XE 070687, RG 319, NA; and Vogt int., 18/7/45, Entry 119A, RG 226, NA.

143   Moglia int., 30/4/45; Dodon int., 14/4/45; 'Parachuting: Commune of Challonges (Hameau de Duyet), Haute Savoie', 3/4/45; 'Renseignement – Goyard, Emile', 9/5/45; and 'Exploitation de l'Affaire Sommer', 26/5/45, all in Entry 119A, RG 226, NA.

144   Stahl, 13–16.

145   Biddiscombe, 'The Last White Terror', 820–21, 838, 840; Chevannes int., 17/1/45; Tostain int., 14/1/45; 'Interrogation Report on 1 officer and 15 EM of Jagdeinsatz Nord FPN 40478', 6/4/45; 'The Maquis Blanc in France', 8/4/45; Dodon int., 14/4/45; Lamblin int., 4/5/45, all in Entry 119A, RG 226, NA; and Gerlach int., 11/8/45, XL 13744, Entry 19, RG 226, NA.

146   Lamblin int., 4/5/45; 'Sabotage Group Operating in France', 4/4/45; and 'The Maquis Blanc in France', 8/4/45, all in Entry 119A, RG 226, NA.

147   Gerlach 11/8/45, XL 13744, Entry 19, RG 226, NA; 'Carlotti, Alban', 6–15/2/45; 'Interrogation Report on 1 officer and 15 EM of Jagdeinsatz Nord FPN 40478', 6/4/45; 'Note de Renseignement', 7/5/45, all in Entry

119A, RG 226, NA; and HP 9220, 12/12/44, UMC, r. 53, NAUK. For maritime landings launched by naval special forces based in San Remo, see DEG 4032, 11/3/45; 4041, 12/3/45; 4048, 13/3/45; 4057, 16/3/45; 4072, 18/3/45; 4093, 21/3/45; 4098, 22/3/45; 4165, 19/4/45, all in HW 19/277, NAUK; BT 3406, 26/1/45 (r. 59); BT 4585, 11/2/45 (r. 61); BT 5575, 24/2/45 (r. 63); BT6088, 2/2/45; BT 6947, 12/3/45 (both in r. 64); BT 6827, 10/3/45; BT 7197, 14/3/45 (both in r. 65); BT 7299, 15/3/45 (r. 66); BT 8225, 24/3/45 (r. 67); BT 9550, 5/4/45; BT 9630, 6/4/45 (both in r. 69); KO 25, 10/4/45 (r. 70); KO 534, 16/4/45; KO 605, 17/4/45 (both in r. 71); KO 1430, 26/4/45 (r. 72), all in UMC, NAUK; and 'Renseignements', 4/4/45, 7P 125, SHAT.

148 Jean de Lattre, *Reconquérir* (Paris, 1985), 157; *Five Years – Five Countries – Five Campaigns* (Munich, 1945), 89; *JNSV*, ii, 576–77; 'Poignet, Jean', 9/1/45; 'Poignet, Jean', 15/1/45; Tostain int., 14/1/45; 'Denjean-Massia', 26/1/45; 'Joel Robert Marcel Denjean-Massia', 9/3/45; 'Sabotage Unit "Einheit Ossfeld" – SS Jagdverband', 13/3/45; Michels int., 14/3/45; Lamblin int., 4/5/45; 'Note de Renseignement: Renoue, Edouard Joseph', 7/5/45, all in Entry 119A, RG 226, NA; 'CIR 4 – The German Sabotage Service', 23/7/45 IRR File XE 070687, RG 319, NA; Gerlach int., 11/8/45, XL 13744, Entry 19, RG 226, NA; 'Ostrich and the Brandenburg Division', 18/1/45; and report on 'Ostrich', 30/4/45, both in CIANF, Entry 86, RG 263, NA.

149 *Daily Mirror*, 11/4/45; 'Extract from Weekly Intelligence Summary dated 19th March 1945'; 'Extract from Weekly Intelligence Summary of 4.4.45 from Strasbourg'; Quirk to ALP/LF 20 War Room, 2/4/45; Clay to WR C.2 (Roland), 6/4/45, all in Entry 119A, RG 226, NA; and report on 'Ostrich', 30/4/45, CIANF, Entry 86, RG 263, NA.

150 P.L. Thyraud Vosjoli, *Lamia* (Boston, 1970), 120–21; Ian Sayer and Douglas Botting, *America's Secret Army* (London, 1989), 197–98; Skorzeny, *Wir Kämpften – Wir Verloren*, 126; 'Renseignements – Alsace-Lorraine', 8/1/45; and 'Renseignements Alsace', 8/1/45, both in 7P 125, SHAT.

151 Gerlach int., 11/8/45, XL 13744, Entry 19, RG 226, NA.

152 *The Washington Post*, 19/7/45.

153 Gerlach int., 11/8/45, XL 13744, Entry 19, RG 226, NA.

154 Kahn, 362–64; and 'The Activity of the German Intelligence Service in France and Belgium', 7/3/45, WO 219/1700, NAUK.

155 *German Military Intelligence*, 290–91.

156 Gellermann, 186, 188; Lucas, 289; Stahl, 233–34, 243–45; Amouroux, 347; *L'Éclair des Pyrénées*, 4/11/44; 'Interrogation Report on Survivors of German Crew', 6/3/45, 120249, Entry 16, RG 226, NA; Morael int., 30/3/45; Prelogar int., 1/4/45; Kurrer int., 30/5/45, all in Entry 119A, RG 226, NA; ULTRA/ZIP/ISK 126503, 27/12/44; 126506, 3/12/44, both in HW 19/215, NAUK; 127137, 2/1/45; 127208, 3/1/45; 127209, 4/1/45; 127354, 2/1/45, all in HW 19/216, NAUK; 127840, 12/1/45; 127883, 11/1/45; 128216, 16/1/45; 128239, 17/1/45; 127888, 12/1/45, all in HW 19/217, NAUK; DEG 3967, 15/2/45; 4130, 28/3/45, both in HW 19/277, NAUK; and 'Notes on Leitstelle III West für Frontaufklärung', 29/8/45, WO 208/3620, NAUK.

157 ULTRA/ZIP/ISK 137225, 25/3/45, HW 19/230, NAUK.

158 'Rapport d'Information', 10/1/45, i, F/1cIII/1206, AN; 'Rapport du 25 Décembre 1944', i, F/1cIII/1207, AN; 'Rapport Bi-mensuel du 25 Décembre 1944'; 'Rapport du 10 Janvier 1945', both in F/1cIII/1210, AN; 'Rapport périodique', i, 11/1/45, F/1cIII/1217, AN; 'Rapport du 10 Janvier 1945', i, xiv, F/1cIII/1230, AN; and 'Rapport d'Information', 25/12/44, 0042 W 0040, ADAHP.

159 Bailly, 387; *Les Allobroges*, 3/4/45; 'Rapport d'Information', ii, vi, 15/3/45, F/1cIII/1206, AN; 'Rapport du 10 Janvier 1945', annex, F/1cIII/1207, AN; 'Rapport Bi-mensuel du 16 Décembre 1944', iv, F/1cIII/1208, AN; 'Rapport Mensuel', 28/3/45, vi, F/1cIII/1233, AN; 'Bulletin sur la Situation dans les Régions et les Départements' 33, 27/1/45, F/1a/4028, AN; 'Additif à Note de Service relative à la lutte contre les parachutistes ennemis', 21/12/44; CTA CRE DRE Police Judiciaire Lyon to CRE Renseignements Généraux en Cion to Préfets Région de Lyon, 24/12/44; 'Lutte contre les parachutages ennemi', 8/1/45; Commissire Régional de la République to the Préfet de la Savoie, 29/12/44; Préfet de la Savoie to the Maires du Département, 5/1/45; de Lavareille to the Préfet de la Savoie, 13/1/45, all in 132–67, CAB K, AS; Comité Départemental to Morin, 30/12/44, 0011 W 0002, ADAHP; Morin to Préfet des B.A., 27/2/45; Préfet des Basses-Alpes to Morin, 2/3/45; 'Ordre de Mission', 29/3/45; and Pons to the Préfet du Département des Basses-Alpes, 28/3/45, all in 0042 W 0011, ADAHP.

160 'Rapport Bi-mensuel' 3, vi, 9 Jan. 1945, F/1cIII/1210, AN; 'Rapport Bi-mensuel', 2/1/45, vi; 16/1/45, vi; 31/1/45, I, vi, all in F/1a/4024, AN.

161 Jacques Delperrie de Bayac, *Histoire de la Milice* (Alleur, 1985), ii, 289; Eberhard Jäckel, *Frankreich in Hitlers Europe* (Stuttgart, 1966), 365; *La France*, 4/12/44; and 'GPG', 20/11/44, FO 898/187, NAUK.

162 Paxton, 293; Delperrie de Bayac, ii, 125; and HP 3194, 13/10/44, UMC, r. 45, NAUK.

163 ULTRA/ZIP/ISK 131638, 15/1/45, HW 19/222, NAUK.

164 Paillole, 556; Delperrie de Bayac, ii, 218–19; *The New York Times*, 1/6/44; *La France*, 20/11/44; 18/12/44; *Daily Express*, 13/1/45; *The Times*, 6/1/45; *Völkischer Beobachter*, 9/1/45; 'Schoennerz, Heinz', 20/10/44; 'Information relative à trois parachutistes agents du SRA', 27/1/45; 'Annex II to the report on Leon Albert

Jacobs', 30/4/45; and Delioux int., 7/7/45, all in Entry 119A, RG 226, NA.

165 Bertram Gordon, *Collaborationism in France during the Second World War* (Ithaca, 1980), 323–24; Delperrie de Bayac, ii, 298; Kurrer int., 30/5/45; Kurrer int., 17/8/45; 'Exploitation de l'Affair Sommer', 26/5/45; and Delioux int., 7/7/45, all in Entry 119A, RG 226, NA.

166 Giolitto, 320; Wolf, 295–96, 360; Delperrie de Bayac, ii, p. 297; Amouroux, 343; Paquis, 64–66, 84–85; *Le Petit Parisien*, 26/1/45; *La France*, 29/1/45; 'Final Report on the Case of Walter Friedrich Schellenberg', IRR File XE 001752, RG 319, NA; 'Paul Lucien François', 11/2/45; 'Synthese des Activités de l'Oberleutnant Hans Johann Philipp Freund, Amt Ausland Abwehr III F3 – RSHA VI/Z', 1/5/45; Waneck int., 11/8/45, all in Entry 119A, RG 226, NA; and report on 'Ostrich', 30/4/45, CIANF, Entry 86, RG 263, NA.

167 *L'Aurore*, 12/6/45.

168 Amouroux, 350–51.

169 Jankowski, 139.

170 Gerlach int., 11/8/45, XL 13744, Entry 19, RG 226, NA. For a description of Schwinn, see Lamblin int., 4/5/45; and Mackert int., 11/5/45, both in Entry 119A, RG 226, NA.

171 For cases of camouflaged *Miliciens* or PPF activists caught re-entering France in repatriation convoys, see Bailly, 384–85; *Combat*, 30/4/45; 23/6/45; *Neue Zürcher Zeitung*, 6/5/45; *La Croix*, 1/6/45; 4/6/45; 7/6/45; 12/6/45; *Rassemblement*, 10/6/45; and 24/6/45.

172 *Le Populaire*, 5/7/45; and *L'Humanité*, 5/7/45.

173 Le Directeur de l'Électricité to l'Ingénieur en Chef de la Circonscription Électrique, 29/5/45, 132–67 CAB K, AS. For instances of suspected rail sabotage, see *Le Populaire*, 20/6/45; 4/7/45; *Libération*, 20 /6/45; Bincaz to le Sous-Préfet, 3/7/45; and 'Procès-verbal constatant l'incendie d'un pont chemin de fer à La Chambre (Savoie)', 2/7/45, both in 132–67 CAB K, AS. For the bombing of a gendarmerie post at Suse, which killed two men and wounded seventeen, see *La Croix*, 26/6/45; *Le Populaire*, 26/6/45; and *L'Aurore*, 26/6/45.

174 *Combat*, 19/5/45; 29/5/45; 8/6/45; *L'Aurore*, 19/5/45; 27/5/45; *Le Populaire*, 19/5/45; 20/5/45; 22/5/45; 27–28/5/45; 30/5/45; *L'Humanité*, 19/5/45; 20–21/5/45; 22/5/45; 23/5/45; 27–28/5/45; 2/6/45; *L'Aube*, 19/5/45; 20–21/5/45; 27–28/5/45; 29/5/45; *Le Figaro*, 20–21/5/45; 27–28/5/45; *Le Monde*, 27–28/5/45; and 29/5/45.

175 Jacques Bergier, *Agents Secrets contre Armes Secrètes* (Paris, 1955), 171–72; and 'A/S d'une activité secrète de l'Allemagne contre la France afin d'y créer un atmosphère troublé', 12/3/45, 109–67 CAB K, AS.

176 *Giustizia e Libertà*, 19/2/45.

177 Biddiscombe, 'The Last White Terror', 853–57, 859–60.

178 Yann Fouere, *La Patrie Interdite* (Paris, 1987), 378–79; Paul Sérant, *La Bretagne et la France* (Paris, 1971), 305–10; Le Buterf, iii, 609–14, 672–85; Déniel, 314–19; and Le Grand and Thomas, 374–81, 383–89.

CHAPTER FIVE: NORTH BY NORTH-WEST

1 Spaeter, 416, 489.

2 Meyers, 257, 265; Van Cranenbroeck int., 21/3/45; Morael int., 30/3/45; Prelogar int., 1/4/45; Bultes int.; Van Cranenbroeck int., 17/4/45; Vanhoeke int.; Vanhoeke int.; Polstra int., 18/4/45; 'Daily Report in the Case of Morael', 19/4/45; Post int., 4/5/45; De Roo int., 28/5/45; and 'Hoppe, Hubertus Josef', 10–11/6/45, all in Entry 119A, RG 226, NA.

3 'The Belgian Bureau of the German Foreign Office', 27/9/45, XL 21124, Entry 19, RG 226, NA.

4 G. Carpinelli, 'Belgium', in *Fascism in Europe* (London, 1983), 305.

5 'CIR 4 – The German Sabotage Service', 23/7/45, IRR File XE 070687, RG 319, NA; Himmler to Kaltenbrunner, 16/9/44, T-175, r. 122, fr. 2648214, NA; 'Henri Morael', 16/3/45; Morael int., 30/3/45; and Prelogar int., 1/4/45, all in Entry 119A, RG 226, NA.

6 'CIR 4 – The German Sabotage Service', 23/7/45, IRR File XE 070687, RG 319, NA; Radl int., 4/6/45; Van Cranenbroeck int., 21/3/45, both in Entry 119A, RG 226, NA; and *JNSV* (Amsterdam, 1981), xxii, 286.

7 Bultes int., Entry 119A, RG 226, NA.

8 Heinrich Hoyer, r. A 3343 SSO-117A, fr. 1208, RG 242, NA; 'Ostrich & the S.D.', 12/1/45, CIANF, Entry 86, RG 263, NA; Morael int., 30/3/45; Prelogar int., 1/4/45; 'Hoppe, Hubertus Josef', 1/5/45; Olmes int.; De Roo int., 28/5/45; De Roo/Weber int., 3/6/45; Hakkenberg van Gaasbeek int., 18/6/45; 'SS Jagd Verband Mitte (and the Fuehrungs Stab of the Jagd Verbaende)', all in Entry 119A, RG 226, NA; and 'Counter Intelligence Report on Werwolf', 31/5/45, IRR File 000417, RG 319, NA.

9 Willy Dethier (fr. 1292); 'Vorschlag für die Verleihung des Deutschen Kreuzes im Gold' (fr. 1294–95, 1298), both in r. A3343 SSO-144, RG 242, NA; Van Cranenbroeck int. 21/3/45; 'Hoppe, Hubertus Josef', 1/5/45; Maggen int., 22/5/45; De Roo and Weber int., 3/6/45; and Hakkenberg van Gaasbeek int., 18/6/45, all in Entry 119A, RG 226, NA.

10 'Note: Agent ennemi envoyé en Belgique par la Suisse', 23/3/45; Huygens int., 30/3/45; Prelogar int.,

1/4/45;'Morael', 16/4/45;'Hoppe, Hubertus Josef', 1/5/45; Hakkenberg von Gaasbeek int., 18/6/45; and 'SS Jagd Verband Nord West', 16/1/46, all in Entry 119A, RG 226, NA.

11 Josef Bachot, r. A3343 SSO-025, RG 242, NA; Van Cranenbroeck int., 21/3/45; 'Translation of the French Statement by Joseph Covent', 28/3/45; Prelogar int., 1/4/45; 'Daily Report in the Case of Henri Morael', 3/4/45; and Hakkenberg van Gaasbeek int., 18/6/45, all in Entry 119A, RG 226, NA.

12 'Agent ennemi envoyé en Belgique par la Suisse', 23/3/45; Corley int., 24/4/45; and 'Morael', 27/4/45, all in Entry 119A, RG 226, NA.

13 Bultes int.;'Interrogatoire d'un refugie: Details sur le SR et CI Allemand Actuel', 29/3/45; and Van Cranenbroeck int., 17/4/45, all in Entry 119A, RG 226, NA.

14 'Morael', 16/4/45;'Hoppe, Hubertus Josef', 1/5/45; De Roo int., 28/5/45; De Roo and Weber int., 3/6/45; Hakkenberg van Gaasbeek int., 18/6/45; and Hakkenberg van Gaasbeek int., 4/7/45, all in Entry 119A, RG 226, NA.

15 Kurt Rathje, r. A3343 SSO-008B, fr. 1327, RG 242, NA; Erich Eklöf, r. A3343 SSO-183, fr. 250, RG 242, NA; Jens int., 16/4/45; Van Cranenbroeck int., 17/4/45; Claes int., 28/4/45; 'Hoppe, Hubertus Josef', 1/5/45; Pott int., 20/5/45;'Note on Danish members of Jagdverband 502', 6/6/45; Hakkenberg van Gaasbeek int., 18/6/45; War Room C2 to Section V, 7/7/45; Jens int., 16/8/45; and 'SS Jagd Verband Nord West', 16/1/46, all in Entry 119A, RG 226, NA.

16 'Translation of Statement made by Carl Göran Edquist on 24 May 1945 at Anacapri'; Edquist int., 3/7/45; and Edquist int., 15/7/45, all in Entry 125A, RG 226, NA.

17 Brohs int., 19/12/45, ETO MIS-Y-Sect. CSDIC/WEA Final Interrogation Reports 1945-47, RG 338, NA; Corlay int., 5/45; Hakkenberg van Gaasbeek int., 18/6/45; Jens int., 16/8/45; and 'SS Jagd Verband Nord West', 16/1/46, all in Entry 119A, RG 226, NA.

18 Morael/Prelogar/Claes/Maggen int. 20/3/45;'Morael', 16/4/45; Bultes int.; Corloy int., 28/5/45; Maggen int., 22/5/45; 'Further List of GIS Personalities & Others', 3/6/45; and Hakkenberg van Gaasbeek int., 18/6/45, all in Entry 119A, RG 226, NA.

19 Morael int., 30/3/45, Entry 119A, RG 226, NA.

20 Charles Whiting, The March on London (London, 1992), 45-58, 65-68, 71-73, 78-79, 88-90, 95-100, 107-12, 143; Roderick de Normann, For Führer and Fatherland (Thrupp, 1996), 81-102, 169-70; de Vosjoli, 121-23; and 'Translation: Otto Skorzeny', 7/12/45, IRR File XE 000417, RG 319, NA.

21 Letter from Wolfgang Herfurth, 12/7/92.

22 Olmes int.; Noakes to CI War Room, 20/8/45; and Schnorr int., 11/10/45, all in Entry 119A, RG 226, NA.

23 Van Cranenbroeck int., 21/3/45; Prelogar int., 1/4/45; Corby int., 25/4/45; Maggen int., 22/5/45;'Further List of GIS Personalities & Others', 3/6/45; and Hakkenberg van Gaasbeek int., 18/6/45, all in Entry 119A, RG 226, NA.

24 Clissmann int., ETO MIS-YSect. CSDIC/WEA Interim Reports, Special Interrogation Reports 1945-46, RG 338, NA;'Mil Amt D – Leitstelle II West fuer Frontaufklaerung – II-Kommandos and Trupps in the West', 17/4/45;'FAT 260', 2/10/45;'FAT 222', 4/10/45; Mareel int., 9/11/44; 104 SCI Unit to HO for VB, 7/3/45; Mesmacher int., 14/2/45; Vogt int., annexes ii, iii, 18/7/45; Bergner int., 8/8/45; and Schlemmer int., 11/8/45, all in Entry 119A, RG 226, NA.

25 Charles Whiting, Ardennes: The Secret War (Spellmount, 2001), 22; 'FAT 363', 22/10/45; Pirmollin int., 2/4/45;'Jean Eustache Pirmollin', 2/4/45; and 'Note on Busmans, Oscar', 12/5/45, all in Entry 119A, RG 226, NA.

26 Brohs int., 19/12/45, ETO MIS-Y-Sect. CSDIC/WEA Final Interrogation Reports 1945-47, RG 338, NA.

27 'CI Report' 5, 24/9/44; 6, 8/10/44, both in vol. 10812, RG 24, Series 90, NAC;'Counter Intelligence in the Present Campaign in the West', 8-11/44, vol. 10704, RG 24, Series 90, NAC; and 'CI Operations', 15/2/45, vol. 10811, RG 24, Series 90, NAC.

28 'CI Report' 5, 24/9/44, vol. 10812, RG 24, Series 90, NAC.

29 'CIR 4 – The German Sabotage Service', 23/7/45, IRR File XE 070687, RG 319, NA; Tinlot int.;'Personal Statements by de Mulder', app. 'A'; Hulsman int., 28/9/44; von Weile int., 2/45; Walgraeve int., 28/2/45; De Roos int., 22/3/45; Huygens int., 30/3/45;'Appendix III to 103/ID/151317 of 30 Mar 45 – Account of Enterprise Henriette'; Huygens int., 15/4/45; De Ridder int., 16/4/45;'SCI Report on Colpaert, Gerard F.A.', 23/4/45; Delphine int.; and 'Sabotage Dump', 13/5/45, all in Entry 119A, RG 226, NA. For the claim about 1000 parachutists in training, see DSO Hut to Section V, 9/2/45, Entry 119A, RG 226, NA.

30 'CIR 4 – The German Sabotage Service', 23/7/45, IRR File XE 070687, RG 319, NA; 'Case Extracts', 17/12/44; LaHaye int., 22/11/44; Desirant int., 2/11/44; 'LaHaye', 8/12/45; 'LaHaye', 12/12/45; 'LaHaye', 13/12/45;'Appreciation of the Case of "E" 2 "F"'; 12700/B to V.BZ, 13/12/44;'Employment of H.H.H. LaHaye, 5th Jan 45', 7/1/45;'Progress Report on H.H.H. LaHaye', 31/1/45; Huygens int., 30/3/45; Morael

int., 30/3/45; and Moreal int., 4/45, all in Entry 119A, RG 226, NA. The enterprise described in 'CIR' 4 as 'Operation Jeanne' was actually 'Henriette'. See War Room C2 to Sands, 2/8/45, Entry 119A, RG 226, NA.

31   Prelogar int., 1/4/45, Entry 119A, RG 226, NA.

32   Claes int.; 'Enemy Intelligence Service Contacts'; Bliss, Paris to Crusade, 6/3/45; 'Henri Morael Group', 7/3/45; Report 231, 16/3/45; Prelogar and Morael int.; Noakes to War Room, 22/3/45; 'Arrestation des Parachutistes', 23/3/45; 'Henriette', 27/3/45; 'Morael-Prelogar-Huygens', 27/3/45; Morael int., 30/3/45; Huygens int., 30/3/45; 'Appendix III to 103/ID/151317 of 30 Mar 45 – Account of Enterprise Henriette'; Prelogar int., 1/4/45; 'Daily Report Morael', 1/4/45; 'Daily Report in the Case of Prelogar', 2/4/45; 'Daily Report in the Case of Morael', 3/4/45; 'Daily Report in the Case of Prelogar', 4/4/45; Claes int., 13/4/45; 'Daily Report in the Case of Henri Morael', 17/4/45; Huygens int., 19/4/45; 'Huygens/Morael', 20/4/45; 'Daily Report in the Case of Henri Morael', 20/4/45; 'Claes and Maggen', 24/4/45; Morael int., 4/45; 'Corloy, Paul', 1/5/45; and Maggen int., 22/5/45, all in Entry 119A, RG 226, NA.

33   Morael/Prelogar/Claes/Maggen int., 20/3/45; 'Agent ennemi envoyé en Belgique par la Suisse', 23/3/45; 'Poppe', 31/3/45; Claes int., 13/4/45; 'Daily Report on the Case of Morael', 19/4/45; SHAEF CI War Room to Noakes, 20/4/45; Corloy int., 25/4/45; and 'SS Jagd Verband Nord West', 16/1/46, all in Entry 119A, RG 226, NA.

34   Schmidt int., 17/9/44; 'Andre Isadore de Haene – Sabotage Equipment found Ypres, Belgium', 23/9/44; Delaet int., 25/9/44; Van Eenaeme int., 15/10/44; Van de Bulcke int., 14/10/44; Van de Bulcke int., 28/10/44; Couvrier int., 28/10/44; MSS Traces on Schmidt, 25/11/44; 'Summary of Traces', 25/11/44; Olsen to Noble, 11/12/44; de Cevlaerde int., 11/5/45, all in Entry 119A, RG 226, NA; 'CI Report' 8, 27/9/44; 10, 27/10/44; 11, 11/11/44, all in vol. 10706, RG 24, Series 90, NAC; 'War Diary', 1/9–30/9/44; 1/10–31/10/44, both in vol. 16397, RG 24, Series 90, NAC; 'CI Report' 7, 25/10/44, vol. 10812, RG 24, Series 90, NAC; and 'Periodical CI Report' 16, 26/1/45, vol. 10704, RG 24, Series 90, NAC.

35   'CI Report' 9, 12/10/44; and 11, 11/11/44, both in vol. 10706, RG 24, Series 90, NAC.

36   'FAT 260', 2/10/45; 'CI News Sheet' 24, 27/6/45; WO 205/997, NAUK; ULTRA/ZIP/ISK 126933, HW 19/216, NAUK; Mareel int., 9/11/44; Bird to Noble, 9/12/44; and Schlemmer int., 12/8/45, all in Entry 119A, RG 226, NA.

37   'Annex II – Agents and Stay-Behind Agents in Belgium', 31/3/45; Macalister to Noakes, 23/4/45; Disteque int.; 'Note on Peeters, Jean', 13/5/45, all in Entry 119A, RG 226, NA; Bosmans int.; and 'Sabotage', 26/5/45, both in IRR File XE 001063, RG 319, NA.

38   'Background Notes', 17/1/45, FO 371/46789, NAUK.

39   Van Cranenbroeck int., 21/3/45; 'Cludts, Guillaume', 31/3/45; Van Cranenbroeck int., 17/4/45; Claes int., 28/4/45; and de Ceulaerde int., 11/5/45, all in Entry 119A, RG 226, NA.

40   'The Belgian Bureau of the German Foreign Office', 27/9/45, XL 21124, Entry 19, RG 226, NA; 'Guillaume F. Hendricx', 27/1/45; Morael int., 30/3/45; 'Daily Report in the Case of Henri Morael', 8/4/45; 'Report dated 15th April 1945 – Morael', all in Entry 119A, RG 226, NA; 'Sabotage School of the Vlaamische Jongeren Corps, Casteel Moretus, Stabroek', 17/1/45, XE 001063, RG 319, NA; and 'Background Notes', 17/1/45, FO 371/46789, NAUK.

41   'CI Report' 9, 12/10/44; 10, 27/10/44, vol. 10706, RG 24, Series 90, NAC; 'Operation of Agents in Ghent-Antwerp Area', 6/10/44, vol. 10812, RG 24, Series 90, NAC; and 'CI Report' 6, 8/10/44, vol. 12176, RG 24, Series 90, NA.

42   John Raycroft, *A Signal War* (Prescott, 2002), 42–43; 'CI Report on Gent', vol. 10812, RG 24, Series 90, NAC; and 'CI Report' 6, 8/10/44, vol. 12176, RG 24, Series 90, NAC.

43   'Operation of Agents in Ghent–Antwerp Area', 6/10/44, vol. 10812, RG 24, Series 90, NAC; 'CI Report' 9, 12/10/44, vol. 10706, RG 24, Series 90, NAC; 'Periodical CI Report' 10, 11/11/44, vol. 10704, RG 24, Series 90, NAC; and 'Guillaume F. Hendricxx', 27/1/45, Entry 119A, RG 226, NA.

44   'Report of Civil Security Liaison Officer/Belgium', 12/11/44, vol. 10704, RG 24, Series 90, NAC; and 'Intrep' 89, 8/10/44, vol. 10821, RG 24, Series 90, NAC. For other instances or possible instances of sabotage, see 'CI News' 9, 12/10/44; 11, 11/11/44; 13, 11/12/44, all in vol. 10706, RG 24, Series 90, NAC; and 'Periodical CI Report' 12, 11/12/44, vol. 10704, RG 24, Series 90, NAC.

45   'CI Report' 7, 25/10/44, vol. 10812, RG 24, Series 90, NAC.

46   *New York Times*, 31/10/44.

47   ULTRA/ZIP/ISK 136036, 18/12/44, HW 19/228, NAUK; Pirmollin int.; 'Arrest of the Group "Waterloo" of Front Aufklaerung Trupp 363', 5/4/45; and 'Notes on the SS Jagdverbaende', 8/4/45, all in Entry 119A, RG 226, NA.

48   *Green Route Up – 4 Canadian Armoured Division* (1945), 42–44; Norman Kirby, *1100 Miles with Monty* (Gloucester, 1989), 94–97; 'ND' 1690, 22/2/45, BC, Robbins Library; 'Background Notes', 17/1/45, FO 371/46789, NAUK; 'Enemy Underground Activities in Liberated Territory', 15/11/44, HS 4/291, NAUK; Report FV-114, 19/10/44, L 48226, Entry 21, RG 226, NA; 'Unit History of CIC Detachment no. 418,

Tactical Reserve Team no. 3';'Monthly Information Report', 4/3/45, both in IRR File ZF 015109, RG 319, NA;'De Vreese', 23/12/44; DSO Hut 3 to Section V, 26/1/45;Van Weile int., 2/45; reports by Mareel on prison life, all in Entry 119A, RG 226, NA;'CI Report' 6, 8/10/44; 8, 24/10/44, both in volume 12176, RG 24, Series 90, NAC; 9, 21/11/44, vol. 10812, RG 24, Series 90, NAC;'CI Report' 9, 12/10/44, vol. 10706, RG 24, Series 90, NAC;'CI Report' 7, 25/10/44; 8, 7/11/44, both in vol. 10812, RG 24, Series 90, NAC; 'Sitrep' 3, 21/1/45; 5, 4/2/45; 6, 11/2/45; 7, 18/2/45, all in vol. 16387, RG 24, Series 90, NAC;'Periodical CI Report' 10, 11/11/44; 17, 27/2/45; 19, 25/4/45; 21, 25/6/45;'Report of Civil Security Liaison Officer (Belgium)', 12/11/44; and 27/2/45, all in vol. 10704, RG 24, Series 90, NAC.

49   'Report of the Civil Security Liaison Officer (Belgium)', 12/1/45, vol. 10704, RG 24, Series 90, NAC.

50   *Contribution a l'Étude de la Question Royale: Événements – Documents* (Brussels, 1945), ii, 354–59; Geoffrey Warner, 'Allies, Government and Resistance', *Transactions of the Royal Historical Society* 28 (1978), 46–54; Martin Conway, 'The Liberation of Belgium', in *The End of the War in Europe* (London, 1996), 123–24;'CI Report' 3, 23/9/44, vol. 16397, RG 24, Series 90, NAC;'Periodical CI Report' 8, 10/10/44, vol. 10704, RG 24, Series 90, NAC;'CI Report' 7, 24/10/44, vol. 10812, RG 24, Series 90, NAC; and 'Report of Civil Security Liaison Officer (Belgium)', 27/10/44, vol. 10704, RG 24, Series 90, NAC.

51   'Report of Civil Security Liaison Officer (Belgium)', 27/1/45; 'Periodical CI Report' 15, 26/1/45; 16, 11/2/45; and 17, 27/2/45, all in vol. 10704, RG 24, Series 90, NAC. For examples of rail sabotage in late 1944 and early 1945, see Kirby, 95–96;'War Diary', 1/45; and 2/45, both in vol. 16387, RG 24, Series 90, NAC.

52   *AdAP*, series E, viii, 559; John Maginnis, *Military Government Journal* (Amherst, 1971), 189; Conway, 'The Liberation of Belgium', 124; *The New York Times*, 27/11/44; and 15/2/45.

53   Warner, 58–59.

54   Whiting, *Ardennes*, 41–42, 46–47, 143–44; *The New York Times*, 5/11/44; *Le Figaro*, 12/1/45;'CIC Monthly Bulletin' 2, IRR File ZF 015109, RG 319, NA;'Translation of Statement of Kurt Goblet, Arrested by CIC Detachment 505 re: Sabotage Ring in Lontzen, Belgium', 17/12/44;'Translation of Statement by Heinrich Cormann, Arrested by CIC Det 505', 17/12/44;'Potential Sabotage Ring in Lontzen', 16/12/44;'Heinmat-treue [*sic*] Front Movement in Lontzen', 11/12/44, all in Entry 119A, RG 226, NA.

55   Kirby, 93–94; Desmond Hawkins, *War Report: D-Day to V-E Day* (London, 1985), 243; Whiting, *The March on London*, 94; Whiting, *Ardennes*, 116, 119;'Diary of First US Army (Courtney H. Hodges)', Papers Related to the Allied High Command, r. 8; and 'Renseignements – Belgique', 17/1/45, 7P 125, SHAT.

56   'Jean Eustache Pirmollin: Preliminary note on interrogation', 2/4/45, Entry 119A, RG 226, NA;'Basacles et Parachutages', 119334, Entry 16, RG 226, NA; and 'Report of Civil Security Liaison Officer (Belgium)', 12/2/45, vol. 10704, RG 24, Series 90, NAC.

57   Whiting *Ardennes*, 85–86; Meyers, 265–66; Eddy de Bruyne, *La Collaboration Francophone en Exil* (Housse, 1997), 175, 183;'CI News Sheet', 1/45, vol. 16393, RG 24, Series 90, NAC;Van Cranenbroeck int., 21/3/45; Morael int., 30/3/45; 'Cludts, Guillaume', 31/3/45; Prelogar int., 1/4/45; 'Preparation of Partisan Warfare', 8/4/45;'Van Cranenbroeck, Leo', 3/4/45; and De Ceulaerde int., 11/5/45, all in Entry 119A, RG 226, NA.

58   Whiting *Ardennes*, 85–86; Meyers, 265–66; De Bruyne, 175, 183; 'CI News Sheet', 1/45, vol. 16393, RG 24, Series 90, NAC;Van Cranenbroeck int., 21/3/45; Morael int., 30/3/45; 'Cludts, Guillaume', 31/3/45; Prelogar int., 1/4/45; 'Preparation of Partisan Warfare', 8/4/45;Van Cranenbroeck int., 3/4/45; and De Ceulaerde int., 11/5/45, all in Entry 119A, RG 226, NA.

59   Martin Conway, *Collaboration in Belgium* (New Haven, 1993), 279; Meyers, 251, 266; Wilfried Wagner, *Belgien in der deutschen Politik während des Zweiten Weltkrieges* (Boppard am Rhein, 1974), 292; *AdAP*, series E, viii, 353–73, 558–60, 628; Prelogar int., 1/4/45, Entry 119A, RG 226, NA; and 'The Belgian Bureau of the German Foreign Office', 27/9/45, XL 21124, Entry 19, RG 226, NA.

60   Meyers, 265; *AdAP*, series E, viii, 536; 'GPG', 25/9/44, FO 898/187, NAUK;'CI News Sheet' 7, 5/10/44, WO 205/997, NAUK;'The Belgian Bureau of the German Foreign Office', 27/10/45, XL 21124, Entry 19, RG 226, NA; 'ND' 1568, 3/10/44; 1571, 6/10/44, both in BC, Robbins Library; 'CI Report' 4, 24/9/44; and 5, 7/10/44, both in vol. 10812, RG 24, Series 90, NAC.

61   'The Belgian Bureau of the German Foreign Office', 27/9/45, XL 21124, Entry 19, RG 226, NA; and *AdAP*, series E, viii, 534–35. For Spaak's observation, see 'Belgium and King Leopold', 143612, 14/4/45, HW 12/313, NAUK.

62   Hal Wert, 'Military Expediency, the "Hunger Winter" and Holland's Belated Liberation', in *Victory in Europe 1945* (Lawrence, 2000), 126, 136.

63   G.L. Cassidy, *Warpath* (Toronto, 1948), 203; 'Counter Intelligence in the Present Campaign in the West – Report 2', app. 'C';'Periodical CI Report' 16, 26/1/45, both in vol. 10704, RG 24, Series 90, NAC; 'By-Monthly [*sic*] Intelligence Report' 13, 22/12/44, vol. 16391, RG 24, Series 90, NAC;'CI Sitrep', 11/11/44; 8/12/44; 20/12/44;'War Diary', 11/44; 12/44, all in vol. 12176, RG 24, Series 90, NAC; and 'CI Report' 15, 11/1/45, vol. 10706, RG 24, Series 90, NAC.

64   'CI Report' 7, 23/10/44; and 8, 6/11/44, both in vol. 10812, RG 24, Series 90, NAC.

65 David Littlejohn, *The Patriotic Traitors* (London, 1972), 116–17, 119, 124–25, 128; and Pieter Lagrou, *The Legacy of Nazi Occupation* (Cambridge, 2000), 86.

66 'CIR 4 – The German Sabotage Service', 23/7/45, IRR File XE 070687, RG 319, NA.

67 Hugo Bleicher, *Colonel Henri's Story* (London, 1954), 165.

68 'CI Report' 17, 11/2/45, vol. 10706, RG 24, Series 90, NAC; Bulang int., 26/6/45; and Niemeier int., 27/7/44, both in Entry 119A, RG 226, NA.

69 S.R. Elliot, *Scarlet to Green* (Toronto, 1981), 334–38; 'CI Sitrep' 11, 3/6/45; 12, 7/6/45; 16, 20/6/45; 17, 27/6/45; 'Monthly CI Report' 4, 19/6/45; 'War Diary', 6/45, all in vol. 16395, RG 24, Series 90, NAC; and Smit int., 5/2/45, Entry 119A, RG 226, NA.

70 'Enemy Propaganda – "Z" Organization in Holland', 29/3/45; Geertz int., 21/7/45; and Schlemmer int., 29/8/45, all in Entry 119A, RG 226, NA.

71 'Sitrep', 25/12/44; 'Periodical Monthly Report', 5/1/45; 'CI Report' 1, 21/4/45, all in vol. 16387, RG 24, Series 90, NAC; 'CI Sitrep' 10, 30/5/45; 14, 13/6/45; 'Monthly CI Report' 4, 19/6/45, all in vol. 16395, RG 24, Series 90, NAC; and 'CI Report' 35, 22/6/45, vol. 10706, RG 24, Series 90, NAC.

72 'GPG', 9/4/45, FO 898/187, NAUK.

73 Gerlach int., 11/8/45, XL 13744, Entry 19, RG 226, NA; 'German Intelligence', 26/12/44, IRR File XE 000417, RG 319, NA; 'Schwarts', 3/12/44; 'Smits, Walther', 2/12/44; 'Smits, Walther', 5/12/44; 'Doorewaard, Anton', 4/12/44; 'Concealment of Arms, Ammunition and Explosives by the Streifkorps for the Use of Wehrwolf', 30/7/45, all in Entry 119A, RG 226, NA; 'CI Report' 13, 11/12/44; and 14, 27/12/44, vol. 10706, RG 24, Series 90, NAC.

74 *Manchester Guardian*, 9/1/45; and Bird to Noble, 11/1/45, Entry 119A, RG 226, NA.

75 'Report on Josef Schreider'; 'De Roo, Louis', 9/6/44; De Roo int., 22/5/45; and Hakkenberg van Gaasbeek int., 18/6/45, all in Entry 119A, RG 226, NA.

76 CSDIC BLA to GS Int, Main HQ, 21st AG BLA, 3/6/45; and Gerlach int., annex, 11/8/45, both in Entry 119A, RG 226, NA.

77 Alfred Hakkenberg van Gaasbeek (fr. 905); 'Beurteilung des SS-Untersturmführers Hakkenberg v. Gaasbeek, geb. 15.4.1920' (fr. 917), both in r. A3343 SSO-054A, RG 242, NA; Post int.; Courage to War Room, 12/4/45; Polstra int.; 'Hoppe, Hubertus Josef', 11/5/45; Post int.; Polstra int.; Wouterson/Hoppe/De Jonghe int.; 'Wouterson, Jan Wijnandus'; 'de Jonghe, Cornelius'; Hakkenberg van Gaasbeek int., 18/6/45; and Hakkenberg van Gaasbeek int., all in Entry 119A, RG 226, NA.

78 G.D. Sheffield, *The Red Caps* (London, 1994), 161; and 'War Diary for Week ending 22 Apr 45', vol. 12176, RG 24, Series 90, NAC.

79 Schmidt int., 17/9/44, Entry 119A, RG 226, NA.

80 Snabel int., 25/10/44; Paques int., 28/10/44; Eggers int., 27/10/44; and 12700/B to VBZ, 24/10/44, all in Entry 119A, RG 226, NA.

81 Casimir int., 31/3/45; De Jonghe int.; Lautenbach int., 28/4/45; Schaefer int., 3/5/45; Weber int., 15/8/45; Schlemmer int., 21/8/45; Schlemmer int., 29/8/45; 'CI Report' 19, 26/3/45; 20, 25/4/45, vol. 10706, RG 24, Series 90, NAC; 'War Diary for week ending 14 Apr 45', vol. 12176, RG 24, Series 90, NAC; and 'War Diary – April', vol. 16387, RG 24, Series 90, NAC.

82 Bergner int., 8/8/45; and Schlemmer int., 23/8/45, both in Entry 119A, RG 226, NA.

83 'Periodical CI Report' 2, 10/11/44, vol. 10704, RG 24, Series 90, NAC; 'CI Report' 16, 27/1/45, vol. 10706, RG 24, Series 90, NAC. For the strange case of Jan Hoes, see 'Counter Intelligence Report' 1, 18/3/45, vol. 16398, RG 24, Series 90, NAC; 'CI Report' 19, 26/3/45; and Hoes int., 21/3/45, Entry 119A, RG 226, NA.

84 Hendriks int., 3/11/44; Wouterson int., 9/5/45; 'Hoppe, Hubertus Josef', 19/5/45; Hakkenberg van Gaasbeek int., 18/6/45; Fuchs int., 17/6/45, all in Entry 119A, RG 226, NA; 'Interrogation Report on PW from 5 Coy, 2 Bn 83 Regt. SS Landstorm Nederland', 12/4/45; 'Intrep on PW from 34 Dutch SS Div Landstorm Nederland', 17/4/45, both in vol. 10685, RG 24, Series 90, NAC; and 'CI Report' 35, 22/6/45, vol. 10706, RG 24, Series 90, NAC.

85 Kirby, 91–92; Cassidy, 233, 242; C.P. Stacey, *The Victory Campaign* (Ottawa, 1960), 555; *The Globe and Mail*, 10/4/45; 'CI Report' 9, 24/11/44, vol. 10812, RG 24, Series 90, NAC; 'CI Report' 12, 27/11/44; 16, 27/1/45; 18, 27/2/45; 35, 22/6/45, all in vol. 10706, RG 24, Series 90, NAC; 'War Diary', 7/1/45; 'Sitrep', 31/12/44; 8/1/45; 'Periodical Monthly Report', 5/1/45; 'CI Sitrep' 6, 21/1/45; 'CI Report' 2, 22/1/45; 'Sitrep' 12, 11/3/45; 'War Diary', 3/45, all in vol. 16387, RG 24, Series 90, NAC; 'CI Sitrep of 031200A', 3/12/44; 'CI Sitrep as of 071100A', 7/12/44, both in vol. 16396, RG 24, Series 90, NAC; 'War Diary', 2/45; 4/45, both in vol. 16397, RG 24, Series 90, NAC; 'War Diary', 3/45; 'CI Sitrep' 7, 4/4/45, both in vol. 16398, RG 24, NAC; 'CI Sitrep' 6, 13/5/45; 9, 28/5/45, both in vol. 16395, RG 24, Series 90, NAC; 'True Spy Stories for the Troops' 1; 'War Diary for Period Ending 28 Apr 45'; 'War Diary for Week Ending 7 July 45', all in vol. 12176, RG 24, Series 90, NAC; BT 2664, 18/1/45 (r. 58); and BT 3601, 28/1/45 (r. 60), both in UMC, NAUK.

86 'CI Report' 20, 25/4/45, vol. 10706, RG 24, Series 90, NAC.

87 'CI News Sheet' 24, 22/6/45, WO 205/997, NAUK; 'CI Report' 20, 25/4/45, vol. 10706, RG 24, Series 90, NAC; and 'CI Sitrep' 2, 22/4/45, vol. 16398, RG 24, Series 90, NAC.

88 'Preliminary Note on de Roo', 22/5/45; Hakkenberg van Gaasbeek int., 18/6/45; Munt int., 23/6/45; and 'Concealment of Arms, Ammunition and Explosives by the Streifkorps for the Use of Wehrwolf', 30/7/45, all in Entry 119A, RG 226, NA.

89 'CI Report' 20, 25/4/45, vol. 10706, RG 24, Series 90, NAC.

90 'CI Sitrep' 12, 20/5/45, vol. 16387, RG 24, Series 90, NAC; 'War Diary', 6/45; 'CI Sitrep' 17, 27/6/45; 'War Diary', 7/45, all in vol. 16895, RG 24, Series 90, NAC; 'War Diary', 7/45, vol. 16394, RG 24, Series 90, NAC; and 'No. 3 Monthly Report of CSLM(H) for the Period 24 June 45–23 July 45', vol. 10704, RG 24, Series 90, NAC.

91 'CI Report' 2, 5/5/45; 'CI Sitrep' 9, 10/5/45; 'CI Sitrep' 10, 14/5/45; 11, 16/5/45, all in vol. 16387, RG 24, Series 90, NAC; 'War Diary', 5/45; 6/45, both in vol. 16394, RG 24, Series 90, NAC; 'War Diary', 31/5/45; 30/6/45; 31/7/45; 'War Diary for Week Ending 1 June 1945', all in vol. 16397, RG 24, Series 90, NAC; 'War Diary', 5/45; 6/45; 'Sitrep' 10, 30/5/45, all in vol. 16395, RG 24, Series 90, NAC; 'War Diary for Week Ending 1 Jun 45'; 'War Diary for Week Ending 9 Jun 45'; 'War Diary for Week Ending 21 July 45', all in vol. 12176, RG 24, Series 90, NAC; 'No. 3 Monthly Report of CSLM(H) for period 24 June 45–23 July 45'; and 'No. 4 Monthly Report of CSLM(H) for period 24 Jul 45–23 Aug 45', both in vol. 10704, RG 24, Series 90, NAC.

92 New York Times, 8/5/45; The Globe and Mail, 9/5/45; 16/5/45; and 'Background Notes', 12/5/45, FO 371/46790, NAUK.

93 Heiber, 290.

94 Burleigh, 459–60; Littlejohn, 72–74, 79–81; 'Martinsen int., 20/9/45; Bovensiepen int., 1/8/45; Pancke int., 6/7/45; Pancke int., 20/8/45; 'Ostrich' int., 2/11/44, KV 2/1327, NAUK; 'Notes Extracted from Lord Rothschild's Interrogation of Nebel', 6/12/44; 'Translation of Statement by Kaltenbrunner handed in on 20.7.45 (no. 23) – The Danish Resistance Movement and German Counter Measures', all in Entry 119A, RG 226, NA; 'Progress Report in the Case of Schellenberg', 17/7/45, IRR File XE 001752, RG 319, NA; 'German Intelligence', 26/12/44; 'Unternehmen Peter'; 'Special Activities of Skorzeny Group', 21/5/45, all in IRR File XE 000417, RG 319, NA; 'Ludwig or Louis Nebel'; Chief to Chief, Foreign Branch W, 7/1/49; [—] to Washf, 7/2/47, all in CIANF, Entry 86, RG 263, NA; and ULTRA/ZIP/ISOS 96567, 14/4/45, HW 19/84, NAUK. For individual cases where Skorzeny continued to train 'Peter' agents, see Jens int., 16/8/45; and Goy int., 29/6/45, both in Entry 119A, RG 226, NA.

95 Maly int., Entry 119A, RG 226, NA.

96 In the spring of 1945, it was Schwerdt who provided the head of the Sipo in Copenhagen, Otto Bovensiepen, with phoney identification papers and a vial of poison for use in case of capture. Bovensiepen int., 1/8/45, Entry 119A, RG 226, NA.

97 'Hstuf. Scwert@Schäfer@Peter', 8/10/45, Entry 119A, RG 226, NA.

98 Andersen int., 20/7/45, Entry 119A, RG 226, NA.

99 Bovensiepen int., 1/8/45; Clissmann int., 15/9/45, both in Entry 119A, RG 226, NA; Himmler to Kaltenbrunner, 16/9/44, T-175, r. 122, fr. 2648214, NA; 'Background Notes', 3/5/45, FO 371/46790, NAUK; 'Northern Region Intelligence Review – Denmark' 88, 4/5/45; and 90, 15/6/45, both in FO 371/47253, NAUK.

100 Pott int., 20/5/45; 'Further List of GIS Personalities & Others', 3/6/45; Golding to Section V, 7/7/45; Jens int., 16/8/45; and Ullrich int., 14/9/45, all in Entry 119A, RG 226, NA.

101 'CI News Sheet' 26, 30/7/45, WO 205/997, NAUK.

102 Littlejohn, 80.

103 Clissmann int., 23/11/45, ETO MIS-Y-Sect. CSDIC/WEA Interim Reports, Special Interrogation Reports 1945–46, RG 338, NA; 'CI News Sheet' 24, 27/6/45, WO 205/997, NAUK; ULTRA/ZIP/ISOS 96565, 14/4/45, HW 19/84, NAUK; Clissmann int., 15/9/45; Falland int., 3/9/45; Hansen int., 5/9/45; Clissmann int., 4/10/45; and Schoeneich int., 31/10/45, all in Entry 119A, RG 226, NA.

104 Manchester Guardian, 19/6/45; Neue Zürcher Zeitung, 19/6/45; and Daily Herald, 19/6/45.

105 FOWPIS 12, Summary 316, 24/10/45; Manchester Guardian, 22/5/45; 31/5/45; Journal de Genève, 31/5/45; The Globe and Mail, 2/7/45; The New York Times, 21/5/45; 15/6/45; 18/10/45; 'Background Notes', 12/5/45, FO 371/46790, NAUK; 'Northern Region Intelligence Review – Denmark' 90, 18/5/45, FO 371/47253, NAUK; and Gallop to Eden, 22/5/45, FO 371/47524, NAUK.

106 Himmler to Kaltenbrunner, 16/9/44, T-175, r. 122, fr. 2648214, NA.

107 'Enemy Expectations, Intentions and Sources of Information (16 March 1945)', WO 208/3616, NAUK.

108 Rose, 129; Hellmuth Romeick (fr. 1169); 'Lebenslauf' (fr. 1188), both in r. A3343 SSO-045B, RG 242, NA; 'Amt VI Resistance Org in Norway', 5/6/45; Olmes int.; memo from VF 19, 12/7/45, all in Entry 119A, RG 226, NA; Saint, London to Saint, Washington, 15/9/45, IRR File XE 000440, RG 319, NA; and 'CIR 4 – The German Sabotage Service', 23/7/45, IRR File XE 070687, RG 319, NA.

109 BT 6410, 6/3/45, UMC, r. 64, NAUK.

110 'Edquist, Carl Goran', 15/7/45, Entry 125A, RG 226, NA. For the Swedish interest in Scandinavian prisoners, see Danziger int., 27/9/45, Entry 119A, RG 226, NA; Felix Kersten, *The Kersten Memoirs* (London, 1956), 187, 226–27; W.M. Carlgren, *Swedish Foreign Policy during the Second World War* (New York, 1977), 216; and Peter Padfield, *Himmler* (London, 1991), 565–66, 578, 591, 594.

111 'CIR 4 – The German Sabotage Service', 23/7/45, IRR File XE 070687, RG 319, NA; Clissmann int., 15/9/45; Hansen int., 5/9/45; and 'FAT 261', all in Entry 119A, RG 226, NA.

112 'German Streifkorps', 9/9/45, IRR File 003688, RG 319, NA.

113 KO 1420, 26/4/45, UMC, r. 72, NAUK.

114 Tore Gjelsvik, *Norwegian Resistance* (London, 1979), 183–84; FOWPIS 11, Summary 278, 31/1/45; 'Fortnightly Directive for BBC Norwegian Bulletins, Feb. 3rd–16th, 1945', 2/2/45, FO 371/46789, NAUK; 'Report on Visit to Finnmark: July 17th–August 7th, 1946'; and 'Visit to the counties of Nordland and South Troms, 30th May–6th June 1946', both in FO 371/56292, NAUK.

115 'Background Notes', 12/4/45; 'Fortnightly Directive for BBC Norwegian Bulletins, April 14–27, 1945', 13/4/45, both in FO 371/46790, NAUK; 'Daily Summary', 12/4/45, Entry 92, RG 226, NA; and 'ND' 1763, 21/5/45, BC, Robbins Library.

116 Gjelsvik, *Norwegian Resistance*, 212; Ralph Hewins, *Quisling* (London, 1965), 338–56; Paul Hayes, *Quisling* (Newton Abbot, 1971), 296–97; Littlejohn, 46–47; FOWPIS 11, Summary 287, 4/4/45; 291, 2/5/45; 292, 9/5/45; *Daily Express*, 5/5/45; *The Washington Post*, 10/5/45; *The Globe and Mail*, 12/5/45; *The New York Times*, 12/5/45; 18/5/45; *The Stars and Stripes*, 26/8/45; 'Background Notes', 3/5/45; 12/5/45, both in FO 371/46790, NAUK; 'Daily Summary' 28, 10/5/45; 30, 12/5/45; 31, 14/5/45, all in Entry 92, RG 226, NA; 'ND' 1757, 14/5/45; 1762, 19/5/45; 1767, 25/5/45; and 1770, 29/5/45, all in BC, Robbins Library.

117 *Washington Post*, 26/6/45; *Daily Herald*, 26/6/45; *Journal de Genève*, 1–2/9/45; *Stars and Stripes*, 19/9/45; *Manchester Guardian*, 23/11/45; *The New York Times*, 21/8/45; 16/9/45; 28/11/45; and 1/12/45.

118 Allen Chew, *The White Death* (Grand Rapids, 1971), 229–32; John Wuorinen, *Finland and World War II* (Westport, 1983), 114–22, 186; and Brohs int., 19/12/45, ETO MIS-Y Sect. CSDIC/WEA Final Interrogation Reports 1945–47, RG 338, NA.

119 Mader, *Hitlers Spionagegenerale sagen aus*, 193–95, 358, 381, 386; Spaeter, 226–33; Stahl, 16; 'Small Unit Actions during the German Campaign in Russia', in *WWIIGMS* (New York, 1979), xviii; and Cellarius int., 23/6/45, Entry 119A, RG 226, NA.

120 Hengelhaupt to Gehlen, 12/5/44, T-78, r. 566, fr. 896, NA.

121 Carl Gustav von Mannerheim, *The Memoirs of Marshal Mannerheim* (London, 1953), 493–501; Mastny, *Russia's Road to the Cold War*, 51; and *Khrushchev Remembers* (Boston, 1970), 156.

122 Chew, 27–28; Eloise Engle and Lauri Paananen, *The Winter War* (New York, 1973), 16, 18, 86, 144; Mader *Hitlers Spionagegenerale sagen aus*, 322; Nevakivi, 90, 96; and Ismail Akhmedov, *In and Out of Stalin's GRU* (Frederick, 1984), 113, 115–18.

123 The New York Times, 8/11/44.

124 *AdAP*, series E, viii, 425; Metzgar int., 14/2/46, ETO MIS-Y Sect. CSDIC/WEA Interim Reports, Special Interrogation Reports 1945–46, RG 338, NA.

125 Gellermann, 110–11; and Brohs int., 19/12/45, ETO MIS-Y Sect. CSDIC/WEA Final Interrogation Reports 1945–47, RG 338, NA.

126 Mannerheim, 502–03; Chew, 243; G.A. Gripenberg, *Finland and the Great Powers* (Lincoln, 1965), xii; Earl Ziemke, *The German Northern Theatre of Operations* (Washington, 1959), 290; Linke to FHO, 9/9/44, T-78 , r. 497, fr. 6485632–33, NA; 'SSD Fernschreiben', 18/10/44, T-77, r. 1431, fr. 291–292, NA; and 'A History of Germany's Campaigns in World War II by Genobst (Col Gen) Heinz Guderian', 26/7/45, WO 208/3148, NAUK.

127 Stig Jägerskiöld, *Mannerheim* (London, 1986), 182–84; Wuorinen, 179–80; Nevakivi, 95–96; Sampo Ahto, 'The War in Lapland', *Revue Internationale d'Histoire Militaire* 62 (1985), 224, 231; Allan Sundström, *Den falska freden* (Örebro, 1997), 34–44; and Reijo Ahtokari, *Asekätkentäjuttu* (Porvoo, 1971), 15–20.

128 *AdAP*, series E, viii, 491.

129 Ahtokari, 25–40, 127–28; Matti Lukkari, *Asekätkentä* (Helsinki, 1984), 19–70, 78–95, 99–192; Sundström, 50–52; Jagerskiöld, 190–91; Pertti Kilkki, *Valo Nihtilä* (Porvoo, 1994), 160–65; and Max Jacobson and Jukka Tarkka, 'Finland's Security Policy after the Second World War', *Revue Internationale d'Histoire Militaire* 62 (1985), 245.

130 Brohs int., 19/12/45, ETO MIS-Y Sect. CSDIC/WEA Final Interrogation Reports 1945–47, RG 338, NA.

131 Ibid.; and Cellarius int., 23/6/45, Entry 119A, RG 226, NA.

132 Chew, 231; *FRUS, 1945*, iv, 608; and Brohs int., 19/12/45, ETO MIS-Y Sect. CSDIC/WEA Final Interrogation Reports 1945–47, RG 338, NA.

133 Metzger int., 14/2/46, ETO MIS-Y Sect. CSDIC/WEA Interim Reports, Special Interrogation Reports 1945–46, RG 338, NA; and Brohs int., 19/12/45, ETO MIS-Y-Sect. CSDIC/WEA Final Interrogation Reports 1945–47, RG 338, NA.

134 'GPG', 2/10/44, FO 898/187, NAUK; *Morgen-Tidningen*, 1/10/44; 'ND' 1567, 2/10/44, BC, Robbins Library; Brohs int., 19/12/45, ETO MIS-Y-Sect. CSDIC/WEA Final Interrogation Reports 1945–47, RG 338, NA; and Gambke/Raupach/Peters int., 15/8/45, Entry 119A, RG 226, NA.

135 Mader, *Hitlers Spionagegenerale sagen aus*, 391–92; Ahtokari, 127; Lukkari, 23, 201–05; ULTRA/ZIP/ISK 120343, 25/9/44, HW 19/205, NAUK; DEG 3672, 14/10/44, HW 19/276, NAUK; 'Translation of statement made by Carl G. Edquist 24 May 1945 at Anacapri'; Edquist int., 3/7/45; 'Edquist, Carl Goran, Albergo Bellavista, Anacapri, Capri, Italy', 15/7/45, all in Entry 125A, RG 226, NA; Brohs int., 19/12/45, ETO MIS-Y-Sect. CSDIC/WEA Final Interrogation Report 1945–47, RG 338, NA; Willy Laqua, r. A3343 SSO-243A, RG 242, NA; Cellarius int., 23/7/45; Horn int., 18/6/45; 'Extract from File no. PF 602,583', 18/6/45; Kraemer int., 23/7/45; Wenzlau int., 3/10/45, all in Entry 119A, RG 226, NA; and 'Notes on Mil Amt C and other Departments of RSHA', 11/9/45, WO 208/3620, NAUK.

136 *AdAP*, series E, viii, 425.

137 Metzger int., 30/1/45, ETO MIS-Y Sect. CSDIC/WEA Interim Reports, Special Interrogation Reports 1945–46, RG 338, NA; Brohs int., 19/12/45, ETO MIS-Y Sect. CSDIC/WEA Final Interrogation Reports 1945–47, RG 338, NA; War Room C2 to VF 20, 17/7/45; Cellarius int., 23/6/45; and Horn int., 18/6/45, all in Entry 119A, RG 226, NA.

138 Brohs int., 19/12/45, ETO MIS-Y Sect. CSDIC/WEA Final Interrogation Reports 1945–47, RG 338, NA; Obladen int., 28/6/45; Cellarius int., 5/12/45; Cellarius int., 18/6/45; Horn int., 18/6/45, all in Entry 119A, RG 226, NA; and 'Notes on Mil Amt C and other Departments of RSHA', 11/9/45, WO 208/3620, NAUK. For the arrest of Fabritius, see *The New York Times*, 25/7/46.

139 Lukkari, 96–97, 211–75; Ahtokari, 37, 49–50, 102–04, 108–09, 125–26; Jagerskiöld, 190–91; and Jacobsen and Tarrka, 245.

140 Elliot, 334; and 'Extract from "Revision Notes no. 1 on the German Intelligence Services" dated 6 Dec 44', WO 204/11839, NAUK.

141 De Bruyne, 183; and Skorzeny, *Wir Kämpften – Wir Verloren*, 112.

CHAPTER SIX: THE TIME OF THE WOLF

1 Skorzeny, *Wir Kämpften – Wir Verloren*, 105–06; 'CI News Sheet' 12, 26/12/44, WO 205/997, NAUK; 'Notes on SS, SD and RSHA/Mil Amt', 10/4/45; and 'Miscellaneous', 20/4/45, both in WO 208/3616, NAUK.

2 'Counter Intelligence Report on Werwolf', 31/5/45, IRR File XE 000417, RG 319, NA; 'Report on Interrogation of Walter Schellenberg', IRR File XE 001752, RG 319, NA; and Gambke/Raupach/Peters int., 15/8/45, Entry 119A, RG 226, NA.

3 Himmler to Kaltenbrunner, 16/9/44, T-175, r. 122, fr. 2648214, NA.

4 Charles Whiting, *Werewolf* (London, 1972), 68–69; 'Counter Intelligence Report on Werwolf', 31/5/45, IRR File XE 000417, RG 319, NA; Radl int., 4/6/45; Olmes int., 18/6/45, both in Entry 119A, RG 226, NA; and Gerlach int., 11/8/45, XL 13744, Entry 19, RG 226, NA.

5 Skorzeny, *Wir Kämpften – Wir Verloren*, 106.

6 'Counter Intelligence Report on Werwolf', 31/5/45, IRR File XE 000417, RG 319, NA.

7 Prelogar and Morael int., 17/3/45, Entry 119A, RG 226, NA.

8 Rose, 28–29; 'Bertelsmann, Klaus – 2. Order for the Recruiting of Werwolf Volunteers'; 12th AG to War Room, 27/5/45; and 'Interrogation report on 1 officer and 15 EM of Jagdeinsatz Nord FPN 40478', all in Entry 119A, RG 226, NA.

9 'Counter Intelligence Report on Werwolf', 31/5/45; Skorzeny int., 19/5/45, both in IRR File XE 000417, RG 319, NA; Gerlach int., 11/8/45, XL 13744, Entry 19, RG 226, NA; Schepers int., 25/3/45; Mueller int., 4/45, both in IRR File XE 001063, RG 319, NA; 15th 'Collated Report on the SS Sonderkommando at the Jagdverband Kampfschule in Tiefenthal', 12/5/45; 'Extraction from 12th AG "Weekly Intelligence Summary" no. 42, 29 May 1945'; Prelogar and Morael int., 17/3/45; 'Notes on the SS Jagdverbaende', 8/4/45; 'Countersabotage Bulletin' 7, 21/6/45, all in Entry 119A, RG 226, NA; 'Ostrich' int., 26/4/45, CIANF, Entry 86, RG 263, NA; and 'Notes on the Brandenburg Division and SS Jagdverbände der Waffen SS', 1/4/45, WO 208/3015, NAUK.

10 Gambke/Raupach/Peters int., 15/8/45, Entry 119A, RG 226, NA.

11 Wenck to the Heeresgruppen and Armeen, 6/2/45, RH 2/1930, BMA; and Winter, Memo from WFSt./ Op.(H)/Ia to Chef WFSt. Stellv. Chef, PO(H), Ia, Ic, Qu, 28/2/45, RW 4/v. 702, BMA.

12 'Notes on the SS Jagdverbaende', 8/4/45; Asbach int., 3/5/45, both in Entry 119A, RG 226, NA; and 'Countersabotage Bulletin' 2, 17/4/45, IRR File XE 070687, RG 319, NA.

13 Gambke/Raupach/Peters int., 15/8/45, Entry 119A, RG 226, NA.

14 Perry Biddiscombe, *Werwolf!* (Toronto, 1998), 64–65; and zu Eikern to Gehlen, 20/3/45, T-78, r. 566, fr. 340, NA.

15 Skorzeny, *Wir Kämpften – Wir Verloren*, 105.

16 Skorzeny int., 19/5/45, IRR File XE 000417, RG 319, NA.

17   Biddiscombe, *Werwolf!*, 14; and 'Report on Interrogation of Walter Schellenberg', IRR File XE 001752, RG 319, NA.

18   'Counter Intelligence Report on Werwolf', 31/5/45, IRR File XE 000417, RG 319, NA.

19   'Report on Interrogation of Walter Schellenberg', IRR File XE 001752, RG 319, NA; and Radl int., 4/6/45, Entry 119A, RG 226, NA.

20   'Special Brief – Twelfth Army Group, SCI Det., Munich – dated 8 July 1945'; Waneck int., 11/8/45; War Room Incoming Telegram AMZON 947, 2/7/45, all in Entry 119A, RG 226, NA; and JBO to Spearhead, AMZON, 30/6/45, IRR File 000417, RG 319, NA.

21   Mundhenke int., 20/7/45, Entry 119A, RG 226, NA; and 'Weekly Summary 13 for White', 15/1/45, CIANF, Entry 86, RG 263, NA.

22   Mader, *Hitlers Spionagegenerale sagen aus*, 133; *HCIC*, xx, 4; 'Leitstelle II Sud Ost'; 'Monthly Summary' 3, 18/6/45; 'Cache of Resistance Supplies found at Mohra', 24/4/45; Huntermann int., 4/5/45; Hilz int., 11/5/45; report on Oscar Kirchner, 5/6/45; Mundhenke int., 20/7/45; Bergner int., 4/8/45; Herrlitz int., 20/2/46, all in Entry 119A, RG 226, NA; 'Historique du FAK 102 de Février 1945 à début Mai 1945', IRR File XE 020652, RG 319, NA; KO 654, 17/4/45 (r. 71); KO 780, 19/4/45 (r. 72), both in UMC, NAUK; ULTRA/ZIP/ISK 139764, 12/4/45; 139981, 14/4/45, both in HW 19/233, NAUK; and 140109, 10/4/45, HW 19/234, NAUK.

23   Rose, 200, 206; Skorzeny, *Wir Kämpften – Wir Verloren*, 99, 188–89; 'CI News Sheet' 26, 30/7/45, WO 205/997, PRO; 'Report on Interrogation of Walter Schellenberg', IRR File XE 001752, RG 319, NA; and letter to the author from Wolfgang Herfurth, 7/12/92.

24   Kirchner int., 3/1/46, XL 40257, Entry 19, RG 226, NA.

25   Otto Skorzeny, *Skorzeny's Special Missions* (London, 1957), 193; 'Skorzeny, Otto', 22/6/45, IRR File XE 000417, RG 319, NA; and 'CIR 4 – The German Sabotage Service', 23/7/45, IRR File XE 070687, RG 319, NA.

26   Rose, *Werwolf*, 205.

27   Gellermann, 102–03.

28   Karol Jonca, 'The Destruction of "Breslau"', *Polish Western Affairs* ii (1961), 329; *Pogranichnye Voiska SSSR v Velikoi Otechestvennoi Voine*, 554–55; 'Leitsätze und Fragen für den Einsatz von Streifkorps' (fr. 366); Thomas to Lindeiner, 14/3/45 (fr. 352), both in T-78, r. 566, NA; 'FAK 202', 23/11/45, IRR File XE 020651, RG 319, NA; and Gambke/Raupach/Peters int., 15/8/45, Entry 119A, RG 226, NA.

29   'General Situation Report' 2, 1/9/45, OMGUS AG Security-Classified Decimal File 1945-49, 350.09 (Intelligence, General), RG 260, NA; and KO 1122, 22/4/45, UMC, r. 72, NAUK.

30   Charles MacDonald, *Company Commander* (New York, 1978), 358, 364.

31   Korbonski, 107; FOWPIS 12, Summary 304, 1/8/45; Summary 305, 8/8/45; *The New York Times*, 29/7/45; 4/8/45; *Stars and Stripes*, 8/8/45; *Neue Zeit*, 25/8/45; 'Summary of Political Events, 25 July–31 July'; and Bulletin of the Czechoslovak Ministry of Information 7, 17/8/45, both in State Dept. Decimal Files 1945-49, 860F.00, RG 59, NA.

32   'CIR 4 – The German Sabotage Service', 23/7/45, IRR File XE 070687, RG 319, NA; Kirchner int., 3/1/46, XL 40257, Entry 19, RG 226, NA; Forras int., 10/12/45, ETO MIS-Y Sect. CSDIC/WEA Final Interrogation Reports 1945-47, RG 338, NA; Heckel int., 28/5/45, Entry 119A, RG 226, NA; and 'Weekly Intelligence Summary' 7, 30/8/45, FO 1007/299, NAUK.

33   'Joint Weekly Intelligence Summary' 3, 20/7/45; 4, 27/7/45, both in FO 371/46611, NAUK; 7, 17/8/45, FO 371/46612, NAUK; 'Security Summary', 16/6/45, WO 204/831, NAUK; 'Weekly Intelligence Summary' 1, 11/7/45; 3, 25/7/45; 7, 30/8/45, all in FO 1007/299, NAUK; 'Joint Fortnightly Intelligence Summary' 3, 23/3/46, FO 1007/301, NAUK; and Dowe and Sokolov int., 8/8/45, Entry 119A, RG 226, NA.

34   *FRUS, 1945*, iv, 729; Warroom, London – Spearhead to AMZON, 19/6/45, IRR File XE 000417, RG 319, NA; Alexander to SHAEF Fwd for G-2, 18/5/45, WO 219/1602, NAUK; and 'Information Concerning the Refuge of the SS Jagdverband in the Ortler Massif (Northern Italy)', 21/5/45, WO 204/12439, NAUK.

35   *JNSV*, ii, 579–80; Gerlach int., 11/8/45, XL 13744, Entry 19, RG 226, NA; 'Information Received from Ostrich', 27/4/45; report on 'Ostrich', 30/4/45; Plum int., 21/5/45; and Michaelis to Holcomb, 4/5/45, all in CIANF, Entry 86, RG 263, NA.

36   Amouroux, 279; 'Bulletin du Renseignements', annex 3, 16/5/45; 'Maquis Allemands'; certificate for A. Gangl, 25/6/45, all in 7P 125, SHAT; and 'Information on Kommandos in Southern Germany', 14/5/45, Entry 119A, RG 226, NA.

37   *The New York Times*, 4/6/45; *The Washington Post*, 4/6/45; 'Information Received from Ostrich', 27/4/45; and Michaelis to Holcomb, 28/4/45, both in CIANF, Entry 86, RG 263, NA.

38   Schnorr int., 30/5/45, Entry 119A, RG 226, NA.

39   Gerlach int., 11/8/45, XL 13744, Entry 19, RG 226, NA; and 'Note de Renseignement: Renoue Edouard Joseph', 7/5/45, Entry 119A, RG 226, NA. For mention of a 'Doriotist' special unit encountered by the Allies at Heidelberg, where *Jagdkommando* 'Wissemberg' reassembled, see *L'Aurore*, 13/4/45.

40   Klaus-Dietmar Henke, *Die amerikanische Besatzung Deutschlands* (Munich, 1995), 947; 'SS Jagdverband SW CSHAF, 21 AGp, 15 Apr 45', vol. 10685, RG 24, Series 90, NAC; Gerlach int., 11/8/45, XL 13744, Entry 19, RG 226, NA; Doerr int., 27/3/45; 'Interrogation report on 1 officer and 15 EM of Jagdeinsatz Nord FPN 40478', 6/4/45; 'Jagdverband Groups in U.S. Uniforms', 6/4/45; 'Notes on the SS Jagdverbaende', 8/4/45; 'Preparation of Partisan Warfare', 8/4/45; 'SS Jagdverbande (Personalities)', 11/4/45; 'Bechmann int., 14/4/45, all in Entry 119A, RG 226, NA; Berndt int., 6/11/45; and 'Extract from III Corps G-2 Periodic Report 105', 26/3/45, both in IRR File ZF 011666, RG 319, NA.

41   *JNSV*, xxii, 286–87, 298; 'Summary of recent Information on SS-Jagdverband NW', 4/6/45; Keller int., 25/4/45, both in Entry 119A, RG 226, NA; and confession by Redel, 18/4/48, OMGUS ODI General Correspondence 080.4, RG 260, NA.

42   De Roo int., 28/5/45; and 'De Roo, Louis', 9/6/45, both in Entry 119A, RG 226, NA.

43   Olmes int., 18/6/45; 'Further List of GIS Personalities & Others', 3/6/45, both in Entry 119A, RG 226, NA; and 'CI News Sheet' 25, 13/7/45, WO 205/997, NAUK.

44   Herold to Officer in Charge, Camp 93(CI), 1/6/45, Entry 119A, RG 226, NA; and letter to the author from Wolfgang Herfurth, 7/12/92.

45   Van Cranenbroeck int., 17/4/45; Corloy int., 5/45; Olmes int., 18/6/45; 'Kraizizek, Walter Paul', 15/6/45; annex "A", 18/6/45; Kraizizek int., 10/45; 'Summary of Recent Information on SS-Jagdverband NW', 4/6/45; Schnorr int., 11/11/45, all in Entry 119A, RG 226, NA; and Kraizizek int., 10/8/45, 141745, Entry 16, RG 226, NA.

46   KO 1122, 22/4/45, UMC, r. 72, NAUK.

47   *HCIC*, xx, 16, NA; 12th AG to War Room, 9/5/45; Schuster/Roederer/Scharf/Kopp/Stohr int., 14/5/45; 'Further List of GIS Personalities & Others', 3/6/45; 'Dethier, Julius', 4/6/45; 'Summary of Recent Information on SS-Jagdverband NW', 4/6/45; 'Arrest Target List', 21/7/45, all in Entry 119A, RG 226, NA; 'Countersabotage Bulletin' 4, 17/5/45, IRR File XE 070687, RG 319, NA; and 'Saboteurs Allemands', 17/5/45, 7P 125, SHAT.

48   Geertz int., 21/7/45, Entry 119A, RG 226, NA.

49   Manfred Bornemann, *Die letzten Tage in der Festung Harz* (Clausthal-Zellerfeld, 1978), 87–88; and Charles Leach, *In Tornado's Wake* (Chicago, 1956), 186–87.

50   12th AG to War Room, 9/5/45; and Schuster/Roederer/Scharf/Kopp/Stohr int., 14/5/45, both in Entry 119A, RG 226, NA.

51   Gerlach int., 11/8/45, XL 13744, Entry 19, RG 226, NA; and 'Assassination of the Mayor of Aachen', IRR File XE 070687, RG 319, NA.

52   Jochen v. Lang, *Der Hitler-Junge – Baldur von Schirach* (Hamburg, 1988), 379; Peter Hüttenberger, *Die Gauleiter* (Stuttgart, 1969), 209–10; 'Amt III (SD Inland) RSHA', 30/9/45, ETO MIS-Y Sect. Special Interrogation Reports 1943–45, RG 338, NA; and Schuster/Roederer/Scharf/Kopp/Stohr int., 14/5/45, Entry 119A, RG 226, NA.

53   'Lehmann, Friedrich', 25/4/45, Entry 119A, RG 26, NA.

54   Rose, 247; and Whiting, *Werewolf*, 179.

55   Schäfer int., 18–23/5/45; 7–8/8/45; Löring int., 13/5/45; 29/5/45; and Beddingen int., 23/5/45, all in Entry 119A, RG 226, NA. British interrogators were suspicious when captured paratrooper-'Werewolves' told them of their connection with Neustrelitz, although the prisoners stridently denied any SS affiliation. When the British learned, however, that the *Jagdverbände* had been recruiting paratroopers at Neustrelitz, this information, they decided, 'provides the link between the Luftwaffe Fallschirmjäger and the SS Jagdverbände'. Pott int., 20/5/45, Entry 119A, RG 226, NA.

56   Skorzeny, *Wir Kämpften – Wir Verloren*, 179; and Mildner int., 11/9/45, Entry 119A, RG 226, NA.

57   Skorzeny, *Wir Kämpften – Wir Verloren*, 178–179, 184, 191; *DDRJNSV*, ii, 765; and 'GPG', 12/2/45; and 18/2/45, both in FO 898/187, NAUK.

58   'Information from: Huhn re: Karl Radl', IRR File XE 000417, RG 319, NA; and 'Summary of Recent Information on SS-Jagdverband NW', 4/6/45, Entry 119A, RG 226, NA.

59   *JNSV*, ii, 578, 602–05.

60   Pott int., 20 May 1945, Entry 119A, RG 226, NA.

61   *JNSV*, ii, 578, 580–85; and Hermann Riedel, *Halt! Schweizer Grenze!* (Konstanz, 1983), 279.

62   *JNSV*, xxii, 287–90.

63   Ibid., xix, 597–602, 604.

64   'Baumann Christian', 11/6/45, IRR File XE 013764, RG 319, NA; Scheidler int., 11/7/45, IRR File XE 000440, RG 319, NA; 'Zeidler interrogation report'; Dunker int., 25/5/45; Olmes int., all in Entry 119A, RG 226, NA.

65   Skorzeny, *Skorzeny's Special Missions*, 195; 'Translation: Train/Telephone Directory', 14/6/45, IRR File XE 000417, RG 319, NA; Olmes int.; 'Otto Skorzeny', 27/4/45; and 'Papadopulos, Panjotis', 23/7/45, both in Entry 119A, RG 226, NA.

66   Weissenrieber int., 11/5/45; and Weissenrieber int., 12/5/45, both in Entry 119A, RG 226, NA.

67   BT 9696, 7/4/45 (r. 69); and KO 1108, 22/4/45 (r. 72), UMC, NAUK.

68   Radl int., 28/5/45, Entry 119A, RG 226, NA.

69   Skorzeny, *Wir Kämpften – Wir Verloren*, 197.

70   Radl int., 4/6/45; and Radl int., 28/5/45, both in Entry 119A, RG 226, NA.

71   Höttl, 310; 'Notes on Mil Amt C and other Departments of RSHA', 11/9/45, WO 208/3620, NAUK; and 'Report on Interrogation of Walter Schellenberg', IRR File XE 001752, RG 319, NA. Julius Mader asserts that Kaltenbrunner issued the final directive for concentration of the *Jagdverbände*. Julius Mader, *Jagd nach dem Narbengesicht* (Berlin, 1963), 136.

72   Melita Maschmann, *Account Rendered* (London, 1964), 170; Höttl, 308; Rose, 311; Mader, *Jagd nach dem Narbengesicht*, 147–48; Girg int., 22/1/46, XL 41372, Entry 19, RG 226, NA; Radl int., 4/6/45; Radl int., 28/5/45; 'Jagdverband Sudost Group', 16/5/45; Dunker int., 25/5/45; 'Preliminary Report', 29/5/45; Pacher int.; 'Arrest Target List', 21/8/45, all in Entry 119A, RG 226, NA; 'CIR 4 – The German Sabotage Service', 23/7/45, IRR File XE 070687, RG 319, NA; and Skorzeny int., 19/5/45, IRR File XE 000417, RG 319, NA. For details on the Mitterberghütten depot, see 'Nipolit in New Forms', IRR File XE 070687, RG 319, NA; 'CI News Sheet' 29, 24/9/45, WO 205/997, NAUK; and 'Weekly Intelligence Summary' 7, 30/8/45, FO 1007/299, NAUK.

73   Ian Sayer and Douglas Botting, *Nazi Gold* (London, 1985), 43–44, 291; 'Leads Meriting Further Investigation in the matter of Oberfuhrer Wilhelm Spacil', 5/7/45, in *Covert Warfare*, xiv; Koch int., 15/5/45; Goettsch int., 4/7/45, both in Entry 119A, RG 226, NA; and Spacil int., 28/8/45, 15135, Entry 16, RG 226, NA.

74   Manfried Rauchensteiner, *Der Krieg in Österreich 1945* (Vienna, 1984), 344; Mader, *Jagd nach dem Narbengesicht*, 149; Girg int., 22 Jan. 1946, XL 41372, Entry 19, RG 226, NA; 'CIR 4 – The German Sabotage Service', 23/7/45, IRR File XE 070687, RG 319, NA; Skorzeny int., 19/5/45, IRR File 000417, RG 319, NA; 'Petter, Herbert', 29/5/45; and Radl int., 28/5/45, both in Entry 119A, RG 226, NA. For the 12th April meeting, see Kaltenbrunner int., 5/6/45 IRR File XE 000440, RG 319, NA.

75   Höttl, 310.

76   'Notes on Mil Amt C and other departments of RSHA', 11/9/45, WO 208/3620, NAUK.

77   'Spot Record on Obst. Georg Buntrock', 7/8/45, Entry 119A, RG 226, NA.

78   Höttl, 310.

79   'Report on Interrogation of Walter Schellenberg', IRR File XE 001752, RG 319, NA.

80   Goettsch int., 4/7/45, Entry 119A, RG 226, NA.

81   Pacher int., 1/7/45, Entry 119A, RG 226, NA; and Girg int., 22/1/46, XL 41372, Entry 19, RG 226, NA.

82   Höttl, 311; 'Meeting between Wirsing and Schellenberg end of April 1945', 25/7/45, CIANF, Entry 86, RG 263, NA; 'Sandberger, Martin', 29/5/45; Sandberger int., 8/7/45; 'Sandberger', 2/8/45; 'Monthly Summary' 4, 23/7/45; Waneck int., 11/8/45; Goettsch int., 4/7/45; 'Spot Report on Obst. Georg Buntrock', 7/8/45, all in Entry 119A, RG 226, NA; 'CIR 3 – Amt VI-E of the RSHA', 21/6/45, IRR File XE 000440, RG 319, NA; and 'Notes on Mil Amt C and other departments of RSHA', 11/9/45, WO 208–3620, NAUK.

83   Sayer and Botting, *Nazi Gold*, 24, 26–27, 28–38; Henriette von Schirach, *The Price of Glory* (London, 1960), pp. 92–93; Simon Wiesenthal, *The Murderers among Us* (New York, 1967), 85–95; Maschmann, 170; 'Diary prepared by Gretl Biesecker covering period 21 Apr–8 May', 5/7/45; Schiebel int., 5/7/45; Biesecker int., 5/7/45; Biesecker int., 5/7/45, all in *Covert Warfare*, xiv; Girg int., 22/1/46, XL 41377, Entry 19, RG 226, NA; Pacher int., 1/7/45; Lermer int., 4/5/45; 'Lemaire, Paul', 12/5/45; Schulz int.; 'Principes Fondamentoux de la Communaute Europeene [sic]'; 'Amt IIIB Underground Movement', 20/7/45; 'Adolf Wulf, official of Abt III Munich and Courier for Sonderkommando Renndorfer', all in Entry 119A, RG 229, NA; 'Amt III (SD Inland) RSHA', 30/9/45, ETO MIS-Y Sect. Special Interrogation Reports 1943–45, RG 338, NA; 'My Knowledge about the Communication Project of Amt III of the RSHA'; Kaltenbrunner int., 8/6/45, IRR File XE 000440, RG 319, NA; 'Intelligence Report', 25/6/45, XL 12705, Entry 19, RG 226, NA; 'CI News Sheet' 26, 30/7/45, WO 205/997, NAUK; and 'Joint Weekly Intelligence Summary' 1, 6/7/45, FO 371/46610, NAUK.

84   PF 601, 960/WR C3/A to 105 SCI Unit, 1/6/45, Entry 119A, RG 226, NA; and Zschunke int., CIANF, Entry 86, RG 263, NA.

85   Manfred Rauchensteiner, *Der Sonderfall* (Graz, 1979), 99–100; Peter Black, *Ernst Kaltenbrunner* (Princeton, 1984), 237–57; John Toland, *The Last 100 Days* (New York, 1976), 289–90; Rodney Minott, *The Fortress that Never Was* (New York, 1964), 41–42, 59–61; Neubacher, 194; Goettsch int., 24/7/45, in *Covert Warfare*, xiii; 'OSS Intelligence Activities with the Russians', 18/8/45, Records of the Joint Chiefs of Staff – Part I: 1942–45 – The European Theatre, r. 3; Kaltenbrunner int., 20/5/45; Kaltenbrunner int., 22/5/45; Kaltenbrunner int., 24/5/45; Kaltenbrunner int., 25/5/45; Kaltenbrunner int., 28/5/45; Kaltenbrunner int., 5/6/45; Kaltenbrunner int., 8/6/45; Kaltenbrunner int., 28/6/45; 'Arrest Report: Ernst Kaltenbrunner', 12/5/45; Spearhead, AMZON to War Room, 30/6/45; Scheidler int., 11/7/45, all in IRR File XE 000440, RG 319, NA; 'Progress Report in the Case of Schellenberg', 17/7/45, IRR File 001752, RG 319, NA; Schulz int.;

12th AG to War Room, 9/6/45; Waneck int., 29/6/45; 12th AG to War Room, 2/7/45; 'Summary of Traces – Spacil', 20/7/45; Goettsch int.; Waneck int., 11/8/45; 'Further on Hoettel, the Reported Split within the SS, and Alleged Desires to Make Peace with the West', all in Entry 119A, RG 226, NA; and 'Japanese Ambassador, Bad Gastein, Reports Conversation with Steengracht', 7/5/45, HW 1/3760, NAUK.

86   Goettsch int., 17/7/45, Entry 119A, RG 226, NA; and Report B-2551 pt., 21/4/45, 126098, Entry 16, RG 226, NA.

87   Toland, 639; Wiesenthal, 91; Höttl, 308–09; *Eichmann Interrogated* (London, 1983), 261–62; Goettsch int., 17/7/45; and 'Special Brief – Twelfth Army Group, SCI Det., Munich – dated 8 July 1945', both in Entry 119A, RG 226, NA.

88   Black, 258–60; Ralph Pearson, *Enroute to the Redoubt* (Chicago, 1958), iii, 230–31; Höttl, 312–13; *HCIC* xxvi, 78–79, NA; 12th AG to War Room, 9/6/45; 12th AG to War Room, 2/7/45, both in Entry 119A, RG 226, NA; Spearhead to Scarf, 3rd Army, 8/6/45; Kaltenbrunner int., 5/6/45; and 'Arrest Report: Kaltenbrunner, Ernst', 12/5/45, all in IRR File XE 000440, RG 319, NA.

89   Skorzeny, *Wir Kämpften – Wir Verloren*, 205–11; Maschmann, 174–75; Donald Taggert, *History of the Third Infantry Division* (Washington, 1947), 372–73; *HCIC* xxvi, 30, NA; *Manchester Guardian*, 16/5/45; *St. Louis Post-Dispatch*, 17/5/45; *Daily Express*, 18/5/45; *The New York Times*, 18/5/45; 'Petter, Herbert', 29/5/45; 'Radl, Karl', 28/5/45, both in Entry 119A, RG 226, NA; US 7th Army G-2 to 12th AG G-2, 17/5/45; 'Arrest Report: Skorzeny, Otto', 19/5/45; Skorzeny int., 19/5/45; 'Skorzeny, Otto', 12/9/46, all in IRR File XE 000417, RG 319, NA; 'Otto Skorzeny', 5/6/51; and 24/9/51, both in CIANF, Entry 86, RG 263, NA.

90   Maschmann, 170–73, 179. On 11 May 1945, SS bands attacked Hungarian troops guarding $25,000,000 worth of Hungarian state treasure, which was stored in a train near Bad Gastein. *Wingfoot* (Weinheim, 1945), 87, 92.

91   Skorzeny int., 19/5/45, IRR File XE 000417, RG 319, NA.

92   Maschmann, 172, 179; and 'Activity Report for week ending 16 June 1945', 18/6/45, CIANF, Entry 86, RG 263, NA.

93   Pearson, iii, 232–33; Schuermann int., 3/8/45; 'Preliminary Report', 29/5/45; Manderschied int., 5/9/45; 'Jagdverband Sudost Group', 16/5/45, all in Entry 119A, RG 226, NA; and 'CI News Sheet' 28, 9/9/45, WO 205/997, NAUK.

94   Skorzeny, *Wir Kämpften – Wir Verloren*, 206.

95   Karl Paetel, 'The Reign of the Black Order', in *The Third Reich* (London, 1955), 674.

96   'Meeting between Wirsing and Schellenberg end of April 1945', 25/7/45, CIANF, Entry 86, RG 263, NA.

97   Skorzeny, *Lebe gefährlich*, 173; and 'Kraizizek, Walter Paul', 15/6/45, Entry 119A, RG 226, NA.

98   KO 1886, 3/5/45, HW 1/3747, NAUK.

99   An Allied assessment noted that 'the local population, though still dazed by the turn of events, appears to be generally friendly and not likely to lend much support at present to any large-scale subversive plans'. 'Joint Weekly Intelligence Summary' 1, 6/7/45, FO 371/46610, NAUK.

EPILOGUE AND CONCLUSION

1   'CI News Sheet' 24, 27/6/45, WO 205/997, NAUK.

2   Olmes int., 18/6/45; Prelogar and Morael int., 17/3/45; Morael/Prelogar/Claes/Maggen int., 20/3/45; Prelogar int., 1/4/45, all in Entry 119A, RG 226, NA; and 'Martin Oberlander', 13/11/47, IRR File XE 000417, RG 319, NA.

3   *Weser Kurier*, 19/4/47; *Neue Württembergische Zeitung*, 22/4/47; letter to the author from Wolfgang Herfurth, 12/7/92; Olmes int., Entry 119A, RG 226, NA; and 'Hans Günther Redel', 18/4/48, OMGUS ODI General Correspondence 080.4, RG 260, NA.

4   'Theatre Commander's Weekly Staff Conference' 28, 2 July 1946; 'Weekly Intelligence Summary' 62, 19/9/46, both in State Dept. Decimal Files 1945–49, 740.00119 Control (Germany), RG 59, NA; 'Skorzeny, Otto', 21/12/46; 31/1/47, both in IRR File 000417, RG 319, NA; 'Security Arrest Report: John, Werner', 12/6/46; 'Translation Organization Boheme', 7/10/46; 'File', 29/10/46; 'Operation Brandy', 6/11/46; BAOR Intelligence Division to USFET G-2, 27/12/46; 'Operation "Brandy"', 7/1/47; 25/1/47; CIB to USDIC signed Wallenborn, 31/3/47; and 'Termination Instructions for Operation Brandy', 18/4/47, all in IRR File ZF 011666, RG 319, NA; 'Skorzeny, Otto', 20/1/47; 24/3/47, both in IRR File XE 000417, RG 319, NA.

5   Lee, 40–41; *Stars and Stripes*, 25/6/47; 'Otto Skorzeny', 27/9/46; 'D-417 Skorzeny, Otto', 21/10/46; 'Operation Brandy', 15/1/47; 'Skorzeny, Otto', 20/1/47; 27/1/47; 25/3/47; Eucom Deputy Director of Intelligence to Deputy Director, Judge Advocate for War Crimes, 7708th War Crimes Group, 23/5/47; 'Otto Skorzeny', 29/7/47; 5/8/47; 13/8/47; 'Weissner, Hilde', 10/8/48; 'Otto Skorzeny', 16/9/48, all in IRR File XE 000417, RG 319, NA; and 'Possible Underground Organization of Former Members of Skorzeny's Jagdverbaende and SS', IRR File ZF 011666, RG 319, NA.

6   *Stars and Stripes*, 10/9/47; 11/9/47; 31/7/48; *Kesseler Zeitung*, 28/7/48; and 'Skorzeny kein Kriegsverbrecher', 10/9/47, IRR File 000417, RG 319, NA.

7   Note the comments of Colonel Clifford Merrill, provost marshal of the Dachau prison compound: 'I congratulated old Skorzeny on getting out of that [trial], because our sympathies were with him… They were fighting just like we were. We were doing the same thing.' <http://www.tankbooks.com/amile/merrill/merrill1.htm>, as of 7/4/98.

8   Skorzeny to Potter, 16/9/47; 'Otto Skorzeny', 23/12/47; Skorzeny int., 19/2/48; 'Otto Skorzeny', 30/4/48; Skorzeny to Freudel, 26/7/48; 'Otto Skorzeny', 5/8/48; and 12/8/48, all in IRR File XE 000417, RG 319, NA.

9   Genrikh Borovik and Phillip Knightley, *The Philby Files* (Boston, 1994), 246–47; and Lee, 42–43.

10 *The New York Times*, 22/7/49; 27/7/49; *Hessische Nachrichten*, 29/7/48; *Giessner Freie Presse*, 29/7/48; 31/7/48; *Marburg Presse*, 30/7/48; *Der Spiegel*, 14/7/49; 'Weissner, Hilde', 10/8/48; 'Special Intelligence Report', 15/10/48; 'Alleged Skorzeny Movement', 28/10/48; Smith to PCO, 4/1/49; 7970th CIC Group to RFDAP, 2/1/49; 'Skorzeny, Otto', 31/1/49; 7970th CIC Group to Ops Branch, 4/2/49; 'Otto Skorzeny', 8/2/49; CIC Eucom to CIC Region IX, 21/2/49; Kelly to L'Heureaux, 11/3/49; 'Skorzeny, Otto', 31/3/49; 17/6/49, all in IRR File 000417, RG 319, NA; 'Otto Skorzeny', 11/5/51; and Deputy Director, Plans to Farrell, both in CIANF, Entry 86, RG 263, NA.

11 Lee, 43–45; and 'Activities of Otto Skorzeny', 11/10/51, CIANF, Entry 86, RG 263, NA.

12 W. Stanley Moss, 'The Quest for Skorzeny', *The Listener*, 28/6/51; *Stars and Stripes*, 15/2/49; and 16/2/49; and 'Nazi Activities: Colonel Otto Skorzeny', 17/2/50, CIANF, Entry 86, RG 263, NA.

13 Wiesenthal, 82; *Die Abendzeitung*, 7/10/49; *Süddeutsche Zeitung*, 8–9/10/49; CIC Liaison Office Heidelberg to 7970th CIC Group, 15/8/49; CIC Group Region IV to 7970th CIC Group, 7/10/49; 7970th CIC Group to Region IV, 7/10/49; JOG to Larned, 24/10/49; 'Otto Skorzeny, Alias Rolf Steinbauer', 5/11/49; and 7970th CIC Group to CIC Liaison Office Heidelberg, 8/11/49, all in IRR File XE 000417, RG 319, NA.

14 Sayer and Botting, *Nazi Gold*, 46–47; Nicholas Goodrick-Clarke, *Hitler's Priestess* (New York, 1998), 181, 186; Lee, 62, 109; Kurt Tauber, *Beyond Eagle and Swastika* (Middletown, 1967), i, 241; *New York Times*, 2/3/54; *Der Spiegel*, 14/7/75, 108; *Washington Post*, 8/7/75; 'Possible Underground Organization of Former Members of Skorzeny's Jagdverbaende and SS', IRR File ZF 011666, RG 319, NA; 'Skorzeny, Otto', 16/6/52, IRR File XE 000417, RG 319, NA; Chief FDW to Chief, 18/1/51; Chief to Chief, Foreign Division W, 2/3/51; 'Otto Skorzeny', 5/6/51; 'SS Colonel Otto Skorzeny', 28/6/51; 'Otto Skorzeny', 24/9/51; 'Skorzeny, Otto, Former Abwehr Personality', 26/6/52; 'Activities of Otto Skorzeny', 13/5/53; 'Recent Activities of Otto Skorzeny', 20/8/54; American Embassy, Madrid to Department of State, 9/9/54, all in CIANF, Entry 86, RG 263, NA.

15 Richard Deacon, *The French Secret Service* (London, 1990), 170; and Deputy Director, Plans to the Secretary of State, 30/6/53, CIANF, Entry 86, RG 263, NA.

16 Miles Copeland, *The Game of Nations* (London, 1969), 87–88; Goodrick-Clarke, 175–77; Lee, 43–44, 76, 133–35, 153–54; Mary Ellen Reese, *General Reinhard Gehlen: The CIA Connection* (Fairfax, 1990), 43; *Letters*, Report 1/60, 5/2/60, 11; Report 2–3/60, 7/4/60, 12; *The New York Times*, 13/1/54; 'Skorzeny, Otto', 22/3/49; 7970th CIC Group to Ops Branch, 12/4/49; 'Skorzeny, Otto, Rumored to Have Been in Salzburg', 20/11/50; 'Skorzeny, Otto', 16/6/52; 'Barnes, Sidney U. Major USAR, O-116600(S)', 18/10/55, all in IRR File XE 000417, RG 319, NA; Berger int., IRR File 000440, RG 319, NA; Pullach to Special Operations, 6/2/51; Chief Karlsruhe to Chief, Foreign Division M, 30/3/51; Special Operations to Karlsruhe, Pullach, 11/4/51; 'Otto Skorzeny', 17/4/51; Berlin to Special Operations, 23/4/51; 'SS Colonel Otto Skorzeny', 28/6/51; 'Activities of Otto Skorzeny in Spain', 16/7/51; 'Otto Skorzeny', 11/7/51; 'Biographic Notes on Skorzeny'; Karlsruhe to Special Operations, 15/10/51; Karlsruhe to Chief FDM, 30/11/51; Hoover to Wyman, 6/12/51; EE/SC to DDP; Chief, Karlsruhe to Chief, Foreign Division M, 3/1/51; Chief, Foreign Division M to Chief, Frankfurt, 16/1/52; Chief FDM to Chief, 1/2/52; 'Soviet Intelligence Service said to be Using Former Abwehr (Military Security), SS (Nazi Elite Guard), Sicherheitsdienst (SS Security Service) and Gestapo', 10/6/52; 'Skorzeny, Otto, Former Abwehr Personality', 26/6/52; 'Comments on Report Given by Gunther Buhn Regarding Otto Skorzeny', 13/1/53; 'Alleged clandestine group engaged in returning former Waffen SS officers to Germany, and planning an anti-American riot in Tehran', 2/3/53; SR Rep Salzburg to Director, CIA, 18/4/53; 'Activities of Otto Skorzeny', 13/5/53; Deputy Director, Plans to the Secretary of State, 30/6/53; 'Skorzeny', 15/7/54; Hoover to Director, CIA, 29/8/55; note on remarks by Skorzeny, 6/10/55; Deputy Director, Plans to Papich, 6/12/55; 'Otto Skorzeny', 17/8/60; Deputy Director for Plans to Deputy Assistant Secretary for Security, Department of State, 20/2/67, all in CIANF, Entry 86, RG 263, NA. For the case of Alfred Skorzeny, see Karner, 34–36.

17 Lee, 61–62; *France-Soir*, 16/11/50; *Morgen-Tidningen*, 18/11/50; 'Col. Otto Skorzeny, Former Aide to Heinrich Himmler', 1/12/50; 'Biographic Notes on Skorzeny'; HICOG, Frankfurt to Department of State, 21/2/51; Pullach to Special Operations, 6/2/51; Chief to Chief, Foreign Division M, 20/3/51; 'Controversy between

Otto Skorzeny and General Hans Doerr', 27/3/51; Chief to Chief, Foreign Division W, 6/4/51; 'SS Colonel Otto Skorzeny', 28/6/51; Chief, Karlsruhe to Chief, Foreign Division M, 30/3/51; 'Otto Skorzeny', 24/9/51; 'Future Plans of Otto Skorzeny', 27/9/51; 'Comments on the Political and Military Situation, and the Consequences Thereof'; 'Activities of Otto Skorzeny', 11/10/51; Deputy Director, Plans to Farrell; 'Colonel Otto Skorzeny', 13/5/53; 'Activities of Otto Skorzeny', 13/5/53, all in CIANF, Entry 86, RG 263, NA.

18   McCloy to Secretary of State, 26/1/51, CIANF, Entry 86, RG 263, NA. See also Dulles to Assistant Director for Policy Coordination and Assistant Director for Special Operations, 7/2/51, CIANF, Entry 86, RG 263, NA.

19   Alistair Horne, *Back to Power* (London, 1955), 58; Lee, 61, 429; Tauber, i, 135; *Bremer Nachrichten*, 8/8/51; *The New York Herald Tribune*, 19/11/54; 'Skorzeny Otto aka Rolf Steinbauer', 10/8/54, IRR File XE 000417, RG 319, NA; 'Cr. Werner Naumann', 1/5/51; 'Activities of General Skorzeny', 13/5/51; Chief, Karlsruhe to Chief, Foreign Division M, 30/3/51; Deputy Director, Plans to Farrell; 'Comments on the Political and Military Situation, and the Consequences Thereof'; 'Some Notes on the Present State of Mind of the People of Western Germany'; 'Otto Skorzeny', 24/9/51; 'Activities of Otto Skorzeny', 11/10/51; 'Skorzeny's Activities', 27/12/51; 'Skorzeny's Neo-Nazi Apparat in Western Germany'; 'Skorzeny's Alleged Austrian Representative', 1/4/52; 'Dr. Werner Naumann', 16/2/53; and 'Memorandum of Conversation', 17/9/53, all in CIANF, Entry 86, RG 263, NA.

20   Simpson, 249–52; Lee, 121, 125–26, 128–32, 135–36, 142; Copeland, *Game of Nations*, 88; Miles Copeland, *The Game Player* (London, 1989), 181; Andrew and Leslie Cockburn, *Dangerous Liaison* (New York, 1991), 53; John Loftus and Mark Aarons, *The Secret War against the Jews* (New York, 1994), 257; *Pueblo*, 2/4/53; *Le Journal d'Égypte*, 14/6/53; 'Otto Skorzeny's Efforts to Supply Arms for Egypt'; 'German Military Experts', 16/4/53; 'Memorandum of Conversation', 25/4/53; 'Otto Skorzeny Mission to Egypt', 25/4/53; 'Guerrilla Warfare Training: Centers under German Direction', 28/4/53; 'Brief file notes on Otto Skorzeny, per our conversation of today', 14/5/53; Deputy Director, Plans to the Secretary of State, 30/6/53; 'Return to Egypt of Colonel Otto Skorzeny', 2/7/53; 'Otto Skorzeny Again in Egypt', 15/6/53; 'Proposed Imminent Return to Egypt of Colonel Otto Skorzeny for Purpose of Training Commandos', 30/7/53; 'Otto Skorzeny', 13/8/53; 'Dr. W. Beisner, Probably Otto Skorzeny's Representative in Egypt', 10/9/53; 'Memorandum of Conversation', 17/9/53; Deputy Director, Plans to Farrell; 'Otto Skorzeny', 'Guerrilla Training', 25/5/55; Deputy Director for Plans to Deputy Assistant Secretary for Security, Department of State, 20/2/67, all in CIANF, Entry 86, RG 263, NA.

21   'Recent Activities of Otto Skorzeny', 20/8/54; and 'Skorzeny Denies Yossef Kidnap Plot', 26/1/56, both in CIANF, Entry 86, RG 263, NA.

22   Lee, 142, 144; *La Croix*, 22/6/56; *Le Monde*, 19/10/56; and 'Arms Traffic to Algerian Rebels', 25/1/57, CIANF, Entry 86, RG 263, NA.

23   Lee, 146, 152, 169–170, 186, 190, 431; Goodrick-Clarke, 183; Ian Black and Benny Morris, *Israel's Secret Wars* (New York, 1991), 198; Yossi Melman and Dan Raviv, *The Imperfect Spies* (London, 1989), 140–41; Walter De Bock, *Les Plus Belles Années d'une Génération* (Berchem, 1976), 59; *The New York Times*, 10/11/58; 4/2/63; 28/4/65; 8/7/75; *The Washington Post*, 26/2/61; 8/7/75; 'SS Colonel Otto Skorzeny', 28/6/51; 'Otto Skorzeny', 7/2/52; 17/8/60; Director, CIA to Munich, 5/1/61; 'Otto Skorzeny', 25/1/62; 'Arrest Order against Otto Skorzeny, Former Nazi SS Colonel of Austria', 2/2/63; AmEmbassy Madrid to Department of State, 27/2/63; Deputy Director for Plans to Deputy Assistant Secretary for Security, Department of State, 20/2/67; and 'Otto Skorzeny', 24/11/71, all in CIANF, Entry 86, RG 263, NA.

24   Lee, 200.

25   Höttl, 311; 'Skorzeny's Trip in Germany', 28/7/51; and 'Activities of Otto Skorzeny', 11/10/51, both in CIANF, Entry 86, RG 263, NA.

26   Sayer and Botting, *America's Secret Army*, 332; 'Girg, Walter, Reported US Informant', 9/12/48; 'Girg, Walter'; Turnip, Lapin to Crusade, 30/4/45; 'Activity Report for Week ending 16 June 1945', 18/6/45; 'Ludwig Nebel@Leo Neumann@"Ostrich"', 28/1/47; [—] to Washf, 7/2/47; Heidelberg to Special Operations, 11/4/47; Chief to Chief, Foreign Branch W, 7/1/49; and Chief, FBW to Chief, 4/2/49, all in CIANF, Entry 86, RG 263, NA.

27   Pullach to Director, 16/11/56; note on Ney; Chief, Pullach to Chief, Germany, 20/11/56; and Chief, Vienna to Chief, EE, 12/4/60, all in CIANF, Entry 86, RG 263, NA.

28   <http://medlem.spray.se/uddasverige/palme.html>, as of 29/04/03.

29   SR Rep Salzburg to Director, CIA, 18/4/53, CIANF, Entry 86, RG 263, NA.

30   'Deva, Xhafer', 24/1/63, CIANF, Entry 86, RG 263, NA.

31   'C' to Cavendish-Bentinck, 16/12/44, Entry 119A, RG 226, NA.

32   Henry Rousso, 'L'Épuration en France: Une histoire inachevée', *Vingtième Siècle* 33 (1992), 103.

33   Pavone, *Una guerra civile*; Rab Bennett, *Under the Shadow of the Swastika* (New York, 1999); and Tzvetan Todorov, *A French Tragedy* (Hanover, 1998).

34   A.J.P. Taylor, *Origins of the Second World War* (London, 1961), 102–03.

35   Warlimont, 471; Hans-Georg von Studnitz, *Als Berlin brannte* (Stuttgart, 1963), 196; and *AdAP*, series E, viii. See also comments by Schellenberg and Canaris, quoted in Lee, 20–21.

36   Maschmann, 170; and 'General Situation Report' 2, 15/7–1/9/45, OMGUS AG Security Classified Decimal File 1945–49, 350.09 (Intelligence General), RG 260, NA.

37   *FRUS, 1945*, iv, 1131.

38   Tony Smith, 'New Bottles for New Wine', *Diplomatic History* 24 (2000), 569–74.

39   *Le Petit Parisien*, 3/2/45; 20/3/45; *St. Louis Post-Dispatch*, 28/4/45; James Chutter, *Captivity Captive* (London, 1954), 215; *Hitler Directs His War*, 131–32; 'Japanese Ambassador, Berlin, Reports German Proposal to Negotiate with Russia', 5/4/45, HW 1/3678, NAUK; 'ND' 1673, 2/2/45; and 1682, 13/2/45, both in BC, Robbins Library.

40   Sartorius int.; Kissel int., 28/6/45; 'Report of Traces – Horst Kopkow', 24/7/45, all in Entry 119A, RG 226, NA. For the case of a Polish Gestapo agent sent behind Allied lines disguised as an operative of the Soviet intelligence service, see 'Jerzy Baldt', 18/6/45, Entry 119A, RG 226, NA.

41   'GPG', 6/11/44; 18/12/44; 22/1/45; 28/1/45; and 19/3/45, all in FO 898/187, PRO.

42   John Wheeler-Bennett and Anthony Nicholls, *The Semblance of Peace* (London, 1972), 294; Thomas, 504–05; and Spencer Warren, 'A Philosophy of International Relations', in *Churchill's 'Iron Curtain' Speech Fifty Years Later* (Columbia, 1999), 99.

43   'CI Report' 3, 6/2/45, vol. 16387, RG 24, Series 90, NAC; and 'CI Report' 17, 11/2/45, vol. 10706, RG 226, Series 90, NAC.

44   Ministry of Foreign Affairs, Berlin to all Stations, 143527, 12/4/45, HW 12/313, NAUK.

45   Bradley Smith and Elena Agarossi, *Operation Sunrise* (New York, 1979), 54–58, 89–124; and 'Statement by Schellenberg re Wolff', IRR File XE 001752, RG 319, NA. For propaganda appeals, see 'GPG', 30/4/45, FO 898/187, NAUK.

46   Greene and Massignani, 229.

47   'Intelligence Summary' 1, 13/2/47, State Dept. Decimal File 1945–49, 740.00119 Control (Germany), RG 59, NA.

48   *Die Welt*, 14/2/70.

49   Tauber, ii, 1109; Lee, 61; Goodrick-Clarke, 183; Chief, Karlsruhe to Chief, Foreign Division M, 20/3/51; 'SS Colonel Otto Skozeny', 28/6/51; 'Latest Interview with and Personalities connected with Otto Skorzeny', 21/9/51; 'Interview between Rumanian Iron Guard Leader Horia Sima and [—]', 31/10/51; and 'Further Activities of Otto Skorzeny', 5/12/51, all in CIANF, Entry 86, RG 263, NA.

50   Chief, Karlsruhe to Chief, Foreign Division M, 14/6/51; FDY (1–2) to State, Army, Navy, Air, JCS, SICDEF, ONI, OCI, AFSA, CIA, 25/9/51; Hoover to Kirkpatrick, 15/1/52; 'Activities of Otto Skorzeny', 28/9/51; 'German Nationalist and Neo-Nazi Activities in Argentina', 31/5/55, all in CIANF, Entry 86, RG 263, NA.

51   Tauber, ii, 1096–97, 1104–06; Lee, 169–76, 180–82; and Goodrick-Clarke, 183.

52   *The New York Times*, 17/7/75; and *The Washington Post*, 17/7/75.

53   Paul Wilkinson, *The New Fascists* (London, 1983), 66.

54   Lee, 188–89, 203, 336–37.

Bibliography

ARCHIVES

Archives de la Savoie, Chambéry
109–67 CAB K; 132–67 CAB K

Archives Départementales des Alpes-de-Haute-Provence, Digne
0011 W0002; 0042 W0040; 0042 W0011

Archives Nationales, Paris
F/1a; F/1cIII

Archivio Centrale dello Stato, Rome
PCM Segreterie Burroca (1943–45)
RSI Segretaria Particolare del Duce – Carteggio Riservato

British Library of Political and Economic Science (Robbins Library), London
Bramstedt Collection, PID 'News Digests'

Bundesarchiv:
Abteilung MA (Bundesmilitärarchiv), Freiburg im Breisgau
RH 2; RH 15; RH 19; RH 19II; RW 4

Abteilung R, Berlin-Lichterfelde
NS 19; NS 19neu; R 6; R 58; R 62; R 70

Lastenausgleichsarchiv des Bundesarchivs, Bayreuth
Ost-Dokumente

Stiftung Parteien und Massenorganisationen der DDR, Berlin-Lichterfelde
NY 4034

Imperial War Museum, London
Office of US Chief Counsel, Evidence Division, Interrogation Branch
Office of US Chief Counsel, Subsequent Proceedings Division, Interrogation Branch

National Archives of Canada, Ottawa
RG 24, Series 90

National Archives of the United Kingdom, Kew Gardens, London
FO 371; FO 898, PID 'German Propaganda and the German', 1944–1945; FO 1007; HS 4; HS 5; HW 1; HW
19; HW 47; WO 201; WO 202; WO 204; WO 205; WO 208; WO 219

Service Historique de l'Armée de Terre, Vincennes, Paris
7P 125

US National Archives, College Park, Maryland
RG 59; RG 165; RG 226; RG 260; RG 263; RG 319; RG 338
History of the Counter Intelligence Corps (Baltimore, 1959)

MICROFILM COLLECTIONS

Berlin Document Center Microfilm, RG 242, NA
Microcopy T-77: Records of the *Oberkommando der Wehrmacht* (OKW), RG 242, NA
Microcopy T-78: Records of the *Oberkommando des Heeres* (OKH), RG 242, NA
Microcopy T-175: Record of the Reich Leader-SS and Chief of the German Police, RG 242, NA
Microcopy T-311: Records of German Field Commands – Army Groups, RG 242, NA
Papers Relating to the Allied High Command (East Ardsley, Wakefield, 1983)
Records of the Joint Chiefs of Staff – Part 1: 1942–1945 – European Theatre (Frederick, 1981)
Ultra Microfilm Collection, 1944–1945, NAUK

PUBLISHED DOCUMENT COLLECTIONS

Akten zur deutschen Auswärtigen Politik. Göttingen, 1966–, Series E
Covert Warfare. New York, 1989
DDR-Justiz und NS-Verbrechen. Amsterdam, 2002–
Documents of Polish-German Relations, 1939–1945. London, 1967
Documents of the Expulsion of the Germans from East Central Europe. Bonn, 1954–1961
Foreign Office Weekly Political Intelligence Summaries. Millwood, 1983
Foreign Relations of the United States, 1945. Washington, 1967
Foreign Relations of the United States, 1944. Washington, 1966
Foreign Relations of the United States, 1946. Washington, 1969
Hitler: Reden und Proklamationen 1932–1945. ed. Max Domarus. Munich, 1965
Justiz und NS-Verbrechen. Amsterdam, 1969–
Pogranichnye Voiska SSSR 1945–1950. Moscow, 1975
Pogranichnye Voiska SSSR v Velikoi Otechestvennoi Voine 1942–1945. Moscow, 1976
Operation Slaughterhouse. Philadelphia, 1970
UPA v Svitli Nimetskykh Dokumentiv. Toronto, 1983–
World War II German Military Studies. New York, 1979
The Trial of Dragoljub-Draza Mihailovic. Belgrade, 1946

INTERVIEWS AND CORRESPONDENCE

Wolfgang Herfurth, 16 February 1992; 12 July 1992; 7 December 1992
Yetven Shtendera, 25 October 1988

MAJOR NEWSPAPERS

Le Figaro	*Morgen-Tidningen*	*Süddeutsche Zeitung*
L'Humanité	*Neue Zürcher Zeitung*	*The Times*
Izvestia	*New York Times*	*Völkischer Beobachter*
Libération	*Pravda*	*Washington Post*
Manchester Guardian	*Das Schwarze Korps*	
Le Monde	*Stars and Stripes*	

PRINCIPAL ARTICLES

Biddiscombe, Perry. 'The Last White Terror: The Maquis Blanc and its Impact in Liberated France, 1944–1945', *The Journal of Modern History* 73, no. 4 (Dec. 2001).
— 'Prodding the Russian Bear: Pro-German Resistance in Romania, 1944–1945', *European History Quarterly* 23 (1993).
— 'Unternehmen Zeppelin: The Deployment of SS Saboteurs and Spies in the Soviet Union, 1942–1945', *Europe-Asia Studies* 52, no. 6 (2000).
Burds, Jeffrey. 'The Early Cold War in Soviet West Ukraine, 1944–1948', Carl Beck Papers no. 1505. Pittsburgh, 2001.
Constantiniu, Florin. 'Victoria Insurectiei din August 1944 si Falimental Politic Definitiv al Garzii de Fier', *Revista de Istorie* 32, no. 8 (1979).
Conti, Giuseppe. 'La RSI e l'attività del fascismo clandestino nell'Italia liberata dal settembre 1943 all'aprile 1945', *Storia Contemporanea* 10 (1979).

Kajcev, Naum and Ivanka Nedeva, 'A Minor Affair or an Important Factor? (IMRO Groupings in Bulgaria after the Second World War)', *Bulgarian Historical Review* 26, nos. 3–4 (1998).

Korovin, V.V. and V.I. Shibalin. 'Gitlerovskii Abwehr Terpit Porazhenie', *Novaia i Noveishaia Istoriya* 12, no. 5 (Sept.–Oct. 1968).

Laurent, Gotti. 'Skorzeny à Malmedy', *Malmedy-Folklore* 57 (1997/98).

Luburic, Vjekoslav. 'The End of the Croatian Army', in *Operation Slaughterhouse*. eds. John Prcela and Stanko Guldesku. Philadelphia, 1970.

Moss, W. Stanley. 'The Quest for Skorzeny', *The Listener*, 28 June 1951.

Potichnyi, Peter. 'The Ukrainian Insurgent Army (UPA) and the German Authorities', in *German-Ukrainian Relations in Historical Perspective*. eds. Hans-Joachim Torke and John Paul Hinka. Edmonton, 1994.

Sevin, Dieter. 'Operation Scherhorn', *Military Review* 46, no. 3 (March 1966).

Weingartner, James. 'Otto Skorzeny and the Law of War', *The Journal of Military History* 55 (April 1991).

Wheeler, Mark. 'White Eagles and White Guards: British Perceptions of Anti-Communist Insurgency in Yugoslavia in 1945', *Slavonic and East European Review* 66, no. 3 (1988).

PRINCIPAL BOOKS

Armstrong, John. *Ukrainian Nationalism*. Englewood, 1990.

— *Ukrainian Nationalism, 1939–1945*. New York, 1955.

Biddiscombe, Perry. *Werwolf!*. Toronto, 1998.

Black, Peter. *Ernst Kaltenbrunner*. Princeton, 1984.

Bower, Tom. *The Red Web*. London, 1989.

Chastrusse, Jean, René Garnier and Louis Vaux. *Le dernier sursaut nazi en Corrèze*. Tulle, 1990.

Cookridge, E.H. *Gehlen: Spy of the Century*. New York, 1971.

Daumantis, Juozos. *Fighters for Freedom*. New York, 1975.

Fatu, Mihai and Ion Spalatelu. *Garda de Fier: Organizatie Terorista de Tip Fascist*. Bucharest, 1971.

Foley, Charles. *Commando Extraordinary*. London, 1954.

Gehlen, Reinhard. *The Service*. New York, 1972.

Gellermann, Günther. *Moskau ruft Heeresgruppe Mitte….* Koblenz, 1988.

Greene, Jack and Allesandro Massignani. *The Black Prince and the Sea Devils*. Cambridge, 2004.

Höttl, Wilhelm. *The Secret Front*. New York, 1954.

Infield, Glenn. *Skorzeny: Hitler's Commando*. New York, 1981.

Korbonski, Stefan. *The Polish Underground State*. New York, 1978.

Lee, Martin. *The Beast Reawakens*. Boston, 1997.

Loftus, John. *The Belarus Secret*. New York, 1982.

Lucas, James. *Kommando*. New York, 1985.

Lukkari, Matti. *Asekätkentä*. Helsinki, 1984.

Mader, Julius. *Hitlers Spionagegenerale sagen aus*. Berlin, 1971.

— *Jagd nach dem Narbengesicht*. Berlin, 1963.

Milazzo, Matteo. *The Chetnik Movement & the Yugoslav Resistance*. Baltimore, 1975.

Minott, Rodney. *The Fortress that Never Was*. New York, 1964.

Neubacher, Hermann. *Sonderauftrag Südost 1940–1945*. Göttingen, 1956.

Pisanò, Georgio. *Storia della Guerra Civile in Italia (1943–1945)*. Milan, 1965.

Reinerth, Karl and Fritz Cloos. *Zur Geschichte der Deutschen in Rumänien 1935–1945*. Bad Tölz, 1988.

Remeikis, Thomas. *Opposition to Soviet Rule in Lithuania, 1945–1980*. Chicago, 1980.

Rose, Arno. *Werwolf. Eine Dokumentation 1944/45*. Stuttgart, 1980.

Schellenberg, Walter. *Memoiren*. Cologne, 1956.

Siemaszko, Zbigniew. *Narodowe Siły Zbrojne*. Odnowa, 1982.

Skorzeny, Otto. *La Guerre Inconnue*. Paris, 1975.

— *Lebe gefährlich*. Königswinter, 1973.

— *Skorzeny's Special Missions*. London, 1957.

— *Wir Kämpften – Wir Verloren*. Königswinter, 1973.

Stahl, P.W. *'Geheimgeschwader' KG 200*. Stuttgart, 1980.

Stephen, Robert. *Stalin's Secret War*. Lawrence, 2004.

Tauber, Kurt. *Beyond Eagle and Swastika*. Middletown, 1967.

Tomasevich, Jozo. *The Chetniks*. Stanford, 1975.

Vanadzins, Ints. *Starp Sarkano un Melno*. Riga, 2001.

Whiting, Charles. *Skorzeny*. New York, 1972.

Index

264, 282, 284, 287, 288, 289,
290, 293, 295, 309, 310, 311,
314, 330, 351
Frontaufklärung units (FAK) 9, 10,
11, 17, 36–38, 40, 54, 58, 59,
64, 66, 69, 79, 86, 88, 95, 96,
98, 108, 110, 113, 120, 132,
140, 141, 155, 159, 160, 166,
167, 177, 182, 189, 190, 193,
203, 205, 207, 274, 304, 305,
313, 315, 329, 331, 333, 334,
335, 356
FAK 102 333
FAK 103 68–69, 83
FAK 104 333
FAK 105 72
FAK 120 203, 333
FAK 130 203, 268, 333
FAK 144 315
FAK 201 108, 109, 153, 154,
166, 167, 171, 173, 174, 175,
176, 177, 181, 182, 183, 188,
190, 193
FAK 202 48, 58, 62, 73–74,
75–76, 77, 78, 80, 98, 99, 101,
118, 334–35; *Einheit* 'Schill'
334–35
FAK 203 58, 62, 66, 83, 86,
96–97
FAK 204 58, 61, 82, 97–98, 324
FAK 205 73, 107–08, 117
FAK 206 48, 107, 108, 109,
116–17, 120, 121, 138
FAK 210 204, 205, 254, 266,
267, 270
FAK 211 203–04, 205, 208,
211, 213, 214, 233, 238, 241,
243–44, 253
FAK 212 58, 98–99, 104,
108, 109, 110, 204, 207–08,
331–32
FAK 213 204–05, 267–68,
284–85, 291–92, 299–300,
303–04, 306, 310, 312, 313;
'*Teilgruppe Norwegen*' 315;
Zersetzungspropaganda
element 299–300
FAK 305 79
FAK 307 285, 333
FAK 311 159
FAK 313 203, 252
Trupp 128 182
Trupp 212 86, 87
Trupp 214 117, 186
Trupp 215 117–18;
Überrollungskommando
'Lovasci' 117–18
Trupp 216 193–94
Trupp 218 111

Trupp 219 109
Trupp 221 109, 155
Trupp 249 344
Trupp 255 238, 243
Trupp 257 233
Trupp 260 291, 304
Trupp 261 315
Trupp 262 331, 333
Trupp 263 285
Trupp 363 296
'Edelweiss' (*Sonderkommando*)
110–12, 368
Frost 273
Fruska Gora (training camp)
107, 114–15, 150
Fucker, Karl 52, 352

Gambke, Gotthard 58, 110, 111,
331
'Gara' (Operation) 182, 185–86
Gasparovic 195–86
Gehlen, Reinhard 39, 46, 95–96,
365
'General Plan for 1945' 12, 13, 31
Georgiev, Ivan 154
Gerhard, Reinhardt 34, 57, 330
Gerken, Richard 204, 268,
284–85, 291
Gerlach, Hans 199, 200, 202, 203,
205, 269, 270, 273, 300, 301,
331, 338–39, 345
Gerullis 66
Gestapo 79, 90, 93, 99–100, 111,
158, 246, 247, 249, 275, 282,
293, 300, 306, 308, 309–10,
342, 370, 435
Giel 57
Giersch 117
Girg, Walter 47, 124–25, 127, 352,
353, 368
Goebbels, Joseph 11, 64, 90, 147,
161, 300, 345, 366, 370
Gohl 253
Golombiefski, Richard 199–200,
300–01, 397
Göttler, Waldemar 64, 84
Göttsch, Werner 332, 353,
355–56, 357, 358
Graff 292
Gragert Wilhelm 204, 254
Grapmanis, Gunars 81, 88–89
Great Britain, British 15, 18, 19,
40, 57, 80, 87, 88, 94, 95,
96, 102, 111, 112, 122, 133,
141, 142, 143, 147, 148, 154,
158–59, 164–66, 167, 168,
170, 173, 174, 178, 179, 180,
181, 191, 192, 194, 196, 204,
208, 233, 235, 238, 243, 251,

283, 290, 294, 295, 303, 306,
307, 311, 312, 313, 336, 342,
346, 350, 355, 356, 363, 366,
370, 396, 431
Greece, Greeks 10, 32, 42, 105,
109, 149, 157–68, 175, 179,
241, 294, 299
Greek National Republican
League (EDES) 39, 157–59,
166, 168, 179; Central
Committee 158
'green' guerrillas 39, 59, 60, 65,
71, 73, 131, 132, 133, 139, 144,
146, 147, 148, 189–91, 238
'*Greif*' (Operation) 48–50
'*Greif*' (Operation) 273
Grossier, Georges 271
'*Guardie ai Labari*' 209–10
'Guiscard' (Operation) 312
Güldenpfennig, Hubert 243
Gunne, Roland 128, 129, 135, 138,
139, 140–41, 146, 147, 148

Haahti, Sakari 319, 328
Hagedorn, Charles 256, 257,
258–59, 262, 264, 265, 266,
352
The Hague (training camp) 25,
55, 96, 191, 255, 256, 257,
284, 286, 287
Hakkenberg van Geesbeek,
Alfred 302, 303, 305
Hallamaa, Reino 321–22, 324,
325
Hamm, Lucien 272
'Hannibal' (Operation) 269–70
Harbig 108–09
'Harbig' (Operation) 108–09, 110
Hardick 48–49
Harispe, Michel 266, 275
Harstang, Fritz 342
Harster 206, 210, 214
Hass 205, 206, 208, 210–11, 214,
371
Hasselmann 86, 87, 88
Heckel, Ernst 336
Hegermann, Gustav 346
Heikkilä 324, 325
Heinze, Wolfram 55, 56, 58, 68
'*Heinzelmännchen*' (Operation)
193
Helanen 319–20, 321, 324, 325
'Henriette' (Operation) 34,
285–90, 304
Heppen 338
Herfurth, Wolfgang 345–46
'Herzog' (Operation) 355–56
Hettinger 200
Heye, Helmuth 40–41, 192

TEMPUS – REVEALING HISTORY

Private 12768 Memoir of a Tommy
JOHN JACKSON

'Unique... a beautifully written, strikingly honest account of a young man's experience of combat' **Saul David**

'At last we have John Jackson's intensely personal and heartfelt little book to remind us there was a view of the Great War other than Wilfred Owen's' **The Daily Mail**

£9.99   0 7524 3531 0

The German Offensives of 1918
MARTIN KITCHEN

'A lucid, powerfully driven narrative' **Malcolm Brown**
'Comprehensive and authoritative... first class' **Holger H. Herwig**

£13.99   0 7524 3527 2

Verdun 1916
MALCOLM BROWN

'A haunting book which gets closer than any other to that wasteland marked by death' **Richard Holmes**

£9.99   0 7524 2599 4

The Forgotten Front
The East African Campaign 1914–1918
ROSS ANDERSON

'Excellent... fills a yawning gap in the historical record'
The Times Literary Supplement
'Compelling and authoritative'
Hew Strachan

£25   0 7524 2344 4

Agincourt
A New History
ANNE CURRY

'A highly distinguished and convincing account'
Christopher Hibbert
'A *tour de force*' **Alison Weir**
'*The* book on the battle' **Richard Holmes**
A **BBC History Magazine** Book of the Year 2005

£25   0 7524 2828 4

The Welsh Wars of Independence
DAVID MOORE

'Beautifully written, subtle and remarkably perceptive' **John Davies**

£25   0 7524 3321 0

Bosworth 1485 Psychology of a Battle
MICHAEL K. JONES

'Most exciting... a remarkable tale' **The Guardian**
'Insightful and rich study of the Battle of Bosworth... no longer need Richard play the villain' **The Times Literary Supplement**

£12.99   0 7524 2594 3

The Battle of Hastings 1066
M.K. LAWSON

'Blows away many fundamental assumptions about the battle of Hastings... an exciting and indispensable read' **David Bates**
A **BBC History Magazine** Book of the Year 2003

£25   0 7524 2689 3

If you are interested in purchasing other books published by Tempus, or in case you have difficulty finding any Tempus books in your local bookshop, you can also place orders directly through our website

www.tempus-publishing.com